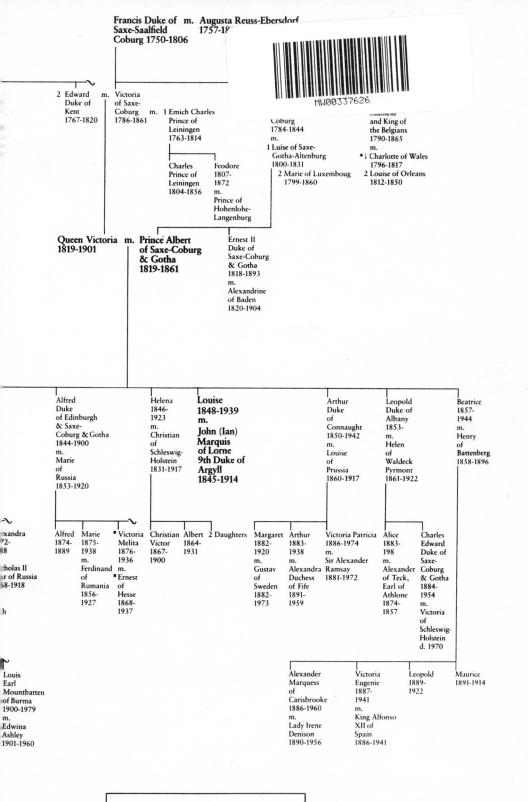

Francis Duke of m. Augusta Reuss-Ebersdorf
Saxe-Saalfield   1757-18
Coburg 1750-1806

2 Edward   m. Victoria
Duke of   of Saxe-
Kent   Coburg   m. 1 Emich Charles
1767-1820   1786-1861   Prince of
                               Leiningen
                               1763-1814

Coburg
1784-1844
m.
1 Luise of Saxe-
Gotha-Altenburg
1800-1831
2 Marie of Luxemboug
1799-1860

and King of
the Belgians
1790-1865
m.
* i Charlotte of Wales
1796-1817
2 Louise of Orleans
1812-1850

Charles   Feodore
Prince of   1807-
Leiningen   1872
1804-1856   m.
                 Prince of
                 Hohenlohe-
                 Langenburg

Queen Victoria m. Prince Albert   Ernest II
1819-1901   of Saxe-Coburg   Duke of
                    & Gotha   Saxe-Coburg
                    1819-1861   & Gotha
                                         1818-1893
                                         m.
                                         Alexandrine
                                         of Baden
                                         1820-1904

Alfred   Helena   Louise   Arthur   Leopold   Beatrice
Duke   1846-   1848-1939   Duke   Duke of   1857-
of Edinburgh   1923   m.   of   Albany   1944
& Saxe-   m.   Connaught   1853-   m.
Coburg & Gotha   Christian   John (Ian)   1850-1942   m.   Henry
1844-1900   of   Marquis   m.   Helen   of
m.   Schleswig-   of Lorne   Louise   of   Battenberg
Marie   Holstein   9th Duke of   of   Waldeck   1858-1896
of   1831-1917   Argyll   Prussia   Pyrmont
Russia   1845-1914   1860-1917   1861-1922
1853-1920

xandra   Alfred   Marie   * Victoria   Christian Albert 2 Daughters Margaret Arthur   Victoria Patricia Alice   Charles
2-   1874-   1875-   Melita   Victor   1864-   1882-   1883-   1886-1974   1883-   Edward
8   1889   1938   1876-   1867-   1931   1920   1938   m.   198   Duke of
                   m.   1936   1900   m.   m.   Sir Alexander   m.   Saxe-
holas II   Ferdinand m.   Gustav   Alexandra   Ramsay   Alexander Coburg
r of Russia   of   * Ernest   of   Duchess   1881-1972   of Teck,   & Gotha
8-1918   Rumania of   Sweden   of Fife   Earl of   1884-
                   1856-   Hesse   1882-   1891-   Athlone   1954
h   1927   1868-   1973   1959   1874-   m.
                            1937   1857   Victoria
                                                                                                                            of
                                                                                                                            Schleswig-
                                                                                                                            Holstein
                                                                                                                            d. 1970

Louis   Alexander   Victoria   Leopold   Maurice
Earl   Marquess   Eugenie   1889-   1891-1914
Mountbatten   of   1887-   1922
of Burma   Carisbrooke 1941
1900-1979   1886-1960   m.
m.   m.   King Alfonso
Edwina   Lady Irene   XII of
Ashley   Denison   Spain
1901-1960   1890-1956   1886-1941

ROYAL FAMILY TREE

PRINCESS LOUISE

Queen Victoria's Unconventional Daughter

PRINCESS LOUISE

Queen Victoria's
Unconventional Daughter

JEHANNE WAKE

COLLINS
8 Grafton Street, London WI
1988

William Collins Sons & Co. Ltd
London · Glasgow · Sydney · Auckland
Toronto · Johannesburg

BRITISH LIBRARY CATALOGUING IN PUBLICATION DATA

Wake, Jehanne
Princess Louise: Queen Victoria's
Unconventional Daughter.
1. Louise, *Princess, Duchess of Argyll*
2. Great Britain – Princes and Princesses
– Biography
I. Title
941.081'092'4   DA559.L6

ISBN 0-00-217076-0

First published in Great Britain 1988
Copyright © Jehanne Wake 1988

Photoset in Linotron Galliard by
Rowland Phototypesetting Ltd
Bury St Edmunds, Suffolk
Printed and bound in Great Britain by
T J Press (Padstow) Ltd, Padstow, Cornwall

FOR WILLIAM

CONTENTS

LIST OF ILLUSTRATIONS

Unless otherwise stated,
all sculpture, paintings and drawings are by Princess Louise

The Black Prince, c. 1873. (*Inveraray Collection; Photo: Carolyne Mazur*).

Princess Louise's Boudoir (Blue Parlour) at Rideau Hall,   191
Ottawa. From Princess Louise's albums, PAC. (*Dr Robert Hubbard*).

Princess Louise, aged 33, 1881 in Venice. Photograph by Vianelli Bros. (*Royal Archives, Windsor*).

Princess Louise, aged 43, 1891. Watercolour by Josephine Swabodow. (*Queen Margaret College, Edinburgh; Photo: Andrew Parnell*).

Joseph Edgar Boehm, 1879. (*Jean van Caloen Foundation, Bruges*).

Between pages
302–303

'*What is most enjoyed!*' Colonel William Probert on the telephone, c. 1902–6. (*Bevills Collection*).

Lorne in Egypt. Photograph by his wife, 1906. (*Bevills Collection*).

Ethel Badcock, 1896. (*Bevills Collection*).

Scenes of the Nile: *Arab Village*; *Group of Arabs under Palm Trees*, 1906. (*Royal Library, Windsor*).

The unveiling of the statue of *Queen Victoria* in Kensington Gardens, June 1893. (*Photo: the Royal Borough of Kensington and Chelsea Arts & Libraries Services*).

The Studio at Kensington Palace. (*Photo: Public Record Office, Kew*).

Detail of the *Memorial to the Colonial Soldiers who fell in the Boer War*, 1903–5. (*Photo: Malcolm Crowthers*).

Self-bust, n.d. (*National Portrait Gallery; Photo: National Portrait Gallery*).

Rosneath Castle from the air. (*Photo: St Andrews University*).

Princess Louise with the Prince of Wales (later the Duke of Windsor) at The Princess Louise Hospital for Children, Kensington, 14 November 1933.

Princess Louise's favourite photograph of herself, 1927. Photograph by Olive Edis. (*Photo: National Portrait Gallery*).

The 9th Duke of Argyll writing a telegram, 1910. After the painting by Sydney Hall. (*Collection of Ian Anstruther*).

Back jacket photo courtesy of Sotheby's.
Endpaper: Royal Family Tree.
Endpaper: Argyll Family Tree.

PART I

The Princess Louise
1848–1871

CHAPTER I

Birth

The year 1848 was not the most auspicious year for a princess to be born. Queen Victoria gave little indication of this in her New Year letter to Uncle Leopold, King of the Belgians. She wrote from Claremont House, of how 'safely and happily housed', she and Prince Albert were 'with our *whole* little family'.[1] The Queen was leading a quiet life because she was expecting the birth of her sixth child at the beginning of March. Her husband's equerry, General Grey, used to see her on his daily walks 'with her waterproof on, & her petticoats held up to her knees, braving the wind and rain' with her children, as they trotted behind clutching their petticoats in emulation.[2]

So, at first, the European menace did not impinge upon her thoughts; nor did it seem to threaten the peaceful shores of Britain. A revolt in Sicily on January 12th was hardly of great significance. Only after reports were received that the Hapsburg Emperor had been forced to abdicate did the British take notice. For not only was a fellow empire threatened, but revolution was edging its way nearer England.

When King Leopold wrote from Belgium, 'What will soon become of us God alone knows; great efforts will be made to revolutionise this country,'[3] Queen Victoria, too, became alarmed. Although Belgium withstood the European menace, France did not. On February 24th, an armed mob marched on the Tuileries to demand the King's life. The Royal Family just had time to escape through the gardens before the mob broke in. When news of the French Revolution reached London two days later, Queen Victoria wrote: "*Je ne sais plus où je suis,*" and I fancy really that we have gone back into the *old* century.'[4] By the 28th, the first members of the French Royal Family had reached the safe haven of Buckingham Palace; the Queen and Prince Albert were shocked by the arrival of their cousin, Princess Clémentine of France, 'in real rags, her *only* clothes half torn off' by the Parisian mob.[5]

Concerned at the effect on her confinement, Prince Albert did his best to calm the Queen, who had become 'sadly agitated' at the sight of the refugees. For, as she admitted to Uncle Leopold, 'God knows we have had since the 25th enough for a whole life – anxiety, sorrow, excitement, in short, I feel as if we had jumped over thirty years' experience at once. The whole face of Europe is changed and I feel as if I lived in a dream.'[6] And, as if this was not enough, the royal couple were now faced with a government crisis.

For the disruption in Europe had diminished trade in England, which greatly increased unemployment. Instead of using funds to combat this, Lord John Russell's Whig Government decided to expand the militia and to raise the necessary money by increasing income tax by 80 per cent. They were now threatened with a revolt by their own supporters. This naturally increased concern about Queen Victoria's imminent confinement. The Queen worried that her unborn child would be sure to turn out 'Something peculiar', since no one born in such turbulent times could possibly be 'ordinary'.[7] As her baby became overdue, the Prince became 'full of misgiving, because of the many moral shocks which have crowded upon Victoria of late'.[8]

It was not until the early hours of Saturday, March 18th, that a group of eminent gentlemen gathered in a sitting room at Buckingham Palace. They had been summoned to witness the birth of the Queen's child: announced by the appearance from the adjoining bedroom of Prince Albert, carrying the babe in his arms. Tradition required the presence of the Home Secretary, the Archbishop of Canterbury, and senior members of the Queen's Household who, as Privy Councillors, could verify that all was in order at the confinement of a reigning Queen.

Childbirth, then, carried a high rate of mortality; indeed Queen Victoria owed her throne to the death in childbirth of Princess Charlotte of Wales in 1817. So, her husband's concern was more than shared by the company waiting in the adjoining room. In such troubled times, it would be no small matter for the Monarch, a symbol of stability and continuity for her country, to be incapacitated through childbirth.

But with that disregard for pomp and punctuality, which was to mark her actions throughout the course of a long life, the child kept the distinguished company waiting. It was not until eight o'clock that morning that the Queen, after a particularly difficult confinement, was safely delivered of a fine, healthy daughter; it was half past eight before the Privy Councillors were allowed to disband. As they drove away in their carriages, a bulletin announcing the birth was posted on to the main gates of the Palace; Londoners elsewhere heard the news by the firing of a twenty-one gun salute at the Tower and in Hyde Park.

The Princess's birth was, however, overshadowed by news of another revolution. That afternoon, as Prince Albert settled down at his writing table to give his brother, Duke Ernest of Saxe-Coburg & Gotha, 'some good news for a change', revolution broke out in Berlin.[9] The reactionary King of Prussia admitted 'we all lay flat on our bellies inside the Palace as bullets whistled about outside'.[10] His brother and heir, the Prince of Prussia, nicknamed 'the grapeshot Prince' for his association with the reactionary party, the Junkers, decided to flee to what had become a royal refugee camp, namely England. As news of the fall of Berlin and the flight of the Prussian prince circulated around London, Mr Disraeli wryly observed that, 'Kings and Princes are turned off as we turn away servants – worse, without character – and nobody resists.'[11]

In fact, Queen Victoria and Prince Albert were expecting the Prince of Prussia but not quite so soon, nor under those circumstances. Although they had wanted him to stand as godfather to their baby Princess, his imminent arrival now placed them in an awkward position. Queen Victoria could not be seen to honour a deposed Prussian prince; such an act might damage future relations with whoever ruled Prussia once the revolution was over. The Prime Minister helped them by officially stating it was 'better the Prince of Prussia should not be the godfather of the young Princess'.[12]

The brothers and sisters of the young Princess wanted to call her 'La Nouvelle', but her parents chose the names LOUISE CAROLINE ALBERTA. It was perhaps a measure of Prince Albert's increased confidence in his role as the Sovereign's husband that, unlike his other five children, Princess Louise was named after people whom he, rather than Queen Victoria, held especially dear.

That Princess Louise was named after Prince Albert's mother, who was also Queen Victoria's aunt, is surprising because Duchess Luise was a disgraced woman. In 1817, sixteen-year-old Princess Luise, heiress to the Duchy of Gotha, had married the thirty-three-year-old Prince Ernest, the Duke of Coburg. Although she was very much in love with her husband, by the time their second son, Prince Albert, was two years old, Duke Ernest had reverted to the promiscuous life he had led before his marriage. Humiliated and neglected, the young Duchess eventually fell in love with a young army officer at Court. After the Duke demanded a separation, she had to leave Coburg in

1824 and was never permitted to see her two small sons again. Divorced in 1826, the year the Duchies of Saxe-Coburg and Gotha were united, she married her army officer, Alexander von Hanstein, but died three years later, in St Wendel, after a long and painful illness. Prince Albert never forgot her and, according to the Queen, 'always spoke with much tenderness and sorrow of his poor mother';[13] now, in 1848, he named his baby daughter after her.

It was to be a singularly appropriate choice of name for Princess Louise inherited some of her qualities and most of her looks from Duchess Luise. While helping General Grey with his biography of the Prince Consort, the Queen told him that Princess Louise 'is said to be like her in face'; the Queen described Duchess Luise as 'very handsome tho' very small, fair with blue eyes – and Prince Albert was said to be extremely like her – she was full of cleverness & talents'.[14]

Princess Louise was named Caroline in memory of the Dowager Duchess of Gotha, Prince Albert's step grandmother, who had died in February, a month before her birth. This formidable but kind-hearted lady had, with Prince Albert's other grandmother, taken charge of the two boys when their mother left Coburg. Prince Ernest and Prince Albert had adored her. A progressive thinker, she introduced the boys to literature and drama. It was through her that the royal children in England learned to garden and drive a miniature cart: for she had introduced their father to these pursuits as a little boy.

Princess Louise was the only one of his five daughters to be named Alberta after her father. To those who knew Prince Albert and all his children, Princess Louise was the child who most reminded them of him. Despite such an appropriate choice of names, during the first few years of her life she was known by none of them: she was always called 'Loo-Loo' or 'Princess Loo-Loo'.

Plans for her christening at Buckingham Palace had been disrupted by news of disturbances occurring in various large towns in England. It was just as Prince Albert had predicted: the spirit of revolution had followed the exiles across the Channel and infected the people of England. A London crowd even broke into Prince Albert's skittle alley in Buckingham Palace, but, far from being belligerent or dangerous, when the leader of the march was arrested, he burst into tears.

Prince Albert wrote to Baron Stockmar the next day: 'we had our revolution yesterday, and it went up in smoke'.[15] He spoke too soon; for much more serious plans for public protest were being made by the

Chartists. Prince Albert feared that the disaffected working classes would unite with the Irish in rebellion and during the winter of 1848, plans for an Irish rebellion had been laid. Its leader, Feargus O'Connor, was also leader of the working men's movement in England, the Chartists, who hoped to improve the appalling conditions in which they lived and worked by peaceful means. Their Charter contained a list of demands ranging from 'one man one vote' to secret ballots.

On April 3rd, the day Queen Victoria ended her confinement, reports reached the palace of plans for a vast, open-air meeting on Monday, April 10th, at Kennington Common. From there the Chartists planned to march to the House of Commons to present a petition bearing the signatures of more than one and a half million people. News of this meeting caused the Queen and Prince Albert to fear for the safety of England and the Queen's throne. Women and children were advised to leave for the country while people living in districts like Pimlico, which was considered dangerously close to Westminster, elected to visit friends or family in safer areas of London. Few underestimated the threat posed by the Chartists. Sir Colin Campbell, the military hero, wrote to his brother that: 'This may be the last time I write to you before the Republic is established!'[16]

As the day of the demonstration grew nearer, the Queen, still suffering from the aftermath of a difficult confinement, became distraught. She had fed, clothed and sheltered the refugee French Royal Family, but who would be left to do the same for her family after Monday's events? she asked. The fate of her children, and especially her fortnight-old baby, seemed so uncertain. Bravely preparing to meet any eventuality, she wrote to King Leopold: 'I always think and say to myself, "Let them grow up fit for *whatever station* they may be placed in – *high or low*." This one never thought of before, but I *do* always now.'[17]

She was secretly relieved when Prince Albert told her that the Government had advised him to leave London. This was no easy matter for the Queen was still very weak from her confinement; women in this condition were expected to remain quietly on a sofa until at least six weeks after the birth of a child.

Early on the morning of April 8th, several hundred special constables were positioned around Waterloo Station; otherwise the station was completely empty. At half past ten, a large party appeared. Prince Albert escorted his wife and children, with Mrs Thurston carrying

Princess Louise, on to the special train. With Queen Victoria safely on a daybed in one of the carriages, the train moved off on its journey to Gosport. The caravanserai then transferred to the royal yacht to cross the Solent, reaching their refuge, Osborne House on the Isle of Wight, at a quarter past two that afternoon. Utterly exhausted from the journey the poor Queen went straight to bed.

The flight, for so it must be called, however orderly a procedure, of the Queen and her family did not pass unnoticed. Prince Albert was rather uneasy about their departure during such a crisis, and even asked an equerry, Colonel Phipps, to remain in London and check the reaction. Thus, on the evening of April 9th, Colonel Phipps wandered about the streets of London to try and gauge public opinion. Prince Albert was relieved to hear that the Queen's 'reputation for personal courage stands so high, I never heard one person express a belief that her departure was due to personal alarm'.[18] Where there was any blame, it fell upon the Government for 'allowing it', but most people tended to support the official view that it was safer to have the Queen out of the way for, 'should any serious disturbance' occur, her presence would be 'an additional anxiety'.

At first the Isle of Wight seemed as peaceful as ever, sheltered from the events disturbing the rest of the world. But, by Sunday, Lady Lyttelton noticed that the atmosphere of crisis had penetrated even this sleepy island. At Matins, the prayer was said 'in case of war and tumult', which had not been heard since the time of the Napoleonic Wars over thirty years before.[19] It was even arranged that the six-year-old Prince of Wales would sleep nearer his parents.

In the event, what Queen Victoria always referred to as 'Our Revolution' was a placid, self-restrained affair. When the leader Feargus O'Connor arrived at Kennington Common, the Commissioner of the Police duly informed him that the demonstration would not be allowed to go back across the river to Westminster. O'Connor simply 'expressed the utmost thanks, and begged to shake [the Police Commissioner] by the hand'; then he proceeded to urge the vast crowd to disperse, and went off in a cab to the Home Office, where he assured the Home Secretary that the Government 'have been quite right'.[20] The Charter with the signatures of 23,000 people, instead of the expected one and a half million, was quietly presented to the House of Commons.

As is often the case in England, the weather proved to be the decisive factor. All afternoon heavy rain had poured down upon the fervent Chartists and their loyal supporters on Kennington Common, and, in the end, soaked to the skin, the bedraggled, disappointed crowd dispersed.

'Thank God!' wrote the Queen after she had received the Prime Minister's telegram, 'the loyalty of the people at large has been very striking & their indignation at their peace being interfered with by such wanton & worthless men – immense.'[21] This did not spell the end of Chartist disturbances; but their support started to wane. However, even the Isle of Wight had to contend with a final scare.

The police alerted Osborne House that a party of men, who had recently arrived by steamer at East Cowes, were revolutionaries in disguise. Such was the jittery state of nerves of the authorities that all menservants, estate workers, even building workmen, were called upon immediately to down tools and bear arms in defence of their Queen. It transpired that this alarm, like many others, was groundless; the so-called revolutionaries were only men on an outing to the seaside.

Nevertheless, the Queen and her family enjoyed their extended stay at Osborne. Princess Louise gave the Queen little trouble, being 'as placid and happy as possible, cries very little, and begins to laugh and even *crow*, which at six weeks old is early'.[22] The Queen's views on babies are well-recorded: until they were at least six weeks, she thought 'an ugly baby is a very nasty object – and the prettiest is frightful when undressed',[23] and, she frankly admitted, this included her own. Yet, she did not dislike babies and chose to have her own with her as much as possible; for an hour and a half during luncheon with the older children, at tea, and then often at bath time in the evening. As she told her eldest daughter years later, 'though I am no admirer of babies generally – there are exceptions'.[24] Princess Louise was one and the Queen was 'extremely proud' of her. As a baby, Princess Louise was 'extremely fair, with white satin hair; large, long blue eyes, and regular features; a most perfect form from head to foot'.[25]

Before leaving Osborne at the beginning of May for Princess Louise's christening, the Queen wrote to one of her closest friends, Harriet, Duchess of Sutherland, 'We are very happy here though the weather is not what it was last year. *Everything* is different in this terrible *48*.'[26] Princess Louise's christening was unusually quiet because foreign Royalties were unable to leave their countries. Instead of the customary four sponsors, as royal godparents are termed, Princess Louise had only three – Queen Victoria's cousin Princess Augusta of

Cambridge, now the Grand Duchess of Mecklenburg-Strelitz, the Grand Duchess of Saxe-Meiningen and the Duke of Mecklenburg-Schwerin – her intended fourth, the Prince of Prussia, not being allowed to stand. The Queen and Prince Albert had always chosen reigning Sovereigns as sponsors for their children but the uncertainty of the times, when it was not known from day-to-day which ruler would keep his throne, now meant that it was wiser to chose rulers of smaller states to whom the Government could not object.

Princess Louise was christened in the Chapel at Buckingham Palace at six o'clock on the evening of May 13th by the Archbishop of Canterbury. It was a glittering state occasion, with a reception in the Throne Room afterwards and a banquet in the Picture Gallery, followed by an evening party in the White Drawing Room. In the absence of her three sponsors, the Duchess of Cambridge, Prince Albert and Queen Adelaide, widow of William IV, stood proxy.

Prince Albert had adapted the music of a chorale, which he had written several years before, to the hymn 'In Life's Gay Morn' (now known as the Gotha tune) which was performed once everyone was seated. Then the Lord Chamberlain conducted Princess Louise who, dressed in the Honiton lace robes worn by her brothers and sisters, was carried by Mrs Bray, her nurse, and Lady Lyttelton, the royal governess, into the Chapel. At the golden lily font, which Prince Albert had designed for the christening of his eldest child in 1841, Lady Lyttelton took the baby Princess and handed her over to the Archbishop for baptism. Princess Louise was exceedingly quiet and good, much to everyone's relief.

However, her christening did not pass without incident. Her five-year-old sister, Princess Alice, fidgeted and the oldest member of the family present disgraced herself; Princess Louise's great aunt, the 72-year-old Princess Mary, Duchess of Gloucester, perhaps reminded of a Coronation, became so confused that in the middle of the service she suddenly left her seat and, in an act of homage, fell on her knees before the Queen. Queen Victoria was greatly shocked: 'Imagine our *horror*!'[27]

Princess Louise may have been baptized into the Church of England, but every one of her sponsors, indeed even their proxies, was German. Although German by descent, she would be English by upbringing. A decision about her education had been reached long ago by her parents. 'The Education of the royal Infants ought to be from its earliest beginnings, a truly moral and a truly *English* one.'[28]

CHAPTER II

Childhood

Prince Albert's predilection for neatness emerges from a letter he wrote to announce Princess Louise's birth; he lamented that the balance between boys and girls in his family was now spoilt: 'if a little boy had come, our children would be quite symmetrical. Now there are four against two.'[1] Princess Louise's position in the family did not, however, entail any change in nursery or schoolroom routine; her own early years simply followed the pattern set by her parents for her elder brothers and sisters.

When young, all Queen Victoria's children were thought remarkable for their soft-heartedness, their high spirits matched by strong tempers and, above all, for their loyalty to each other. There was never any question of tale-telling or breaking ranks; when one was punished the others rallied round with sympathy. Thus, the Prince of Wales, when one of his sisters was banished for being naughty, would 'steal to the door to give a kind message, or tell a morsel of pleasant news, his own toys quite neglected'.[2]

Of the six children, the most dominant was the eldest, Princess Victoria or 'Vicky', the Princess Royal. Undoubtedly her father's favourite child, she was considered something of a child prodigy; saying, at the age of six, 'Poor Roger Bacon! So hard on him to have been thought wicked because he was so clever as to invent gun powder!'[3] She might well have turned out an insufferable prig, but was saved by her mischievousness, soft heart and great curiosity.

It was, however, unfortunate for the rest of the children that she was the trail blazer; for she shone in lessons and read and wrote well from an early age. Her parents were entranced by this clever, amusing, little girl and, although in theory Prince Albert recognized that they were unlike each other 'in looks, mind or character',[4] in practice he invariably compared them with the Princess Royal. As a little girl Princess Louise tended to hero-worship this much praised, older sister, who did everything so well, but whom she rarely saw.

The two children who most suffered from comparison with the

Princess Royal were the next two in age, Prince Albert Edward, Prince of Wales, and Princess Alice. The Prince of Wales, usually described by Queen Victoria as 'Poor Bertie', was emotionally scarred by the relentless pressure exerted upon him as heir to the throne. He developed a stammer and was consumed with rages when he would scream and stamp, yet his affectionate, very lovable nature meant that the younger children were always loyal to him, however much provoked.

His favourite sister, Princess Alice, was also Princess Louise's favourite. For her brothers and younger sisters, Princess Alice's position was like that of the sun around which they, as satellites, revolved; it was she who mothered them and soothed their troubles. Whereas the Princess Royal was abrasive, she was approachable and never made her younger sisters feel inferior. She assumed the role of mediator between the children and their mother, a role which sometimes earned Queen Victoria's displeasure. The Queen, nevertheless, called her 'good amiable Alice' for her obedience, gentleness and quiet charm.

Two children shared the nursery with Princess Louise. The older, Prince Alfred, or 'Affie' as the family called him, was then nearly four. Since the Duke of Saxe-Coburg was without an heir, Prince Alfred would eventually succeed to the dukedom. However, as he was also second in line to the British throne, it seemed essential to give him an English upbringing. He was by far the most handsome of the boys, having inherited his father's blue eyes and all the Coburg dark good looks. Worshipped by his younger sisters, who later made a great fuss of him during his leave from the Navy, he had a great passion for ships and loved to tinker with steam engines. He was undoubtedly the son dearest to Prince Albert's heart.

Princess Helena, the second member of the nursery, was always linked with Princess Louise. Although only twenty months separated them, they were far apart in temperament. Known in the family as 'Lenchen', Princess Helena was a straightforward, placid child. She adored horses and longed to be a boy so as to avoid riding side-saddle; she was, however, protective of her younger sister, who was much less robust. Princess Helena grew into rather a gauche, stolid girl who lacked the charm that Princess Louise possessed; the Queen's ladies called Princess Louise 'our dove' and cooed over her pram. Everyone agreed with Lady Augusta Bruce, who said 'the delicious Baby – it *is* a delight and a beautiful creature'.[5]

Princess Louise's first birthday was celebrated by her brothers and sisters dining *en famille* with Queen Victoria and Prince Albert. General Grey described the 'Princes in black velvet jackets and silver buttons and Royal Stuart Tartan kilts and the Princesses in Royal Stuart Tartan silk dresses – laced in front in the Swiss fashion, with diamond crosses and pearl necklaces.'

'The more I see of the Royal domestic life,' he wrote, 'the more I am in admiration of it and I am convinced so pure and exemplary a Court never before existed.'[6] Prince Albert would have been well-pleased with this comment, for it was his intention to improve the atmosphere of both Court and Society. His first step had been to reorganize the royal nurseries and, in 1842, to appoint a Lady Super-intendent. The first to hold this position was the Dowager Lady Lyttelton. She was, from the first, a great success with both parents and children; the latter giving her the nickname of 'Laddle'. Her son George always referred to her as the 'Governess of England' and she did much to train the nursery staff, as well as to bring up her royal charges whom she called 'Princessy' or 'Princey' except for Princess Louise who, as the youngest then in the nursery, was always 'Princi-pina'. Lady Lyttelton was an influential figure in the lives of the eldest children; but she retired when Princess Louise was barely three.

The next Lady Superintendent, Lady Caroline Barrington, known to her charges as Lady Car, had held the position of Lady-of-the-Bedchamber since Queen Victoria's accession; present at the Queen and Prince Albert's marriage, she was one of the six people still at Court when they celebrated their twenty-first wedding anniversary in February 1861. The daughter of the second Earl Grey and a sister of General Grey, her personal life had been sad; three of her children died young and her husband, Captain George Barrington RN, died insane, leaving her a young widow with two children.

Lady Car was like a second mother to Princess Louise when she was of schoolroom age. Before then, the Head Nurse, Mrs Thurston or 'Turty', took first place, even before Queen Victoria, in the Princess's affections. Mary Ann Thurston was a widow with one daughter when she entered royal service in 1844; she remained in the nursery until the last child moved into the schoolroom in 1867 and she gave Princess Louise unstinting affection. As the Princess later wrote to her: 'You have been a dear true loving friend to me all the days I can remember . . . God bless you . . . for the motherly love (I may say) you gave us always.'[7]

Although Queen Victoria declared 'I love to hear the little feet and merry noises above',[8] this was said in retrospect, well after the nursery was empty; at the time, she was not the most affectionate of mothers, mainly because she felt the children came between her and Prince Albert. When leaving on a visit while the children were still young, Queen Victoria was touched at the sight of them lined up at the door to say farewell. 'Poor little things', she thought, not because she felt sorry to leave them but because she felt sorry *for* them.

Lady Car commanded a platoon of three governesses, three nurses and the nursery domestics, and supervised day-to-day affairs under the meticulous instruction of Prince Albert. She looked after the children's health and diet, bought their clothes, and taught them their first simple lessons. Mrs Thurston looked after the babies, dressed and fed them, nursed them through any sickness and slept with them in the night nursery in case of bad dreams or intruders.

This last was no idle threat for unauthorized people had been caught wandering about the royal apartments. The Prince took great precautions for the safety of his children, to which the Lady Superintendent bore witness: 'The last thing we did before bedtime was to visit the access to the children's apartments to satisfy ourselves that all was safe . . . Threatening letters of the most horrid kind aimed directly at *the children* are frequently received.'[9]

Their lives were just as protected during the daytime. Although the royal parents stated that 'the Children should be brought up as simply and in as domestic a way as possible',[10] they were defeated by the special position into which their children were born. Thus, the most simple walk became a ceremonial procession: 'I met the Queen walking in the garden yesterday,' wrote Eleanor Stanley, a maid of honour, 'without the Prince, but with the two eldest children, one in each hand, Princess Alice following in a sort of go-cart with Mdlle Grüner, besides three footmen, one to draw the cart, one to carry cloaks, &c., and one with scraps of bread for the swans and ducks.'[11]

Princess Louise also had to be taught to put out her hand to be kissed by people she met, be they interrupting her games in the corridor at Windsor or crossing her path in the gardens. 'Just seen the Princess Louise in the gallery', wrote the 45-year-old General Grey, 'and kissed her hand, 16-months-old and a bit – toddling along.'[12] Furthermore, she had to learn to distinguish between family, courtiers, visitors, indoor staff, outdoor staff and 'familiars' like Turty and Lady Car. In a letter home, Eleanor Stanley described how after lunch 'there was an exhibition of the children, which seems now to be rather the customary thing on Sunday'.[13]

The royal parents were not showing off their children, proud of them though they were, nor, as in former ages, proving their continued existence to the Court; they were simply trying to prepare them from an early age for their later royal and public role. Princess Louise had to learn to be at ease in the company of her elders, by whom for most of her childhood she was surrounded. From the age of three she was regularly presented to visitors and family guests after dinner, before being taken off to bed. Innumerable railway journeys also provided opportunities for learning to acknowledge the officials who greeted her family at the railway stations. Princess Louise, like other well-born children of her day, was much travelled from birth; her year being divided among the four family houses. The first railway journey she had made was to Osborne when barely three-weeks-old; the next was to Scotland.

In September 1848, having withstood the trying months of that spring, the Queen and Prince Albert had felt in need of an autumn holiday. The air of Osborne was not felt to be bracing enough to act as a restorative, and so they had taken, sight unseen, a four-year-lease on Balmoral in Aberdeenshire. Thus was inaugurated the tradition of passing the autumn at Balmoral. Queen Victoria and Prince Albert were enchanted with this simple shooting lodge and impressed by its isolation. Unfortunately, the old house proved too small and informal for the entourage; Prince Albert estimated that one hundred-odd people would have to be housed there at any one time. The lack of sitting rooms meant that a Minister-in-Attendance had to discuss affairs of State in his little bedroom with the Queen perched on the edge of his bed.

Nevertheless, in 1852, she purchased the house and its 17,400 acre estate for 30,000 guineas and Prince Albert found an Aberdeen architect builder, Mr William Smith, to transform the shooting lodge into a Scottish baronial castle. This new castle, built of local gleaming white granite, is set one hundred yards from the original house. The estate itself forms a little township: Prince Albert built cottages for the tenants, schools at Crathie and Glen Girnock, a library to serve the district, a shop, a savings bank and a cottage-based weaving industry besides the two already established main houses. One of these, lying ten miles away, is the little eighteenth-century dower house of Birkhall, which was used as an overflow for the royal Household and royal relations.

To reach Crathie Kirk, which lies half-way between Balmoral and Birkhall, from Balmoral the family used to cross the Dee by walking across a swaying suspension bridge. Three miles up the Dee from Balmoral lies that old Gordon stronghold, the dour little fortress of Abergeldie which was dark, low-ceilinged and possessed only one sitting room.

The children loved Abergeldie, despite its austerity; what they loved most about it was the excitement of crossing the Dee by an old-fashioned, open-sided cable-car. This was really three wooden planks connected by iron bands, which ran on two iron wheels along a roped cradle thrown across the river. The Abergeldie gardener worked it, taking two children across at a time. He would place one leg across the knees of his passengers to keep them steady while they held on to the wooden rounded bar above their heads, their legs dangling over the sides.

The interior of Balmoral was all Prince Albert's work, with its 'cheerful un-palace-like rooms', furnished with sporting trophies and Landseer engravings and covered everywhere with Royal Stuart or green hunting tartan. The 'tartanitis' was broken by the loose covers which were of thistle-patterned chintz. There was, as ever, method behind Prince Albert's tartan madness; he used so much of it in order to revive a depressed industry.

The whole Royal Family adopted the life of a Scottish laird as their own; the Queen, especially, became more Scottish every year and, oddly, more Jacobite. One of her Prime Ministers, Lord Salisbury, found, 'It was a sort of passion with her, and her descent from the Stuarts was what she valued most.'[14]

The children were taught to reel so they could join in the reeling parties held at home or at neighbouring lairds' houses. Catherine Paget remembered her first one at Abergeldie with '30 or 40 Highlanders carrying huge torches of pine wood . . . the bagpipes started on a lively tune and all danced reels in the courtyard. I never saw anything so picturesque or so exciting. The strangest flashing effect lit up the dark background – the blue moonlight enhanced the firey red of the torch flames as the Highlanders wildly and recklessly waved the great flaming logs till sparks fell all over them and on every side shrieking and howling at intervals and finally throwing down all the torches together so as to make a huge bonfire, round which they danced more wildly than ever.'[15]

Princess Louise used to go with her brothers and sisters, on the sturdy little Highland ponies they always rode at Balmoral, to visit the crofters on the estate, taking them flannel petticoats and baskets of provisions in panniers strapped across the ponies' backs. Their hosts always offered them cakes and 'a wee dram' which, regardless of their age, they were expected to drink. One of their favourite pastimes was the obligatory visit to the Merchant's: 'a paradise of granite, cairngorms and tweeds' where they always had to buy something on each visit.

Princess Louise's early upbringing was otherwise happy but strictly regimented. Every moment of every day was accountable, whether playing hide-and-seek or reading a book. Her parents rigidly followed the directive from their *éminence grise*, Baron Stockmar, that 'Whenever a child left the room, somebody must go with her and she must never be left alone.'[16] The allegations of extravagance, incest and dissipation made against some of George III's children disturbed Queen Victoria and Prince Albert; they feared that their children might develop, or at least be accused of, similar tendencies unless constantly watched by the large staff who surrounded them.

Baron Stockmar had devised a plan of education for the children, which was followed to the letter by their over-anxious parents. Before she was five, Princess Louise had started lessons in reading, writing and counting as well as in French and German; painting and music were added a year later. Like other well-born children, she did not really live with her parents but visited them at fixed times of the day; usually at breakfast and tea time. She had plenty of fresh air, with riding lessons or skating in the morning and a walk in the afternoon.

When she was six, arithmetic, geography, history and grammar were added and she joined her parents for lunch, after which progress reports would be read out by Prince Albert. At seven, she was given her own maid but continued lessons under specialist governesses while her brothers were given their own tutors, a valet and a separate establishment.

It has been claimed that this system was too harsh, especially in relation to the Prince of Wales. Certainly, when he got into difficulties, adjustments could have been made and the curriculum lightened. However, his brothers and sisters followed the same curriculum without

ill-effect and it was noticeably lighter than that endured by many of
their contemporaries. The Duchess of Sutherland's eight-year-old son
had 'lessons all day long from 7 am till 7 pm'.[17]

Parents and teachers seem to have confused slowness with laziness.
This particularly applied to the Prince of Wales who was expected to
perform well in everything and, when he did not, was more severely
chastised by Prince Albert and his tutor than were his brothers.

Although Princess Louise did not have the same pressures on her
as her eldest brother did, her inability to master spelling earned her
bad reports, which incurred her father's displeasure. In fact, Princess
Louise remained a bad speller throughout her life and her private letters
are scattered with misspelt words; later, her official letters were always
checked at her request by a member of her Household. Both children
needed encouragement and sympathy. Instead, the Prince of Wales was
given too much attention while Princess Louise was not given enough.
As a result, he became more disruptive and she more withdrawn.

Her governess for English was 'Tilla', Miss Hildyard, a 'sensible
quiet woman', and the daughter of a clergyman. She could be authoritarian and impatient, sometimes adopting what Queen Victoria called
'her most particularly dry and unpleasant way'[18] with Princess Louise,
who tended to become bored and lose her concentration during lessons
she disliked. 'Tilla' was not, of course, a trained teacher. Although she
was the Princess Royal's favourite governess, this was not the case with
Princess Louise, who always retained a deep affection for the French
governess, Mlle Rollande de la Sange, or 'Rolly' as the princesses called
her.

Princess Louise did well at her French lessons, which no doubt
eased her path with 'Rolly', and she used every opportunity to practise
French and remained fluent all her life. In the course of teaching her,
Mlle Rollande became all too familiar with Princess Louise's spitfire
temperament, which she likened to the English weather: a perfectly
clear, sunny sky suddenly marred by a thundercloud which rapidly
dissolved to leave no trace.

Major Elphinstone, Prince Arthur's tutor and later his Governor,
was especially fond of Princess Louise and amused by her precocity in
French. It was the custom on Christmas Eve for the Household to be
called to see the royal presents. Each prince and princess had his or her
her own table laden with presents. On 24 December 1858, when the
Major entered the room, he found the children in ecstasies over their

presents, which he considered to be far more than they could properly appreciate. Princess Louise watched the Major examine each table a little disapprovingly and then shyly whispered to him, '*Vraiment un peu trop extravagant*'.[19]

At this stage her greatest dislike was reserved for the German lessons taught by Fräulein Bauer; she was described by one pupil, Louisa Grey, as a 'dried-up, withered little lady, but behind her rather acid manner and blunt remarks she had a kind heart'. After one lesson in which Princess Louise had been extremely naughty Fräulein Bauer insisted she accompany her outside. Princess Louise always remembered this walk when she was in 'such disgrace'. As the sturdy little German stalked on ahead, Princess Louise deliberately tarried behind to fill her elastic-sided boots with sand. But Fräulein Bauer simply walked on without paying the slightest attention, for which, even at the time, Princess Louise respected her.[20]

Although she was occasionally naughty, until Princess Louise was seven the Queen always referred to her in her Journal as 'dear good little Louise'. As the youngest and prettiest daughter she was much petted but never spoilt. But, as the baby of the family, her reign was short-lived for, when she was barely two, her brother Prince Arthur was born. An obedient, interested, little fellow he was undoubtedly the Queen's favourite child, her 'precious love'. Prince Arthur over-shadowed his younger brother, Prince Leopold, born in 1853. Compared with Prince Arthur, the Queen thought Prince Leopold rather an ugly child and he was, in fact, an invalid as he suffered from the bleeding disease, haemophilia. It is said that the royal children were never allowed kittens as pets in case Prince Leopold was scratched.

The Queen and Prince Albert made their worst mistakes in the upbringing of their family with the older children; the younger ones benefited from a less strict regime. By the time Princess Louise and Prince Arthur were in the schoolroom, Prince Albert was insisting that much might be learnt out-of-doors through looking at plants and collecting pebbles, and that lessons should be adjusted to suit a child's capacity.

But this more flexible curriculum was offset by the fact that the younger children saw less of their parents. The Queen used to see her elder children bathed and put to bed every night; she might not see Princess Louise and Prince Arthur in the same way for three or four months, if not longer. The Queen regretted this but said there was no time for it. When the eldest children were young, it was usually Prince Albert who played with them during his constant visits to the nursery, but Princess Louise's time in the schoolroom coincided with her father's increasing preoccupation with public affairs. The fun-loving father of the Princess Royal's schoolroom days was almost unrecognizable to Princess Louise; he was increasingly the Victorian paterfamilias, an over-worked, harassed disciplinarian. Years later she told a great-niece that, much as she loved Prince Albert, he had been 'too strict'; when, for example, she practised at the piano, he would rap her knuckles at *every* wrong note and make her play the piece over and over again.[21]

The Prince could be unduly severe with his children, especially if they were untruthful, and he was very particular about their table manners. When the Queen wrote down some reminiscences about their home life, she mentioned how at meals he always sat next to one of the younger children: 'He could *not* bear bad manners & always dealt out his dear reprimands to the juveniles & a word from him was instantly obeyed.'[22] But when he did find time to enter into their games and family celebrations, help them with *tableaux vivants* or build a sand castle, he lost his stiffness and reserve and treated them as equals; but their love for him was tempered always by awe and sometimes by fear.

As she grew up, Princess Louise saw less and less of her father; by 1853 even the Queen was complaining that he never had time for her. The Prince became associated only with punishment and difficulties. Princess Louise probably never knew of the deep affection he bore her; his early death denied her the opportunity of becoming closer to him as her elder siblings had. For, as they grew up, the Prince would set aside an hour of his busy day to spend with each one individually. It was the Prince, and not Queen Victoria, who discussed marriage and the 'facts of life' with their daughters.

Princess Louise's relationship with her father was not made easier by the Queen's continual comparison of her children with their father. '*None* of you can *ever* be proud enough of being the *child* of SUCH a Father who has not his equal in this world . . . so great, so good, so faultless.'[23] Assailed by constant criticism and comment, the Princess began to feel that she was inferior. When Lady Augusta Bruce congratulated a grown-up Prince of Wales on the excellent behaviour of his children at dinner, he said it was marvellous not to have to be always at them for, 'We were perhaps a little too much spoken to and . . . we thought we could never do anything right anyhow.'[24]

From an early age Princess Louise had to accept frequent admonish-ments, punishments and whippings for misbehaviour. Whereas the Lady Superintendent naturally hesitated before beating the princesses, the Queen knew no such qualms. When the Duchess of Kent remon-strated that it was upsetting to hear a whipped child cry, she retorted, 'Not when you have 8, Mama – that wears off. You could not go through that each time one of the 8 cried!'[25]

The Queen preferred her children when they were between three-and six-years-old; then they were like human dolls and she could love and play with them like any ordinary mother. But once they were six, the Queen felt she could no longer treat them so intimately; her relationship with them changed as they were made aware that their mother was also their Queen. To maintain her position, the Queen believed she had to keep them in order and therefore not become too intimate with them.

Prince Albert, who treated his children as their father and not as the Prince Consort, wrote to her, 'It is indeed a pity that you find no consolation in the company of your children. The root of the trouble lies in the mistaken notion that, the function of a mother is to be always correcting, scolding, ordering them about and organising their activities. It is not possible to be on happy friendly terms with people you have just been scolding.'[26] But it was only in later years that the Queen would admit that she had over-emphasized discipline: 'too great care, too much constant watching leads to those very dangers hereafter, which one wishes to avoid'.[27]

These years indelibly marked Princess Louise's character. As she progressed through the schoolroom, she changed from the merry, outgoing child of Queen Victoria's 'good little Louise' into the over-sensitive girl of Queen Victoria's 'poor, backward Louise', (meaning that Princess Louise was reticent and hung back, rather than that she lacked in intellect). Her crippling shyness even prevented her from accepting thanks for a present which she had given. A member of the Household wrote: 'That sweet little Princess Louise sent such a pretty chair watch-stand and when I tried to thank her, she modestly ran away to avoid receiving them.'[28]

The emphasis in Princess Louise's upbringing was intended not only to produce the normal Victorian ideal – a submissive, gentle lady-like girl – but also to produce a princess whose mother was Queen of England. When the Princess Royal reproved one of her daughters for not behaving like a lady, let alone a princess, her children's outspoken French governess corrected her: 'Don't say, and don't think, that a princess is brought up to be lady-like, a lady is taught to think little of herself, to take the lowest place, be unselfish and put herself in the background but a princess is told "go, my dear, put yourself in the best place, before everybody".'[29] Unfortunately for Princess Louise, she always thought like a lady but was forced to behave like a princess.

It was bewildering, at first, to understand her mother's position; that 'Mama' was called 'Mam' by people like Lady Car and 'Laddle'; that Mama was Queen but Papa was not King; that they as children must kiss Mama's hand, never Papa's, but that other people kissed *their* hands. Confused, the children sometimes overreacted to their exalted status. During a drive with Mary Ponsonby, Princess Alice was 'rather obstreperous behind, and as I [Mary Ponsonby] was resisting her whims she said, "Really Mary don't you know you must do what I tell you?"'[30] The children were not allowed by their parents to get away with such behaviour, but this episode illustrates the anomaly of their position. They were taught never to consider themselves above others, especially servants and others less fortunate in life; yet they were treated as if above the rest of humanity.

The contradictory duties of being a lady and a princess are again evident in the lessons which formed part of Princess Louise's 'Royal' instruction. On the one hand, she was supposed to be a demure Victorian lady who kept silent and did not fidget; on the other, a dazzling princess who took the initiative socially and shone in company. One of her brothers-in-law often repeated a family saying, 'Royalties must learn to be bored with dignity'[31] and, like its European counterparts, the English Court provided a good training ground.

As a Royalty she would be expected to *cerclé*, to enter a room and move around it, speaking to each of the assembled company; her task was to make each one feel at ease and believe that she liked them and was interested in meeting them. In her youth at Weimar, the Princess Royal's future mother-in-law had been trained to '*cerclé*' by walking round the garden and speaking a few polite words to each tree and bush. Princess Louise used to practise '*cercléing*' with her sisters and assorted chairs strategically placed about the schoolroom.

Another lesson which formed part of her education was memory training. Every evening Princess Louise would be questioned about the visitors she had met, their names, positions and titles, their clothes or uniforms, and other personal details. With time, this exercise became almost instinctive, thus enabling Royalties to retain an internal-filing-system from which they could extract details at will. Although the vaguest member of her family, during a hospital visit late in her life she learnt that a doctor presented to her came from Kintyre. Although she had only visited Kintyre once, sixty years before, Princess Louise immediately asked after an old farmer she had met there; to the doctor who was born and bred in the district the farmer was but a dimly remembered name!

However, life for Princess Louise did not consist entirely of lessons since she went to Osborne in May for her mother's birthday and again in July and August. She always said that the happiest days of her childhood were the summer holidays at Osborne. The Queen and Prince Albert had always longed for a country house of their own where they could 'walk about anywhere [by themselves] without being followed and mobbed', as occurred when they stayed at Brighton Pavilion,[32] and, in 1844, they had purchased the Osborne estate on the Isle of Wight, deliberately paying for it with the Queen's own personal money, so that it belonged jointly to the Queen and Prince Albert. The house was a new but not especially grand villa, as foreign to England as its occupants sometimes appeared to be. A mixture of the Victorian idea of an Italian villa and a Belgravia town house, it stood in lovely grounds with gorgeous views. Unfortunately, it was an inconvenient place to reach. Although visitors from London journeyed in a special connecting train and steamer, or royal launch, to East Cowes, in 1845 the train journey took two and a half hours and the crossing at least one hour; moreover, in uncertain weather, crossings were often delayed.

In hot weather all the doors and windows were left open and the children used to dine and take tea in the gardens and run about to their hearts' content. The atmosphere, even for adults, was relaxed, with time for pleasant tête-à-tête rambles along the quiet public roads, 'a thing that would make everybody's hair stand on end at Windsor'.[33]

Every day during these idyllic summer holidays Princess Louise used either to walk across the sloping lawns and through the fields, where wonderful mushrooms grew, to the beach; or she would drive there in the big 'waggonette', past hedges full of honeysuckle. It was a private beach of 'beautiful white sand' with, at the end, a small semi-circular pavilion. Here, on a wooden seat, the Queen and her ladies would sit to watch the children as they played on the sand. However, the children were not allowed to walk barefoot on the sand, nor to paddle in the sea; they had to remain fully clothed while they built their moated castles and dug up shells.

Fully clothed, they also, unusually for the period, learnt to swim. Prince Albert filled an iron bath with sea water for the timid beginner. Once their fears were overcome they graduated to the swimming bath; this was a ship with canvas walls and a bright blue painted hull, which was anchored in the bay. The children were rowed out to it in a lifeboat from Osborne pier by two sailors from the royal yacht. On the ship was a dressing room astern from which a narrow platform ran round the inside of the canvas walls, railed off from the perforated floor in the centre of the ship. It was a perfect bathing place, as the floor could be raised or lowered to change the depth of the water.

The children were on holiday at Osborne, so lessons were of a different kind. The Prince was keen that his children should be brought up with some practical knowledge of housework, carpentry, cooking and gardening, a belief in direct contrast to the established mores of the period. Most aristocrats were brought up to do little for themselves; they would not dream of adding a log to the fire but would ring for a footman to perform the task.

In order to give his children some practical knowledge and to make such lessons fun for them, Prince Albert had thought of giving them a miniature chalet, known as a Swiss cottage, and, in 1854, he had the cottage erected at the end of the high walk near the sea in the grounds at Osborne.

A little house of dark wood, it had a balcony round the upper storey and a low, sloping roof. The house-warming party took the form of a birthday tea for Queen Victoria, held in the sitting room. Besides a dining room and a dressing room, the cottage had a blue and white, tiled kitchen filled with cooking utensils and miniature pots and pans. It was here that Princess Louise learned to cook, becoming a dab hand at baking cakes and buns which she would then invite her parents to eat for tea.

The idea of a Swiss cottage was by no means unique; what was unique about the Osborne one was the way in which Prince Albert used it to provide his children with practical experience of running their future domestic households. In later years, Princess Louise would delight in taking her house party at Kent House over to Osborne for a tour round the Swiss cottage. She would show them the kitchen and describe how she had learned to cook there. She would then show them the toy grocer's shop, which she and her sisters had been taught to run. It was about a foot square and bore the name 'Spratt'. On the shelves they kept all the usual ingredients, including sugar, jam and tea. They were expected to keep accounts in a little cash book which Prince Albert would go over at the end of the holidays. The cottage also had room for a little workshop where they learnt carpentry and mechanics.

Finally, she would conduct her friends round the little strips of garden laid out in front of the cottage which, in 1927, were still kept as the royal children had left them, with the same plants and designs. Like children everywhere, the first thing she always used to do on arriving home would be to dash into the garden to pick and guzzle the ripe gooseberries, strawberries and fresh green peas. Then she would go and see how everything was developing in her own individual garden plot. Each child had been given a plot to grow fruit, vegetables and flowers. Whenever the under-gardener judged their potatoes or artichokes, for example, to be ready, he would present a certificate which was given to Prince Albert who would buy the produce at the current market price.

Gardening was considered a 'practical subject', so most well-off Victorians knew nothing about it. The knowledgeable amateur gardener, now so quintessentially English, did not then rule over every garden in the land. Mid-Victorians considered it decidedly odd that the children of the Queen should be labouring away in the garden instead of allowing the gardeners to do the work.

Next to the children's gardens was a summer house which contained their gardening tools and wheelbarrows, each marked with the owner's name. Today they still stand, ready for use by their owners, relics of a long-ago childhood.

CHAPTER III

Early Sorrow

Until 1862 Princess Louise's birthdays always occurred when the family were at Buckingham Palace. Her birthday celebrations, therefore, reflected the more formal atmosphere found in her mother's London house. Despite its grand façade, however, there were not enough rooms to accommodate the royal children, who had to sleep in the attics. After an unrelenting campaign by Prince Albert, Parliament eventually voted a grant and the renovation work, begun when Princess Louise was about two, was completed shortly after her eighth birthday in 1856.

From the outside, Buckingham Palace is set symmetrically round four sides of an inner courtyard. Inside, however, it is a rabbit warren on a grand scale, with innumerable narrow passageways, marble halls and staircases, a vast throne room and ballroom, burrows of bedrooms and sitting rooms and acres of red carpeting: 'Everything is so straggly,' wrote one queen in despair, 'such distances to go and so fatiguing.'[1]

Queen Victoria and Prince Albert ensured that family birthdays were special fête days, beginning with the table laden with toys and pieces of jewellery, which was the first sight to greet the birthday child as the Queen led her into the breakfast room. On Princess Louise's second birthday, Aunt Mary Gloucester started a pearl necklace for her, as she had for each princess, adding a pearl every year. After her death in 1857, the Queen and the Duchess of Kent contributed the pearls which eventually formed part of the magnificent necklace Princess Louise always wore in later life. After tea Prince Albert would organize a magic lantern show which was a great favourite with all the children.

On her fourth birthday, the Queen thought Princess Louise was ready for more sophisticated festivities and organized a children's ball in her honour. The Victorian equivalent of present-day tea parties, children's balls usually started at nine o'clock in the evening and ended well after midnight. Formal evening dress, or sometimes fancy dress, was obligatory, and parents and members of the Household attended, accompanying a young partner in the dances. Children under six were allowed to leave at half past ten after a supper of ices and wine and seltzer.

Otherwise, these balls were conducted as replicas of adult ones; guests mounted the grand staircase to the gallery where they waited until after the National Anthem was played. Then Prince Albert would lead in the birthday child and, followed by the Queen and the Royal Family, they would process into the Throne Room for the ball. Despite such formal surroundings, these balls often resembled grand romps with the dancing master endeavouring to maintain order.

Beforehand, all the royal children had attended dancing classes, under Monsieur Deplanche, held either at the Palace or at Stafford House with some of the invited children. In this way they began friendships with little Sutherlands, Argylls, Devonshires, Russells, Pembrokes, Lytteltons and Seymours. Some dreaded the ball; 'feeling that the severe eye of the terrible Deplanche was upon us, we almost lost all enjoyment and nearly trembled to think that we were insufficiently throwing out our toes'.[2]

Unlike Monsieur Deplanche, the Queen did not hold herself aloof and critical but, since she loved dancing, entered into the occasion with gusto: 'it was rather nice,' wrote a maid of honour, 'to see the Queen fussing about getting partners for her little girls and arranging them in the quadrilles just like any of the other Mamas, and then taking a turn in the waltz with the Prince of Wales'.[3] She also helped children who found themselves in difficulties. When, without the faintest idea of how it was done, little Mary Gladstone tried to head a country dance, the Queen ran across and showed her how to pirouette.

The royal children were the stars of these children's balls, not because of their status but because they all danced so well and looked so pretty. Prince Arthur and Princess Louise were usually judged the loveliest, an opinion seconded by their mother who wrote to an absent daughter after one ball: 'Your sisters and little brothers looked very pretty, particularly Arthur and Louise.'[4] Even other children described Princess Louise as 'pretty'.[5]

During the parliamentary session, from February to the beginning of August, the Royal Family were based at Buckingham Palace, where they often saw other children. The afternoon games period would include anything from skating to hide-and-seek. Lord Ronnie Leveson-Gower noted in his diary that two or three afternoons a week he and Lord Lorne and Lord Archie Campbell would go to play with the princes at Buckingham Palace while their sisters went to play with the princesses. On Thursday, 2 March 1855 they played blind man's bluff in the study as it was raining, while on the 6th they went to Buckingham Palace for riding, followed by football and a game called 'prisoner's base', which they played in the garden as it was fine.[6]

Riding lessons were also taught with other children in the riding schools at Buckingham Palace and Windsor Castle. At fourteen months, Princess Louise was started on a quiet, sturdy, little pony, later progressing to Webster, on whom all the royal children learnt to ride. For a girl, riding was fraught with obstacles so it is not surprising that Princess Louise longed to be allowed to ride astride like a boy. Because she could only ride side-saddle, the full-skirted habit she wore was always gathering on the wrong side of the saddle; underneath the habit she wore loose, divided, skirt-like trousers fastened under the stirrup foot with a strap, which was always breaking so that the trousers would ride up and rub her legs raw. Nevertheless, Princess Louise became an excellent rider and she always tried to start the day with a morning ride wherever she was. She also learned carriage driving in the little barouche drawn by a shetland pony, which Queen Adelaide gave to the children.

One of Princess Louise's first public appearances was at Buckingham Palace on 20 February 1854, when in the early morning she stood with her family on the balcony, watching a line of drummer boys leading the march past of the Guards on their way to embarkation for the Crimea. On March 28th, war was formally declared. For the next few years the events of the Crimean War riveted the attention of the nation.

The royal children were brought up, in emulation of their parents and regardless of their sex, to have a special interest in all matters military; their mother thought of herself as head of the army, which fought and won battles for her foremost and the country second. Thus, any war was seen in personal terms by the Monarch and her family.

To make things interesting for his children, Prince Albert asked Lord Cardigan, who had led the Charge of the Light Brigade, down to Windsor. When the children met him, they plagued him with questions about the war. Prince Albert also had various charts on which the position of the armies was shown and he would explain the battles of the Alma, Balaclava and Inkerman to his attentive children and their friends. From their journal entries it appears that they thought of little else but the war: 'Snowing the whole day,' reads one such entry, 'The wind blows furiously from the East. I hope the soldiers in the Crimea have all got their winter coats.'[7]

The horrors of war were not hidden from the children. In May 1855, they accompanied the Queen when she awarded the first Crimean medals to injured soldiers, many coming forward on crutches or in bath chairs to receive their awards. Princess Louise also accompanied the Queen and her sisters on visits to Chatham Hospital, where the conditions were cramped and often dirty, insanitary and cheerless. Still, as the Queen pointed out: 'It is very gratifying to feel [that what] one can do easily, gives so much pleasure. It is one of the *few* agreeable privileges of our position & it certainly *repays* us for many disagreeable ones.'[8]

It was with increased zeal that Princess Louise returned to the task of knitting endless woollen stockings, scarves and mittens for the 'poor' soldiers in the Crimea. A constant supply of such items was sent forth from the schoolrooms at Buckingham Palace and Windsor; and at Christmas energies, which would normally have been expended on producing presents for the family, were divided equally beween family and soldiers at the front, for whom parcels were packed and sent out.

Christmas was always a busy period for Princess Louise: 'how much there is always to be done at Xmas time,' she wrote to a girlfriend, 'a tree for the poor people, one at New Year's Day for all the servants in this house, and presents to them besides, Ladies and Gentlemens presents, all our Family's presents, it is hard work but it pleases people, and that is our greatest pleasure.'[9]

She would have spent the previous months making these presents herself. 'No end of surprises of work',[10] as one member of the Household put it, such as drawings or an illustrated poem, pieces of needlework, crochet and cross stitch, even essays in composition. Princess Louise especially liked to give albums of pressed leaves or flowers, matched on the opposite page by her own minutely detailed drawings. Sometimes, the savings from the children's one shilling a week pocket money would not be enough to frame a picture or to set a piece of decorative work; a kindly tutor or governess would then appeal to a higher authority for assistance in making up the difference.

At Christmas, after exchanging presents in the family, they would walk over to the riding school where plum pudding and alms to the poor were distributed by Queen Victoria. They would also learn special pieces of music to perform or verses to recite on such festive occasions;

sometimes they joined together to put on a play in French or German. 'Tomorrow the Royal Children are to act their little play,' Eleanor Stanley informed her mother, 'Lady Caroline . . . says Princess Louise will look very pretty in one scene where she comes on as a fairy. It is the old story of Little Red Riding Hood, in German, improved, or, some people say, spoilt by . . . the German governess.'[11]

In her father's lifetime, Christmas was always spent at Windsor Castle. Although very old, it had been completely renovated by George IV. For the children and grandchildren who lived there, Windsor was memorable for its special sounds and smells and for the games they played over the years in the long corridors. The terraces looked out on stately trees in which rooks perched. The sounds which the children always associated with Windsor were the tramp, tramp of the sentinels and the caw, cawing of the rooks. Then 'there was a special Windsor Castle smell,' remembered one grandchild, '– old furniture kept very clean, [and] flowers'.[12] But what all the children remembered most about Windsor were the marvellous romps in the towers, staircases and long corridors, which were a paradise for hide-and-seek.

For the Princess Royal, these memories became all too soon part of the 'bright happy past' of childhood. On 25 January 1858, at the Chapel Royal, St James's, she was married to Prince Frederick William, 'Fritz', of Prussia, son and heir to that Prince of Prussia who had attended Princess Louise's christening as a refugee from Berlin, but who was now ruling Prussia on his brother's behalf. It was a grand dynastic alliance and the Palace was full of royal guests. Although the Princess Royal, who was only fifteen at the time, had become engaged in 1855, it had been kept secret from the rest of her brothers and sisters; surprisingly, they were not told until April 1856 and even then the Queen kept it a little longer from Princess Louise and Prince Arthur 'as they would not understand'.[13]

On the wedding day, Princess Louise, with her elder sisters, headed the bride's procession; all three were much moved by the occasion. After the wedding and a brief honeymoon at Windsor, all the children cried their eyes out when their eldest sister, so long their leader, departed for Germany. They were much happier a year later at the news of the birth of a son, Prince William, 'Willie', to Princess Frederick William in Germany. When it was announced Princess Louise cried out triumphantly, 'We are not Royal Children, we are uncles and aunts', and nine-year-old Prince Arthur ran round the Castle like a town crier announcing to any footmen he encountered: 'I am an uncle you know, I am an uncle.'[14]

Their nephew had one English aunt who was only twenty months older; this was Princess Beatrice, the 'Baby' of Queen Victoria's family, who had been born in 1857, when Queen Victoria was preoccupied with choosing a trousseau for the then Princess Royal. As the youngest of a large family, Princess Beatrice was thoroughly spoilt. She was a vivacious, outspoken, little girl. She always insisted that, since she was two years older than Prince William, he should call her 'Aunt'; this he was disinclined to do. Annoyed by her repeated reminders, he finally hurled out: 'Aunt Baby then!'[15]

The first years of Princess Beatrice's life coincided with a difficult period in Princess Louise's childhood. She was now ten-years-old and no longer the youngest daughter and she felt a certain sense of rivalry, compounded by jealousy, at all the attention Princess Beatrice was receiving. It seems, as a result, that Princess Louise became naughtier and started suffering from bad dreams and restless nights; the Queen had to arrange for either a governess or maid always to be near her, but it was Princess Beatrice who now slept in the night nursery with 'Turty', and Princess Louise felt excluded.

On a short visit to Penrhyn in Wales in the autumn of 1859, the Queen's instructions for their sleeping arrangements demonstrate the care taken with Princess Louise and the extent of the children's entourage, which consisted of two governesses, one tutor, five maids, two valets and a nursery cook. The princesses would need their own sitting room and a bedroom each; Princess Louise would have her maid sleep in her room and Fräulein Bauer had also to be near in case she needed help during the night; the other children, however, could sleep alone in their rooms unless there was a shortage of space when they could double up with their tutors or each other.

That Princess Louise was not easily managed was made more evident by the exemplary behaviour of Prince Arthur. In a letter written to Princess Frederick William at this period, the Queen is full of praise of Prince Arthur, 'Really the best child I ever saw'; of Princess Louise she could only say 'very naughty and backward, though improved and very pretty, and affectionate'.[16]

The Queen, however, was more preoccupied with Princess Alice's future. In 1860, Princess Alice emerged from the schoolroom to make her debut. During the spring and summer various eligible suitors presented themselves for inspection at Windsor and Buckingham Palace. One of them, Prince Louis of Hesse-Darmstadt, made a favourable impression and was asked back to stay at Windsor in November. The 'great Alician event', as her father described her engagement to Prince Louis, came off on November 30th to everyone's satisfaction; this time Princess Louise was included in those who were told the news. Thus, the family gathering at Windsor Castle for Christmas was made merrier than usual by the addition of 'our dear young lovers'. It was, however, but a happy prelude to the sad year of 1861.

On March 16th, the Duchess of Kent died at the age of seventy-six. Although other members of the scattered family had died during Princess Louise's lifetime, they had been distant both in terms of relationship and geography. 'Grandmama' Kent's death was the first to affect Princess Louise, for she loved her grandmother, and would miss the treats and little attentions she had always received from her.

This was the Queen's first attendance at a deathbed and her reaction was severe. Princess Louise's birthday two days later passed without the customary celebration at Buckingham Palace. The Prince eventually packed off his wife and children to stay first at Osborne and then at White Lodge, a comfortable house set in the middle of Richmond Park. Despite such tranquil surroundings, the Queen complained at the least noise or talking; she could not bear the children's high spirits and squabblings. They hardly saw her since she passed her time almost entirely alone. The death of their grandmother had affected all of them, but the children would soon have got over it and accepted their loss had not the Queen's continual expressions of grief meant that they lived through the next six months in an atmosphere of gloom and foreboding.

It was a miserable year for the overworked Prince: his wife was absorbed in her grief; eight-year-old Prince Leopold was very ill; the political situation in Prussia was causing him concern; and his health was affected by the cumulative strain. He began to have insomnia and to suffer from his old enemies: toothache, neuralgia and depression. On November 6th, telegrams arrived from Portugal announcing the illness and death from typhoid of two, much-loved Coburg cousins, King Pedro V and Prince Ferdinand. Princess Helena told the Archbishop of Canterbury six months later that her father 'felt so deeply the death of the King of Portugal', that she never saw him smile again.[17]

A week later the Prince caught a chill from attending a function at Sandhurst in the pouring rain. He was already worried about the Prince of Wales's dalliance with an actress, Nellie Clifden. The Prince was told by his father that 'no forgiveness could restore him to the state of innocence and purity which he had lost, and he must hide himself from the sight of God'.[18]

By November 27th, Prince Albert was clearly unwell and should have been confined to bed by the doctors, but he continued to struggle on with everyday duties. On December 2nd, Dr Jenner warned the Queen that the Prince would probably develop a fever. Although upset, she was determined not to alarm the Prince especially as he had said, 'that if he got fever he should die'. The Queen therefore cautioned Jenner 'not to let the Prince on any account suspect what he feared'.[19] By the 8th, Dr Jenner had confirmed the diagnosis as gastric fever but stressed that 'there was no cause for alarm'. Unfortunately, the constant repetition of this phrase resulted in the Queen forgetting that gastric fever was only another name for the much feared disease of typhoid, which was then usually fatal.

As far as Princess Louise was concerned, little of this drama penetrated the refuge of the Windsor schoolroom. She had not seen much of her father but then that was not unusual. Only on December 8th was it decided that the younger children were on no account to see him for fear of infection, and they should be told that he was unwell. On the morning of December 14th, the schoolroom buzzed with the news that the Prince of Wales had suddenly returned from Cambridge. The day before there had been a crisis in Prince Albert's condition and Princess Alice had telegraphed for the Prince of Wales, who had no idea of the dangerous condition of his father until his arrival at Windsor at 3 a.m. The public bulletins, now issued hourly, remained optimistic, but Prince Albert lay dying.

Princess Louise saw her father for the last time between eight and nine o'clock that evening before she went to bed. The Queen was worried that the children might agitate him but such fears were groundless: 'Alice came in and kissed him, and he took her hand. Bertie, Helena, Louise and Arthur came in one after the other and took his hand', the Queen later wrote in her Journal.[20] Princess Louise and Prince Arthur barely understood the gravity of the situation, which had been entirely kept from them.

Princess Louise saw her father lying down, his bed pushed out from the wall into the middle of the room. The Queen sat quietly at his side with Princess Alice. Sadly, Prince Albert 'was dozing and did not perceive them',[21] so that there was no real leave taking for Princess Louise to look back upon. She and Prince Arthur were soon taken away to bed, leaving the Prince of Wales and Princess Helena behind in the room.

Towards half past nine that evening the Queen 'had another burst of misery' and left to talk with the Dean of Windsor. Shortly afterwards, Princess Alice fetched the Queen back to the bedside where she took hold of Prince Albert's left hand and knelt by him. The Prince's breathing grew quieter and quieter as 'Two or three long but perfectly gentle breaths were drawn, the hand clasping mine, & . . . *all all* was over.'[22] It was a quarter past ten.

The Queen stood up, kissed the Prince's forehead and called out in a bitter, agonized cry, 'Oh! my dear Darling!', dropping on to her knees in numb despair, unable to utter a word or shed a tear. She was helped up and taken to the Red Room. The children ran into her arms to comfort and be comforted. Then the Gentlemen of the Household came in, knelt down and kissed the Queen's hand. She begged each one, 'You'll not leave me, you'll stay with me, to help me?', and other, similar, entreaties. Princess Alice sat on the floor at the Queen's side supporting her, Princess Helena stood sobbing violently behind her and the Prince of Wales stood silently at the foot of the sofa.[23] Later, the Queen had 'strength enough to go up to the Nursery to see her unconscious, sleepy children before she lay down to get 3 hours sleep. Princess Alice remained on a couch in her room.'[24] Both found it difficult to sleep and they talked and wept for a few hours.

It was not until later, on that morning of December 15th, that Princess Louise was told of her father's death. She then went, with 'Baby' and Prince Arthur, to see the Queen in bed, where she blurted out to her mother: 'Oh! why did not God take me. I am so stupid and useless.'[25]

CHAPTER IV

A House of Mourning

All over England Prince Albert's death made a deep impression. 'Never was there a more universal grief!'[1] Harriet Sneyd wrote from Staffordshire, while in London her sister reported, 'everybody almost is in deep mourning and *no* one seems inclined to be gay. The poor people and the shopkeepers all seem to feel it as a *personal* grief, as well as those in a higher class.'[2] The grief, however, was not so much for Prince Albert, never an especially popular figure, as for the Queen. At Windsor, the Household could not imagine how she would carry on without him. Neither could she, who never did anything without him and whose first words were always 'Ask the Prince'.

The death of her father was to alter the tenor of Princess Louise's life; the first of the many changes in her routine came with the evacuation of the Royal Family to Osborne for the Queen had agreed to go there. According to one maid of honour, King Leopold, then on his way to England, was such a hypochondriac that he believed he would catch Prince Albert's fever if he came to Windsor.[3] King Leopold was merely a man of his times: the fear of infection was universal; moreover, he was right to suspect Windsor since much of the blame for the Prince's fever lay with the Windsor drains.

The day of departure was fixed for December 18th when that atmosphere of muffled noise, grief and gloom, which had surrounded the Princess since the day of Prince Albert's death, was pierced by the hustle and bustle of packing and the loading of vans. Suddenly, at seven o'clock that evening, an order came to stop and, like mechanical toys in need of rewinding, everyone jerked to a standstill. The Queen had decided not to leave until the following morning. She could not bear to tear herself away, 'as long as she felt that He was still in the room near her,' the Queen explained to George Grey, 'She could not feel that she had lost His support!'[4] She was no better the next morning, so only the younger princesses were sent off to Osborne.

It was a sad return to their holiday home; there were only bare trees, beaten by wintery sea winds and set in a colourless landscape.

Osborne had that bleak appearance of a seaside resort caught in the wrong season: deserted, melancholy and grey. Princess Louise had never been to Osborne in the winter time; the white, airy house with its great glass windows looking to the sea had been built to withstand the heat of summer. When Fräulein Bauer asked Princess Beatrice what windows were made for, she received the immediate reply: 'To let in *wind*.'[5] Princess Louise also hated the cold; on her way north one year she wrote despairingly to a friend, 'We leave all the beautiful green trees and flowers, for snow and frost. "*Chacun à son gout*" – I prefer the former.'[6]

Princess Louise did not attend her father's funeral on December 23rd. The only members of the family present were the Prince of Wales, representing Queen Victoria as chief mourner, and Prince Arthur; the other sons being abroad. In those days funerals were usually male events as women were judged too weak to bear their grief in public. Even so, the Prince of Wales's eyes were red from weeping and 'poor little Prince Arthur' stifled 'his sobs by biting his pocket handkerchief' – both so overcome they had to be led gently away by two elderly Cabinet Ministers.[7]

This year, Christmas was passed at Osborne. The presents so carefully made were left for another, happier year; instead the staff received pictures of the Prince while the family were given lockets containing his hair. The Queen barely noticed the event, writing, 'What a year! What an Xmas! I hardly know it – and I hardly know the day of the week or the month! All pass alike in darkness.'[8]

She literally surrounded herself by darkness, the darkness of black mourning clothes; black blinds half drawn; and of black cloth draped over everything, even the pews in Osborne's local church. Throughout Queen Victoria's reign, the footmen continued to wear black armbands in memory of Prince Albert; even in rural areas beehives were draped with black crêpe. Children did not escape the 'shrouding in black' and Princess Louise was already more than accustomed to wearing black clothes; by the end of 1861 Court mourning had been declared on seven different occasions.

Immediately after the Prince's death, the Queen was so upset that she could not bear to sleep alone. It was arranged that either Princess Alice or Princess Louise would always sleep in the room with her, on a couch at the foot of her bed. This lasted until the beginning of February. Even then Princess Alice continued to bear the brunt of the

Queen's grief. 'What she has to bear,' wrote Lady Augusta Bruce, 'the anguish of the present and such anxiety!'[9] In the absence of an official private secretary, Princess Alice helped the Queen with the political correspondence which had previously been the Prince's responsibility. With the Queen pretty much *hors de combat*, Princess Alice now tried to manage everything but, in the process, she became 'thin and wan' from the hard work. 'This is indeed a house of mourning,' the experienced Colonel Phipps wrote, 'for never, I believe, did so irreparable a loss fall on a family. Already every hour questions arrive and decisions are sought – and there is no head to judge – no authority to decide.'[10]

It was undoubtedly a struggle for Princess Alice to accomplish everything herself. She did not, however, delegate some of the simpler tasks to Princess Helena; instead she chose Princess Louise. Victoria Stuart Wortley wrote, 'I am so glad to hear Princess Louise is now of great use helping Princess Alice; she has much the same character';[11] while Eleanor Stanley noticed how Princess Louise had suddenly grown up as a result of her father's death: 'Princess Louise strikes me as improved.'[12] Princess Alice found that Princess Helena, who had seemed the obvious choice as helpmate, tended to break down in tears, whereas Princess Louise, who had always been thought the more sensitive of the two, possessed the greater resilience.

Princess Louise also had to adjust to Queen Victoria's belief that life from henceforth would be one long homage to Prince Albert's memory. Everything must be done in strict accordance with her interpretation of his wishes; more significantly for her family, everything was to remain the same. Thus, because Prince Albert had planned a journey to Palestine and the Near East for the Prince of Wales, the Queen now insisted that he travel there. On 6 February 1862, he left on his journey and was replaced by Princess Frederick William, now the Crown Princess of Prussia, who arrived from Berlin on February 14th and was met by Princess Alice on the pier; both sisters cried a good deal. Yet General Grey told his wife, 'I . . . feel sure that the Queen will soon fancy the Princess Royal's manner too unconcerned. She *has* felt the death deeply – but has struggled against giving way to it.'[13]

Soon it became evident to the Queen's children that their style of mourning differed considerably from their mother's. She wished to emphasize the blank in their lives and to ensure that they never forgot it. They wished to incorporate the loss into their lives, continuing their former activities with only spontaneous pangs of remembrance. The two positions were irreconcilable and the Queen came to resent her family's inability to accept and adopt her attitude. The hushed voices and whispered conversations adopted in 1862 were demanded by the Queen of her children and Court for many years after the event which had inspired them. Even in the 1890s visitors and newcomers at Court remarked on the hushed tones, which they considered an intrinsic part of the atmosphere surrounding royalty. Few recalled that this had not existed before 1862.

Princess Louise had an open way of 'always talking about dear Papa', which the passage of years did nothing to change. She was intrigued by his fatalism and wondered how he had known he would die young. Unfortunately, her natural, affectionate way of chattering about her father was restricted by Queen Victoria's insistence upon her children adopting an unnaturally devout attitude whenever his name was mentioned. The Queen was already slipping into the habit of putting herself and her own comforts first. There was no one to check her now Prince Albert was dead. Only a few weeks before he died, he had told Queen Victoria: 'My advice to be less occupied with yourself and your own feelings is really the kindest I can give.'[14] Her daughters, sadly, had nobody to help them in coping with their mother's grief, which seemed to increase as the reason for it grew more remote.

On March 6th, the Royal Family left Osborne for what the Queen called the 'dreadful return' to Windsor, where they would remain until Easter. The reason for their return was that on the 15th the Queen would lay the foundation stone for the Mausoleum at Frogmore. It was not until she returned to Osborne at the beginning of April that Princess Louise was reunited with little Prince Leopold on his return from convalescence in the South of France. It was a great joy for her to have him home again but Queen Victoria, although pleased to see him, was full of trepidation at the thought of her lively nine-year-old son breaking into the hushed atmosphere of Osborne, a house which 'seems like Pompeii, the life suddenly extinguished'.[15] Before his arrival, Major Elphinstone had received instructions from the Queen 'to take care and make poor little Leopold understand that . . . he comes back to a House of Mourning and that his poor broken-hearted Mother cannot bear noise, excitement, etc'.[16]

The Queen soon admitted that her children were but the remaining 'poor half' of her life and 'their company . . . is no support'.[17] She used them as receptacles for her unbounding grief, pouring it out in every letter and on every occasion, in tones of remorseless self-pity and heedless of the effect upon her younger children. Their problems were secondary *always* to her own grief.

This period was a trying time for all of them, but especially for the younger ones like Princess Louise. As the immediacy of their grief waned, the Queen's efforts to crush their rebounding spirits strengthened. Even the pet of the family, four-year-old Princess Beatrice, whose childish prattle amused the Queen, slowly had the life crushed out of her. 'I had such a funny thought today,' she told Mrs Bruce, 'just for my own amusement, but it turned out an *unproper* thought so I would not let it think.'[18] Not surprisingly, she began to lose her endearing charm and turned into a solemn, quiet, little girl.

It was, of course, an onerous task for the Queen to supervise the education and upbringing of the younger children on her own. There were many trivial domestic matters which Prince Albert had always overseen, but which now she had to cope with alone. Luckily, she had simply to follow the educational curriculum initiated by Prince Albert. A blind may have been drawn on social activities for the royal children but lectures and readings by guest speakers were permissible, as the Prince had always considered them an essential part of their education. Thus, Professor Max Müller from Oxford lectured them on the 'Origins of Language'. Used to teaching undergraduates rather than thirteen-year-olds, he started by tracing the primeval languages to one source; not surprisingly, the children preferred Professor Owen's lecture on 'Fishes' and Princess Louise thoroughly enjoyed a lecture on 'Chemistry'.

Problems inevitably arose. The first schoolroom dispute concerned 'Rolly's' successor as French governess, one Madame Hocédé. Queen Victoria had found her unreliable; somewhat reluctantly, for she was loath to part with anyone 'who had lived with us in former, happy times', the Queen had to pension her off. She had discovered that Madame Hocédé had been giving Princess Helena and Princess Louise 'unsuitable books', by which she meant novels, to read. When questioned about this, Princess Louise loyally tried to protect her 'Govie' by claiming she had not been given the novel, but had found it lying about. The Queen, who treasured truthfulness above all qualities, was very upset and blamed Madame Hocédé. 'I have terrible governess troubles,' she confided to the Crown Princess, 'I find out . . . that she has done Louise a terrible deal of harm, made her deceitful and has disobeyed orders.'[19]

Holidays, too, were divided up in quite a different way. Princess Louise celebrated her fourteenth birthday quietly at Windsor; instead of Osborne in May for Queen Victoria's birthday, they went to Balmoral where it rained on their arrival and for many days thereafter. The Queen was continually reminded of Prince Albert and convulsed with grief: 'the agonised sobs as I crawled up [the stairs] with Alice and Affie! The stags heads – the rooms – blessed, darling Papa's room – then his coats – his caps – kilts – all, all convulsed my poor shattered frame!'[20]

The bustle in the mornings, when the ponies and dogs, ghillies and pipers mingled with the family before everyone set off on their various expeditions, was no more. Princess Louise's drawing master, William Leitch, noticed the difference from the year before. Now 'the whole place is changed. Everything very quiet and still . . . All is gone with him who is the life and soul of it.'[21] It was a miserable holiday: Queen Victoria felt her loss more here than anywhere else, Princess Alice went to bed with an awful cold and Princess Louise had a nasty stye on her eye. It was with some relief that they left Balmoral at the beginning of June to prepare for Princess Alice's wedding, on 1 July 1862, at Osborne.

It was only because the wedding had been planned by Prince Albert that it was not now postponed. The ceremony, which began at one o'clock, was in great contrast to the Princess Royal's wedding, which had been a formal state occasion. The dining room was converted into a chapel and entirely draped in black; the Archbishop of Canterbury read the service with tears pouring down his cheeks. 'This poor unhappy marriage,' wrote Queen Victoria, 'is more like a funeral than a wedding!'[22] Princess Louise started the day in black, changed into her white bridesmaid's dress for the wedding and plunged back into black directly after the bride and groom left on honeymoon. It seemed to Princess Louise as if a chapter in her life was over; for Princess Alice had done much to encourage her and bring her on.

Princess Helena had been confirmed earlier that year and so was considered to be out of the schoolroom. She could thus be groomed to succeed her sister as the Queen's right hand. This left Princess Louise even more isolated. Prince Arthur would leave the schoolroom in September, for his own establishment at Blackheath; Princess Beatrice was only five, so Prince Leopold was her nearest companion but, though fond of him, there is a considerable difference between a nine-year-old boy and a fourteen-year-old girl.

Nevertheless, Princess Louise did have something to look forward to that autumn. She was going on a long journey to Germany via Brussels. Before he died, Prince Albert had decided, sight unseen, that Princess Alexandra of Schleswig-Holstein-Sonderburg-Glücksburg, daughter of Prince Christian, heir to the Danish throne, would make the best wife for the Prince of Wales. However, the Queen wanted to meet Princess Alexandra or 'Alix' as she was usually called, before the Prince of Wales actually proposed. The meeting was fixed for September 3rd at Brussels, where the Royal Family stayed with Uncle Leopold at Laecken Palace.

Still in deep mourning, the children had to confine themselves to the Palace grounds. At half past one, the Queen with Princesses Louise and Helena went down to the drawing room for a brief meeting with Prince and Princess Christian and their two daughters. There was only time for a short, rather formal introduction before luncheon. But, afterwards, Princess Louise was able to chat with Princess Alix and her sister while their parents talked alone with Queen Victoria. Princess Louise was charmed with Princess Alix; she was so pretty and sweet and not at all stiff or shy.

The next day the Royal Family travelled to Reinhardsbrunn in the Duchy of Gotha, arriving on September 6th. It was here that they received the news from Brussels of the Prince of Wales's engagement to Princess Alexandra. It was arranged that she would visit them in England in November, by which time the children would have settled in after their long holiday.

Eight miles outside the town of Gotha lies the childhood home of Prince Albert, the Schloss of Reinhardsbrunn, hidden in the midst of forest, where the family stayed. Here, Prince Albert had collected the various specimens of plant and rock which he had used to start the children's museum at Coburg. Princess Louise carried on the tradition and gathered many flowers and plants to take back to England. Such outdoor occupations helped her to withstand the stifling atmosphere caused by the Queen's continued attempts to dampen her children's spirits. The Queen made it painfully obvious that she could not endure any chatter at meals and complained, 'what I suffer often at dinner when jokes go on and my heart bleeds!'[23]

From Reinhardsbrunn the Royal Family travelled to Coburg to see

Duke Ernest and to visit the Rosenau, the summer house outside Coburg in which Prince Albert had been born. They were enchanted with their father's small garden, so like their own at Osborne. Finally, on October 16th, the Queen tore herself and the family away from 'dear, dear Coburg' which was 'so full of precious recollections' and they travelled home, reaching Osborne by October 26th.

Having been away for nearly two months, Princess Louise struggled to settle back into the routine of life at Osborne. She hardly saw Princess Helena, who was helping Queen Victoria. Princess Louise felt completely left out and ignored by the family; even 'Baby' Beatrice had their mother to herself for an hour every morning. Worse was to come. Princess Alix was arriving at Osborne for a three-week visit on November 5th. The day before, Princess Louise learnt that only Princess Helena, who had a bad cold, and Prince Leopold, as the only male member of the family at home, were to meet Princess Alix at the pier. Furthermore, Princess Helena alone was asked by the Queen to do the honours on her behalf and look after Princess Alix during her stay. It seemed so unfair to Princess Louise, and, in the heat of the moment, she complained bitterly. Queen Victoria gave Princess Louise short shrift and told her that, since she was still in the schoolroom, she could not possibly dine with the party on the night of Princess Alix's arrival.

Princess Alix arrived at about half past eight on the night of the 5th. Nine-year-old Prince Leopold felt overwhelmed by his important role in the proceedings. He had agonized over the problems of simultaneously introducing himself, presenting a bouquet and greeting the beautiful Princess; but, before he could do anything, the pretty, graceful Princess stepped lightly on shore, took the great representative of the House of England in her arms and kissed him.[24] Everyone at Osborne fell in love with her, especially the children, who hero-worshipped her. Princess Alix did her best to slip away to visit Princess Louise in the schoolroom and to suggest walks with her in the afternoon.

Years later, Princess Alexandra described 'the . . . alarming character of her visit to Osborne "to be inspected" a few months before marriage . . . She had not even a lady in waiting and was "terribly frightened at the process".'[25] Left alone at Osborne by her father at the Queen's request, Princess Alix clung to Princess Louise and Prince Leopold. Used to the company of her own younger brother and sisters, she found these two members of the English Royal Family by far the best company, for with them she could relax.

Even the Queen seemed to notice the beneficial effect of Princess Alix's presence on Princess Louise. She wrote to the Crown Princess that Princess Louise 'behaves as well as possible . . . and keeps quietly, and without grumbling, in her own place'.[26] It was the more astute Lady Augusta Bruce who sensed the reason for Princess Louise's improved behaviour: 'Dear P[rincess] L[ouise] is very darling at present. She is so happy to be a little made of.'[27]

For Queen Victoria, however, the forthcoming marriage loomed as a threat. As the family became more excited by the preparations, she became more depressed. She asked the Crown Princess to do the honours in her place and to help her in 'checking noise, and joyousness in my presence'. The reason for her attitude was that she felt guilty if she or anyone else enjoyed themselves for it meant they had forgotten Prince Albert: 'I shall be unable to join in family dinners, when the sad part gets overlooked for the moment and high spirits of youth get the better of everything else.'[28]

When Princess Alexandra and the Danish contingent arrived at Gravesend on March 7th, they were welcomed by vast crowds. Her reception by Londoners was equally ecstatic. Princess Louise, with her brothers and sisters, had planned to watch the procession with 'Uncle George' Cambridge at Gloucester House. The Queen, however, refused to allow any of her children to go to London since it would constitute an appearance in public. In spite of their fervent pleas that they would not be appearing in public but only peeping out from behind windows, the Queen ruled that they must all remain at Windsor. There was, as one lady-in-waiting put it, 'Great grief'.[29]

It was late that evening by the time the Prince of Wales and Princess Alix reached Windsor Castle; yet Princess Louise and Princess Helena had long kept vigil at the main door and rushed out into the darkness and pouring rain to welcome them, leaving the Queen and Princess Alice, who was about to be confined with her first child, inside at the top of the staircase. Princess Alix jumped out of the carriage and kissed the young Princesses before being led inside by the Prince of Wales to greet the Queen, who was in low spirits, missing Prince Albert terribly: 'all were there with their Husbands. Where was Hers?'[30]

The next two days were crammed with family parties and the bustle of preparations. Princess Louise was even allowed to help the Crown Princess arrange the wedding presents for exhibition. Then, on Tuesday, March 10th, the wedding was held at St George's Chapel, Windsor.

Eight days later the Queen would record Princess Louise's birthday with the words 'Today is poor Louise's 15th birthday. These days are so sad now.'[31] For once, however, Princess Louise felt anything but poor and sad. She was thrilled with her new sister-in-law and she thoroughly enjoyed the wedding and the accompanying festivities. For the first time she was allowed to wear her grandmother Luise Coburg's beautiful pearl necklace which everyone had admired; to be noticed, especially on such an occasion when the focus of attention was naturally on the bride, was an added and unusual pleasure for her.

The advent of Princess Alix, who now assumed her official title of the Princess of Wales, did much to improve the quality of Princess Louise's life. Having come from a warm-hearted and loving family, the Princess of Wales brought from the first a spirit of loving intimacy to her relations with the English Royal Family. She also brought back glamour to the Court by her manner and character, and by her taste in clothes. Since Queen Victoria was notoriously uninterested in her own clothes and those of her children, it was from this sister-in-law that Princess Louise learnt the rudiments of dress sense. In later years Princess Louise was, after the Princess of Wales, the member of the Royal Family consistently described as the most 'elegantly turned out'.

The Prince and Princess of Wales seemed so happy and in love that Princess Louise was much affected by them. In her letters, the Princess of Wales addressed her as 'My own dearest Louise' and begged her to 'think sometimes of the sister who loves you'.[32] Princess Louise felt that she had found the perfect older sister; one whose position ensured that she would never desert her by going to live abroad. Anxious to please her, Princess Louise sent the Princess of Wales little presents of china pugs, after she had confessed to liking them, and saved her best drawings and needlework for her.

William Frith had been commissioned to paint the group wedding portrait and when Princess Helena and Princess Louise sat for him, he thought 'they would be considered most charming girls anywhere; none of their photographs do them justice. The difficulty is to keep in mind in whose presence you are – they laugh and talk so familiarly, and still sit well.' While he was working, the Princess of Wales, the Crown Prince and Princess and Prince Willie of Prussia with Princess Beatrice came in 'and of all the rows! those children shouting, laughing, and romping with the Princesses'.[33]

Unfortunately, the wedding had done nothing to change Queen

Victoria's attitude. On their second public appearance since the death of their father, the Royal Family attended the unveiling of a statue of Prince Albert in the Royal Horticultural Gardens, in the summer of 1863. Mary Gladstone, aged sixteen, recalled the event in her diary: 'the Royal Family, all looked so grave'.[34] The Queen would not have agreed; on the contrary, she thought the children displayed 'unseemly' high spirits unwarranted by such a solemn occasion. They were told the ceremony was 'not one to be joked about, for of course it was very painful to Mama'.[35]

On 15 November 1863, the Princess of Wales's father succeeded to the throne as King Christian IX. He immediately found himself at war over the Duchies of Schleswig and Holstein with the Crown Princess's father-in-law, King Wilhelm of Prussia. Bismarck, Prussia's new Chancellor, had taken the opportunity to gain more territory for Prussia as a first step in his plan for Prussian dominance over Germany and Europe.

This crisis immediately made itself felt in the Queen's family. The Queen was strongly pro-Prussian because, as she told Mr Gladstone, Prince Albert had supported them. She spoke about this 'with intense earnestness and said she considered it a legacy from him'.[36] Thus, when some of her family disagreed with her, she took it as a direct personal attack on the Prince. The Crown Prince and Princess were also then at Windsor; Queen Victoria reported to King Leopold that 'Fritz is very violent' in support of Prussia, though 'Vicky is sensible' about it.[37] Since the Prince and Princess of Wales were rabid about Denmark, discussions between the two camps inevitably evolved into heated arguments. By the end of November, the topic was taboo as 'the Queen became so worried, that she has had to stop talk on the subject'.[38] Other members of the family, however, took up the cudgels. Princess Helena was pro-Prussia, but Princess Louise wholeheartedly Danish; not for political reasons but because it tore at her heart to see her 'beloved Alix', who was expecting a baby, weeping and worrying about her family and their probable defeat. As a result, Queen Victoria considered Princess Louise more naughty and 'contrary' than ever.

Princess Louise, having found a legitimate outlet for her rebellious spirits, now immersed herself in politics for the first time. She would study the newspapers every day in the schoolroom; at luncheon she would pick up the latest information on the war; then, in the afternoon, full of self-importance, she would rush over to confer with her Danish ally, Sybil Grey, who was General Grey's eldest daughter. February 22nd was 'a sad day' for the two Danish supporters, as Sybil Grey recorded: 'Princess L[ouise] called. The Danes are beaten but will not surrender. Have tea in the nursery.'[39] However, their absorption in the war had already been interrupted unexpectedly by the premature birth of an heir to the Prince of Wales.

The baby Prince, christened Albert Victor but always called 'Eddy', had been born on January 8th with a complete absence of ceremony. None of the seven doctors, 'who had been quarreling for months',[40] was there; in the absence of a cradle and clothes, the wadding in which Miss Knollys's jewels had been packed was used to wrap up the babe. When the news reached Osborne, the Queen and Princess Helena immediately started for Windsor Castle. Although downcast at being left behind, Princess Louise was thrilled to be an aunt again, as Lucy Lyttelton recorded when she dined with the Household: 'the evening much helped by Prss Louise showing Miss Bowater and me her photographs, and laughing and talking gaily'.[41]

A few weeks later, the Queen commissioned a christening cup from Mr Corbould, the royal drawing master. He had just completed a painting of Prince Albert, represented as a Christian knight clad in medieval armour, sheathing his sword; the cup was a version of this picture, in the form of a statuette of Prince Albert. On February 16th, Queen Victoria recorded in her Journal that she had been to see Corbould and that 'Louise has also been helping & shows great taste'.[42] The cup was finally given to Prince Eddy at Christmas and Princess Louise was not a little pleased to have had a hand in its construction, especially since the Waleses were delighted with it.

Edward Corbould was the first friend Princess Louise made from outside Court circles. He was a 'tall, fine-looking man',[43] and she came to value him greatly. Prince Albert had offered him the post of teaching his children and 'Cobby', as they called him, was an immediate success mainly due to his belief in 'free' drawing with its emphasis on ideas and imagination rather than technique.

It was owing to him that Princess Louise learnt to draw so well and to observe the people about her, quickly committing their likeness to paper in a hasty but accurately characterized sketch. He suggested that, instead of sitting unoccupied through dreary evenings, she should use the time as part of a secret drawing class. Eventually, Princess Louise became known for never appearing without a little sketch pad or scrap of paper and pencil. Mr Corbould thought she 'possessed artistic talent in a striking degree from an early age',[44] while the Princess always claimed she owed to him her interest in art, which became 'the foundation of all things' in her life. She kept up with him long after he had finished teaching the youngest royal child. Years later, she wrote, 'You have been one of my *few true* friends that I have looked up to all my life and from whom I have . . . learnt much besides art.'[45]

In the nineteenth century, drawing and sketching were fashionable pursuits for otherwise unoccupied young ladies. They drew and painted to chronicle their lives; their draughtsmanship was excellent, their eye for colour and detail often superb. Today, many of them would not be considered amateurs but, in those days, no lady would wish to be considered anything else. Princess Louise inherited an artistic talent from both sides of her family; from Queen Victoria she inherited a gift for a quick, lively likeness boldly executed, but it was from her father that she learnt to take art seriously. He enjoyed drawing but, when he wished to learn etching or modelling, he turned to the top professional artists of the day to ensure he was properly taught. Princess Louise was given her first crayons and colouring box at three years of age and started regular lessons at four. And, according to Frederick Leighton, the Crown Princess's and Princess Louise's work compared favourably with that of professional artists.

Whereas Edward Corbould encouraged Princess Louise's originality, William Leitch emphasized technique. Leitch was a watercolourist much influenced by Turner and he taught Princess Louise the principles of composition and of light and shade during their expeditions to places of scenic beauty. He described one such expedition at Balmoral: 'H.M. sitting in the middle of a country road, with a great rough stone out of the river to put her paint box on; Lady Churchill holding an umbrella over the Queen's head and I seated near her so that she could see what I was doing. The Princess Louise was on my right hand, sitting on a big stone, and working away at her drawing, and the Highlander – . . . John Brown – with the pony in the background . . . There was lots of talking and laughing and nearly 2 hours passed away very soon.'[46]

It was their mutual love of sketching and of being outdoors which brought Princess Louise and her mother together. In the past, the Queen had never spent much time with this daughter. Indeed, the Queen admitted she did not find the adolescent mind an easy one to understand. She was, therefore, rather surprised to find how much she enjoyed these sketching expeditions with Princess Louise. After several artists had praised her daughter's abilities, the Queen began to take her work seriously. As she told the Crown Princess, Princess Louise 'is decidedly cleverer (odd though she is) than Lenchen and has a wonderful talent for art'.[47]

Something of a perfectionist and apt to be extremely self-critical, Princess Louise was always very humble about her work. When sending Louisa Knightley a present of a picture, she added the following note: 'Here I send you this unhappy little drawing. It is not worth for anything but to be kept in your drawer to look at it there sometimes and think of the one who failed doing it as she wished.'[48]

Unfortunately, in 1864, the Princess's artistic activities were curtailed by severe illness. She had never been an especially healthy child, being increasingly prone to catching colds and coughs. Like her brothers and sisters, she had succumbed to scarlet fever, measles and chicken pox. Much more debilitating were the constant headaches, acute neuralgia, giddiness and fainting spells from which she suffered as a girl. The Queen even retained a German doctor, Doctor Bulen, specifically to treat her: 'he is quite necessary to Princess Louise', the Queen informed General Grey, 'for some years'.[49]

The Victorian attitude to sickness was very different from our own: it was then fashionable to be ailing, so that sickness and delicacy in a woman were considered attractive features; robust health was looked upon as vulgar. Victorian women often took to their sofas with an imaginary illness; some in order to escape further childbearing, others through boredom. Partly as a consequence, illness in young girls was often diagnosed and treated perfunctorily by male doctors as 'hysteria', regardless of the symptoms.

In the winter of 1864, Princess Louise had a series of colds and was laid up with sickness and severe headache. During the autumn visit to Balmoral, her condition suddenly deteriorated. She had been complaining of headaches ever since her arrival but now they had become incapacitating. Sybil Grey heard that 'she can't ride, fond as she is of it, for it shakes her so. She can't draw though there is nothing she likes so well, nor read. No noise. Scarcely the rustling of a silk gown can she bear nor the light either and I afraid she is vy. unwell.'[50] Doctor Christison, an Edinburgh physician, was sent for and he duly diagnosed neuralgia, with no treatment apart from rest. Neuralgia was the

Victorian female illness *par excellence*; the Queen and all her daughters suffered badly from it. The Queen's belief in fresh air, open windows in winter and drives in open carriages in the middle of a downpour, even a blizzard, often led to attacks of neuralgia and colds for her daughters.

When Princess Louise's condition worsened, Dr Sieveking, physician to the Prince and Princess of Wales, was sent for on October 19th. He decided she was seriously ill and diagnosed 'meningitic complications', in this case a euphemism for tubercular meningitis, which often led to infertility in adolescent girls. Princess Louise was told to rest in a darkened room, since the light hurt her eyes. Thus, she was confined to her room and the Royal Family's departure from Balmoral was further delayed until October 28th. Even then, the poor girl was so unwell that she had to be carried off the train at Carlisle, where she remained overnight. Once at Windsor Castle she was put to bed, where it was not until December that she was able to move her head without pain, and to receive the odd visitor in her bedroom.

Her illness had naturally worried her mother, but, once Princess Louise was out of danger, Queen Victoria was able to view her condition more philosophically. With a haemophiliac son, whose health was a constant source of worry, she tended to minimize illness unless it threatened life. Her concern was whether Princess Louise would ever be fit enough to become her companion when Princess Helena married. She told General Grey in a written memo that 'Princess Louise's illness has made Princess Helena almost my only companion – and the Physicians declare, that with her [Princess Louise's] peculiar constitution of brain, I can never rely on her as an assistant or a companion.'[51]

Sighing over the perversity of nature, the Queen noted that, even taking into account her ill-health, Princess Louise possessed all the attributes so esteemed then. She was 'so handsome (she is so very much admired) and is so graceful and her manners so perfect in society, so quiet and lady-like, and then she has such great taste for art'. But Princess Louise was not the daughter for whom Queen Victoria now had to find a husband; and Princess Helena, although in perfect health, was not the Queen's most marriageable daughter: 'Poor dear Lenchen, though most useful and active and clever and amiable, does not improve in looks and has great difficulties with her figure and her want of calm, quiet, graceful manners.'[52]

During the autumn, while Princess Louise had been so ill, the search for a husband for Princess Helena had been going forward. Before his death Prince Albert had left a memorandum on the subject, which assumed that Princess Helena would marry at the age of eighteen or nineteen. This presented the Queen with a dilemma; she had to choose between keeping her unmarried daughter at home, as she wished, or obeying the Prince's plan for a foreign marriage. In the event she decided that Princess Helena should marry, but on condition that she and her future husband lived with the Queen. While Princess Louise lay in her darkened room, the Queen and Princess Helena were occupied in scouring Europe for a Protestant prince who would accept this proviso.

Although Princess Louise continued to suffer from headaches, by August she was well enough to accompany the Queen to Coburg where they were to meet a candidate. The Royal Family made their headquarters at the Schloss Rosenau just outside Coburg. The peaceful town was overflowing with Royalties, courtiers and their suites, as all nine of the Queen's children were there for the unveiling of a statue of their father. The weather was extremely warm, which agreed with Princess Louise, and she felt much better than she had done for over a year. In a letter home she described how much she was enjoying her stay in Germany: 'in such a lovely place, and every spot associated with my father's youth'.[53]

Princess Louise loved staying at the Rosenau, as it was homely, informal and somehow different. For a start, it possessed only one staircase which everyone, be they guests, the Queen, or servants, had to use; then all the rooms opened on to each other and, instead of passages, there were huge, cool, dark landings lit both night and day by candles. But, undoubtedly, the most extraordinary part of the cold Schloss was the glorious loft, which ran under the length of the roof. It was a high, shaded place and thrillingly haunted by bats. Whenever Princess Louise and her brothers and sisters went up there in the daylight, the bats would be dangling in neat rows from the rafters; if disturbed by a thrown ball, they would whirl about noiselessly.

It was at the Rosenau that Princess Louise began a lifelong habit of sketching from windows. The view from her room was glorious and the air smelt delicious, scented by the masses of roses, pinks and delphiniums, which surrounded the Schloss. The tranquillity of such surroundings did little to soothe the Queen, however. Having defeated Denmark, Prussia had now concluded an agreement with Austria whereby they divided the Duchies between them: Schleswig to Prussia and Holstein to Austria. Prussia's claimant to them, the Duke of Augustenburg, was roughly pushed aside by Bismarck and made stateless. This naturally upset Queen Victoria, for not only was the Duchess of Augustenburg her niece but Prince Christian, whom she had come to vet for Princess Helena, was the Duke's younger brother.

The Queen had invited Prince Christian and the Duchess to meet her at the Rosenau at the end of the month, but she was asked to hold the meeting earlier because Bismarck had been threatening to arrest the Duke and he would hardly have 'the audacity to lay violent hands on the Prince [Duke] of A while his wife is visiting the Queen'.[54]

On paper, Prince Christian did not appear to possess the qualities which would appeal to any romantically inclined princess. He seemed older than his thirty-five years and was rather bald and stolid. Even the Queen wished 'he looked younger'.[55] But, as a stateless prince, he was the only candidate who would positively welcome the Queen's condition that he make England his home. Her nerves 'quite shaken' by the end of the visit, Queen Victoria was thankful to leave Coburg and remove to the peace and cool, autumnal air of Balmoral.

By the middle of October, however, even the Highlands could offer her little refuge from the family row over the marriage prospects she had arranged for Princess Helena. By announcing that a marriage was being negotiated between Princess Helena and Prince Christian, the Queen set off a fuse which burned through her family during the autumn and, by the time of Prince Christian's first visit in December, had severely strained the loyalty which bound them together.

The Crown Princess reacted favourably to the idea of Prince Christian as a future brother-in-law, since she knew and liked him. The Prince and Princess of Wales, however, were hurt that the Queen could even have considered him when his Augustenburg family were the sworn enemies of Denmark. Prince Alfred and Princess Alice supported them. Princess Louise felt torn between the two camps. While her sympathies naturally lay with the Waleses, she felt unable to abandon Princess Helena, whose fate might well be her own in the not too distant future. She confided to a friend how sad these days were for her.

After Princess Helena ignored his attempts at peace-making, the Prince of Wales declared his side of the family could 'not take part from henceforth in any family matters'.[56] It was thus in a state of some tension that, at the end of November, the family went their separate ways: the Waleses to Marlborough House and everyone else to Windsor Castle where Princess Alice, who had been with the family at Balmoral, now took up the fight.

The Queen's way of dealing with opposition was to disparage her opponent. Thus of Princess Alice, the beloved daughter, who had supported her through her early widowhood at great cost to her own health, Queen Victoria now wrote 'Alice is vy unamiable . . . sharp, grand and wanting to have everything her own way'.[57] Similarly, when Princess Louise dared to voice a differing opinion, the Queen would immediately classify her as 'trying', 'difficult' or 'wayward'.

Yet for the Prince of Wales, who had never had the Queen's confidence, and for Princess Alice, who had previously had it but now saw it transferred to Princess Helena, it was a galling prospect to imagine an otherwise unoccupied Prince Christian enjoying a more powerful influence over the Queen than they had. It may be thought that the Royal Family were overreacting to the spectre of Prince Christian as the power behind the English throne but, at the time, they were deeply concerned about the Queen's attitude to her public duties; her reluctance to appear in public was increasing, and the growing republican movement at home and the wars abroad were fraying her nerves. She needed someone to lean on and was just as likely to chose Prince Christian as anyone else, having consistently rejected the Prince of Wales.

However, despite the campaign to prevent Prince Christian's visit to England, he duly arrived at four o'clock on December 1st at Windsor. Sybil Grey, whose informant was Princess Louise, recorded that 'he is to propose this evening I believe. Princess Helena has only seen him for one night – at the Rosenau . . . The Press has got hold of Princess Helena's marriage – though it is not really settled as it is just possible they may *not* fall in love with each other, as they are expected to do!!!'[58]

Nonetheless, that evening Prince Christian did propose and was accepted by Princess Helena. It was a better fate than remaining unmarried and no other suitors had appeared to claim her. As for Prince Christian, he found himself in a most uncomfortable position for the Prince of Wales initially refused to meet him and threatened to boycott his wedding. It took an appeal by Princess Helena to the diplomatic General Grey to bring about a rather stiff *rapprochement*

Princess Alice, Princess Helena and
Princess Louise at Osborne, July 1858.

Carte de visite of Princess
Louise, aged 12, 1 March
1861.

Lord Cardigan at Windsor, 1855, describing the Charge of
the Light Brigade.
Left to right:

Prince Alfred	Prince Arthur
Prince of Wales	Princess Royal
Lord Cardigan	Princess Alice
Prince Albert	Duchess of Wellington
Princess Helena	Lord Rivers
Princess Louise	

*Dancing lesson with
M. Deplanche*, n.d., pencil.

Prince Albert's death:
Princess Louise's dream of her parents'
reunion in heaven, 10 February 1862,
watercolour; and mourning him with
Queen Victoria at Windsor,
28 March 1862.

between them, although the Princess of Wales continued to keep her distance.

Upon being told of her sister's engagement by the Queen, Princess Louise suggested that 'Lenchen like Herodias should ask for B[ismarck]'s head' as a wedding present from the King of Prussia. The Queen wrote to the Crown Princess: 'She is so very amusing and original.'[59]

Princess Louise found it less easy to be amusing and original when she considered her sister's fate. To be married off to an unknown, middle-aged, balding man is a horrific idea to a romantic seventeen-year-old girl. The Queen did not help by remarking, 'We think him looking older this time even . . . And his manners and movements are so old.'[60] Nevertheless he was a 'worthy, good sort of man, of no brilliant talents'.[61] It was not a description which inspired Princess Louise to look forward to her own marriage.

The first change came on Princess Helena's birthday; as her last unmarried birthday, it was the first to be celebrated, since Prince Albert's death, by a tea dance held in the Orangery at Windsor for the servants' children. Louisa Bowater was amazed to find that Princess Louise, Prince Arthur and Prince Leopold were allowed to attend since they were suffering from whooping cough. The Queen looked on – 'an immense step gained' – while her children danced with the servants until twenty to eight. They dined with the Queen at nine o'clock and 'dear little Princess Beatrice . . . proposed "dear Na's health (her name for Princess Helena) and many happy returns of the day, as it is her last birthday at home"', a sentiment which was received with shrieks of laughter, resulting in a simultaneous burst of whooping-cough from Princess Louise, Prince Arthur, and Prince Leopold. 'It was a horrid shame, but it was impossible to help laughing!'[62]

Just before Princess Helena's wedding, Prussia launched an attack on her former ally Austria; the ensuing war divided the English Royal Family even more deeply. Prince Louis of Hesse joined the Austrian Army, while the Crown Prince of Prussia commanded the Prussian troops in Silesia against the Austrians. Despite the fact that two of her daughters were, to all intents and purposes, at war with each other and unable to attend, the Queen decided to continue with the marriage on Thursday July 5th.

At breakfast on the wedding day, the Belgian Minister received news of the defeat of the Austrians at the Battle of Sadowa and of serious injuries to the brother of the new Queen of the Belgians, who was present. Queen Victoria, however, decreed that she should not be told until after the wedding was over. Archbishop Longley, who took the service in the family chapel at Windsor, felt rather nervous, 'knowing as I did, all the feelings that were stirred from the depths in the family circle on that occasion . . . His [Prince Christian's] position will be a peculiarly difficult one.'[63]

After Princess Helena had left on her honeymoon abroad, the Royal Family travelled down to Osborne. From there, on July 20th, Princess Louise wrote in despair: 'I feel low and sad and sit in my room and cry which you know is not a usual thing for me.'[64] Feeling lonely and misunderstood, Princess Louise believed for a while in that summer of 1866 that nothing would ever improve.

CHAPTER V

The Queen's Right Hand

'I have too much anxiety, too much worry and work,' Queen Victoria wrote on 21 July 1866, a fortnight after Princess Helena's wedding, 'and I miss Lenchen terribly as I can't speak *à coeur ouvert* to Louise (though she does her best) as she is not discreet, and is very apt to take things always in a different light to me.'[1] The Queen always considered any form of change irksome and now, as her 'right hand' for the last four years started a new career, she automatically turned to Princess Louise.

The Queen had grown accustomed to relying upon her daughters for help. She operated a ratchet system of employment complete with its own hierarchy. In 1861, Princess Alice had been at the top as 'right hand' with Princess Helena occupying the notch below as part-time clerk. With Princess Alice's marriage, Princess Helena had moved up and Princess Louise was shunted into the number two place. Now, Princess Louise moved up to occupy the vacant top position. Unfortunately, as Princess Beatrice was too young to help, she alone worked for the Queen. To make matters worse, the Queen did not believe Princess Louise possessed those qualities desirable for the post, as she wanted another Princess Helena who was frightened of displeasing her. Princess Helena was an obedient daughter who had always put 'Mama' and 'Mama's wishes' first: she was an 'Angel in the House'.

This image of the dutiful daughter came to symbolize Victorian femininity. Submission to the will of their parents was unquestioned by all Victorian children; parents ruled over nineteenth-century households, rich and poor alike. The unmarried daughters of the rich had no independent position in Society; they were considered to have no life outside the home and no desire other than to look after their mothers as unpaid companions, sometimes for life. Queen Victoria herself assumed that this would be the case with Princess Beatrice. When Lady Lytton praised a daughter to Queen Victoria, the Queen replied, 'Oh, you must not say that, children ought never to think they can do enough for their parents.'[2]

Princess Louise, however, was 'decidedly cleverer' than Princess

Helena and keen to express her own opinion. Far from automatically accepting the Queen's plans and propositions, she ruffled Queen Victoria by offering alternatives. The Queen became indignant. She considered the Princess's 'disobedience' added to the burdens of her own working life. The Queen found Princess Louise sensitive to unintentional slights rather than sensitive to *her* wishes. So she had to check herself not to upset Princess Louise; it was just one more thing to worry about. For example, after the Crown Princess had asked Prince Arthur to be godparent to her fourth child in April 1866, Princess Louise 'nearly cried' at being forgotten. 'She is very sensitive, thinks no one likes her (and Alice makes such a fuss with her),' wrote the Queen to the Crown Princess, 'I should be very sorry if you overlooked her.'[3]

Nor did Queen Victoria measure up to Princess Louise's idea of a perfect mother. Her constant criticisms and admonitions (what the Prince of Wales called 'Jobations') made Princess Louise feel unloved and inferior. The Princess at first believed that the Queen's low opinion of her must be true. It was only after Princess Alice, the Crown Princess and Aunt Feodora had praised and encouraged her, that she began to question her mother's judgement.

Nevertheless, it was brave of Princess Louise to stand up not only against the standards of her day, but against the Queen. Just as the Queen, when a child, had refused to be cowed by her own mother, so Princess Louise now refused to be cowed by hers. She was a perfectionist and, hating unfairness, was led to interfere in order to put matters right. Moreover, the family's differences with the Queen over the past year had given Princess Louise the impetus to argue with her. Whereas the Crown Princess considered herself at least the Queen's equal if not superior, Princess Helena and Princess Beatrice always considered Queen Victoria as their Queen and themselves as her subjects. Princess Alice and Princess Louise, however, thought of Queen Victoria as their mother first and foremost and dealt with her as such.

Moreover, Princess Louise's dissatisfaction was increased by the adolescent certainty that she was an injured party. When she wrote 'there are so many things I know ought not to be as they are,'[4] one of these was that, instead of making her debut into Society, as other well-born girls of eighteen were doing that summer, she was sitting in seclusion at Osborne, not so much an 'angel in the house' but a 'poor cinderella'. Yet she had been confirmed and was thus considered out of the schoolroom. Confirmation was one of the rites of passage of adolescence and it normally occurred just after a sixteenth birthday; Princess Louise was almost seventeen, the delay being caused by her long illness in 1864.

When her father was alive, the confirmation of her elder brothers and sisters had been celebrated not just as an important family event but as a royal occasion. Because of the Queen's mourning, Princess Louise's confirmation at Whippingham Church was conducted as a private family ceremony.

She had received her first religious instruction when, as a three-year-old, she had knelt to say her prayers at bedtime in the night nursery with 'Turty' beside her. At five she had started going to services in the private chapels at Buckingham Palace and Windsor Castle; when she was eight she had begun to attend public services at Whippingham or St George's Chapel, Windsor.

The Princess had been receiving instruction over the winter of 1864–5 from Canon Prothero of Whippingham but she underwent her first ordeal on 20 January 1865, when he examined her for an hour in the presence of Queen Victoria. She had to go through the catechism and then state and explain the Creed. Apart from a walk later that afternoon, she had to pass the rest of the day alone in her room studying the Bible so that, as the Queen put it, 'the right atmosphere shall not be disturbed'.[5] The Waleses had arrived that afternoon specially to attend the confirmation ceremony; yet Princess Louise was only allowed a word with them after her walk and before retiring to her room.

The next day was a 'lovely bright day with a hard frost'.[6] Princess Louise, who wore a plain, white, silk gown trimmed at the cuffs and hem with wide bands of swansdown, started for the Church at a little before midday with Queen Victoria. The Greys and the other courtiers were seated in the Queen's pew at the front and all the Osborne servants were there. The Queen with the rest of the Royal Family sat in a semi-circle round the altar, while in their midst stood the white, slim figure of Princess Louise looking, Sybil thought, 'so nice and pretty'.[7] Princess Louise's appearance belied her feelings: she was extremely nervous about forgetting the responses.

Once she had got through the responses word-perfectly, the Archbishop of Canterbury delivered his confirmation charge. It is difficult not to see the hand of Queen Victoria in the opening part of this address since he cautioned Princess Louise against desiring to have her own way, telling her that 'a meek, a quiet, a submissive spirit' was what would please God. He also warned her about the dangers of Court life where 'those who are . . . surrounded by the splendour and luxury of a Court may be in some danger of being fascinated by its witchery, and tempted to set their heart on the pleasures of the world'.[8] Princess Louise may well have been puzzled by this portrayal of her humdrum existence, which seemed remarkably unexciting compared to the Archbishop's description.

She admitted to Sybil Grey that she had nearly fainted from excitement and fright after the ordeal was over. 'When we returned from the Church,' the Queen recorded in her Journal, 'I took Louise up to her dear Father's room where I gave her, in both our names, the Victoria and Albert Order and the necklace and earrings in diamond "*châlons*" similar to her sisters, but alas! no longer chosen by my beloved one, which Lenchen's was . . .'[9]

Since reception by the Church as a life-long member was considered the official prelude to reception by Society as a young lady of marriageable age, Princess Louise naturally now looked forward to her first Season. Unfortunately, her appearances in London were confined to the few ceremonial functions the Queen chose to attend and the odd family ball.

Queen Victoria did agree, however, to hold two receptions for the *Corps Diplomatique*. She found them 'a great bore', an opinion Princess Louise would later share.[10] But the first reception was a special one for her, being her formal debut in Society and her first attendance, as a young lady, upon the Queen. As a special concession, Princess Louise was allowed to wear the customary debutante ballgown of voluminous tulle with the addition of a long train; the bodice of white satin coming to a sharp point below her small waist and the short, puffed sleeves falling off her shoulders to leave them bare. Her confirmation present of large diamond earrings were in evidence, while round her neck hung a magnificent, triple-row, pearl necklace fastened by a sapphire and diamond clasp. She also wore a small ornament of feathers on her head and carried a white fan in her hand. The Queen felt quite the proud mama, recording the event in her Journal: 'I was glad that Louise's 1st appearance in a train and feathers should be with me.'[11] But, for the next day's reception, Princess Louise had to wear mourning dress.

Now that she was officially 'out', Princess Louise was expected to attend the Queen at ceremonial functions. Due to the Queen's mourning, however, the only Court affairs she attended were the Drawing Rooms, which took place at three o'clock in the afternoon in the Throne Room at Buckingham Palace. They were the *bêtes noires* of every Victorian debutante: 'a chilly unbecoming performance [that was] very trying for old and young ladies with very low necks, *very* low, great plumes of feathers and long white veils with huge tiaras . . . , and heavy trains four yards long sweeping on the ground'.[12] Such occasions, tiresome as they were, often provided amusement for the Royalties, who had to stand throughout this interminable parade of ladies. People often panicked and one despairing lady even stuck a large hair pin into an old admiral's arm because he was blocking her way.

Princess Louise always found it difficult to keep a straight face when the untoward happened. After hearing that Louisa Bowater would be attending her first married Drawing Room as Lady Knightley, Princess Louise promised her, 'I shall be so pleased to see you at the Court, and will try and behave very well when you pass, because I have always an inclination to laugh when I see anyone I know.'[13]

Once the novelty had worn off, Princess Louise came to share her family's dislike of such functions. Although she had long been accustomed to standing about when people outside her family were present, she never got used to it. Non-royal guests, even courtiers, were frequently struck by the stamina needed. Princess Louise often admitted to her friends, 'I am so awfully tired from the long day's standing.'[14]

The life of a normal debutante in the mid-sixties was 'a perpetual round of pleasure and excitement'. Princess Louise, however, was bitterly disappointed at not being allowed to attend the balls held in the great London houses, as she loved dancing and longed to join in the fun. The only balls she could attend were those given by her family. In the absence of the Queen, the Waleses led Society and gave many Court balls as well as the one which marked the beginning of the parliamentary session. This was seen as the first great event of the year and Princess Louise attended it for the first time on 10 March 1865. Her experience was notably different from that of the other girls. Whereas they could be partnered by any man present, she could only dance with other Royalties. Nor could she waltz, even though it was the latest, most fashionable dance, with no reversing, just 'a few quick turns, a pause for breath and then another plunge into the throng'.[15]

In addition, as a Royalty, Princess Louise was forbidden to dance the supper dance which was the young people's favourite. Instead, she sedately joined other members of the Royal Family for supper, always taken separately from the other guests. In those days, a girl only danced once with a partner who then returned her to a chaperone. Sitting out a dance was 'not done' and, if it had been, it would have been tantamount to announcing one's engagement. Nevertheless, most girls present would have been able to exchange a few words with any new and interesting partner, whereas the nearest Princess Louise came to dancing with someone new was at a Court ball when she might be led out in the opening quadrille by an aged ambassador or cabinet minister. Far from proving the experienced, distinguished sort of partner likely to impress an ingénue, they were often so out of practice that a young princess had to prompt and almost push them through the various figures.

The only other dance Princess Louise attended during the Seasons of 1865 and 1866 was the servants' dance given by the Queen before Princess Helena's wedding in July. She was not even allowed to attend an informal dance for Sybil in May, despite being a close friend, and, when the Greys' gave a large ball for Sybil on June 15th, Prince Alfred was allowed to attend whereas Princess Louise was not. She felt even more of an injured party, since her brothers were allowed to take part in the entire Season. Knowing that she longed to join them, they or their Governors would send her descriptions of balls they attended. After receiving one of these, she wrote, 'I [am] much touched that you should have thought of me, it would have been a great pleasure if I could have been present, but, – so I had to be satisfied with the accounts.'[16]

Although Princess Helena had not been allowed to go out in Society either, four years had now elapsed since Prince Albert's death; yet the Queen made no exceptions to her family's mourning. She held no dances for them and made no allowance for her daughters' desire for some frivolity and fun. All this despite the fact that Queen Victoria herself had adored dancing and, as an eighteen year old, had often left a ball at sunrise. It would have been quite natural for the Queen to have asked the Princess of Wales to chaperone Princess Louise to them. The Queen, however, adamantly refused to allow such a thing; indeed she continued to prevent Princess Louise from spending any time at Marlborough House, much to the latter's dismay. Even if she could not go out at night, Princess Louise would have loved to join the Princess of Wales for her afternoon drive in Hyde Park.

Although Princess Louise longed to play her part in the Season, which was all the more appealing for being forbidden, she had to be content with the carefully guarded, dull days which constituted her life at home. That autumn of 1866, when most other well-born girls of her age were going to their first house parties, Princess Louise was tucked away, first at Osborne and then at Balmoral, with only the society of her mother, younger siblings and courtiers. Lucy Lyttelton, who passed much of her time in-waiting, accompanying Princess Louise on walks or rides, 'could not help pitying all these Royal people who are never allowed to go out of their own domain'. She and Louisa Bowater spent most of their rides raving about country house visiting. "'I *should* like it!", said the Princess, half hesitatingly, "Ah, that is one thing we are deprived of."'[17]

Country house life for seventeen-year-old Princess Louise consisted of prayers followed by breakfast with Queen Victoria, who was surprised at how much she was beginning to enjoy these tête-à-tête sessions with her 'difficult' daughter. 'These quiet breakfasts with dear Louise . . . ,' recorded the Queen, 'are very comfortable.'[18] After a ride or walk, Princess Louise would go to help Queen Victoria with her vast correspondence. Part of her daily task was to copy out letters from one absent member of the family to send on to another; in this way news from Prince Alfred at sea would reach Princess Alice in Darmstadt, and so the family would always remain in touch. Since her family was both large and scattered, Princess Louise was never underemployed; indeed some of the Queen's ladies privately expressed their concern at how 'cruelly overworked' the princesses were, 'the Queen having no notion how . . . mind and body are strained'.[19]

Luncheon at two o'clock was strictly a family meal, with Queen Victoria and any of her children who were at home; no one else was present except, of course, for the butler, groom of chambers, under butler and footmen in livery. In the afternoon Princess Louise had time for some sketching, either outdoors or in her studio. Sometimes, she would drive her little pony carriage to visit cottagers or crofters on the estate, when she would leave a basket of provisions as her calling card. She always had to return by four in case she was required to accompany the Queen on a drive.

Instead of tea in the schoolroom, she now joined Queen Victoria for tea with the ladies, after which she worked at correspondence or industriously embroidered or sketched until it was time to change for dinner. Usually, Princess Louise dined with the Queen *en famille* with only ladies of the Household present; but sometimes they would be joined by a visiting Cabinet Minister or clergyman and gentlemen members of the Household. Princess Louise infinitely preferred their livelier company. As one courtier noticed, 'Poor little Princess Louise! She loves coming out of her dull schoolroom [atmosphere].'[20]

When Sybil left Balmoral in September 1866 to pay more country house visits, the Princess was upset; she was fond of Sybil and hated losing her company. In 1864, Lucy Lyttelton had noticed how 'Prss Louise sent for Horatia [Stopford, a maid of honour], and cried and sobbed at the thoughts of losing her . . . , after their long bit at Osborne together.'[21] Sybil's departure affected Princess Louise even more because she was her best friend.

The Queen herself had brought them together by suggesting to General Grey in February 1863 that 'Sybil would be a charming *companion* for Princess Louise', and she invited Mrs Grey and Sybil to join General Grey at Balmoral that autumn.[22] However, Queen Victoria did not hope that Sybil's presence would lead to a friendship with Princess Louise; on the contrary, Her Majesty's choice of the word 'companion' was deliberate. She desired *only* that Princess Louise should have another girl of the same age to join in her walks, drives and teas, especially since Princess Helena then passed most of her time with Queen Victoria. The Queen was adamantly opposed to outside friendships for any of her children or grandchildren, and made her views abundantly clear when she warned one granddaughter: 'You are right to be civil & friendly to the young girls you may occasionally meet, & to see them sometimes – but *never* make *friendships*; girls friendships & intimacies are very bad & often lead to great mischief – Grandpapa & I never allowed it.'[23]

The Queen believed that closer relations would lower the barriers between commoner and royalty, as the friend would be in a position to influence the princess. In short, she saw friendship as leading to an impermissible relationship of equality. Thus, the few chosen companions were usually the children of courtiers who, because of the position of their parents, could more easily accept the difference between the royal children and themselves.

Sybil Grey met the Queen's requirements perfectly. She was the same age as Princess Louise and, as the eldest daughter of General Grey, had grown up at Court side-by-side with the princesses. Her

younger sister, Louisa, remembered her 'small, oval face very serene in
expression . . . full of kindness and understanding'. Princess Louise,
despite the Queen's strictures, came to love Sybil dearly, and Sybil,
'more of a listener than a talker', heard all the Princess's confidences
and kept them to herself.[24]

The Whitsun and autumn holidays at Balmoral were much more
enjoyable for Princess Louise now that she had Sybil to share them.
They went off riding through the glens, then had tea together with
Princess Helena in the Grey quarters, after which Princess Louise
usually took Sybil back to her rooms for dinner. During the warm
weather they would go out for an after-dinner walk in the gloaming
until nearly ten o'clock. Sometimes, after tea, Princess Louise would
drive Sybil over in the waggonette to watch General Grey or Prince
Arthur fish the Dee for salmon; but they could not participate themselves because fishing was not considered a suitable occupation for
young women.

Through her friendship with Sybil and her affection for Lady Car,
Princess Louise became much attached to the whole Grey family. But,
as she became closer to them, she became more dissatisfied with her
own lot: the emphasis in the Grey family was entirely on the children,
in contrast with the Royal Family where it was on the Queen. Looking
back on her childhood, one of Sybil's sisters wrote that '"Don't" was
a word we hardly ever heard, for there was no undue fault-finding, or
restraint or interference at home, where our parents made us their first
object.'[25]

Princess Louise was only allowed a growing intimacy with the Grey
family because Queen Victoria considered them such superior people
and placed every confidence in General Grey. The Queen used to lean
on him to cope with matters normally outside the scope of a secretary.
At a time when no lady admitted to wearing cosmetics, a young
lady-in-waiting appeared at court rather made-up. 'Dear General Grey',
said the Queen, 'will tell her.' Though, when the message was conveyed
to him, he was heard to murmur: 'Dear General Grey will do nothing
of the kind.'[26]

Nevertheless, he was invaluable to Queen Victoria. 'Good, excellent
Grey,' wrote the Queen, with 'His great worth, honesty, cleverness,
charm of conversation and his great experience.'[27] William Gladstone
too found him a man of high integrity, who never abused 'his peculiar
situation by playing the courtier'.[28] Years later, Princess Louise told

his daughter Louisa, 'He was so dear and kind to me. I quite looked on him as a second delightful father.'[29]

As she became involved in the political affairs of the country through her unofficial role as personal secretary to Queen Victoria, Princess Louise turned to General Grey for guidance; this he was well-qualified to give. He had brought to his position at Court considerable political experience, gained in the first instance from acting as private secretary to his father when Earl Grey's Reform Bill was going through Parliament in 1832. He had been appointed equerry to Prince Albert in 1837 and then his private secretary in 1849.

These years of the late sixties were overshadowed for Princess Louise and all the Royal Family by the mounting problem of the Queen's almost complete withdrawal from public life. The nation had been sympathetic to the natural desire of a widow to observe mourning. However, what was seemly behaviour in the years immediately after Prince Albert's death, was no longer so four years later. It was an issue which bubbled up occasionally in the years 1862–5. It came to the boil in 1866 and simmered on until the end of 1871, when the Prince of Wales's illness reinstated the nation's innate good feeling for the Royal Family and put out the flame of republicanism.

The longer the Queen remained in seclusion, the more criticism grew and, more importantly, was expressed in all quarters. As the eldest daughter at home from 1866, Princess Louise was unavoidably involved in the struggle to force the Queen to attend to the representational functions of Monarchy. This, inevitably, brought her into greater conflict with her mother.

Although the Queen had early and repeatedly stated that she would never appear in public again, such remarks were ignored by those about her. But in October 1863, after General Grey had innocently remarked that he looked forward to the time when Her Majesty would reappear in public, she immediately set him straight, 'The Queen wd certainly *not* wish her loyal people *not* to *wish* to see her, but it is *utterly* useless for Them *ever* to *expect* she will *take her place as before* . . . There *may* be *special occasions* . . . when she may *come* forth in her weeds . . . but surely the General . . . *never cd* expect or *wish* her to appear weak & shattered as she is, trembling & *alone* at Courts, and Parties and State occasions, without her *Sole* Guardian and *Protector?*'[30]

The press, unlike General Grey, displayed no sympathy for her position. On 4 December 1863, *The Times* launched an attack on the

Queen's absence from London. She was flabbergasted, as one of her maids of honour reported: 'the Queen spoke with me about the Article last night in such terms of indignation, that any *logic* was utterly useless; one could only *calm* (as best one could!).'[31] The Queen justified her seclusion on account of 'her *hard*, slavelike labour *for* the Country,' which she considered far more important than '*mere ceremonials*'.[32]

But her refusal to open Parliament, or to appear in London during the following year of 1864, led a more influential figure to add his voice to the clamour. In a letter to Sir Charles Phipps, Sir James Clark expressed his anxiety that 'time appears to effect no change in HM's views regarding her position'. Since it was now three years after Prince Albert's death, he wrote, 'If the Queen does not make some change . . . matters may become worse.'[33] As one of her oldest confidants, he had great influence and, as her senior doctor, he was in the best position to judge the state of her health. He believed that it was her nerves, rather than any illness, which caused her to shrink from the public gaze. 'I feel at times uneasy regarding the Queen's mind, unless she is kept quiet,' he had written in his diary in 1856, 'Much, very much depends on the Prince's management . . . [to] keep the Queen free from all mental irritation.'[34] As always, the difficulty lay in getting the Queen to do anything she did not want to do.

Queen Victoria was afraid of resuming her old way of life for, in doing so, she believed she would be acting as if nothing had changed, whereas everything had changed irrevocably for her. Then, when she occasionally did forget her grief enough to enjoy herself, she felt guilty afterwards. This was the key to her seclusion, as Princess Alice had explained to General Grey during the visit to Germany in 1863: 'the Queen *is* very well. She got through her luncheon of 18 to the Emperor of Austria perfectly, talked a great deal, and was interested, running to the window etc to see him drive away,' but, Princess Alice continued, 'the Queen owned to her she was afraid of getting too well as if it was a crime! and that she *feared* to begin to like riding on her Scotch pony etc.'[35]

In 1865, as the older members of the Royal Family began to express their concern, the Duke of Cambridge 'was most outspoken about it, and said, she was endangering the very principle of Monarchy'.[36] Princess Louise was deemed old enough to participate in the endless family discussions about the Queen's seclusion.

On 6 February 1866, the Queen opened Parliament in person

for the first time since 1861. It was, therefore, Princess Louise's first opportunity of attending this state ceremony. She drove to the Houses of Parliament in a carriage seated next to Princess Helena and facing Queen Victoria. The Queen thought it was a 'dreadful' ordeal, but after it was over, she wrote that her daughters 'were a true help and support to me – they so thoroughly realised what I was going through'.[37]

Unfortunately, this single appearance did not stem the discontent. A government crisis in the summer of 1866 over Reform brought the Prime Minister into the fray, joined at last by General Grey. The Queen's absence from Windsor during the parliamentary session meant that General Grey's worst fears were realized when the Habeas Corpus Act was suspended in Ireland, and the Queen's signature was immediately required. On 18 February 1866, he wrote to Osborne to warn her of the 'great danger of Your Majesty's proper Constitutional authority being weakened should the Ministers find a reasonable excuse for neglecting . . . to obtain Your Majesty's sanction before taking some important step'.[38]

In February 1866, William Gladstone introduced a controversial Reform Bill in the Commons. The Queen, however, dreading another 1848, could think of nothing but 'this wretched Reform', which threatened to disturb her holiday plans at Balmoral. She wrote to General Grey, 'There certainly seems to be a system of *frightening* the Queen both on Home and F. Affairs every 10 days! *Wolf* is really cried *too often*.'[39] The Queen was completely out of touch and self-absorbed; Prussia and Austria were about to declare war over the division of the Schleswig and Holstein duchies, and, on Monday June 20th, the Government was brought down in Parliament.

In the absence of the Queen, the House was adjourned for a week, as the Government could not resign without communicating with the Sovereign. Once it was learnt that the Queen did not intend to return until the 26th, public opinion swung strongly against her. From now on General Grey relentlessly prodded the Queen to resume her duties. In this campaign, he was aided and abetted by Princess Louise.

After seeing the Queen on the 26th, the Liberal Government resigned and Lord Derby was called upon to form a Conservative Government with Mr Disraeli as Chancellor of the Exchequer. Lord Derby persuaded the Queen to open Parliament again by using the crisis of Reform as justification for the presence of the Monarch. Sybil Grey was there to see Princess Louise enter the House of Lords with the Queen on February 5th 1867, when 'it rained in torrents'. Princess Louise dressed in a long, white, satin gown stood on the left of the throne. One observer commented that 'they might have been statues, so motionless were all'.[40] The accounts of the Royal Family's reception differed; according to the Grey camp they were much cheered, whereas the Queen noticed a sea of 'nasty faces' hissing and groaning 'Give us reform'.[41] She felt that at such a time 'the Sovereign should not be there'.[42]

In the autumn of 1867, the charged political atmosphere for once succeeded in penetrating the peace of Balmoral. In September, a group of Fenians had tried to rescue two of their men from a police van, killing a policeman in the process. Their latest plot was to kidnap the Queen. When Princess Louise awoke on the morning of October 14th, it was to find the Castle preparing for a state of seige by troops. For once that year, the Queen spoke for all her family when she said, 'Too foolish',[43] writing to Major Elphinstone, '*She* believes the danger *entirely* an *exaggeration* and that the *precautions* were really not *necessary*.'[44] Still, in the face of the wettest weather for years, the scare enlivened the time necessarily spent indoors: 'we want something of this sort', wrote General Grey to his wife, 'to keep us alive for we are dull and monotonous here to a degree'.[45]

The Fenians again disrupted the Royal Family's holidays, this time over Christmas passed at Osborne. News of another plot to kidnap the Queen was greeted with panic by the Government, who asked the Royal Family to leave. The Queen refused to budge, commenting, 'There has been a great deal of nonsense and foolish panic, and number-less stories which have proved sheer inventions!!'[46] When Princess Louise went out for a morning ride, she was stopped on her return: no one, she was told, was allowed to come into the house without a pass. 'Who ever took a pass out on a ride?' she asked.[47] It was indeed little better than being, in the Queen's words, 'a *State* prisoner!'

Unfortunately, the Fenian episodes strengthened the Queen's con-viction that her obstinacy over remaining away from London was justified. Princess Louise, now much closer to her, took a different view. She actively began to campaign against her mother's seclusion because she believed Queen Victoria was shirking her duties; clearly influenced by General Grey in her beliefs, she now looked to this 'second father' to support her.

CHAPTER VI

A Determined Young Lady

One cold January day in the year 1868 a liveried messenger delivered a note to Mrs Tyler, who lived at Ventnor. Written by Princess Helena, it invited Mrs Tyler, her two daughters and their friend, Miss Catherine Paget, to pass the day with the Royal Family. At a quarter to one, on January 23rd, the Tyler carriage entered the gates of Osborne House. Welcomed by a housekeeper and escorted by a footman up to the first floor, they were shown into a large sitting room.

Ten-year-old Princess Beatrice was the first to greet them. She was very quiet and self-possessed in all her movements, but had, Catherine Paget fancied, 'rather a nervous way of speaking and laughing'. She gratefully accepted Mrs Tyler's present of a doll's dressing case and fetched two of her dolls to entertain the youngest visitor, Lellie Tyler. Meanwhile, Princess Helena had knocked at the door and come in to kiss Mrs Tyler, shake hands with the girls and sit down at the writing table. She wore half mourning clothes of black skirt and grey wool jacket which Catherine Paget thought 'was not a very becoming dress'. After a few minutes general conversation, she made way for Princess Louise who, as usual, was the last to arrive, her appearance in dramatic contrast to her elder sister's.

This in no way detracted from the effect Princess Louise had upon the visitors, who thought her the perfect young lady. 'Tall and graceful in figure more than any other of the Royal family,' Catherine Paget found, 'she is also far the most perfect in beauty – and, were she no princess, everyone would praise and delight in her noble, handsome face – so refined and well proportioned in every feature.' The nineteen-year-old princess wore her luxuriant, fair hair coiled in a thick plait around the back of her head and pinned with two simple hair pins.

In place of her sister's drab costume, Princess Louise wore a rich, brocade dress trimmed with satin, which fell in long, heavy folds and swept the ground behind, as she gracefully crossed the room to kiss Mrs Tyler. The contrast between the dark, blue brocade and the simple, beaten-silver cross, which hung from a little chain round her neck, was stunning and uncommon in that era of fussy, fringed and beribboned costume. Catherine Paget, who had never seen such an ornament before, described it as 'a curious cross of dead silver'; in fact Princess Louise had designed and made it herself in the studio at Osborne.

There is no doubt that Princess Louise made a tremendous impression upon the Tyler party. Catherine Paget later wrote of her 'most delightful manner – gentle, anxious to give pleasure yet . . . gracious all the time. She took more pains to make our time at Osborne pass happily, gave us more of her time and attention than anyone there. I shall never forget how truly kind she was.' The Princess, of course, was delighted to have some company.

Later in the day, on being summoned to the Queen's presence, the party aligned themselves so that they faced the door and waited with a feeling of apprehensive awe. In this case they were not put at ease by the imperious, germanic hissing of Fräulein Bauer: 'The Queen will come in by one of those doors . . .', 'we must all bow at once,' and, finally, 'She is not at all likely to give you her hand but if she does you may kiss it.' A few minutes later, after the party had collected their breath, Princess Louise 'with her kind, beautiful face' re-entered, followed by 'the little black-robed lady' who approached them 'with rather a pretty shy manner, smiling, moving quickly'.

Catherine Paget was disappointed that the Queen was not beautiful to look at: 'She is short, and getting now, stout and broadshouldered which no art of dress is employed to hide . . . Her face looked younger than I expected. There is still pink colour in her cheeks . . . It is not a face to impress itself on one's memory, but, looking at it I thought how pleasant and womanly it was.'

Afterwards, Princess Louise took them on a tour of the house, which ended upstairs in her own pretty, bright, little boudoir. This housed an astonishing array of 'endless photographs, brackets and ornaments' and Princess Louise took a delight in showing them an excellent photograph of the Prince and another of the Princess of Wales. Mrs Tyler, noticing some unusually large violets on a round table, asked for one or two as a souvenir. Princess Louise immediately gathered up the whole bunch and gave them to her, saying 'I would have offered them to you, but that they are not worth your acceptance.'

They remained talking until Princess Louise said she had to get ready to go out with the Queen and reluctantly took her leave. The Tyler party watched the Queen start on her drive and then they themselves started from Osborne at four o'clock and 'talked with great delight and gratitude of our happy day all the way back to Ventnor'. The Royalty whom they liked the best was undoubtedly Princess Louise. Catherine Paget would meet her again over the years and would always remember her 'face and look' and her 'gentle attentive kindness with no touch of patronage or condescension about it'.[1]

It was, of course, this kindness combined with a sympathetic, modest manner which made Princess Louise appear so appealing, especially to people who expected to be confronted by a rather stiff, formidable princess. The Tylers probably believed that she passed most of her time in a round of social activity; little did they realize that their visit had been a rare occurrence for her. She always remembered it with fondness, believing that *they* had done her the honour, rather than the other way round. Indeed, all her life she remained surprised to find that people actually enjoyed her company.

Despite being one of those princesses whom Lord Clarendon had described as 'The poor little birds in royal cages [who] do love a day of liberty and to try their own wings,'[2] Princess Louise had come to the conclusion that there was no point in moping about her lonely life. By 1868 she had thrown off those feelings of abject self-pity, which had earlier coloured her attitude to life. Her two years as 'right hand' to Queen Victoria had thrust her into a position of some importance in the arena of national affairs: a rare situation in which to find any nineteen-year-old, unmarried, Victorian girl.

This had had the effect of strengthening her character. She was no longer content to sit about waiting for something to happen. Although everyone had failed to persuade the Queen to undertake more public engagements, Princess Louise continued to try to prise her mother from seclusion. Despite such proddings, she remained in high favour with her mother, who wrote in her Journal on Princess Louise's twentieth birthday, 'She has much character, such originality, such an affectionate heart, also possesses a great taste and talent for art.'[3]

As the parliamentary session of 1868 began, Princess Louise not only read the daily press reports criticizing the Queen's absence from London, while she was precising the main news items for her, but also heard from General Grey of the dissatisfaction felt by Ministers. With the resignation of Lord Derby in February, Benjamin Disraeli had become Prime Minister. Two months before, William Gladstone had succeeded Lord John Russell to the leadership of the Liberal party.

This meant that, for the first time, the two main parties were led by men from the Commons. In May 1868 a parliamentary crisis involved Princess Louise once again with the question of the Queen's attitude to her duties. Disraeli was steering a supplementary reform bill for Scotland through the Commons when, not unexpectedly, at a single sitting, the Government were twice defeated on critical points of the bill.

The Queen again ignored the signs and departed as planned for Balmoral. Before leaving she had received conflicting advice. Princess Louise had suggested the Queen remain at Windsor for a few days, whereas Princess Helena thought she was right to go. Princess Louise had consulted General Grey. He, as the Queen's secretary, was in close touch with leaders of both parties, as well as with other courtiers. Princess Louise undoubtedly tended wise advice but the Queen was only too ready to believe Princess Helena, whose conflicting advice suited her own wishes. As one Londoner, Lady Hardy, wrote: 'the very night she went off to Balmoral, her Ministers were again defeated and all yesterday and today no one knows what the result will be. There were placards all over the City calling on her to abdicate since she herself seemed to think her presence of so little consequence.'[4]

This further absence was too much for the sorely tried patience of the House of Commons. One MP handed in the following notice for Question Time on May 21st: 'To ask the Prime Minister, as the Queen's health appears to be so weak that she cannot live in England, whether he has advised her to abdicate in favour of the Prince of Wales?'[5], and notice of it duly appeared in the newspapers.

On May 20th Princess Louise had confidentially asked General Grey to write to Disraeli about the Queen's stay at Balmoral, in the hope that he could persuade her to return to London. If only 'her Ministers had said a word,' Princess Louise told Grey, she 'could not have come!'[6] and she blamed the Government entirely for not insisting that the Queen should remain at Windsor.

The Princess here showed considerable maturity and understanding of her mother's character. She believed it was useless to manœuvre Queen Victoria into a position from which she could not retreat without appearing to have given in, since this would only make her more obdurate. Thus, it was much better for the Government, rather than anyone else, to make the request, for it provided the Queen with a strong reason, a constitutional one, to accede to it gracefully. Princess

Louise had realized that the Queen felt that if she once gave way to General Grey or the Family, she would be setting a precedent.

Although the Prince of Wales and Princess Louise initiated an approach from Disraeli, his influence over Queen Victoria was not then as great as it was to become. The Queen remained at Balmoral but, goaded by some disagreeable discussions with Princess Louise, she decided to indulge in some public relations work. She sent Dr Jenner, as her emissary, to see the Home Secretary and win him over to her side.

William Jenner had been introduced into the Royal Household by Sir James Clarke, who was now eighty and in poor health. Unlike Sir James, he was unable to stand up to Queen Victoria and this, combined with a somewhat autocratic manner, did not endear him to some of his royal patients. Princess Louise had always felt his daily visits to her and Prince Leopold were 'somewhat tiresome', as he tended to fuss too much.[7]

The Home Secretary's account of Jenner's visit on 5 June 1868 shows how successful the Queen's lobbying exercise had been: 'Speaking medically he [Jenner] looks at her nervous temperament, time of life, easy excitability . . . He described the state of agitation in which at times he found her in her private room, and the violent headaches and sickness to which she is subject. Amid all this her hard work on papers etc. . . . Poor Queen, she feels lonely and desires at least to know that those about her sympathise.'[8] Unfortunately, the Queen looked the picture of health. Sybil Grey noticed her complexion was 'even more robust and healthy looking than when I saw her last. She, however, complains of not being well.'[9]

During the summer of 1868, Princess Louise had been able to discuss the Queen's health and seclusion with other members of the Family for, in August, she had accompanied the Queen on a holiday to Switzerland. It was a great adventure for her, because they travelled incognito and rented a small villa, the Pension Wallis in Lucerne, where they lived 'completely together like a family'.[10] The Queen travelled as the Countess of Kent, something she had not done since a carefree expedition made with Prince Albert in the Highlands in 1861.

Princess Louise took immense pleasure in mischievously asking people like Major Elphinstone to write to her as 'Lady Louise Kent'. 'The view from the House is beyond all our expectations,' she wrote from Lucerne on 8 August 1868, 'and the heat is not greater than it was in England and Mama has not complained of it since we are here.'[11] The Pension Wallis stood, as it still does, on a hill overlooking Lucerne, set against the St Gothard range of mountains and looking on to the lake. It was so tiny for a royal residence that, of necessity, they had to live informally. Luckily, the novelty appealed to all of them. Moreover, it became a centre for other relations to visit.

Princess Louise thoroughly enjoyed the boating expeditions on the lake, climbing the glaciers and sketching the glorious scenery. The warm climate agreed with her and she returned to England in September feeling quite restored after the trying early summer. Meeting her on the stairs at Balmoral, General Grey thought her looking very well, 'Princess Louise is in gt good looks . . .'[12]

The Princess was quickly involved in Court affairs. The tutor of her younger brothers, Mr Jolly, had left royal service but the expected pro-forma appointment as Queen's Chaplain had failed to materialize and Princess Louise was asked to help. Since she realized this was a genuine oversight, she set about rectifying the omission by casually asking her mother, in the course of conversation, 'what had become of Mr Jolly?'[13] This led to Queen Victoria discussing the matter and coming to a decision unaware of any interference from her daughter. The Princess was learning that the best way to succeed in such matters was to employ the indirect approach.

She also took the initiative over more official questions of patronage. Whereas Princess Helena only wrote at her mother's explicit request, Princess Louise wrote in anticipation of a subject requiring the Queen's decision. She believed she could only act as her mother's right hand after she had consulted other advisers and heard their views. It was because of such initiatives that, in later years, she would often be accused of interference and 'meddling'. Sometimes, being young and inexperienced, she did not clearly understand the issues involved but she never took offence at being corrected. Writing to Dean Wellesley about some church appointments the Queen would shortly have to make, she sounded him out about Dr Temple for the Bishopric of Exeter, having heard the Queen praise him but forgetting that a Prime Minister does not usually appoint men linked to the Opposition, even if they are clergymen. In his reply, the Dean reminded her of this and suggested men who would be acceptable to Mr Disraeli.[14]

In the middle of November, the Princess learnt that Queen Victoria was planning to keep her next year's engagements to a bare minimum.

Princess Louise was glad of the opportunity to confide in the Crown Princess, over on holiday from Germany. She tried to persuade her sister to add her name to the list of family, who were actively working to end Queen Victoria's seclusion. General Grey, however, advised them to wait; he knew the Queen hated anything that smelt of a plot.

On December 3rd, Princess Louise and the Crown Princess again consulted General Grey about the Queen. The Crown Princess, who had not been in London since 1865, had been horrified to hear hissing from the crowds and shouts of 'Down with Royalty'.[15] She now realized that her younger sister was not overreacting and that her fears about the growing popularity of the republican movement were sound. She joined Princess Louise in trying to persuade Queen Victoria to undertake more public engagements in 1869. By the end of December, the Queen could be heard expressing 'much dissatisfaction with Prussians and [the] Crown Princess'.[16] Despite being the ringleader, Princess Louise escaped her mother's wrath because Queen Victoria had a habit of always blaming the eldest child involved whenever her children displeased her.

The Queen was full of dissatisfaction at this period; not only with her family, but also with her new Prime Minister, William Gladstone, of whose proposed legislation to disestablish the Irish Church she strongly disapproved. Losing Disraeli was also a blow to the Queen. They had got on so well, partly because he sent her letters full of gossip about parliamentary and other affairs. She had daily sung his praises to her family. Since he had done little to tackle the problem of the Queen's seclusion, Princess Louise thought everyone seemed far too enthusiastic about Disraeli.

Besides, the Princess was not really a natural Tory because the people who were most influential in her life were all Liberals. Princess Alice was perhaps the person most responsible for instilling Liberalism into Princess Louise, but the Crown Princess was also a Liberal. In addition, those closest to Princess Louise at Court were all Liberals. General Grey and Lady Car were staunch Whigs as were the Queen's greatest friends, the Duchess of Sutherland, the Duke of Argyll, the Westminsters, the Clarendons and Lady Augusta Bruce. Of the Princess's particular circle, Sybil Grey and Lucy Lyttelton were Liberals, as was Louisa Bowater until her marriage to Sir Rainauld Knightley, an ardent Tory. The Princess felt the Royal Family had a duty to appear impartial, and tried to suppress her Liberal inclinations as much as possible but she also treasured fairness; as she saw a Tory bias emerging, so she felt obliged to champion her true cause and, as Princess Helena became more rabidly Tory, Princess Louise became more radically Liberal.

Princess Louise found even more of her time taken up by the seclusion issue in 1869. At the end of May, the visit to England of the Pasha of Egypt caused a major row. It broke out as a result of an innocuous telegram, received by the Foreign Secretary, which asked about arrangements for the Viceroy's visit, the assumption being that as a State visitor he would stay with the Queen of England. This coincided with an article in *The Times* tantamount to an announcement that he would be staying at Buckingham Palace. Despite the Pasha's recent generous hospitality to the Waleses in Egypt, the Queen refused to house him, saying, 'The Queen cannot say *how* indignant *She* feels at the way in which the Cabinet disposes of *her* Palace!! To make it an Hotel, is too cool!'[17]

Coincidentally, General Grey had just received several articles sent anonymously to him about Queen Victoria; one of these, headed 'Another Highland Fling' and couched for the first time in offensive language, gave a list of all the State offices and functions rendered useless by Her Majesty's absence from London. General Grey felt obliged to tell the Queen that, if she refused to entertain the Pasha, the Government would have to ask Parliament for the necessary funds. This would provoke public discussions about the large grants she received from Parliament.

The Queen gave way about the Pasha but not without writing to her Prime Minister: 'The Queen must strongly protest against the pretension raised, that she should, at her *own expense*, in the *only* Palace of her *own*, which she may come to at any time, and which is constantly used for her family – entertain all foreign Potentates *who chose* to come here for their own amusement.'[18] Much has been written about the Queen's truthfulness; yet in this letter she is clearly dissembling. She rarely used Buckingham Palace; moreover she often refused to allow her family to stay there, while it was empty. Princess Helena even had to cancel an engagement because the Queen said 'she cannot have us and does not wish us to come this week – we have nothing else to do but to be obedient'.[19]

On the same evening, as Queen Victoria dashed off this letter to Mr Gladstone, Princess Louise sent for General Grey and again asked whether something should not now be done to push the Queen more into the public eye. She 'had heard so much of the feeling excited by the Queen's continual seclusion, that she was anxious to help in any way to put an end to it'.[20] Unfortunately, events once more conspired against Princess Louise. She was advised to do nothing because the Queen had just given in about the Pasha. The General pacified Princess Louise by telling her that he thought the Prime Minister would now take up the cudgels and force the Queen to do more. So the Princess suppressed her inclination to confront the Queen and accompanied her to Balmoral for the Whitsun break.

When Prince Arthur joined them, he brought Princess Louise further evidence of their mother's growing unpopularity. He told Princess Louise that at the Royal United Service Club, into which he often went, 'he could not help hearing many remarks whether meant for him or not he could not say, which were very disagreeable'[21] about Mama.

Princess Louise was 'seriously alarmed' by this information. General Grey found her, on May 31st, '*very* decided as to the ability of the Queen to meet any *fatigue* – and is most indignant with Jenner for encouraging the Queen's fancies about her health'.[22]

General Grey passed on these views to Gladstone, in the hope that they would strengthen the Government's case against the Queen, but, although Gladstone was prepared to ask the Queen to perform a function in the City in July, he was not prepared to bring the weight of his office to bear in the struggle to end a poor widow's seclusion. The General now turned to Princess Louise, who reiterated that 'the Government *alone* had the power to put a stop to a system of running away from her duties', for the Princess saw this struggle to end the Queen's seclusion as a crusade to save the Monarchy.

Apart from General Grey, Princess Louise was in the best position to judge whether the Queen was overwhelmed by work. Her unequivocal support of General Grey's assertion that Gladstone had an exaggerated opinion of Queen Victoria's workload is, thus, of some importance: 'In *very* short notes; in shorter interviews, Her Majesty gives me her orders to "write fully" on this or that subject; and beyond reading the letters or despatch . . ., she has no further trouble, except to approve of the draft which I submit to her. It is only on a question, such as that of entertaining the Vice-Roy [pasha] which affects her own comfort or inclinations, that she is at the trouble of writing herself! Pray . . .

dismiss from your mind, any idea of there being any "weight of work" upon the Queen; and this, Princess Louise, emphatically repeats.'

The Princess also insisted her mother was wonderfully well. She had spoken to the Queen several times about putting off her Osborne visit on July 7th in order to perform the City function, but Queen Victoria would not listen to her. In order to forestall what she predicted would be the Queen's next move, that Jenner said she was too ill to attend, Princess Louise tackled Jenner about it. All he could do in answer to her accusations was to admit the truth of her remarks about the Queen: 'the Government should speak "authoritatively", as of a thing it was absolutely necessary Her Majesty should do, and she could do it' and disingenuously ask her, 'Why don't they do it?' To which Princess Louise shrewdly answered, 'What's the use of your asking why they don't when you go to them and tell them they *mustn't*?' As he began to protest, she added firmly 'You *know* Sir William, you do.'[23]

However, despite the badgering of Princess Louise and General Grey, the Queen went straight from Balmoral to Osborne. When Gladstone finally suggested, through the Dean of Windsor, that she remain at Windsor during the difficult passage of the Irish Disestablishment Bill through the Lords, the Queen nonchalantly replied: 'the Queen has had repeated Crises *there* [Osborne], in the *PRINCE's time*,'[24] but, when he finally submitted a formal request directly to the Queen for her presence at Windsor, the result was that she left Osborne.

It may be wondered why Princess Louise did not speak plainly to Queen Victoria, instead of deferring to the General's opinion; by doing so she might have succeeded in changing the Queen's attitude. Yet, when faced with anything unpleasant, the Queen either became agitated or ignored it. Frequent references were made both by her family and courtiers to the Queen adopting 'the usual course' of escaping into 'a dogged silence' so that the person concerned was 'sent to Coventry' over a particularly disagreeable issue.

Princess Louise was well aware of an immediate fall from grace should she continually contradict the Queen about her seclusion; after all, the Princess had been in that position *vis-à-vis* her mother before. The danger, as Princess Louise saw it, was to go so far that she lost her position of influence with the Queen altogether. Instead, she chose to work gently but steadily; she also chose to rely upon the General's judgement and experience. Princess Louise, more than most of the Royal Family, might try to deal with Queen Victoria as an errant mother, who was not doing her job properly, yet this mother was also the Queen and no one, including Princess Louise, could ever completely forget this fact. 'All, high and low, dread the chance of a disapproving nod,' wrote Henry Ponsonby, 'yet you tell me that she has no power.'[25] Princess Louise was one of the very few about the Queen willing to stand up to her on matters she considered important. But she constantly had to be on her guard against accepting everything Queen Victoria said, since her mother's views were changeable at the best of times. Thus, over Windsor, one moment she liked it and the next 'she can't endure it and feels more wretched and lonely in that large State Prison than anywhere else'.[26]

Furthermore, Sybil Grey was no longer available to listen to her tales of woe and help her through this difficult period. A few days before Princess Louise's nineteenth birthday, Sybil had become engaged to the Duke of St Albans. She was '*very*, very happy' she told Princess Louise on her return visits to Windsor and Osborne. Having spent much of the past year and a half away from Court, it was even more apparent to Sybil how boring and constricted life was for Princess Louise. When she and St Albans dined with Queen Victoria after their engagement was officially announced, she found it heavy going: '5 of one family sitting all together [the Greys] and 4 of the Royal family also together does not promote conversation and it was heavier and duller than ever.'[27]

Their marriage took place on 20 June 1867 in St James's Palace, where the Greys had an apartment. Although best friends, Sybil could not simply invite Princess Louise to her wedding but had to wait, as etiquette demanded, for the Princess to signify her intention to attend. Princess Louise, anxious not to miss out on such an event, made a special journey with Lady Car to St James's Palace. There she told Sybil she would like to be invited; it was only afterwards that she told Queen Victoria. Permission to attend was granted.

But, with Sybil married, Princess Louise, more on her own than ever, continued to lead a life of dullness and routine. Her duties were not merely ornamental, as she worked hard and continuously. Although her mother felt that these duties should make for a full and happy life, her only position was as the eldest daughter at home. She needed more than this to satisfy her. Circumstances prevented her from seeking the answer in the outside world so she had to look to her own resources.

She possessed an imaginative, active mind, a talent for sketching and natural intelligence. Full of energy and high spirits, she wanted to do something which she could call her own, and she found her consolation in sculpture.

She had become interested in sculpting through sitting for two lady sculptors. The first was Susan Durant, who had been commissioned by Queen Victoria to do medallion portraits of the royal children for the Albert Memorial Chapel at St George's, Windsor. She started work in the winter of 1864 and passed the next three years staying regularly at Windsor and Osborne. Princess Louise took to her at once and the Queen allowed her to study with Miss Durant, who unfortunately became ill with cancer and was soon unable to continue her instruction.

The second lady sculptor was Mary Thornycroft, who was appointed to teach Princess Louise in 1867. Mary Thornycroft had long received her share of royal patronage. She was an excellent teacher, being an 'unpretentious artist who loved her work', despite being much lionized as almost the only woman sculptor of her time. Both she and her husband were great admirers of Prince Albert, believing that by his patronage and interest, he had done much to encourage the growth of Victorian sculpture.[28]

The Prince had encouraged his children to model as well as draw and etch; unfortunately, Princess Louise was too young to benefit from his encouragement as she only took up sculpture after his death. Her more fortunate, eldest sister, the Crown Princess, had always shown her work to him, sending home bas-reliefs of historical subjects like Henry VIII. Prince Albert had expounded his views on sculpture in a letter written to her on 13 April 1859: 'As an art it is even more attractive than painting, because in it the thought is actually *incorporated*; it also derives a higher value and interest from the fact that in it we have to deal with the three dimensions, and not with surface merely, and are not called upon to resort to the illusion of perspective.'[29] He placed the greatest importance upon realism and, in her works, Princess Louise strove to achieve realism, but did not always succeed.

The Prince placed great emphasis upon his children learning to sketch, weave, sew, spin and model because he believed that they could neither appreciate nor judge the works of others until they fully grasped the creative difficulties involved. He saw his children as future patrons of the arts and not as future creators; as he told Lady Bloomfield, 'I consider that persons in our position of life can never be distinguished artists. It takes the study of a whole life to become that, and we have too many other duties to perform';[30] but what seems certain is that, despite his words, he would, had he lived, have encouraged Princess Louise and been pleased by her ability. The same cannot be said of Queen Victoria.

The Queen considered sculpture 'unnatural' for a girl and not a suitable pastime for a young princess; sketching was a much more sensible occupation. The Queen had expressed her views to the Crown Princess when she had tried to discourage her from modelling and painting in oils: '. . . watercolours always are nice and pleasant to keep in books or portfolios'.[31] Like her eldest sister, Princess Louise chose to ignore Queen Victoria's advice. As a consequence, she passed more, rather than less, of her spare time with a mallet and chisel in hand during these years of the late sixties.

To be fair to Queen Victoria, sculpture was generally considered to be heavy and unnatural work for a woman.[32] Its attention to anatomy immediately made it an unsuitable occupation for Victorian women. Prevailing attitudes stressed that any talent should be used as 'the means of home enjoyment', never as 'a medium of display'. As the author of a best-selling, Victorian, advice manual enquired, 'who would wish a wife or daughter, moving in private society, to have attained such excellence in music as involves a life's devotion to it?'[33] Learning and, especially, achievement were the province of the Victorian male. So there were very few women sculptors, two exceptions being Princess Louise's tutors.

The Queen changed her mind about Princess Louise's new 'pastime' once she saw the quality of the work her daughter produced. Most of Princess Louise's early work was done as presents for birthdays or Christmases. One of her first attempts in sculpture was a marble bust of Princess Beatrice which, at the age of sixteen, she gave to Queen Victoria for her birthday in 1864. It took pride of place among the Queen's presents and, in her Journal for 24th May, the Queen wrote 'Louise's bust of Baby is charming and so like.'[34]

Princess Louise followed this with a bust of Prince Arthur, which she gave to her mother for her birthday in 1867. The Queen thought it 'excellent', and good enough to be given in 1868 to the Royal Military Academy at Woolwich, which Prince Arthur attended. Princess Louise had first executed a preliminary sketch of Prince Arthur's head, from which she made a small sketch model in clay to show to Mary Thorny-croft for criticism and advice; she had then constructed a full-scale model, from which a plaster model had been cast, before producing the final version in marble, which was given to Queen Victoria.

Although the Princess used rooms next to Mrs Thornycroft's as her studio at Windsor, her main studio was at Osborne. Here Prince Arthur had come for his sittings in 1867 and it was here that he and Princess Louise brought some acquaintances who had expressed an interest in seeing her studio: 'begging us to excuse a room in a mess', Princess Louise showed them her bust of Princess Beatrice 'life size and not only a perfect likeness but very graceful and pretty in expression', recorded one of the party. Over the mantelpiece in her studio, Princess Louise had a copy of her favourite picture, Leonardo's 'Last Supper', as well as photographs of other Italian masterpieces.[35]

The Queen was also becoming the proud mama as regards Princess Louise's work; she thought highly enough of it to ask her to try and improve on the work of other sculptors, including Matthew Noble, one of the most eminent sculptors of the day. Regarded by establishment art critics supporting the Chantry School, as a man of 'great ability', his work was condemned by an up-and-coming art critic, Francis Palgrave, as 'dead dullness'.[36] Whether Queen Victoria knew of this is not certain but, on 7 December 1867, she wrote to the Crown Princess, 'Poor Noble . . . is devoid of all real genius and has a horrid, colossal statue of me for India which Louise is going to try and greatly alter.'[37] The statue, complete with Princess Louise's alterations, was erected in Bombay in 1872. The Queen was now beginning to turn to Princess Louise for advice on, and help with, artistic matters.

They had become closer as a result of a project which Princess Louise had embarked upon in February 1868. This was a bust of Queen Victoria started at Osborne. While sitting for Princess Louise, the Queen was able to draw or chatter with her daughter and thus these afternoons passed in quiet companionship; she now realized that her daughter was no longer a child but a person with a mind of her own. Moreover, she was excited by watching the progress of the work and noted the sittings each day in her Journal; thus, on February 25th, 'Sat to Louise, who is doing a bust of me, & getting on wonderfully well.'[38] When the Court moved to Windsor the sittings continued. The bust was a huge undertaking for the Princess and it would not be finished until March 1869.

The Queen was thus more inclined to accede to Princess Louise's extraordinary request, made early in 1868, to attend classes at an art school, and so become the first princess to be educated publicly. For the Queen to agree to such a proposition meant that she accepted her daughter's determination to take art seriously, at a time when Princess Louise was in high favour with her. The Princess enrolled in the National Art Training School, where 128 students attended a variety of classes as part of an art teacher's certificate course. However, Princess Louise only attended the modelling classes. Sitting next to her was Henrietta Montalba, who later became a professional sculptress and was one of four sisters, all of whom became well-known Victorian artists and great friends of the Princess. Thus, these classes were important to Princess Louise because they enabled her to make friends with people she would not normally meet.

Her attendance at South Kensington was sadly erratic, not even on the basis of a weekly class, for she always had to fit in with her mother's arrangements. This undoubtedly affected her progress. Although the Princess was unable to attend regularly, she had ample reason to practise at home, through the family custom of giving works of art as presents. Birthday tables usually supported a mixture of pictures, sculpture, sketches, photographs and albums. In a large family, opportunities for output were endless and, at times, her studio must have resembled the production line in a factory.

She had eagerly adopted the fashionable custom of decorating her photograph albums, which contained *cartes de visite* (card-sized portraits). People collected and swopped them rather like stamps. Princess Louise's letters are full of requests for photographs or, more often, apologies for forgetting to send ones of herself. Arranging them in albums was no simple chore, for they were not just stuck on to a page; elaborate borders and designs were conceived for each *carte* and each album became a work of art in itself. Princess Louise drew a window surrounded by climbing roses with a birdcage at the side as one frame, while another, for the artistic Lady Waterford's photograph, was an artist's easel.[39]

Another outlet for Princess Louise's artistic talents was to design the scenery required for family charades and *tableaux vivants*. In these mid-Victorian years, amateur theatricals became popular as a means of entertaining guests at country house parties, which had become more popular with the spread of the railway system. Prince Albert used to organize performances but, after his death, the Queen stopped such celebrations. Then, in 1865, she was persuaded by Princess Helena and

Princess Louise to allow their younger brothers to enact one for New Year; the Queen slightly spoilt the event by becoming upset at watching it without the Prince by her side.

By the beginning of 1868, however, she had accepted such productions. That year Princess Louise was the prime force behind a charade, and a tableaux. Fräulein Bauer told a friend, 'Princess Louise looked lovely, talked a clever patois of Italian, German and French and sang a song with great charm . . .' In addition to being the star of the show, Princess Louise had designed most of the scenery. The tableaux set was 'a distant view of the city of Jerusalem, beautiful palm-trees at the sides – and a rough wooden cross lying in an opening broken through the boards of the stage in front. *All* the scenery which looked beautiful and effective even by daylight was the work of Princess Louise's own hands.'[40]

The Princess's active interest in the arts brought about a thaw in the Queen's strict adherence to her mourning. When Princess Helena had been the Queen's chief companion, she had not dared to play the piano or sing without first asking the Queen, whereas Princess Louise would play a few bars in front of her mother or quietly hum a refrain, and it was through her that the Queen's singing voice was again heard at Windsor.

The Princess's attempts to broaden her mother's outlook, whilst making her own life more interesting, had the support of Dean and Lady Augusta Stanley, who were concerned by the Queen's lingering seclusion. Lady Augusta, as Lady Augusta Bruce, had been the lady-in-waiting of Grandmama Kent and, after Prince Albert's death, had lived almost *en famille* with the Royal Family: 'She is like a *Sister* to the Queen to whom she cd say anything.'[41] Loathe to lose such a confidante, the Queen was most upset when, in 1864, Lady Augusta unexpectedly married Dean Stanley, formerly Regius Professor of History at Oxford. They made the Deanery at Westminster a centre towards which eminent Victorians gravitated; Lady Augusta's tea parties became well-known as gatherings of the literary, ecumenical, musical and scientific worlds. It was through the Stanleys that Princess Louise became acquainted with the latest books, music and social movements. In 1868 she heard through them, and their great friend the Duke of Argyll, that Longfellow was visiting England. The Princess persuaded her mother to receive him at Windsor. The Queen 'was much pleased with him and he had a few words with Pr. Leo and Pss Louise besides,' Lady Augusta informed her sister.[42]

In the winter of 1868–9, another poet, Robert Browning, had recently published a volume of poems entitled *The Ring and the Book*, which had been widely reviewed and well-received. Princess Louise hatched a plan with Lady Augusta to meet him. Since she could only meet company in the presence of an older member of her family and with the Queen's permission, she and Lady Augusta arranged a special tea party for the Queen, where she would meet representatives of the artistic and scientific life of the country.

Surprisingly, in view of her known wariness of 'intellectuals', Queen Victoria agreed to the scheme, as one she had talked of herself! However, Princess Louise's plan of just 'popping in' to meet people at a simple tea party foundered owing to the etiquette involved in entertaining royalty. Far from being an informal gathering, it became a stiff function where guests were too self-conscious to give any evidence of their brilliant reputations.

On Thursday, 4 March 1868, long, narrow strips of red cloth were laid between the archway leading to the Deanery and the House itself and at five o'clock that afternoon, the Stanleys stationed themselves at the door. The Queen arrived punctually, having left without Princess Louise, who was not ready and had to make her own way. Accompanied by the Duchess of Atholl, the Queen glided into the drawing room where 'drawn up in a circle with their backs to the fire stood *four men & two women*! a dead silence! you might have heard a pin drop for a second & then in whispers they were each successively presented,' reported the Duchess. 'It was so *drôle* – I could have laughed.' Although the conversation 'at last got quite consecutive – I mean constant not cheerful', it was heavy-going.[43]

The one person who thoroughly enjoyed herself, once she had found her way there, was Princess Louise. Despite the Queen's eminence, the Princess was the star attraction. The assembled company found that conversation with her was anything but stilted or trivial. The Princess made a great impression upon Carlyle, who thought her 'decidedly a very pretty young lady, and clever too, as I found out in talking to her afterwards'.[44]

Delighted with her afternoon, the Princess hoped that, now the ice was broken, the Queen would consent to further outings. Although Queen Victoria had described Princess Louise on her nineteenth birthday, as 'very handsome, full of talent' with 'a very affectionate heart',[45] she continued to find her daughter's wish for outside stimulation and

Family group at Coburg, where Queen Victoria had come to vet Prince Christian, August 1865.

Key:
1 Prince Louis of Hesse
2 Prince Alfred
3 Princess Helena
4 The Princess of Wales
5 The Duchess of Saxe-Coburg & Gotha
6 The Prince of Wales
7 Princess Beatrice
8 The Crown Prince of Prussia
9 Princess Louise
10 Prince Leopold
11 Duke Ernest of Saxe-Coburg & Gotha
12 Princess Alice
13 Prince Arthur
14 The Crown Princess of Prussia

One way of passing the Queen at a Drawing Room, Buckingham Palace, March 1866, pencil.

The Marquis of Lorne at Inveraray, c.1869.

independence difficult to tolerate. As she grew older, Princess Louise chafed even more against the Queen's domestic tyranny.

On innumerable occasions, the Queen exercised her power over Princess Louise by arbitrarily withholding permission for her to have tea with a courtier or visit a neighbour, for no apparent reason other than whim. On 11 December 1867, Princess Louise had to send her excuses for the following evening to Mrs Grey, because 'the Queen seems *not* to *wish* me to *leave* her; therefore I have to asked to be excuse, but not without expressing my great disapointment at not being able to come.'[46] Furthermore, she was expected to be grateful when Queen Victoria said she might go another time. On another occasion, when the Dufferins were at Osborne, with the Queen's permission, they had invited Princess Louise to join them for a sail but, suddenly, this did not suit the Queen, despite the lack of other plans for her daughter. Princess Louise had to decline the invitation, writing 'I need not disguise from you my disappointment.'[47]

She irritated Queen Victoria even further when she expressed interest in an issue of the day that Queen Victoria refused to condone or support. This was the matter of women's suffrage, as it was then called. It was through the Greys that Princess Louise became interested in the movement. Although neither of them supported women's rights, their cousin, Josephine Butler, was actively involved in it and thus came to Princess Louise's attention. Josephine Butler had become involved in the women's movement after she went to live in Liverpool, where she also became President of the North West of England Council for Higher Education of Women. Many women fell under her spell: 'Mrs Butler was like a flame . . . she was one of the very great people of the world,' wrote a younger suffragist, Millicent Fawcett[48].

The first public meeting held in support of votes for women occurred in April 1868 at Manchester and attracted great publicity. When the Crown Princess paid a visit to England that year, Princess Louise spoke so excitedly about women's rights and of her wish to help the organizers that she managed to persuade the Crown Princess to write on her behalf to Josephine Butler to offer her support. Knowing how busy Mrs Butler must be, Princess Louise felt too shy and useless to approach the lady herself, whereas she felt her eldest sister had a known position and a great name to bring to bear. When Mrs Butler wrote to Princess Louise to ask for her support in the rescue work of prostitutes in Liverpool, Princess Louise was thrilled and flattered. In her answer to Mrs Butler she remarked: 'I do take great interest in the happiness and well-being of women, and long to do everything that I can to promote all efforts in that direction,' and concluded: 'I feel pleasure in thinking you will let me know whenever any question arises in which my assistance and sympathy could be of any use to you.'[49]

Princess Louise, in common with other young ladies, met strong opposition from her family. Although she had the sympathy of both the Crown Princess and Princess Alice, their residence abroad meant that they were of little practical help. The Princess could support women's rights and pronounce on the sufferings and ambitions of other women, but the reality of her situation was that the only rights she possessed were those the Queen allowed her. Knowing how utterly opposed to women's suffrage Queen Victoria was, Princess Louise tried not to antagonize her mother unduly; she nonetheless felt obliged to defend women's rights in front of her, in the hope of tempering the Queen's views.

J. S. Mill's proposal to give the vote to women had moved Queen Victoria to anger: 'It is a subject which makes the Queen so furious that she cannot contain herself.'[50] Despite this, Princess Louise knew enough of her mother to judge that she would be as mercurial on this issue as on others. She never questioned her *own* ability to rule as Queen, although women were definitely 'the weaker sex . . . in need of the protection which man was intended to give'.[51]

Along with the Queen, the country in general and Society in particular were against the idea of educating women to be equal to men and giving them the vote. Admitting that Elizabeth Barrett Browning was a 'woman of great genius', a fellow writer, Edward Fitzgerald, nonetheless asked, 'but what is the upshot of it all? She and her sex had better mind the kitchen, and their Children and, perhaps, the Poor.'[52]

His view was shared by many whose voices were raised in the outcry against Lady Amberley, a signer of Mill's petition, who gave a public lecture on the 'Claims of Women' to be educated, to join the professions and to vote. Whereas Princess Louise wrote to support Lady Amberley, the Queen wrote asking Sir Theodore Martin 'to join in checking this mad, wicked folly of "Womens Rights" with all its attendant horrors, on which her poor feeble sex is bent, forgetting every sense of womanly feeling and propriety. Lady – [Amberley] ought to get a good whipping . . .'[53]

As the issue was aired in the press, Princess Louise became concerned that the publicity would harm the movement. Writing to Mrs Butler about starting an *International Women's Review*, she suggested that, since the whole issue of women's rights had 'become so tedious to the eyes of so many whose support it would be an advantage to gain,' it might be wiser to omit the word 'Women' from the title, 'as I think all appearance of exclusiveness should be avoided as it is after all only with the cooperation of the cleverest men that we can hope to succeed'.[54]

Another aspect of the women's rights question, about which the Princess felt strongly, was the law banning women from entering the professions. She believed that since women could be nurses they ought to be allowed to train as doctors; such a suggestion, increasingly voiced by women from the late eighteen sixties and seventies onwards, met with tremendous opposition. The case against female doctors was based upon the Victorian concept of femininity as incorporating purity and innocence – in other words, ignorance. The medical profession believed women were 'naturally' barred from membership and the *Lancet* even claimed that no one would want to marry a woman doctor because she would be 'impure in *l'âme*'.[55] Opposition also existed on social grounds. Since doctors were rarely received in Society, well-born women would be placing themselves outside their hereditary position by joining their ranks.

One young lady, who was named by the *Lancet*, was Miss Garrett who practised as the first woman doctor in Britain. Yet she had to go to Paris to gain her MD, since no British institution would accept her as a pupil. In 1866 she had settled in London as a consulting physician for women and children. Through Sir James Paget, news of Miss Garrett reached the ears of the Princess of Wales and Princess Louise.

There were several links between Princess Louise and Miss Garrett: they both corresponded with Mrs Butler; they both knew and dined with Dean and Lady Augusta Stanley. Having heard so much of Elizabeth Garrett's work, the Princess longed to meet her, but she was far too shy to summon Miss Garrett to Buckingham Palace; moreover, her mother's views on female doctors were so unfavourable it was unlikely she would consent to receiving one at a royal residence. So Princess Louise seized the opportunity of a visit to London and, with Emily Cathcart in attendance, turned up on the doorstep of 20 Upper Berkeley Street, 'a house discreetly on the fringe of fashionable medical

London'. She was admitted by a parlour maid and passed upstairs to the front drawing room where a communicating door led to the consulting room. Here the flustered maid opened the door and announced, 'Her Royal Highness the Princess Louise'.

Elizabeth Garrett was, according to her children, actually on a stepladder practising economy by hanging her own wallpaper. 'There was no need to apologise for old clothes, piles of books or the articulated skeleton laying on the desk,'[56] for Princess Louise paid no attention to them but straightaway launched into conversation, talking eagerly and without restraint. 'A pleasant visit followed and Elizabeth . . . treasured every word the Princess uttered.'[57] Upon taking her leave, however, she asked Miss Garrett, *please* not to tell [the Queen] she had called, as she would not approve'.[58] It is said that Queen Victoria learnt of the visit and was extremely annoyed. Whether she forbade Princess Louise to have anything to do with Miss Garrett is not known. The visit was never repeated, but, in later years, the Princess would work with Elizabeth Garrett Anderson to raise funds for her hospital for women.

Whatever she said about the incident, the Queen was clearly disturbed by Princess Louise's increasing 'restlessness' and her dalliance with such a dangerous movement as women's rights. It was certainly time, the Queen decided, for her daughter to settle down.

So, once more, she took up the role of matchmaker. True to form, Princess Louise's marriage would be different to those of the rest of the family. She might not be able to change Society's perception of women's rights, but she would change its perception of royal marriages.

CHAPTER VII

In Search of a Husband

In 1869 Princess Louise was twenty-one. Her wide, expressive, blue eyes were framed by thick, curly, fair hair, which always smelled of the honey-wash with which it was brushed. Mary Ponsonby admired her elegance: 'Princess Louise looked lovely; she contrives to put on her things like a picture.'[1]

She was not only charming to look at; she was also a most agreeable companion, a 'sweet, amiable girl with no nonsense about her',[2] one with 'lots to say', who was 'not at all stiff'.[3] When called upon to perform any public duty, such as her first one, the opening of Inner Temple Hall on behalf of her mother, she 'fulfilled it so well' and always appeared 'so very amiable', according to the great woman philanthropist Baroness Burdett-Coutts.[4] Even the Prime Minister thought her 'most kind', with such 'a charming manner'.[5] There were many who agreed with his assessment.

Earlier that year, the Radical MP, John Bright, whose recent appointment as President of the Board of Trade had displeased the Queen, was received at Osborne for the first time. Queen Victoria was extremely nervous and had a bad headache as a result. Princess Louise was a great help and chatted away to Mr Bright, so that even Queen Victoria thought the dinner went off 'extremely well'.[6]

The painter, Sir Edwin Landseer, was also there and the two visitors travelled back to town together. One of the topics of conversation was 'pretty, vivacious' Princess Louise. As they warmed to their subject, Sir Edwin exclaimed, 'If I were a young man and a Prince I should never rest till that lovely girl had promised to marry me!'[7]

Queen Victoria was equally aware of her daughter's attractive qualities; she judged accordingly that it would be much easier to find a husband for Princess Louise than had been the case with Princess Helena. Nevertheless, her terms had not changed an iota since those stormy days. She was now exceedingly dependent upon Princess Louise's companionship and wanted to find her a husband who would reside nearby. Not that Queen Victoria would admit that this was *her* wish; rather she expressed it as being the desire of Princess Louise, who would wish to 'stay with her when she cd be of use . . .'[8]

Princess Louise, however, had no intention of being palmed off with another Prince Christian. She wanted to chose her own husband, as her mother had done. The question of Princess Louise's marriage had already been raised by various members of the Royal Family. Over at Marlborough House, the Princess of Wales hoped to arrange a match between her eldest brother, Crown Prince Frederick of Denmark, and Princess Louise. Aware of the tastes and nature of this favourite sister-in-law, the Princess of Wales surmised that she would suit the informal, quiet, family life of the Danish Court and make an admirable future queen. But, in May 1868, when the Danish newspaper *Dagestele-graphen* printed a report of their engagement, it was immediately denied by *The Times* the next day.

The Queen had long been opposed to another Danish marriage. When Prince Frederick came to study at Oxford in 1863, the Queen had decided this was another Danish effort to capture Princess Helena or Princess Louise in marriage. The British Minister in Copenhagen was instructed to inform the Prince's father that 'Her Majesty can *never* entertain a question of marriage [between] the young Prince and any of her Daughters.'[9]

When, in the early summer of 1869, the now Crown Prince Frederick visited the Princess of Wales, she naturally tried to throw her brother and Princess Louise together. But the Queen's antipathy towards the Danish Royal Family could not be overcome.

The Queen of Holland was another who had decided that Princess Louise would do '*admirably*' for her eldest son, Prince William of Orange. She liked her better than any of Queen Victoria's daughters and sang her praises to Lady Westmorland. Not only was Princess Louise 'graceful, handsome, very attractive', but she had 'a cultivated mind'.[10] Unfortunately, Queen Victoria did not feel the same about the Prince of Orange or 'Citron', as he was nicknamed. He had been vetted as a possible husband for Princess Alice at Windsor in 1860 and found wanting. Since then, he was known to have lived openly in Paris with a *demi-mondaine*.

Of the thirteen remaining princes whose names were in the *Almanach de Gotha* in 1869, only seven were eligible—that is, Protestant and healthy with an independent position and fortune. The Queen then, for various reasons, pared the list down to just one name, that of

Prince Albrecht or 'Abbat' of Prussia, who might agree to live in England.

Delighted, the Crown Princess urged his claims to Queen Victoria and Princess Louise at every opportunity. Prince Albrecht was a nephew of the King of Prussia and a close cousin of the Crown Prince. Immensely impressed by England after attending the Crown Princess's wedding in 1858, he had decided to marry one of her younger sisters. He had also been considered by Prince Albert as a future husband for Princess Helena. The Crown Princess realized that the best chance of success for Prince Albrecht lay through Princess Louise, so she began to praise him to her and enlisted the support of Princess Alice, whose word always carried weight. The persuasive Crown Princess described the Prince as 'so nice', 'so good looking' and told endless stories of how good and kind he was. Moreover, Prince Albrecht was immensely rich even by royal standards. A giant of a man, he outstripped Bismarck, who was said to wear the largest-sized helmet in the Prussian Army.

Princess Louise became rather intrigued by the idea of this Prussian prince and, encouraged by the Crown Princess, even mentioned his name to her mother. However, Prince Albrecht had refused to reside in England. Determined not to have Princess Louise living abroad, the Queen was furious that the idea had been suggested to the Princess without her permission. She 'bitterly complained' about the Crown Princess raising the matter 'even behind my back with Louise. Alice also.'[11] General Grey advised the Crown Princess to say and do nothing further. Instead, he suggested that Princess Helena should persuade the Queen to invite Prince Albrecht over to make Princess Louise's acquaintance. Although the Queen agreed, she stated she would not conceal her wish to prevent the marriage from anyone, including the Prince.

Princess Louise passed the afternoon of November 18th with Sybil St Albans. As the two girls walked in the grounds of the Home Park at Windsor, their talk turned to Prince Albrecht. Princess Louise was in 'quite a state' about it and began to 'let out some of her griefs'. Sybil St Albans thought it best for Princess Louise to wait. After all, this was what she had done with her own husband. Her father had refused his first proposal but, in the end, she had married him. As the girls turned towards the Castle, they agreed that it was an awful dilemma for the Princess.[12]

Over the next few days the Princess also sought the counsel of the Princess of Wales, who might have been expected to pour scorn on any loathsome Prussian marriage. Instead, she warned her sister-in-law: 'Pray don't let yourself be guided by so many!!!', and advised her, 'better go straight about that kind of thing to your Mama'.[13] Thus, although it was not easy for Princess Louise to ignore the arguments put forward by her rather domineering eldest sister, the combined forces of Queen Victoria and the Princess of Wales won the day, and she decided against the match. In retrospect, she was wise to follow her mother's advice; the unpunctual Princess Louise, who was described by Queen Victoria as 'devoid of all pride and is vy fond of going among the poor people & the Peasantry,'[14] would never have felt at home at the Prussian Court where 'bowing and heel-clicking', and a 'stiff and "correct" attitude' were the order of the day.[15]

The difficulty now facing Queen Victoria was that, for political reasons, she could not summarily reject Prince Albrecht without a plausible explanation. As a result, when the time came for the Crown Princess to return to Germany in December 1868, the Queen sent a message with her to the effect that Princess Louise was not yet ready for marriage; this gave the Queen time to find an alternative suitor and Princess Louise some respite.

There were, however, no other eligible princes available, let alone any who would consider living in England. This led the Queen to consider the novel idea of a non-royal suitor for her daughter. In Princess Louise's own words, 'the only way of putting a stop to [this Prussian affair] has been that the Queen should have no opjection to a subject . . .'[16] For someone who in 1851 had written a letter, 'couched in uncompromising terms of anger and dismay,' to protest against the marriage of Prince Alexander of Hesse to the commoner Countess Julie Hauke, it was indeed a volte-face to propose a marriage for her own daughter with a commoner.[17]

A problem, which neither Queen Victoria nor Princess Louise seem to have considered, was that an eligible subject might not welcome the honour of entering into a royal marriage. Whilst the Queen could accept that foreign Royalties might refuse her conditions, it never crossed her mind that eligible British noblemen, with estates and responsibilities of their own, might also prove reluctant to live with or near the Queen.

The Monarchy was unpopular with the British nobility in 1869. Many of them would have agreed with Bagehot, when he wrote, 'From causes which it is not difficult to define, the Queen has done almost as much to injure the popularity of the Monarchy by her long retirement from public life as the most unworthy of her predecessors did by his profligacy and frivolity.'[18]

The Queen suffered from a further disadvantage in arranging such a marriage: she did not go into Society herself, nor did she allow Princess Louise to do so. The previous year, when Gladstone had presumed to request the Queen's permission for Princess Louise to dine at his house with the Prince and Princess of Wales, the Queen had replied smartly, Princess Louise 'never dines out except at Marlborough House.'[19] It was, therefore, difficult for her to meet suitable noblemen without causing undesirable speculation. Anyway, the Princess, like other girls, would not have been able to make more than a passing acquaintance with any suitor before marriage. For it was not thought necessary by Victorian parents for young people to know each other before marriage, let alone be on terms of familiarity, or in love. As Louisa Antrim explained, 'Respect and mild affection were generally accepted as the best basis for married life, whereas romance was regarded as distinctly dangerous.'[20] Indeed, to prevent 'romance', the ruling convention of the period was that unmarried men and women were never left alone together, which made courtship extremely difficult. If a man came into a library or sitting room where a girl was reading or writing alone, she was expected to make her excuses immediately and leave, as staying was forbidden.[21]

Now, in consequence of Queen Victoria's scheme, Princess Louise was about to be thrown into competition with other well-bred girls, who, like her, had been reared for marriage; the idea that a 'suitable' marriage was their natural destiny in life was so deeply ingrained in all Victorian girls that, in the eighteen sixties, those who failed to marry were considered 'redundant'.[22] Thus, girls were kept conspicuously under glass cases as exhibits for eligible young men to examine, approve and select, in the full knowledge that whomever they finally chose as a wife had always been pure, innocent and ignorant and would therefore be utterly dependent upon them.

Unlike other girls, Princess Louise was not going to be placed under a glass case; the plan was for eligible British noblemen to be placed under her own glass case so as to examine their suitability as prospective husbands. To expedite this, Queen Victoria's rule of keeping Princess Louise out of Society was to be broken, in order to arrange 'sightings' of suitors.

Somehow, the Queen had to find a British assistant marriage-broker. Normally, she would have used General Grey, but she no longer deemed him worthy of her confidences. His efforts to prise her from seclusion had banished him from her inner sanctum. Princess Louise could now only seek his counsel secretly.

In place of General Grey, the Queen used two other advisers. Gerald Wellesley, the Dean of Windsor, was a much tested counsellor and close friend of Queen Victoria. The other member of the Queen's team and her chief scout was Earl Granville, then Secretary of State for the Colonies. He had acted as an intermediary between the Palace and the Liberal Government since 1859 and had become a great favourite with the Prince and the Queen. A charming, cultured, old-fashioned gentleman and witty raconteur, he was admirably suited to the position of royal matchmaker since he kept abreast of Society gossip and so knew the worst about prospective suitors; more importantly, he was related to, or connected with, most of the British nobility.

*   *   *

While the Queen was consulting her advisers over 'the personal & delicate subject' of the Princess's marriage, Princess Louise had pushed all thought of marriage to the back of her mind.[23] She was preoccupied with the completion of the bust of her mother, which had to be finished before the opening of the new Royal Academy in May, since her mother wished to present it to the Academicians. Her task was made easier, because of the constructive criticism and encouragement she was receiving from her new sculpture tutor, Edgar Boehm.

A handsome, debonair, 35-year-old Hungarian with 'sparkling, dancing blue eyes', Boehm had been brought up in Vienna.[24] He had settled in England in 1862, but, with a young family to support, he soon found it impossible to make a living at sculpture. Using the then unfamiliar material of terracotta, he made his reputation in the fashionable world with an equestrian statuette of a lady 'that became the rage' and assured his financial success.

Princess Louise had met him at Osborne in January 1869, when she sat to him for a similar equestrian statuette. As a quick sketcher, the Princess was fascinated by the speed of Boehm's work and by the flow of 'elegant and witty conversation' which accompanied it.[25] Later, the Princess asked the Queen if Boehm could give her some lessons.

Flattered by what was, in effect, a royal command, Boehm accepted the position and took on Princess Louise as his first pupil.

The arrangement was a success from the first and Boehm gave Princess Louise the confidence to complete her work. The Queen was impressed, finding him a 'gentleman-like, clever, and excessively modest quiet person . . .'[26] The Princess was equally struck by his skill. From him she learnt to model in bronze, to produce the statuettes which he had popularized, and to portray much more realistically the texture, fit, drapery and trimmings of dress in her work. 'Treat a coat-sleeve, a woman's gown, *con amore*, ennoble it by art,' he admonished her and other young sculptors.[27] Undoubtedly charmed by him, the Princess, like many a nineteenth-century art student, fell a little under the spell, and much under the influence, of her art master.

On 12 May 1869 Princess Louise accompanied her family to the opening of the new Royal Academy at Burlington House. Ten rooms had been given over to the Academy and, in the Octagon room, in a position of honour, was placed Princess Louise's marble bust of the Queen.

*   *   *

Impatient to begin the process of seeing eligible noblemen before the Crown Princess again pressed Prince Albrecht on them, the Queen decided in July that she could wait no longer for her advisers to report on the constitutional position of marriage with a subject. She had already stipulated that a candidate must possess the three F's of family, fortune and fine position; and, in the early summer, Lord Granville had sent her reports about two young peers who perfectly met her requirements.

On July 16th, the Queen invited the first of them to dine with her at Windsor. Henry Petty-Fitzmaurice had succeeded his father in 1866 as the 5th Marquess of Lansdowne. In keeping with family tradition, Lord Lansdowne was following a political career and, by 1869, he was Lord of the Treasury in Gladstone's government.

In appearance and manner he seemed more French than English; this was not surprising for he had inherited his looks from his mother, Emily de Flahault, the granddaughter of Talleyrand. The Queen thought him 'a remarkably nice young man – with such good manners, and very good looking'.[28] Unfortunately, just when the Queen had ascertained from Princess Louise that she might like to see him again, rumours reached Osborne that he was engaged.

This news gave 'Louise really *quite* a *shock*'.[29] With Lansdowne's removal, she began, with the perversity of youth, to wonder whether anyone else would suit her as well. The Queen was more philosophical; 'we must not lament over what cannot be changed,' she told Lord Granville, agreeing that for Princess Louise at this early stage 'there can be *no real* feeling' and, added as a little joke 'tho' 1st night after does wonders!'[30]

The Queen now hastened to ensure a smooth path for the other eligible candidate. She instructed Lord Granville to 'just mention' to the Lord Chancellor that she was considering 'the possibility of occy [occasionally] returning to the old & perfectly loyal position of marriage with a *subject* . . .' At first, the Lord Chancellor displayed the caution associated with his profession and stressed the difficulties of such a novel arrangement for a princess of the royal blood. Queen Victoria would have none of it, arguing: 'The Queen believes th. only reason wh. made George III make that law was because his brothers married objectionable people . . .'[31] Having reprimanded the Lord Chancellor, the Queen instructed Lord Granville to ensure that the next candidate was not attached to anyone.

John (usually called Ian) Douglas Sutherland Campbell bore the courtesy title of the Marquis of Lorne as the eldest son and heir of the 8th Duke of Argyll. As John Bailey remarked, a duke in Victorian days 'however simple his nature might be, . . . could not escape being treated, even by his family and friends, as a kind of being apart from the rest of the world' and, from birth, Lord Lorne had been destined to succeed to the estates of Argyll and to the position, pre-eminent in Scotland, of Chief of the Clan Campbell.[32]

Moreover, his family had long been intimates of Royalty. As a little girl in Kensington, Queen Victoria had been enchanted by his beautiful grandmother, Harriet, Duchess of Sutherland. 'She saw me begin life,' Queen Victoria said of her, 'and was with me in all the happiest and most eventful moments of my life . . .' The Duchess was with the Queen on her wedding day, was her Mistress of the Robes and saw much of her privately because Prince Albert shared the Queen's fondness for her: 'Few were as beloved or highly regarded as she was and few had more friends.' She was also with the Queen 'in the saddest and hardest' moment of her life, 'in that chamber of Death in December

1861'.[33] She had become for the Queen: 'one of our dearest, kindest, truest friends'.[34] Thus, it was not surprising that the Queen showed such interest in Lord Lorne and, from the beginning, inclined towards him as a future son-in-law.

Furthermore, Lord Lorne himself had long been acquainted with the Royal Family. The story is often told of Queen Victoria's first sight of him at Inveraray Castle, the Argyll seat in Scotland, in 1847. 'Outside stood the Marquis of Lorn [sic], just two years old, a dear, white, fat, fair little fellow with reddish hair, but very delicate features, like both his father and mother,' the Queen wrote in her Journal. She was delighted with this wee imp: 'he is such a merry independent little child,' and, enchanted, she 'took the little fellow by the hand and lifted him up and kissed him'.[35] Lord Lorne was often teased with accounts of the Queen's affectionate greeting but he was unable to recall it. It appears that, from an early age, he was far more interested in soldiers than Sovereigns. He admitted it was difficult 'to know why the Queen made no impression at all on my youthful mind, but the tent and armed men a deep one!'[36]

There were, however, plenty of other meetings with Royalty which Lord Lorne did remember. As a child, he was often asked to Buckingham Palace to play with the young princes and, from the age of three, he had attended the children's balls there, quite at ease in such surroundings, which he could probably hardly differentiate from those of Stafford House. His mother noticed that, when she took the boys to see Queen Victoria, 'Archy chose to be stupid but Ian was quite comfortable,'[37] as he continued to be throughout his life with every sort of person in whatever circumstances; always charming, courteous, easy-going and sympathetic.

The Queen learnt more about Lord Lorne from Lord Granville, who was related to him on both the Sutherland and Argyll sides, and missives flew between Osborne and the Colonial Office: in one breath, 'Would Lord Granville ascertain Lord Lorne's position?', in another, Lord Granville must not 'let a soul know about it'. Reports followed – Mrs Wellesley has told the Dean how much praised Lord Lorne was at Lady Essex's; and urgings – Lord Granville must realize that 'no time shd be lost'. Finally, the Queen humbly admitted, 'she fears she is adding greatly to Ld Grs work by these confidential communications'.[38]

In fact, the affair was progressing nicely. The Princess had been pleased with Lord Granville's report on Lorne and was willing to see him, mainly because she had 'the gtst admiration & respect for the D of Argyll' whom she had known from girlhood.[39] She had also seen Lord Lorne just before her twenty-first birthday, when she and the Queen had called on the Duchess of Argyll at their London home in Kensington. Lord Lorne had happened to be there and he had shown her some of his brother's caricatures but, as he noted in his diary, 'had not much talk with her' as they were only together a few minutes.[40] Having seen a book he had written, and read the recent accounts in *The Times* of his speeches in the House of Commons, Princess Louise feared that she was '*not* clever enough' for him.[41]

The Queen, however, had no fears and gushed about how wonderful the Argylls were: 'their family is so admirable – the rank & name is so *high* that one could not wish for anything better'. Eager to ascertain the Argylls' inclinations, she asked Lord Granville 'as a *friend* to undertake the 1st breaking of the ice . . .' Recognizing that the Argylls 'wd be so shy & embarrassed, as to be unable to say *what* they felt' and admitting 'not to *say* how awkward & difficult it wd be for the Queen,'[42] she thought Lord Granville should speak to them before they came to stay at Osborne for a Saturday to Monday.

The couple who landed in the Isle of Wight on the afternoon of August 7th were quite used to the journey. The Duke of Argyll had undertaken it on many previous occasions in his official capacity as Queen Victoria's favourite Liberal Minister-in-Attendance; the Duchess had also done so, either when accompanying her mother, Duchess Harriet, or in her own capacity as Mistress of the Robes.

Although only forty-three years of age, Elizabeth Argyll bore the appearance of an older woman. Queen Victoria, who had known her since childhood, always said 'dearest Elizabeth's' frailty was the result of over-exhaustion from having twelve children, the youngest only four years previously. As a young woman 'Libby' Argyll had attracted attention by her intelligence and vivacity rather than by any extraordinary beauty. Now, as a matron, she had an air of stateliness and dignity. To those who did not know her well 'she was rather formal in manner, and kept one somewhat at a distance, though at the same time very kind and considerate'.[43] Her family and friends, however, adored her, and admired her knowledge of 'books, events and politics'.[44] As Lady Frederick Cavendish wrote: 'The Duchess of Argyll's wonderful cleverness is delightful to listen to.'

The Duchess was nervous, not of Queen Victoria, but of the

outcome of their discussions. She felt that it would be disadvantageous for Lorne to be so closely connected with the Court; her husband agreed. His main concern was how the Queen could react to his objections to such a match. A small, wiry man, he nevertheless had a commanding presence. His most remarkable features were a pair of piercing blue eyes and a huge mane of thick red-blonde hair, which he brushed straight back over his head and kept slightly long so it fell below his collar.

In 1869, the Duke was considered by many to be the finest speaker in the House of Lords. However, he was apt to become extremely excited and, throwing caution to the winds, would wildly overstate his case in words of flowing rhetoric. It was on one such occasion that Cobden likened him to 'a canary-bird firing off a big cannon'.[45] His temper and indignation flared up and as quickly evaporated, but his family and Cabinet colleagues were quite used to his 'impulsive and fizzing' temperament.[46]

The Duke was a man of wide interests; after reading his journals and letters, a grandson remarked upon their varied content: 'Political, yachting, birds, trees, all topics . . .'[47] In Scotland, the Duke was respected as the Mac Cailein Mor and a landlord of varied talents. An Oban innkeeper shrewdly observed, 'The Duke of Argyll is in a verra deeficult poseetion whaterva. His pride of inteelect will no let him associate with men of his ain birth, and his pride of birth will no let him associate with men of his ain inteelect.'[48]

Princess Louise liked and admired him. She even admitted to her mother that, if it was the Duke rather than his unknown son who was being offered as a prospective husband, she would have accepted him immediately.

At the first meeting with Queen Victoria, the Duke raised every objection to the match he could think of, in order to retain as much freedom as possible for Lorne in the future. The next day, the Queen told the Duke that she had considered many people but had come across none she would like so well as Lord Lorne and asked whether he was free and if the Duke thought it was possible. The Duke mentioned other possibilities: but all were rejected. The Queen had gone through the whole *Peerage* and found none as well-suited as Lord Lorne. 'But would not Society be very jealous?' asked the Duke. 'Yes – perhaps – but Society is *not* the Country.'

At this point, the Duke said he could not commit Lorne without first consulting him and requested the Queen's permission to do so. The Queen asked for time to consider and later agreed. 'Under the seal of secrecy', the Duke was 'formally authorised' in writing to tell Lord Lorne. Although this might seem perfectly normal, it had great significance; by informing Lord Lorne of the prospects of marriage with Princess Louise, 'a very formal step' would be taken in the Victorian quadrille of courtship. It implied that he 'was to have *an early* if not the first chance of gaining the prize . . .'[49]

The Argylls hurried back to London, where the Duke, 'fizzing' with excitement, told Lord Lorne the moment they arrived home: 'I saw at once that he was much taken with the idea – assuming that he was not to be kept hanging about a Court.'

Having asked for time to think about it, Lord Lorne told his father the next day that 'he wished to try', on condition he was not kept 'long in suspense' and that the matter would be settled soon, 'one way or another'. The Duke understood the outcome of the Osborne talks to be that Lord Lorne and Princess Louise would meet at Balmoral. If they liked each other, they would marry but if not then neither was under any obligation but was free to look elsewhere.[50]

Lord Lorne, therefore, answered through his father that he felt deeply touched by the Queen's kindness but 'perfectly unworthy' of the Princess. The Duke sent off Lord Lorne's acceptance of the conditions, behaving as if the matter was almost finalized – but Lord Lorne took a more cautious view; he could not believe 'that anything will come of these extraordinary negotiations'.[51]

Greatly relieved to have survived the ordeal of two such frank conversations with the Duke, the Queen also thought that the affair was more or less settled. But when told by the Queen of the outcome of the meetings, Princess Louise replied that she was in no hurry to marry and would rather wait. This was the last thing Queen Victoria wanted, since she had precipitated the Lorne affair in order to discourage and refuse the Prussian prince. Telling Princess Louise, 'If you go on delaying always you will lose everybody,'[52] the Queen confided to Lord Granville that she sometimes thought Princess Louise would never marry – 'as she is *so* very *difficile* . . .'[53]

Princess Louise's indecision had been fostered by Princess Helena, who had urged her sister not to hurry into any arrangement and to see all the other eligible people first. Princess Helena now turned her attention to the Queen. Playing her trump card, she reminded the

Queen that Princess Beatrice was still too young to take Princess Louise's place as companion; it would thus be more convenient for the Queen if Princess Louise's marriage was delayed.

As the Dean told Lord Granville, not only was Princess Helena anxious to avoid 'any speedy settlement' of her younger sister's marriage prospects but she, along with others in the family, wanted 'to put off Louise's marriage on their own accounts'.[54] With Princess Louise married and living away on some nobleman's estate, the Queen would turn to the only older daughter available: Princess Helena, who was living nearby at Frogmore House.

To avoid the Prussian match, the Queen had proposed a marriage with a subject in the hope that it could be arranged as quickly as possible; hence her speedy invitation to the Argylls. Now that Princess Helena had reminded the Queen of her dependence upon Princess Louise, she changed her mind about seeing Lord Lorne in the autumn.

When she received the Duke's letters, their implication that the outcome was likely to be decisive 'rather alarmed her'. The Dean urged her to agree to a meeting at Balmoral but the Queen sought refuge in silence and did not reply. 'This is her way when she disagrees or is otherwise influenced,' the Dean told Lord Granville on August 15th.

Princess Louise also confided to the Dean that she thought a meeting at Balmoral would be difficult for her because 'of more observation in the small circle there than at Windsor . . .' Nevertheless, she admitted to the Dean that, while she had not seen enough of Lord Lorne to know him, she 'liked very much what she had seen'. The Queen and Princess Helena, however, wanted to prevent the Princess seeing more of Lord Lorne; 'She and the elder sister don't want the Princess to marry yet', the Dean complained, 'till it will be too late . . .'[55] One way of ensuring this was to allow Princess Louise to see other noblemen over the next two years. Allowed some say in the matter at last, Princess Louise seized the opportunity of being a party to the selection of a husband.

Having led the Argylls on, the Queen now wrote to them to discourage the match. She said she would like Princess Beatrice 'to be a *little* older' before she could think of losing Princess Louise, and that Princess Louise must see other people first.[56] Since the Queen felt that if Princess Louise was going to marry anyone 'no other English connection' but the Argylls 'would please her nearly so well', she agreed to a November 'sighting', but insisted that Lord Lorne was absolutely free to marry someone else in the meantime.[57]

Since a woman's aim in the nineteenth century was to marry at all costs, not to choose the best husband, Princess Louise's decision to see many peers in order to discover whether she wished to make any nearer acquaintance, and then to conclude whether she liked the person enough to want to marry him, was an extremely unusual one. The Duke naturally thought this unfair to his son; while not wishing to threaten to forget the whole affair, he did not wish Lorne to be kept 'Dangling' indefinitely, especially since he had 'pretty much nearly his own pick and choice of all ranks *below*' the Princess. The Duke wanted to see his son and heir settled and feared that if Lord Lorne thought the project doubtful he would 'fly off at a tangent' and rush abroad.[58]

Lord Lorne himself was quite fatalistic about the affair: 'God only knows how this strange story will turn out,' he wrote in his Journal. Feeling unworthy of the good fortune he was told it would be if Princess Louise became his wife – 'this is only from hearsay for I know her too little as yet to wish for it' – he was happy to leave the matter in the hands of 'the Supreme'. His only anxiety was the disappointment his parents would feel if 'things went wrong', but better that than a loveless marriage with any princess.[59]

On August 21st Lord Granville brought the Argylls up-to-date with royal thinking. The Queen was 'abstractedly in favour of the marriage with Lorne'; it was now Princess Louise who was alarmed. The meeting with Lord Lorne in November would place her in exactly the same position as she would have been in if Prince Albrecht had come to England. Mistrusting her own resolve, she knew that the pressures of such a meeting would undoubtedly force her into agreeing to marry Lord Lorne, regardless of whether she liked him or not.

Queen Victoria's mistake had been to allow the Duke to tell Lord Lorne of her plans, which had advanced the courtship game into the second half, while the players were still struggling in the first. The Princess felt so upset about it that she told Queen Victoria she could not marry anyone until all the fuss had died down. She was 'afraid of having matters discussed by others, without having full opportunity of deciding for herself'.[60] To meet Lord Lorne now, when each knew about the other, would be mortifying for her.

Nevertheless, after a month's respite at Balmoral, the Princess had to steel herself to face Lord Lorne's visit and her first meeting with his father since Osborne. The Duke passed a night at Balmoral for a Council on October 9th. Princess Louise felt shy of him at first but he behaved so nicely about everything that they were soon back on their old footing. The Duke did notice one change in her mode of life, which he considered a great improvement. She was now allowed to remain all evening with the company, playing billiards and talking. Queen Victoria had decided that, if her daughter was going to marry a subject, then she must gain some experience of meeting them socially.

However, nothing in her life so far had prepared Princess Louise to interpret the advances of men; she had never been alone with a man, not even a brother for a moment. Such ignorance left her at a great disadvantage when it came to choosing a husband. She could discuss government policy with the Prime Minister but she had no idea what to say to a suitor. Inexperienced and over-protected, the Princess was still in many ways young for her twenty-one years. She was, indeed, luckier than many girls of her age in that she was always able to confide in her married sister-in-law, the Princess of Wales. But, unfortunately, she was absent when Princess Louise met Lord Lorne on November 18th.

The visit was not a success. The Princess's acute shyness and stilted conversation gave Lord Lorne the impression that she did not really like him. She was trying to behave graciously without appearing to encourage or discourage him, but the effect was of an unnatural reserve.

Given no encouragement, Lord Lorne assumed that she must either care for someone else or be rebelling against maternal pressure. He concluded that it was the Queen rather than Princess Louise who wished for the match. Nevertheless, he did not want to give up the idea and was prepared to wait until she had made up her mind for he admired and liked the little he had seen of her.

Having decided to see other peers, the Princess refused to enter into any discussions of marriage with Lord Lorne. She wanted to keep her options open; he, whose options had always been open, wanted to confine them to her. Nonetheless, she refused to allow the Queen formally to reject Lord Lorne as a possible husband. The Queen felt there was something in Princess Louise's character which 'will always disincline her to take a great decision'.[61] So, at the end of 1869, the confused, hesitant, 21-year-old Princess was no further forward than she had been twelve months before. The question of whom she would marry remained unanswered.

CHAPTER VIII

A Husband Found

Queen Victoria began the year of 1870 with a new reference book at her side; the *Almanach de Gotha* had been replaced by a thick, leather-bound copy of *Burke's Guide to the Peerage and Baronetage*. 'The Peerage', as the Queen called it, became quite a hobby; though invaluable in her search for a husband for Princess Louise, it proved to be the bane of Lord Granville's life. The Colonial Office was bombarded with enquiries about eligible young men whose names the Queen had found in her daily sorties through the *Peerage*. Having asked him to make 'full' enquiries about some unsuspecting eligible, the Queen would suddenly object to an obscure relation she had discovered lurking among the pages of Burke's. Or, as in the case of the rich Lord Douglas, she would object to the churchgoing. 'The High Church tendency wd be a gt objection,' she told Lord Granville, 'as *none* of the Queen's family cd go against the Estab [lished] Church of the Country in Scotland . . .'.[1]

When Lord Granville took the initiative and submitted the name of Lord Cowper, he received, by return of messenger, the Queen's very definite opinion: 'Lord Cowper is *out* of the Question,' because her *bête noire*, Lord Palmerstone was his step-grandfather. Moreover, Lord Cowper was already thirty-four, had been about in London '*so long*' and was 'personally *not* agreeable to either' of them.[2] Although the Queen invoked Princess Louise's name in support of her opinion, the Princess had not actually met Lord Cowper. When she did so at Marlborough House in the beginning of March, he made 'a most favourable impression' and she persuaded Queen Victoria to ask him to dine at Windsor on March 21st.[3]

The Dean reported to Lord Granville that Princess Louise, who liked Lord Cowper's shyness, good looks and position, was more impressed with him than anyone else; he was amused that the Queen, who previously would not hear of it, now had to let him take his chance, 'still nevertheless unwillingly'.[4] At dinner, Queen Victoria found Lord Cowper 'quiet & gentlemanlike & agreeable' but also very thin and delicate looking. When the Dean reported that Princess Louise had pleased Lord Cowper, the Queen, seeing a chance of happiness for her daughter, chose to forget her recent objections. She scribbled off a note begging for Lord Granville's help: 'it wd *not* do quite at so early a state for Lord C. to know the Queen wished it'; on the other hand, would it be possible to find out whether he would consider it?[5] After what had occurred with Lord Lorne, the Queen did not wish to approach him directly.

Queen Victoria felt guilty about Lord Lorne. She was reminded of him again when she and Princess Beatrice went to see the Duchess of Argyll in London in March. It was rare for the Queen to visit people in their own houses and was a mark of favour reserved for those of whom she was especially fond.

Four months previously the Duchess had suffered a stroke, which left her paralysed and weak. As a result, she had resigned her office of Mistress of the Robes. Lord Lorne had been summoned back from Italy so that, while the Queen was having tea at Argyll Lodge, she saw him and remained as impressed by him as ever. It seemed such a shame Princess Louise '*feels* she could *not like* him enough (tho' she thinks him very clever & agreeable) to let it go farther'.[6]

Upon her return from Argyll Lodge, the Queen told Princess Louise that she must make a decision about Lord Lorne; it was not fair to keep him in suspense. Princess Louise, still uncertain about Lord Lorne and attracted to Lord Cowper, agreed that it was now unfair to ask Lord Lorne to wait indefinitely. He should be told to look elsewhere. This the Queen told the Duke, who thought her letter most kind. It put an end to the rather unsatisfactory state of affairs for Lord Lorne, who was now free.

Having despatched Lord Lorne for the time being, the Queen and Princess Louise awaited reports on Lord Cowper. Queen Victoria had quite made up her mind to accept him, as the position 'was a very good one' for the Princess. But her hopes were quickly dispelled by Lord Granville's next letter. It seemed, once again, that Princess Louise's hopes were to be 'cruelly dashed', for Lord Cowper was about to become engaged to Lady Katie Compton. Both Queen Victoria and Princess Louise were intensely disappointed; Princess Louise, especially, became 'extremely annoyed' that her hopes had been raised only to evaporate upon closer investigation. Queen Victoria returned to the *Peerage*: 'there are others surely to be found' there.[7]

As they breakfasted together, the Queen would mention fresh possibilities but she soon noticed that Princess Louise was becoming more critical; so much so that the Queen wondered whether she would ever marry at all. The Princess's mood was not improved by other developments in her life. On March 26th, she had gone over to Claremont to help the Queen arrange some pictures. Whilst engaged in this enjoyable task, a messenger arrived bringing the sad tidings that General Grey had been seized with convulsions that morning and had had a bad stroke, which left him in a dangerous state.

This news was made all the more painful for Princess Louise because she knew that Sybil St Albans was about to be confined with her second child in the room next to his at St James's Palace. The General died after six days' unconsciousness and the poor Grey family had to dissemble about his death to Sybil until she had recovered. So did Princess Louise, who came to see them the next day, and again the following day, 'bringing his favourite flowers [lilies of the valley] to cover his coffin. She was so unhappy.'[8]

For Princess Louise, his death could not have come at a worse time. She had always gone to him with her troubles; now, when she most needed his advice, he was no longer there. As time passed, she missed him more rather than less, writing to Mrs Grey from Osborne on April 29th: 'I do miss the beloved General so dreadfully here I can hardly bear passing his room.'[9]

While mourning General Grey, the Princess learnt that the Queen had decided to replace Prince Leopold's Governor, Mr Duckworth, with a doctor. The Revd Robinson Duckworth had first come to the attention of the Royal Family through Dean Liddell of Christ Church. A brilliant scholar, Mr Duckworth had taken a first in Greats and gone on to take holy orders before becoming a Fellow at Trinity College. It was while at Trinity that, one hot day in July 1862, he rowed a ten-year-old girl and her two sisters from Folly Bridge three miles up river to Godstow for tea. Also manning the oars was his friend and maths tutor at Christ Church, Charles Dodgson. As the boat glided along the waters of the Thames, Charles Dodgson entertained them by telling the story of a girl's adventures down a rabbit hole. Published as *Alice in Wonderland*, Lewis Carroll, alias Charles Dodgson, included his friend 'Robin' Duckworth in the book, as the Duck.[10]

In 1866 Robin Duckworth was appointed by Queen Victoria as Instructor to Prince Leopold and, the next year, he was promoted to

Governor. By then he had become a great favourite with Royalty. Queen Victoria herself described him as 'a really most talented and charming person'.[11] He also possessed a beautiful voice and was a great addition to the evening gatherings held during the winter months at the Greys' cottage at Osborne. Princess Louise and Sybil Grey would often join him in duets and accompany him when he sang.

As a shy, sheltered, seventeen-year-old, Princess Louise had developed a schoolgirl crush on Mr Duckworth. Originally drawn to him through a shared concern for the well-being of Prince Leopold, she had come to know him better when preparing for her confirmation. His sympathetic, encouraging manner and fascinating, dark, good looks were irresistible; he was her first girlhood love.[12]

There is no doubt that, at thirty-three, he was an extremely handsome, charismatic, man. It is possible that Queen Victoria believed Princess Louise had rejected prospective suitors because she had been comparing them with Robin Duckworth and thus decided to dismiss him. Prince Leopold was dreadfully upset and could not understand why Mr Duckworth had to leave him: Princess Louise's sympathies were with her brother. Since Duckworth had not displeased in any way, she could only conclude that the Queen wanted to appoint a doctor to keep Prince Leopold more under her control now that he was growing up: 'he is to be nothing but his keeper, not his governor' the Princess complained to Colonel Elphinstone on April 12th.[13]

Before Duckworth left in the summer, the Princess and Prince Leopold gave him a ring she had designed. It contained forty-three stones of ruby and diamond for his initials and two of lapis lazuli, for Leopold and Louise. On the inside it bore the inscription: 'Forget us not. Le. Lo. 67'.[14]

Queen Victoria was still immersed in the *Peerage*. A procession of the best of British noblemen passed under the gateway of Windsor Castle during the season of 1870, to be reviewed by their Sovereign and her daughter. Based upon Queen Victoria's random, if increasingly desperate, forages through the *Peerage*, it was rather a makeshift, royal, vetting system. The attempt to maintain secrecy could not be upheld, as more people at Court were consulted. The Dean commented that it was as if a proclamation had been made that Princess Louise 'is to be held up as a prize to the most forward bidder . . .'.[15]

In order to give Princess Louise a wider choice, the Queen had stretched the rules of eligibility to include those of a lesser rank for, as she remarked, they could be raised to *any* rank if necessary. The three F's had been replaced: '*Character* & an *independent* future *are the* really important thing.' This let in men, such as thirty-year-old Henry Strutt, whose father was only the first Baron Belper, though belonging to an old Derbyshire family whose fortune came from coal. The Queen had heard him 'vy highly spoken of' and, more importantly, that 'he will be *very* rich'.[16]

The Princess rejected Mr Strutt sight unseen; if she was to live in Derbyshire, there was only one possible residence, Chatsworth, and Lord Hartington, the heir to Chatsworth, was unmarried and thus available. Unfortunately, the Princess had been told, Lord Hartington was 'not suitable'; for, as all the world knew, he was enamoured of another Louise, who was married to the Duke of Manchester. Princess Louise was simply teasing her mother by suggesting Lord Hartington, a great friend of the Prince of Wales and thus anathema to Queen Victoria. It was just such incidents that caused the Queen to complain how '*difficile*' Princess Louise was.

Another more suitable peer drummed up for Princess Louise was Tommy de Grey, heir to Lord Walsingham, with three country estates as well as Walsingham House in London. Unfortunately, he was also a friend and Norfolk neighbour of the Prince of Wales. As it turned out, it was lucky for Princess Louise that Queen Victoria decided against him, for he eventually had to sell his estates, his London house becoming the Ritz Hotel, and ended his days abroad in relative impoverishment.

By the beginning of May, four new names were being considered: Lord Camperdown had the disadvantage of a mad father, although the Queen felt that two places in Scotland must help; Lord Ailsa, whom Lord Granville considered ugly but was corrected by Queen Victoria: 'Lord Ailsa is *not* ill looking & vy gentleman like'; Lord Gosford seemed eligible but the Queen thought he might be poor; and Lord Rosebery, whom the Princess had mentioned but whom Queen Victoria rejected because 'At one time he was inclined to go on the Turf' and he was a friend of the Prince of Wales.

Then the Queen was told by Lady Waterpark that he had given up the turf; suddenly he became steady and amiable and, of course, 'Dalmeny *IS* is a lovely place.' So Lord Rosebery dined at Windsor on May 14th and pleased the Queen, but Princess Louise refused to commit herself. Queen Victoria sought refuge in the fact that, as he was young, he might not be in a hurry either.[17]

On the following evening, Lord Gosford dined and again Princess Louise refused to commit herself about whether she liked him. While the Queen sat at Windsor, uncertain of her daughter's real feelings, the Princess had been unburdening herself to Colonel Elphinstone in a series of *cris du coeur*: 'The few people I shd have cared for here are just married,' she had written on April 12th, 'so I do not know what is going to happen: meanwhile everyone is speaking, either for or against this & it is most uncommonly unpleasant, & I am to decide without a proper chance of knowing anyone.' She then added, 'I leave it to you to judge what a delightful position I am in . . .'[18] She felt that she was being forced to make a decision that was impossible; for how could she possibly tell who would make her happy? There was no one she knew who could advise her; and, now that everyone knew the plan, she was 'the cynosure of neighbouring eyes'. Poor Princess Louise was like a hind at bay, surrounded by Family, Ministers and courtiers all urging her to run in different directions. As far as she was concerned: '*I* am in no hurry or wish for another life – but it is that I *am* hurried on all sides which is painful.'[19]

Even at Balmoral, basking in the early summer weather, the Queen was busy arranging further dinners for their return to Windsor. 'It is very essential to get on,' she urged Lord Granville.[20] Normally, Princess Louise would have been delighted by the prospect of dining out during the London Season; now, however, the thought of such engagements oppressed her. For the first time, she longed to stay hidden away at Balmoral. She reiterated her refusal to marry without at least feeling *some* affection for her intended husband; otherwise she would remain unmarried. Somewhat exasperated, Queen Victoria nonetheless had to admit that Princess Louise was being sensible: 'She takes the *right view* of *not* wishing to marry for *marrying's sake* wh. is but too common among Prince's and Princess's & everyone in the higher classes,' the Queen informed a weary Lord Granville.

Princess Louise returned to Windsor to discover that the Cambridge family had been busy selecting their own candidate. The bearer of these tidings was Princess Helena, who had never been over-fond of that branch of the family and was only too happy to show them up. Queen Victoria always reacted to the Cambridge family as a Geiger counter does to radioactivity. She immediately turned for support to Lord

Granville, now her new Foreign Secretary. On June 19th, she let him know her views of the Cambridge idea: 'We hear . . . that the *whole Cambridge* family are *determined* to try and force Princess Louise to marry Adolphus of Mecklenberg S.!!! The Queen is most indignant at such a proposterous & impertinent notion . . .'[21] Queen Victoria was, of course, overreacting to what was merely a suggestion. If Princess Louise had refused Prince Albrecht, she could hardly now marry a less important German princeling. The Prince of Wales, however, wanted a non-Prussian royal marriage so the Mecklenberg-Strelitz one suited him.

The Queen's case was not helped by the fact that Prince Adolphus of Mecklenberg-Strelitz had always been a candidate worthy of consideration. Prince 'Doppus', as he was known in the family, was a healthy, nice looking, Protestant heir to a duchy which assured him an independent position. There were, in fact, distinct advantages to such a match for Princess Louise. Not only would she retain her royal position but she would be marrying into a family she knew. For her great-grandmother Queen Charlotte, wife of George III, came from Mecklenberg-Strelitz and the present Duchess was the Queen's first cousin and Princess Louise's godmother. Her ties with England had remained extremely close, since she passed part of every year in London. Thus, Princess Louise could easily have lived in England for most of the year, apart from the three-month period of January to March which formed the Season in Strelitz. Having seen how difficult Queen Victoria made it for the Crown Princess and Princess Alice to come home for holidays, Princess Louise had already stipulated that, if she married abroad, it would be written into her marriage contract that she would reside in England for so many months of the year.

Although people sneered at the *kleinstädtisch* court of Strelitz, Princess Louise would have enjoyed its *gemütlich* atmosphere: where all the entertainments would pivot round her; where there were endless opportunities to take charge of the theatre and opera houses and arrange art exhibitions; and where there was scope to start and organize schools and hospitals and go amongst the people.

The Queen, however, refused to discuss such a marriage with Princess Louise and, afraid of further suggestions from the Cambridge quarter, she urged the Princess to choose Lord Gosford or Lord Rosebery. The Princess had met Lord Gosford at Lady Clifden's and then at Lady Granville's on July 8th. Under pressure, she said he was 'rather nice'; however, Lord Gosford was poor – he had an income of £6,000 a year out of which his establishment had to be kept and his mother receive a jointure of £3,000 a year.[22] The Queen said she could not consent to it: 'I don't think *riches* make happiness, or that they are necessary,' she wrote on another occasion to a granddaughter, 'but I *do* think a certain amount is a necessity so as to be independent.'[23]

Since the Princess had objected to Lord Lorne having an income of £4,000 a year with the prospect of £40,000 a year eventually, the Queen did not feel she was being unfair to object to Lord Gosford's income, which held no prospect of increase. £2,000 a year was then considered by the nobility to be the absolute minimum upon which to marry.

Although there were still more names on her list of eligibles, the Queen was becoming distraught. The Princess would not hear of Lord Dalrymple, three months younger and shorter than herself, and declared 'she would not even *see* Lord Coke as she would not marry a boy'. Queen Victoria decided that '*no* notice must be taken of Princess Louise's fancies' and she would no longer consult her. In despair, she urged Lord Granville, 'We must *search* the Peerage in all its different Degrees'; and, in desperation, she wailed of one unknown hopeful, 'will he *ever* have £100,000 a year?' Princess Louise was 'so vy wayward & unreasonable,' that they would soon have exhausted the list of candidates.[24]

Then, the unexpected happened. At the beginning of July, Princess Louise had been allowed to attend one of the Gladstones' famous breakfast parties. Here, at noon, some of the leading statesmen, churchmen, literary men and artists, as well as friends and family, gathered in the beautiful drawing room of 11 Carlton House Terrace, looking across St James's Park to the Horse Guards. The person who made the most favourable impression upon the Princess was none other than . . . Lord Lorne. He contributed to the interesting talk and seemed so nice and good looking that she found him singularly appealing. Since all talk of marriage between them was dead, they were relaxed and natural in each other's company and this, no doubt, contributed to the mutually favourable impression they now made upon each other. Having seen him again, Princess Louise was now even less disposed to like the other candidates; but how could she admit the real reason to her mother.

But the Queen was quick to sense something in the Princess's account of the breakfast party and asked her lady-in-waiting, Lady

Clifden, a cousin by marriage of the Duchess of Argyll, surreptitiously to mention Lord Lorne again to Princess Louise. Lady Clifden reported back that she seemed more inclined to take Lord Lorne than anyone else being considered.[25] Lord Granville was immediately alerted to this extraordinary development: 'Such things have often succeeded,' the Queen wrote, reminding him that 'the young lady is singularly . . . unreasonable.' Lord Granville, overwhelmed with Cabinets and correspondence in consequence of an outbreak of war between Prussia and France, could hardly believe that the Queen was about to disinter the Argyll affair. He, therefore, replied somewhat shortly, that he understood the matter to be at an end and not worthy of re-opening.

Queen Victoria, nevertheless, proceeded with her latest plan. Under the pretext of inviting companions for Prince Arthur to Balmoral in September, she instructed Lord Granville to issue invitations to five noblemen: Lords Lorne, Rosebery and Henry Fitzroy with Prince Arthur's friends, Lord Stafford and Albert Grey. The Queen informed Lord Granville that Princess Louise had asked for Lord Lorne to be invited and, with a quick thrust, reminded him that he had 'always said . . . he was sure the Princess *would* see how far superior Lorne was to all the young men when she had seen others . . .'[26]

Having arranged everything satisfactorily, the Queen was now free to attend to foreign events for, during the hot, summer days of June and July, a European crisis had precipitated a war between Prussia and France. The Government maintained their stance of strict neutrality, which the Queen supported in public. In private her sympathies were blatantly Prussian. 'My whole heart and my fervent prayers are with beloved Germany!' she told the Crown Princess on July 20th from Osborne.[27]

Once again the Queen's family were divided. Not surprisingly, Prince Christian and Princess Helena were wholeheartedly German. Prince Christian wanted to enlist in the German Army but the Queen dissuaded him: 'as he is nationally my son-in-law and as we are neutral it was thought better he shd not, as it might lead to difficulties and complications'.[28] The Princess of Wales, however, desperately hoped the Prussians would be annihilated by the French.

When war broke out, Princess Louise's thoughts were focused upon how she could help the wounded. Her heroine, Florence Nightingale, had helped to start the National Society for giving Aid to the Sick and Wounded in the War, an organization which acted as a neutral agency and sent supplies to both sides. Princess Louise set to work collecting old sheets and linen, which were torn to shreds to make what was then called 'charpie'. This was used to staunch and dress wounds. All the Household were put to work making charpie or scouring the glens for thistledown, picked to stuff pillows for the wounded. Princess Louise longed to join the war effort, as a nurse or helper but, of course, her position prevented it. She had to be content with 'doing things and sending off boxes for the good of the sick and wounded'.[29] She also donated several pictures in aid of the Fund for the Sick and Wounded.

As the war progressed, the Princess's sympathies for France increased, as did her desire to live in England and remain English. She began to realize the wisdom of the Queen's plan for her to marry a subject.

The war was not only being fought by the Prussians and French on the battlefields of Sedan and Metz; it was also being fought by Royalties and by the Household in the sitting rooms of Osborne and Balmoral. Meals were often delayed, owing to the arrival of a telegram with reports of the latest battle. The Queen could get no sleep, she was so anxious for news of her two sons-in-law; Princess Louise kept having headaches, she was in such constant suspense. She also had to try and keep peace in the Household between the French and German factions. Poor Mlle Norèlle, the 'unfortunate French governess' as Lord Halifax described her, was sadly sat upon by the triumphant Herr Sahl and Fräulein Bauer.

French reinforcements were soon brought up for Mlle Norèlle with the arrival of the Princess of Wales. On September 2nd, a telegram arrived with the news of a French victory at Sedan, which so cheered the Princess of Wales she went around beaming and pulling faces at the Germans. The next day, however, news came from the King of Prussia announcing the surrender of the French Emperor; the sad Princess of Wales wandered around almost in tears, while poor Mlle Norèlle would not even appear at luncheon. Herr Sahl was 'more triumphant than ever!'[30]

These dramatic events on the Continent disturbed the tranquillity of the Royalties, but not the routine of their autumnal holiday. The outward appearance of a typical Balmoral autumn was belied by the discreet entries in the Court Circular of the names of some of the most eligible bachelors in the land, who, this year, had chosen to break the hectic social and sporting round of autumn visits with a quiet week at

Balmoral. The attentive Society observer would have noticed, among the entries of the daily drives and walks, the distinguished names of Lords Rosebery, Stafford, Fitzroy and Lorne.

Lord Rosebery was at Balmoral for a week at the beginning of September, but Princess Louise did not feel she liked him enough to marry. Having found that he '*requires* to feel he *ought* not to give his opinions quite so decidedly upon things in the presence of older people . . .', Queen Victoria asked Lord Granville to pass on a few hints to Lord Lorne about how he should behave if he wanted to succeed, with her at any rate. 'Lord Granville shd advise him being quiet & not talking too much or talking too loud or taking the lead too much at the Queen's small Dinner Table.'[31]

On Friday, September 29th Lord Lorne arrived at Balmoral. That evening he dined with the Queen, Princess Louise, Princess Beatrice, the Lord Chancellor, Lady Jane Churchill and the Ponsonbys. Wearing what one courtier described as 'a wonderful costume, consisting of a black velvet tunic studded all over with silver fish, the distinctive mark of the Campbells' and the kilt, Lord Lorne looked very much the handsome young laird he was.[32] Of slim build and medium height, he had an uncommonly fair complexion, 'the most marvellous piercingly bright blue Campbell eyes',[33] the whole 'crowned by a wreath of yellow gold hair', which he wore long like his father.[34]

Mary Ponsonby thought Lord Lorne's modest, self-effacing manner 'perfect'.[35] The Queen could not determine what her daughter thought about him, but she was only too happy to tell Lord Granville that Lord Lorne was 'vy pleasing & agreeable' and not at all forward. Admitting that his high-pitched, nasal voice was slightly against him, she concluded he was 'vy amiable'.[36]

On the following morning, while Lord Lorne went out stalking, the Queen plotted how to throw him and Princess Louise together that afternoon. She consulted Mary Ponsonby and Lady Jane, eventually deciding, 'I think Mary might go with the tea & the Lord Chancellor & meet them accidentally at the Garralt.' That afternoon, a large riding party consisting of Princess Louise, Prince Arthur, Lady Jane Churchill, Mary Lascelles, Lord Lorne, the Lord Chancellor and the Ponsonbys set off. But the Queen had reckoned without the Lord Chancellor who, according to Mary Ponsonby 'wasn't to be done out of *his* flirtation' and 'in a swallow tail coat and black hat ambled contentedly by the Princess in full conversation the whole way'. Since this was hardly the object of the exercise, Henry Ponsonby had to try and draw him away from Princess Louise, once the Garralt was reached; he eventually succeeded in pinning the Lord Chancellor into a corner by asking him an involved question about Scottish law, which gave Lord Lorne 'room for a little devotion'. Closely watched by all the courtiers 'in the know', it cannot have been the most spontaneous or easiest of wooings.

That evening, the party was joined by Dr Norman Macleod, who was to preach at Crathie Kirk the next day. Lord Lorne knew him well and had been confirmed by him. Much more at his ease by now, Lord Lorne charmed the company with his interesting conversation and courteous manners. The Queen might wish for silence, but her daughter and the Household preferred pleasant talk. Although seated some way from him, Princess Louise was still able to overhear Lord Lorne's remarks; from comments she later made to Mary Ponsonby, she was impressed by his having opinions and views of his own upon different topics.[37]

The Queen took the opportunity of asking Dr Macleod privately on Sunday evening for his opinion of Lord Lorne, naïvely thinking him unaware of her motive; when he replied that he knew '*no* young nobleman who was so thoroughly good or promised so well as Lorne',[38] the Queen was well on the way to embracing Lord Lorne as her future son-in-law. It only needed Princess Louise to adopt the same attitude and all her hopes would be realized.

When Lady Jane Churchill and Mary Lascelles left Balmoral on Monday morning, the great question occupying everyone was still '*Oui ou Non*'[39] to Lord Lorne. It seemed to Queen Victoria, however, that Princess Louise had already more or less made up her mind; at breakfast, the Princess begged her to ask Lord Lorne to stay two more nights, saying she thought him so very nice. This the Queen gladly did. Later that morning, the Queen wrote to Lord Granville and, at last, admitted: 'The Queen *herself thinks this is to be*,' especially since Lord Lorne had arrived on the day the Crown Princess had become engaged.[40] Princess Louise had her own superstitions. That morning she carefully chose only one ornament to wear; it was a cross the Duke of Argyll had given her.[41]

That afternoon, the Queen arranged matters so that, while she, Princess Beatrice and Mary Ponsonby drove along the south side of the Dee, Princess Louise and Lord Lorne were despatched under the chaperonage of Lady Ely and the Lord Chancellor to the far off Dhu

Loch. Although it was a heavenly afternoon with crisp, clear, autumnal air and the sun reflecting upon the snowcapped peaks and russet colourings of the wooded hills, the Queen's choice of the Dhu Loch was not a romantic one.

The party rode to the loch and dismounted to find a small, dark, rather sinister-looking loch, lying deep amongst grim barren hills. The surroundings did not seem to dampen the spirits of the younger of the two couples, however. After having tea at the bothy, they walked to the Upper Loch, Princess Louise and Lord Lorne in front of Lady Ely and the Lord Chancellor. Lord Lorne and Princess Louise walked much faster up the hills than the other two and soon outdistanced them so that, although they remained in sight, they were out of earshot.

Brandishing 'Your Royal Highness's' more than ever before or since, Lord Lorne declared his love and, saying that he was utterly unworthy, he asked Princess Louise to marry him.[42] The Princess surprised herself by the certainty with which she instantly accepted him. She explained to him that she could not say yes before, as the Queen wanted her to do, when they had only met formally a couple of times: 'You could not have respected me if I had made up my mind without knowing you.' Lord Lorne then said he would not have wanted to marry her without further acquaintance, much as he admired her.[43]

They stood together talking in a 'very affectionate and dear' way, until Lady Ely and the Lord Chancellor caught up and then they started for Balmoral, where they arrived at half past seven. Lord Lorne had asked the Princess to promise to tell the Queen at once, since 'she was very shy' about doing so. This the Princess did.

At dinner Lorne could see that Her Majesty 'knew all'. As he told his father that night, 'She was *much pleased* but told L that I ought to have first told her what I intended – "just as I told you she would", L said'.[44]

It was not until two days later, on October 5th, that Queen Victoria announced the engagement to the long suffering Lord Granville. 'The Queen feels anxious and yet satisfied – for she likes Lorne extremely. And Louise seems perfectly happy.' The Queen also complained of the suddenness of the engagement. Her attitude may seem perverse, in that she had been plotting to throw them together for days, but this was only so that they would have a chance to talk to one another. Queen Victoria had no idea events would move so fast *without* her knowledge and, more importantly, her permission. The Queen had thought that any proposal would be made later in the South. 'It is therefore Lorne's and not *our* fault th. the thing came so suddenly . . .'[45]

But having waited for over a year for an opportunity to know and talk to Princess Louise, Lorne was determined to find out what her true feelings for him were.

As impulsive as his father, he knew what he wanted and seized it. The fact that his beloved was a princess did not deter him. After all, as he wrote in his Journal: 'It is no novelty that a Scottish Noble shd be related to the Sovereign. Such a marriage would be the return to old ways.'[46]

CHAPTER IX

A Bold Experiment

'You will be glad to hear that another of your children is going to be married – which is me,' Princess Louise told her beloved, old nurse Mrs Thurston, proudly adding, 'but to no German Prince but . . . an English (a British I suppose I ought to say) *nobleman*, the Duke of Argyll's son. He is one of the *cleverest* and *best* young men of the day, admired and appreciated by everyone.'[1] The Queen agreed with her daughter; indeed, as she was quick to remind everyone, she had been the first to recognize Lord Lorne's fine qualities. Writing on 6 October 1870 to the Duke, the Queen admitted that, although the event had come upon her faster than she expected, she not only 'highly approved', but 'quite rejoiced about it'.[2]

The news of their son's rather precipitate proposal had filled the Argylls with great anxiety for, aware that Lorne was deeply in love but uncertain of the Princess's feelings, they could think only of the risks attached to such a match. As *The Times* drily observed, princesses of the blood royal have been instinctively more obedient to family laws and customs than princes; the last marriage to occur between a daughter of a reigning Sovereign and a subject was in 1515.

Although in the nineteenth century royal and aristocratic marriages were seldom love matches, the Argylls' marriage had proved an exception; they had been extremely happy together for twenty-six years. It was their firm belief that if their son's controversial marriage was to work, it must be based upon the strongest mutual affection. On October 10th, the Duke confided to his old friend, Mr Gladstone, that he had received 'the most affectionate and *excellent* letter from Princess Louise saying she had often yearned for the Consels [sic] of a Father and hoping to be a good Daughter to us'. Still, the Duke cautioned, 'it is rather a bold experiment and one cannot but rather tremble lest it should not succeed'.[3]

The Queen, anxious to see the Duke alone, had invited him to Balmoral on October 13th, two days before Lorne returned. As soon as Princess Louise learnt of this arrangement, she asked the Duke to

see her immediately he arrived. At Ballater station, the Duke was given
a note from Queen Victoria to the effect that *she* wished to see him
first and would do so after she came in from an afternoon drive. On
reaching the Castle, however, the Duke found a note on his table from
Princess Louise saying that the Queen was out and *she* would see him.
The Princess wanted to be the first to welcome him and discuss
the marriage arrangements before the Queen could settle everything
without her. Caught between two rival Royalties, the Duke plumped
for the more senior. 'I thought it was time to begin playing the Papa
and enforcing filial obedience' was how he described his decision to
obey the Queen. The Princess, therefore, had to wait in an adjacent
room until the Queen sent for her. When the Princess came in, 'very
shy', to greet the Duke, she was embraced by him. He had received
the Queen's permission for this relaxation of etiquette beforehand:
'Well, Mam I hope you won't be shocked if I embrace her?' he had
asked. 'Oh, certainly not,' answered Queen Victoria, who at the time
seemed 'vastly pleased with the whole thing'.[4] This episode introduced
the second act of the comedy known as 'the Familiarity Row'.

At first all was well. The Queen was 'in immense spirits' at dinner
and 'most affectionate' to the Duke throughout the discussions.[5]
Having pointed out the obstacles and risks during a long talk alone
with Princess Louise on the 15th, the Duke could report that he found
her charm 'no *varnish* – but the index of a high and noble character'.[6]
However, instead of being delighted by his evident high regard for
Princess Louise, the Queen refused to allow her daughter a moment's
glory. At dinner on the last day of the Duke's visit, the Queen looked
very grave and did not utter a word; it was apparent to everyone that
something was wrong.

Afterwards, Lady Ely told the Duke that 'it was only a little natural
feeling of some jealousy'. The Queen felt that Princess Louise was
receiving too much attention at her expense. These feelings had been
exacerbated by Lorne's return and by a letter sent to Princess Louise
by Prince Ernest of Leiningen in which he congratulated her upon
getting a '"Happy Home of Her Own" – as if her mother's home had
not been happy,' Queen Victoria had sniffed.[7] Unable to fault Princess
Louise, the Queen turned on the Duke and Lorne; their familiarity
with Princess Louise provided the excuse for her surly behaviour.

'I believe Eliza [Queen Victoria] is a little nervous about the whole
thing,' Henry Ponsonby told his wife. 'Is not accustomed to the

intimacy with a subject'.[8] The Queen found it difficult to accept the familiarity inherent in her closer relations with the Argyll family. Lorne might be 'most amiable, clever and gentle', but he was the first young man who was neither relation nor Royalty, yet with whom she had to discuss family matters.

'There are *little* things in *his* manner – like that of all the young Englishmen,' she complained to Lord Granville, 'wh a little startle the Queen who has never *been* on familiar terms strange to say . . . with *any* but foreign' young princes. Moreover, in replying to her letter, Lorne, no doubt unthinkingly, had committed a dreadful error; he had called the Princess, 'dearest Louise'. The Queen immediately asked Lord Granville to make it clear to Lorne that her daughter must be called *Princess* Louise.

The Duke must also be cautioned as he was '*wanting* in tact' and had 'a little shocked the Queen by wishing to bring the Princess too much *down* to his own *level*, and by at *once* treating her as tho' she was already his daughter-in-law . . .'[9] The Duke was well aware of Princess Louise's difficult position and, as an experienced courtier, smoothed matters over with Queen Victoria by writing a little note saying he knew how low she must be feeling about parting with a daughter. Touched by his kindness, the Queen responded by confessing her sins; she could not conceal from him what a trial Princess Louise's marriage was for her and declared it would have been hypocritical of her to have behaved otherwise.[10]

Lorne and the Duke had always called the Princess, 'Princess Louise'. The fact that, apart from that one occasion of the embrace, there had been no 'demonstrativeness' by the Duke or Lorne, who had always called the Princess 'Your Royal Highness' or 'Princess Louise' before others, made no difference to Queen Victoria.

Nevertheless, the Duke was pleased with the outcome of his visit to Balmoral, particularly 'with *our* Princess' for she 'is the greatest Duck I ever saw'.[11] Princess Louise was equally delighted with the Duke and behaved most affectionately towards him when out of her mother's sight. 'I really think the Union promises every happiness with God's blessing,'[12] the Duke wrote. 'They seem desperately in love with each other,'[13] and the Princess 'seems not only clever, and affectionate but eminently sensible . . .'[14] He and the Duchess felt able to face the response of royal and public opinion with much more equanimity.

There were, however, members of the Royal Family who were to share neither the Queen's pleasure nor the Argylls' satisfaction. Lorne had left a Balmoral deep in the 'fever of secrecy'. The Queen had skilfully arranged for prospective suitors to visit Balmoral at a time when key members of her family were elsewhere. She wished to present her family with a *fait accompli*. It was, thus, imperative to keep the engagement secret until she had made certain of the Argylls and spoken to the Lord Chancellor.

When, on October 17th, a blissfully happy Lorne, brimming over with the news of his engagement, arrived at Alnwick Castle, he was forced to 'play the hypocrite to Princess Christian',[15] who was staying there with his sister, Countess Percy, and pretend that nothing had happened. In the privacy of his rooms he found consolation in the long letters sent to him by Princess Louise. 'Lorne is desperately in love and her letters look as if she were *ditto*,' the Duke commented after seeing some of their correspondence. It seemed to be a love match after all.[16]

Having consulted the Lord Chancellor, the Queen announced the engagement to the Family and the Household on October 10th. 'It seems to give great pleasure,' the Queen recorded in her Journal that night,[17] and Princess Louise was encouraged by the initially favourable response. Queen Victoria, however, feared a hostile reaction from Germany, so she had written to the Crown Princess on the day of the engagement to prepare the way – 'I have changed my opinion of Lord Lorne since I have got to know him . . . I think him very pleasing, amiable and clever . . .,' but she made no mention of the engagement. It was only later that she broke the news and admitted: 'I know well that abroad such a marriage, until it is thoroughly understood, may startle people . . .'[18]

Queen Victoria's assumptions about the German reaction were absolutely valid. Lady Ely reported to Disraeli that the Queen was 'rather nervous and low',[19] as neither the Crown Princess nor Princess Alice liked the marriage. Although Princess Alice had written kindly and affectionately to Princess Louise, the Crown Princess highly disapproved and had written 'a *vy* unamiable' letter.[20] The King of Prussia was 'most displeased' that the Princess should prefer to lead a quiet, domestic life with a commoner rather than hold a position at the Berlin Court through marriage to his nephew.[21] Lorne, the proud son of Mac Cailein Mor, was unperturbed: 'Mam', he said, 'my forefathers were Kings when the Hohenzollerns were parvenus.'[22]

Princess Louise had expected criticism from her sisters in Germany but she was unprepared for the response from Marlborough House. The Princess of Wales, who, like the Crown Princess, had championed her own candidate, wrote a rather cold letter, barely concealing her disapproval, although ending affectionately, 'you know my pet, in me you will always find a true friend, whatever may happen'.[23] The Prince of Wales also objected and made the Queen '*most* indignant'.[24] He complained that he had not been consulted, which was quite true though he had been told that several commoners were being considered, and he announced that Lorne had been half-engaged to one of Lord Shaftesbury's daughters and that the family were furious that he had thrown the girl over.[25] In fact, while Lady Victoria Ashley-Cooper may have hoped to be Lady Lorne, she had never received any encouragement. 'It is "most shameful",' the Queen told Lord Granville. 'The Queen *cannot* write a kind word after this' to the Prince of Wales.[26] The Argylls were not seriously offended. They had already decided that the 'real bore and drawback of the whole thing' was the connection with the rest of the Royal Family. The Duke declared, 'I mean to be as stiff as a poker. I should be quite glad if it makes them more stiff.'[27]

The Prince of Wales's initial attempt at sabotaging the engagement heralded a more straightforward protest against the choice of bridegroom, whose position would inevitably cause political and social difficulties. It was certainly 'a bold experiment', for the Queen's future son-in-law was the Liberal Member of Parliament for Argyllshire, with a father who was a Cabinet Minister. The danger was that such a close connection would identify the Crown with a political party and lead to accusations of Liberal partisanship.

Moreover, the Princess would be marrying into a family connected with trade, banking and stockbroking. Lady Frederick Cavendish noted in her diary: 'astonishing news . . . a really good *precedent* . . . but they had better have chosen somebody with fewer belongings and more money. Fancy Princess Louise with such a tribe of brothers-in-law, one of them a Liverpool merchant!'[28] By no means everyone shared her views; Lady Caroline Charteris, an old friend of the Argylls, returned from a visit to Alnwick to report 'the Lorne marriage meets with universal disapprobation'.[29] The Queen of Holland bluntly declared it to be a *mésalliance*, always made worse where the wife 'stoops and renounces'.[30]

When the idea of a British marriage for Princess Louise had been discussed in 1869, Queen Victoria had envisaged '*no* difficulty whatever;

Louise remains what she is, and her husband keeps his rank – only being treated in the family as a relation when we were together'.[31] Lorne did not agree. He felt Princess Louise should be treated as Royalty in her mother's house and on state occasions but otherwise as Lady Lorne. Many people in Society would dislike 'the notion of red carpet spreading, doorway receptions and the other usual rubbish, and say that as she has chosen to marry me they will not ask her to their house, if they are to go thro' all that humbug'. Lorne did not care 'a rush' about precedence but he did not want Princess Louise to suffer any social ostracism on account of her marriage.

Lorne wanted an official pronouncement on their position, since both he and Princess Louise believed that their case would be 'the first in all probability of a series of marriages' between Royalties and subjects.[32] The Duke believed that Society would take its lead from the Princess: 'Her own dignity of manner, which is great, will always protect her from snobbish familiarity . . .'[33] In the event, the Princess kept her 'HRH', but was received in Society and informally as the Marchioness of Lorne. The difficulties were to centre not upon her position but upon Lorne's.

Nevertheless, her brother's disapproval upset Princess Louise. It is no wonder that she wrote: 'I do not delude myself that my life will be a cloudless one.'[34] But opposition only strengthened her determination to overcome the obstacles raised by her family: 'I think we shall be very happy, and we shall have pride in overcoming the difficulties which everybody places before us, every position has its difficulties, why should we be without them.'[35]

She was pleased that Lorne was back with her for the public announcement of the engagement on October 14th. The coverage of the event by the national press was immense. Most papers treated the engagement simplistically, as a triumph of love over tradition. *Punch's* caption, with the Franco–Prussian War in mind, was 'This betrothal is a real German defeat!' Potted histories of the Campbell Clan were numerous and the correct spelling of Mac Cailein Mor taxed the resources of most reporters. A Glasgow firm received orders for 60,000 photographs of the Marquis, 'the most talked of man in three Kingdoms'.[36] The exhumation of the Royal Marriage Act of 1772 in the newspapers corrected one misconception; namely that a royal marriage with a subject was illegal.

The Princess was delighted with the enthusiastic praise of Lorne at

Balmoral. Charming and courteous, Lorne pleased everybody, especially her. She had thought him 'very clever and amiable' at first[37] but now, as she saw more of him, she was becoming very attracted to him. 'There is no one like Lorne, you rightly say,' she told Lord Dufferin, an 'Arthurian Knight so exactly describes him'.[38] Seeing the handsome pair together, the Household were agog to know her real feelings. Mary Ponsonby wished the Princess was more in love but decided, philosophically, that it would not last even if she was.[39] The Queen, of course, was quite decided: 'She does *not* think the Princess "desperately in love" she is thankful to say . . .'[40]

Not surprisingly, Lorne held a different opinion. There might be 'no sort of flirtation' in public or in front of the Queen, but the couple had a doting ally in Lady Ely and they used to meet in her sitting room where, according to Lorne, 'we are as private as in the backwoods'.[41] When asked by one of his sisters about it, Lorne replied, 'if she does not show true affection, I do not know anything of human nature'. He was extremely definite that 'it is not a *mariage de convenance*' and that they were incredibly happy together.[42] As soon as the time came for Lorne to leave Balmoral, Princess Louise became noticeably upset and cried; even Queen Victoria found the Princess 'fretted' over his absence.

Lorne had left to attend various functions elsewhere in Scotland. The Campbells from the West and the Isles were jubilant over the engagement, not because a princess had chosen a Scot as her husband but because the son of their Clan Chieftain was to be wed. At Inveraray, twins born to the schoolmaster were christened Lorne and Louise Smith. The tenantry on the Argyll estates celebrated the engagement in inimitable Highland style: reeling, speechifying and drinking. The Queen's secretary inadvertently referred to Lorne as an Englishman when he congratulated her on the engagement. He was at once corrected: 'Colonel Ponsonby speaks of his being a young Englishman, but he is *not*, he is a Scotchman *and* a Highlander.'[43]

The Queen had realized that there was some sense in the Prince of Wales's objection to the match on political grounds. Her solution now was to suggest the creation of a peerage for Lorne. The scheme was masterly: it simultaneously solved the difficulty over Lorne's rank and removed him from the House of Commons, since only as a peer in his own right, rather than by courtesy as eldest son of a Scottish Duke, would he have a seat in the House of Lords. The advantages of sending him to the Upper House were manifold, according to Queen Victoria.

It would prevent Lorne from being too closely associated with Gladstone and the Liberal party, which, as the husband of the Queen's
daughter, 'would clearly be vy objectionable'; it would raise him above
'a mere Commoner'; and, most importantly, it would remove the
necessity for Lorne and thus Princess Louise to pass most of the year
in London, where Queen Victoria imagined they would fall under the
sway of the Prince of Wales's 'fast set'.[44]

However, the Queen's plan was thwarted by an alliance between
two unforeseen adversaries: Princess Louise and the Duke of Argyll.
The Princess voiced her strong conviction that Lorne should 'take
nothing in the way of Court favours'; he must retain an independent
position and follow his old pursuits. The Duke thought her 'as sensible
as any man about it all'.[45] Vehemently opposed to the scheme and
with Lorne's support, he directed Gladstone not to give the Queen's
wish a moment's encouragement. The Duke did not want Lorne's
marriage to be the ruination of his political career. He argued that
Lorne had not yet done anything to warrant the reward of a dukedom;
anyway, as a family 'proud of one of the most historical of all Scotch
titles', they had no wish for the heir to the Argyll title to have any new
one.[46] In fact, the wishes of the Duke and the Princess prevailed,
although the issue was by no means exhausted: it would resurface in
1883 and in 1892.

Queen Victoria gave her consent to the marriage in Council on
October 24th. She told the Crown Princess of the deed, which she said
'has called forth a great burst of delight. People call this "the most
popular act of my reign"'.[47] Celebrations opened at Balmoral with a
bonfire followed by a ball in the servants' hall. The ballroom, a long,
low, white-washed room, was devoid of any ornamentation save for a
few sprigs of fir put up for the occasion. The orchestra consisted of
Willie Blair, the head fiddler, and his son 'with the most awful squint
on record'.[48] Dr Poore entered into the spirit of the occasion, wearing
a kilt lent by his patient, Prince Leopold, but commented as an
Englishman that 'it was a fine sight to see the lads in their kilts
a-dancing, though me thinks there be more fitting costumes than that,
for some do kick their heels mighty high . . .'[49] The company consisted
of servants and villagers but 'everyone danced with the exception of
the Queen . . . & although the room was hot, dirty and as odorous as
a sailor's chapel, Her Majesty remained until 12.30 . . . It was very
funny to see the Duchess of Roxburghe, dressed in lace and with about

a thousand pounds worth of diamonds on, dancing a gig and all the ghillies in the room striving for the honour of facing her.'[50]

Absent from the dance floor was the person in whose honour the ball was held. Princess Louise had hurt her knee. Professor Lister, the pioneer of antiseptic surgery, put her leg in a splint and prescribed complete rest, which prompted Queen Victoria to postpone the return to Windsor.

Lorne was already in London 'devising ornaments for his Beloved'[51] and prepared to return to Balmoral. This placed the Queen in a predicament. She was worried that the Princess's condition would not only delay the marriage but that any permanent disability would affect her marriage prospects: 'no Mother wd allow their daughter much less the daughter of the Queen . . . to marry in a state wh wd make her a *burthen* to her Husband and herself . . .'[52]

The Princess wanted to return South to see Lorne. She knew perfectly well that, if she had been laid up at Windsor just before leaving for Balmoral, the Queen would have insisted on packing her into any form of transportation in order not to miss a day at her beloved Balmoral. When she told the Queen as much, Prince Leopold was much amused by the fuss: 'Oh! What a row!' he exclaimed.[53] Queen Victoria decided Princess Louise's obstinate behaviour was entirely owing to her engagement. At the best of times, the Queen had, as she expressed it, 'a *particular* aversion' to the presence of a betrothed couple; it always reminded her of former happy days and, in her present state, she felt *de trop*.[54]

When Princess Louise asked permission for Lorne to travel over to be with her, the Queen refused, 'it is *quite impossible here* & *as she is now*'.[55] Since *she* had already lost Princess Louise's society out of doors and at meals, the Queen did not wish to compete with Lorne for the remaining available time. The Duchess of Argyll sympathized with her son; 'Poor Ian thinks he ought to be at Balmoral,' but realized, 'He is begining [sic] his life of small disciplines . . . the take it easy line will not be possible.'[56]

In addition, the Queen was becoming seriously alarmed by Lorne's habit of repeating stories he had heard in London to Princess Louise. At the beginning of November, the Prince of Wales stayed at Stafford House for three days when the Duke of Argyll was also there. Notwithstanding the Duke being his sister's future father-in-law and the brother-in-law of his host, the Prince never asked to see him once. 'He hates the marriage very naturally but still this is carrying his dislike too far,' Sybil St Albans wrote in her diary.[57]

Princess Louise then complained to Queen Victoria 'how stupid & ill natured & silly' her brother and sisters were in their attitude.[58] Queen Victoria was concerned about the mischief and '*bad blood*' which could ensue. So, poor Lord Granville was ordered to caution Lorne 'for with *our* large family and *his own* enormous one, it might become serious!'[59]

The Court moved to Windsor on November 24th and the next day Princess Louise saw her future mother-in-law for the first time since her engagement. 'I was very happy,' wrote the Duchess; there was 'Something very confiding and restful about Princess Louise.'[60] Several days later a family party consisting of the Duke of Argyll, the Westminsters, Lorne and his sister Lady Libby Campbell, whom Princess Louise asked to be chief bridesmaid, arrived at Windsor Castle. Lorne stayed until December 17th, before going on to Cliveden for Christmas. Princess Louise, now walking on crutches, left two days later for Osborne where she passed the customary, quiet, family Christmas and New Year; the last, as Queen Victoria was quick to remind her, as an unmarried daughter.

The improvement in Princess Louise's lameness enabled the Queen to set a date for the wedding, March 21st, despite calls for its postponement by foreign members of the family because of the war. Although the Princess's marriage would not be a state occasion, the consideration of her foreign relations as guests inevitably drew the event into the arena of political affairs. The Queen had heard from her Ambassador, then Odo Russell, at Versailles, that everyone from the King of Prussia downwards was hostile to England because she had sold arms to France in the recent war, and that even Princess Louise's marriage was interpreted 'as a hostile demonstration!'[61]

It was also after the New Year that Queen Victoria began to voice her anxiety over the forthcoming provision for Princess Louise in Parliament. This was to be in addition to the Queen's personal marriage settlement by which the Princess was given the same as Princess Helena; that is, a capital sum of £100,000 paying 4 per cent per annum interest as income. The Queen would also provide a housekeeper, two housemaids and help towards furnishing a house. The Princess's income of £4,000 per annum would be supplemented by the public provision of a £6,000 annuity and a £30,000 dowry. Although large by most standards of the day, such an income was judged to be extremely small for a royal establishment.

The source of the Queen's concern was the opposition by working people to the granting of any dowry at all. At meetings held in the various boroughs of London, and all over the country, MPs were questioned persistently about the way they intended to vote and hissed if it was in favour of the dowry. At one such meeting, the workmen were told it was 'the duty of Englishmen to look after their own pockets and not to give the contents to German Princes like Teck or Christian or Scottish noblemen who did not need them'.[62] The marriage of Princess Louise and her dowry provided the pretext for protest: behind it was the issue of the Queen's seclusion.

In view of the controversy, it was decided that the Queen would open Parliament in person two days after the Court returned to Windsor on February 7th. This did little to appease critics; it merely provided evidence for the belief that Queen Victoria only opened Parliament when provision for her children was at issue. During the second reading of the Provision Bill, several speakers in the House of Commons opposed the resolution; an unusual occurrence since provision debates were considered to be mere formalities. In the event only three MPs went through the 'Noes' lobby.

Once 'that wretched dowry business' was over, Princess Louise could turn her attention to the more enjoyable side of the wedding preparations. Sybil St Albans found her 'very full of herself and her prospects' at Windsor on February 13th.[63] As preparations advanced, so public interest increased. The newspapers gave daily reports of deputations received at Windsor and wedding presents given. 'Louise keeps receiving no end of presents, such lovely things from so many people,'[64] the Queen noted and '*quite* unequalled in the case of *any* of our daughters. It is vy gratifying to her & to me to see her so beloved & so *universally* popular. She will be *sadly* missed.'[65]

Queen Victoria's obsession over the loss of a daughter to marriage, 'like a lamb to the slaughter', increased with each wedding. 'One may see them as often as one likes afterwards,' she lamented, 'and there may be but short separations – but one's Child is *no longer* one's own, when she has a husband who claims not only *equal but more* affection from one's Child.'[66] By March 18th, Princess Louise's birthday, the Queen admitted to feeling unwell: 'I can't deny I dread the 21st March for to lose one's daughters, *one* after the other [the last being five years previously!] is a very cruel thing. To Louise the time is very trying when she has to leave her Home. Saturday is her *last* unmarried birthday!'[67] As such it was a very special twenty-third birthday and began early: the band of the 2nd Life Guards played a selection of the Princess's favourite music under her bedroom window at 7 a.m. The Royal Salute was fired at one o'clock in the Long Walk and the bells of churches rang out in her honour; all of which increased the excitement of the thousands who had streamed into Windsor to see the wedding preparations. A huge crowd gathered outside the railway station to see the bridegroom arrive, but he managed to give them the slip.

During the morning of the wedding day, the bride had invited the Campbell children to the Castle. One of them, the ten-year-old Lady Frances, could always recall that exciting and blissfully romantic moment when she first caught sight of Princess Louise, dressed as a bride, coming down the Long Corridor. 'A vision of beauty', she looked like a princess out of a fairy tale to the enraptured child: 'I fell in love with her at once, and resolved to give her a piece of my knitting.'[68]

Outside, so vast was the crowd, that, for the first time, policemen had to form chain barriers to keep control. The south side of the route was lined with about nine hundred boys from Eton waiting to give a special cheer to the Old Etonian bridegroom.

The marriage was celebrated at St George's Chapel, transformed from a place of worship into a devotional palace. Carpets were especially woven for the occasion, only to be consigned to a storeroom at the end of the day. A temporary platform, erected in front of the communion rails, was covered by a blue carpet woven with a pattern of Tudor roses encircled by the Garter and *Honi soit qui mal y pense*.

For reasons of precedence and logistics, waiting-rooms had to be constructed to contain, for example, Lorne who, as a subject, must arrive before the Royal Family but, as a bridegroom, must not take his place at the altar until they were seated. A bridal bower was created for Princess Louise on the off-chance that she might need to readjust her dress when she arrived at the Chapel. An arched doorway, hung with looped muslin curtains, opened on to white silk walls, panelled with magenta-striped gauze, decorated with gold beading at the corners and even on the skirting boards. It had been thoughtfully furnished to meet every conceivable bridal need with a satinwood dressing table, gilt chairs and large mirrors.

When the wedding guests reached the Chapel, they were required to show their tickets to the policeman. Presently, a grand carriage drew up from which stepped the Duke and Duchess of Northumberland, the latter 'bearing diamonds worth a King's ransom'. 'Tickets, Mam!' demanded the policeman, oblivious to the glittering array of diamonds on display before him instead of proper tickets.[69] Only after a uniformed officer in the 91st Argyllshire Highlanders had acted as a 'pew opener' were they allowed to enter, to find 'the whole place . . . a blaze of uniforms, jewels, gala dresses and magnificence'.[70]

At noon Lorne, in the uniform of the Royal Argyllshire Artillery Volunteers, was shown into his waiting-room in the Bray Chapel. Although he was a commoner, as this was a royal wedding he was accompanied by two supporters, Earl Percy and Lord Ronnie Leveson-Gower, rather than the customary best man. Shortly before half past twelve the Royal Family arrived. The Princess of Wales, beautifully dressed in blue satin with a train of velvet edged in lace and a head-dress of feathers, pearls and diamonds, almost upstaged the bride.

Once the Royal Family were in their places, a flourish of trumpets announced Lord Lorne and his two supporters, 'upon which everyone looked at each other,' according to Sybil St Albans, 'not knowing whether to get up or not'.[71] The Princess of Wales gave the lead and rose to her feet, whereupon the congregation followed her until Lorne was in his place. Once the Royal Family were seated, the bridegroom stood alone at the altar, his supporters sitting behind him. A long delay of ten minutes meant that he was left, a handsome but rather vulnerable figure looking, his father said, 'so manly and noble'.[72] In that position, Campbell of Islay decided there were two things a man could do, one was to look sheepish, the other to look cocky. Lorne did neither and won the admiration of everyone for standing quietly, and looking as if he did not know everyone was staring at him. Two days before, he had confided to his Aunt Dot that he felt 'rather sad as I turn from independence to – we know what!'[73] It must have been a poignant moment for him, a subject and an outsider, yet the focal point of this royal pageant.

Finally, a heavy crimson curtain, concealing a doorway, was dramatically swished aside as, to the sound of trumpets, the procession of the bride appeared. Princess Louise looked very pale but nonetheless lovely, with the Queen on her right and the Prince of Wales and Prince Alfred on her left. She wore an off-the-shoulder, white, satin dress, embossed with the English rose, Scottish thistle and Irish shamrock; its deep flounces of Honiton lace were trimmed symbolically with cordons of orange blossom for the bride, white heather for luck, and myrtle for Germany and the Campbells. Her veil, also of Honiton lace, was worked to her own design and was held in place by two diamond daisies given her by Prince Arthur, Prince Leopold and Princess Beatrice; with Lorne's present of a chain of diamonds holding an enormous sapphire, which matched the colour of her dark blue eyes, she looked the perfect Victorian bride. Her dress may seem overburdened by all these symbols of position but each was considered necessary; their absence would have provoked comment.

The Princess's eye for design and colour was evident in the dresses and jewels worn by her eight bridesmaids; instead of the customary pastel colours and flowers, she had achieved a dramatic effect by substituting large, red roses on plain, white, silk dresses. Around their necks they wore the lockets given and designed by the bride; almost pre-Fabergé in concept and formed of an oval of rock crystal carved with miniature, enamelled roses and forget-me-nots, each one was topped by a tiny, gold coronet studded with rubies and emeralds.

The Princess's pallor was not surprising, since she had caught a bad cold, which left her 'looking pulled' and had resulted in earache. The Queen thought she seemed tired and not as beautiful as usual. At the door of the Chapel, the Princess stopped for a moment to give the Queen one last word of love and then, with a half nervous smile, started along the aisle towards Lorne 'with a great deal of gentle maidenly grace and self-possession' so that few realized how nervous and unwell she felt.[74]

In contrast to Princess Louise, the Queen looked 'positively radiant – her whole face beaming with smiles'.[75] On this occasion the Queen's severe, black, mourning dress was relieved by the crimson of rubies and the blue of the Garter; she was giving the bride away because, in the absence of Prince Albert, no one else could take his place, certainly *not* the Prince of Wales. At the end of the ceremony, the Queen kissed Princess Louise, and Lorne, now a member of her family, courteously kissed the Queen's hand. When the couple left the Chapel, prolonged cheering accompanied their drive back to the Castle for the wedding breakfast, held in the Waterloo Gallery.

When Princess Louise and Lorne had thought about their wedding day they both knew that, far from being a private affair, it would be a long day passed in the gaze of the public eye; much of it would be tedious as, 'besides the ceremony in the Chapel, there is afterwards much to be gone through', Lorne admitted to his family.[76] Both of them were nervous of the unknown life that lay before them: the Princess leaving her family for a man she barely knew; Lorne leaving the life of a private citizen for one of ceremony and public attention.

Yet, amidst all the formality, there was time for some private moments. One occurred directly the couple arrived at the Castle, when the Queen gave Lorne the Order of the Thistle: 'Lorne made vy little resistance and his *wife*, mother-in-law and brother-in-law Arthur took him by storm' and, amidst much general embracing, Princess Louise was embraced for the first time by her husband.[77]

PART II

The Marchioness of Lorne

1871–1900

CHAPTER X

Homecoming

It was not until four o'clock that an open carriage drawn by four horses and accompanied by a royal escort assembled in the Quadrangle. Presently, amid 'a regular wedding chatter', the Marquis of Lorne with his new Marchioness, emerged to be met with a shower of rice and satin slippers 'like a snow storm in a gale of wind, and cheery happy voices giggling as human beings do when they are off stage'. Then, as the cortège swept down Windsor Hill, the Eton boys cheered 'till they were black in the face' and flowers rained down upon the Lornes from balconies and windows: 'The British lion was purring over one of its pets and welcoming one who may grow to be another.'[1]

One disadvantage to marriage with a princess quickly revealed itself during the drive to Claremont: Lorne was not able to exchange a private word with his bride. Even after the Lornes had left Windsor and had changed horses at Chertsey, they had to converse affably in front of the escort and were unable to engage in a little marital flirtation on the two-hour journey. At Claremont, they found Lady Jane Churchill and Colonel McNeill, who had been sent over by Queen Victoria to attend them, even at meals; their opportunities for being alone together remained proscribed.

The next morning Lorne wrote his first letter to the Duchess of Argyll, telling her that a friend had sent them 'a pair of turtle doves! And Frisky [Princess Louise's little dog] is always getting up upon the chair to look at them which makes them uncomfortable and is emblematic of the public and ourselves!'[2] As near strangers, it is hardly surprising that they felt self-conscious with each other. When the Crown Princess stayed at Windsor and occupied the rooms used on her honeymoon in 1857, she remembered 'how we sat here – two young innocent things – almost too shy to talk to one another'.[3]

The Lornes occupied the 'bridal suite', which had been designed specifically for their four-day visit; even the bridegroom noticed the 'wonderful orange blossom carpet', which had been specially woven for the lovers.[4] But they had barely settled into these surroundings when, after only two days, their honeymoon was interrupted by a visit from Queen Victoria. On the afternoon of the 23rd, she drove from Windsor and climbed the twenty steps to the entrance hall, in order to satisfy her maternal curiosity as to how her 'beloved Loosey' was taking to married life. The Queen's visit was a signal for the newly-marrieds' return to normality; on the 25th they left Claremont for Windsor, where once more they were rarely left alone together. A short stay at Windsor before going abroad was planned by Queen Victoria so that she could advise the couple and smooth over any troubles arising from the marriage.

The Princess's changed status did not prevent the Queen from continuing to employ her as a personal secretary. On March 28th, Queen Victoria went to Buckingham Palace to hold a drawing room, which was as over-crowded as the Princess of Wales's first married one had been in 1863. The reason for the queue of carriages halfway down Birdcage Walk and the fearful 'pushing and squeezing' was that Princess Louise was expected to attend. However, the Princess was at Windsor where she was dutifully employed with the Queen's correspondence, as a backlog had developed.

The following day Princess Louise emerged to attend the Queen at the opening of the Albert Hall. As a 'newly married' Princess with 'all the light of new found love and enjoyment of life on her brow', her appearance for once out-shone that of the Princess of Wales. It was also the first time Lorne experienced the splendours of his new position as a sort of honorary member of the Royal Family. Mary Gladstone noted the 'magnificent sight', when Queen Victoria 'arrived about 12.30, the first in the gorgeous procession in which Princess Louise shone eminent in dazzling white from top to toe'.[5]

After this brief appearance, only allowed because the event was connected with Prince Albert, the Lornes were once more enveloped in the cloak of seclusion then considered seemly for a newly married pair. In their case, the period was passed abroad on a honeymoon tour. The day of their departure was 'indeed a sad one and leaves a terrible blank,' the Queen told the Duchess of Argyll; '. . . their journey so different to anything she has undertaken before – makes me anxious. Still I quite approve of it and *think it is* in every way desirable.'[6] This was not strictly true but perhaps sentiment had caused Queen Victoria to forget that, initially, she had strongly opposed the Lornes going abroad at all.

Horrified at the thought of her daughter wandering about a war-torn Europe, she had tried to enlist Lord Granville's opposition. She had objected to their plan of travelling without chaperones: 'Were they going with another *couple* the Queen would never have *said anything* or been alarmed but one of her daughters totally unaccustomed ever to go about alone, never travelling except with the Queen and a Lady, having been little abroad' worried her. And since Lorne was 'totally unaware of *what* a Pss is accustomed to or ought not to do', he obviously needed the guidance of an experienced courtier.[7]

Lorne, however, refused to change his arrangements. He saw the journey as a romantic adventure with his beloved and he wanted to be alone with her. The honeymoon issue was the first battle in his campaign to play down his connection with royalty and to ensure their independence from Court life in the future. Princess Louise was placed in a difficult position. She agreed with Lorne that they should travel as privately as possible; but she also realized that her mother was genuinely concerned that their unorthodox marriage should begin well. She suggested a compromise. They should take M. Kanné with them and when in a large town she would ask one of the Embassy ladies to accompany her. Determined to obstruct Princess Louise's plans, the Queen intimated that Kanné was neither suitable nor available. Prince Arthur then asked Colonel Elphinstone to recommend another courier and a Mr Reibolds was suggested. On January 29th, Princess Louise wrote to ask that Reibolds present himself in London.

Three days later, however, Princess Louise had the services of two couriers rather than one; for, sensing defeat, Queen Victoria told her daughter that she had sent for Kanné after all. An exasperated Princess Louise broke the news to Colonel Elphinstone: 'You know I told you the Queen would *not hear* of my taking Canée abroad with me this spring. I waited a long time before I asked you about Reibaut (I forget how the name is written) as I know how often the Queen changes [her mind], but at last something had to be done.'[8] However, taking both couriers would offend their professional pride. The Colonel, who knew Queen Victoria's ways, smoothly arranged another position for Reibolds.

So it was that on April 3rd the Prince of Wales accompanied the Lornes to Charing Cross Station to see them board the train for Dover. At nine o'clock the next morning, they embarked for Ostend: 'We start with every good sign as to health, wind & weather,' Lorne wrote to his mother.[9]

'Training it' through Ghent and Cologne, Lorne and Princess Louise made their way down to Darmstadt to see her sister, Princess Alice, but were only able to meet for ten minutes at Darmstadt station. Their words of greeting and congratulation were punctuated by the shunting of troop trains, and other signs of the war. Prince Louis was on leave from the Front and Princess Alice, who had just had her third child, was more occupied with nursing wounded soldiers than babies. Very anxious about her sister's welfare, Princess Louise had hoped to be able to stay and help her. But Queen Victoria, who resented Princess Alice's influence over Princess Louise, used the war as a pretext to curtail the visit. So the sisters merely had time to glimpse each other, but this was long enough for them to decide to try to arrange another meeting on the return journey. However, the long arm of Queen Victoria reached her children wherever they were; her permission had to be obtained before any of them could meet. Princess Alice, as the elder sister, was deputed to write and ask the Queen 'if you would allow them quite incognito on their way back to pass a day here, it would give both Louise and me the greatest pleasure'.[10] This, their 'Mama' allowed.

Despite travelling as Lord and Lady Sundridge, Lorne noticed 'we are recognised everywhere on the lines of rail but get about quickly by our selves in the towns!' He also learnt that the Queen expected to receive daily reports containing details of their every movement. 'We get numbers of telegrams from Osborne,' Lorne complained to his mother, 'so are well posted in everything that goes on and heard of the Princess of Wales's confinement and death of the child as soon as she did herself . . .'[11] Given such a correspondence, the Lornes often completed each other's letters. From Bologna, Princess Louise wrote to the Duchess: 'Lorne began but did not go on so I do so, knowing you like to know about your darling Boy. He is enjoying himself very much, looks well and happy.'[12]

On April 18th they arrived in Florence. Lorne had wintered there in 1867 and was thus able to show Princess Louise his favourite haunts. Their first days were passed wandering about, buying copies of their favourite pictures and the odd terracotta bust, discovering each other's taste and 'getting stuff for Venetian blinds, curtains and portières and some good shutters'[13] with which to furnish their first home in

England. Florence was full of the charm of the unfamiliar for the Princess. She had never stayed in an hotel, never been surrounded by jostling strangers without a buffer of officials or courtiers, and never been shopping in a foreign city. Lady Paget, wife of the British Minister in Florence, was detailed to accompany 'this lovely young Princess'. She found that Princess Louise's 'great amusement was going out and shopping with me alone'.

At an Embassy party, some elegant Florentine ladies were presented to Princess Louise. In the midst of the party, however, she 'suddenly became shy or tired, or both, and insisted on beating a retreat' through Lady Paget's bedroom. Although Princess Louise had passed much of her childhood longing to be the centre of attention, the reality of finding herself in such a position far away from home brought on an acute attack of shyness; overwhelmed by the novelty of her new life, she bolted, with Lorne at her heels. Wally Paget sympathized with the Princess, whose behaviour was so 'like the Queen and the Princess Royal, subject to fits of shyness'.[14]

The next morning Princess Louise sent her the following note: 'Dear Wally, would 12.30 do, it is rather dreadful the King wishing to meet us: as this is the case would you and Sir Arthur Paget kindly go with us to the gardens: I do not think the Queen would like me to meet His Majesty without you.' Princess Louise had never met a foreign king on her own before. She was not only nervous but knew that etiquette required she be attended. Years later when Wally asked her if she could publish this letter, Princess Louise asked to see a copy of her 'foolish little note' first, 'for fear of its being too foolish for you to put in your book'. She afterwards remarked at its 'naïvety' which she thought must have greatly amused the cosmopolitan Pagets at the time.[15]

After twelve glorious days in Florence, the Lornes travelled leisurely on to Venice for a ten-day stay at the Hotel Danieli.[16] Their first evening was a fine one, so they walked to the Piazza San Marco to watch the crowd and hear the band playing. Unfortunately, the weather changed to heavy rain, so that thereafter they had to make sorties enveloped in mackintoshes and umbrellas, and travel in enclosed gondolas during the day. This gave Lorne the idea of bringing home the top part of a gondola to be fitted on to a Loch Fyne rowing boat: 'such a protection would be so useful in wet weather' as it had windows at the side, but could easily be removed in fine weather.[17]

They left Venice with reluctance, for the journey home through Germany. They stayed at Darmstadt with Princess Alice, who sent Queen Victoria a report of their visit: 'Louise and Lorne are just gone, and it rains & blows & is dreadful. Their visit was so pleasant, so *gemütlich*, and I think Louise looks well & happy.'[18] By the time Queen Victoria received this report, Princess Louise was safely tucked up in bed in London, where she and Lorne were staying with the Argylls.

When the maid drew back the curtains and opened the windows in Princess Louise's bedroom, on the morning of June 10th, she not only let in the sun, which streamed into the room, but also the sound of bird song. For a moment it must have seemed to Princess Louise as if she were still in the German countryside rather than in Argyll Lodge on Campden Hill in Kensington. This was not so strange, for in those days, Kensington was considered by Londoners to be a village in the country. A turnpike even lay between Westminster and Kensington, with green, open meadows bordering the muddy lanes.

In his autobiography, the Duke of Argyll describes his purchase of the house in 1853: 'It had four acres of land about it, beautifully planted, and two very old oaks in the grounds, which would have done no discredit to any ancient chase in England. It was next to Holland Park, and absolutely removed from all noise of traffic. We went to see it, and the first thing I saw out of the late Duke of Bedford's room was a fine lawn covered with starlings, hunting for grubs and insects in their very peculiar fashion . . . Flycatchers and warblers were also visible to my accustomed eye. There were objections; distance was to be considered. But the birds settled everything . . . it seemed quite a subordinate consideration that the lawn would be perfect for the children, and perfect too for breakfast parties. I returned to town and instructed my agent at once to purchase Bedford Lodge.'[19]

The Duke loved Argyll Lodge, above all, for the bird life, his family for the gardens. On Princess Louise's first day there, they were at the height of their beauty, 'the May trees covered with red and white flowers', one of Lorne's sisters, Lady Mary, wrote, 'and the laburnum, especially the Scotch one at the end of the lawn, like a shower of gold . . .'[20] A vast chestnut tree provided shade for summer teas, Sunday gatherings and the great breakfast parties the Duchess held during the Season.

On honeymoon, the Princess had expected everything to be new and different; once in England, she had thought that everything would be familiar and comfortable. However, though Lorne had written from Baden-Baden to his mother that 'Louise . . . is looking forward very much to being in the same house with you,'[21] the Princess found herself unprepared for the gulf which lay between her old life and her new one. Just as she and Lorne had been plunged into a false intimacy at Claremont, so she now found herself on familiar terms with his family, most of whom she barely knew. Moreover, her first night at Argyll Lodge was also the first she had passed in Britain in a non-royal residence. Her status further exacerbated the situation, since it meant that the initiative in dealing with the Argyll family always had to be taken by her.

Her own family were at Balmoral, so all she had to ease the transition were the footmen and her maid – and Lorne. In a way, this situation worked to his advantage for she clung to him more than she might have done had they first gone to Windsor or Osborne. The Princess had not only to adjust to married life, but also to the change from a world of courtiers to a world of commoners.

From the moment she left her bedroom on the first floor of Argyll Lodge, she must have noticed how the Argylls kept 'open house' for the family. In the summer months, they gathered on the south-facing, wide verandah, which was full of geraniums, basket chairs and dogs. Here, scattered members of the large Sutherland–Westminster–Blantyre–Carlisle–Leinster–Northumberland clan came to join them, to exchange news and learn of the latest political events. Here, the Argyll family, regardless of age, passed most of the day, moving inside to the white and gold drawing room for the evening. It was the sort of informal family life, which Princess Louise had seen and envied with the Greys, yet which had never been a part of her own home life.

The most remarkable difference for Princess Louise was the way in which the Argyll children were included in everything. Unlike her childhood, theirs was passed mainly with their parents and any visitors. This amazed and delighted the Princess. The children were brought up hearing general conversation; furthermore, they were expected to take part in such conversation and were never excluded or made to feel childish, unless they interrupted an elder or said something silly. In conversation, their talk was often heated, yet always interesting. *En masse*, they could appear formidable, but not to Princess Louise, who soon got used to the romps and talks. Because she appeared such a beautiful and romantic figure to the Campbells, they were fascinated by her and went out of their way to welcome her into the family.

The Princess had been brought up to be an early riser; this was not the case with her husband or his family. The Duke never held family prayers in London, so the family did not assemble for breakfast until ten o'clock. After a leisurely breakfast, they moved on to the verandah. The younger children went to the schoolroom under the roof for their lessons or, if too hot, they would remove to the lawn. Here the Duke might venture, lying on a plaid, while other members of the family grouped around him. Lunch was held at two o'clock, after which Lorne, as an MP, would leave for Westminster. Parliament met at 4.30 p.m. for its first session and sittings habitually continued until very late. Despite being considered 'on honeymoon', Lorne took his duties seriously, and did not intend his marriage to interfere with his parliamentary career.

Dinner was at 7.30, rather earlier than Princess Louise had been accustomed to dine at home. Often notes would be sent by hand to invite friends or relations to dine that evening. Despite the stately supervision of Mr New, the butler, and the gleaming of gold plate and the great, silver candelabra, the atmosphere was anything but formal, since all attention was focused upon conversation rather than ceremony. To Princess Louise, used to the dreary *sotto voce* suppers of her mother's table, the contrast was striking. Mary Gladstone described one such evening in her diary: 'some of the talk was good – on Darwin's theory & about the war; a discussion as to how far Garibaldi helped the French. The room was like fairyland when we arrived, so dim, sweet and mysterious, lovely elfs with golden hair in various picturesque positions, beautiful contrasts of colour.'[22]

In keeping with Scottish custom, at ten o'clock, after Lady Libby had played some music, the tea table with its white cloth was set out and the eldest daughter at home presided over it. By eleven o'clock, guests and relations started to leave and, after a little talk, the family retired to bed.

This was the way in which Princess Louise passed the next ten days at Argyll Lodge. On June 15th, an exception was made when she joined the Argylls at a breakfast party, given by Mr Gladstone at Carlton House Terrace. Owing to Queen Victoria's instructions, Princess Louise did not participate in the Season. No sooner had her engagement been announced than Queen Victoria had told Lord Granville of her plans for the Lornes' first year of marriage: 'they ought to be almost entirely absent from London (which is normally the case for a young married couple) as the Princess is most anxious to avoid great parties the 1st year and if she were in London & did *not go out*, everybody would say her position was so untenable she could not do so. The Queen means to insist on this.'[23] So, as many Victorian brides did, Princess Louise remained quietly at her new home.

Before leaving Balmoral for Windsor, on June 19th, the Queen wrote to the Duchess of Argyll that 'Louise writes delighted and astonished at your kindness and I am truly happy to hear that she is a good and amiable daughter amiable to you both,' adding in the way mothers can, 'Don't spoil her for that would not be good for her.'[24] Two days later, Princess Louise and Lorne exchanged the informality of Argyll Lodge for the circumspection of Windsor, when they were reunited with the Queen. A week later they returned to Argyll Lodge where they were henceforth based. They were also invited to visit Dublin at the end of July.

The Prince of Wales was to represent the Queen at the installation of Prince Arthur as a Knight of the Order of St Patrick, and to open the Royal Agricultural Show. With the Princess of Wales still convalescent after losing her baby, the Prince invited one of his sisters to accompany him on this state visit. To Princess Helena's dismay, he chose Princess Louise. The Lorne marriage had been so well-received that their presence in a politically volatile Ireland was seen by the Prince of Wales as a means of ensuring a friendly reception. Princess Louise had never been to Ireland, so she was delighted to join her brothers on, what now became, a family outing.

For Lorne, however, this visit created a conflict of interests. Although officially required to vote in the House until the recess in August, his absence would normally have been easy to arrange. But Prince Arthur's Annuity Bill was expected to be opposed by Radical MPs. It was feared they would use the issue to attack the Monarchy. The vote would be no mere formality: and so Lorne put his duty to his party first and refused to go to Ireland with the rest of the Royal Family.

Princess Louise had already accepted the invitation and knew that her eldest brother would be annoyed by Lorne's decision. Although she quite understood Lorne's wish to do his duty, she hoped he would come by finding a Pair. Lorne, however, felt that his new family connections should not interfere with his ability to vote. Fast becoming adept in the art of compromise, the Princess indicated she was ready to go alone, but she had reckoned without Queen Victoria, who strongly objected. Henry Ponsonby wrote from Osborne to Lord Granville on July 28th, 'If they go separately there will be all sorts of stories. Nor will it do for both of them to go later . . .'[25] In the event, royalty gained an easy victory on this occasion and Lorne joined the royal train for Holyhead.

The party were given a splendid welcome; there followed five days of functions conducted at a hectic pace. Princess Louise had accompanied her mother to the odd, public function, but she had never passed several days on continuous public display and found it immensely tiring. Lorne was more than happy to take a back seat. He saw his Irish relations, the Leinsters, and was deputed to write to 'Madam and Dear Mama', as he addressed Queen Victoria, with reports of their activities. On previous visits, Lorne had been free to roam about at will, but this time his movements were severely restricted, so he did not enjoy himself.

Meanwhile, the Argylls were supervising the arrangements for the six-day 'Homecoming' reception at Inveraray, to welcome the heir and his bride. Meticulous planning was essential since the numbers to be entertained encompassed the family, their personal guests, the county, the township, the tenantry, the local militia, estate people and staff. The Duke had to commandeer the whole of his inn, the Argyll Arms, as an overflow for his guests. It was domestic, rather than colonial, issues which caused the Secretary of State for India to toss his leonine locks impatiently and sit scribbling missives to clarify such weighty issues as where to house the visiting servants, or how best to disguise the earth privies to be erected in the grounds – perhaps fir spruce bushes placed around them would hide them sufficiently, yet allow them to be used. The whole township of Inveraray had to be cleaned and white-washed. Finally, the Castle itself had to be overhauled; a pavilion erected nearby to house the ballroom; and, in case of rain, a porch built over the main entrance to the Castle.

The Argyll arrangements also had to incorporate the problems caused by the desire of 'the Royal Mama', as they now called Queen Victoria, to attend. To stable the Queen's horses, for example, they would have to oust their own. The Queen was not insensitive to the trouble her attendance might entail, 'Please also to ascertain whether the Argyll's *really* wd wish us to come or *rather not* this year at all. Or whether 20th or 21st September *wld* do,' she asked Lord Granville on the 10th. 'The Queen is most anxious *not* to be in their way or to cause an unnecessary Expense tho' she would be sorry not to go at all this year.'[26] Despite such consideration, the Queen was unable to limit the amoeba-like encroachment of her retinue on any household she visited; her visits always involved 'a fuss' according to Princess Louise. Meanwhile, Mr Gladstone was preoccupied with another sort of royal 'fuss'. On the grounds of ill-health, the Queen had refused to delay her journey to Balmoral until after Parliament was prorogued. She had used this excuse so often, no one believed her: even Jenner admitted, 'Isn't it better to say the Queen can't do so and so because of her health – which is to a certain extent true – than to say she won't?'[27]

For once, however, the Queen really was unwell after being 'painfully stung' on her right elbow on August 4th. On the 18th, she was clearly quite ill: 'the Queen is going to put off her visit – which will be dreadfully inconvenient,' the Duke moaned. 'I am feeding the whole County till she comes.'[28]

Because of the Queen's illness, the festivities at Inveraray finally occurred without the added attraction of 'the Royal Mama'. Family guests, including Ian Campbell of Islay, began to arrive at the Castle on August 20th. He was soon put to work hanging flags in the new ballroom, 'a very grand wooden building 140 foot by 50 lighted with Gas'.[29] Yachts began to arrive in the bay and, the next day, guests and visitors flooded off steamers crowded with goods and passengers; for the whole of the County of Argyllshire was *en fête* and heading for the little eighteenth-century township of Inveraray. The Duke's fourth daughter, Lady Victoria, 'V', Campbell, who had been left crippled after an attack of infantile paralysis, kept watch from a window in the Ardkinglas turret room in the Castle. 'Everybody was busy all morning,' she reported to her absent Aunt Dot, 'people kept crowding up to the Castle' past the Halberdiers, in kilts, who kept the garden gates.[30]

It was a wet day and the wind was blowing hard from the south as the Lornes journeyed north to Arrochar, a little village at the head of Loch Long, which they reached at noon. Here, they were given a taste of what lay ahead; a guard of honour lined the pier, a piper played 'The Campbells are Coming', bouquets were presented and addresses read before the Lornes were allowed to enter the carriage and post to Inveraray.

In those days, the journey required steely nerves and a disregard of discomfort and danger. As the Lornes' carriage left Arrochar, they crossed the humpback bridge which divides the counties of Dumbarton and Argyll. The carriage then began the slow climb through the bleak pass of Glen Croe. At the summit, 860 feet above sea level, the horses were changed, and Lorne showed Princess Louise the white stone which marks the top and bears the words, 'Rest and be Thankful'. They then began the twisting descent to Inveraray.

The Princess's first view of her Scottish home was from the opposite side, as they rounded the head of Loch Fyne. In the foreground, indenting the opposite side of the loch was a small bay, crowded with yachts and smaller craft, all decorated with bunting. On the left lay the neat little township of Inveraray, set apart yet close enough to the Castle to serve as a reminder of a time when Campbells were safest within bowshot of their Chief's fortress. To the right of the township stood the Castle, a gaunt, grey block with turrets at the corners, and dominated in the centre by a square tower, rising above the main building. Behind rose the conical hill of Duniquaich, capped by a watch tower on the summit. Beautiful, wooded hills formed the immediate background and, encircling the whole scene, lay what Queen Victoria described as 'a fine range of mountains – green, pink and lilac',[31] framed by a glowering sky.

As the Lornes continued on around the loch and approached Frew's Bridge, suddenly, the yachts started firing a welcome and, in the ensuing panic, everything erupted into movement. 'Nobody was quite ready,' said the Duchess later, 'as it was an hour before it was expected.'[32] The Duke had calculated their arrival for four o'clock, but they came at three and caught everyone unprepared. From her turret window Lady V commented, 'the carriage looked as if it were just ploughing through the people, and such a noise as sounded! There was a total lack of order, but people comforted themselves by the enthusiasm which was shown.'[33]

Many of the invited guests were forced to leave their luncheon unfinished at the inn, and hasten to the Castle to try to reach the porch before the carriage. Amidst cheers and a royal salute, the crowds pressed against the four horses leading the carriage, so that the Lornes' progress was impeded. Eventually, the porch was reached. Lorne jumped out to help Princess Louise alight, and she was kissed by the Duke and Duchess. She 'looked remarkably well and wore a white muslin dress with blue bows, blue sash and a lace bonnet trimmed with blue.'[34]

Lorne told the assembly that Her Royal Highness had asked him to thank them for their warm welcome to Inveraray. A slight delay ensued while everyone looked for Provost MacArthur, who was one of those trying to make his way through the crowd in order to read the address. After this was delivered, Princess Louise and Lorne retired inside so that he could don his uniform. Ten minutes later, with the rain still falling, Lorne emerged to inspect the Argyllshire Volunteers, and to present them to Princess Louise and the Duke of Argyll, who were standing with him in the wet.

After a rest and some tea to steady her for the ordeal ahead, the Princess went along to the saloon, where a large number of Campbells had assembled to present her with the Clan wedding present of a necklace. Sir Donald Campbell of Dunstaffnage read the address from a roll of parchment, illustrated by a border of the English rose and Scottish thistle, intertwined with orange blossom. Standing between the Duke and Lorne, Princess Louise read the reply; it was her first effort at public speaking and the presence of her father-in-law, considered to be the finest orator of the day, made her extremely nervous. One clansman present, John Campbell of Kilberry, wrote in his diary that Princess Louise was 'very pretty and has a very charming manner. She made a little speech thanking us for the Clan present but was rather embarrassed and did not speak very well.'[35] Luckily, it was the only speech Princess Louise had to give during the festivities as Lorne made the rest on her behalf.

The following night the Duchess gave a ball in the pavilion, and the Princess thoroughly enjoyed herself dancing the country dances and reels, just as she had always done at Balmoral. She charmed everyone with her friendliness, from the Duke to the oldest estate worker, MacIntyre, who said he had 'never seen her, except at the ball, where she behaved as humble-like as anybody, and that she seemed a verra *pleasant* ladie'.[36]

The great regatta was held on the third day. Postponed for an hour, in the vain hope that the weather might improve, the regatta eventually got underway. 'The Yacht race turned out to be no race at all as through some mismanagement, only two Yachts entered and one of them was knocked out,'[37] commented Campbell of Kilberry. The nearest to a race was when seven or eight fishing boats decided to make for port during a heavy downpour, and Lorne's brothers placed bets on which of them would get home first. As one of the Argyll girls said: 'the arrangements were rather a failure . . .'[38]

It was not until the last day that the weather cleared and Princess Louise saw Inveraray for the first time in all its glory. She and Lorne strolled through the grounds in the morning and joined the rest of the family at noon to watch the cricket match, which went on until 6.30. That evening, the Tenantry ball for 710 people brought the official homecoming festivities to a close.

From then on the fine weather enabled the family to live the outdoors-life they loved. Princess Louise was introduced to one of the Duke's favourite occupations, trawling, or dredging Loch Fyne with a net. He used a small launch for this form of cruising, crewed by two Highlanders, who spoke Gaelic. At a loss as to how to address Princess Louise, one of them eventually plumped for 'Yer Royal Soverin'. His companion then nudged him and explained in Gaelic, 'Hoot mon. You're all wrong. She's n'are a Royal Soverin – she's only half a soverin.' The Duke, who spoke Gaelic, translated for the Princess, who burst into peals of laughter.[39]

All too soon it was time for the Lornes to begin their marriage tour. On the evening of September 21st, they arrived at Campbelltown Loch, aboard the *Columba*. They had deliberately chosen to arrive the night before they were to be officially welcomed, so that the Princess would have time to recover from seasickness. Lorne had hoped to include a short sail over to Ireland for lunch with Lord Dufferin at Clandeboye, but had to write, 'The Princess is such a bad sailor, I am ashamed to say that she would be unable to do anything after crossing, if there is much sea.'[40]

Princess Louise was looking forward to visiting Kintyre, for the house that the Duke had given them as part of their marriage settlement was here. Kintyre is the Scottish equivalent of a tropical island, with its beaches, lush farmland, excellent sport – and delicious, wild mushrooms, which the family always eagerly rushed out to pick.

On Friday, after a calm night, Princess Louise and Lorne disembarked at Campbelltown to a reception unlike any they had so far encountered. The people of Campbelltown had tried to emulate the mainland, but their isolation and size made it difficult; instead of a grand pavilion, the Princess found a little wooden hut erected by the local carpenter; instead of bunting and welcome arches, people waved their handkerchiefs and threw flowers along the Princess's path. As

The Marriage of
HRH Princess Louise
to the Marquis of
Lorne, March 1871.

The Marquis and
Marchioness of Lorne
on honeymoon,
spring 1871.

ey:

1 The Queen	27 Lady Archibald Campbell
2 HRH Princess Louise	28 Lord Colin Campbell
3 The Marquis of Lorne	29 Lord Archibald Campbell
4 The Bishop of London	30 Prince Edward of Saxe-Weimar
5 The Bishop of Oxford	31 The Duke of Sutherland
6 The Dean of Windsor	32 The Maharajah Dhuleep Sing
7 HRH The Prince of Wales	33 The Maharasee Dhuleep Sing
8 The Duchess of Cambridge	34 Lady Elizabeth Campbell
9 The Duke of Saxe-Coburg	35 The Duchess of Westminster
10 HRH Princess Mary	36 The Duke of Westminster
11 HRH The Princess of Wales	37 Lord Granville
12 HRH Prince George of Wales	38 Lady Granville
13 HRH Prince Albert Victor	39 The Duchess of Leinster
14 The Count of Flanders	40 The Duke of Leinster
15 HRH The Duke of Connaught	41 Lord Salisbury
16 HRH Prince Leopold	42 The Duke of Richmond
17 The Duke of Cambridge	43 Mr Gladstone
18 HRH Princess Beatrice	44 Mr Cardwell
19 HRH Princess Helena	45 Dr Guthrie
20 Prince Christian	46 Lord Beaconsfield
21 The Duke of Teck	47 Dr Norman McLeod
22 Earl Percy	48 Lady Dudley
23 Lord Ronald Leveson-Gower	49 Sir Albert Woods
24 The Duchess of Argyll	50 Mr Planeli
25 The Duke of Argyll	51 Earl Sydney
26 The Countess Percy	

George, 8th Duke of Argyll.

Elizabeth, Duchess of Argyll.

Fishing the Aray, part of the wall decorations in the library at Inveraray Castle, c. 1872.

The Archie Campbells: clockwise Lord Archie, Janey in theatrical costume, Niall, and Elspeth (Niky) as a debutante.

church bells rang, the Lornes made a triumphal progress to the town boundary. From here they continued their nine mile journey through windy lanes and undulating country down to Southend, which lies on the south coast by the sparkling sea.

Outside the little parish church, a platform had been hurriedly erected upon which the Lornes sat while a tenant read an address of welcome. The Macharioch tenantry then succeeded in unharnessing the horses of the carriage and dragging the Lornes to their new home, Macharioch House, where the whole party were given a dinner by Lorne at the Home Farm. Princess Louise was so touched by the warmth and simplicity of her reception that she spontaneously made an impromptu speech of thanks, and proposed a toast to 'the health of the tenantry' and 'the prosperity of Kintyre'.[41]

It was not until the next day that Princess Louise turned her attention to Macharioch House. The Duchess had described it as 'tolerable' but 'very ugly . . . and the grounds very neglected looking'.[42] Although the Argylls had improved the house, a great deal more needed to be done, since the roof was not even water-tight. This did not deter Princess Louise, for Macharioch was the only house which was hers and so could satisfy her strong, nesting instincts. She hired an architect, George Devey, to enlarge and modernize the house by adding some bathrooms. Her flair for landscape design came to the fore. Undergrowth was hacked down, walks cleared and gardens laid out so that the sea, which she loved, would be visible from every room of the house. Fuchsias grow in great profusion in Southend, and Princess Louise successfully planted a long fuchsia walk, which still connects the house to the beach. Her head whirled with ideas for improvements and she sketched away, furiously committing them to paper.

Yet, even in this Campbell stronghold, they could not escape being stared at by crowds; most of whom were not locals, but came from elsewhere to try to see the Princess in church on Sundays. One week, the small local church was so crowded she and Lorne could hardly enter. The following Sunday, determined to beat the crowds, they arrived half an hour before the bells were rung. When the congregation came in, only the backs of two seated figures were visible. At the end of the service, the minister arranged for them to slip out by a side door; he also let it be known that the Lornes would not be in Kintyre for much longer. In fact, Princess Louise liked 'this curious lovely spot' so much that she and Lorne decided to remain until October 6th. The next Sunday, the crowds kept away so that the Lornes were able to go to church in peace.

These carefree Macharioch days were nevertheless sad ones for Princess Louise. She was grieving for her dearest friend, Sybil St Albans. On August 21st, Sybil had been safely confined with a daughter at a house in Cromwell Road, rented specifically for her confinement. Despite taking precautions, within two days, she had developed puerperal fever, caught from defective drains. There was no known cure, and on September 7th, aged only twenty-two, Sybil died.

Princess Louise was stunned. Sybil was so much a part of her life. Since her marriage she had seen less of her, but now that she, too, was married, Princess Louise had looked forward to seeing more of her old friend, especially in London, where they could go about together. Sybil, who always listened sympathetically, who was 'the brightest and most winning of creatures', so unaffected and beloved – it was impossible to grasp that this dear person was gone from her life.[43]

She immediately telegraphed an offer of help to Mrs Grey, now left in charge of two, motherless, young children and a two-week-old babe. In the bleak days that followed, Princess Louise considered ideas for a memorial, perhaps in the little church at Bestwood which Sybil had built. After the funeral, she wrote to Mrs Grey asking, 'if you and the Duke would let me try to do a recumbent statue of darling Sybil? I have an idea in my head as to how I should like to represent her. It might be carried out in marble but only if quite, quite suited to your Tastes, and the Duke's idea of what he wanted.'[44]

Having drawn up some preliminary sketches for the work, Princess Louise wrote again from Macharioch with her proposals. Mrs Grey thought her designs lovely, but her only son, Albert, was opposed to Princess Louise having anything to do with his sister's memorial. Admitting he had not even seen the bust Princess Louise had done of his father, he nevertheless wrote that everybody said 'a more fearful thing was never executed'.[45] He suggested that Boehm should be asked to do it.

Albert Grey's opinion carried the day. Princess Louise was tactfully told that the family had decided to erect a Wayfarers' Repose for Travellers, outside Bestwood church, with a bust of Sybil done by Boehm. Delighted that her tutor and friend should have the commission, Princess Louise was at pains to let Mrs Grey know that she had only offered her services out of affection, rather than a belief in her own sculptural abilities. In fact, she privately modelled a medallion of Sybil's head for Mrs Grey, which remains in the church at Bestwood today. Mrs Grey held a much higher opinion than her son of Princess Louise's work.

Once the Princess had organized everything at Macharioch, it was time to travel South. Yet they had no sooner settled into Argyll Lodge, when it seemed as if Princess Louise was to lose another person dear to her. On November 21st, the Prince of Wales had succumbed to a feverish attack at Sandringham. The family were put on alert two days later when his illness was diagnosed as typhoid. On December 7th, his condition became critical. Absent family members were telegraphed for, including some of the Danes. The Queen, with Princess Louise and Prince Alfred, 'drove in deep snow and hard frost up to S. Nobody at the door but Lady Macclesfield, who said dear Bertie was *very bad*.'[46]

As his condition worsened and the rest of the family arrived, it was soon evident that there were far too many people there. Sandringham heaved with activity as Royalties sent conflicting messages and orders flew between them, the Household and doctors. Conditions were also exceedingly cramped – so much so that Princess Louise and Princess Beatrice had to share not just a room, but a bed. Princess Louise was kept busy acting as her mother's link with the Government, writing to Mr Gladstone on the morning of the 13th: 'My dear brother's state is unchanged and his life is hanging on one slender thread . . .'[47]

It was, as she said, 'a fearful existence', especially, since the Prince's ravings were impossible to ignore. Many of the subjects aired in his delirium were those with which he was preoccupied when well, such as the autumn manœuvres: 'he constantly refers to these and talks about the dress and about his spurs being the correct pattern! etc. etc. dress is a sort of mania with them all,' wrote one courtier.[48] The Queen, in particular, was sure that the awful 14th would claim her eldest son, as it had her husband.

However, as the family apprehensively gathered in the library and the hall that morning, the doctors issued a cheerful bulletin. By the 15th, only the Queen, Princess Louise and the Hesses remained in the House: 'All the rest are gone,' the Queen recorded with relief. Since there was still cause for anxiety, Queen Victoria decided to spend Christmas at Windsor, which, she told the Crown Princess, 'I never have done since '60 and which will be painful.'[49]

So it was that the Lornes passed their first married Christmas, somewhat unexpectedly, at Windsor Castle. It was very quiet, with only one tree for the whole Royal Family, and no great celebrations or dancing. Perhaps as a result of the strain of the last anxious weeks, Princess Louise became unwell and was unable to throw off her bad cough. A quiet Christmas was all that she could manage. Lorne, worried by this, now insisted that they go abroad again.

CHAPTER XI

Early Married Life

When the doctors had suggested the South of France as a suitable place for Princess Louise to 'get rid of her . . . horrid winter cough'[1] and ease the rheumatism in her knee, she jumped at the chance to pass the dreary, winter months in a place with 'nice mild bright weather which I love'.[2] Now that the Prince of Wales seemed to be out of danger, the Queen urged her to delay no longer. Queen Victoria never mollycoddled her children. Her real concern was that if Princess Louise developed bronchitis, it would interfere with her wifely duties and diminish the possibility of any 'hopes'. Queen Victoria might denigrate the process of childbearing, but she was as conscious as any Victorian mama of the necessity for her daughter to produce an heir.

Lorne's beloved Aunt Dot, more formally Lady Emma Campbell, had married Sir John McNeill, an old friend of the Duke's, six months before the Lornes' wedding. When the Lornes decided upon the South of France, the McNeills invited them to stay in their villa at Cannes. However, the Christians had also taken a villa in the South of France. Since Princess Louise did not want to offend her sister by staying elsewhere, she and Lorne decided to be independent and stay in an hotel.

They arrived at the Hôtel Bellevue in Mentone in early February 1872. They had chosen Mentone because it was then considered the best health resort in the South of France. Mentone had become like a foreign annexe to an English convalescent home: there was a saying 'Cannes for living, Monte Carlo for gambling and Mentone for dying'.[3] There was more truth in this than intended, for its level of hygiene was not that usually associated with a health resort; certainly, it did not measure up to Princess Louise's standards: 'This hotel is not nice in any way,' she wrote home, 'noisy, public, dirty and uncomfortable, beds dreadful and no baths! But,' she added, 'we make the best of it and get on very well.'

The main comfort was the weather, which really was 'quite beautiful, the sea an everlasting blue'. Walks, however, were not such a success.

Princess Louise was a great believer in exercise and had looked forward to following a regime of long daily walks. Lorne was less enthusiastic. 'I make him walk as much as I can,'[4] she told his mother, but she was prevented by the position of the hotel which, according to Lorne, 'clings to the steep hillside . . . so that there is no walking about it except along little sharp steep terraces and the carriage road zig zags down to the door from the highway.'[5]

Their easy companionship added extra enjoyment to expeditions. Princess Louise started to collect plants and take cuttings of rosemary, thyme, juniper and geraniums for Inveraray, although Lorne was afraid they would find themselves out of their element in Scotland. The Lornes also experimented with woodcarving in order to make the inlaid work they saw manufactured locally, and Princess Louise was rarely without a sketch pad. As Lorne wrote to the Duchess, 'we have plenty to do when not out . . . I am writing a Journal, reading French and English light literature & we mean to take lessons in Italian,' while Princess Louise was also trying to finish working a pair of slippers for Lorne.[6]

They also had to call on the other English residents, including the Shaftesburys. Princess Louise reported to the Duchess that one of the Shaftesbury girls, 'Hilda, never took her eyes off me – as she did on the *Cumberland*.'[7] During her visit to the *Cumberland* training ship in September 1871, the Shaftesbury family, who were old friends of the Argylls, had been staying at Inveraray. Both Princess Louise and the Duchess had noticed how Lady Hilda had stared rather obviously at Princess Louise, something they put down to unspoken Shaftesbury hopes of an alliance between her sister and Lorne. An admirer of Lord Shaftesbury, Princess Louise now felt slightly uncomfortable about being with his family; even the present of a box of *marrons glacés* did not sweeten Lady Hilda's gaze.

Marrons glacés were the Lornes' great discovery and they were mad about them. 'Have you ever eaten marrons glacées [sic]?' Lorne asked the Argylls. 'We live on nothing else – and if you do not know what they are like, do order them from Fortnum and Mason.'[8]

On their return to England, the Lornes went straight to London and their house at Number 1, Grosvenor Crescent, off Belgrave Square. Belgravia was then the fashionable area for houses, rivalled only by the even more expensive Mayfair. Lorne had taken this house from his Uncle Westminster to tide them over until they bought a house.

Although Princess Louise would happily have lived at Argyll Lodge, Lorne preferred to be independent.

Unlike most gentlewomen of her day, the Princess had an excellent grasp of financial matters and did not consider them to be the sole province of her husband. Never inclined to be extravagant, she was able to exercise caution when the need arose, without ever being mean or too thrifty. Her early training with the accounts book at the Swiss cottage stood her in good stead; she paid bills promptly and her bank books always balanced. It was the Princess, rather than Lorne, who exercised fiscal restraint in their marriage. Not that Lorne was profligate, but his impulsive, generous nature sometimes involved them in unforeseen expenses.

Fully aware of the cost of decorating a house – having discussed it with Princess Helena, who had refurbished Frogmore House – Princess Louise was prepared to be frugal over Grosvenor Crescent, since it was not to be her permanent London house. 'I fancy papering is less expensive than painting and looks just as well,' she told the Duchess. 'We must not do all at once as we shall only require part of it. The expense will be great, but we will try to be as careful as possible.'[9]

For a house that was merely a 'stop-gap', Grosvenor Crescent did the Lornes proud; it stood comparison with most of the town houses occupied by the great landed families during the Season. The entrance faces Belgrave Square and leads into a spacious marble-floored hall. With nine good reception rooms on the ground and first floor, and their two bedroom suites on the second floor, let alone eight more bedrooms with dressing rooms on the third and fourth floors, Princess Louise was right to think they would only need to use part of the house. Its beauty lay in the large, oval rooms, which were a feature of each floor; Princess Louise turned one into a drawing room and another into her boudoir. Having made the house habitable, the Princess was ready and eager to enter London life in the Season of 1872.

Her knowledge of London was, of course, extremely limited since she had been there so rarely before her marriage. As a result, London was associated in her mind with treats – visits to the theatre, opera or an art gallery – or with duties – courts, drawing rooms and accompanying Mama to the opening of Parliament. Now, for the first time, she was able to explore it at leisure. London was then much quieter, its radius limited for the inhabitants by the capacity of their horses and the comfort of their equipages. The Princess's carriage and horses were stabled in her mews in Wilton Row.

So, when on a spring afternoon in 1872 she appeared at the open doors of her house, she would be met by the sight of a beautifully appointed carriage waiting motionlessly with the coachman. The carriage was a brougham if she was going on an errand, and a swinging barouche if she was going on an afternoon drive. In either case, the Princess would not be venturing further than Belgravia, Mayfair or St James's, unless she was going to Kensington; in 1872, everyone she knew lived within this tiny area, though the charitable and artistic circles she now began to frequent slowly expanded her geographical knowledge of London.

For the moment, however, she contented herself with afternoon drives in Hyde Park, before calling on members of the family; sometimes in warmer weather, she would take the fashionable route back from the Park through Berkeley Square, where her carriage would draw up under the trees while her footman brought out a tall glass of delicious, cooling, pink strawberry ice from Gunters.

The Princess often preferred to walk rather than drive. In those days, people thought nothing of walking five or six miles to see someone. Living in Grosvenor Crescent was extremely convenient for her. At the other end of the street was the wall surrounding Buckingham Palace. She had a key to the door in it, so she could slip into the grounds and walk up to the Palace to see any visiting family. On other occasions, she would cut across Green Park to Bond Street, where she would visit the art galleries.

Apart from 'taking the air', walks and drives had a function in a Victorian lady's life. It was while on these excursions that she would participate in the 'card-and-call' ritual, which regulated social life in the nineteenth century. Etiquette decreed that, after meeting, a lady could leave her card and two of her husband's with another lady. If the lady of the house wished to start an acquaintanceship, she in turn would leave her cards. The preliminary steps in this dance of friendship having been executed successfully, the ladies glided into the next turn, which involved a short call of less than fifteen minutes, which was then returned. Only now could either of them issue an invitation to tea and then dinner.

As royalty, Princess Louise did not have to leave cards, though others had to leave them with her, but she did have to pay and receive calls incessantly. Before going away or abroad, and upon her return, she had to visit other members of the family and close friends, just as they did her. This ritual took up much of Princess Louise's time. Although, according to Lord Ernest Hamilton, the main objective of Society in those leisured days was to kill time rather than to save it, Princess Louise found that she never had enough time at her disposal.[10] As the years passed, she came to look upon the ritual as 'The lonely monotony [which] kills me – & the incessant messages & letters & calls!' It was to combat this grinding routine that she urged exercise upon herself and her Household: 'at least twice in the day & breaks & changes above all things & runs to the country'.[11]

But the pressure of work was relatively light in the early days of her married life. Not yet involved in many public duties, and released from her duties as companion to Queen Victoria, she was left with an unaccustomed freedom of choice over the way in which to pass her time. She usually passed the mornings at home with Lorne, employed with letters or plans for the day; sometimes a member of their large family would drop in at noon and stay to lunch, which she always took with Lorne; after lunch she would sketch or work on a model for an hour or so. Then, at about three, she would go out, sometimes returning home with friends for tea. Lorne would leave for the House in the afternoon, but usually returned to dine with her. They paid several visits a week to Argyll Lodge and Stafford House, and she saw the Princess of Wales as often as possible.

The Lornes also began to entertain. 'I liked seeing her receive for the first time. It seems only the other day we were all girls together,' wrote Louisa Knightley after attending one of Princess Louise's first dinner parties on 15 May 1872.[12] Parties then were large, stately affairs, where guests inevitably knew each other. The Lornes found them dull, ostentatious, and much too formal. They decided to entertain in quite a different way and gave 'a small but very new and amusing party'.[13] This was considered very daring.

It is difficult, over a century later, to realize just how rigid and small London Society was in the mid-Victorian years. It was a caste system of nobility and gentry. Thus to mix painters, musicians and literary men, and even include theatrical and medical people not normally received in Society, with established Society at small dinner parties of ten or twelve people, was revolutionary. To a certain extent, Princess Louise was following her father's example, when he had invited distinguished professional men to Windsor, much to Queen Victoria's discomfort; but the relaxed atmosphere of Princess Louise's parties was more conducive to conversation. She did not uphold the convention that royalty must open a conversation before anyone else could speak. She much preferred an easy exchange, and in later life would win a reputation as an amusing, interesting conversationalist.

Unfortunately, all the other evening entertainments she attended were of the conventional, formal kind. Indeed, during the Season of 1872 the Lornes dined out at all the great London houses and Northumberland, Stafford, Devonshire and Grosvenor Houses welcomed Princess Louise as a new member of the family.

Although the Princess enjoyed the Season, she had no intention of being trapped into an ornamental, useless existence. From the first days of marriage, she and Lorne had received a stream of letters from individuals and organizations, begging for their patronage and financial help. When the stream threatened to become a river, Princess Louise decided they needed the help of a secretary. According to Lorne, another reason for employing a secretary was 'L [Louise] much objects to my answering all begging letters myself as she has heard of the possibility of their being sold as autographs!'[14] Such an idea was alien to Lorne, but he agreed to use one of the Duke's secretaries from the India Office for official letters.

The majority of these begging letters, as the Lornes called them, asked no more than permission to use the Princess's name to further their cause. While she was usually happy to give it, she wanted to be more than a figurehead. She had gained organizational experience as the Queen's right hand for four years, and grown used to exercising some power. Moreover, she had long wished 'to be useful' in some way, and marriage provided her with a platform from which to launch herself into public life.

Her first attempt was a dismal failure. Ever since their initial correspondence in 1869, the Princess had followed Josephine Butler's work with increasing interest. By 1871 Mrs Butler had embarked upon her work with prostitutes and her crusade for the repeal of the Contagious Diseases Acts. 'I am abhorred by everyone above the middle classes who happens to know anything about it,' she admitted.[15] Her campaign caused a national uproar and deep divisions among women, some of whom considered that support for her would harm other campaigns for better education and conditions, which were of more concern to most women. Princess Louise had no such compunction and fully supported Mrs Butler's home for 'unfortunate girls' in Liverpool. However, her inexperience had led her to choose far too controversial an issue as her first venture into public life.

She had expressed great interest in Mrs Butler's book, *Women's Work and Women's Culture*, and the author gladly sent her a copy. After Lorne casually mentioned it to Lord Granville, there was a great fuss, not so much because the book dealt with women's suffrage, as that it came from a controversial woman. The decision was made that Princess Louise must return the book; for to keep it would identify her and thus the Royal Family with a political question. It was even more important for Princess Louise to seem impartial about public issues because of her marriage to a Liberal MP.

So the Princess returned the book but sought a way to explain that this was not her personal decision but a political one. She was extremely anxious that Mrs Butler should not think that she had acted 'in a cold-hearted manner' for she wished 'to assure Mrs Butler of her entire appreciation of her high-minded and unselfish labours, and of her regard for her personally'.[16] Mrs Butler understood and sympathized with the Princess's predicament. Princess Louise had flown the Court nest only to discover that her wings were clipped.

Undaunted, Princess Louise soon found another related but less controversial cause to promote. She had been interested in education ever since she had heard the debate on the Education of Children Bill in 1869. The Bill proposed to extend compulsory education to cover not only children in workshops and factories, but all children. Surprised by the defeat of such sensible legislation, Princess Louise began to discuss the issues with General Grey and Dean Wellesley and to read up on the subject.

As it happened, this coincided with a national debate on public education and, in particular, the education of women. When the School's Inquiry Commission of 1864–7, headed by Lorne's uncle, Lord Taunton, had been appointed, Emily Davis had seized this opportunity to prove that girls were just as capable of learning as boys, but were hampered by both the lack and quality of teaching. She somehow managed to persuade the Taunton Commission to examine girls' schools.

Maria Grey afterwards called the Commission's report the Domesday Book of Women's Education – because it was so damning in its indictment of 'the general deficiency in girls' education'.[17] News that money collected specifically for a girls' school had been diverted to an already endowed boys' school sparked off Maria Grey's campaign. Not only did she write to *The Times* about it, while Princess Louise was on honeymoon, but she read a paper to the influential Society of Arts.

In this paper Maria Grey unfolded her plan for a National Educational Union for Women with its own Charter, which would recognize their equal right with men to the best education. Although the Education Act of 1870 gave compulsory free elementary schooling to all children, regardless of their sex, there was no such provision for secondary education. What Maria Grey proposed was to establish secondary schools for girls, which would give them, in Lorne's words, 'a most excellent and cheap education'.[18]

The warm reception given to Mrs Grey's paper led to the formation of a general Committee and the recruitment of influential people, like Princess Louise, to promote her 'National Union for the Education of Girls of all Classes above the Elementary'; a title soon shortened to the Women's Education Union or W.E.U. Princess Louise became its first President and, at her request, on a November day in the dining room of 1 Grosvenor Crescent, a meeting was held, which included such figures as Dean Stanley, Lady Stanley of Alderney, Lucy Cavendish with her father Lord Lyttelton, Mrs Maria Grey and Miss Emily Shirreff, former Mistress of Girton. Their aim was to open a public day school for girls in Kensington or Chelsea.

Sir Wyndham Dunstan, who later served with Princess Louise on this Committee, wrote that she became 'a real enthusiast' about setting up the schools: 'To her indefatigable work and influence was largely due the emergence of a strong council of persons ready to work for the cause and the raising of the necessary capital.'[19]

The Princess insisted upon her right to be consulted on all major questions. Lorne wrote to Mrs Grey on 23 April 1872 to remind her that 'Nothing should be regarded "as final" without the President's sanction.' Furthermore, she wanted to receive the minutes of all meetings and to have the right to state an objection if need be. Should the Union propose a 'striking' change of plan, the Princess wanted the power to call a special meeting at which she would have the right to vote, though she would always concede to the majority vote on any issue.

Princess Louise was lucky to have a husband who not only fully supported her interest but who became actively involved as a member of the Committee, which now resolved to form a Company. On 7 June 1872, Lorne attended a public meeting in the Albert Hall at which the plan was unveiled in a prospectus, with an accompanying letter from Princess Louise. In it, she called attention to the 'great need for really good schools where girls could obtain a sound education at moderate cost'. In order to provide these Schools, a Girls' Public Day School Company or G.P.D.S.C. would be launched, for which the funds would be raised in shares of £5 each by means of a Limited Liability Company.[20]

The W.E.U. soon successfully raised £12,000. The Committee was transformed into an executive council and Princess Louise became Patroness of the Company's schools. On 21 January 1873, the first school was opened at Durham House in South Street, Chelsea. She met the school's twenty pupils in March 1873 and was entirely happy about their progress. Yet there remained many who did not share her views.

Despite the President's support, there was passionate opposition from those who were suspicious about granting girls the same academic opportunities as boys. 'I was always hearing that girls could be turned into boys by studying the same subject,' recalled the headmistress of Cheltenham Ladies College in 1888.[21] One of the most vehement opponents was the Duchess of Northumberland, a connection of the Princess's by marriage. She believed that 'Schools for women are in themselves, in their very nature, bad, and to be avoided as much as possible.' Her argument was based on the supposition that a man's home would be made uncomfortable by the presence of an educated wife. One man, who was asked to support the W.E.U., endorsed her view when he bluntly replied that 'women were getting out of hand and wanted instead of help "to be taken down a peg"'.[22]

Yet more controversial were the two principles upon which the schools would be based: they would be non-denominational and there would be no class distinctions. Again, there was much prejudice against this policy. Princess Louise and the founders of the W.E.U. had to stress time and again that the schools were not godless. Opposition also continued to be voiced against the idea of socially mixing classes at a public school. The surgeon, Louisa Martindale, remembered the dismay felt by her mother's friends when she was sent to a Girls' Public Day School. Mrs Martindale protected her daughter's gentility by employing a governess to accompany her to school. To protect themselves against charges of encouraging unsuitable friendships, the schools introduced a rule that girls would only be allowed to walk home together if both sets of parents gave their permission.[23]

Louisa Knightley was another who, despite her intelligence, was disturbed by the concept of social mixing. 'This whole movement for the education of girls is no doubt an experiment,' she wrote after Princess Louise had arranged for her to visit the Chelsea school on 17 July 1873. There, she heard a lecture on Political Economy. But her wistful conclusion – 'I only wish I had received such training in my youth!' – was an echo of Princess Louise's own attitude to education.[24] Aware of the academic gaps in her own knowledge, and the inflexibility of her own education, she was determined that other girls should not suffer the same fate and should have the opportunity to be well-educated. Years later she said, 'Luckily the habit of moulding all children to the same pattern has gone out of fashion. It was deplorable. I know, because I suffered from it. Nowadays individuality and one's own capabilities are recognised.'[25]

Although Princess Louise would be involved in other philanthropic endeavours, the G.P.D.S.C. was the cause closest to her heart. She helped start the movement, nurtured it and watched it grow to thirty-five schools, most of which still exist. Moreover, it embodied beliefs she held dear, such as progress for women through teaching, the opportunity to learn regardless of family income, and the abolition of class distinctions.

During the early seventies other matters competed for Princess Louise's attention. Her first tasks included the organization of her Household. Determined to have a simple Household, the Princess chose only one lady-in-waiting, Lady Sophia Macnamara. One of the Earl of Listowel's ten children, she already had connections with the Court. She had married Captain Arthur Macnamara, a Bedfordshire gentleman, in 1854, but there were no children, so she possessed the essential qualification for a courtier – namely, availability. Known in the family as 'Aunt Smack', Lady Sophie was tiny with dark, curly hair framing a plain face. 'Lady Mac is here. She is as jolly as ever,' a fellow guest at a houseparty wrote.[26] She shared Princess Louise's sense of humour and remained the Princess's only Lady until ill-health forced her to retire at the turn of the century.

To begin with, the Princess only needed a part-time Comptroller and chose a friend of Lorne's, Major Frederick Campbell. The rest of the staff were similar to those found in any large London household in 1872. Henry Ponsonby mistakenly thought Princess Louise would be unable to manage domestic matters, or to understand her married position, owing to a comment she made about her footmen: 'I don't want an absurd man in a kilt following me about everywhere and I want to choose the men at once or I shall have some others thrust upon me . . .'[27] Although she was more than happy to employ Scottish servants, like James Tait, who came to her aged fourteen in the 1890s and was with her until 1939, she adhered to the custom that the kilt was left behind in Scotland once the border was crossed. Highland servants in their kilts were fine, as ghillies and outdoor men, but she had no intention of emulating the Queen and bringing them indoors.

Used to unfettered bachelorhood, Lorne was unprepared for the appendages of a married establishment. He found 'Travelling with womenkind is too frightfully expensive.'[28] Now, a retinue accompanied the Lornes on every journey, whatever its duration. Although large to Lorne, it was nothing compared to Princess Louise's excursions with her mother. On the Lornes' autumn visits to Inveraray, they took only the butler, three men servants, a ladies' maid, a laundry maid and a housemaid.

The recollection in Inveraray today is that Princess Louise neither visited the place nor liked it. Yet, up to the mid-eighties, she passed most of the year based at Inveraray. It was only in later years that she did not stay there, owing to changes in the Argyll family which prevented even the Campbells from treating Inveraray as their home.

In 1872, Princess Louise left London for Inveraray at the beginning of August to celebrate Lorne's birthday on the 6th. Apart from short trips away, she stayed there until the second week of March 1873. The weather was so lovely that August that the Duke decided to bring forward a cruise he had planned for September 'to show all our Island Glories to our Princess'.[29] It was during this cruise that Princess Louise astonished the family by taking charge of the galley and teaching the chef how to cook various dishes. She was probably forced into action by the poor quality of the food; something the Argyll family hardly seemed to notice. The Duchess thought the Princess showed great pluck since she was 'a terribly bad' sailor.[30] Seasickness was considered par for the course by the Argylls since all the female side suffered – indeed weather was judged in terms of such sufferings; a day would be described as a 'spewing' day.[31]

During her three-week visit to Queen Victoria in October, Balmoral, in contrast with life at Inveraray, seemed more oppressive than ever to Princess Louise. There was a 'severe dreariness' about the place.[32] Conversation at meals was punctuated by prolonged silences, since so many topics could not be mentioned before fifteen-year-old Princess Beatrice. For instance, marriage could not be discussed in case it put ideas into her head.

In contrast, there was an easy-going informality about Inveraray which the Princess treasured. As at Argyll Lodge, it was a family life which included the tenantry and estate people. Furthermore, it was not run on the well-oiled lines of a Court. Unpunctuality in the Argyll households was no sin; in fine weather, sport and outside interests always prevailed over meal times, although meals were served at set hours, regardless of whether every member of the family had returned home. That autumn and winter of 1872, Princess Louise was woken at eight o'clock each morning by Ross, the Duke's piper. A housemaid then brought tea and bread and butter into the bedrooms. The Duke always rose then, and worked in the drawing room for an hour, after which he would walk through the Saloon into the Green Library. At nine o'clock, or thereabouts, the family met in this room for prayers. The servants stood in a line down one side and the family sat on the green, leather chairs which faced a table, upon which was placed the Bible. The Duke would read a psalm in his fine, educated, Scottish voice, say a prayer and pronounce the benediction. Whereupon the family hastened into the large, tapestry dining room to tuck into a hearty breakfast. As little Campbell nephews and nieces left the nursery, they ate at a separate, round table made of coloured, Iona marble, and quietly amused themselves, while Princess Louise and their uncles and aunts made plans for the day or discussed politics with the Duke.

From the dining room, Princess Louise would migrate with the rest of the family to the porch. Although it had only been erected for her homecoming, as a temporary protection against the weather, it soon came to play the same role as the verdandah at Argyll Lodge: a gathering place for the whole family. Along the walls of the glass-roofed porch and ranged horizontally upon hooks, were much-used salmon-rods. The men of the family 'would be busy with fly-hooks and baskets, guns or rifles. The whirr of fishing-reels sounded through the chatter of voices. Outside on the gravel, the ghillies waited, and the gamekeepers, surrounded by panting, pink-tongued dogs.'[33] That autumn of 1872, it was Lorne and his two younger brothers, Lord Walter and Lord Colin, who stood there in their kilts and tweed coats, filling their pockets with baps of cold grouse, which constituted their lunch out on the hills.

Meanwhile, Princess Louise, who had never been allowed to fish at Balmoral, eagerly joined the ranks of Campbell fisherwomen. Lorne had given her a rod and after a few lessons, she used to run down to the loch, only five minutes away, to land a grilse or sea trout. Old Sandy McKellar, the Duke's fisherman, taught her with Lorne's help to fish. He had a fine, strong face which Princess Louise used as a model for her drawings. He lived in a croft, practically on the shore of the Dhbu Loch, where the Princess and Lorne's sisters used to visit him and sit on the seat outside his 'wee hoose'.

Those not out stalking on the hills would regroup at the Castle for lunch, which was the schoolroom children's main meal. Princess Louise was amazed to find that her parents-in-law were as quick as her mother over their meals and was dismayed to learn that the Campbell children often went hungry and were never allowed 'sweet things'. The Duke often finished eating before the servants had put food before the youngest child at table. Oblivious, he would rise from the table with the Duchess, thereby ending the meal.

After lunch, Princess Louise might go riding with Lorne, if the weather was fine. Sometimes, she accompanied the Duke and Duchess on a drive along the lochside or through the woods to 'the Douglas Water' which was 'all clear and brown and foaming, running fast to get down to the loch'.[34] Several afternoons a week, she would call on people living about the estate and sit with the sick.

The old clan system, combined with the simplicity of Highland life, fostered an intimacy between people which was, for the most part, unknown or misunderstood south of the border. In England, the feudal relation of the Big House with the village people was, however kindly, a relation of superior to inferior. In Scotland, to belong to a clan was to belong to a family. The landlord or chief was simply the head of the family and responsible for them all. Dean Baillie, whose family hailed from Inverness-shire, reiterates, 'there was to be found in Scotland the most aristocratic democracy and the most democratic aristocracy in the world. I was always conscious of a quality of mutual respect which was quite different from what I was likely to find south of the border.'[35] With these people, Princess Louise, like her mother, was able to relax and forget her position; indeed, to them she was simply 'another wummin'.

She would often drive herself to the township to call on Jessie MacArthur, wife of the schoolmaster, or Miss Margaret McGibbon, an old resident, before lunch or tea. As Mrs Baldwin recounted in a letter to her son, when Miss McGibbon fell seriously ill in 1875, 'Princess Louise came here and, not being allowed by the Doctor to see Margaret, she sat with me some time, asked if she could send anything from the castle that she would like, and was so nice and friendly.'[36]

If it was a wet day, then Princess Louise would spend it with the young Campbell girls, sketching or reading aloud with them before tea. She showed them how to string their own shells and little stones into necklaces. Years later, she delighted to relate to one of Lady Frances's daughters how she had to teach Lorne's sisters the correct way to sew on a button which had fallen from the Duke's coat. 'They hadn't an idea of it,' she explained. 'They put it on quite flat. Oh, your poor grandfather!'[37] At the time, Princess Louise was rather surprised, if not shocked, by such deficiencies in their education and set about remedying this deplorable state of affairs for the Campbell girls.

'Nothing in life will ever be so merry and jolly as our sisterhood,'[38] was an opinion shared by all the Campbell girls, although here uttered by Lady V in a letter to Lady Frances. They were fiercely protective of each other. In 1872, the sisterhood really comprised Lady Libby, aged twenty, Lady V aged eighteen, Lady Evey aged seventeen, Lady Frances aged fourteen, and Lady Mary aged thirteen. Of the other two sisters, Lady Percy, or 'Edie', was married and Lady Connie was only seven and considered the 'Baby'.

All the sisters had warmly welcomed their brother's bride into the family, noticing that people listened to her and did things for her and that, although she rode beautifully, she could not fish. But as she began to introduce changes into their lives, their 'Hieland' blood would out, and some would cling to the auld ways. Princess Louise's bustling reorganization was rather like medicine to them – the idea of it was all right but, when swallowed, it often left a bitter taste. Much as they loved Princess Louise, they did not always submit to her rule, but learnt to rearrange matters quietly to suit themselves.

Little Lady Mary (she was under five foot) was rather a pet of the Duchess's and later became Lorne's closest sister. With a pink and white complexion, fair hair and the marvellous Campbell eyes of a piercing, deep blue, she was strikingly pretty.[39] Like all the sisters, she was possessed of great determination. So, when Princess Louise set about arranging the family books, which had been scattered among four or five rooms, into the Study and Green Library with some for the new library room, which she and Lorne were creating off the Great Hall, little Mary led the resistance.

'Louise is determined to get everyone of the children's books into the study,' Lady Mary warned her absent sister 'Fa'. But Princess Louise, fired with enthusiasm, did not intend to stop there; as Lady Mary related, 'then she came upstairs to arrange the books in the shelves, I was in despair when I saw them filling up all the rooms'. Undaunted, Lady Mary mounted a rescue operation of her own. She stealthily crept upstairs afterwards and removed some of these books to the general shelf in the room she and Lady Frances shared. 'Then I took Evey's, Libby's, Victoria's books to a little cabinet in Libby's room, because Louise pulled out of the cupboard in the Study all Evey's best bound books.'[40] Far from being cross when she discovered Lady Mary's counterraid, the Princess was amused and sympathetic; she won Mary's heart by apologizing for having moved their cherished books.

While the sisterhood might baulk at some of Princess Louise's suggestions, the Duke and Duchess welcomed them, since they recognized her good taste. The Lornes redesigned a suite of rooms to form the Gallery Library, off the Great Hall. Princess Louise also designed the wrought-iron scrollwork for the rails enclosing the gallery, which circled the room. Her design incorporated a sequence comprising the Galley of Lorne, her coronet, the Argyll coronet, and linked 'A's. On the walls of the passageway, and on the doors leading into the Gallery Library, she drew frescos of Inveraray and of her honeymoon tour in Italy and the South of France, which remain there today.

The Duke also used Princess Louise as an in-house art consultant, much as Queen Victoria did. When his stepmother died in London, various Argyll pictures were returned to Inveraray and their hanging caused a massive rearrangement of the family pictures. 'We have borne in mind Louise's fancies and advice,' the Duke wrote, 'she will be glad that her special spite – the 1st Duke – is down. We have put Lord Bellenden there.'[41] At Princess Louise's suggestion, the Duke added 'a new wardrobe combining the loo', which was a great improvement. She had been put out to discover, that in a residence of twenty-one bedrooms, there were only two bathrooms; one on the first floor and one on the ground floor. She suggested that the Duke employ the estate carpenters in adding lavatories to some of the dressing-room wardrobes – as had been done in her mother's houses.

Princess Louise also improved the quality of life for one of the sisterhood. Lady Frances suffered from a diseased hip, which left one leg shorter than the other and obliged her to wear a special, built-up boot. Yet she was, if anything, the most active and energetic, both intellectually and physically, of the sisters, despite being short-sighted. This did not pass unnoticed but was firmly ignored. Princess Louise discovered her short-sightedness when she first saw the end result of an afternoon's sketching in the gardens. A massive splodge of green with jaggedy edges depicted the beautiful, widely-spaced, stately cedar trees. She immediately saw to it and gave Lady Frances her first pair of spectacles which, naturally, 'transformed her existence'.[42]

Music was strangely missing from the accomplishments displayed by the daughters of the house. Used to the numerous Bechsteins and Steinways which proliferated in royal houses, Princess Louise was disappointed to find that Inveraray possessed only one piano, which stood in the Great Hall where it was no match for the attractions of the neighbouring billiards table. The painter, William Richmond, who was working at Inveraray in 1867, wrote home: 'I pine for music. There is a piano but no one has the smallest feeling for anything but "the pipes".'[43] As Richmond discovered towards the end of his stay, 'Lady Elizabeth was the only musical member of the family.'[44] As the eldest daughter at home, Lady Libby was a natural companion for Princess Louise, and a shared love of music cemented their friendship. Taller than her tiny sisters but less pretty, 'she had,' Lady Frederick Cavendish noticed, 'a better figure and very delicate features' in a small, pointed face.[45] Her daughter Lesley later described how 'she used to laugh and kick her tiny shoes off and dance about'.[46]

Whenever the Princess had to attend a local function or distribute prizes to Lorne's Volunteers, it was Lady Libby who accompanied her as an unofficial maid of honour. On returning from any such function, Princess Louise was met in the entrance hall by Mrs MacPhail, the housekeeper. The children remembered her as 'always smelling of sweet biscuits' which she surreptitiously doled out to the younger generation of Campbells.[47] The entrance hall led into the large vaulted Great Hall whose ceiling extended to the roof. It was here that Ross would play the pipes at seven o'clock to mark the 'dressing' hour before dinner at

7.30. High up round this hall, and level with the first floor, was a gallery, out of which most of the bedrooms opened. The red plush curtains behind the balustrade allowed people, who were standing there, to see, without being seen. The more timid of Princess Louise's nephews and nieces would peer through the rails 'to see all the ladies in their evening gowns . . . and Grandpa and all the Uncles in their lovely kilts and watch them all going two by two into dinner like animals into the Ark';[48] while the naughtier, braver ones, like Lord Archie's children, would hurl missiles down at the heads of their elders. In 1884, Lorne teased one of the culprits, eleven-year-old Niky, 'We dine in peace in the Old Library now, no more shots with balls on one's head from the gallery – such a blessing!'[49]

After dinner, the family would be absorbed by billiards. The Duke had loved the game so much in his youth that his old tutor used to stand in the gallery above and plead with him to return to his interrupted studies 'at the end of a break'.[50] Lorne and his siblings played by instinct rather than great skill. Strangely enough, Lorne did not like Princess Louise to play billiards. Although all his sisters had been brought up on the game, he thought it undignified for women. Lorne might be forward-thinking about women's education, but he was old-fashioned about his wife's image even at home. Nor did his attitude change over the years. Holidaying in the South of France in 1905, Princess Louise's lady-in-waiting reminded her husband, 'HRH is very afraid of your telling HG [Lorne] *she* played billiards – so don't say so.'[51]

The Lornes passed their second Christmas at Inveraray. Despite cold, wet weather, Princess Louise found, as another guest wrote, that 'The roaring and splendid fires, crackling luminous and joyous, made the indoor sun, and the happy life lived at the Castle made up for defects of Climate.'[52] The Castle hummed with the news of the second son Lord Archie's great good fortune. In what the Duchess called 'an odd mixture of romance and business,' Baroness Burdett-Coutts had offered him a junior partnership in Coutts Bank.[53] Princess Louise, who loved the Archies, was glad to have them closer to hand in the South.

By the second week of January, the Argyll party had broken up. 'I am accused of attending to nothing but marital duties,' Lorne jested to a friend after he and Princess Louise had decided to remain on at Inveraray until March. Lorne maintained that 'nothing of consequence is expected for some time longer in Parliament, and so Inveraray and a good conscience are still comfortable'.[54] The same could not be said a month later when they returned South to witness the defeat of the Government over the Irish University Bill, which caused a ministerial crisis since Disraeli refused to form a minority government and Gladstone had to resume office.

The following year great consternation was felt on both sides of the political spectrum at an announcement in *The Times* on 24 January 1874. Mr Gladstone had decided to dissolve Parliament and call a general election. The Lornes had received the news by telegraph at Inveraray, where they had been resident since Christmas. In their letters, the Argylls commiserated with Princess Louise about being left, for much of the next few weeks, with only the company of her little dog, Spark. For she could not accompany her husband on his electioneering sorties about the County – much to her disappointment. Lorne's jest a year ago about devotion to marital, at the expense of parliamentary, duties had come home to roost. He now found himself having to defend his seat at extremely short notice. On January 31st, the *Glasgow Herald* declared that Lorne had no chance of being re-elected because he had not attended Parliament 'but a few times' during the past session 'and had never visited the district since the last election'.[55]

Three days later, at the important Oban meeting, he answered those who criticized his silence in the House. 'It was not always desirable for young men to say too much in their first session,' Lorne told a somewhat sceptical crowd, 'and many men said far too much in every session about subjects they knew too little about. Silence on many occasions was better than talk; and in the last Parliament, work would have been done more effectually and more speedily perhaps had the talking element in the House been greatly abridged [hisses and applause].'[56]

Lorne had spoken twice in the House since his election as an MP in 1868; as a supposed Liberal 'high flyer' it was a dismal record and Princess Louise and his parents constantly urged him to take a greater part in debates. However, Lorne was a good constituency MP and he had done much to promote local affairs in the last Parliament. He was also a desultory MP because his heart was not in parliamentary life, and he was not ambitious to achieve high office; he had wanted to be a soldier, and he would make a fine administrator, but never a good politician.

Lorne was lucky to be re-elected as Liberal MP on February 5th, for the Conservatives increased their Scottish seats from seven to nineteen in their landslide victory. The election also saw the emergence of a Home Rule party in Ireland at the expense of the Liberals. The Duke of Argyll realized that this would strengthen the Radical wing of his party; he was almost glad to be out of office: 'as I am not a Radical, and many of the extreme joints of our tail had been wagging too much'.[57]

Princess Louise was delighted by Lorne's win, though sorry about the Liberal defeat, unlike some of her family. The Queen felt it showed 'how little he [Gladstone] is trusted and how unpopular he is!'[58] while the Christians crowed over Disraeli's victory. Princess Louise had remained more tolerant of Disraeli's policies than Princess Helena was of Gladstone's. Whereas Gladstone saw the world in terms of issues, Disraeli saw it in terms of people. Thus, it was Disraeli who always helped the royal children with Queen Victoria, and who, in the spring of 1874, helped to smooth matters over for Princess Louise in the 'precedence row'.

CHAPTER XII

At Home

In the spring of 1874, Princess Louise was occupied with two very different marriages: her brother Alfred, Duke of Edinburgh, had contracted a grand alliance with the most eligible Princess in Europe, Marie of Russia, while Lorne's brother, Lord Walter Campbell, was marrying a cotton spinner's daughter, Olive Milns. Royalties were longing to see how this grand princess would adapt to the ways of Queen Victoria's Court. The Queen of Holland thought with difficulty: she remembered the transition from feudal splendour to comparative simplicity of her Russian sister-in-law, who simply 'could *not* understand everyone and everything *not* submitting to her sway . . . Should the Duchess of Edinburgh have the same feeling, how will she be able to exist in England . . . surrounded by people who are no slaves!'[1]

Although observance of precedence was comparatively relaxed in England, it was rigidly followed elsewhere, especially at the Russian Court. To the Tsar's stipulation that his daughter be called Imperial, not Royal, Highness, Queen Victoria retorted that she did not care which was used, so long as the English title came first; so poor Princess Marie was saddled with both, being known as Her Royal and Imperial Highness. But the use of Imperial was of significance, for those of Imperial took precedence over those of Royal rank. Thus, the Tsar expected Princess Marie to take precedence over all the English royal ladies except the Queen. This Queen Victoria would not allow and Lord Granville was instructed to inform the Russians that 'the Grand Duchess is to take her place as the Wife of one of *my younger Sons after my Daughters*. The Princess of Wales being the only one who goes *before them*.'[2] This meant that on official occasions she would be placed after the youngest daughter of the Queen present, usually Princess Louise.

None of this was allowed to spoil the arrival of the Edinburghs at Windsor Castle on March 7th, when Princess Louise was there to greet them. After a family luncheon, all the Royalties returned to London, since the Queen wished to have the Duchess of Edinburgh to herself.

Before leaving, the Prince of Wales made a point of speaking to Queen Victoria about Lorne's nebulous position at Court, which would have to be formalized before the Queen's official banquet two days later. This would be the first state occasion to include the Lornes since their marriage. As a commoner, Lorne could not enter the dining room with the Royal Family, but only far behind, after members of the Government and Opposition; nor would he be allowed to sit near his wife at dinner. The Prince of Wales saw this as an anomaly and an insult to Princess Louise. Although Queen Victoria agreed, with her first banquet since 1859 looming ahead, she did not want lengthy family discussions over problems of precedence.

So, on March 8th, she appealed to her Prime Minister, with the suggestion that Lorne should take precedence at her Court over all but ambassadors and princes. At twenty-four hours notice, Mr Disraeli smoothed matters over with the Lord Chancellor to ensure Lorne walked into St George's Hall with the Family, rather than at the rear of the procession.

Lorne did not care a 'hoot' about precedence; nor did Princess Louise. The Queen, however, had always believed that the only solution was for Lorne to accept a dukedom or some honour which would elevate him to the proper position for her son-in-law. Lorne, to her annoyance, continued to oppose the idea: 'as Lord Lorne seems anxious *not* to have anything selected for honours,' the Queen sniffed to Disraeli on March 17th, 'she will *at present* leave the question open for him to do as he likes'.[3]

The Queen had wanted to give Lorne a dukedom on Princess Louise's birthday but he had once again refused it. Despite his obduracy, the Queen had nothing but praise for his wife: 'It is dear Louise's 26th birthday today,' she wrote to the Crown Princess, on March 18th: 'It is a pleasure to see her so happy and so satisfactory, so good and sensible in every respect! She is adored in her husband's home.'[4] Well-beloved by the Argylls, Princess Louise was in the best position to help them over a crisis concerning their third son, Lord Walter Campbell.

The announcement of his engagement six months previously had upset his family. It was a *mésalliance*, sweetened only by money. Lorne hoped Mr Milns would give his daughter an adequate fortune, 'as we cannot otherwise be in favour of the marriage'.[5] Since Lord Walter was over twenty-five and had seen 'something of the world', the Duke was not disposed to stop the match, although he made his displeasure known by referring to Olive as 'a young lady whom we had not the pleasure of knowing'.[6] Enquiries about the family drew a blank, as Lorne recorded: '. . . of course it has been difficult to find out anything about the family, who for all the world knows are and might have been wrapped up in a cotton ball all their lives'.

Such worldly considerations carried little weight with the female members of the family. Aunt Dot was the couple's first champion, though Lorne scoffed 'One cannot trust Dot's account of the girl as she is enthusiastic about all marriages.'[7] He scoffed less when he learnt that Aunt Dot's accomplice was his own wife. Although he was abroad at the time of her marriage, Princess Louise had come to know Lord Walter well during their long spells together in Inveraray. He was amusing and, like Lord Archie, an excellent mimic; when he imitated a cat stuck in the chimney of the Great Hall, the Duke was so concerned that he sent for the estate carpenter to rescue the poor creature. Princess Louise was soon captivated by his charm and general outrageousness.

She had never met Olive, but Lord Walter had produced a photograph of his beloved, whom she thought looked 'very pretty'.[8] It seemed straight out of a nineteenth-century, romantic novel: the dashing young Lord riding across the glens to pay secret court to the beautiful cotton-spinner's daughter. Princess Louise spoke out in favour of this love match and her word carried weight with the Argylls. From Inveraray she wrote to Lord Archie, 'The dear boy is so happy it does one good to see him so. I do hope all will be satisfactory about the parents, and that the Duke and Duchess can welcome the young lady with an open heart.'[9] This the Duchess eventually did and, by February 1874, she was writing to her old friend, Lord Dufferin, that her son was 'very fortunate'.[10] The irrepressible Lord Ronnie Gower, however, delighted in reporting that Mr Milns had said he hoped '"there'd be no 'itch on the occasion"'. Nor was there.

After the wedding, Princess Louise had to supervise the packing up of Grosvenor Crescent. The Lornes had decided to try and let their London house: 'If you hear of any nice rich people who are wanting a house in London,' Princess Louise had written to Lord Archie in February, 'you can mention that 1, Grosvenor Crescent is to be let furnished, for 3 years from the 1st May.'[12] A tenant had quickly been found and the Lornes moved into Argyll Lodge by the end of April.

The weather was so lovely in May that Princess Louise persuaded

Lorne to give a breakfast party. As the four hundred guests arrived, 'Alas, alas rain began at 6 o'clock with thunder and altho many people were good enough to come – all crowded the verandah and would hardly move,' Lorne told his absent mama. Princess Louise was in despair and believed her first large party was doomed to failure. How could she move people from the verandah, she asked her experienced sister-in-law? The Princess of Wales came to the rescue and sallied forth from the verandah; she walked leisurely across the lawn, stopping here and there to admire the shrubbery, until she reached the large tent. Others immediately followed her example, despite Lord Ronnie Gower's jokes about discovering the Kensington water gardens, and Princess Louise's reputation as a hostess was saved.[13]

She was soon able to even the score with Lord Ronnie. A mutual friend and great hostess, Marion, Lady Alford, gave a masquerade ball where he was fascinated by a beauty, bejewelled and befeathered in a wonderful mask. 'I was much puzzled as to the identity of a lady whom I took to supper; and only discovered, on her taking off her mask, that it was my august relative, Princess Louise!'[14]

But the summer was not all frivolity. The Duke had asked Princess Louise to persuade Lorne to speak in the House of Commons. At the beginning of June, the Duke had led a Liberal revolt against Gladstone, and had spoken in the Lords in support of a Bill for the Abolition of Church Patronage in Scotland. A yachting holiday in the Western Isles towards the end of June did not deter the Duke from bombarding Lorne with letters about the imminent third reading of the Bill in the Commons. 'I do hope you will come out on the Patronage Bill. There will be *plenty of opportunity*,'[15] he wrote on June 24th. On the same day he wrote separately to Princess Louise: 'I want Lorne so much to speak on this question.'[16] When Lorne asserted that Gladstone talked 'irrelevant stuff and nonsense' on Patronage, Princess Louise asked if he would refute him in the House. But Lorne merely laughed and said it would not matter either way.

In the seventies, parliamentary debates were conducted mainly by the Front Benches. It was not until the advent of a strong Irish party and the subsequent domination of Home Rule affairs that backbenchers came to play a prominent part in debates. The exception was over matters of especial local importance, but Lorne felt his father was the more influential representative of Argyll. Thus, it would seem presumptuous of him to interfere and would only be interpreted as supporting his father. In the event, Argyll was victorious, but Lorne did not speak at all in the final debate. Princess Louise was disappointed, though more for the Argylls' sake than her own; the Duke was upset enough to write to Lorne on July 15th, 'What is the use of a man having brains and a tongue if he won't speak?'[17]

She had always respected Lorne's parliamentary judgement, and was conscious of his difficulties in trying to represent constituents, yet never offend royal relations. Now the Princess began to compare him with other parliamentarians, including his father, and, for the first time, she questioned her husband's abilities. Her perceptions began to change and her 'darling boy's' glittering halo grew a little tarnished.

Once the family fuss over patronage had died down, Princess Louise was able to devote herself entirely to what she called 'our *small* country place',[18] Dornden, near Tunbridge Wells. These words were not meant to be disparaging, since it was precisely the small size of the house, which had attracted her in the first place. She loved the cosy rooms with their mullioned, stained-glass windows and rich, oak-panelled walls. The dining room was so small that Lorne wondered how to seat a family party of the Walters, and the Crown Prince and Princess of Prussia and suite; he concluded that one guest would have to sit on the windowsill.

Despite its size, Dornden was the last word in Victorian luxury; it had such effective central heating that, to their amazement, the Lornes found the house too warm; Blenny, Princess Louise's spaniel puppy, became drowsy after only an hour in the house. Dornden also possessed 170 acres of land; the grounds included an archery, a rockery, a pinetum, a lake with its island and rustic boat-house, an orchard, a fencery, a vinery, a wood, magnificent stabling and four cottages apart from the Home Farm. Princess Louise found the place somewhat overdone. As she wrote to Lord Archie on 24 February 1874, 'You must come and see the small place and not laugh too much at its pretension.'[19]

The Princess grew attached to Dornden and thoroughly enjoyed managing it with the help of seven male and ten female servants. She expected a high standard of service from staff, not so much because of her royal upbringing, but as a result of her practical training at Osborne. If a dish did not succeed, then she would demonstrate how it should be cooked; if a skirt was not properly washed and ironed, she would walk across to the laundry room and, with her own hands, show the laundry maids how the work must be done.

On his first visit to Dornden, Lord Ronnie was struck by Princess Louise's happy domesticity; 'it's pleasant to see the busy German housewife strongly developed in her,' he recorded in his diary, 'bustling about looking after and superintending all the domestic arrangements, caring and making herself generally useful'.[20]

The Lornes happily remained at Dornden until they travelled to Argyll where, on September 9th, Princess Louise attended her first Argyllshire Gathering. This was the County meeting held over four days in Oban, with Highland games, a regatta and several balls. The idea for this had grown out of the county lairds coming together to organize the subscription for a wedding present for the Lornes. They had formed a Committee and had elected Lorne as their first President. That evening, wearing the Clan Campbell necklace and an Argyll sash, Princess Louise led off the first country dance at 9.30 with the senior Baronet of the County. More people were there than ever before, probably owing to her presence. Lorne, who had sprained his side and been confined to bed two weeks before, refused to miss the fun and insisted upon reeling.

When the Cavendishes stayed at Inveraray that September, Lady Frederick Cavendish noted: 'Princess Louise very pleasant and easy; seems comfortable with them all.' Remembering their days together at Court, she was struck by the informality of the Princess's life at Inveraray. 'We have hardly any Royal proprieties with HRH – an occasional "Mum" from us visitors, and a very feeble pretence at getting up when she comes in late for breakfast, is about all.'

Lucy thought her so contented and happily married; Princess Louise seemed 'very much devoted to her husband: jumped up from the floor where she was playing with the little Percys when he came in from shooting, saying "Oh, I must go and see about his clothes or he will never change!"'[21]

Always unconcerned about dress, Lorne was described by a niece as 'a little odd in his behaviour, he would wear a Norfolk jacket for a formal occasion and at other times appear at breakfast wearing the Order of the Garter'.[22] When they were first married, Princess Louise found this endearing and amusing; but with the passage of time she became less tolerant and even wondered sometimes whether he was not deliberately trying to provoke her, especially since the Prince of Wales always noticed and complained to her, not Lorne, about it.

The Christmas festivities at Inveraray were marred in 1874 by the news that Prince Leopold had fallen ill. Princess Louise's first thought was to go to him. She knew that, however minor the original complaint, there would be complications owing to his haemophilia. But, although Princess Louise was a married woman of twenty-six, she could not simply take the next train South to be at her brother's bedside, without first obtaining her mother's permission. No such invitation was forthcoming. Queen Victoria merely telegraphed back that Prince Leopold had only caught a cold, so there was no cause for alarm. The Court was not even told that he was ill until December 28th, when Henry Ponsonby informed the Prime Minister: 'Prince Leopold has caught a bad cold – and is I believe, *very* ill.' Two days later, the doctors' original diagnosis was confirmed: 'I may mention – it is secret – that P. Leo's illness is typhoid . . . Heavy sorrow here.'[23] The sorrow was even heavier at Inveraray where, fed by secret reports from Prince Leopold's Governor, Major Collins, Princess Louise lived in torment as she awaited news of her brother's illness.

She was particularly close to her two young brothers: 'I watch over those two boys, as if they were my very own, I would do anything for them' and had an especial, almost maternal, tenderness for the invalid Prince Leopold, whom she had often nursed through the most dreadful attacks of bleeding. He, in turn, had relied upon her and confided in her from childhood.

Princess Louise never forget what he had said to her in 1866. Queen Victoria had decided that Prince Leopold was becoming too attached to Princess Louise, since he paid more attention to his sister than to his mother. So Prince Leopold was stopped from passing a couple of hours every day with his sister, when she used to encourage his reading or help him to sketch. It was a great grief to them both and thirteen-year-old Prince Leopold had said: 'Loosey, I don't know what would happen to me if you ever went away, all would be over for me then.'[24]

Major Collins knew that Princess Louise's presence would be a great boost to her brother's morale and a support in the sick room. The bulletin on 3 January 1875 was: 'Pr Leo not so well last night, that is to say he was weak and exhausted.'[25] The Queen still refused to send for Princess Louise; Major Collins could not believe her hard-heartedness. He wrote, Prince Leopold 'knows so well that it is useless to ask the Queen on ordinary occasions to have this or that relative . . . to come and see him that he never did more during the earlier part of his illness than say to me how much he should like to see her.' Collins had conveyed this wish to the Queen who had ignored Prince Leopold's request: '. . . but when the first gush of haemorrhage came,' continued Collins, 'and he knew at once the danger that awaited him, and was stunned . . . at what he (not unreasonably) supposed was the approach of death, he made me promise that she would be sent for. The Queen delayed doing it.'[26]

Princess Louise was kept waiting for a month in an agony of apprehension. At last, on January 18th, the summons came. Travelling overnight, she and Lorne reached Osborne the next day to find Prince Leopold in 'a very precarious state'.[27] Major Collins had been 'in an agony that she would be too late'; the contempt he had long felt about the Queen's behaviour to her children now became 'a loathing dislike, with difficulty concealed'.[28]

Despite being at Osborne for the sole purpose of being with Prince Leopold, Princess Louise was only allowed to sit with her brother for an hour twice a day. Fortunately, the doctors turned a blind eye to the Queen's orders. 'I am a good deal with my poor brother,' Princess Louise wrote to Lord Archie on January 23rd, 'he looks still very ill, but is gaining strength daily, and can now eat more. He takes interest in all that goes on and likes being read to.'[29] By the end of January, Prince Leopold was considered to be out of danger; as soon as Queen Victoria decently could, she sent Princess Louise away.

Major Collins echoed Prince Leopold's disappointment at Princess Louise's departure. 'It was an immense pleasure to him to have his sister sitting with him,' Collins wrote on February 7th. 'Alas! She is gone again. The Queen was I think waxing jealous – at any rate she wouldn't let her tarry longer.'[30]

Queen Victoria could be an impossible mother. What made her system of control mortifying for her children was the employment of a third party as executioner. Thus, the Queen would ask her secretary to tell Prince Leopold that he must leave Osborne the day Cowes Regatta and all the fun began; or she would instruct a lady-in-waiting to inform Princess Louise that she must come to Windsor on a particular day 'as she had no other day', regardless of the fact that the Princess had a long standing engagement, which she would otherwise have greatly enjoyed.[31] And the Household undoubtedly resented being used by her as buffers. Henry Ponsonby moaned, 'Will the Queen never find out that she will have ten times more influence on her children by treating them with kindness and not trying to rule them like a despot?'[32]

Yet her children continued to flock to her side: they never broke completely with her, despite periods of coolness; they always turned to her in times of real trouble, when she never failed them. She dominated their lives completely, but did not want them with her for they disrupted her routine and interfered; hence, she wrote to them every day, yet baulked at inviting them home. She knew everything about them and any change in their lives was of immediate interest to her.

Thus, on the afternoon of 10 March 1875, Queen Victoria set off with Princess Beatrice and Lady Jane Churchill from Buckingham Palace in a carriage and four, heading westwards across the park to Kensington: '. . . getting out in the inner Court at the Palace,' she noted in her Journal. 'Louise took me upstairs to her sitting-room, where I had never been.' Princess Louise also showed them the spare bedrooms. 'Though quite unfurnished,' the Queen commented, 'when I went in and saw the well known look out, the doors etc. where I spent 16 years of my life everything came back again so vividly to my mind!'

Going back downstairs the Queen noticed 'The Dining room is also v nice, but a great deal has still to be finished.' After tea, she expressed her satisfaction, though she remarked that the long corridor had still to be cleaned and left with her party at a little before six o'clock.[33] Princess Louise could now regard herself as officially settled into her rooms at Apartment No. 1, Kensington Palace.

'Keny-Paly' or 'The Pally', Lorne's nicknames for their new residence, had been given to Princess Louise by Queen Victoria in September 1873 after the death of the Duchess of Inverness. When Princess Louise, with plans in hand, was shown round the rooms in November 1873, she was surprised at their sorry state: 'They are very dirty at present, not having had anything done to them since George IIIs time,'[34] she wrote. There was no gas to use for lighting; some of the lovely spacious rooms had been partitioned; and the drains were bad. It was now that Princess Louise came across that great bugbear of English Royalties, the Ministry of Works. Nothing could be done to a royal residence without Ministry of Works approval. By the end of January, work had still not begun, though the Princess remained hopeful it would 'start soon'. By the beginning of February she had ascertained that the delay was caused by the Treasury quibbling over

The Fire at Inveraray Castle:
The Great Hall with the equestrian
statue of The Black Prince,
27 October 1877.

The Black Prince. c.1873, bronze.

Princess Louise's Boudoir (Blue Parlour) at Rideau Hall, Ottawa, showing her painted door, 1879.

Princess Louise, aged 33, in Venice, April 1881.

Joseph Edgar Boehm, 1879, pencil.

Princess Louise, aged 43, by Josephine Swabodow, 1891.

the cost of the alterations. They were prepared to grant £370 for the drainage improvements, but bickered over the costs of structural repairs and maintenance.

The Lornes only moved into Kensington Palace in February 1875, and spent that month arranging their apartments. But building work was still underway and much remained to be done, finances permitting. 'We must be very careful,' wrote Princess Louise to Lord Archie, 'as our pockets are very empty and will be I fear for some days to come.'[35]

The Lornes migrated North for the autumn and were at Inveraray to welcome the Queen, who came to stay for a week at the end of September. This visit was a brilliant edition of Princess Louise's homecoming: 1871 had been the chaotic dress-rehearsal for the smoothly managed display of 1875; even the weather obliged. The Duchess had assumed the Queen would use the 'best room', the State bedroom on the ground floor, but Princess Louise, certain her mother would prefer a more secluded set of apartments, willingly gave up her own set of rooms in the Ardkinglas turret. Before the Lornes came North, the Duchess had them redecorated: 'the rooms for the Queen look well. The willow paper we chose is rather dark,' she wrote to Lorne on July 14th.[36] The Duke, as usual, was more concerned with where he was going to put everyone; once again he had to commandeer the Argyll Arms 'as I don't see how I can ask any County people even to drink – as they will be unable to get accommodation if the Hotel be filled with *starers* from Glasgow and elsewhere'.[37]

With the Duke, Duchess and Princess Louise busy organizing everything, Lorne thought the best policy was to keep out of the way. As far as he could see, the only benefit of the Queen's visit was that at last the Duke had been persuaded to change the awful sherry. 'The sherry here has improved,' he told Lord Archie on September 4th, 'but unless condemned after analysis by Sir William Jenner, it won't kill any courtier or guest.'[38]

On a bright, sunny, Wednesday morning, Lorne and Princess Louise met Queen Victoria and her entourage at the head of Glen Aray, and escorted them to Inveraray. The welcoming strains of the pipes stationed at Frew Bridge were heard by those at the Castle, only to be drowned by the band striking up the National Anthem as the Queen's sociable, followed by Lorne on horseback, and Princess Louise in her phaeton, came round the corner of the Castle and stopped in front of the porch.

'The Duke and Duchess took us upstairs at once to our rooms, part of which are Louise's,' wrote the Queen in her Journal, 'very comfortable, not large but cheerful, and having a beautiful view of Loch Fyne. It was one when we arrived, and we lunched at two, only Louise, Beatrice and Lorne, in a nice room . . . with tapestry at the foot of the stairs . . . After lunch we went to the large drawing room, next door to where we had lunched in 1847 . . . And now I return, alas! without my beloved Husband to find Lorne my son-in-law!'[39]

The usual routine of the Queen's visits to her favoured subjects was followed at Inveraray so that the agreeable monotony was broken only by meals and the company invited to meet her. The Queen's custom of having meals separately during her visit was misunderstood by her private secretary, Henry Ponsonby: 'Evidently, the Queen considers herself as paying a visit to Princess Louise, the rest of the family being merely accidental. She occasionally sees the Duke and Duchess and even Lorne.'[40] Certainly, the Queen breakfasted solely with her daughters in her sitting room but, when Lorne lunched at home, he lunched with her rather than his parents. In other words, the Queen was behaving exactly as if she was at one of her own houses.

The evening was the time the Queen set aside for being sociable. At Inveraray she did the same; inviting one or two of the house party to dine with her and either the Duke or Duchess, the one who did not dine presiding over the remaining members of the house party in the Saloon. The Argylls, of course, were familiar with Court life and were not surprised by the Queen's behaviour. Though, as the Duke admitted to Gladstone, it helped enormously 'having the Daughter here – who knew all Her ways'.[41]

After an enjoyable dinner, enlivened by the conversation of Lord Dufferin or Dr MacGregor, the house party would assemble in the Saloon to await the Queen. The moment she was announced, the Argylls would receive her at the door, everyone would rise to their feet, and the ladies, despite the sharp weather, would hastily discard their scarves and shawls and hide them underneath cushions, while the drawing-room windows would be thrown open, instantly reducing the room to freezing temperature. Not surprisingly, total silence fell. The Queen would move about talking to everyone and, shortly afterwards, withdraw for the night.

Even so, the other members of the house party contrived to enjoy themselves. After the ladies had retired to bed, the gentlemen adjourned to the smoking-room where Lord Dufferin, Campbell of Islay and Dr MacGregor regaled them with a series of blood-curdling, ghost stories. Occasionally, the Queen would unbend and join in the fun. As the company sat in great formality over their tea before retiring, Princess Louise nervously knocked over a vase of flowers. Like some knight errant, Sir William Thomson, later Lord Kelvin, leapt to her rescue and 'in an excess of loyalty' mopped the water with his handkerchief. At a loss to know how to dispose of the soaked hankie in front of Queen Victoria, he desperately stuffed it into a teacup. The Queen found this hilariously funny and stayed in the drawing room much later that evening.[42]

Queen Victoria was delighted with the whole visit, which she felt owed much to Princess Louise's care. 'Dear Louise,' she wrote in her Journal, 'so kind and attentive, so anxious I and all my people should be comfortable, thinking of everything.'[43] Princess Louise even remembered her old friend, Miss MacGibbon, who was dying, and arranged for her to meet the Queen.

So it was that Margaret MacGibbon and her Cousin Anna were taken to the billiards room to await the Queen. Princess Louise, the Queen and Princess Beatrice, 'looking shy and startled, with her shoulders up to her ears', came into the room. After Miss MacGibbon was presented, she remarked to the Queen: "We are all so fond of the Princess; she is a great pet," and Princess Louise said, "I have told the Queen that Lord Lorne is your pet," upon which Miss MacGibbon said, "Yes, he is and so you are a double pet."[44]

On the morning of her departure for Balmoral, the Queen was feeling sad. 'I took leave of the whole family,' she wrote in her Journal, '. . . and, with a heavy heart, of my darling Louise.'[45] Queen Victoria felt especially tender and protective towards Princess Louise because she knew all was not well. Worries over personal matters involving the Argylls were upsetting the Princess and she had talked them over with her mother and Lady Jane Churchill. Word of this had somehow reached Henry Ponsonby in a gossipy, roundabout way. As a result, he portrayed Princess Louise as a 'mischief maker who plays old Harry with every household or person she touches' and as a complaining, authoritarian, spoilt, young woman.[46] Yet two weeks before, someone else on a visit to Inveraray, Louisa, Lady Ashburton, depicted an entirely different Princess Louise. 'I am quite bewitched by her – so much intelligence, fun, high feeling and distinction in all ways,'[47] she had told Thomas Carlyle.

Henry Ponsonby's letters to his wife were written not with a view to posterity but to amuse. Thus, he could mislead and was often guilty of light-hearted exaggeration. In one entertaining but nonetheless overstated letter, he wrote that Princess Louise had been 'pouring out her grievances', which he then enumerated. Her supposed complaints were 'that her rooms were not good enough, that she could not dine alone when she wished, that the Ladies Campbell did not treat her with becoming respect', and of 'the company the Duke asks to Inveraray: Professors and Presbyterian Ministers'.

Yet Princess Louise considered her rooms good enough for her mother to use, indeed that she would prefer them to any others at Inveraray. The Argylls did not mind when or where she dined. The Campbell girls were well-bred and not at all pushy, especially to their elders. All the evidence shows that Princess Louise got on well with her young sisters-in-law, and that they treated her with every respect. As for the Princess's complaint about the Duke's preference for clergymen as company, Ponsonby was wrong. If it was anyone, it was Lorne who objected to a surfeit of the Church, and he and Lord Archie always joked about how 'Meenisters' outnumbered even the Campbells at the Castle.

Where Ponsonby was nearer the mark was when he wrote, 'she complains that she hasn't got a separate country house. The Duke built one for them but in an uninhabited desert and they "can't abide it".'[48] For Princess Louise was extremely worried about losing Dornden. Lately, Lorne had been complaining that it was too expensive. Lord Ronnie had recorded in his Journal how 'Lorne talks of parting with this place, finding it too expensive to keep up, which seems a pity as the Princess is much attached to it.'[49]

The Princess should have been in a position of strength. Under the terms of her marriage settlement, the Duke was obliged to provide Lorne and his bride with a house. The Queen raised the matter with the Duke in her thank you letter, written from Balmoral on October 2nd. In his reply, the Duke stated: 'There is one sentence in Your Majesty's letter which I must confess gave me some annoyance when I first read it . . . I refer to the passage which implies that Your Majesty thinks I have not fulfiled some understanding with you as to the provision of a country residence for Lorne and the Princess.'[50]

The Duke had given them Macharioch, and had supplied funds to redecorate it; but even he had to admit it was too inaccessible for a permanent house. Princess Louise loved it but could not regard it as her own home, as it continued to be used as a holiday house and yachting base by the Argyll tribe. The Duke claimed that he could not afford to provide Lorne with anything else. Yet the Lornes' wish for a decent house was hardly untoward by Victorian standards. Lorne was, after all, heir to a dukedom and large estates.

Princess Louise would not have had Dornden at all if she had not provided half the purchase price of £30,000. Lorne had borrowed half from his father which he and the Princess repaid in full: 'we send you the last instalment of our debt with the interest – which I think you will find correct to 2½%,'[51] Lorne wrote to the Duke on 13 January 1876. The fact that the Lornes had somewhere to live in London owed everything to Queen Victoria's generosity, and nothing to the Duke of Argyll. So, when Lorne threatened to sell Dornden, Princess Louise raised the whole issue of the Duke's responsibilities to his heir.

However, of greater concern to the Princess than a country house, or indeed anything else, was her inability to have a baby. She had always been an affectionate, warm-hearted person, she was happily married, and she longed for a baby of her own to make her happiness complete. Major Collins, who met her at the Opera with Prince Leopold during this period, described her as 'charming'. 'She really looked tremendously jolly – composed, loving, tender, sympathetic, slightly sad – a beautiful type of womanhood.' He came away wishing 'she could have some fine healthy children'.[52]

During the first two years of her marriage, she had been busy organizing her houses and settling into Argyll family life. Now that the marriage was established, her longing, resentment and bewilderment over not having a baby, intensified with every passing year. Lorne was exceedingly sympathetic and tender, despite his own disappointment. It had never occurred to him that he would not father children; only now did he realize how much he wanted them.

While Lorne was at Inveraray in the autumn of 1873, Princess Louise had gone to Germany with Lady Sophie to take a course of baths in the hope of improving her health, and thus her chances of conception, but still there were 'no hopes' of her own two years later. The Argylls naturally entered into their daughter-in-law's feelings on the subject. The Duchess was wonderfully understanding and hopeful; she believed that their marriage would survive this tragedy, writing that Princess Louise was 'a great pleasure in our lives'. 'I wish – I wish – But however that may be, I think their happiness is safe. She is full of charm, intelligence and occupation.'[53] The Duke, however, tended to be more impatient. Although it was some comfort that both Lord Archie and Lord Walter had sons to secure the inheritance, the Duke was touchingly interested whenever Princess Louise was indisposed. Frantic notes and telegrams would be sent to Lorne asking for details of 'dearest Louise's condition'.[54]

When Queen Victoria came to stay at Inveraray, she brought along her most senior physician, Sir William Jenner, rather than the usual junior doctor-in-attendance. He came to discuss the Lornes' childlessness with the Argylls and to advise Princess Louise and Lorne on the delicate subject of conception. The doctors did not seem to have thought it necessary to examine Lorne; all their attention was focused upon his wife. It was thought that Princess Louise's difficulties were due to the meningitic complications she had suffered when she was sixteen. The only treatment a Victorian doctor could prescribe was to take the waters at a German spa.

So it was that over the next twelve years Princess Louise would journey to Kissingen or Homburg or Marienbad in search of a cure that would give her children. She and Lorne first stayed in Kissingen for this purpose in August 1876. Many of the patients were there to lose weight rather than to recover from an illness. Lorne noticed what a prosperous set of persons the Brünen drinkers were, 'fat corporations are most conspicuous'.[55] On her way back from the baths, Princess Louise was amused to see weighing machines strategically placed along the path and always in use.

The Lornes returned to Kensington Palace on 18 September 1876. Two days later, Lord Ronnie lunched with them and found them looking well: 'she having been drinking the Kissingen waters, but I doubt if the desired effect will be produced'.[56] Sadly he was correct – there were no 'hopes' that year.

On the 25th, the three of them travelled to Inveraray specially to see the Duchess, who had suffered two strokes during that year. By the time they arrived, she was able to walk a little, but remained very weak.

From the mid-seventies, the Duchess had been an invalid and often extremely ill. On the whole, she bore the constant pain and discomfort like an angel, but her family had to bear the brunt of her occasional bursts of fractious 'worriting'. At such times, Princess Louise was often the one to soothe the Duchess. She, in turn, appreciated Princess Louise's kindness and loved her. Her affection shines out of this letter, one of many written in September 1877 to Lorne, who was meeting Princess Louise at Edinburgh on her return from taking yet another 'cure': 'it makes my mouth water to think of your both being so near – you will tell me about Louise as soon as you can. Best love to her . . . My darling, how happy you will be to be with Louise again.'[57] A week later, the Lornes were back with her at the Castle.

Between three and four o'clock on the wild and stormy morning of 12 October 1877 an old fisherman of Inveraray, resisting the entreaties of his wife to go back to sleep, insisted upon going out to the pier to ensure the fastening of his boat. As he emerged from the shelter of the houses clustered about the pier, he saw a glare of light and huge flames leaping from the roof of the Castle. His shouts gave the alarm and the townspeople ran up the short road and drive to the Castle to hammer and pound upon its great locked doors. 'It was dreadful, they said, to see all the place quiet with the house in flames.'[58] Immediately, the alarm was given inside the Castle but, despite the danger, the rules of decorum were strictly observed. The Clerk of Works ran to the State Bedroom where the Duchess had been moved since her stroke the previous year. Stopping outside the door, he ceremoniously knocked and shouted: "Get up, my Lord Duke, the castle is on fire and you can't pass through the hall!"[59] Roused, the Duke jumped out of the huge tapestry bed, gently got the Duchess up, and walked her through to the inner hall. He stopped to grab his Ulster coat and put it around the Duchess, who wore only her nightdress. While he was struggling to do this, the Lornes joined them. Princess Louise immediately started getting the Duchess's arms into the sleeves of the greatcoat in case she caught cold.

Meanwhile, Mr New, the butler, had raced upstairs to wake the sleeping Campbell girls and their maids and governesses. 'The first we knew of it was by Mr New . . . hallooing at the top of his voice,' thirteen-year-old Lady Connie recalled; 'we all got up in a dream'. Lady Frances and Lady Mary remembered to release their parakeets from their cages and, holding the birds inside their dressing gowns, they all got out to the gallery where 'we had the choice of two staircases, so Frances, New, myself and Mrs B went down one while Mary by mistake got separated and went down the other where she, poor wretch, found herself . . . in the middle of havoc'.[60] For, as Lady Mary said, 'the heat and glare were dreadful, and the shouts of men and the hissing and roaring of the flames quite deafening, while burning glass and plaster wrapped in sheets of flames, together with molten lead, were falling in all directions'.[61] With difficulty she found her way safely to where her parents stood with Princess Louise. Lorne, who had gone to bring down Lady Car Charteris, arrived at the same time.

Amidst the noise and darkness, the Duke now took a roll call. To their horror, Lady V and Mrs Campbell were missing. Lorne immediately darted away through the blazing hall, ignoring his father's order to turn back. As the Duke with Lady Mary and Lady Connie ran to the door to call him again, the gas chandelier that hung from the top of the hall ceiling began to sway, 'then we saw a perfect avalanche of fire and then all was dark for a moment, followed by an awful crash' and the whole roof fell in.[62] It was the longest eight minutes of her life before Princess Louise knew Lorne had escaped by dodging through the side door. He returned, leading the blind Mrs Campbell of Islay and saying, 'Victoria is safe!'[63]

As the Duke prepared to lead the Duchess out of the Castle, it was noticed 'the Princess had gone!' Everyone shouted for her but there was no reply.[64] A minute later Princess Louise, practical to the last, reappeared clutching a candle to light their way in the darkness. Their procession to the stables was certainly a sight. 'We started barefoot and bareheaded in . . . any loose wrap we could find for the stables,' wrote Lady Mary. 'The night was very cold, the hills white with snow, and the ground wet and constant hail showers.'[65] Leaving the bedraggled women and children safe in the stables, Lorne and the Duke returned to the Castle. The fire was spreading so fast that it appeared the Castle would be lost. The cry went up 'Save all you can.' The townspeople, workmen, and servants set to, tearing down pictures and tapestries and flinging out books and furniture. In this way, most were saved.

Having ensured that the Duchess was as comfortable as possible, Princess Louise, with Lady Frances in tow, returned to the Castle to help. Although a great effort was being made to save the family treasures, she realized that no one was attempting to put out the flames. Seeing the schoolmaster, she suggested they form a human chain to the loch and pass up buckets of water to the Castle. This was immediately and successfully done. Since the schoolmaster was also the local reporter for the *Oban Times*, news of Princess Louise's 'heroism' leaked out and was widely reported. The Lornes thought the credit should rather have gone exclusively to the townsfolk who 'worked too gloriously,'[66] but the Duchess wrote that 'Ian and Louise were admirable at the time'[67] and 'I cannot say enough in praise of his dear Wife, Louise.'[68]

CHAPTER XIII

Tragedy and Transition

It would be many months before the roofless wreck of Inveraray Castle could be fit to live in. Princess Louise went across from the Argyll Arms every day to help with valuations for insurance and to re-hang pictures, and push furniture back into place. It was dirty, eerie work 'in those darkened, begrimed rooms listening to the wind howling through the roofless Hall, sending wood and glass down in crackling showers, then to stand and watch the rain drifting in . . . where we have so often sat round the fire, a happy party, now a scene of desolation'.[1]

On the day of the fire, the Duke had repeated his grandfather's remark in a similar situation: 'Thank God I have another House to go to.'[2] Leaving Inveraray to the mercy of architects and builders, he removed his family to Rosneath Castle for the winter. The uprooting was scarcely a hardship, since a return to Rosneath was always welcome. This generation always thought of Rosneath as their true home. It was to Rosneath that, in 1844, the Duke had brought his bride, who had a 'special love for her honeymoon home' which was *like no* other *to her*.[3] Here they had made their home until, in 1864, the Duke had decided that it would be more fitting to use Inveraray which, over the centuries, was the principal seat of the Mac Cailein Mor. He, nonetheless, always preferred to stay at Rosneath when in office, because he could reach London overnight. For the children, it always held a special place in their hearts. 'Oh the joy of coming back to this beloved old home,' wrote Lady Libby after the fire, 'to which I and all the others too are devoted. It is quite lovely and every rock or tree or walk is haunted by some dear old childish recollections.'[4]

The family always said it was like living in a luxurious ship, since they were almost surrounded by water. Sir Walter Scott called Rosneath an island in his book, *The Heart of Midlothian*, but, in fact, it is a narrow, heathery peninsula, eight and a half miles long, which separates the stern desolate scenery of Loch Long from the gentler, almost dreamy loveliness of the Gareloch.

Below the village, on the 'Green Isle' promontory, lay the Castle; not the original one which burnt down in 1803, but the architect Bonomi's extravagant Italianate phoenix. The 6th Duke planned it on a monumental scale, which the Argyle estates could ill-afford; dying suddenly, he left massive debts and a half-finished castle. The Duke, like his father, could not spare the funds to complete it; but this did not prevent him and the Duchess from making it their home.

The Castle was built around a central tower. Nine spacious, public rooms opened off a broad, stone-flagged corridor which ran through the house. As the verandah was the centre of family life at Argyll Lodge, so the library was at Rosneath. Occupying the ground floor of the central tower, it was a delightful, lofty, circular room, fitted with bookshelves around the walls, an Aubusson carpet on the floor and finely-leaded windows looking onto the gardens. Here, with only the light of wax candles, and two or three oil lamps, Princess Louise joined the family after breakfast to read and talk; here, they all gathered around a large, oak table in one corner for tea, while the Duke read aloud at his pleasure.

On the morning of 10 November 1877, Princess Louise sat down in this library to write to Lord Dufferin out in Canada as Governor-General to keep him *au fait* with home news: 'we came here soon after the fire . . . The change seems to suit the Duchess very well. It is very delightful living so near the sea and Lorne has felt like a child again, coming back to all the old haunts of his boyhood, and going over them all carefully again and showing them to me.'[5]

Sad as she was to leave the ailing Duchess, Princess Louise had to be back in London by the end of November to prepare for Christmas. This year she also had to supervise the operations of a cottage industry she had founded and funded in Sloane Street, known as the Ladies' Work Society (L.W.S.). It aimed to provide employment for impoverished gentlewomen, that forgotten class of Victorian womenfolk, who were considered too well-bred to earn their living as domestic servants, if they were unable to find work as governesses. Princess Louise taught them to make items, from simple pocket handkerchiefs to intricate embroidered altar frontals, which they then sold in the shop, and to repair everything from children's clothes to old tapestries. Christmas was naturally a busy time in the shop and Princess Louise went there every day. She was also its best customer and bought some of her

Christmas presents there to supplement the ones she continued to make at home.

Queen Victoria normally left for Osborne just before Christmas to escape memories of 'former, happy times'. It is a measure of the change in her attitude towards monarchical responsibilities since 1870, that the Queen was so absorbed in the Eastern Question that she remained on at Windsor because of 'the very critical state of affairs which obliged me to see Lord Beaconsfield and to communicate rapidly with him'.[6]

Quite a family party gathered at Windsor. Princess Helena was still recovering from the shock of giving birth to a stillborn son in May, after the death of a month-old son born the year before. The Queen, who wanted to give her a memorial to these babies, had asked Princess Louise to commission a statue for her. Princess Louise had suggested Aimée-Jules Dalou, a French artist whose work she greatly admired. In the weeks before Christmas, she regularly visited his studio at Glebe Place in Chelsea. She brought Lorne to see the work in progress on December 5th: 'Dalou is doing a very pretty thing of an Angel with small children,' he wrote the next day.[7]

Jules Dalou was a romantic figure. He had fought as a Communard in the 1871 Paris uprising, miraculously escaping to England afterwards; a death sentence was still on his head. He was then befriended by Lorne's cousin, George Howard, who introduced Princess Louise to the artist. The realism and intimacy which Dalou achieved in his terracotta busts, and mother and child groups, soon brought him much admiration. However, it was not the royal patroness who called at the Chelsea studio, but the eager young pupil, who came *'en bonne cama-rade'* to learn from a master.[8] The Princess was able to put to use what she had learnt on a work in clay which she intended to exhibit at next summer's show at the Grosvenor Gallery.

Opened on May 1st, as an *avant-garde* shop window for those artists who refused to produce conventional pictures of Highland cattle or families at tea for the Royal Academy, the Grosvenor Gallery was an immediate success. Landseer and Frith now took a back seat to Watts, Whistler and Burne-Jones. Here, on the corner of New Bond Street, the rebel forces of reborn Pre-Raphaelitism and the new aestheticism attacked the ramparts of Burlington Street. 'To believe in it and to profess it became a stamp of artistic sensibility,' wrote one Victorian; it became 'a sort of religion to the highly cultured'.[9]

The force behind this temple to aestheticism was Sir Coutts Lindsay of Balcarres, who founded the gallery. His policy was to invite artists, as well as amateur friends, to exhibit. He had spared no expense in the Italianate decoration of his gallery, and the ceiling by Whistler was of a clear blue sky, powdered over with stars and phases of the moon in silver. Underneath the picture rooms was the restaurant which provided a banquet for the opening night, which Princess Louise attended. She knew many of the people there and joined the Archie Campbells, Boehm, the Mitfords and Lord Ronnie Gower, in frequenting the Bohemian, cultured circles which, in the late eighteen seventies met, in the words of a Gilbert and Sullivan opera, at the 'greenery-yallery Grosvenor Gallery'.

Princess Louise was at her happiest and most relaxed in such surroundings. Her official, royal existence was only a background, it was never her life. Her cultural horizons had been broadened through marriage to a man who had already produced a published *Book of Psalms* and several well-received volumes of poetry. The Princess had come to know many of the leading literary figures of the day through him and the Argyll circle.

When George Eliot was at the height of her fame, after the publication of *Middlemarch* and *Daniel Deronda*, Princess Louise finally achieved her wish to meet her. It was difficult for the Queen's daughter to know a woman who had deliberately flouted convention by living with George Lewes, a married man. However, by 1877, George Eliot's status had made her socially acceptable; invitations to the Lewes's Sunday gatherings were eagerly sought.

When invited to dine at the Goschens on 15 May 1877, Princess Louise specially requested that George Eliot be present. On arrival, the Princess made no attempt to hide her great regard for the writer. Instead of waiting for her to be presented, as etiquette demanded, the Princess immediately asked to be introduced and was taken up to her, whereupon she sat down beside her and entered into a long, friendly chat. It was at dinner, when George Eliot and John Bright were discussing women's suffrage, that Princess Louise asked, "But, you don't go in for the superiority of women, Mrs Lewes?" Her vehement reply "No!" elicited the comment from another guest, the scientist Huxley, "I think Mrs Lewes rather teaches *the inferiority of men*."[10]

Such meetings remained rare occasions for the Princess, who continued to be hampered by the barrier created by her royal status. With her romantic nature and her unsatisfied desire for children, Princess Louise was still searching for some sort of fulfilment to colour her existence. It was the world of the Grosvenor Gallery which provided her with the opportunity to form friendships with amusing, intelligent people.

In the early part of 1878, Princess Louise was doing her best to live the life of a lady artist. She was sitting to Blanche Lindsay, Sir Coutts's wife, for her oil portrait and passed many an afternoon at 5 Cromwell Place. She and Blanche became friends and the Princess often stayed on to dine there in the company of other artists. She was also modelling a terracotta statuette of the beautiful Violet Lindsay, later Duchess of Rutland, who regularly came to sit at Kensington Palace; as a work, it owed much to the influence of Dalou and was eventually exhibited at the Grosvenor Gallery in 1879. At the same time, the Princess was trying to finish a clay relief of *Geraint and Enid* in time for the Summer Show.

This was her second imaginative work; the first was the bronze equestrian statue of the medieval Black Prince in armour, which she had done for the Argylls in the early seventies and which had escaped the fire at Inveraray. The title of her second work, *Geraint and Enid* is from a poem in Tennyson's *Idylls of the King*. Tennyson's ideal of womanhood is represented by Enid, the loyal wife who serves her unreasonable husband, even though he humiliates her from a ground-less belief that she has been unfaithful to him. The passage that Princess Louise chose to depict was of Geraint ordering Enid to drive six horses: 'And said to her "Drive them on before you through the wood!" He follow'd . . .'[11] Geraint is shown as an equestrian knight in armour, following a beautiful maiden with flowing tresses. The influence is Pre-Raphaelite in its romantic evocation of the medieval past and attention to detail.

Both of these works were equestrian. This was because the Princess, as a Victorian girl, had been unable to study anatomy or attend life classes. Consequently, she had little idea of the mechanism of human movement or the interaction of bodies. However, as a student of Boehm, a master of the equestrian statue, Princess Louise had learnt a great deal about the equine form, where she knew little of the human one. She was, therefore, more comfortable working with equine and clothed, immobile figures.

With such preoccupations, it was hardly surprising that, when Disraeli dined on 3 March 1878 with Princess Louise at Percy and

Madeline Wyndham's in Belgrave Square, he found 'all the talk about pictures and art and Raffaello, and what Sterne calls "the Correggiosity of Correggio"'. It was decidedly an 'aesthetical' dinner, although Robert Browning, whom Disraeli found 'a noisy, conceited poet', was there.[12] Princess Louise had not met him since the tea-party at the Deanery in 1869, and she found him as handsome as ever, though aged.

It was entirely owing to her marriage that Princess Louise met artists socially, rather than as a royal patron. Thus, through Lord Ronnie she had met Frank Miles, who lived below his great friend, Oscar Wilde. Frank Miles was the first to immortalize Lily Langtry, whom Princess Louise had then introduced to Prince Leopold long before the Prince of Wales ever knew her. Through the Archies, Princess Louise was introduced to the aesthetic movement and frequented the Grosvenor Gallery. Lord Archie's work at Coutts was not so onerous as to prevent him from escorting Princess Louise around the galleries after lunch, or taking her and his wife skating with William Richmond and the composer, Hubert Parry, among others. Lord Archie had considerable artistic talents, but he was unable to study art because he was a banker. Princess Louise knew he was bored and unhappy and that he was drinking too much.

Usually the most considerate of brothers, drink made Lord Archie reckless. He had unwittingly placed Lorne in a dreadful position over Christmas. 'Fancy Archie telegraphing to me at Windsor from London in German, as if that were an unknown language at Windsor, "Will there be peace or war? Please answer",' Lorne exclaimed to his mother. How could Archie expect him to give out that kind of information to the City? The 'suspicion that I dabble in the stocks and use any knowledge that I picked up while with the Queen for those purposes,' would obviously seriously damage his standing with her.[13] The Lornes eventually persuaded the Duke to send Lord Archie off to the family doctor, who forbade all stimulants. The warning had the intended effect and he remained an abstemious drinker thereafter. At the root of his troubles lay his turbulent marriage with the adorable, bewitching, yet infuriating Janey Callander, whose eccentricities were legendary.

In the summer, Janey wore a huge, round, straw hat with an upturned rim, around which a tiny monkey incessantly ran, and where he slept. She would arrive at a dinner party without her husband and drawl, 'Oh Archie cannot come, his shirt has not come home from the wash.'[14] She used her deep, musical voice to great effect in the amateur productions she staged in their country house at Coombe, when Whistler and Godwin did the sets, and her friend Ellen Terry helped with the acting. The epitome of aestheticism, she drew Princess Louise into that circle. Janey's style saved her from ridicule; however, unlike Princess Louise, she could get carried away. One day, deciding that she wished to live 'under the sea', she draped the sitting room with a coloured fish net from which dangled shells of mother-of-pearl, silver fish, and green seaweed. Some samples were despatched to Princess Louise, who returned them saying firmly, 'they are very cleverly done but I am not requiring anything of that kind'.[15] But Princess Louise was used to her sister-in-law's 'whimsies' and, not having to live with them, found them endearing. Princess Louise introduced her to the Prince of Wales and he often joined their parties to the opera or theatre, which led to speculation that he and Janey were lovers. The Prince of Wales was undoubtedly attracted to Janey, but she had no wish to become his mistress.

Wally Paget attended one of Janey's typical dinner parties at Beaufort Street, with the Lornes, Disraeli, Signor Tosti, the Italian singing master, and the Henry Somersets, among the other guests. Lord Archie received them in 'the little pink-and-brown drawing room, painted all over with large white birds, hung with hundreds of gilt palm leaves. Every candle was carefully shaded by a green butterfly, and the room was very dark.'[16] Whistler, the painter, would have approved but Disraeli, the Prime Minister, certainly did not; he found the house hardly 'fit for an elder son', since 'great nobles have great houses to receive the world in and not such hugger-mugger as I had to endure'.[17]

Distracted by the increasing number of social diversions in the spring, Princess Louise fell behind with her sculpture. With the deadline for the delivery of her relievo to the Grosvenor Gallery looming, Lorne insisted they keep to their original plan of attending the opening of the great Paris Exhibition at the end of April. The visit could not have come at a worse time. After putting considerable effort into *Geraint and Enid*, she now had to finish it in a tremendous hurry. She arranged for her old tutor, Boehm, to help her out by supervising the baking stage in her absence.

Unfortunately, the work was not dry enough so that, in the process of moving it from Kensington Palace, a large crack appeared and Boehm had to patch it up. He did not relish telling her about 'these little misfortunes'[18] which could not be prevented, but which were caused by too much haste. The trouble was that, caught between leading the life expected of her and the life she wanted, she inevitably compromised. Projects were often left unfinished once the momentum and concentration were lost.

∗   ∗   ∗

Princess Louise returned from Paris on 7th May to find the Duchess was giving cause for concern. Lord Ronnie did not think her well, 'the stare in her eyes and general abstractedness of manner very apparent'.[19] On the evening of May 24th, the Lornes were dining out at Marlborough House. Shortly after ten o'clock they were summoned urgently to Carlton House Terrace. There, amid sad bewilderment and confusion, they found the poor Duchess, utterly unconscious, covered with blankets and lying on a mattress.

Lucy Cavendish told the Princess all. She had greeted the Duchess who said, 'I'm afraid I shall be troublesome', but her next words were indistinct.[20] At dinner the Duchess sat next to her old friend, William Gladstone, but it was plain to everyone, she was in the throes of another stroke. The Duke helped carry her into the study where she was laid on the floor. Mrs Gladstone cut off her clothes, and William Gladstone gently lifted her on to a mattress close by. Within half an hour, four doctors and two nurses were doing their best to contain a brain haemorrhage.

At about one thirty, Dr Radcliffe, thinking the end might be prolonged, begged everyone to get some rest. So Princess Louise and Lorne left for nearby Stafford House. At about three o'clock, the Duchess began to breathe heavily and Ross, the piper, ran all the way to Stafford House for the Lornes, who returned just in time 'to kneel behind Mama and see the life ebb away from her dear body'. It was half past three on a May morning, which dawned as 'one splendid crimson glow'.[21]

After helping Mrs Gladstone cover the Duchess with white flowers, the Princess tried to comfort Lorne's sisters. At half past five, she and Lorne took the Duke home to Argyll Lodge and stayed with him while he rested. It was not until mid-morning that Princess Louise, feeling tired and numb, returned to Kensington Palace. Yet even here, rest and a little time for her own grief eluded her. After a change of clothes, Lorne returned to Argyll Lodge to start organizing the funeral, leaving

Princess Louise to deal with the innumerable telegrams, messages and notes, which poured in over the next ten days.

She urged Lorne not to remove the Duchess's body to Argyll Lodge as she knew this 'would be painful' for the Duke.[22]. Instead, it was taken to St Faith's Chapel in Westminster Abbey where, on May 27th, Dean Stanley conducted a short, private service for the family. Afterwards, Princess Louise returned to stay at Argyll Lodge because the Duke could not bear any of them to be away from him. The arrangements for the Duchess's burial were complex and time-consuming. She was to be buried in the family mausoleum at Kilmun in Argyll, which entailed an eighteen-hour train journey to Rosneath.

The burden of the arrangements had fallen largely upon Lorne, who coped admirably, but had to struggle not to break down altogether. He felt, in Princess Louise's words, 'the loss of his mother terribly, he was so devoted to her'.[23] 'I am so glad,' Princess Beatrice wrote in sympathy, 'that dear Louise is there all the time, as she is so calm and full of feeling.'[24]

Ten days later the funeral party boarded a night sleeper for Scotland. Princess Louise observed prevailing etiquette and remained behind. But all her thoughts were with those at Rosneath. She and Lorne wrote twice a day and he telegraphed to her at every opportunity. In the early afternoon of June 4th she wrote, 'Dearest Lorney – so glad to get your telegram at lunch time . . . I have been thinking so much of you my poor little Boy'; how she missed him: 'My thoughts will not leave you all day tomorrow – poor darling you must bear up you know – try to think of her alive and not dead, her speaking to you and laughing at your feeble jokes!'[25]

The grieving Princess tried to occupy herself with making sketches of the Duchess's face for a bust. At three o'clock on the afternoon of the funeral, she sat down at Lorne's writing table in his study and wrote to him, 'All is over now I suppose. . . . My thoughts have been continually with you, grieving for you poor darling. . . . Your Papa wrote me a dear little heartbroken letter. I have written to him to take courage. I hope it is not a stupid letter?' Earlier, she had called on Lucy Cavendish, 'it was terrible going into that house again, it brought that night all back to me'.[26] In turn, Lorne told her how beautiful Kilmun and the Holy Loch had looked in the glorious sunshine. The Duke 'bore up wonderfully well until he broke down when he lent over the coffin just before leaving the vault'.[27]

On June 8th, Lorne was reunited with his loving 'Wifey' at the McNeills' house in Edinburgh, and escorted her to Rosneath. 'It was a lovely evening when we arrived here,' Princess Louise wrote to Aunt Dot. The Duke 'dreads being alone at all, so we always manage to be 2 or 3 in a room that he can speak to us if he likes'. On wet days, Dr MacGregor frogmarched him up and down the library, saying 'Ye must keep the body going.'

The longer the Princess was there, the more she missed the Duchess. At Rosneath, more than anywhere else, 'Everything speaks of her, one can hardly believe she will not come into the room in another moment.'[28] For Princess Louise, as well as for the Argylls, the death of the 'good Duchess' heralded a parting of the ways. It became clearer with every passing year, that the cohesion of such a disparate, high-spirited family, owed everything to her calm, affectionate management. While the Duke 'fizzed' and strutted, it was 'her strong and vigorous mind' which made the decisions or worded the official letters.[29] She steadied him, just as she sustained their children. Her care and interest would have smoothed many a rough passage in the years ahead.

While Lorne prepared to join the Duke on the *Columba*, the Princess returned to London to supervise her latest project: the building of a proper studio at Kensington Palace. She had long wanted a studio of her own, which would be convenient yet inaccessible enough to deter the constant interruptions which befell her when she worked at home. A site at the end of her private garden perfectly met these requirements. She gave the commission to the architect Edward Godwin, who was currently building the White House in Tite Street for Whistler. The Princess had met both men through the Archies.

When Whistler was decorating the dining room of 46 Prince's Gate for the Leylands in the summer of 1876, the Archies and Bertie Mitford, who lived next door to Whistler, had told Princess Louise about the creation of a 'dazzling masterpiece' in the form of a room decorated in blue and gold. Her curiosity piqued, Princess Louise had called to see the ultimate in aesthetic decoration: 'Willie has told you of the visit of the Princess Louise to the "Peacock Palace"',* Whistler wrote to his

* The Peacock Room (1865–7) has since been reconstructed in the Freer Gallery of Art, Washington, D.C.

mother, 'and her delight in the "gorgeous loveliness" of the work'.[30]

The Princess remained an admirer of Whistler's despite the public outcry which greeted his pictures. His portrait of Carlyle was condemned by art critics, while the public believed he had insulted a great author. Princess Louise, however, thought it technically admirable, with its total absence of colour. Whistler later sent a proof of his engraving of Carlyle to the Princess for her 'approbation'.

It was in June that Whistler sought her help with his new house. The simple, three-storey building was faced in white Portland stone with a green slate roof; the door and woodwork were painted a peacock blue. Unlike the other houses in Tite Street, it was deliberately unadorned by mouldings, cornices or parapets and it had windows where Whistler needed them, rather than where windows were usually found. The Metropolitan Board of Works refused to grant a builder's licence unless some ornamentation was added, and the architectural critics wrote hostile reviews of Godwin's 'stark' work.

During a visit to Bertie Mitford's, Princess Louise was told of Whistler's problems and she suggested they send next door for him. Whistler found that 'she greatly sympathised'. Never one to miss an opening, Whistler plunged in to suggest if HRH 'would only drive past and say how beautiful she thought the house that, of course, would put an end to the whole trouble. She laughed saying that she didn't believe her influence was as strong as that!' Nonetheless, she later mentioned reflectively that 'Lorne knows Sir James, I think . . .'[31] As a result, Lady Hogg was persuaded to see the house and Whistler was subsequently told that, although Sir James Hogg, the Commissioner, did not have complete control, she thought Whistler would be successful, which he was.

The Princess had, in fact, seen the White House while building was in progress; for she passed it on her frequent visits to the Victoria Hospital for Children, also in Tite Street. For her, the role of patroness was not a symbolic gesture of adding her name to the subscription list; rather, it involved assuming responsibility for the hospital and overseeing its operation with, if necessary, frequent personal intervention to maintain standards. The board of the hospital soon learnt that their Royal Patroness's wishes could never be ignored. Hence, Tite Street saw a good deal of the Princess.

Whistler was so grateful for her help that he sent her a little picture of the Thames near Battersea Bridge, which, for once, did not represent the riverside clothed in mist. 'In it, I would timidly hint,' he wrote to her, 'that, while I recognise Nature's . . . use of fairy fog – "when the evening mist clothes the riverside with poetry, as with a veil" – I still do love to look at her, when she is beautiful without it.'[32] According to the artist, Princess Louise was enchanted and 'so delighted' with his picture and thanked him 'very many times'.[33]

As a consequence of her friendship with the Bohemian fringe, Princess Louise lent its members a certain respectability, which staider Victorian Society resented. It was felt that members of the Royal Family should not know controversial people like Edward Godwin, who had run off with G. F. Watt's child-wife, the actress Ellen Terry. Eschewing marriage, they lived together while she bore him two children, but he thereafter philandered uncompromisingly. The Victorian Establishment deemed him utterly unworthy of a Royal Commission. The Princess ignored such views; she chose the controversial architect because she liked his work. On April 8th, the Board of Works and the Lord Chamberlain officially approved the site of the studio, but only after they had learnt of Queen Victoria's consent. The Princess's word might sway the Metropolitan Board of Works, but only the Queen's could propel the Commissioner of Works and the Lord Chamberlain into action.

The studio was a low, one-storeyed building, consisting of a model's dressing room, lavatory, sitting room and large studio room. Built of red brick to blend in with Kensington Palace, the only detail was provided by the windows and graduated slates of the roof. Delighted with this diversion, Princess Louise was, however, unable to work there for two more years.

While yachting in the Hebrides in July of 1878, Lorne had a vision, startling in its clarity, that he would be offered high office overseas. Like all good Highlanders, the Argyll Campbells believed in second sight. Princess Louise decided to keep an open mind until evidence surfaced to support Lorne's case. In the event, she had not long to wait.

At the beginning of July, Lord Dufferin had refused the Government's offer to extend his period of office as Governor-General of Canada. The Colonial Secretary, Sir Michael Hicks Beach, thought the appointment of the Queen's son-in-law could be used to illustrate the greatness and unity of the British Empire.

During a three-day visit to Osborne, Disraeli proposed the appointment to the Queen. She was divided in her feelings; on the one hand, she felt satisfaction at the distinction for Lorne and the 'fine independent position' for Princess Louise; on the other hand, she felt sure that the Princess did not want to be so far from all her family and interests. The Queen had to admit that 'The thought too, of parting from her for so long was v. painful.'[34] Certain of their refusal, she wisely decided it would be unfair to withhold permission.

Mid-morning on 24 July 1878, Lorne, comfortably ensconced in a large, red leather armchair in 10 Downing Street, listened to the Prime Minister offer him the position of one of 'our great Viceroyalties'. Disraeli impatiently brushed aside Lorne's suggestion that there were other, better men with administrative experience; no, he was most anxious that Lorne should take it, since he had 'abilities'. After asking for time to discuss it with his wife, Lorne made his bow and left.

Princess Louise forgot all about Lorne's vision in the excitement which followed the news of Disraeli's offer. Lorne told her that he would only accept the office if she favoured it. At first intrigued by the prospect of a journey to an unknown land, which seemed a great adventure, Princess Louise soon had second thoughts. She knew little about Canada and turned to the Prince of Wales and Prince Arthur for information. The first disadvantage, she discovered, was the intense cold, which is agonizingly painful for sufferers from facial neuralgia such as herself.

However, she was much more concerned at the thought of being so far from home; especially as the normal term of office for a Governor-General was five years, which seemed like an eternity to her. As a Royalty, she was even more likely to suffer from homesickness than other Governor-General's wives. In the Queen's words, 'it will be, for *her* in *her* particular position – *with* no absolute equals – a vy trying & isolated one'.[35] Then, the thought of being so far away in an emergency, involving say Prince Leopold, distressed her. It would take at least ten days travelling to return home by which time she might be too late.

Nevertheless, the Princess had to consider her husband's wishes. In the endless discussions that ensued, it became increasingly clear that Lorne desperately wanted to go to Canada. Rarely was such a position offered to an inexperienced 32-year-old. He said he would not even have considered it if his mother had been alive; now, he felt he could go 'with less anxiety' and with the wholehearted support of the Duke. The

Princess agreed with Lorne that it was their duty to go. 'I thoroughly feel,' he wrote on July 29th, 'the great necessity of keeping all bonds of Empire closely knit, and the duty of all to do their utmost to that end.' Lorne, of course, knew that an appeal to duty was guaranteed to carry the day with Princess Louise, especially in the absence of any maternal pressure.

Four days after seeing Disraeli, Lorne formally accepted the Governor-Generalship of Canada. With the Queen's consent, he stipu-lated that they should have annual home leave and that the initial term of office should be three years, subject to renewal if the Princess liked it. Lorne was more than aware of the great responsibilities involved. Writing to Dufferin, who had made a brilliant success of the job, Lorne admitted, 'I am told that it is impossible to succeed you worthily, and in the same breath that I shall be shirking my duty unless I make the attempt. So I shut my eyes, shudder and say "I'll try" and rely on your goodness to give me all the help you can.'[36]

The date of their arrival in Canada proved difficult to settle. It was felt Lorne's arrival ought to coincide with his predecessor's departure in the autumn. Elections were due to be held in Canada on September 17th, which Lorne felt should be over before he arrived. He was also averse to festivities, since he was still in deep mourning for his mother; an arrival in, say, November would avoid this nicely. Princess Louise was not so pleased. Anxious to avoid the worst of the winter, she also wanted to be in England for her brother's wedding in early February. Prince Arthur was engaged to pretty Princess Louise of Prussia, a niece of the Crown Prince of Prussia. The Princess asked the Queen to plead her case with the Prime Minister.

Lorne's suggestion was that he should go alone and let her follow. The Queen immediately scotched this idea: 'if Lord Beaconsfield can let them stay till Feby – so much the better – but if not they must *both* go in Nov: for he cld *not* arrive *without* her'.[37] Disraeli entirely agreed that they must arrive together, but doubted whether the date could be delayed until February without creating a bad impression. Princess Louise's case was lost when Queen Victoria decided on July 30th that if the departure could not be delayed beyond November, 'it *cannot be helped*, after all there will be plenty of the family here & Louise *knows* her future sister-in-law'.[38]

Difficulties did not end there. Princess Louise was dismayed to learn that all the Canadian newspapers referred to their stay as being for five or six years rather than three. She foresaw that the Canadians would be upset when they left after three years: 'they will think it is because we were dissatisfied and we may be seeming not to recognise all their kind feeling towards us. I shd be very sorry if there were any misunderstanding of this sort.' Would her mother straighten this out for them? A missive, ordering Lord Beaconsfield to 'take *care* & *set* this *right at once*', left with the next messenger from Osborne.[39]

The Prince of Wales was also busy on Princess Louise's behalf. Sensing that the opportunity might never arise again, he raised the old question of a dukedom for Lorne. Since Lorne was no longer in the House of Commons, he could hardly refuse elevation to the Lords on the grounds of his parliamentary career. It would be much more fitting for his sister to be a duchess and would prevent Lorne from seeking re-election as an MP on his return from Canada. Before anyone could deal with this issue, the Prince had fired off another salvo. The salary of £10,000 per annum for a Governor-General of Canada was not really commensurate with a royal appointment. He had been the recipient of sumptuous viceregal entertainment in India and expected his sister to be granted the same facilities in Canada. When the Prime Minister referred this to Sir Michael Hicks-Beach, he was told that 'the first thing Lord Lorne said to me was an expression of his strong desire that *no* increase to the pay of the Office should be asked for: and this he has frequently repeated since.'[40] The penny-pinching Colonial Office supported Lorne, but Royalties took it as yet another instance of Lorne practising 'Scotch economy'.

Lorne was concerned about meeting the extra expenses of office out of their limited incomes; so he now seized his chance to sell Dornden. Its sale caused the Princess distress, although Lorne promised her that the proceeds would be put towards the purchase of a higher-yielding estate on their return from Canada.

Instead of increasing Lorne's salary, the Colonial Office persuaded the Dominion Government to make up his salary by providing free 'perks'. Thus, all the expenses of housing, extra staff, and travel would be paid for by Canada and not by Lorne.

After a German holiday, the Lornes went to Balmoral where the Princess tackled the Queen about the Edinburghs who, she said, 'are very anxious to know what is to become of them'.[41] The Duke was in disgrace for having entertained Prince Alexander of Battenberg, then ADC to the Russian Commander-in-Chief, on *HMS Sultan* at a time when the British Government was threatening to go to war with Russia over Turkey. Even after Britain and Russia had reached a settlement at the Congress of Berlin in June, he was kept in exile aboard another ship.

Matters came to a head when he threatened to resign if he was not allowed home. It was common knowledge in the family that Queen Victoria was refusing to allow Prince Alfred to come home and was peeved with his pro-Russian attitude. At Balmoral, Princess Louise provided the perfect solution: she suggested he supply the royal escort on her journey to Canada. The sorely tried Prime Minister hoped this 'shipping affair' was now ended, but on 4 October 1878 the Admiralty received a telegram from Balmoral: 'What is meaning of statement in papers that *Sarmatian* and not *Northampton* takes out Lord Lorne?'[42]

Queen Victoria wanted Princess Louise to arrive in Canada as the Queen's daughter in one of the Queen's ships, but when the owners of the Allan Line offered the use of one of their mail steamers, the Lornes accepted because it would be more comfortable than any naval ship. The Queen was annoyed that Lorne had not referred the matter to her, and the Admiralty and the Prime Minister were drawn into a lengthy correspondence about a minor detail. Not surprisingly, the Prime Minister wrote from Hughenden, 'I am sick of this business.'[43] The Queen's fussing was related to the imminence of Princess Louise's departure. What had seemed to her a 'fine distinction' and 'an honourable position' in July was 'a banishment' and 'a real cruelty' in November.

For Princess Louise the tearful partings, first with her mother at Balmoral, since the Queen would not alter her routine and return South earlier, then with the Duke at Rosneath, followed by the Waleses at Sandringham, made her miserable. Her last two weeks at Kensington Palace sped by in a whirl of packing and entertaining, though she still managed to give superb dinner parties. When she and Lorne dined at Alford House on November 5th, the house was very cold with feeble fires and dull food. But on the 7th, when she gave a dinner party at Kensington Palace for Disraeli, he deemed the food 'exquisite', 'too many luxuries' if anything, including truffles swimming in champagne sauce, which Prince Leopold blithely tucked into, regardless of his sister's protestation that they were far too rich for his delicate digestion. It was a small party for her close friends, the Coutts-Lindsays and the Mitfords; nevertheless, the socialite Prime Minister enjoyed the 'rather amusing' evening though he noticed the difference in the Lornes' attitude to Canada. Princess Louise was 'in low spirits but her spouse (His Excellency) rampant'.[44]

Lord Ronnie and the Archies lunched with them on the day of their departure: 'she very sorry to go and looks forward apparently with great dislike to her life there', Lord Ronnie noted in his diary.[45] At a quarter to twelve that night, Princess Louise, with Lorne, Prince Arthur and Prince Leopold, boarded the Liverpool sleeper at St Pancras Station. As the clock chimed midnight, the train steamed out of the station. The Princess retired to her compartment soon afterwards and was not woken until half past five that morning. She was distressed to learn that, when the train had stopped at Stockport at four o'clock, the Mayor, dressed in his robes of office and bearing an address, had been turned away, because the royal party were asleep. Orders were given that such treatment must never be repeated.

They reached Liverpool in the moonlight and went straight to the Adelphi Hotel for breakfast. At ten o'clock they made their way to the pier via the Town Hall where the Mayor presented an address in front of cheering crowds. The leave-taking on board the ship was the most affecting of all. As Princess Louise kissed and hugged her two beloved brothers over and over again, uncontrollable tears streamed down her face.

At twenty minutes past eleven, the *Sarmatian* moved off as Prince Arthur and Prince Leopold returned to the pier, where the bands were playing such cheerful airs as 'Will ye no come back again' and 'Friends far from home'. On board, Lorne was left to comfort Princess Louise as best he could; while she dwelt upon their sad departure, he could think only of their arrival in Canada. 'It is curious,' he wrote to Lord Dufferin, 'that the Princess should be the first daughter of her house who has ever had the opportunity of landing on the shores of America.'[46]

CHAPTER XIV

A New World

The *Sarmatian* was considered the crack ship of the Allan Line, whose fleet regularly plied the Atlantic. Having been specially refitted for the Princess's journey, she had been transformed into what Victorians regarded as the ultimate in luxurious transportation. The hardy, old bar-saloon had become a palatial drawing room, panelled in white and gold, and supported by fluted columns of ebony; wire baskets overflowing with flowers and ferns, hung from the ceiling above crimson velvet sofas and walnut sideboards. In one corner stood a new piano, placed there solely for the Princess's use. Two staterooms on the starboard side had been knocked into one to form the Princess's cabin, which housed a berth specially designed to remain steady in rough seas. This was of particular interest to her as were the special pillows which felt as soft as feathers, but were as buoyant as cork, so that they doubled as lifebuoys.

Accompanying the Lornes were the members of their suite: Lady Sophie; their Comptroller, the Hon. Richard Moreton and his wife as second lady-in-waiting; their two ADCs, Captain the Hon. Charles Harbord and Captain Veron Chater; Dr Andrew Clerk; and Colonel John McNeill. Their secretary, Major de Winton, had travelled ahead with his family. Twenty-five servants, including their seventy-year-old piper from Tiree, were also aboard.

The Princess, however, was unconscious of both surroundings and companions; her next ten days passed in a nightmare of terror and seasickness. Once the ship left the coast of Ireland, it encountered storms, varied by a hurricane which tore away foresail and mainsail as well as seats fixed to the deck. In addition to the roar of the waves and the interminable rolling and pitching of the ship, it was so bitterly cold that the cabin portholes became frozen on the inside; with no internal heating it was impossible for those lying prone, like the Princess, to keep warm.

She was so ill that another bunk had to be constructed for her; it was suspended by ropes from the cabin ceiling so as to minimize the effects of the rolling of the ship. In the next cabin, little eight-year-old Evelyn Moreton could still hear Princess Louise 'alternately groaning and loudly praying to all the Saints'.[1] Everyone, including Dr Clerk, was unwell except for Lorne. After the first few days, he happily promenaded on deck and paid visits of commiseration to the seasick.

The *Sarmatian* was encountering rougher seas partly because it was not following its usual route. On November 1st, the Foreign Office had received a despatch from Washington about a Fenian plot to seize Lorne and the Princess en route to Canada. The Admiralty had ordered the *Sarmatian* to be navigated off her usual course and a man-of-war to meet her fifty miles from land and convey her to Halifax.[2]

On November 22nd, instead of steaming into the calm waters of Halifax harbour, the Captain, hoping to establish contact with the warship, decided to lie to fourteen miles away, 'to the disgust of the ladies who have another night of rolling . . . before them'.[3] After waiting in vain the next day, in rain and rough seas, the Captain took pity on the suffering ladies and ran into harbour. Almost immediately, a steam launch bearing Prince Alfred from the *Black Prince* came out to the ship. The Princess was woken and, in her dressing gown, ran into Lorne's cabin for a joyous reunion: 'Then there was much conversation in my cabin,' Lorne recorded, 'to the wrath of Dr Clerk, who wanted L to go to bed.'[4]

On a cold, bright Monday afternoon, the Lornes crossed the water from the *Sarmatian* to the pier. 'The landing was the prettiest sight imaginable – the town looking its best in bright sunshine, with its many steeples, and houses covered with flags,' Lorne recorded.[5] They set foot on Canadian soil to the familiar sound of a royal salute, the national anthem, and loud cheering from the crowds. Lorne had stepped out first, followed by the Princess, to be met by Prince Alfred and the usual volunteers and local dignitaries. Halifax looked more like a Hampshire port than an unfamiliar Canadian town. As the only British military and naval base in North America, its streets were brightened by uniforms and lined with clubs and it offered visitors a pleasant social life. Only the wooden buildings and pavements, the presence of Red Indians and Blacks and the sound of strangely accented voices, showed they were not still in England.

The Princess looked thin and drawn; ten days of seasickness had taken its toll upon her appearance and strength. Her pinched white face was accentuated by the unrelieved black of her silk dress, trimmed with jet, for she was still in mourning for the Duchess. The only unintentional touch of colour was provided by a bouquet which had been presented to her.

Through streets gay with bunting and arches proclaiming '*Ne Obliviscaris*', they drove to the Parliament Building where Lorne was sworn in as Governor-General of Canada. The Chief of the Micmacs had asked permission to walk in the procession behind the daughter of the great White Queen. So, duly and colourfully protected, the Lornes drove back through the town to the eighteenth-century Admiralty House.

Princess Louise looked 'quite lovely' and 'every inch a Princess' according to the ladies of Halifax, as she received them at the Drawing Room, her jewels and orders sparkling against the rich, black velvet of her gown. Standing on the centre of a dais in the drawing room of Government House, from nine thirty until after midnight, and bowing to what seemed like the whole population of Halifax, the thirty-year-old Princess was, for the first time in her own right, fulfilling the role for which she had been trained; ten days of seasickness were thrown off and she played her part to perfection.

After two days in Halifax the Lornes set off on a train journey which was the formal inauguration of the new winter route into Canada. Had they arrived the year before, they would have had to cross into the United States and pass through Maine to reach Montreal. The Inter-Colonial Railway provided the eastern link of the railway, which was to run between the Atlantic and the Pacific coast of Canada. The journey to Montreal took longer than its usual thirty-six hours because they stopped to receive addresses at wayside stations overflowing with spectators and illuminations. As the train entered the French-speaking province of Quebec, Princess Louise saw the first signs of a Canadian winter: snow had begun to cover the vast plains which stretched far away into the horizon. There, and in Ontario, apart from a few big granaries and the odd, little, wooden farmhouse, there were no other signs of human habitation. So, for what seemed like one interminable day after another, the train ploughed through this deserted, white, land.

On November 29th, four weary days after leaving Halifax, the train steamed into Bonaventure Station. The Lornes' reception by the people of Montreal was tumultuous; a continuous shower of flowers fell upon their carriage as they drove in state to Victoria Square. It was alarming, after their incarceration in the train, to be suddenly exposed to so much noise and so many people. The horses of their carriage became so nervous that a number of bystanders had to remove the traces and, in emulation of a 'homecoming' ceremony, draw the Lornes' carriage to their temporary Montreal home, the magnificent Windsor Hotel.

At half past ten that night, the Princess opened the St Andrew's Ball when she partnered Lorne's old school friend, Russell Stephenson, in a foursome. Described by one observer as 'acquitting herself with fascinating grace and an old time air at once delicate and charming', the Princess felt at her best since landing in Canada.[6] She might be in an unknown city, but her immediate surroundings seemed strangely familiar: for the spartan ballroom, the swirling kilts and the sound of the pipes resembled a tenants' dance in the pavilion at Inveraray.

The next day was spent by Lorne in granting audiences and receiving addresses. Although her part was secondary, the Princess was kept busy with activities of her own. In the morning, as one newspaper put it, 'the address business which has become a perfect nuisance was pleasantly relieved' by the Ladies' Educational Association of Montreal.[7] Having learnt that the Princess Louise was an active supporter of women's education in England, they now asked her to become their patroness in Canada. In her reply, the Princess warned: 'The fruits of education are so attractive that we are often tempted to force them prematurely without sufficient tillage' because of losing sight of the true object of education, which 'consists much more in the development of the intellect than . . . in cramming'. Much better to give a broad, thorough grounding which pupils would always retain: 'Knowledge thus got never dies; knowledge got otherwise never lives.'[8] This was a far cry from her embarrassed attempt at public speaking at Inverarary in 1871. Since those days, she had not only mastered the art of delivery but, in this case, had written the speech herself.

At last, on December 2nd, the Lornes reached their journey's end when the train steamed into Ottawa. The torchlight procession had to be postponed for two days on account of the incessant rain. The Princess, therefore, was greeted by drenched soldiers and civilians and driven under sagging arches and dripping flags two miles northwards to her new home.

Thus, her first sight of Rideau Hall, the official residence of the Governor-General, was not made under the most favourable circumstances; not that fine weather would have altered her impression. Lord Dufferin had written: 'it is a dull grey building without any architectural pretensions, in the middle of an ill-kept shubbery'.[9]

The Lornes' immediate verdict was no better: they found the house 'hideous'.[10] This rambling, two-storeyed, stone building had begun existence in 1838 as a Presbyterian Scotsman's idea of a neo-classical villa. His Rideau Hall of eleven rooms, basement and attic was known as 'Mackay's Castle' since it was a 'princely mansion' compared to the surrounding log houses. In 1868, the Government purchased it outright. It had long been overwhelmed by the piecemeal additions, undertaken by successive Governor-Generals, when Princess Louise first saw it. But ugly though it might be, its homeliness and comfort would be valued by the Princess. Rideau Hall was like a trusted old friend, whose faults come to seem, with the passage of time, endearing and somehow precious.

The Lornes were touched by the warmth of the welcome given them by the public and unprepared for the display of sentiment from the more hard-boiled politicians. Leaders of deputations concluded their addresses with swimming eyes and choked voices, while Lorne was soon suffering from that royal condition, crushed hands, since MPs then 'nearly shook one's hands off'.[11] The Princess escaped such injuries since she had only to acknowledge by a bow of her head their greetings. But her stamina was well-tested at her first big dinner for the Cabinet, followed by a long Drawing Room at which she had to stand and bow for nearly three hours.

The Princess also tackled the unpacking and ordered alterations and repairs. Although basic furniture was provided at Rideau Hall, there were no pictures, books, or ornaments in the house, so that the overall effect was depressing. Princess Louise had never had to move into an empty house before and she found it dispiriting. Lorne, as usual, was all cheerfulness: 'Here we are settling down in this big and comfortable house,' he wrote that day to his father, 'which I tell Louise is much superior to Kensington, for the walls are thick, the rooms are lathed and plastered . . . and there is an abundant supply of heat and light.'[12] Such comparisons were meant to cheer up the Princess but they did little to assuage her homesickness. Nonetheless, determined to create a home from such unpromising material and with the carpenter in tow, she soon set 'everybody to work their arms off, all through the house'.[13]

The ground floor rooms were decorated in colour schemes chosen by the Princess, but progress upstairs was delayed because she and Lorne could not agree on a choice for their bedroom and dressing room. Although by December 7th some of their beautiful old tapestries were up in the drawing room, the process of making Rideau Hall comfortable was 'a slow one'.[14] 'I hope the Princess will settle down to a half liking of the life at all events,' Lorne wrote to Lord Dufferin.[15] Sadly for the Princess, events at home prevented any immediate enjoyment of life in Canada.

Her reunion with Prince Alfred at Halifax had already been tinged with sadness for he had reported the death from diphtheria of their youngest Hesse niece. Thus, her first few days at Rideau Hall passed in an agony of waiting for the mails and telegrams to arrive from home. On December 9th, she heard that her favourite sister, Princess Alice, had also caught diphtheria. It was all she could do to keep going for, as Queen Victoria wrote, 'the anxiety is terrible, wearing and to be so far away is agonising!'[16]

On the morning of December 15th, Lorne broke the news to his wife: Princess Alice had died the previous morning. 'We feel so for Princess Louise,' wrote Russell Stephenson's wife, Gwen, 'it is most unfortunate happening you may say on her arrival and as we hear she is very homesick, she will feel double so now that she has this sorrow to bear.'[17] It was a sad introduction to life in Canada; the first months of her stay filled with grief, separated as she was from those who most shared it and understood her.

Princess Louise felt bitterly her absence from home at such a time. She wrote to Lady Cadogan, 'I was indeed deeply touched by your . . . thought of me, in this far off country, at this sad time, when this sudden sadness has come upon us. It has been doubly hard to bear, not being at home and not being able to comfort the dear Queen.'[18] As the wretched year of 1878 drew to a close and the New Year dawned, Queen Victoria's thoughts dwelt upon the loss of 'our darling precious Alice, one of my five beloved daughters', and upon 'my poor dear Loosy far away in a distant land, in another quarter of the globe!'[19]

CHAPTER XV

Queen of Canada

The Princess's first Canadian Christmas passed very quietly owing to mourning for Princess Alice. This meant that she relied more than ever upon the companionship of the viceregal staff who, in effect, became surrogate members of her family. Living together in a strange land amongst strange people, sharing the same house, the same meals and the same amusements day after day, as if on a country house visit that would never end, it was inevitable that they should cling together.

They breakfasted together around a large square table in the dull-red dining room so typical of its period, with Winterhalter portraits of Queen Victoria and Prince Albert and Dutch landscapes on the walls, and a pair of black walnut sideboards, which groaned with gold salvers, claret jugs and stuffed duck shot by Lorne. Afterwards, the group dispersed for the morning. Lorne either drove into Ottawa to his office or went to his study, which overlooked the aviary and the skating rinks, and from which a narrow door opened into Princess Louise's workroom, used by Lord Dufferin as a studio. She was 'extremely touched' by his thoughtfulness in leaving casts for her use. Lorne told him that she was looking forward to having a workroom in which 'she can make an artistic mess'.[1] Half the room was given over to easels, tools and palettes, while the other half housed a day bed and tripod table sheltering behind a screen, and a piano. Myriad photographs, miniatures and portraits of her family occupied every available surface. However, this did not lessen her output; on January 5th, Lorne wrote 'Painting has been going on, Mr Sydney Hall [a painter friend] and Captain Chater and an old Frenchman having all sat to the Princess.'[2]

She usually divided her mornings between the workroom and her boudoir, where she had replaced Lady Dufferin's pink hangings with peacock blue paper and curtains, peacock feathers *à la* Whistler, and old tapestries. She furnished the room with chairs covered by antimacassars, which she had embroidered with pink and blue daisies, a piano, portraits of Grandmama Kent, and the Waleses, and a photograph of Queen Victoria. One journalist, who was given a tour of it, wrote: 'Evidences of the aesthetic taste of its royal mistress are everywhere visible, from the dead gold panels and their blood red flowers, to the linnets and canaries warbling in quaint and picturesque cages, from choice and elegant literature in many languages to the quantity of woman's work lying on ottomans.'[3] Wherever she was, the Princess was seldom idle and Canada proved no exception.

After lunch, the viceregal party would sally forth to experience the delights of the Canadian winter. The Princess, who had dreaded the cold climate, was surprised to find how much she enjoyed winter life. Although the thermometer registered 22° below zero twice in January alone, she was not conscious of the temperature. The sunshine and crisp air and the hard exercise made her feel physically exhilarated. Walks were made on snowshoes up the Ottawa River, which lay to the west of Rideau Hall, to the Chaudière Falls; this led to a great many tumbles and much laughter by those who remained upright. Like all well-dressed women and children, Princess Louise bundled up in a sealskin coat, her head shrouded in a white woollen muffler, always called a 'cloud', which she wore over a hat to protect her ears. Evelyn Moreton specially remembered the more sedate walks on Sunday afternoons, 'headed by Lorne, talking in his high pitched nasal voice, with Princess Louise, young and beautiful by his side'. Princess Louise nicknamed her 'Little Seal' 'because she said I was seal coloured all over – eyes, hair, coat'.[4]

The Princess was also introduced to 'the glory of Canadian winter life – good sleighing'.[5] As the roads were impassable, drives were taken in sleighs whose bells jingled in the crisp air, their occupants tucked up in heavy buffalo skins and bear skins lined in gay colours, gliding along under fir trees which held the snow like blossom. The Princess delighted in this form of transport and, with the addition of runners, her carriage was easily turned into a sleigh.

Although she had skated as a child at Osborne, she soon realized that skating in Canada bore no relation to a quick turn round an English village pond. At Rideau Hall there were two skating rinks, which had frozen to an even blue-green expanse. The favourite rink was about one hundred and fifty yards from the house where, to one side, almost on the ice, stood a little wooden hut which contained a burning stove. This was always kept alight for the spectators, who sat there, and the skaters who changed there. Princess Louise joined everyone for lessons in figure skating so as to be proficient for the skating parties she would give during the Season. She also tobogganed and was often the first to go down the slide, an arm clasped round a child sharing her toboggan. 'On a fine frosty day the thing goes down at a tremendous speed, the snow rising in dust clouds behind it,' wrote Lorne, 'and when at the end of the course there is an upset, the cedar thickets ring with laughter.'[6] Afterwards, everyone trooped back to the warm house, shed their outer clothes and sat by the roaring fire while Princess Louise poured out tea.

On 10 January 1879, the British Minister at Washington, Sir Edward Thornton, and his wife arrived on a private visit to Rideau Hall by invitation of Lorne, who felt that it would help to get to know his neighbour. Sir Edward had last travelled to Canada in August when, as an unknown passenger on the railways, he had taken the opportunity to learn what Canadians really thought about Lorne's appointment as Governor-General. He reported back to his chief, Lord Salisbury, that they seemed universally 'gratified and flattered by the appointment and by the prospect that HRH Princess Louise would honour Canada by residing there'.[7] Despite these diplomatic words, Sir Edward had reservations about the wisdom of appointing such a young man to reign in Canada. He thought Lorne far too inexperienced for the position, especially after the great success of Lord Dufferin. The fear was of American encroachment upon Canada to the detriment of British interests. Thornton's concern was that Lorne would not prove a strong enough ally, because of his political inexperience.

In the event, the Thorntons' visit passed off remarkably well. They were 'delighted' with the Lornes and Sir Edward told his staff that the Princess was 'already a great favourite'.[8] Before they returned to Washington, a plan was made to meet up at Niagara Falls on January 21st which they subsequently did.

After registering at the hotel, the Lornes wandered out for a look at Niagara before dark. Victorian tourists visiting Niagara were warned of two hazards: guides and gratuities. 'Every other man you meet is, or professes to be, a guide and . . . every bit of scenery has its money value,' wrote one visitor.[9] Princess Louise, however, found a third hazard: 'We could not take our walk in peace,' Lorne recorded, 'as three reporters followed us all the time and remained within hearing of all we said.' Still, he and Princess Louise had their revenge when 'One of them to our joy, fell into a little grove and got up covered with snow.'[10]

On their return, the Lornes were occupied with preparations for their first Season in Ottawa, which began in February to coincide with the opening of Parliament. The Princess gave her first uniquely Canadian entertainment, a skating carnival, on the evening of February 11th. Rows of coloured chinese lanterns and flaming torches lit up the grounds and fringed the rinks. A military band played for the skating dances, but the intervals were frequent, since the brass instruments had to be thawed out at a large stove, kept nearby for this purpose. The guests themselves provided a colourful contrast to the white snow and the black of night. The men wore coloured blanket coats, knicker-bockers, blue stockings and moccasins, while the ladies' coats were green or blue, piped with red. Everyone wore red sashes, blue knitted hats, 'tuques', with red tassels.

Supper was served in a long, covered, curling rink to the north of the house. Since the temperature was the same as outside, well below zero, the footmen waited in heavy fur coats and caps. In place of flowers on the table, frozen silver vases held branches of spruce and fir; even the menu had to be planned carefully, since any dish containing liquid, such as a mousse, would freeze immediately. Lorne's favourite meringues froze into 'uneatable cricket balls'.[11]

On 13 February 1878, Princess Louise drove into Ottawa for the opening of Parliament at the magnificent gothic Parliament Buildings around which the township clustered. Seated to the left of the Governor-General's throne, upon her own red velure throne specially constructed and intricately carved for her, Princess Louise had a clear view of the Senate Chamber. This was the first time she had ever been able to watch such a procession, since at home she had always accompanied her mother and been the last to enter. Here, however, Lorne's procession was met by the Black Rod, who walked backwards into the Chamber, bowing all the way and Princess Louise, like every-one else, stood up until the Governor-General requested them to be seated. For in Canada, Lorne as Governor-General always took precedence over her. As at Westminster, the Commons were sent for and Lorne read the speech in French and English.

During the session, the Princess observed for herself the way the French speaking MPs drew attention to the inability of many MPs of English or Scottish extraction to speak or understand French. During debates, a French-Canadian would insist that a very Scottish sounding Member repeat his remark in French, then the House would break into howls of laughter. The Princess was less amused by the 'disgusting habit of spitting in all directions', which the viceregal ladies found rather sickening.[12] However, the institution of little Pages found great favour with them.

In order to meet all the MPs, the Lornes decided to give bi-weekly dinners of fifty people. Cultural differences soon became apparent. At dinner one evening, the Princess asked a member of the Government whether he thought Whistler had been unjustly treated by the English art critics. Replying that he knew the Whistler case well, the Minister said that flogging him was an outrage that would forever stain the British Army. The Princess was taken aback. It turned out that it was not Jimmy Whistler, but one Alexander Somerville who, writing under the *nom de plume* of Whistler in Canada, had been flogged forty years previously for his political views.

Princess Louise often found these dinners heavy going, as did many in her party. Lady Sophie had 'to stalk round the women and talk to them after dinner. They are too dreadful some of them with a "I'm as good as you" sort of manner when one begins a conversation.' When her niece, Mrs Langham's turn came, she reported she would much rather talk to her maid as 'she has ideas anyway'.[13] Everyone seemed to be 'on the lookout for being neglected, or not given their place',[14] to the extent that even the theatrical rehearsals were marred by the 'great jealousy shown' because the Princess tried to help a fellow actress with her part.[15]

Observing the differences between England and North America, the novelist Henry James said there was no such thing as Society in America: 'It is an auxiliary – an accident – an occasional diversion', whereas in England, 'It is the business of life.'[16] This was certainly true of Ottawa which, unlike the older cities of Quebec and Montreal, had no resident aristocracy and, consequently, no Society. Canada, in the late eighteen seventies was still a frontier country. Former Premier Mackenzie was originally a stonemason, and one senator had been an axeman, living in a lumbering shanty on $12 a month.

Such men rarely had cultured wives but hoped to produce daughters in that mould. Lorne's sister, Lady Frances, found the women 'ignorant, commonplace to the last degree . . . but one does see in them the beginnings of something better than their mothers aspire to'.[17] She also complained that no woman ever mentioned politics or books. Lady Frances, already displaying matriarchal tendencies at the age of twenty-one, found it necessary to reprimand the pretty daughter of a distinguished judge: 'I could not have Billingsgate language in my presence.'[18]

The Lornes, nevertheless, followed the pattern of entertainment established by the Dufferins: in effect, open house for everyone who called at Rideau Hall and who could afford the clothes to attend viceregal functions. The visitor would be requested by a footman to inscribe his name in the visitors' book before retiring 'impressed by a subdued sense of awful – because unseen – grandeur'.[19]

Many of these names were sent invitations to the first state ball Princess Louise gave on February 19th. The Lornes received their guests in the ballroom. When Lord Dufferin had added on the ballroom to Rideau Hall, he had an area cordoned off with silken ropes to enclose the viceregal party when they danced the quadrille of honour. Princess Louise was dismayed at the idea of being segregated from her guests in such an obvious way; she ordered them to be taken away at once.

At midnight, Lorne's piper led the way to supper across the hall and into the red and white, striped, tent room, where shields bearing the arms of the various provinces were interspersed with ninety-four gas burners, blazing with light around the walls. Although the supper and dancing were a success, Princess Louise's first official ball was marred by various mishaps. A fire nearly broke out while she was at supper, caused by a half tipsy bandsman pulling a curtain over a gas lamp. Then some of the guests were obviously drunk. Neither Lorne nor the Princess were used to seeing their guests, six according to Lorne, literally carried out by footmen and put into sleighs.

Some guests complained about the status of others. One story, often recounted, told of the ambitious grocer who, after making a delivery, walked round to the front entrance and signed the visitors' book. A customer was horrified to be dancing in the same set with him at the ball: 'Why, that is our grocer!'[20] Such tales were not without foundation: 'an old lady was asked by 2 maidservants permission to go out on a certain evening and it was discovered that they were going to the ball'.[21]

The balance between stuffiness and informality proved hard to strike. In preparation for the first Drawing Room at Montreal, held shortly after their arrival there in November 1878, Colonel Littleton had issued orders that ladies should appear in low-cut, evening dresses, as they did in England on such occasions. Canadians did not wish to have to incur the extra expense of dress for them. The only drawback to Lorne's appointment had been the prospect of the establishment of a royal Court in Canada. When Colonel Littleton's instructions were made known, it seemed to ordinary Canadians as if their worst fears had been realized.

Papers representing the whole political spectrum in Canada reported that a terrible mistake had been made and 'it caused a great row'. Lorne was not unnaturally annoyed, since Littleton had purposely been left behind to guide and advise him about the customs of the country. He ensured that, in future, only 'Evening Dress' should be stipulated in the official announcement of evening receptions: 'and then let people come as they like,' he told Lord Lansdowne, 'I shdn't care if they came in blankets!'[22]

Despite the memory of this contretemps, Princess Louise always enjoyed herself in the more cultured atmosphere of Montreal. It was marvellous to be able to attend concerts and recitals again, and she tried to hear as many as possible during her short stays. The Lornes visited the city in May 1879 to open the new gallery of the Arts Association at Phillips Square. Founded in 1860 by a group of private citizens, this was the oldest arts association in Canada. The arts at that time played no part in Canadian life and there was little demand for pictures or beautiful buildings or appreciation of design in industrial arts and manufacturing. Princess Louise had recognized the need for action and urged Lorne to found a Royal Canadian Academy of Arts.

On opening the gallery, Lorne proposed the foundation of an Academy managed by artists, along the lines of the Royal Academy in London, which would develop all branches of Canadian art. His suggestion was well-received by his audience and by the Canadian press. Over the next two weeks, the Lornes composed a set of guidelines for such an organization and stressed the importance of exhibitions, prizes and designs for 'all sorts . . . of useful things, from wearing apparel and embroidery to . . . new stoves and implements'.[23]

The Princess's own artistic endeavours had been prodigious. She had invited her friends, Clara and Henrietta Montalba, to spend three months painting and sculpting with her in Canada. She used to pass many an hour sitting at an upstairs window with Clara Montalba to sketch what continues to be called 'the Princess's Vista',[24] a view of the Ottawa River. Reid, the carpenter, was asked to build her a sketching-box on wheels, which could be moved about the grounds.

One side of it was a sheet of glass so she and Clara Montalba could sit inside and sketch away, regardless of the weather. The Princess also painted on to the doors of her boudoir 'charmingly placed' boughs of crab apple trees in leaf, laden with fruit. One of these extremely pretty painted doors still survives at Rideau Hall, a record of her attempt to beautify the house. She also began working on two oil portraits, one of Clara as the Dark Lady, and one of Russell Stephenson.

On June 4th, the Lornes arrived in Quebec and lost their hearts to the old French city. Lorne described it as 'the most charming place in Canada',[25] while the Princess told Minnie Paget, 'I like Quebec very much, the country . . . is lovely.'[26] Following the precedent set by previous Governor-Generals, the Lornes made their summer home at the Citadel. Evelyn Moreton remembered 'What a great moment it was, when we first drove up through the tortuous road to the Chain Gate round hairpin bends, to the beautifully arched and tunnelled entrance.'[27] The Citadel stands in a barrack square, where a regimental band plays and sentries tramp and present arms, so that it is rather like a little Frenchified Windsor; it has all the charms of a fortress with the amenities of a country house.

The Lornes' first six months in Canada had been painful and exhausting. They looked forward eagerly to the arrival of some family, and three weeks salmon fishing. In June, the Duke of Argyll arrived with Lady Libby and Lady Mary. The party set off for the Metapedia River and arrived at the Indian House Pool, thirty miles from civilization, on June 19th, when the Princess landed her first salmon, a twenty-eight pounder, that afternoon. All the fishing was from canoes, as the Duke explained in a letter to Lady Frances: 'The bark canoes are delicious; you must sit quiet and they are poled or punted or paddled up the river by half breed Indians.'[28] He concluded that, given the women's success rate (for Princess Louise landed three salmon in one day), fishing in Canada required no skill.

A *Toronto Globe* reporter managed to track them down and reported that the Princess 'exhibited the same inimitable look of . . . fearless self-possession which she displayed on state occasions';[29] her impassive face was, no doubt, due to the presence of an obtrusive intruder.

'Here we are, some of us in tents, others in cabins on a barge . . . and all of us eaten up by three kinds of fly,' the Duke wrote home on June 22nd.[30] Yet even this could not detract from everyone's enjoyment of the beautiful rivers, the water clear as the purest crystal, with great pools half a mile long, and marvellous birds: 'I saw the great white-headed eagle catch a salmon and lift it clear out of the water,' exclaimed the Duke.[31] At night, when the canoes were drawn on to the ground and the tents were lit up by camp fires, it was difficult to remember that they were living in the nineteenth century. The Duke wrote of the Princess, 'She seems in good health and able to rough it – sleeping in tents and in barges where the changes [in temperature] are very trying.'[32] The newspaper reporters were most impressed by the Princess and commended her in print for 'roughing it in the bush'.[33]

On June 28th, the party broke up. The Argylls left for America and the Lornes for the Citadel, where they rested in preparation for their tour of the Maritime Provinces; the first stop was St John in New Brunswick, then south to Fredericton. It was an extremely tiring tour. To travel from Fredericton to Prince Edward Island, they had five hours up the river to St John where there was 'a duty drive' through the town, followed by a three and a half hour sail to Shadiac where an official reception awaited them; then an overnight crossing to Picton in Nova Scotia, where they passed the day. Another overnight sea journey finally brought them into the harbour of Prince Edward Island the next morning.

Everywhere there were Drawing Rooms and Levees to hold and Lorne had to reply to many addresses, but their reward was in their rapturous reception by enormous crowds. They were astonished to find so many Highlanders settled in this part of Canada, 'over 300,000 of them and there is often more Gaelic heard than English,' Lorne recorded in his Journal. They realized the extent of their popularity after learning that many 'came twenty-five or thirty miles at half a day's notice' in the middle of the harvest to see them.[34]

In September, the Princess and Lorne paid a long awaited first visit to Toronto. The 'Queen City of the West', as Toronto was then called, showed, even in 1879, its proximity to the United States in the lay-out of the streets to the American grid-plan. It possessed well-paved streets, excellent shops, fine public buildings, even a university, 'looking like Glasgow University though on a smaller scale and like it a tower unfinished for lack of funds'.[35] In short, it was a thriving, English, country town, designed by an American.

Unfortunately, Toronto was the home of the anti-Court spokesman, Goldwin Smith, an Oxford professor, who had settled in Canada. From Boston, where he had fled to avoid the visit of Princess Louise, he wrote: 'Toronto is just now in a paroxysm of vulgar flunkeyism. . . . We left all our neighbours (literally) practising presentation bows and curtsies for a monkeyish imitation of a "Drawing Room".' Respected as a professor, his message was assured of an airing in the North American press. He was opposed to Canada remaining dependent upon the mother country and thus to Lorne as Governor-General. The advent of the Princess he thought ridiculous and wrote, 'at the State Ball at Ottawa a number of people were drunk, including a Minister of State, a Chief Justice and a Bishop. Thus does Royalty refine and elevate Colonial Society!'[36] Such utterances were often reported in the anti-British New York press. It was apparent, however, to those who stayed to witness the visit of the Princess to Toronto that the Torontonians were overjoyed by her presence.

Ontario seemed to be populated exclusively by people from home. Visiting an institution in Toronto, Lorne found the Lady Director remembered his father and Aunt Dot as children; McKellar, the head ghillie at Inveraray, had a cousin who was High Sheriff of Hamilton, and Princess Louise met the grandson of Grant, the Balmoral game-keeper: 'At every turn one meets people from the old country who knew members of the families, and your arms are emblazoned in every street,' Lorne wrote to his father from Toronto.[37]

While Lorne was beginning to feel that Canada was, indeed, his second home, the Princess wanted to return to her real home for a holiday. 'So many of my friends and acquaintances have died since I left home! that it makes me often sad,' she told Minnie Paget, and she was anxious to see everyone again before some fresh tragedy occurred.[38] On October 6th, Lorne informed Lord Dufferin that 'The Princess goes to England, as all good Canadians do, and will be back for the opening of Parliament.'[39] Lorne had decided to stay in Canada for Christmas: 'I have been spending so much money that I mean to live economically here for the next few months,' he told Lord Archie on September 22nd.[40] In fact, he had already overspent his salary by £400, largely owing to the endless claims upon him and the Princess for subscriptions.

'We see in the papers that you are coming home for Christmas but *because* it is in the papers suppose it is not true,' Lady Mary teased Lorne.[41] The press had proved inaccurate yet again; Lorne remained behind to spend a second Christmas in Canada, when he entertained Sir John and Lady Macdonald. On a visit to England in September,

Sir John had stayed overnight at Hughenden. He gave Disraeli the impression that Lorne, 'though he tries hard', had not made the Canadians forget Lord Dufferin. However, it appeared that Lady Dufferin was considered 'reserved and dry', whereas Princess Louise was 'a great success in Canada, which was a toss-up; but she is extremely gracious, speaks to everybody and is interested in everything and skates divinely!'[42]

CHAPTER XVI

An Accident

The Princess passed her time at home with the family. The Christmas festivities were spent with the Queen at Osborne, followed by trips to Sandringham, Inveraray and Windsor. She used Buckingham Palace as a base and, to make up for what she had missed, she threw herself into the cultural life of London. Accompanied by Prince Leopold or Lord Ronnie, she went to exhibitions, theatres, concerts, operas and galleries. Shopping expeditions were mandatory, as she now knew what to buy for Canadian life and Lorne had also given her a long list.

On 3 February 1880, having donned her Canadian winter uniform of fur hat, silk jacket lined with fur and her 'cloud', the Princess, looking pale from seasickness, stepped ashore to resume her duties as 'Queen of Canada'. Without lingering in snowy Halifax, the Lornes boarded the train for Ottawa, stopping overnight in Montreal on their way through. The Princess was full of enthusiasm for the forthcoming art exhibition of the proposed new Canadian Academy. During her absence, both the Ontario and Montreal Art Societies had adopted Lorne's proposals as a preliminary constitution, so that plans were by now well-advanced for the opening of the Academy. The Princess was very pleased with the way in which Lorne had organized matters. Even the press had supported his proposals and the author of a hostile letter was 'nearly torn to pieces for his unpatriotic depreciation of talent and worth'.[1]

The first exhibition was planned for the middle of the month, in the rooms of the Old Clarendon Hotel, in Sussex Street. Since they needed many pictures to fill the exhibition, a large audience to view them and much financial support, the Lornes started lobbying everyone they knew. Even the most democratically-minded of Canadians found it impossible to refuse a royal appeal for support in building up an institution designed to discover local talent, and infuse energy into the artistic life of Canada.

Before going home for Christmas, Princess Louise had drawn up some designs for the decoration of the interior of the Houses of

Parliament which had been accepted by the Canadian Ministry of Works. Since the decorations remained unfinished, the Princess had to superintend the stencilling of her designs to ensure their completion by the opening of Parliament on the 12th. Her aim was to 'take off the bare cold look' of the interiors, which were in such contrast to the picturesque exterior of these fine buildings.[2]

The Princess welcomed such occupations since they helped to overcome her pangs of homesickness. To provide some variety at Rideau Hall, there were several new faces in the Household, as Lorne tried to change the staff annually. Apart from a music master and a new cook, Princess Louise had also brought out Captain Arthur Collins, brother of Prince Leopold's Governor, Robert Collins. As new ladies-in-waiting, two young widows, Mrs Eva Langham and Lady Lilian Pelly, had come to pass a year in Canada.

In a letter home, Eva Langham gave a description of her duties with HRH: 'I deliver messages of contrary descriptions, write to the Queen every week, pen other documents for HRH, talk to the bores, parliamentary and otherwise, sketch a little, stand about a good deal and make myself generally useful.'[3] She found Government House 'very comfortable' and English, with its bright, chintz-covered sofas and great open fireplaces. Other expatriate visitors agreed; an invitation to stay was much appreciated by the homesick British Embassy staff in Washington. One young attaché, Victor Drummond, told a colleague 'the life at Rideau Hall . . . is like the best kind of English country house'.[4]

There were some English visitors who, used to Court life at home, found the lack of ceremony strange and the Princess's position stranger still. Marie de Bunsen, accompanied her father on a visit: 'the Court struck me as odd,' she decided. Etiquette was kept to a minimum. All the honours were paid to Lorne, the Queen's representative, while the Princess, who was, after all, the Queen's daughter, 'played second fiddle on every occasion'. She not only rose with everyone else when Lorne came into a room and remained standing until he was seated, but also entered a room behind him.

Marie de Bunsen has left a description of the Lornes, as they appeared to her in February 1880. Lorne was the more straightforward of the two: 'A fair, cheery man, not a personality, but keen and with many interests.' The Princess was more difficult to fathom: 'tall and slight, a handsome figure in black velvet with diamonds and emeralds in the evening. She was clever and had artistic tastes, but was even shyer than most of the Queen's daughters and, although most likeable, without our Crown Princess's charm of manner.'[5]

The winter of 1880 had been an unusually treacherous one. On the evening of St Valentine's Day, three sleighs left the front entrance of Rideau Hall for the Houses of Parliament, where the Princess was to hold a Drawing Room. Princess Louise was seated in the last covered sleigh with Mrs Langham on her right, opposite Colonel McNeill and Lorne. Turning left into the main road, the horses took the corner too quickly, so that the sleigh skidded violently out to the right, over a bank of snow, and was turned over on to its right side. The coachman and footman were thrown out and the frightened horses bolted, dragging the overturned sleigh behind them.

The Princess was tossed head-first sideways against one of the iron bars supporting the roof; she was knocked unconscious for a second by the blow and her head slipped on to the ground. Mrs Langham, being on the right side to begin with, was dragged along with her body only partially protected from the ground by the leather roof. Remaining conscious throughout, she remembered for ever after 'that horrible night' with the 'horrid broken glass rushing past my face'.[6]

It was the Princess who saved her from much worse injury. 'If it had not been for Princess Louise's wonderful presence of mind my face must have been cut to ribbons,' she told her Aunt Cecy, 'but directly the sleigh overturned she seized me around the neck and held my head back' from the ground.[7] The Princess's body lay across Lorne, who was trapped underneath her, unable to move, expecting 'the sides of the carriage to give way every moment', which would have killed them.[8] Colonel McNeill was able to steady himself and push his left hand under the Princess's head, in order to support it. He could feel his hand and arm becoming damp and then wet, as they bumped along.

What was extraordinary about this scene was that it took place in complete silence. Not a sound escaped the lips of the four occupants as they rattled through the darkness. Gradually, the horses began to grow calmer and slacken their pace, as they overtook the sleigh ahead. One of the ADCs, Mr Bagot, jumped from his sleigh with a groom, and managed to run beside and clutch at the horses' heads. The alarm was raised at the lodge and an empty sleigh was sent to convey the injured back to Government House. On arrival there, Princess Louise and Mrs Langham were helped inside and supported as they slowly climbed the stairs to their bedrooms.

Dr Grant arrived shortly afterwards. He found that Princess Louise was severely concussed and in shock; it was judged 'a wonder that her skull was not fractured'.[9] If she had been hit directly, Dr Grant declared, she would have been lucky to remain alive. The dampness, Colonel McNeill had felt, was caused by Princess Louise's injured right ear, which bled so profusely that it saturated his whole sleeve. One of her earrings had caught in the side of the sleigh and, as her head was thrown forward, the earring was pulled out of her ear, tearing her lobe in two.

The Princess suffered the most serious injuries, although Mrs Langham's shoulder and side were badly bruised and her nerves remained fragile for some months after. Lorne had only a few bruises, whilst Colonel McNeill escaped injury entirely. Mr Bagot, who pulled up the horses, was hurt about his knees and legs. Writing about him five years later, Queen Victoria was much grieved 'to think he shd continue lame from the dreadful accident in Canada when he contributed to save dear Louise's life'.[10]

At nine o'clock next morning, a medical bulletin was issued: 'H.R.H. much recovered from shock. Ear slightly cut and the side of the head bruised. . . . H.R.H. passed a good night and at present is progressing most favourably.' Over the next four days, the twice daily bulletins stressed that her 'condition was much improved' and that she was recovering well.[11]

The wording of these bulletins reflected a deliberate policy to minimize the Princess's condition. Not only were the bulletins couched in over-confident terms, but the Canadian press was muzzled. News of the accident, nevertheless, spread quickly round Ottawa. Canadians naturally felt concern for the Princess and were anxious to learn about the extent of her injuries. However, Major de Winton not only refused to hold press conferences, he also refused to allow any overseas telegrams to be despatched without his permission.

With Government House under siege by press and well-wishers, the Major had panicked. It was claimed later that the press was gagged to ensure that Queen Victoria would not be alarmed by exaggerated reports. The Major's policy, though no doubt well intentioned, was 'stupid and ill advised'.[12] Knowledge of her true condition would have won her great sympathy from the Canadian people. As it was, most people believed the accident was trivial. 'Except the cut in the lower part of the ear I think there was no injury done worth mentioning,' wrote one MP.[13] When the Princess cancelled her engagements, they thought she was malingering. From this, rumours spread that she disliked Canada and its people and that she was unhappy there. The mistakes made by Major de Winton, and presumably sanctioned by Lorne, caused irreparable harm to the Princess's reputation in Canada.

Details of her injuries were also favourably coloured for Queen Victoria. In a letter to the Crown Princess, dated February 18th, she wrote that Princess Louise was 'going on quite well' and improving.[14] She was, nevertheless, annoyed with the Duke of Argyll's 'curious want of feeling and tact in making no enquiries after the Princess Louise after her recent accident'.[15] The apparent lack of concern from the Campbells was entirely owing to the sanguine reports in English newspapers. It was not until later that they learnt the truth: 'we were much shocked afterwards to find how serious it was,' Lady Mary lamented from Milan.[16]

The Senate and Commons of Canada were asked to delay sending the usual message of sympathy in case it might 'increase the general alarm'.[17] However, de Winton was unable to use similar tactics on Queen Victoria. In March, the Queen gave *The Times* a detailed account of the accident for publication. Unfortunately, this was too late for Canadians, whose concern had long since waned.

By March 11th, the Princess was still on the couch in her bedroom, and suffering from excruciating headaches, shattered nerves and insomnia. As a special treat on her thirty-second birthday, she came downstairs and went out for a short walk in the grounds. Lorne noted that 'Any fatigue, and almost anything gives her fatigue, brings on much pain in the injured side of her head' and also noticed that, when tired, she became rather deaf.[18] It would have been easy to slide into confirmed invalidism, as many Victorian women did; the Princess, however, was determined to try to lead a normal life again.

She had been extremely disappointed to miss the opening of the Canadian Academy. From her couch, she insisted that Lorne bring up nearly every one of the large collection of pictures so that she could see them. Lorne gave her an account of the opening ceremony on his return. $500 was taken at the doors, and subscriptions, including a substantial donation from themselves, came to $2,000. The Princess was pleased to hear that some of the money was going to be used to start an Ottawa art school.

One visitor she had especially looked forward to seeing, but whose visit was marred by her accident, was Arthur Sullivan, then touring America with *Pirates of Penzance*. He had arrived at Rideau Hall on February 24th, and was soon busy with the music for a 'Dominion Hymn', written by Lorne as a proposed national anthem for Canada. Lorne described it as 'a rumtidum, glory and gunpowder affair' but it never caught on.[19]

Unfortunately, the more the Princess began to do, the more tired and the more depressed she became. At the end of April, in order to reassure an anxious Mrs Thurston, she wrote, 'I am all right again now, but do not feel strong.' The truth was that the smallest thing tired her and she was plagued by insomnia. Nevertheless, she continued to hope that 'when I get away from this the 2nd week in May, I daresay I shall get myself again.'[20]

Used to being active and keeping engagements, the Princess was trying to do too much too soon. By the middle of May, she was exhausted. Increasingly aware of her precarious health, Lorne and the Household hoped that a change of air and the arrival of Prince Leopold would boost her morale and help her recovery.

It may seem strange, in view of her feeble condition that, three days after Prince Leopold's arrival, the pair of them should set off on a tour of the United States. However, it was only after a long battle that Queen Victoria had reluctantly given way to Prince Leopold's wish to visit his sister in Canada. The Prince longed to escape the restrictions of life at home and to find adventure. Since his frail health might prevent him from undertaking such a journey again, the Princess could not bring herself to disappoint him because of her own ill-health.

Thus it was that they took leave of Lorne, who was going fishing with the newly arrived Lord Archie, and boarded the train for Toronto. Robert Collins was distressed to find how changed Princess Louise was. 'She has not wholly recovered from her accident,' he wrote to Frederick Myers, 'and is unstrung and restless at times, but as happy probably as her nature will ever allow her to be.' He hoped that his brother's cheerful character might 'even improve her view of life'.[21]

Quite unexpectedly, the Princess took Prince Leopold along to the Toronto General Hospital to visit the patients. After a tour of all the wards, which took a long time since the Princess insisted upon speaking to every patient and chatting at length with those she recognized from two previous visits, the royal pair were escorted round the new Eye and Ear Infirmary. Such visits did much to enhance the Princess's popularity.

After seeing Niagara Falls, the party travelled on to Chicago. If asked during that day what she thought of Chicago, the Princess would have found it difficult to reply; from half past eight that morning until a quarter to three in the afternoon, she rested in her hotel room after the tiring journey. Her brother, however, made the most of his short spell in Chicago; nothing could contain his exuberance as he visited the Republican Party Convention, currently in session, where he learnt from *The Times* correspondent of the death of the Empress of Russia, and sat scribbling telegrams of condolence while surrounded by a gesticulating, yelling mass of politicians and delegates.

Since accommodation was at a premium owing to the Convention, the royal party had to stay elsewhere. Chicago, to which they returned on Sunday June 6th, was, at that time, the boom town of America. By 1882, over 400,000 people lived in the city and its suburbs. People would often come to Chicago simply to stand and marvel at the great bustling city, which had come to symbolize the growth and progress of America. As one English tourist remarked, 'America is energetic, but Chicago is in a fever.'[22]

The Princess was staying in the Palmer House, Chicago's most palatial hotel. It was immense, with seven hundred rooms; she was told proudly that it had cost £450,000 to build and £100,000 to furnish. To a princess brought up in real palaces, the surroundings were not as impressive as they would be to everyone else. What did impress her was that the daily board cost only twelve shillings, while a meal of many courses could be had in the fine restaurant for forty cents.

Two days were given up to sightseeing. The Princess was surprised to find miles of broad carriage drives, bordered by trees, in the South Park and along the boulevards; the Mayor was pleased when she told him it reminded her of Paris. She also made the six-mile journey to see the famous Chicago Stock Yards, where everything was done by machinery, except for the herding of the cattle. The Princess was fascinated by the Mexicans and cowboys on high peaked saddles, with pistols in their holsters, high jack boots, knives in their belts and rifles slung on their backs, dashing down the crowded streets at full gallop.

The people and press of Chicago were surprised by the normality of their visitors and nonplussed by a princess who dressed 'neatly and stylishly in plain colours' and was 'rather pretty' and 'quite girlish in her actions'. Prince Leopold was even more of a disappointment; 'he is as far removed as possible from what is known as the English snob or "cad". He is not even a Swell,' complained the *Chicago Tribune*.[23]

The Household considered the American press coverage distasteful in its familiarity. On June 10th, Lorne wrote to his father, 'L and party return tomorrow. . . The vulgarity of the Yankee papers about them surpasses belief.'[24] Yet Princess Louise found the reportage highly amusing, and even sent an article headed 'Vic's Chics' home to Queen Victoria, who was riveted by her children's escapades in the States, and pleased by their reception.[25] The Queen would not allow any disparagement of Americans. It was, after all, only Queen Victoria's grandfather who had 'lost' America, so that she always thought of it as being almost British and, hence, worthy of respect.

The Princess and Prince Leopold rejoined Lorne and Lord Archie at Quebec, on June 11th. Although pale with fatigue, the Princess thought the trip well worthwhile. 'Prince Leopold,' she wrote to Minnie Paget, 'has really enjoyed himself, everything being new to him.'[26] From Quebec, they all travelled northeast for some salmon fishing. The year before, Lorne had purchased the rights to thirty miles 'of the best salmon river in the country',[27] and had brought the materials all the way from Quebec to build a log cabin, Cascapedia Cottage, in the wilderness for his wife. She was delighted with her new toy house and its situation. Surrounded by firs, birch and maple trees, with the scent of pines in the air, beside the river, which coursed over rocks to form miniature waterfalls, it was idyllic and completely isolated.

However, Lord Archie spoke for all of them when he broke out into disjointed plaints of, 'oh dear, lovely, most lovely – but, dear me – *quelle profonde misère*! Delicious wilderness, but quite savage – bears making dung almost over one's breakfast-cloth, and ants as big as the knife handles.'[28] The worst of Cascapedia was the ubiquitous insects.

When Princess Louise rose between four and five o'clock in the morning and when she went out again in the evening to fish or sketch, she donned a defensive armour over her clothes. She attached a gauze veil to her straw hat and secured it with elastic around her neck. Long, holland gauntlets had been sewn on to her gloves, which she now fastened above her elbows with elastic. Gaiters had to be fitted over her boots and leggings worn to protect her legs underneath her long skirts. In addition, she had to rub black tar oil over her face and neck to repel the sandflies. As one of her ladies asked, 'who would recognise the graceful form and lily complexion of . . . [a] fair English damsel in the flannel clad figure swathed in holland and gauze with a face apparently smeared over with treacle!'[29]

'We are catching v. fine salmon. . . The River is lovely, almost beyond belief,' Lorne wrote to Lord Granville from Cascapedia on July 2nd, 'and were it not that the Princess is not feeling strong, and that the flies are odious, our happiness would be perfect.'[30] Having struggled gamely to keep going for the last three months, the Princess was defeated by a combination of exhaustion and pain. Lorne had realized as long ago as March that there would be 'nothing for it but long periods of rest and quiet in England' to restore her health.[31]

The party were already deeply concerned about her condition, when Prince Leopold fell over while fishing a salmon. 'Poor Uncle Leopold was imprudent and overdid it fishing and had both legs bad!' Queen Victoria told a granddaughter.[32] Dr Sewell had to be summoned urgently to attend the Prince, and it was decided to return to Quebec. The obvious solution was for Prince Leopold to accompany the Princess back to Britain. The announcement of her departure was made public on July 18th. Lorne expected that his wife's state of health would be misunderstood, for 'she looks so well, and is so vivacious in talk that no one will believe she suffers'.[33] His prophecy proved all too true; in the months that followed her departure, she became the victim of much unsubstantiated innuendo.

CHAPTER XVII

Halfway between Heaven
and Balmoral

On a January day in 1881, those Canadians who read their newspapers learnt that their Vicereine, or 'Vice Queen' as one Canadian newspaper had unfortunately christened her, would return to Canada in May. Princess Louise had been convalescent in England since October, yet Canadians had not been allowed to forget her, for innumerable reports were published about her every month. Yet no official statement had been made by Government House; nor any refutation of some of the rumours about the Princess which circulated during the Canadian Season.

Those who had returned recently from Europe, brought the news that she was still unwell in spite of having taken a long cure in Germany. Courtiers, who had seen the Princess over Christmas, described her and Prince Leopold as 'both looking very ill'.[1] At Windsor, on December 15th, Lucy Cavendish spoke to Princess Beatrice, who 'gave rather a dismal account of poor Princess Louise, who has never recovered from her ghastly sleigh-accident'.[2]

Little of this percolated through to the Canadian public. Instead, they were fed a diet of scandal: the Princess had quarrelled with Lorne; she hated Canadians; she had left Canada in defiance of Queen Victoria's wishes. Yet Lorne did not think that she was ready to return for she 'always *looks* well, but still suffers from headache and sleeplessness and is very thin. I am advising extract of malt and iron.'[3] He believed that the Princess would grow weaker in the wintery weather and, more importantly, her safety would be threatened if she returned to Canada. Not only were reports of Fenian disturbances being received, but also threats that 20,000 Fenians were coming to kidnap him as a hostage until their leader, Davitt, was released by the authorities in London.

May passed without her arrival. Although she wanted to return to Canada to undertake a viceregal tour of Manitoba, Lorne was convinced that such an arduous expedition in the heat of the summer would be 'too fatiguing'. 'Flies, heat, dust and long drives across the prairie would knock her up.'[4] The issue of the Princess's return was so mishandled that, even after her doctors, Sir William Jenner and Dr Weber, let it be known that they did not consider her equal to the rigours of the journey and wanted her to remain in the more moderate English climate, the public continued to think that the Princess was malingering. Although Lorne talked to friends about the Princess's health, they thought he was being loyal to an errant wife. Rumours even spread that Lorne was resigning his position and that Princess Louise would *never* return. From London, the Princess firmly scotched this idea. When Lord Ronnie Gower called on her she told him there was 'no truth in the reports' they were 'giving up Canada'.[5] Princess Louise now hoped to join Lorne in August.

However, this tour was extended to include the remote North West Territories up to the edge of the Rocky Mountains; Lorne would be the first Governor-General to visit 'this wild and woolly West'. He wrote to Sir Edward Thornton on May 17th: 'I shall be in the North West all the autumn, but fear from what the Doctors say that I can't allow the Princess to have her wish in accompanying me, the journey being necessarily a very fatiguing one.'[6]

This it certainly proved to be. Leaving Ottawa on July 13th, Lorne and his party, which included reporters from British newspapers, did not reach Winnipeg until August 1st and this was the easiest stage of their journey, in the days before the Canadian Pacific Railway. Crossing the prairies by waggon and fording the rivers by raft, the party pitched camp 350 miles from Winnipeg at Hudson Bay Fort on August 11th for a great Indian pow wow with Chief Sitting Bull of the Sioux tribe, who had fled over the border after Custer's last stand at the Battle of Wounded Knee. It was here that Lorne saw an Indian who resembled Mr Gladstone. As he told Princess Louise: 'On inquiring we found that the name of this Chief was Way-wa-sa-ka-po, or "the man who is always right"!'[7]

A trading post, which had become the capital of the province of Saskatchewan in view of its proximity to the planned Canadian Pacific Railway, was called Pile O' Bones. Here the quantities of bleached bones, skulls and skeletons of the buffalo, which lay thickly over the surrounding prairie, had been gathered into heaps in order to be able to lay the railway line. Since the name 'Pile O' Bones' was not considered suitable for the capital of Western Government, Sir John Macdonald had asked the Princess for a new name. As 'Victoria' was already in use in British Columbia, the Princess suggested the latin word for queen: 'Regina'.

On this landmark tour, Lorne was travelling through territory which bore no name and did not appear on maps. It had been Lorne's idea to name the unknown province beyond Saskatchewan after the Princess. The existence of Louisiana ruled out Louiseland, while Lu-lu-land was too childish; so the Princess's second name, Alberta, was chosen. The capital, Calgary, had even less to offer weary travellers than Pile O' Bones. It was then literally only a name, without people or settlement.

On returning to Ottawa after an extremely successful Western tour, the first ever made by a Governor-General, Lorne learnt that the Queen was anxious for Princess Louise not to spend the winter in Canada. Apart for over a year, the couple were naturally anxious to see each other; therefore, it was decided that Lorne would travel home for Christmas. At last, Lorne publicly responded to the critics and used the occasion of his leave-taking, on November 7th, to refer to the recent campaign against the Princess by *Truth* newspaper: 'She will, I know, also share my contempt for the awkward attempt made by some . . . to turn her shattered health into a weapon against your invincible loyalty,' he said.[8]

Once in England, Lorne saw for himself that the Princess was still in 'very weak health'.[9] The doctors believed that the accident had brought on attacks similar to the meningitic complications from which she had suffered as a girl; the same symptoms of severe headaches, neuralgia, vomiting and insomnia were present. Yet none of this was publicized, and even some of the Argylls found it difficult to believe the Princess could still be unwell.

When, in January 1882, Lorne sailed from Liverpool without the Princess, gossip was rife. Sir Henry Ponsonby passed the gist of it on to his wife. Lorne would not force Princess Louise to return because 'he is apparently happy without her'.[10] Lorne, however, told Aunt Dot that Louise was 'still very weak and good for nothing', and that he was not prepared to subject her to the rigours of a Canadian winter.[11] It would make a much worse impression if she returned to Ottawa, but was unable to undertake any duties.

By March, the Princess was feeling stronger and the headaches were fewer; she hoped for a clean bill of health from the doctors. As of old, Jenner was cautious and refused to commit himself. The Princess grew impatient over his 'shilly-shallying' and, as she told Lord Ronnie on March 11th, 'resolved to return to Canada whether the doctors permit it or not!'[12] She would have booked her passage on the next sailing but for Prince Leopold's marriage to Princess Helen of Waldeck on April 29th at St George's Chapel. His wedding was full of poignant moments for Princess Louise; watching him limp down the aisle, it seemed extraordinary that this beloved invalid brother, upon whom she had lavished an almost maternal affection, should have a wife on his arm.

Free to rejoin Lorne, the Princess caught the next boat, which sailed on May 25th. She left behind a worried Queen Victoria. The last few months had seen increased violence in Britain and the Queen was much concerned for her daughter's safety. On May 6th, the Irish Secretary, Lord Frederick Cavendish, was murdered with his Under-Secretary in Dublin's Phoenix Park by Fenian terrorists. The Queen became nervous about the close proximity of New York, the headquarters of American Fenianism, to Princess Louise in Canada and instructions were issued that every precaution be taken for HRH's safety.

None of this impinged upon the Princess's enjoyment of her first three weeks in Quebec, where she landed on June 5th. She rode out on her pony with Lorne every morning and together they made expeditions to the Montmorency Falls or to Tadoussec. The Princess had brought out a copy of the spring issue of *Good Words*, which contained an article on Quebec with pictures by her and verse by Lorne. Although Lorne described it as 'our gushing' on 'my blessed Canada', Princess Louise had sent a copy of his verse to the poet, Frederick Locker-Lampson, whose favourable opinion naturally pleased Lorne.[13]

They were also occupied with Lorne's 'other Canadian child', the Royal Society for Literature and Science. During his summer tour, Lorne had come across an expedition from the Smithsonian Museum in Washington, who were collecting Indian relics on Canadian soil. In order to stop such American plundering, Lorne enlisted the support of McGill University to found an institution to bring together learned men in Canada and publish their works. After preliminary discussions, it was agreed that the Governor-General should nominate the first members, including a fair proportion of French-Canadians. However, the publication of Lorne's list created a furore. While the French-

Canadians were in favour of the Royal Society, English-speaking Canada was opposed to it.

That persistent critic, Goldwin Smith, believed there was a strong feeling against 'anything savouring of exclusiveness or artificial distinction', and the *Toronto Globe* referred to the new institution as 'a mutual admiration society of nincompoops'.[14] Lorne judged the situation perfectly. He ensured meetings went ahead as planned to organize the Society regardless of the critics. For the first time in Canada's history, its notable scholars came together in a body, which went on to become an established institution.

As the Season drew to a close, Quebec began to empty for the summer and the Princess and Lorne planned to go to Cascapedia Cottage for ten days' fishing. On June 22nd, Lorne received a telegram in code from the Home Office in London, which warned of a plot to abduct Princess Louise. 'I have received . . . a nasty Fenian warning of an attempt against the Princess, and must take precautions as the devils are mad enough to try anything,' Lorne hastily informed Sir John Macdonald, before leaving for Cascapedia.[15] The Princess refused to take seriously such threats. Sir John Macdonald, however, acted immediately to place security forces on the alert and sent the *Druid* to the Bay de Chaleurs.

Confirmation of the plot to abduct the Princess was not received until July 12th. It came through the British Consul at Philadelphia, who had an informant in the Fenian camp in New York. He reported that at a meeting on July 5th, a man code-named the 'Canadian quail' had boasted of how he had sent explosives to Canada without detection; apparently, men were ready to seize the Princess on her fishing expedition and hold her hostage on the Grand Island, Lake Edward. According to the informant, a definite timetable had yet to be made.[16]

Despite the threat of kidnap, Princess Louise enjoyed the fishing. The only reference to the Fenians occurred when the Princess insisted the Queen should not be told about the threats in order to spare her worry. Lorne was inclined to agree with the Princess and ignore the Fenians. However, their imminent tour to British Columbia by way of the United States raised the problem of safety and Sir John advised Lorne to postpone the journey. Lorne sent Major de Winton to Washington to discuss it with General Sherman, an Argyll family friend. The General offered a military officer as ADC and the Foreign Office provided two detectives to accompany the party through

America. 'Although I do not believe much myself in the rumour being more than bluster,' Lorne told Sir John on August 13th, 'yet after my cousin's cruel murder in Phoenix Park, it is evident our friends will stop at nothing.'[17] Nor could Princess Louise forget how Prince Alfred had been shot in the back by a Fenian in Australia; it was said he was saved by his braces. Reassured by the presence of specially trained security men, the Lornes set off on their West Coast journey on 1 September 1882.

They were not visiting America for a holiday. In the days before the Canadian Pacific Railway, the route from the east to the far west of Canada was by train to Niagara, southwest to San Francisco and by boat up the Pacific Ocean to Vancouver. Thus, Princess Louise's home for the next seven days was a pullman car. She slept in a small, square cabin called a 'drawing room', which communicated with another used by her two new ladies-in-waiting. The Princess had asked Aunt Dot's niece, Miss Ina McNeill, out to Canada to help her to recover after the death of her fiancé, who had died on the day they were to be married. She was judged 'nice but very sad, quiet and depressing'.[18] Her other lady, Miss Augusta Hervey, was much more lively and an accomplished pianist. According to Gwen Stephenson, she was 'a giggling young old lady, who shaves daily' and has 'a marked blue line'.[19]

They all entered into the novelty of boiling kettles on a copy of Queen Victoria's tea-burner, just as Princess Louise used to do when out in the glens at Balmoral. They preferred to have tea and breakfast in this style, but lunched and dined at the 'eating stations', there being no 'hotel car', as a dining car was then called. Otherwise the Princess sat and read, wrote letters, chatted the time away or walked to the observation car. In the early evening, they played whist or other games and usually turned in early. On September 7th, she watched the train cross the grand Mississippi River and head due west across the middle of America, crossing the Missouri River at Omaha. Steaming slowly 'at an easy sort of jog-trot', the train passed alongside the Platte River, which was the old emigrant trail west through Indian country. On the third day, after dining at Grand Island, where the ice cream was judged better than at Gunters in Berkeley Square, the party turned in for the night. The train began its long, slow ascent of the Rockies and entered territory typical of the Wild West.

The Princess rose early the next morning in order to see Julesburgh, the first ghost town visible from the train. Formerly a railway terminus with 4,000 inhabitants, it was now almost deserted except for the odd, wild dog. Yet its name lived on as 'the wickedest town' in America, where gambling and whoring were universal occupations and 'a day seldom passed but what they had a man for breakfast'.[20]

The great Indian Wars had occurred only five years before and Chiefs, like Sitting Bull, were still attacking 'the White man'. As Princess Louise's party traversed the Indian heartland, still considered extremely dangerous by the rest of America, the fears of Lorne and the Canadian Government about Fenian attacks appeared rather ridiculous. The detectives sent by the Foreign Office could provide little defence against an attack by hostile Indians with tomahawks. It was an extraordinary journey for a British princess to be undertaking.

The train crossed the snow capped Rocky Mountains to reach Sherman, which, at 8,263 feet above sea level, was at a greater altitude than any other railway station in the world, before descending to Evanston in Wyoming, the halfway mark of their journey, on the fifth day. Here the Princess saw her first Chinaman. It was at a point nearby, in the desolate Utah landscape, that two locomotives from opposite directions had met in 1869 to link up the Central Pacific and Union Pacific Railroads which bridged the United States. As the Chinese workmen were about to put the last piece of rail in place, the photographer had shouted to his assistant: 'Shoot!' and, used to hearing such commands from cowboys, the Chinese had dropped the rail and fled.[21]

From Evanston they travelled through the magnificent scenery of the canyons, whose red stone was 'twisted and tilted . . . into every sort of strange form', before reaching Ogden, a town in Mormon country.[22] One of the chief tourist attractions was the house of a Mormon Bishop, famous for his eight wives and forty children. They were also interested in the system of timekeeping at Ogden, which had no time of its own but kept eastern time for trains going East and western time for trains going West. Ever since he had met the Canadian engineer, Sanford Fleming, Lorne had become an enthusiastic and influential advocate of Fleming's 'cosmic day' system, by which the adoption of a common meridian and the division of the world into twenty-four time zones would regularize the measurement of time around the world. The acceptance of this system in Europe was largely due to Lorne's efforts, as he promoted the scheme to all the European Royal Societies.

The Princess woke early on the morning of September 13th to find herself in California with the most hair-raising part of the journey still ahead. Just before reaching the town of Colfax, the train rounded the precipice of Cape Horn, where Princess Louise could look straight down into the valley far below with nothing to protect the train from falling off the line into it. Although the railway line from Colfax to Sacramento is a miracle of engineering, since it descends seventy-five miles in six thousand feet and is carried along the edge of precipices and through steep perpendicular rocks, Princess Louise had every right to be nervous as they crossed the swaying skeleton bridges, which were built without the protection of barriers and did not seem capable of bearing the weight of the train.

At six o'clock that morning outside Oakland, a *Chronicle* reporter from San Francisco had just boarded the train and was talking to Major de Winton when, with a crash of crockery and glassware and the sharp crackle of splintering wood, the two men found themselves catapulted through the air. After a great lurch and a few screams, all was quiet. The train had collided with a freight train; the engine was left completely wrecked and the cowcatcher and brass buffers were demolished.

Fortunately, the injuries sustained by the viceregal party were slight, with the exception of the Princess who, standing in front of her dressing table when the accident happened, had been thrown against it and had received a severe bruise to her left shoulder and a cut over her eye. After an hour's delay, the train set off for San Francisco. Despite the shock and injuries, the Princess had to carry on.

The Lornes were received at Oakland station by the British Consul and General McDowell, who commanded the Federal Armies during the Civil War. Although battered, the Princess managed to look respectable in a striped, black and grey, silk dress 'of no very recent fashion' and a dark, straw hat bound with a red ribbon.[23] A crowded ferry boat took her and Lorne across the Bay. A southern, pink haze veiled the surrounding dry, bare hills, the islands and the wide sweep of the bay.

On landing at San Francisco the Lornes were driven to the Palace Hotel, where a crowd of several hundred people had waited two hours to greet the first princess ever to visit California. It was built around a vast courtyard into which guests, wandering along the corridors above, could look down and watch the carriages drive up to deposit passengers. When Princess Louise arrived the courtyard was bedecked with flags while some of the one thousand people staying there cheered and waved at her.

The highlight of the Princess's stay in San Francisco was her visit to Chinatown and the Chinese Theatre that evening. The party were seated in a gallery box overlooking a pit full of Chinamen and a stage bare of wings and scenery. Since the play was unintelligible, the interest was in watching the spectacle provided by the costumes: gold and embroidered satins, brightly coloured head dresses, and enormous drooping feathers, which were twirled as if they were moustaches. Since Chinese plays could last for up to six hours without an interval, and the audience came and went as they pleased, the viceregal party did not stay until the end but went on to a Chinese restaurant illuminated by coloured lanterns. Upstairs they found music and gambling and saw opium pipes everywhere. Although there was a Chinese community in London full of opium dens, thought to be centres of vice, they were quite beyond the Princess's ken. Yet, here in San Francisco, the Princess could go where she could not at home.

From here the party were driven to the Temple of Yung Wo on Brooklyn Place where a service had begun in honour of one of the Chinese gods. The Princess 'viewed the oriental scene with wonder and asked numerous questions' about the service and the gods.[24] It was the nearest she ever came to the wonders of the Orient.

After four days in San Francisco, the Lornes were due to travel to Canada on board H.M.S. *Comus* at half past eleven on the morning of September 16th. An hour before embarkation, the Captain received an anonymous threat that the ship would be blown up by a torpedo as soon as the Lornes stepped on board. The distressed Captain appealed for help and a squad of marines arrived to make a thorough search of the *Comus*; soon afterwards the viceregal party arrived at the dockside. After several minutes of consultation between Lorne and the Captain, the party boarded the *Comus*, which weighed anchor at noon. However, a second ship followed the *Comus* for some distance out to sea to ensure her safety.

In the early evening of September 19th, the *Comus* sailed into Esquimault harbour in British Columbia. It had been a rough passage and the Princess, as always, had suffered but, as she told the Captain, 'there is only one remedy, and that is to stay at home and then I should see nothing'.[25]

Pre-railway British Columbia was a land of primeval forest, deep canyons and fjords where elk, bear and beaver were familiar sights within a mile of Victoria or Vancouver; a land where villages still contained Indian tepees, whose smoke curled up into the air over the banks of unexplored rivers; yet also a land where the sweep of the blue Pacific Ocean, across which many Chinese had sailed to find new homes, links the occident with the orient.

The many different people of this land gave the Princess a tumultuous welcome. As she entered the Governor's home, Cary's Castle, the royal standard floated proudly over Government House in Victoria for the first time in its history. Despite the pioneering atmosphere of Victoria, entertainments given by the Lornes were of the formal kind. On the Monday following their arrival, the Princess held a Drawing Room in the Parliament Buildings, which went off extremely well. In a black and white silk and appliqué lace dress, her diamonds, and her hair gathered into a simple knot and decorated with roses from the garden, she 'looked very beautiful' to the two hundred settlers who passed before her.

Since the gardens were still full of flowers, the Princess decided to hold an open house garden party at Government House on September 26th. A reporter from the *Colonist* decided that 'The Governor-General and Princess Louise are winning all hearts by their affability and kindness.'[26] The Princess told Mrs Cornwall that she felt as if she was in England; certainly she led an intensely English way of life in Victoria. She gave a series of small dinner parties; she walked into town every day and strolled about undisturbed; she visited the hospitals and schools and attended flower shows and charity bazaars; and she sketched as much as possible.

Yet, despite an upper stratum of 'intensely British Englishmen', as Lorne described them, the anglicized way of life was surprising, given the extraordinarily mixed set of people who inhabited the province, which was still, in reality, frontier country. The Hudson Bay Company's trading posts remained the centres of civilization for many who regarded a visit to Victoria as a rare and exciting pleasure. The fur traders, the lonely pioneers, the gold-diggers, the half-civilized trappers and the half-breeds who journeyed into Victoria swelled the resident population of Indians, Chinese, and White settlers to form an exotic society very different from any the Princess had known elsewhere in Canada.

Nevertheless, she felt at ease in Victoria, with its simplicity of life and lack of pretension. Moreover, the people were not over-sensitive as they were in Ottawa; she could enjoy the novelty of British Columbian society without having to guard against making a spontaneous remark to one person and not to another. When the Colonial Secretary visited the Queen at Osborne, she told him that Princess Louise 'was delighted with British Columbia'.[27] It reminded her of an exotic Scotland; indeed, she described her three months there as 'halfway between Heaven and Balmoral'.[28]

Lorne was working hard to prevent the province from carrying out its threat to leave the Dominion. British Columbia had only joined Canada on condition that a transcontinental railway would be built by 1881. Unfortunately, political intrigue and corruption had delayed its construction. When Lord Dufferin had visited Victoria in 1876, secessionist feeling ran high and he had failed to get the railway completed. However, Lorne succeeded. He encouraged Sir John's measure to award higher grants to a new consortium; through his friendship with three eminent Scotsmen – Lord Strathcona, Lord Mount Stephen and Mr Angus – the finance was raised. An agreement was drawn up, and the Canadian Pacific Railway would be completed ahead of schedule in November 1886.

Lorne's policy of visiting as much of Canada as possible was followed in British Columbia. On September 28th, he and the Princess sailed over to New Westminster on the mainland, where they landed to the cheers of thousands of people, including three thousand peaceful Indians, who had come many hundreds of miles to welcome the daughter of their Great Mother, the White Queen. As they came out into Bishop Stillitoe's colonial gardens, full of rambling English roses, about forty chiefs dressed in brightly coloured dresses and blankets, their banners fluttering in the breeze, greeted them. Each Chief was presented, his hand shaken, and several speeches were made, after which the wife of the Chief of the Seebeldts presented Princess Louise with baskets, a silver ring and a bracelet as a token of good will. The woman was overcome when both the Princess and Lorne shook her hand; a courtesy rarely shown towards the Indians by White people.

Having lingered in Victoria far longer than their original intention, the Lornes finally left for San Francisco on December 7th. The Princess had become so popular and beloved in Victoria that Premier Beaver is said to have suggested that British Columbia should secede from the Dominion, and become a separate kingdom with Princess Louise as its Queen. 'By numerous little acts of thoughtful kindness, by an invariable graciousness of manner added to her exalted position, she won all hearts in this colony and in so doing, has added to that loyal feeling to the Imperial Government of Her Majesty, another powerful link,' ran one editorial in a Victoria newspaper.[29] Indeed, the Princess had admirably performed the role which Prince Albert had envisaged for his children; she had successfully served the crown in the colonies.

CHAPTER XVIII

Far Afield

'It is a great change,' Lorne wrote, 'to come as we have done, in sixty two hours' from the glorious autumnal russets and dampness of British Columbia 'to the South-of-Spain-like atmosphere and dryness of San Francisco.'[1] Since the Princess always preferred a sunny climate, she was quite content, but Lorne complained of the heat and longed for the cool, damp air they had left behind; Princess Louise merely put this down to his preference for everything Canadian. At the Palace Hotel, the red-coated marines on duty outside her apartments were made miserable by the constant enquiries about 'the Princess' or 'the Marqiss' from curious guests. Replies about 'His Hexellency' were patiently received by the ladies, who really hoped to catch sight of the Princess. To one insistent enquirer, a marine explained, 'They hare hall in the bawth, you know, mum.'[2]

Since the Lornes did not have to return to Canada until the opening of Parliament in February, they decided to linger in California. Two American friends, Minnie Paget and Lady Randolph Churchill, had recommended a place south of San Francisco called Monterey. When the Lornes arrived there, on 15th December 1882, they were not disappointed. The Del Monte Hotel was surrounded by beautiful, tropical gardens, which overlooked the Pacific Ocean. The magnificent cedars and cypress groves were separated from the beach by a luscious terrace of green turf. Gathering up her skirts, the Princess joined Lorne in exploring the coves where they found shells, previously known only from collectors' cabinets. The 'wonderful colours of prismatic mother-of-pearl shone at every yard', while in every rocky pool, the Princess found pieces of red coral.[3]

From Monterey they went to Los Angeles which, in the eighteen eighties, was famous as a health resort and for wine and oranges. Princess Louise was taken to a vineyard, something she had never done in France or Italy, and tasted a wine called 'El Dorado'. Walking through Los Angeles was rather like strolling through the grounds of a tropical country estate. Every street was bordered by red-berried, pepper trees, castor bean plants, and big bushes with crimson flowers which straggled along the ground. However, their stay was short since they sailed to the tiny village of Santa Barbara on Christmas Eve.

Although far from home, they found congenial company in Judge Fernald, the Mayor of Santa Barbara, and General Dibblee, whose daughters associated the coming of the Princess on Christmas Eve with fairy tales. They pestered their governess to allow them to talk to 'a real live princess'. Their wish came true when the Princess visited their parents; far from finding her a 'magical' Princess, they came away disappointed: she was 'only a sweet lady after all'.[4] The Franciscan priests, however, found the Princess so unlike other ladies that they broke with tradition and allowed her to become the first woman ever to enter their Sacred Garden, behind the monastery walls of what is now the Old Mission building in Santa Barbara.

The original plan had been for Lorne to accompany Princess Louise to Charleston, in South Carolina, where she would pass the winter in a warmer climate than Canada. But the Princess preferred to pass the next few months on British soil where she could be of some use, rather than remain on as a tourist in America. She chose Bermuda.

Furthermore, Lorne had been informed of new Fenian threats on the Princess's life. It would be more difficult to protect the Princess in Charleston, on the American mainland, than in Bermuda, a British island. Although he would have to send two detectives to guard her, he could 'feel quite free of anxiety about L there as no one can move on the islands without being watched'.[5]

Yet, in order to be out of reach of Fenians, Princess Louise had to travel through the most dangerous part of the American Wild West, ruled by Mexican bandits and Indians. Several trains on the route across the 'cowboy haunted' plains of Arizona and New Mexico had recently been stopped and robbed by desperadoes. Afraid that the presence of royalty on one of these trains might attract unwelcome attention, General Schofield, commanding the United States Western Army, provided them with an escort of troops.

As Princess Louise looked out of the train window on to the 'most awful desert, sand, stones, little cactus and scrub', mostly without a sign of habitation for two hundred miles, she was no doubt reassured by the protection of her escort. Between Yuma and Tucson in Arizona, the ladies were advised not to undress when they went to bed 'because of the scare of Indians'.[6] Only three weeks before Princess Louise travelled along this route, the Apaches had murdered two Englishmen and about thirty White settlers.

The Lornes saw the last of the American Indians at Santa Fé, where the train headed over the prairies on its long journey eastwards. By now, the warmth of California had given way to the snow and ice of a Southern winter. 'Dear Old Virginia we found looking very white,' Lorne told his father from Richmond on 16 January 1883.[7] Lorne's Southern partisanship in the Civil War had not entirely disappeared since his Virginian tour in 1866, and he now looked forward to showing Princess Louise the sights of its capital city.

They put up at the Exchange and Ballard Hotel, where the Prince of Wales had stayed in 1860. In appearance, a strange rambling building, connected by a covered wooden passage – it seemed appropriate that Edgar Allan Poe read aloud 'The Raven' there in 1849; in atmosphere, it was very like an old-fashioned English inn with open fires in the rooms instead of the steam pipe heating used in the northeast and Canada.

On January 18th, the Lornes boarded the southbound train for Charleston, which they reached two days later. From here, the Princess would sail to Bermuda. Because of Fenian threats, her travel plans were kept secret for as long as possible. On January 28th, the newspapers brought the startling information that she was due to land in Bermuda the following day. Unfortunately, the 28th was a Sunday and in the eighteen eighties the sabbath was sacred. A compromise was reached that preparations for her arrival should start at one minute past midnight on the 29th so that all would be ready for the Princess's reception.

From Hamilton, the Princess drove to the nearby hamlet of Paget, where the Hon. James Trimingham was waiting in the entrance hall of 'Inglewood' to welcome her, and place his house at her disposal. The chief attraction of the spacious house was the high, double-storeyed verandah, where the Princess loved to sit and sketch. Although these were winter months, the thermometer registered a steady 60° to 75°; doors and windows were left open, roses and oleanders were in full bloom, and people donned their straw sunhats. As another Canadian exile in search of good health wrote to Sir John Macdonald, 'it is a great place for *rest* from *Work*. Mails only once a fortnight and no cable.'[8] It was exactly what Princess Louise needed.

Despite being isolated from the outside world, the Princess found that bad news had a way of invading her privacy. Some New York newspapers, like *The World*, had continued their campaign to denigrate her. In addition to fabricating remarks made by Lorne in New York – he was reported as stating she was in good health but preferred to live in Bermuda rather than Canada – they had now decided that the Princess's absence was due to the existence of bad feeling between her and Lady Macdonald, who had supposedly ordered Princess Louise about in Canada.

When the Lornes first arrived in Canada, the American press, despite themselves, had been intrigued. Had they been the usual examples of Victorian nobility so often found in colonial service, American interest would have faded rapidly. But, from the first, an aura developed around this glamorous young couple, who were considered extremely newsworthy; then, as so often happens, the 'honeymoon period' was replaced by the 'mud-slinging' period.

The so-called 'row' between Princess Louise and Lady Macdonald was also widely publicized in Canada. The fact that the two ladies had not seen each other for eight months was not allowed to spoil the story. Poor Lady Macdonald, though she had the strength of character to cope with a brilliant husband who was prone to alcoholic sprees in public, was nevertheless deeply upset by the calumnies. As soon as Princess Louise heard about the press reports, she wrote to the Macdonalds to sympathize and reassure them about her unchanged feelings of friendship for them. When the Princess returned to Canada, she made a point of appearing at the Opera House in the company of Lady Macdonald who, at her request, stood beside her to acknowledge the applause from the audience.

The Princess suffered less from this episode because she was tucked away in the peaceful atmosphere of Bermuda, where she was extremely happy. However, even in Bermuda, mishaps occurred. Water was scarce on the island and rain water was collected in tanks. When a fire broke out in the Princess's bedroom one night, the scarcity of water to douse the flames created great excitement. The Princess was not injured, but the damage to her room was extensive. She already knew of the water shortage, as a result of calling at a cottage for a glass of water. The woman of the house, who had some distance to go to obtain water, was reluctant to do so because she had to finish her ironing. When the Princess offered to continue ironing while the water was fetched, the woman refused, saying, 'I can't trus yu – yu doan luk sif you cud iron,' adding, 'I in a hurry t'git dis doan s'as t'go tu San Georges t'see de Princess.'

Once the Princess realized she was unrecognized, she egged the poor woman on. 'Haven't you seen the Princess?' she asked. 'Yus I seed her ven she cum,' the woman replied. 'Do you think you would know her if you saw her again?' demanded Princess Louise. 'Ah think so, but I aint rightly sure,' the woman admitted. 'Well take a good look at me now,' the Princess announced, 'so you will be sure to know me tomorrow at St Georges.'[9] The Princess, indeed all her family, might cling to privacy and try to go about unrecognized yet, whether passing themselves off as humble folk in the Highlands or Bermuda, they took immense delight in revealing themselves afterwards as Royalty. It was the ultimate royal charade.*

The Princess did not only appear in public on official visits, she also attended prize-giving events of local importance, like school sports days. She was conscientious about entertaining and seeing people who called, whatever their station. When a Mr Jones from Ottawa called and left his name at Government House and at Inglewood, an invitation to dinner was forthcoming from the Princess, whereas the Governor had 'not noticed us'.[10]

With the approach of warm weather in Canada, the Princess began her return journey. She was given a tremendous reception by the people of Ottawa when she arrived on April 18th, looking 'happy with cheeks aglow with health'.[11] She was full of energy and ready to take up her duties as 'Queen of Canada'. But, on the day of her arrival, a suspicious character was seen lurking around Government House; detectives combed the house and grounds for weapons and explosives and the Household was put on alert.

During the next week, several anonymous letters were received, threatening the lives of the Lornes. The fact that the fire-hose had been cut, despite the presence of armed police, made everyone feel jumpy.

---

* Princess Louise's desire to remain unrecognized, particularly when travelling incognito abroad, has been misunderstood. The incognito was used not because she had something to hide but because it was a royal rule of behaviour. For example, as he left an Italian church, the King of the Belgians recognized his cousin, Princess Louise, approaching; yet, when she raised a parasol to screen her face from him, thus showing that she was incognito and could not be recognized officially, he understood that she was in Italy without her official escort, her husband, and so travelling privately and under another name. This prevented her from having to make official calls and incur the expense and tedium of official entertainments. However, in this century, members of the British public, not knowing the etiquette of the incognito, asked to be presented if they saw her abroad.

The Princess resisted attempts to dissuade her from walking into Ottawa, until four revolver shots were fired from a grove adjacent to Rideau Hall. Lorne now insisted upon a detective accompanying her everywhere. When Gwen Stephenson went to stay in the middle of May, she found Government House in a state of siege. 'Lorne is awfully scared about Fenians,' she wrote home; he had a bodyguard called Carpenter for travelling, and a detective, Sheffington, assigned to the Princess.[12] The male staff thought Lorne a bit of an alarmist, as he was full of tales which, according to Josceline Bagot, 'would curdle your blood'.[13]

Lorne had armed himself 'with knives and revolvers' in preparation for an attack by Fenian assassins. Not surprisingly, the ladies of the Household became convinced that every outside noise was that of an intruder breaking in: 'there is a policeman in every flower bed and gas lamps all round the outside of the house,' Gwen Stephenson noticed, and 'HRH is not allowed outside the gates without a gentleman', which did not please the Princess, who felt that Lorne was fussing unnecessarily.[14]

Her sharpness towards Lorne surprised Gwen Stephenson, who wrote of her: 'She was most affectionate and gracious to me, but she is an odd woman and nothing would induce me to be her lady-in-waiting.'[15] The Princess was behaving 'oddly' because she was angry with Lorne. On May 21st, a telegram had arrived from Lord Derby, the Colonial Secretary, announcing that Lord Lansdowne had been selected as Lorne's successor; he would take up his appointment when the Lornes left Canada in October.

Until this telegram arrived, the Princess had no idea that they were leaving Canada: 'I have been much worried and troubled by Lorne sending in his resignation without consulting me a little, or even telling me a word about it, till Lord Derby's answer came,' she confided to Lord Granville.[16] She could not believe that Lorne would make such an important decision about their future without discussing it with her first; after all, his acceptance of the Governor-Generalship had rested upon her approval. Lorne had first raised the issue of returning home when the Princess was away in Bermuda. Sir Robert Herbert, the Under-Secretary, had noted on the bottom of Lorne's letter, 'Lord Lorne is mistaken: hope he will remain till the end of his term November 1884': and had cabled that the length of Lorne's time in office was six years.[17]

In his letter to Lord Derby, Lorne stated that he had come to Canada 'on the understanding that after 5 years I might turn to something else, and I wish to abide by that arrangement'. He hoped not to be officially asked 'and compelled to refuse' to stay on, since it would not only give offence to Canadians, but also set a precedent for longer terms of office, which he believed a mistake; 'a new broom is a very good thing for this country after 5 years'.[18]

Lord Granville had already received a letter from Queen Victoria, in which she pleaded Lorne's case for the Viceroyship of India, insisting that it would be impossible for him to remain another year in Canada. 'The Princess's health has suffered gtly from the gt cold, the fearful accident from wh she has *really never entirely* recovered – & from the Dreadful sea voyages almost all of wh have been vy bad' was the Queen's contention; she seems to have forgotten that journeys to India involved even longer sea voyages than those to Canada.[19] No one, however, had told the Queen that Lorne had decided to leave Canada. She was simply preparing the ground for the Government's consideration of candidates for Viceroy, since she knew that Lorne would like the position.

The Canadian Government also knew about Lorne's plans before the Princess. In April, the Prince of Wales had stipulated that he would only accept the Presidency of the British Association meeting in Montreal in 1884, if the Lornes were going to be there. In answering, Lorne had told Sir John Macdonald about his plans. The Canadian Government were disappointed and officially stated their wish for Lorne to remain another year.

Unfortunately, by the time the Princess heard about it, Lord Lansdowne had been officially appointed. The Canadian response was lukewarm, if not hostile, and the Princess was blamed for Lorne's early retirement. This resulted in the Princess having a great row with Lorne. Distressed by his lack of consideration for her feelings, and by the Canadian accusations that she did not want to stay in Canada because she disliked the people, the Princess turned to Lord Granville for help.

In a letter dated June 5th, she asked him to see if Lord Lansdowne would be prepared to wait until after the New Year to take up his appointment and, if so, whether he would then ask Lorne to remain on in Canada. She explained that it was not true that she wanted to leave Canada: 'All these most annoying circumstances wh have kept me away from this country . . . are supposed to be of my free choice, and the continual abuse I have received from the press, has made the people here really believe it. I do not think any woman has ever been placed in such a cruel and unfair position, and Lorne does not see this.' Nor was Lorne's reason for leaving, because of her ill-health, valid: 'I am never strong anywhere,' she told Lord Granville. Of the two winters she had passed in Ottawa, there had been scarlet fever during the first, and 'that tiresome accident' during the second. She did not want to leave Canada under a cloud: 'I don't care for myself what is said. I have been too much unfairly abused to mind that,' she wrote, 'but having been sent here as one of the Queen's children, I do care for the sake of my family, and I do wish to show the people that I do recognise their kindness to me,' especially since they had been led to believe that 'I do not care for them whereas I do'.[20]

Having sent this letter off to Lord Granville, she followed with a *cri du coeur* to her mother: 'I have always tried my best and I am anxious not to leave this Country till I have proved them this . . . Everyone is asking me to stay. And I feel so foolish having always to say "I am too ready to stay. You must ask His Ex?" Then they say, "Off course he will do what you wish".'[21]

Although the Queen had originally told Lord Granville that Lorne could not remain in Canada because of Princess Louise's health, she had done so only in order to qualify him for another job. Once she learnt of her daughter's feelings, and the Canadian reaction to Lorne's resignation, her opinion changed completely. The Indian position was not yet under consideration, and until such time as it was, Lorne should remain in Canada. She supported Princess Louise, not only out of maternal loyalty, but because she believed the Princess was right to object to Lorne's decision.

Having decided to support the Princess, Queen Victoria spared no punches. 'As a *profound secret* the Queen *must* tell Lord Gr . . . that L is *vy* jealous of his wife & can't bear *her* to be thought popular – but only *he*,' went one letter. 'He is *too* proud, to admit her being there, was such a *help to him* wh it was.'[22] This was rather unfair to Lorne, who was universally judged a great success in Canada; indeed, Queen Victoria herself had written 'Lorne has done admirably in Canada & made himself vy popular there,' but this opinion was swept away, in doing battle for her daughter.[23]

The combination of Queen Victoria and Princess Louise should have been effective. Lord Granville hesitated to interfere for political reasons. 'It's all Lorne's fault,' was the Queen's response. 'Nothing can equal the pride of the Campbells.' All the Queen could do was try to ensure Canadians understood that 'it was not poor Louise's fault that she did not go back 2 years ago. *We* prevented it as she was *so unwell* still from the effects of that dreadful accident.'[24]

The Queen was not pacified by the reasons Lorne gave for leaving Canada: 'I fear more time here would spoil me altogether for England.'[25] He enjoyed Canada so much that he believed that if he did not get away then, he would emigrate permanently, which would obviously affect his wife and family. Equally, he was determined not to succumb to 'petticoat' government. He was amused by the consternation expressed about the appointment of Lord Houghton to the Lord Lieutenancy of Ireland. It was held to be a difficult position without the help of a wife. 'I don't think so,' commented Lorne. 'A Viceroy thus gets rid of "female complications".'[26] Having made his decision, however impetuously, he would not be swayed from it by his wife, whose ill-health had been an important consideration. The Princess could not forgive Lorne, whose continual praise of everything Canadian only made matters worse; there was a coolness between them.

The Lornes' last months in Canada flew by in a flurry of visits and farewells. Mr Clemens, alias Mark Twain, arrived at the end of May. He ended up staying with them for five entertaining days. 'There's plenty of worse people than the nobilities,' he told Dean Howells, 'I went up and spent a week with the Marquis and the Princess Louise and had as good a time as I want.'[27] Although he invited the Lornes to Hertford where he would 'hang out the flag and also the latch key'[28] for them, it was in London that he again met the Princess. He noticed 'how natural and pleasant she was, and interested in everything going, and taking more trouble for other people than she did for herself.'[29]

On October 8th, Lord Melgund arrived at Government House, as the advance guard for Lord Lansdowne. He found the Lornes 'most cordial. She looking very well and pretty.'[30] Lady Melgund, who was Sybil St Alban's youngest sister, soon met the Princess. Remembering how homesick she had felt on her arrival five years before, the Princess went out of her way to look after her and show her round.

'Nothing can have been nicer than both Lord Lorne and Princess Louise were to us,' Mary Melgund wrote home.[31] She went to see the Lornes off at Ottawa station on October 15th. A large crowd had assembled to give them a cheer as they left the station. 'Poor Lorne was deeply affected. He wept like a child. Tears streamed down both his cheeks,' Albert Grey, who was there with the Melgunds, wrote to Mrs Grey. 'He says his five years here have been the happiest years of his life and that they have gone like 5 weeks.'[32]

On October 29th, the *Sarmatian* sailed out of Quebec, watched by enormous crowds; this time the tears rolled down Princess Louise's cheeks. She had seen more of the New World than any other member of her family and, although there had been 'trials', she was leaving behind friends and a way of life, which had grown strangely familiar. Nevertheless, as the ship edged its way into Liverpool, in the early hours of November 7th, she was full of happiness. As a friend, Lady Collier, wrote, having made the same journey, 'Nothing ever looked more beautiful to me than the gleams of gold and silver light on the Mersey, and the irregular outline of the dingy town of Liverpool.'[33] The Princess was no longer 'Queen of Canada', but she was home.

CHAPTER XIX

A Hopeless Family

Princess Louise passed the first months at home in a state of euphoria. It was marvellous to see the family again and to be told all the news. There was also a great deal to be done to restore Kensington Palace, which had been closed up for five years, to its former comfortable state. Once she had paid visits to Windsor, Sandringham and Argyll Lodge, the Princess was able to take stock of the changes which had occurred in her absence; she found much that was different. Lorne agreed, saying that Windsor was the only old home he found unchanged.

Certainly, Inveraray and Argyll Lodge were startlingly different. This was to be expected since they had a new chatelaine. The Lornes had first heard tell of her from Lady Mary, who had written in February 1879 from Cannes, about a new friend, 'one of the pleasantest people in the wide world is the little Mrs Anson'.[1] A niece of Lord Dudley's and the daughter of the Bishop of St Albans, Mrs Anson had remained in Cannes after the death of her invalid husband.

By that summer, rumours about the Duke were rife, not least amongst the family. 'His hobnobbing with Mrs Anson is much discussed and who can wonder', Lord Archie informed Lorne in July;[2] 'The lady is only 35 . . . so there may be no end of family – 10 or 15 perhaps? What is to become of us!' Lady Archie speculated to Disraeli.[3]

Reports of the attachment had even reached the New World. American and Canadian newspapers related that the Duke had proposed by telegram, while staying in Canada with the Lornes; furthermore, that he had little to say to reporters, because he was occupied with 'this electric lovemaking'. 'It all makes one very sick,' Lorne wrote home, adding 'I certainly shall never go near the place [Inveraray] if Mrs Anson is to rule the roost.'[4]

His reaction could have been expected. The memory of his mother was sacred; she had only been dead a year and he could not accept that anyone else might occupy her place. Princess Louise, who had loved the Duchess, shared Lorne's feelings; she felt the Duke's behaviour was unseemly and insensitive to his children's feelings. Nevertheless, she thought Lorne was being rather extreme when he said that he would never see Inveraray or Argyll Lodge again.

When the Duke announced his forthcoming marriage, he admitted to Lord Dufferin: 'this has been a trial to my Children,' but he hoped, 'things will come all right in time'.[5] The wedding, on 13 August 1881 was a sad occasion; conspicuously absent were the Argyll family, apart from Lord Colin and Lord Ronnie, who noticed that the small congregation consisted 'principally of maidservants'.[6]

Duchess 'Mimi', as she was always called, was a sweet, intelligent woman, who soon convinced most of the family that she was worthy of their father and eager to look after his children. Princess Louise persuaded Lorne that, as the eldest, he should set the example for the others and accept her, not as a surrogate mother but as his father's wife. Princess Louise's affectionate sympathy and encouragement did much to help the family during a difficult time. At a stiff, family, dinner party Duchess Mimi gave, so unlike the gatherings of old, Lord Ronnie noticed that it was Princess Louise who made it pleasant for everyone.

The arrival of a stepmother, however nice, also meant that Princess Louise and the Campbells could no longer use Argyll Lodge as the centre of family life. Their spontaneous way of wandering in and out with relations and friends now had to become more formal since they did not really know the new Duchess, who dispensed hospitality and made arrangements for the Duke.

The Princess also had a host of new relations by marriage to get to know. She liked some of them more than others. Lord George, a funny, endearing little fellow, rather like a cocksparrow and exactly like the Duke, had married pretty Miss Sybil Alexander, later an heiress, but Princess Louise did not see as much of them as she did of Lady Frances and her husband Eustace Balfour, who had settled nearby in Addison Road. A tall, dark, good-looking man, he was a great contrast to his short, red-haired wife. He would have been ideally suited to the lordship of a great estate, 'with nothing to do but improve it and the people on it', but, as the youngest son of a family of eight, he had to make his way in the world and chose architecture.[7] It was through him that Princess Louise came to know 'Ned' Burne-Jones and William Morris, and to work with the Society for the Protection of Ancient Buildings.

Family deaths had conspired against the marriage prospects of her other sisters-in-law. 'Poor Libby, I wish a Lord Libby would appear and take her away,' Janey's sister, Molly, had said in 1878. The only

Lord Libby on the horizon, a Mr Gillett, was considered unsuitable, and after he persuaded Lady Libby to elope with him, the Duke heard of it and squashed it. She then met Major Edward Clough-Taylor, but the Duke was strongly opposed: 'He is penniless – a most foolish affair altogether.' However, as time passed, he came to believe that at twenty-eight, 'she is too old to dictate to & I do wish to see Her married'.[9] Lord Ronnie wrote of their marriage that though 'desperately in love', he looked 'feeble, she poor dear well, as someone said, like a very poor pre-Raphelite picture'.[10] After their sojourn in India, she and the Princess drifted apart.

Lady Mary, however, had kept in close touch with the Lornes during their time in Canada; she had great charm and warmth of heart and was, undoubtedly, the beauty of the family. In 1882, she had become engaged to Edward Glyn, the clergyman son of Lord Wolverton. Although Lord Ronnie thought such a match 'a more sensible arrangement than most of those made by the young ladies of her family', the Duke was disappointed.[11] Mary's marriage does not *satisfy* me,' he wrote. Teddy Glyn was 'a vy good fellow and vy popular in his Parish,' but he would 'never set the Thames on fire'.[12] Certainly, compared to the Campbells, he was moderate in his ecclesiastical views. The Duke found some consolation in the thought that it was, therefore, all the more likely that he would be made a Bishop (which he later was). He was a rich man since his people were the Glyns of Glyn's Bank, yet Lady Mary did not benefit as much as she might have done. According to the family, he gave away most of his shares, saying 'I am a Lord Spiritual and not Temporal.'[13]

Princess Louise came to know and like him very much. A lovable man with a cheerful outlook on life, he had a 'hopelessly infectious laugh'.[14] Since Kensington was his parish, and he and Lady Mary lived at the Vicarage, so conveniently near Kensington Palace, she saw a great deal of them. As Lorne's favourite sister, Lady Mary was always popping into Kensington Palace for 'a cosy Druid talk' – Campbellese for a tête-à-tête.[15] As with the Balfour children in Addison Road, the Princess was a popular aunt, and gave the Glyn children the love she would have given her own children.

Ensconced in this Kensington enclave, the Princess tended to see less of her own family. There were still regular visits to the Queen and calls upon Princess Helena. The Waleses she did not see as much as previously, mainly because they were so busy. Prince Arthur was serving with the army and Princess 'Louischen' was much engrossed with her new baby, 'the long looked for son'.[16] The most extraordinary change was that Prince Leopold had a little daughter, Princess Alice, born earlier in the year. This birth, perhaps more than any of the others, brought home to the Princess how much she missed babies of her own.

The return from Canada had not eased relations between her and Lorne, which left her unhappy and depressed. Lorne, however, was preoccupied with hopes that he might become Viceroy of India. Lord Granville had warned Gladstone back in April, that Prince Leopold for Canada and 'Lorne for India, are coming on [I] fear'.[17] Sure enough, the next day, the Queen had suggested to Lord Granville that Lorne 'wd do excellently for India'; he was 'most anxious' for employment and 'is very desirous to go', besides which 'the presence there of a daughter of the Empress wd have an immense effect & she wd be almost an Empress herself'.[18] The Prince of Wales had also lobbied the Prime Minister.

On May 19th, Lord Granville had had an audience at Windsor, when she 'touched (lightly) upon Lorne for India'.[19] Lord Granville, in an attempt to leave his Chief room for manoeuvre should he not want Lorne, had told her 'it was the most important appointment she had to make, as much or almost more so than that of the Prime Minister'.[20] What he had omitted to say was that the reasons Lorne had given in his unofficial application seemed scarcely suitable or sufficient. Lorne wanted the position mainly for financial reasons, and had written diffidently that 'it would probably suit Princess Louise's health and enable him to buy a country house at the end of the term'.[21]

Aware of the uneasy state of affairs between the Lornes after their return from Canada, the Queen was anxious for Lorne to have an occupation. 'If only we cd give him some employment,' she wrote to Lord Granville on October 11th. One solution was to make him 'a Peer & a *Duke* as a mark of her approbation of his service'.[22] Unfortunately, the Duke remained adamantly opposed to a peerage for Lorne. 'I hope Your Majesty will not think this too proud,' he wrote, 'but I cannot help it. It [the Argyll title] is one of the most historical of all the Scotch titles and it has not been associated with any other by property.' The Duke then put forward another reason. He wanted Lorne to remain in the House of Commons to resist 'the advance of Radicalism'. 'It is the only place where one can experience real *power* now,' he told Queen Victoria.[23]

Lorne agreed with his father and so, once more, the Queen had to accept defeat. Yet she was perhaps the only one to realize that this would make it very difficult to know what to do with Lorne. She did not wish him to sit in the House of Commons, the Duke did not wish him to sit in the House of Lords, and Princess Louise did not wish him to go to India.

In her New Year letter to the Crown Princess, the Queen wrote, 'I do always pray for strength, patience and courage to "fight on" for life does become sadder and sadder and harder.'[24] These words could not have been bettered as a description of what Princess Louise felt about life in 1884; it was a most unhappy year for her.

A week after staying at Windsor for her thirty-sixth birthday, Princess Louise, with Lorne, went to dine and sleep at Claremont. There she found her old friend Lady Knightley, who was now in-waiting on Princess Helen, who was expecting her second child. Princess Louise still could not believe Prince Leopold was a family man. 'Dear me,' she said to Lady Knightley as they came down to dinner, 'it seems so odd to come to Leopold's house and see Leopold's child!'[25]

Princess Louise saw her brother again briefly before he went off on his annual spring holiday to Cannes. On the morning of March 29th, Lorne came into the Princess's boudoir at Kensington Palace and broke the unbearable news of Prince Leopold's death. He had died quite suddenly after a brain haemorrhage, at two o'clock that morning, after having slipped, mounting the stairs in his club. Dr Boyle had put his leg in a splint and sent him to bed at six o'clock, feeling that there was no cause for alarm.

The Princess was heartbroken. She immediately joined the Queen at Windsor and travelled with her to Claremont to be with Princess Helen.

Princess Helen was wonderfully composed and resigned; as Princess Louise told Aunt Dot, 'The coming baby seems such an absorbing interest to her and the sweet little girl a great comfort, that she luckily does not to the full realise her great loss now.' For Princess Louise, there was no such consolation to mitigate her grief: 'he was, and we were to each other in fact the dearest friend we each had'.[26] She had lost the best of brothers and 'the joy and object of a lifetime'.[27]

When Princess Louise visited Princess Helen at Claremont on May 14th, Lady Knightley recorded in her Journal 'Poor Princess Louise! No one loved Prince Leo better, and to no one is he a greater loss.'[28]

The passage of time did little to heal her sorrow. After lunching at Kensington Palace on July 22nd, Lord Ronnie found that Princess Louise was in a bad way; she had 'much lost her looks, has grown too very sallow'. Lorne asked him 'not even to allude to the death of Prince Leo – as she had been quite "upset" ever since'.[29]

Lord Ronnie also noticed that she seemed 'somewhat irritable' with her Household. Her old enemy, insomnia, had returned with a vengeance and it made her at times very difficult to live with. The pains of neuralgia and rheumatism, and the sleeplessness left her exhausted and depressed. There was also the realization that it was now improbable that she would ever have a child. For years she had pinned her hopes on the example of Mrs Grey, who had taken twelve years to have Sybil. In the summer of 1884, Princess Louise was in her thirteenth year of marriage; she could now summon up little hope.

The dynamics of a marriage can change and, in the Lorne's case, the balance had swung away from him to her. The long spells apart and their clashes of opinion had changed Princess Louise's perception of Lorne; she now saw the stubborn side of his character and began to be irritated by him. Although, whenever this happened, she would be sorry and try to be kind to make up for the feeling, it took its toll upon her nerves. She was very like her sister, Princess Alice, in temperament. In Princess Alice's words, they had 'things to fight against, and to put up with, unknown to those of quiet equable dispositions, who are free from violent emotions, and have consequently no feelings of nerves – still less of irritable nerves'.[30]

In any marriage, the continuous dashing of 'hopes' about a baby must place an additional strain upon it. Although Princess Louise would have tried to make a success of any arranged marriage, she had succeeded with Lorne because she loved and respected him. They were very close and she even, as in 1878, showed him her dresses. When Minnie Paget brought a grey dress from Paris for her, Princess Louise tried it on for his approval: 'At first Lord Lorne thought I looked a little bit like a stable boy in it, but now he likes it very much.'[31] However, by 1884, she had fallen out of love with him, and the lack of any children to tide her over this change meant that her affection for him was threatened.

If Princess Louise had not cared for Lorne, if she had been indifferent to him, it would have been easy for them to lead separate lives, attending the odd social or public function together in order to maintain outward appearances. This was the *modus vivendi* thankfully adopted by other couples, such as the Archies. Unlike them, the Lornes had found much more happiness in their marriage. Princess Louise did care deeply for Lorne but just needed to be away from him for a while, for she found it difficult to adjust to a marriage of companionship when it had been so much more before.

The Lornes, like their contemporaries, were seldom alone; they were continually surrounded by people: maids, valets, dressers, footmen and, in their case, equerries and ladies-in-waiting. The dictum 'not in front of the servants' was strictly observed. This is not to say that during this difficult period there were no rows; there were, but they were fewer because they rarely took place face to face. Scribbled notes were the vehicle used to convey a cross word, accusation or apology. Lorne's easy-going attitude and wish to avoid troublesome issues often precluded intimate discussions with Princess Louise. There was no question of a formal separation or, still worse, divorce. Both were taboo in royal and social circles. In any case, the Princess did not want a divorce or a formal separation. All she needed was time to recover from her breakdown and to adjust to the changes in her relationship with Lorne. Meanwhile, having spoken to her mother about it, she would try to live amicably with him.

Queen Victoria had been marvellously understanding. Aware of the Princess's unstable state, she had tried to ease the pressures on her, while 'feeling very much' for Lorne, who was also remarkably understanding and patient with his wife.[32] His manner to women was said, by his sister Frances, to be 'if anything, too chivalrous'.[33] He still thought of Princess Louise as his beautiful wife; he was still in love with her, but it was a courtly, rather than a passionate, love. Even at the height of Princess Louise's unhappiness, they kept in close contact and wrote daily. He thought of her constantly, writing to the Duke in May of that year from Inveraray, 'I wish Louise cd see this place again at this time, when the spring beauty is so fresh and lovely.'[34]

On September 21st, Lorne decided that matters between them would be helped if he and Princess Louise went away quietly together. He asked Queen Victoria if they could join the Crown Princess on her holiday in the Tyrol. The Queen thought it an excellent idea, only stipulating to the Crown Princess that she must make allowances for Princess Louise's weak health: 'you must not make her do the third part of what you can do'.[35]

The Crown Princess was disturbed to see Princess Louise so unwell. 'It did *grieve* me more than I can *say* to see her looking so ill,' she wrote afterwards to Lorne, 'and to perceive how the *slightest* exertion, *noise* or excitement made her suffer from pain in her *head*, and altogether upset her.' She praised Lorne for his patience with the Princess, since, 'Men can hardly quite understand how much a woman can suffer – whose health and nerves are out of order! both mentally and physically.'[36]

During the summer of 1884, the Queen continued to try to 'find something for poor Lorne to do'. She knew he needed the additional income since the Argyll estates had suffered in the agricultural depression of the seventies, and the burden of another duchess and marriage settlements for the children had further depleted the coffers. The Queen thought 'some sort of commission to report on the state of some of the Colonies wd be the very best,'[37] but Lord Granville was unable to appoint a commission solely for the purpose of providing Lorne with a job; nor did he have a spare one lying around waiting for a chairman.

A peerage was again discussed, this time by the Government. Lorne had asked for an inexpensive constituency, but there was no point in allocating one to him if he was to be made a peer. Edward Hamilton, one of Gladstone's private secretaries, believed the Queen's son-in-law 'ought to keep clear of political contests'.[38] Lorne declined to accommodate Hamilton and refused a peerage again.

Then, in August, Lorne was considered for the Governorship of New South Wales, which would not fall vacant until 1885. Lord Derby felt the only drawback to this appointment was that it was a demotion from Canada. However, the Princess refused to accompany him to Australia. She could not face the thought of the long sea passages, of homesickness and of her dependency upon Lorne for society.

His name was also floated as a candidate for the Berlin Embassy, in succession to Lord Ampthill. Although Gladstone wanted Lorne, the Queen, after hearing from the Crown Princess, wisely ruled him out completely. In desperation, Queen Victoria even suggested the Commissionership of New Guinea. Lord Derby quickly scotched the idea: 'it was out of the question, as the place required a man of great experience with Savage natives';[39] Lorne was no doubt relieved to have escaped so dangerous a fate.

In December, the Lornes tried to resume their life together. They went Christmas shopping and saw family and friends as of old. Lord Ronnie called at Kensington Palace, on December 10th, and thought Princess Louise 'much better for her time in Germany'. Nevertheless, when he called on Mary Ponsonby at Windsor she seemed to think that Princess Louise was 'in a very uncomfortable, unstable state'. The Princess remained restless, nervous and unhappy. 'If she had married the Archangel Michael,' Mary Ponsonby remarked, 'it would have been all the same.'[40]

There was, however, one unexpectedly bright spot in an otherwise harrowing year. Princess Beatrice had persuaded Queen Victoria to allow her to marry Prince Henry of Battenberg. They had met the previous summer in Darmstadt at the marriage of Princess Alice's eldest daughter, Princess Victoria, and Prince Louis of Battenberg. Princess Beatrice had not told the Queen of her wishes until their return home. Nothing had prepared Queen Victoria for such an eventuality, and she refused to countenance it. As was her wont over disagreeable matters, she resorted to silence on the subject and behaved as if it had never been raised.

The Queen had expected her youngest 'Baby' to remain with her in permanent attendance; yet here was her shyest, most submissive daughter telling her whom she would like to marry. It was only after the relentless intercession of the family that Queen Victoria gave her permission. They had to agree to live entirely with her, so that Princess Beatrice could continue to act as the Queen's secretary/companion.

Queen Victoria admitted to Lorne that she could never have given her consent otherwise, for 'at my *age*, in my position, and after the many sad losses I have sustained, I cd *not* live without one of my own *Children* being continually with *me*'.[41] The years had not changed the Queen's insistence that her comfort should be considered before everyone and everything else.

Conversely, Princess Louise found nothing to cheer her on the Argyll side of the family. In these years of the mid-eighties, Lorne's brothers were proving an anxiety, and a drain upon the Lornes' financial resources. Since the Duke found it difficult to manage family affairs, the burden of responsibility was borne entirely by the Lornes. Even Lord Archie had been excelling himself. His latest fad of keeping on a pair of black gloves at all times was harmless enough; less so were the debts he regularly incurred which, but for Lorne's intermediacy, would have cost him his position at Coutts. Nor could he rely upon his wife for help. Part of the reason for the Archies' increased expenditure, or 'extravagance' as the Duke called it, was the theatrical productions they were staging at Coombe Hill Farm. Janey was 'madder than ever about her acting and can think of nothing else', Lord Archie attested.[42] In *As You Like It* she played Orlando before the Waleses and Princess Louise; Jimmy Whistler's first depiction of Janey was in his miniature, *Note in Green and Brown: Orlando at Coombe.*

The Walter Campbells, however, were in much more serious straits. In 1879, Lady Walter had been 'very much admired in London', and seemed happily married with two children, Douglas and Lilah.[43] Yet, in May of that year, Lord Ronnie had observed 'Schouvaloff and Lady Walter C the latter great friends. His Excellency apparently being quite smitten with her rather improper style of beauty.'[44] The affair between the cotton-spinner's daughter and Count Peter Schouvaloff, the Russian Ambassador to Great Britain, caused comment in Society. Lord Ronnie found her wild, 'smuggly red faced and debauched looking' in September, and prophesied that 'Olive's exceedingly high spirits will make her commit an act of folly some day'.[45] This proved all too true.

Princess Louise had also heard, in no uncertain terms, from the Queen about Lady Walter. On 11 March 1880, Lady Agnes Wood had attended the Drawing Room where Lady Walter 'was such a sight, no word but *disgusting*, as Ld Hertford confided to me, wd apply. He said the Queen's face was a caution as Lady W went by. The only clothing from half way from her waist seemed to be yellow roses.'[46]

At this stage, Lord Walter was a steady man and only prepared to take risks in his capacity as a stockbroker. Initially, a successful investor, Lord Walter lost not only his own, but also the family and Lord Dufferin's money in the Egyptian crash. He had turned to Lorne for help and, to try to recoup his losses, now began to take even greater risks, usually with disastrous results. Never one to censure people unduly for their misfortunes, the Princess bore these trials philosophically. Her condemnation was reserved almost entirely for Lorne's youngest brother, 31-year-old Lord Colin.

When Lorne was appointed Governor-General, this brother contested his Argyllshire seat in the election that summer and won it. 'Colin is now the great MP and fully takes it in as one watches his slow and solemn movements,' Lady Frances teased.[47] He was looked upon as a young man to watch, and was appointed to a Commission to settle Turkish affairs after the Congress of Berlin. Then, quite unexpectedly, he had informed the Duke that he wished to marry a Miss Blood. Lady Evey told Lorne: 'the girl is certainly not pleasing but really none of us know her'; he had literally seen her over three days. As the youngest son, Lord Colin had very little money to marry upon: 'you know C has no notion of money and is besides so cool,' Lady Evey continued, 'he talks as if he had but to ask and Papa must fork out a certain quantity'.[48]

Lord Ronnie heard about it from the Prince of Wales. 'She is 6 ft high and broad in proportion and speaks 5 languages. What odd boys these Campbells are.'[49] After hearing this news at a dinner party, a 'certain' duke remarked to the Prince of Wales 'what very odd people all Argyll's sons do marry!' To which the Prince laughingly replied, 'I am sorry you think so badly of my sister.'[50]

The Lornes thought Lord Colin 'a donkey' for throwing himself away on a woman with nothing 'more satisfactory than much flesh and stature'. Lorne, especially, felt it was unfair to expect the family to bear the expenses of his parliamentary career for ever, when he could have married well. Instead, he had proposed to 'a pennyless and groatless grenadier of a girl'.[51] Despite his father's opposition – 'She will flirt. His temper won't stand that and there will be a blow up' – Lord Colin married Miss 'Gertie'.[52]

When the Lornes returned from Canada they learnt that Lord Colin's marriage was faring badly. In March 1884, Lady Colin brought a petition for a judicial separation upon the grounds of Lord Colin's cruelty, which was granted, but he appealed. The Colin Campbell case 'has been creating a great interest' read Edward Hamilton's diary entry on March 30th.[53] For the details of the marriage now emerged in a blaze of publicity, more familiar to the twentieth than the nineteenth century. Lady Colin's case was that Lord Colin had intercourse with her while suffering from venereal disease. Lord Colin's case was that she had consented to the non-consummation of their marriage for at least six months, owing to his illness, and had informed her parents, who had still insisted the marriage take place. Only after receiving medical advice was the marriage consummated. Lord Colin's appeal was dismissed on 21 July 1884.

Princess Louise had been shocked when the Prince of Wales had been subpoenaed to appear as a witness in the Mordaunt divorce case in 1871. These feelings were as nothing compared to the shame and revulsion she now felt, as a result of the sordid details which were widely disseminated. It was 'unspeakable' and 'unforgiveable'. Princess Louise never received Lord Colin again.

Lorne did his best to help his brother. When he learnt of further legal proceedings and that Lord Walter had lost more money, his growing fears were confirmed: 'It's a very hopeless family!'[54]

CHAPTER XX

Political Life

In 1885 and 1886, Princess Louise's interests were almost entirely chan-
nelled into the world of politics. Like most of her contemporaries, she
was caught up in the fever of the Home Rule debates, which, since
'the world of politics was still also' that 'of Society', dominated both.[1]
To those who could recall the turbulent atmosphere of fifty-six years
ago, it was as if they had returned to the days of the First Reform Bill.

The position of a Victorian Lady in such proceedings had not
greatly advanced in the intervening years. Her influence was still
confined to the drawing room. Nevertheless, at the height of the Home
Rule controversy, such an influence had considerable impact. Princess
Louise was more qualified than most Victorian women to exercise such
an influence, yet her royal position prevented her from doing so and,
even, from helping her husband to fight an election.

Lord Colin's involvement in scandal had made it impossible for
him to retain his position as MP for Argyllshire. It was naturally
assumed that Lorne would wish to represent it again. However, the
high costs of fighting an election made it impossible for a poor man to
stand, unless financed by a wealthy patron or association. 'At present
all I have goes to the necessities of the family – and there is nothing in
the Till,' Lorne explained to Lord Archie.[2] If the Liberals wanted him
to stand, they would have to contribute at least £1,000. This they were
unlikely to do, and Lorne suggested William Mackinnon of Ballinakill,
'a very nice little fellow, and wealthy,' as the Liberal candidate.[3]
Although Lorne was disappointed at not returning to his old constituency, he had chosen a good man and one with whom he and Princess
Louise would be much involved later on.

Lack of funds did not preclude Lorne from seeking a parliamentary
seat: it merely narrowed his choice to a London constituency where
the cost of electioneering would be less than in the widely spaced
constituency of Argyllshire. By a stroke of good fortune, he was told
that Hampstead needed a candidate and that the Liberal Committee
would pay almost all his expenses. His only hope of adoption was to

unite the moderate and radical strands of Liberalism; in this he was successful and was adopted as the Liberal candidate for Hampstead.

In 1885, Gladstone's Government was unexpectedly defeated. Electioneering started in September for Lorne, whose address was in favour of the reform of the House of Lords by 'the infusion of elected members' and of other 'advanced' measures.[4] 'No one will complain of it as weak-kneed,' Gladstone wrote.[5] Lorne was standing, not on the right of the Liberal party, like his Whig father, but on the left as a Radical. The son of Sir William Richmond remembered the unfriendly, local cobbler, who was 'that terrible thing a "Radical"' and a Radical then was 'more reprehensible even than a communist today'.[6]

The Radical leader, Joseph Chamberlain, wanted to change the Liberal party. He sounded the first, unharmonious notes of class-war ever delivered by a Cabinet Minister when he attacked Lord Salisbury as coming from a class grown fat from the land, yet 'who toil not neither do they spin'.[7] His aim was to force the Whigs out of the Liberal party by capturing urban seats. He launched an 'unauthorized' election programme, which was anti-landlord and demanded, 'What ransom will property pay for the security it enjoys?'[8]

This proved disastrous for Lorne, who was really a Whig with Radical tendencies on specific issues. Whilst he had moved to the left, as a result of Chamberlain's campaign to push the Whigs over to the Tories, Lorne wanted to offer an alternative to Chamberlain and, once elected, become one of the 'pendulums to moderate the pace of the new clock'.[9]

On November 21st, two days before polling, Charles Parnell came to an understanding with the Conservatives and ordered the Irish in Great Britain to vote Conservative. The defection of the Irish vote, the Chamberlain scare, and the memory of Gladstone's failure to rescue General Gordon combined to turn London and the towns against Gladstone and Radicalism. Lorne was defeated by the Conservative, Mr Holland, by 875 votes.

Owing to her position, Princess Louise had been unable to campaign for Lorne, but she had followed his progress carefully. She was very disappointed. 'I do feel it very much that Lorne has not got in, much more than he does,' she told her friend Constance Flower. She was relieved that for once, 'At any rate I have not been Lorne's stumbling block, as I have kept so carefully out of the way all the time.'[10]

Fully aware of how much 'our peculiar position' affected his career, Princess Louise had tried from the first days out in Canada to sink her name 'so that he shd not feel that I am put in a line with him in any way'.[11] It was hard to have to make herself invisible when she longed to be of use and active. Unable to electioneer, she now tried to help him find another seat. His threat 'to settle under another name in America' alarmed her.[12] They were also concerned about the Duke's political position. After being out of office since April 1881, when he resigned over the Irish Land Bill, the Duke's opposition to the Liberal party had increased. Lorne hoped that the Duke would be given office in a future Liberal Government; otherwise he might lead his followers into the Tory ranks.

Christmas festivities that year brought little respite from the widespread concern about national affairs. 'Never did one feel so utterly ignorant as to what a day may bring forth,' Lady V wrote from Inveraray.[13] After only two months in office, Lord Salisbury's government was defeated by an alliance of Liberal and Irish votes. Parnell had changed sides and the fight for Home Rule had begun in parliamentary circles. On January 31st, Gladstone was summoned to Osborne and invited to form a ministry. Princess Louise thought him 'very nervous'; during his interview, Gladstone asked for the Queen's permission to offer Lorne office, to which she raised no objection.

He then had a long talk with Lorne and invited him to join his Government as Under-Secretary of State for the Colonies under Lord Granville; a parliamentary seat would naturally be found for him. It was an offer that Lorne would not normally have considered refusing, but, in the present political climate, he said he 'shd like a little more light on the subject of Ireland'. To this Gladstone replied evasively, 'that is a question of enquiry and examination, and nothing need be determined now'.[14]

Unfortunately, for Lorne's own career, it was the crucial issue in determining whether he would be able to accept Gladstone's offer. The Queen had instructed Henry Ponsonby to send the Prince of Wales a detailed summary of the political discussions, which did nothing to dissuade the Prince from his fierce anti-Home Rule stance. This meant that the Prince, formerly an ally in Lorne's search for a job, was now strongly opposed to the offer of the Under-Secretaryship.

'I hardly think that the Queen's son-in-law should form part of the Government,' he wrote on February 2nd, 'no matter what party is in

power. And how could he form part of a "Home Rule" Government?'
It would place Lorne in 'an utterly false position', and he could hardly
imagine that Princess Louise would wish for it.[15] Princess Louise,
however, remained insistent that Lorne be free to do whatever he
wished in terms of a career. Furthermore, unlike the Prince of Wales,
Princess Louise *was* in favour of Home Rule. Having seen the system
of government in Canada, she believed that Ireland should be governed
in the same way. Thus, the Princess was *not* opposed to Lorne taking
office in Gladstone's Home Rule Government.

Queen Victoria, herself against Home Rule, was easily persuaded
by the Prince of Wales that it was impossible for Lorne to take office.
On February 3rd, she wrote to Gladstone that 'Ld Lorne finds it difficult
to accept office at present but should a vacancy occur later and the
Govt be likely to go on he wd be disposed to do so.' Through Henry
Ponsonby, she told Lorne that it was not the moment to join an
administration, 'the salient feature of whose policy is believed to be
concession to Parnell's demands. Your taking office would lead people
to think that the Queen had been "won over" or that you were acting
in opposition to her.'[16]

Lorne was also considered by the Cabinet for Viceroy of Ireland,
despite his belief that 'a national parliament should not be granted',[17]
which was the central tenet of Home Rule. Lorne did intimate that,
even if Queen Victoria had wished for it, he should not have accepted
it. He was, as Mrs Gladstone realized, too poor for so expensive a post.

Discontent with Government as well as Monarchy was also evident
in the streets of London. After the opening of Parliament on January
21st, the Queen had been loudly booed by an angry mob. Princess
Louise was not with her because she had taken to bed with a bad attack
of influenza. However, the Princess was soon able to see for herself
that the English working man was unusually discontented.

It had been a hard, bitter winter and unemployment was especially
high in London. Yet the attention of government was almost entirely
focused upon Ireland. On the afternoon of February 8th, a large
meeting of the unemployed assembled in Trafalgar Square to publicize
their grievances. At the same time, about eight thousand members of
the Social Democratic Federation held a meeting on the steps of the
National Gallery. The unemployed dispersed quietly after their meeting
ended; the Socialists, fired by the oratory of their leaders, who had told
them 'hanging was too good for capitalists and landlords . . . sitting in

comfort, careless whether the poor starved or not,' unfurled a large red flag and chanting, 'Unless we get bread they must get lead', marched westwards through London.[18] The procession passed through the most fashionable quarters: Pall Mall and St James's to Hyde Park where they attacked carriages, hauled out their occupants and robbed them.

After holding a short meeting in the park, the mob passed into Grosvenor Square, where they attacked the imposing houses of the rich, one of which belonged to the Percys. The Percys' butler thought it was the Salvation Army, so he stood on the steps, with the door open behind him, waiting for them to arrive. Suddenly, the crowd hurled a volley of stones at the windows and the butler fled back inside the house. Holding pillows to their heads, Lord Archie and Lady Percy peered out to see who was attacking them. Lady Percy sent a message through the mews to Kensington Palace for help. Princess Louise received it and immediately sent help, and a message to Lorne, who was at a Geographical Society meeting. By the time he rushed over 'to protect Edith' and her children, the mob had moved on to Oxford Street.

London was at the mercy of rioters for over three hours; next day the police advised shops to close and people to remain at home and special constables were called out for the first time since the Chartists. When the Lornes drove from Kensington Palace that evening to dine with the Edinburghs, they avoided the park and approached from Pimlico. They remarked how quiet the streets were despite the smashed windows and riot debris. The thick fog, which engulfed the city, served to heighten its desolate appearance.

While waiting for the introduction of Home Rule legislation, the question arose of Lorne succeeding as Governor of the Cape. Lord Granville thought 'he would do' and Lorne seemed 'to be biting at it', but Princess Louise did not favour the idea as she dreaded the sea voyages.[19] Circumstances conspired against Lorne ever taking high office again. If it was not the opposition of the Queen and the Royal Family, it was the Princess's health and reluctance to live abroad; if it was not the state of Liberal party politics, it was his father's opposition to a seat in the House of Lords. Although considered by his contemporaries as worthy of high office, since he had the reputation of having done extremely well in Canada, it was denied him by the machinations of his family.

On April 8th, in a masterly speech, Gladstone took three and a half hours to introduce the Home Rule Bill amid spectacular excitement inside a crowded House of Commons, where all the gangways, passages and spaces were packed with chairs, and where Royalties, including Princess Louise, sat over the clock and in the Ladies' Gallery. The Home Rule Bill proposed to set up a separate Irish Parliament in Dublin to enact domestic legislation. Conservatives, Whigs and many moderate Liberals objected to it because they believed that a separate government for Ireland would lead inevitably to independence and the dissolution of the Union. The fight over Home Rule thus simplified itself for the public into those who wished to 'save' the Union and those who wished to render justice to Ireland.

It was a fight that divided families and Society, and the influence of the drawing room made itself felt. Home Rulers were received only by the wives of their own political friends. The mass exodus of peers from the Liberal party, despite ties extending back over generations, meant that Home Rulers were no longer received in many of the salons of the great London houses. When the Gladstones attended a ball at Grosvenor House that summer, Lady Frances noticed how 'Gladstone was wandering about rather forlornly, not many people there he cared to speak to, and no one very keen to speak to him.'[20] But Princess Louise remained loyal and continued to treat him as of old. He had been a personal favourite with her since the mid-sixties, when he would come and tell her of the hymns he liked after the service at Balmoral and she always enjoyed listening to his wide-ranging conversation. Later he asked her to help him explain things to the Queen to make matters easier between them. He and Mrs Gladstone came for tea just before the Home Rule Bill was introduced. Lorne thought him looking 'very nervous'.[21]

It saddened all of them to see the Argyll friendship for the Gladstones founder. For Gladstone's Home Rule Bill forced the Duke out of the Liberal party; in this, to Princess Louise's regret, he eventually was followed by Lorne. The dissentient Liberals had decided to vote with the Conservatives, which made for some strange bedfellows. Chamberlain, whom the Tories loathed, was now cheered by them as a long-lost friend. The Home Rulers were much more bitter with these seceded 'friends' than with the Conservatives.

During the first week of the debates, a great coalition meeting was held at Her Majesty's Theatre. Lord Hartington and Lord Salisbury sat together in symbolic solidarity between their parties, the new Liberal

Unionists and their allies, the Conservatives. The Duke never formally joined this party, but the next election Lorne would fight would be as a Liberal Unionist.

The final debate on the motion for the second reading of the Home Rule Bill took place on 7 June 1886. It was an occasion of unparalleled excitement. The second reading was defeated in a full house by 343 votes to 313. Ninety-three Liberals had voted with the majority against their old party. All over England post offices had remained open till the news came in. 'Long and late it was before the candles were taken up' for bed in many a household in the land.[22]

The General Election that followed was fought on the issue of Home Rule alone and the result was a landslide victory for the Conservatives and Liberal Unionists. Lorne failed to get elected, as Princess Louise predicted to Lady Salisbury, 'I . . . fear there is not much likelihood of his getting in.'[23] So ended, as one historian wrote, the most dramatic thirteen months in modern English party history.

Unable to get away as usual to avoid the severe winter months, the Princess had contracted influenza and a series of coughs, so that she looked and felt 'pulled'. Lorne decided to take her off to Venice in April, a holiday they both enjoyed. It was their first return since their honeymoon days. 'Louise sends her love,' Lorne wrote to the Duke on April 27th, 'She has slept better lately and the sea air seems to do her nerves good.'[24]

In May, the Princess was soon busy with the opening of a new out-patients' wing at the Victoria Hospital in Tite Street. This had long been a pet scheme of hers. In the winter of 1881–2 she had written to Lord Cadogan, the President, with her proposals for the next committee meeting. When she had inspected the out-patients' department, she had found it 'very defective'. There were no treatment rooms for children, who needed to stay overnight; no ward or bathroom for them and no extra rooms for expansion. A new department would have to be built.

The Committee had argued that there were not adequate funds. Princess Louise soon persuaded them otherwise; with the result that on June 30th the new department was to be opened by the Prince and Princess of Wales. Lord Cadogan had assumed that Princess Louise would accompany the other Royalties on the occasion but, luckily, he consulted her about the arrangements. She had quite different ideas. 'I wd like to meet the Pc and Pss at the Hospital with you and Ly

Cadogan,' she told him, 'and to be looked upon as one of the Patronesses on that occasion.'[25]

That autumn, Lorne and Princess Louise realized they would have to postpone their search for a country house yet again. Lorne was worried about the poverty of the Argyll estates. As usual, his father was occupied with a new book he was writing and seemed unaware of his financial position. 'I'm told that not one farthing can be borrowed on the estate as it cannot pay its way as it is,' Lorne wrote to Lord Archie on September 22nd. 'Such is the pride of landlordism! Mere territorial beggary for all and sundry'.[26] The Duke's only response was an admission that 'I am beginning to think how I can *reduce*.'[27] One way would be to stop keeping open house for the family. But Lorne preferred to borrow more from Coutts than ration the family to one annual helping of their beloved Inveraray.

Princess Louise had spent three weeks taking the baths at Aix-les-Bains. She returned on October 7th and was met with the news that Lord Colin's divorce case had come to court. Whenever the Duke was asked for Lord Colin's whereabouts, he told them his youngest son's address was: '*En l'air, Partout, En Europe*'.[28] It was a joke with more than a grain of truth; Lord Colin had been invisible to Society, an 'unmentionable' disgraced by scandal, since 1884. Discreet adultery was condoned by Victorians; divorce was not. Queen Victoria could never receive divorced people at Court, as a matter of Court etiquette, while Princess Louise, who was usually understanding about other people's misfortunes and was considered 'advanced', remained entirely a woman of the nineteenth century in her attitude to divorce. Even in the nineteen twenties, she would not attend a family wedding because one of the guests, Neville Lytton, was divorced. In private she might sympathize and support women like Lady Henry Somerset, who had divorced her homosexual husband; in public she never saw them.

The same convention covered ladies who openly cohabited with their lovers, such as Ellen Terry, who lived with Edward Godwin. When she was to act before the Queen at Sandringham, Princess Louise felt that her mother must know she was 'very improper', but the Prince of Wales called this 'nonsense'.[29] Lady Frances laid most of the blame upon women: 'Too modest to openly speak to their sons, not too modest to openly condone the lives of many a man they know of'.[30] It seemed that in her family, no one had spoken to Lord Colin. Nor at the height of his divorce case did they speak of him. When Lord

Ronnie called on the Glyns at the Vicarage, he found the Duke, who was staying with them during the case. 'The talk was all of other subjects and didn't roll once on the C.C. business.'[31]

Lord Colin's divorce became a *cause célèbre*; he had petitioned for divorce on the grounds of Lady Colin's adultery with four men, including Lord Blandford, while Lady Colin counter-petitioned on grounds of his adultery with his housekeeper, Mary Watson. After three days of the most unpleasant publicity, Lady Colin lost her case against Lord Colin's adultery with his housekeeper, who was found to be a virgin, while her husband lost his against her. It was said afterwards that the jury believed a lady could have one lover, but not four.

The costs of the case were enormous, said to be over £15,000, and Lord Colin had to declare bankruptcy. Unable to afford the hundred guineas to read with a barrister in good chambers, he nevertheless hammered away at the Bar so that he would be able to practise abroad. Whistler's 'lovely Leopard', Lady Colin, now hopelessly *déclassée*, adopted the eccentricity of wearing a 'moving' necklace: 'I always wear a live snake round my throat in hot weather: it keeps one's neck so cool,' she told an astonished observer.[32] Ostracized by everyone and without any financial support, she became a professional journalist. She had a weekly column in *The World* and eventually became editor of *The Ladies' Field* magazine.

It was an immense relief for the Lornes to escape from London to Malta, where they would not be so bothered by the 'divorce business'. Princess Louise had not been able to sleep for ten days and her suffering wrung Lorne's heart: 'There is nothing so horrible as the torture of sleeplessness,' he wrote home on 26 January 1887.[33] Prince Alfred was stationed at Malta, where he had established his family in San Antonio Palace. He and his Duchess were more than delighted to welcome the Lornes on a ten-week visit, which the Princess thoroughly enjoyed.

On April 3rd she travelled with Lady Sophie to Aix-les-Bains. Her arrival was welcomed by those of the Household, who were finding the holiday with Queen Victoria tedious. Princess Louise's conversational gambits were original and sometimes 'a little beyond the rules'.[34] When a Schleswig-Holstein niece had been taken by the Christians to lunch at Windsor, she found it 'very solemn and still', except for the 'fresh and lively' Princess Louise who recounted, in the most amusing manner, the story of a man who committed suicide because he did not want to take a bath every day.[35]

As laid down by the unwritten laws of the dinner table, conversation then revolved around the simple, generalized topics of food, health, and weather. Lord Ernest Hamilton recalled how 'Few indeed in mid-Victorian days had the temerity to exploit original ideas. The intellectual level of the day did not demand it and any such attempt was eyed suspiciously.'[36] Princess Louise, however, rarely chose prosaic topics. After reading an article in *Nineteenth Century* on the Indian Army, she discussed one or two of the more obscure military points with Henry Ponsonby. The Princess had been part of the minority, who had supported Lord Ripon's efforts in India to introduce reforms and encourage better relations with the Indian populace. She thought this could only be good for England for 'if advanced and joined to the British they would support and maintain the Raj and not plot against us'.[37] 'I don't know what I should do at these long dreary evening parties, if it were not for her [Princess Louise],' Ponsonby confessed to his wife from Aix-les-Bains. Whatever others said about her 'I must say she is charming'.[38]

Now, Queen Victoria had come to Aix-les-Bains for a quiet holiday before the tiring Jubilee celebrations which lay ahead. She did not, therefore, encourage her daughter's attempts to enliven the atmosphere of her somewhat staid dinner table; a dull, hushed atmosphere was much more pleasing and restful in her opinion.

CHAPTER XXI

A Search for Direction

For Princess Louise the years from 1889 until the end of the century were ones of aimlessness and wandering. Denied a family of her own, she had also lost the company of those she held most dear: her favourite sister and brother, her mother-in-law, her best friend and her 'second father'. Since she could not utilize her abilities and intelligence in a career, her life seemed without purpose; she would seize upon new ideas or causes in the vain hope of finding something useful to do. Unhappy and frustrated, she sought refuge either in travels abroad or with her mother, the one unchanging fixture in her life.

Although she and Lorne had settled into an easy companionship, she could not rely upon him for direction. For she had married a man who, in 1871, had 'a fine independent position' and 'great expectations' yet who, in 1889, lived in a house provided by her mother and who was unable to offer her any position independent of her family. Thus the Princess, unlike most women of her period, could not anchor herself in the sea of life through her husband; she had to chart her own course.

It was not easy for either of them. Like the Prince of Wales, Lorne also lived for over fifty years in the shadow of an overpowering parent. But where the Prince had a large income, innumerable functions and a country estate with its attendant interests and responsibilities, Lorne had none of these. Duchess Mimi welcomed the Lornes to Inveraray, but only as family visitors; the permanent residence there of Lady V meant that there was little left for Princess Louise to do. Her absence in Canada after Duchess Elizabeth's death had upset the natural pattern of handing on local responsibilities; it was Lady V who, needing occupation, had taken on many of these duties.

Princess Louise certainly felt the lack of such things in her life. While staying with the Queen at Balmoral, she had visited her Wales niece, the newly married Princess Louise, Duchess of Fife. Princess Louise might have set the precedent for marrying a subject, but the Waleses had ensured that their daughter not only gained a husband but a great position from the beginning. 'I shd be dancing over the hilltops had I a 1/4 of her luck,'

Princess Louise wrote to Constance Battersea. 'Fancy marrying a man you love *and* living in that beautiful property!' Princess Louise envied her niece for she was 'the little mistress of all around her'. It was 'what one reads of in *books* but never comes true as a rule'.

From Balmoral she joined Lorne at Inveraray, where they had been asked for two weeks. 'How I wish I cd show you Inveraray,' Princess Louise told Lady Battersea, 'but you see I am a stranger there now, or have to be, so its impossible.'[1]

Princess Louise had been summoned there by the Duke for a family meeting to discuss the sad affairs of Lord Walter. Having run up fearful debts in the City, he had been sent out to America, but had misread the market and been ruined. It was decided to send him to Johannesburg, where people were making fortunes in the South African gold mines. Eager to start again, he had sailed from Southampton in January without his wife and children, Douglas and Lilah. In 1888, when Lady Walter had gone to winter in Biarritz with Lilah, he had discovered that she was cohabiting with a lover, Mr Allan Gordon, and had to remove Lilah. In the train to Paris, Lilah always remembered how her father had 'sobbed like a child', yet had said nothing to her of what had passed and she, of course, understood nothing of what had happened.

Lord Walter had no intention of causing the family further distress by involving them in another divorce case. He merely lived apart from Lady Walter and legally appointed the Duke and Lorne as guardians of his children, who would be brought up at Inveraray until he could again provide for them. Then, on 1 May 1889, a telegram had arrived from South Africa to say that he had fallen ill with dysentery. He died far away from his own; as Lorne said, 'His is a sad story.'[2] As his executor, Lorne had to settle the estate, which was declared bankrupt, so the family were again involved with the law courts.

Although Douglas and Lilah could have been brought up by the Lornes, it was decided to leave them at Inveraray in familiar surroundings, rather than uproot them yet again after their extremely unsettled childhood. This may seem a strange decision given Princess Louise's desire for children. Yet at ten and eight they were no substitute for the babies she wanted, since they were already marked by the trauma of their early years.

The family also decided that Lady Walter's demands to have her children back should be refused in accordance with Lord Walter's wishes, expressed in his will, that they be kept away from her. It was made clear that, should she press her claim in the courts, the Argyll family would produce evidence of her co-habitation. Poor, foolish Lady Walter did not want to harm her children and dropped her claim; she never saw them again. After marrying Mr Gordon in 1890, she died in 1892 at the age of only thirty-seven, having led a 'sad, wasted, useless life'.[3]

Despite her participation in these serious family discussions, Princess Louise was able to enjoy being at Inveraray again because of the presence of umpteen nephews and nieces. She threw herself into organizing treats, interfering with their schoolroom routine and taking them off on visits. The children adored their Aunt Louise: 'she was always full of fun and so charming as well as very good looking', remembered one niece and they had plenty of opportunities to be amused by her antics.[4] One of the familiar faces at Inveraray was Dr McDonald, who came to the Castle every morning 'by way of looking after the books'. Princess Louise developed severe toothache and the old doctor declared the tooth must come out then and there. Unfortunately, his dental skills were not quite up to the mark and he had great difficulty in extracting her tooth. She tried to escape but the doctor refused to let go, with the result that she dragged him round the room with her. Lorne immortalized this painful and primitive performance in a little sketch, to the delight of the children.[5]

The girls were especially gleeful when she disagreed with their governesses, which their own mamas rarely did. Lilah recalled 'laughing till I could hardly stand' when Princess Louise, resplendent in the Campbell tartan coat and skirt she always wore in Scotland, tried to get through the popular song, 'O for the Wings of a Dove', with the German governess. They could not agree on the tempo and, after a few bars, Princess Louise broke off to correct the governess 'Ach, fräulein, das ist *nicht zusammen!*'[6]

It was during these years that the Princess began to assume a more public role. Apart from the spell in Canada, she had lived a quiet and private family life since her marriage. In the main, her outside interests had centred upon art and a few chosen charitable organizations. Now, she started to spread her net more widely. The sense of duty inculcated in her pushed her on to overcome shyness and a dread of 'being stared at'. But she found the work deeply satisfying; it enabled her to combine practicality with creativity and gave her endless opportunities to use her talent for organization. And, of course, it was the only work open to her as a woman and a princess.

Lady Battersea, who worked with her in many of these ventures, wrote: 'the Princess was the heart and soul of many popular and charitable movements, she had unbounded energy that often outran her health and strength, and never grudged giving time and attention'.[7] Princess Louise preferred helping women and children. She followed her mother's convention of not giving her name to any society until it was established, and tended to favour local, Kensington or Scottish, groups. The Princess helped the disabled but, as she told Lord Ronnie, 'I always set my face against incurables as I think it so cruel to do all one can to prolong their misery which no doubt these institutions do,' adding, 'if I were an incurable I shd pray to be helped out of this world'.[8]

Her pet project that autumn was evening classes for girls, and later boys, in the East End. This had seemed to her a natural progression from the day schools, which poor girls left at ten, and also something which could be of use to older girls, who had to work in the day. In 1885 Princess Louise had met Dr Paton, Principal of a Congregational College at Nottingham, who had come to her with his idea for a national association of evening classes. Princess Louise had agreed to become President and had persuaded Lorne's old Cambridge friend, Cyril Flower, now Lord Battersea, to become Chairman. Considered one of the most handsome men in London, he was said to be the original Eric of *Eric or Little by Little*. Princess Louise had first met his wife through her sister, Annie de Rothschild, who had married Eliot Yorke, equerry to Princes Alfred and Leopold. As a result, Princess Louise's friendship with her was much more intimate than it would otherwise have been. Connie Battersea joined the Committee and worked with the Princess to promote the Recreative Evening Schools' Association (R.E.S.A.), which was the forerunner of the present day evening classes run by local educational authorities throughout Britain.

Although keen to promote the study of the arts in these classes, Princess Louise urged that the teaching of art should not hold too prominent a place in the curriculum. She saw the risk that the Radicals and Socialists would denounce the promotion of art as 'one of the foolish luxuries of the upper classes'. Thus, 'the idea of art teaching should creep along with the scheme rather than be pushed forward by itself and so risk attracting adverse public criticism'. The Princess believed that these classes should teach practical subjects, which would enable people not only to pass their evenings in interesting occupations, instead of in dreary monotony, but also to find work. 'I want the people to understand we want to teach them good useful trades', she told Cyril Battersea.[9]

While at Inveraray the Princess was in correspondence with Dr Paton and Lady Battersea about an exhibition of pupils' work at the Batterseas' town house. She was also making arrangements to lead a deputation to the London School Board to persuade them to allow the R.E.S.A. to use its school buildings for evening classes. Another plan was to establish extension classes at the London Polytechnics; a grant from the Charity Commissioners would enable the R.E.S.A. to set up Social Institutes to provide technical instruction and recreational classes under the auspices of the Polytechnics. These Institutes, now known as Adult Educational Institutes, are in existence today to provide further education.

Much of these advances lay in the future but, in 1889, after four years of work, Princess Louise was pleased at the interest shown by girls and boys from such poor areas of London as Bermondsey, Nine Elms and Holloway. She was delighted when a policeman said that, where formerly two policemen had been required to patrol the streets in the district of the schools, a young girl could now walk alone in safety. Princess Louise hoped that in the nineties the R.E.S.A. would have a presence in every town in the land.

Another development in her working life during the nineties was the increase in the number of her public engagements. Not only was Lorne unable to provide Princess Louise with a position, but he was beholden to her for one. In contrast to their early married life, he was being drawn into a royal career. He now always accompanied the Princess on her functions. He still did not like the idea of his wife speaking in public; ladies then simply did not utter so much as an audible 'thank you' from a public platform. So he accompanied her in order to make the speeches and thank the audience on her behalf. By the 1890s, Princess Louise was perfectly capable of carrying out functions on her own, but it had become impossible to change such a long standing custom. Anyway, it gave Lorne some occupation although he always protested that he disliked such functions.

After a short spell in town, the Lornes had hoped to pass the early autumn at Inveraray but the installation of electricity and the Princess's health delayed their visit. 'I got violent tic all down the side of my head & face & oh! Connie dear,' she wrote on 10 September 1890 to Lady Battersea, 'the pain for now over a fortnight and never a wink of sleep at night – far worse than Sir Joshua's "tortures" or anything read of in history . . . The pain has been like red hot pincers twisting out the nerves of my face and ears.'[10] The only treatment then prescribed was rest and 'feeding up' which did little to help the patient. Unfortunately, her convalescence at Overstrand was short-lived; on her return to London she had another attack of neuralgia and then neuritis in her left hand. On doctor's advice she went to Eastbourne, where the mild sea air helped: 'I have been here *quite* incog so that there shd be no botherings and less expense and it has done me good,'[11] she informed Connie Battersea on October 6th before she joined the Queen at Balmoral at the end of the month.

While some courtiers liked the dull, safe atmosphere of 'Balmorality', others welcomed the arrival of the Princess, who breathed fresh, stimulating air into the place with her enthusiasms and entertaining stories. As one of her protégés, Charlie Warr, wrote: 'Her mind was always full of creative ideas. She was widely read and unusually well-informed on the political, cultural and social issues of the times.'[12] She could be relied upon to introduce the latest topics in a vain endeavour to interest the Court in the outside world, just as she had done before her marriage.

She launched the latest Society clique, the 'Souls', as a topic of conversation at one of the ladies-only dinners the Queen now held regularly. Although not a Soul herself, the Princess knew most of the group, who included Arthur Balfour, the Wyndhams and Violet Rutland, and they exchanged visits, so she naturally defended them at Balmoral. Their name, the Souls, originated because, to non-intellectuals, they were supposedly always talking about each others' souls. Queen Victoria had little time for such pretensions and said, 'they really should be told *not* to be so silly!'[13]

Nor did the Princess confine herself to Society chatter; her wide-ranging interests encompassed even African affairs. Indeed, one cause which engrossed her was the scramble for Africa. She had not only read up on Africa; she had also learnt about it from Lorne. He was an active Director of the British East African Company, which helped to secure British territorial claims to Kenya and Uganda, and served as President of the Royal Geographical Society. The adventures of the great Victorian explorers, Livingstone, Stanley and Speke, had captured her imagination, as well as that of her countrymen, and exposed the horrors of the slave-trade and cannibalism.

It was through Lorne and Princess Louise that Stanley had been invited to Windsor in May 1890 to discuss his latest two-and-a-half year expedition in Africa. After dinner, everyone had assembled in the White Drawing Room on chairs drawn up opposite a large map of Africa and listened to the small, brown-skinned man with snow-white hair and piercing blue eyes recount details of his last expedition, expound on the state of Africa and warn them against the aggressive policy now being adopted by Germany.

By the following month Lord Salisbury had begun his successful negotiations to divide up Africa through treaties between the European Powers. On the east coast, Zanzibar became a British protectorate in exchange for the ceding of the British island of Heligoland to Germany. Lord Salisbury had sent out a new Consul-General to Zanzibar, but a former member of the viceregal staff in Canada, Sir Francis de Winton, who was now serving in Africa, wrote to Princess Louise to abuse this official, Ewen-Smith, with whose policies he disagreed. De Winton told Princess Louise that it was essential Britain had a sound man there, and Ewen-Smith should be removed by the Queen.

The Princess thus began to try and interest Balmoral in the affairs of the Colonial Service and Zanzibar. She discussed it with the Queen, who was not especially interested in this private quarrel. She then talked to Sir Henry Ponsonby and his assistant, Colonel Bigge. Not surprisingly, they cared little for such matters and neither knew who Ewen-Smith was, nor why Zanzibar was important: 'Really Princess Louise's political intrigues are beyond me,' Sir Henry confessed on November 1st.[14]

The Princess was delighted with the idea when Colonel John Grey advised her to write to the German Emperor to suggest he demand the recall of Ewen-Smith. Sir Henry Ponsonby luckily pulled her up before any damage was done. To give the Princess her due, she immediately saw the truth of his words, admitting, 'Well, perhaps it would be better not to.'[15] Sir Henry had to explain that, although she could talk to her German relations privately, not only was it not in the Emperor's powers to remove a British Consul-General, but it would be quite unconstitutional for him to interfere or, indeed, for her to do so.

De Winton, of course, had used the Princess to further his own purposes and she, out of loyalty to him for his work for her in Canada, had misguidedly tried to help. Longing to be involved actively in events, she had rushed ahead without sufficient forethought. Yet her causes were never lightly dismissed by the more intelligent courtiers;

they knew that she had a grasp of domestic and foreign affairs, often went straight to the heart of the matter and always, according to Sir Henry Ponsonby, discussed a question or issue 'most capitally'. Her weaknesses were a tendency to be indecisive, and to be carried away by her own enthusiasm. Princess Louise did not just discuss her ideas; she usually tried to persuade courtiers to follow them through. This was not always popular, as Sir Henry intimated: 'While at one moment one complains of Princess Louise, the next one is fascinated by her.'[16]

The Princess now felt at home in the world outside the Court and was full of the latest developments in current affairs. When she tried to introduce topics to the Household, they censured her for being 'meddling' or 'dangerous'. William Jenner had once told Sir Henry how bad it was both mentally and physically to be long at Balmoral; 'he found himself excited about small things which when he got away he didn't care a damn for'.[17] The Queen herself was known to react against the monotony by making rows out of sheer boredom. Connie Battersea wrote after a stint at Court: 'I feel inclined to scream when I am with that depressed household.'[18] Princess Louise did not scream, she merely did her best to widen their interests to include the outside world.

Back in London, the Princess called, somewhat unpunctually, on her old friend Sir Edgar Boehm. He had asked her to call in the afternoon specifically to give her 'valuable advice' on a design he was preparing. At a quarter to six, while they were talking, her adored old master suddenly collapsed unconscious on to the floor. The dazed Princess tried to revive him; she unfastened his collar and felt for his pulse, which did not appear to beat; then, remembering that moving a person's arms backwards and forwards was said to restore life, she moved his arms 'but there was only a gurgling noise in his throat'.[19] She needed help, so she ran out of the studio, along the covered corridor which linked this complex of artists studios, and knocked at the door of Alfred Gilbert's studio. He rushed back with the Princess to try to revive the unconscious Sir Edgar and sent for his doctor. Then, realizing that Boehm must be dead, Gilbert 'begged her not to remain as, it would be unpleasant to have to give evidence at an Inquest'.[20]

The next morning, December 13th, the news of Sir Edgar Boehm's death was widely reported in the newspapers, with widely varying accounts of the circumstances. London buzzed with rumour, especially when it became known that a member of the Royal Family was involved. Lady Abercromby, who had been in his studio on the 11th, declared Princess Louise had found Sir Edgar 'sitting in his chair in a faint' and, while she called for Mr Gilbert, he had 'passed away'.[21]

Rumours about a liaison between the Princess and Sir Edgar also circulated; later fuelled by the oft-repeated gossip related to Wilfred Blunt by the Victorian *poule de luxe*, Skittles, whose friendship with the Prince of Wales lent a semblance of authenticity to it.

According to Skittles, who retold the story in 1909, Boehm spent three months at Balmoral in 1869 working on a statue of John Brown, and he and Princess Louise 'became intimate' though not lovers. Queen Victoria heard of the attachment, sent Princess Louise to Germany and then tried to marry her off to Lord Cowper and Lord Hartington. Eventually, she married Lord Lorne but it was not a success, so Princess Louise took other lovers, including Boehm. 'While he was making love to her Boehm broke a blood-vessel and died actually in the Pcss's arms.' She had sent her lady-in-waiting away and there was nobody about, so she took the key of the studio out of Boehm's pocket and, 'covered with blood', got a hansom cab and drove to Sir Francis Laking. They returned to find Boehm dead, and made up a story that he died lifting a statue. Skittles ended her tale with a flourish: the Princess was so shocked 'that she has not since had a lover'. Apparently, Boehm told her of his liaison with the Princess, and the Prince of Wales knew all about it as well.[22]

Equally erroneous was the first account of Boehm's death to reach Queen Victoria 'that poor Louise had found him dead,' which she soon learnt was not true.[23] It is not known whether the account of Boehm's death in the Queen's Journal is the original version told her by Princess Louise at the time, or the edited transcript version made years later by Princess Beatrice, who then destroyed the originals. Princess Louise's own account of what happened adds much to the account in the Queen's Journal: 'It was a terrible shock, doubly so as he was quite well when he met me in the long passage: as you see I did not go (unattended and unannounced) as all the papers pleased to say. Lady Sophia and I were talking to him some 20 minutes and then Sophia said "as your carriage will be here in a minute I think I will walk home" and in much less than 5 I heard that awful cry. Sir Edgar had carried a bust to show me wh I entreated him not to, also pushed some heavy things & must have overexerted himself. It was found to be aneurism of the heart.'[24]

Sir Edgar was a delicate man and, as the Queen pointed out at the time, suffered much from asthma and bronchitis. 'I work like an engine' he once said[25], and Princess Louise believed overwork had killed him. 'He often complained of pain and difficulty of breathing for many years,' she told the Duchess of Atholl. 'Really I think (only we must not tell the Queen) that that very big statue of "the Prince" he did for the Windsor Park was the cause of his death.' Boehm had told her that he had not had dry clothes on his back for six weeks, owing to the constant stream of water necessary to keep the work moist; he also complained of chest pains after having to stretch up for a long time when working on a large statue. The Princess found 'the shock and the whole thing made me very ill, I am not yet strong and am haunted by the whole, wh all passed like a flash'.[26]

No evidence exists to corroborate the story of a liaison between Sir Edgar and the Princess. After his death, the executors burnt his papers and studio accounts; during the Great War two trunks of family papers were burnt and the family changed its name to the less foreign sounding Boteler. The evidence, that remains in letters and memoirs, shows that, far from being hidden, the close and long-standing friendship between the Princess and Boehm was known to everyone. She was in and out of Boehm's studios and house; she gave innumerable books and presents to his wife and children, and her relations with all of them were extremely visible.

Everyone knew, as the Queen herself wrote, how upset Princess Louise was, for Boehm 'was a very kind friend of hers and she was his pupil'.[27] Burne-Jones wrote of Boehm after his death, 'His was a nice face, wasn't it, and a personality that was fascinating; the brightest company and dearest way of laughing.'[28] He was yet another loss from the diminishing group of those Princess Louise held most dear.

On December 20th the Princess, breaking with precedent, went to his funeral service at St Paul's with Colonel Bigge, who represented the Queen. Afterwards they told the Queen it 'had been touching and impressive and largely attended'[29] for, as Sir Frederick Leighton wrote to Watts, 'he was a most loveable man and many will mourn him'. He was buried 'in his working clothes, as he fell'.[30]

In need of a spring break, the Princess went to stay with Alice de Rothschild at the Villa Victoria in Grasse. Lady Battersea's Cousin Alice was also hostess to Queen Victoria, who came every day from the Hôtel to use her spacious grounds. Lady Battersea was now Princess

Louise's most regular companion. She found being a courtier a 'strange experience' and Court life so '*kleinlich*' and narrow; like Princess Louise, she preferred to keep a distance from it. Nevertheless, she noted that Princess Louise, too, could be impossible at times: 'HRH is very tireing [sic] and *rémuanté* [sic] and will *not* be punctual which simply drives Alice wild.'[31]

Lady Battersea was, however, very fond of the Princess and thought her 'a truly attractive and gifted woman'. She only regretted that she could not 'obtain the influence for good' over her restlessness that she would like. 'It is impossible,' she wrote home. 'I think the Pss's health has something to do with her queer and capricious character'; there were so many contradictions apparent in it.

Lady Battersea noticed that the Royalties had made themselves extremely popular with 'the lower orders', particularly Princess Louise who 'walks into the laundry, irons the linen and jokes with the laundry maids'.[32] Since Princess Louise behaved like this in her own homes, she thought nothing of doing the same at Court. That she found the maids more interesting than the courtiers, naturally excited comment from the Household.

When she gamely tried to make the best of a boring holiday and inject some fun into it, her attempts met with opposition. After meeting a young lieutenant 'with fine grey eyes and beautiful teeth', who was bored to death and 'evidently much struck with HRH', the Princess had the grand idea of arranging tea in the garden for all the officers: unfortunately, the by-now exhausted Cousin Alice did not seem at all enthusiastic.[33] Used to arranging impromptu tea-parties with the Argylls at home, Princess Louise forgot that at Court, even in the South of France, such an event involved extra care and organization to conform to her royal position, especially with Queen Victoria in the vicinity.

As the most interesting, lively person about, Princess Louise was a favourite topic in the diaries and correspondence of courtiers. Her every word and deed was written up for posterity. When the Royalties became rather bored and bickered, such trifling moments were immortalized by courtiers as major rows. Marie Mallet, in attendance on the Queen, wrote: '. . . the rival Psses have already begun to tease each other, what a time we shall have between the two!'[34] because Princess Beatrice wanted to try the harmonium for the Sunday service and Princess Louise wanted the usual organ. 'A Battle Royal' ensued and 'the poor old Queen who heard the end of it was made quite miserable'.[35] But the Princess Louise, who emerged from the pen of Marie Mallet, is very different from the Princess the Argylls and her old friends knew. As a maid of honour with little experience of the world, Marie Mallet's view of Princess Louise was more that of rather a sanctimonious schoolgirl fascinated by the older, sophisticated Princess, than a mature observer. One moment Marie found Princess Louise 'a fascinating woman', who turned 'the heads of all men', yet the next she '*cannot* speak the truth, she tells more lies in 10 minutes than most people do in 10 years!', and then again 'Princess Louise gives us quite enough to think and talk about, she loves intrigue and we all have to be on the alert in order to cope with her'.[36]

Marie Mallet seems to have expected Royalties to be perfect and above displaying any normal characteristics: '*Royal* human nature seems so small, so mean, so unworthy, it disgusts one,' she wrote, adding 'though after all perhaps one is no better oneself!'[37] The public, who rarely came into contact with royalty, longed to see the human in them; whereas the Household, who saw them on a daily basis, wanted to excise their human tendencies. Ethel Smyth found that courtiers all had an air about them of 'distinguished boredom'. The Household displayed 'no ups or downs of moods . . . no enthusiasms, no individual opinions, and for Heaven's sake no originality!'[38] It is no wonder that many of them were so critical of Princess Louise for she possessed all these characteristics to a marked degree.

Marie Mallet wrote that Princess Louise was 'amiable enough but never have I come across a more dangerous woman, to gain her end she would stick at nothing! One would have given her a wide berth in the sixteenth century, happily she is powerless in the nineteenth'[39]; yet all Princess Louise did on this holiday was bicker with her sister over an organ and play Halma all day.

It is noticeable that the members of the Household who liked and got on with Princess Louise, were those whose sense of values and intelligence were the least affected by the practice of continual deference at Court and the inevitable inventory of petty 'bickerings and jealousies',[40] which were part of the life there and always shocked outsiders and non-courtiers. The Princess was 'dangerous' only in the sense of being different from the run-of-the-mill royalty; Henry Ponsonby, a far more experienced courtier than Marie Mallet, found the Princess 'v pleasant', but then he liked her giving him 'a stir up' and was sorry whenever she departed.

CHAPTER XXII

A Public Commission

In the early months of 1892, Lorne was appointed to the honorary office of Governor and Constable of Windsor Castle. He had already earned a considerable reputation as a man of letters through his verse, fiction and prolific contributions to periodicals; he now began a history of Windsor Castle. Unfortunately, his appointment did not escape the notice of Henry Labouchère, the editor of *Truth*, whose violent attack drew national attention to it. The appointment was a disadvantage in the election campaign Lorne was fighting as a Unionist in Bradford, his latest constituency. Lorne remained philosophical since 'I am certain of a beating there anyway.'[1] It was considered such a hopeless constituency for the Unionists, owing to the huge Irish population, that they had been unable to find anyone to take it on for five years. Once again, Lorne was unlucky. The General Election, held in July 1892, saw the return of a Liberal majority, and Lorne was defeated.

The Queen tried to help by consulting Lorne on political matters and appointing him a Privy Councillor. He, with Princess Louise, attended the Queen at the swearing in of the new Privy Council at Osborne. Queen Victoria was very displeased that Gladstone had won a fourth innings as Prime Minister at the age of 82; she had no intention of making his Government feel comfortable, as Lorne related to his father. The new men 'came in very shamefacedly in single file', while the Queen 'sat facing them on a yellow satin sofa, a table with notepaper in front of her'. Lorne thought it was exactly like a scene in a dames' school with a group of schoolboys having to face their Head Mistress. The swearing in began and the absurdity of the scene struck the Lornes greatly. When five or six of the new Ministers went down on their knees 'most clumsily' around the table in front of the Queen, it was like 'little boys pleading not to be whipped'. Then Lord Houghton, who was nearest to the Queen, was sworn and, instead of rising from his knees, shuffled sideways on them to allow the next man to kiss hands, who also 'tried to walk on his knees'; Lorne 'felt inclined to give the whole posse a shove when they would all have gone down like ninepins'.[2]

He thought they looked 'a mournful crew'. The Queen, however, thought they were distinctly dangerous; she had already refused to countenance Mr Gladstone's appointment of the Radical MP, Henry Labouchère, to his Cabinet. His scurrilous articles about her family in *Truth* rendered him ineligible for any position, which made it necessary for her to meet him. Lorne was much teased about the fact that 'Labby' was his cousin.

Princess Louise saw other members of the Clan on October 14th, when she joined Lorne at Aunt Dot's in Edinburgh, in order to attend two functions on Tuesday the 18th; even here, Lorne's occupation was through his wife. The Old Parliament Hall in Edinburgh Castle had been restored and she had been asked to re-open the building. At that time, the regiment stationed in the Castle was the 91st Argyllshire Highlanders which, since April 1872, were styled 'The Princess Louise's Argyllshire Highlanders' and bore on their regimental colours the Boar's Head and the family motto of the Argyll Campbells and the coronet and cypher of Princess Louise. She had also become Honorary Colonel-in-Chief of the regiment, which in 1881 had amalgamated with the 93rd Sutherland Highlanders.

The Princess's interest in the regiment was by no means that of a mere figurehead. Sketches of her designs for the buckle, keepers, tongue and buttons of their uniform still remain at Stirling Castle to bear witness to her abiding interest. The buckle for the sword belt and the cap badge, which are still worn, are also those designed by Princess Louise. After reviewing the regiment on an especially gusty day, the Princess had also suggested and instituted an embroidered weighted tab, designed to hold swirling kilts in place.

After her morning function on October 18th, the Princess was delighted to join 'my Regiment' for lunch, followed by the presentation of Colours. The ceremony took place on the Esplanade where she 'briefly and earnestly' told the soldiers she was proud of the regiment bearing her name. Janey Campbell was with her and Lorne, and afterwards told Niall about the ceremony: 'The presentation of the new Colours to the 91st by Aunt LooLoo was very pretty,' but '. . . did you see how absolutely hideous we all looked in the *Graphic*? . . . Aunt LooLoo looked like a cook out of place, Uncle Ian like an alderman gobble and Nicky and I most provoking.'[3]

Princess Louise might not look her best in photographs, but she always looked lovely in the plays and *tableaux vivants*, which had become a feature of the New Year festivities at Osborne. The nineties ushered in a stream of concerts, recitals and theatricals at Court, all watched avidly by a benevolent Queen. This owed a great deal to Prince Henry of Battenberg, whose influence with her had resulted in the re-introduction of such entertainments. It was activities like these which drew Princess Louise back into the royal fold.

When Lord Ronnie saw Lorne in London in January 1893, Lorne was 'very full' of the *tableaux* at Osborne, and the plans to perform *She Stoops to Conquer*. Having dealt with a scene from Shakespeare, the family cast of Battenbergs, Lornes and Connaughts, supported by the Ponsonbys and Queen Victoria's Indian servants, were growing ambitious. Under the tutelage of Arthur Collins, Princess Louise and Princess Beatrice with the two Ponsonby sons and Major Bigge were soon in rehearsal.

Queen Victoria attended, which made some of the younger members of the cast extremely nervous, and she exercised the royal prerogative as director. In the part where young Fritz Ponsonby was supposed to mistake Princess Louise for the barmaid, he familiarly chucked her under the chin. Queen Victoria considered this overdone, and sent a message requesting him to abstain from any chucking. So, at the next rehearsal he kept his distance, only to receive another message that he was overdoing it the other way.

Although Princess Louise and Princess Beatrice acted well, they kept forgetting their lines. The rest of the cast used to prompt them but there was one scene when they were on alone together; 'of course they stuck, each thinking it was the other's fault'.[4] The audience tried to help by giving a round of applause to muffle the prompter's words but the princesses were unable to continue, so the stage manager quickly let the curtain down. In spite of such thespian disgrace, Princess Louise retained fond memories of the play. She even gave Fritz Ponsonby a silver cigarette box as a memento; it was inscribed inside 'from Kate Hardcastle'.[5]

The Princess was back at Kensington Palace for her forty-fifth birthday. Her favourite present was a silver head of William IV given by Lord Ronnie, who the following week accompanied the Lornes on a holiday to Italy. The Princess was especially keen for him to accompany them because he had long been in low spirits. What she did not know was that, since the early eighties, he had been struggling to contain the secret of his homosexuality.

Much as she loved him, Princess Louise had always thought Lord Ronnie 'rather effeminate' and restless, but homosexuality was not a subject that people thought about, let alone discussed in those days. She and Lorne were unaware of the real reason for Lord Ronnie's erratic behaviour. Lorne put it down to too much drink: 'He writes sensibly . . . during the day, but 2 letters written from his club in the evening seem to have been written in an almost dead drunk state.'[6] He believed club talk did not matter in the least 'if there is nothing of truth in the stories'. Lorne's proposed solution was for Lord Ronnie to 'marry some fair Republican and settle in the US for a while'.[7]

There were, however, others who knew the truth; in particular, the circle of homosexuals and bohemians who frequented Venice in the late eighties and nineties. A young Roger Fry had written to a friend from Venice, in May 1891, of the 'most extraordinary company I ever met'. This included Lord Ronnie, 'a middle-aged man with a splendidly finely featured aristocratic face not yet quite brutalised by debauchery, the most perfect manner, easy and affable, perhaps a little too indifferent. He talked very well about Greek sculpture and Giorgione and so on.'[8] Another homosexual, J.A. Symonds, wrote disapprovingly to Edmund Gosse of Lord Ronnie's peculiarities as being 'of the rankest most diabolical kind'.[9] When Oscar Wilde's novel *The Picture of Dorian Gray* was published, the Venice crowd instantly recognized Lord Ronnie, as the original of the decadent Lord Henry Wootton.

The Princess had to be back in London for the unveiling of her statue of Queen Victoria at Kensington on June 28th. The idea had been formulated by Princess Louise and Teddy Glyn at the time of the Jubilee in 1887. They had wanted to commemorate the Queen's childhood association with the parish of Kensington and, since Princess Louise lived in Kensington and was both a sculptress and the Queen's daughter, it had seemed entirely appropriate that she should undertake this memorial. Teddy Glyn had become Chairman of the Committee of the Kensington Jubilee Memorial to raise funds for it.

Princess Louise had decided to depict her mother as a young woman of nineteen in her Coronation robes, seated on the throne and holding the sceptre. Although the Princess was a quick, hard worker, she could only devote limited spare time to the project. Those who did not know her tended to assume that she was an amateur and heavily dependent upon expert assistance. Alfred Gilbert, who was going to superintend the erection of the completed statue, said that public

'*What is most enjoyed!*' Colonel William Probert
on the telephone in his office at Kensington Palace,
c. 1902-6, pencil.

Ethel Badcock, 1896.

Right:
Lorne in Egypt, photographed by his
wife, 1906.

Scenes of the Nile: *Arab Village;*
Group of Arabs under Palm Trees,
watercolour, 1906.

Princess Louise greeting her mother at the unveiling of her statue of *Queen Victoria* in Kensington Gardens, June 1893.

The studio at Kensington Palace, showing clockwise: *Self-bust*, n.d., terracotta; sketch of an angel for the *Memorial to Prince Alfred and Prince Leopold;* sketch for the *Effigy of Mrs Erskine Wemyss*, c.1895-7, marble; a *Horse's Head*, n.d.; *St George Slaying the Dragon*, n.d., bronze.

Detail of the *Memorial to the Colonial Soldiers who fell in the Boer War*, 1903-5, bronze.

Self-bust, n.d., terracotta.

Rosneath Castle in 1935. Sold in 1940 and left roofless by developers, it was condemned and demolished in 1961. The grounds are now a mobile home park.

Princess Louise with the Prince of Wales (later the Duke of Windsor) at The Princess Louise Hospital for Children, Kensington, 1933.

Princess Louise's favourite photograph of herself, taken at Kensington Palace, 1927.

The 9th Duke of Argyll (Lorne) writing a telegram, 1910.

opinion would inevitably decide that the work had been carried out by another hand. This was exactly what happened. 'People said of course that her master, the sculptor Boehm, had the chief hand in it,'[10] wrote Caroline Holland.

However, her studio assistants emphasized the Princess's independence, as well as her aversion to accept any but mechanical help. 'She is the master and enforces her ideas; and though distinguished artist-visitors may always be ready with suggestions, she never accepts a hint unless it . . . satisfies her own convictions,'[11] the art critic Spielmann wrote. Lady Sophie told Caroline Holland that the rumours about Boehm were 'utterly untrue'. Sir Edgar had 'criticised and advised of course, but the Princess was so determined to do the whole thing herself that she would not allow him so much as to lay a finger upon it'.[12]

The Queen had first seen the statue in July 1890. 'Louise's statue is a fine thing now, and admired by all who have seen it, including the Queen,' Lorne had written to Lord Archie on July 13th.[13] Three years later, on June 20th, the statue was in position on the Broad Walk in Kensington Gardens and protected by a tarpaulin cover. However, the involvement of the 'dreaded' Board of Works had added considerably to the Princess's workload. They were quite prepared to lay down gravel on the footway to prevent the Queen's horses slipping, when entering the gardens for the unveiling, but when it came to the erection of the statue, they were prepared only to dig a hole in the ground. The cost of the concrete foundation, the ballast and cement, and any other materials of labour must all be borne by the Princess, yet carried out by their own contractors at the scheduled rates.

Finding that the planned unveiling ceremony was too formal for her tastes, the Princess decided to include a group of twenty-four, small children, whose presence would symbolize the Queen's childhood in Kensington and the innumerable children who played in Kensington Gardens every day. One of these was Lady Libby's six-year-old daughter, Lesley Clough-Taylor. 'Whereas most people are presented to their Sovereigns when they come out at 18,' she wrote afterwards, 'I made my curtsey to her when I was 6, dressed in a little white silk frock with lace on it, in an overtrimmed white hat with feathers on it, and black silk stockings on my legs.'[14] Julian Grenfell and the other boys wore frilly muslin shirts and white linen knickerbockers. The children had previously rehearsed in Princess Louise's garden, so they were well-prepared for the great event, which was held on the anniversary of Queen Victoria's Coronation.

Early on the afternoon of the 28th June, Princess Louise walked across her garden and out through the studio gate into Kensington Gardens to watch while the tarpaulin was removed from the statue, and to supervise the draping of a Union Jack in its place. Stands had been erected on the Broad Walk facing the statue with several tents nearby and seats for the band: all was in readiness for the unveiling.

Just after five o'clock the Queen with Princess Beatrice and Prince Henry of Battenberg arrived at Addison Road Station and drove in an open landau past Holland House and into Kensington High Street. 'My old native town was beautifully decorated, though unfortunately just when we were in the middle of the High St, a most violent storm, almost like a waterspout came on & we had to shut the carriage,' Queen Victoria recorded.[15] The Queen arrived in the Broad Walk in the middle of this downpour, so there was a hurried consultation of dripping officials and princesses in waterproofs. Most of the large audience had put up their umbrellas, but mamas and nannies had to hurry across to protect their children, who stood in a line in front of the statue.

Then the rain stopped, the mamas returned to their seats, the Queen's carriage was opened, Princess Louise removed her waterproof and advanced to welcome Queen Victoria, and out came the sun. The MP for Kensington read 'a vy nice address' to which the Queen replied, 'It gives me pleasure to be here on this occasion in my dear old home, and to witness the unveiling of this fine statue, so admirably designed and executed by my daughter.'[16]

Princess Louise then handed Queen Victoria the silken cord attached to the flag covering the statue; the Queen handed it on to the Prince of Wales who pulled it. The flag was drawn aside and the old Queen, with Princess Louise by her side, gazed at the semblance of herself fifty-five years before. Henrietta, Lady Stanley of Alderley, later told the Princess: 'Few besides myself' were still alive who 'had assisted at that glorious spectacle' of the Coronation and 'As for Y.R.H.'s great work allow one who remembers very perfectly the lovely young Queen to thank and congratulate Y.R.H. on your truly wonderful representation of your great Mother.'[17]

The children then moved forward and began their act. They were supposed to lay their bouquets at the foot of the statue but some of the boys, in their enthusiasm, clambered up and placed their flowers on the top of the Portland stone pedestal and quickly had to be brought to order. After members of the reception committee had been presented, the children walked hand-in-hand to the Queen's carriage and made their farewells. One little girl, Esther Canzioni, was almost in tears because she thought this meant she had to go to live with the old Queen.

Next day's newspapers were full of praise for the Princess's skill. 'There is no gainsaying that a true artist had been born in the Royal Family,' declared one columnist; it was 'a labour of love' said another, linking the Princess's name with that of Rosa Bonheur, as examples to women and art students.[18] Victorian art critics admired the statue for the movement of the Queen's flowing robes, the accuracy of the details and the likeness to Queen Victoria as she was in 1838. Mr Spielmann praised 'the setting up of the figure, the arrangement of the drapery, the modelling,' and concluded that, 'This statue would have done credit to some sculptors who enjoy considerable reputations.'[19] In a more recent listing of London statues, Arthur Byron writes, 'we find Princess Louise producing a very professional statue of her mother'.[20]

After the unveiling, an iron railing was built to enclose it and a night watchman set to guard it. However, by August, Inspector Hogan was asking the Board of Works for permanent protection as the night park keeper was prevented from patrolling the park by having to stand on guard at the statue all night. Apparently, in 1893, 'the rough and mischievous element' was 'very plentiful indeed'. In the winter, Inspector Hogan had seen fifteen hundred people leave the skating pond 'roaming about in all directions and a great percentage of them were only too ready to injure anything that can be injured, just for the pure mischief of the thing'. He had no doubt that statue would be vandalized if 'not constantly protected' since sculptures in St James's Park and Kensington Gardens had already been attacked.[21] However, constant surveillance required manpower, which required funds of seventy-five pounds per annum from the Treasury. Characteristically, the official decision was: 'we must run the risk' of injury to the statue 'for a time at least'.[22] This portrait of a mother by a daughter, so admired by Victorians, can still be seen today, with its back to the private garden of Kensington Palace, gazing serenely across the Broad Walk to the Round Pond.

CHAPTER XXIII

A Long Apprenticeship

'I think this year must have been the last we were all together at Inveraray in the old family party,' Lesley Clough-Taylor said of 1894.[1] Already one face was missing from the family gatherings; Aunt Dot had died suddenly the previous summer. She had left Argyll Lodge on a hot Saturday morning for Bournemouth and had caught a chill sitting in the garden. 'It rushed to both lungs at once' and on Monday she was dead and much missed by Princess Louise, who was devoted to her.[2]

Now, in the New Year of 1894, another change came upon the family. The strain of continuous asthmatic attacks had finally told upon Duchess Mimi, who slid almost gratefully into death on January 6th. She had been goodness itself to her stepfamily but, owing to ill-health, had made little impression upon Inveraray. The estate people never really knew her. Only the Duke could truly feel that he had lost 'the light of my House and Home during my later years'.[3]

Although it would have been quite normal for the Duke's heir and his wife to have taken up their residence with him after he was widowed, an obstacle prevented it; for, during what the family came to call 'The Interregnum', the household was ruled by the spinsterish Lady V. Princess Louise had never been close to Lady V, whom she thought much too pious and zealous, so, during her reign, she kept out of the way. Nephews and nieces also learned to flee when they heard the tap, tapping of Aunt V's stick on the floor of Argyll Lodge. Only the Duke must needs remain and bow to her domestic rule. He made no secret of his views. 'I have no Home except in a Wife's love and devotion,' he told Lord Dufferin after Duchess Mimi's death. 'Children do not, for me, supply that.'[4] The family said that he would marry again to escape from Lady V. The only difficulty they could foresee was to find the lady.

While the family were busy speculating, Princess Louise was pre-occupied with the arrangements for her niece's debut in May. The Archie Campbells' only daughter Elspeth, always known in the family as 'Niky' or 'Nika', was more like a daughter than a niece and treated Kensington Palace as a second home.

The family, that is Niky's aunts, Princess Louise and Molly Dawkins, had decided that Janey, for all her charm and beauty, was far too 'eccentric and cranky' to be relied upon to arrange her daughter's first Season. It was agreed that, until Niky was decently dressed and her hair was not done 'by the hens in the farmyard', she would never look her best. It was the Princess who now took Niky in hand.

She taught her how to walk into a room gracefully and to *cerclé* as she had been taught all those years ago at Osborne and Windsor; brother Niall was ordered up from Oxford to act as her partner; dressmakers and hairdressers were consulted so that Niky had some pretty frocks and large, picture hats. The family tomboy was well on the way to becoming a poised, beautiful, young lady.

Princess Louise also arranged for Niky to be presented to Queen Victoria and to be given the *entrée*, which made her debut much more comfortable. Niky was obviously 'to be all white satin and silk' but the design was left to her guardian Aunts. Janey was mercifully too 'immersed in her *own* Drawing Room dress!' to attend to Niky's.[5]

On the afternoon of May 10th, a box of a house in Hill Street received a great many visitors. They called to see a young debutante in her presentation frock and Molly Dawkins admitted that 'dearly as I love her I never before realised *how* beautiful she is'. Niky was faultlessly dressed, her curly, almost black hair beautifully done, her lovely aqua-marines and diamonds 'exactly matched her eyes,' yet, in her manner, she was 'as calm and natural as if she was with her guinea pigs'. Janey was in pink, with shells on her shoulders and a girdle of white scallop shells around her stomach: 'she will put on such weird and outlandish ornaments,' complained Molly Dawkins, 'sitting . . . on a rock they would be lovely but on a velvet train and feathers and veil they looked *wrong*'.[6]

At her first ball at the Duchess of Abercorn's on May 23rd, Niky made 'a tremendous sensation'. The story is repeated in the family that, upon seeing her, Arthur Balfour stood silent and then said 'That is not a girl, that is an angel.'[7]

As chaperones, her guardian aunts were undeniably strict and fussy. Niky was not allowed to go to any 'scruffy balls' – nor did she need to when 'all the big houses' were 'at her feet' and she was under the wing of royalty; she could not go to any of the '*nouveaux riches* sort of sale and master places'; nor was she to be contaminated by the 'brutes of women' who were thought by Princess Louise and Molly Dawkins 'to infest the smart set'.[8]

The reason for Princess Louise's protective attitude lay in the Cust Affair. In 1893 Harry Cust had been accused of compromising an unmarried girl, Nina Welby-Gregory. She had reported she was with child by him to Arthur Balfour. The rules had been broken. Despite Harry Cust's protestations of innocence, he was forced to marry her. As a result, mothers with unmarried daughters were even more on the *qui vive* during the following Season. For, in those days, affairs were confined exclusively to married women: 'they know the game, & can play it either way,' Lady Frances wrote to Lady Salisbury just before Niky's debut, 'but not so the girls'.[9]

Lorne was so excited over Niky that he planned an Argyll Lodge ball. Without waiting to discuss details with his womenfolk, he impulsively had foundations dug in the garden, bought an enormous iron framed 'supper room', made Princess Louise and Mrs Dawkins compile lists and generally behaved as if 'it was going to be tomorrow, instead of [the] end of June!'

The family, however, were still in mourning for Duchess Mimi. 'Low! and behold someone (probably Mimi's people) suggests to the bereaved widower that it was indecently soon,' with the result that the Duke told Lorne to postpone the ball for a year and instead hold a garden party. Lorne 'rampaged' and wired to the Duke, 'Perfect nonsense not to have ball.' The Duke wired back, 'Forbid that ball be given.' Mrs Dawkins thought it 'too funny altogether'. The ball would have been given in Janey's name but at Lorne's – in reality Princess Louise's – expense.[10]

It was the Princess who smoothed matters over by arranging to give several parties for Niky at Kensington Palace. She did not want family squabbles to mar Niky's first Season. The Princess's imprint upon the whole business was nowhere more evident than in Niky and Niall's manners, which became 'the topic of London'. Both children had proved apt pupils. 'They *bow* and are so stately, and so courteous' and were 'always nice to everyone,' wrote Mrs Dawkins in July. When Edward Clough-Taylor pre-empted Lord Archie from occupying a family cottage, Mrs Dawkins admitted, 'It amuses me to hear Nika giving him, in her stately princess sort of way, a terrific back hander.'[11]

The family were also concerned with Argyll finances: 'The Duke's money matters are worse than ever,' reported Mrs Dawkins, and 'the old boy very foolish about making them any better.'[12] It was sad to see him looking 'so old and worn and worried' but the decision (never implemented) to put Argyll Lodge up for auction had to be accepted. Such a drastic step was in response to recent Government legislation, which Lorne predicted would put an end to all Highland estates, including the Argyll one. In the Budget of 1894, the Liberal Chancellor of the Exchequer had introduced a new direct tax namely, death duties. This could not have come at a worse time for Lorne. The Duke's life expectancy was short, the estates were overburdened and the rents low, due to crofter legislation and the agricultural depression.

The Budget was, however, the only success for the Government in 1894; the existence of a vast Tory majority in the Lords blocked all other legislation, eventually forcing Gladstone to retire as Prime Minister in favour of Princess Louise's erstwhile Liberal suitor, Lord Rosebery, now a widower. It was the anything but Radical Lord Rosebery who, in October 1894, called the House of Lords 'a great national danger' in need of reform. His speech drew an immediate response; predictably, the Tories denounced it as treason; Queen Victoria thought it 'mischievous in the highest degree' and 'disloyal'.[13]

Princess Louise, however, believed that the Lords should indeed be reformed: not weakened, but strengthened by the addition of Life Peers. When the Princess went to join the Queen at Balmoral on 1 November 1894, she found herself in a Tory camp. None of this was new to her; it came as an unpleasant shock, however, to the token Liberal, the Minister-in-Attendance, Henry Campbell-Bannerman. He and the Princess were old friends, having met over the years at Marienbad where Princess Louise and Mrs Campbell-Bannerman took the cure. 'CB', as he was known to his friends, was immensely relieved to have a friendly face and political ally at Balmoral. 'It is really', he said, 'a different thing when the Princess L is here.'[14]

The Princess realized how important it was for her mother to hear some authoritative Liberal opinions on the subject of reforming the Lords; she now did her best to bring about a meeting between the Queen and CB. This was no easy task, for Queen Victoria always avoided discussing disagreeable matters and she was 'very ill pleased with Archie [Rosebery] for making that speech presaging a revolution'.[15]

The Princess felt her way slowly. At dinner on November 2nd the

Queen hardly spoke and afterwards said nothing about politics to CB. Princess Louise, as usual, was 'noisy and talkative' and kept the party going. It was the same the next night. 'After dinner I had great games with little MacGregor and Princess L about Spain, architecture, Chartres . . . & all about the Scotch church, in chaff,' CB wrote. The Queen still never mentioned politics.[16]

The next night, she again confined herself to generalities, but Princess Louise told CB she had already asked the Queen to speak to him about the Lords. The Princess mentioned how much she favoured Home Rule and that 'so many people would be delighted' to see it happen. As for the Lords, she roundly condemned their action in killing Liberal legislation. 'Really it was quite marvellous,' CB wrote to his wife, 'and I think her influence will have the best effect.'[17]

By Monday evening the Princess had won the day. Arthur Bigge informed CB that the Queen would like to see him to discuss the House of Lords the next day. They then rehearsed the audience together. 'It is very ticklish and indeed critical and I hope I shall come well out of it,' CB confessed to his wife.

Queen Victoria had sent Colonel Bigge a note in which her opinions appeared to be 'irreconcilable to the last degree' to Liberal hopes of reform. She thought the Liberals were 'better called destructives' and their measures 'subversive'. 'I could not have believed it,' CB wrote home, 'and Bigge said you must remember what the Queen is, how apart she is, how little she knows of what goes on, and above all who her grandfather was.'[18] The Queen 'dreads on argument' so he had to be careful not to be 'too contradictious'. 'It is the Princess L,' he wrote, 'who is the divine influence here.'[19]

When the Queen finally saw CB, she made it uphill work. She admitted that the Lords might require reform, but stressed the need to avoid agitation and public meetings. There must be a check against the House of Commons and the 'shocking people' in it, since Lord Beaconsfield's 'most unfortunate Act,' widening the franchise. But having strongly expressed her opinions, the Queen was prepared to hear the opposition. And, as she listened, her common sense prevailed enough to admit the validity of some of his points. The pity of it was that the Queen so rarely had frank discussions with anyone; she heard one-sided views expressed around her and believed them for want of anything else. This was what Princess Louise, almost single-handedly, did her best to fight against.

The Queen had misjudged Lord Rosebery's speech; she had considered forcing a General Election on the issue and had even written to the Opposition leader about it. Solely due to pressure from Princess Louise, she had agreed to see CB and, in consequence, was saved from making an ill-advised move of intervention.

The Lords continued to be a matter of deep concern in the political life of the country. Lord Rosebery delivered another speech at Glasgow on November 14th, which caused the Duke of Argyll to throw his cap into the ring. 'I shall give it to Rosebery as hot as he can support it,'[20] he told Lady Frances, who was delighted. The rest of the family were less enthusiastic; the Duke's last speech of one hour and forty minutes had been a *tour de force*, but it had left him exhausted.

Every place was crammed in Glasgow's City Hall on 18 January 1895, but the audience were denied the Duke's defence of the House of Lords. Shortly after he started his speech, he collapsed. Lady Frances was with him and he was taken to Lord Kelvin's house in what appeared to be a dying state. His first conscious words were to telegraph Lorne 'I am not ill,' and he did, indeed, recover. But he realized that his political career was over: 'I am too old for the exertion.'[21]

The Lornes went to Inveraray and cared for him during his convalescence. Princess Louise stayed on after Lorne left for Manchester where he had political meetings. He had been adopted as the Unionist candidate for the South Manchester constituency and was eager to win the next election, before it was too late ever to sit again in the House of Commons.

While Lady Frances had been looking after the Duke, she had written to her sister-in-law, Lady Betty Balfour, 'I know the whole scattered family is feverishly wondering whether I am looking after him properly, and *what* marriage I am encouraging!'[22] Lord Ronnie saw him at Argyll Lodge on May 24th and wrote, 'to judge by his manner and briskness that morg I shd not be at all surprised if he were to . . . marry again'. The family were perturbed but could neither believe it would happen nor imagine who the lady would be.

When, on May 27th, the Duke announced his third marriage, the shock felt by Princess Louise and the family was caused, not so much by the event, though 'that a man of 72 shd feel it necessary to go on marrying does seem passing strange'[23] Lord Ronnie decided, but by the choice of wife. For the third Duchess was someone Princess Louise knew well and had employed in Canada.

'Received a rather startling letter from D of Argyll, telling me he had proposed to Ina McNeil [sic],' the Queen wrote in her Journal.[24] The Duke had plucked 'Poor Ina', as the Campbells called her, from under the noses of the Lornes, for she and her brother John regularly lunched at Kensington Palace. The friendship owed everything to Aunt Dot, a McNeill aunt by marriage. Princess Louise had felt sorry for 'Poor Ina', who was now little short of fifty and who, since the death of her fiancé in 1880, had seemed consigned to spinsterhood. Aware of her impoverishment, the Princess had obtained the position of Extra Woman of the Bedchamber for her; since 1893 'Poor Ina' had been employed as a reader to the Queen and assistant on the secretarial side.

Lord Ronnie, who hastened to Argyll Lodge to inspect her, found, 'She is handsome and tall and high bred looking' but hardly, as the Duke described her, 'beautiful'. He also found that the family were strongly opposed to the marriage.[25] It was a shock that a poor relation should suddenly be elevated to such a position. Princess Louise, who had been hoping to spend more time at Inveraray, now found herself back in the old position of having to wait for an invitation. Not surprisingly, she spoke 'rather bitterly' of the marriage to Lord Ronnie; after all she had done for Ina, she felt almost betrayed. Financially, it was a great disadvantage for the estates since provision now had to be made for a third duchess.

The Duke could not see what objection his children could have to his remarriage, nor did he attempt to find out. The children boycotted the wedding and relations did not improve afterwards; for life in the Argyll households suddenly became very different. Duchess Ina set about smartening up everything. The auld ways of the far grander, yet simple living, Duchess Elizabeth were not good enough for Duchess Ina. Now the family coachman and footman had cockades put on their hats, knee breeches were introduced and hair powdered. The old Duke was made to wear the Order of the Garter and pumps, which was unheard of since he was notoriously uninterested in dress. Dinner parties with flowers everywhere and the famous Blue Hungarian Band playing on the lawn were regular events.

At first, the family joked that invitations to Argyll Lodge should really read to the Court of St Ina. But, when the same regime was instituted at their beloved Inveraray, they took fright. Lilah Campbell, who was still living with the Duke, noticed how formal Duchess Ina's friends were. 'They seemed always to be changing their dresses which amused me very much, especially when one of the maids of honour to the Queen came down in long kid gloves in the morning.'[26] Lilah could not wait to escape to the old Inveraray life of books and fishing the loch.

Duchess Ina made no attempt to conciliate or retain the friendship of her stepfamily. Her manners became even more stiff and, like the duchess in *Alice in Wonderland*, it was a case of 'off with their heads' if her wishes were not carried out. It was not so much Duchess Elizabeth whom Duchess Ina was trying to outdo, as her stepdaughter-in-law over at Kensington Palace. Princess Louise was upset to discover that Duchess Ina had immediately started to tackle all those projects which she had mentioned in her presence, as being improvements she would like to carry out once Lorne became Duke. She gave Lord Ronnie the latest news: 'I hear Duchess McNeill is now redoing the Parish Church . . . I have often spoken to her how I hoped once to build it up in future days,' adding, 'I have much studied architecture and I do not know that she has.'[27]

Relaying some Court gossip, Harriet Phipps told Marie Mallet that 'Argyll Lodge and *all* the family' living nearby 'are not on good terms so that anyone who gave news to Argyll Lodge would find black looks at KP!'[28] Lord Ronnie passed a sad day in August 1895, when he paid his Campbell nieces a farewell visit at Argyll Lodge, 'as they intend leaving the old home definitely on account of their father's marriage'. More upsetting was the inevitable distancing of the Duke. It revealed itself particularly over a family death. Lord Colin, who had been doing well in his lawyer's life out in Bombay, died suddenly from pneumonia. Lord Ronnie found the family gathered at the Vicarage. It was a shock to learn that the Duke was so engrossed with his marriage that 'his boy's death does not seem to have affected him at all'.[29]

Although the Lornes continued to behave normally in public to the new Duchess, Princess Louise rarely saw her in private and Lorne not at all that summer. But then he was preoccupied with electioneering, which took him to Manchester a good deal. The Liberal Government had been forced to resign; so Lord Salisbury had formed a Conservative Government which, for the first time, included five Liberal Unionists. A General Election was called for July 1895. The large Conservative and Unionist majority was expected and included Lorne as the new Member for South Manchester. He was naturally delighted to have a seat again in the House of Commons; it was, however, the last election to send a son-in-law of the Sovereign to the House of Commons.

That autumn, Princess Louise went to Balmoral. Marie Mallet was back in harness and soon gave vent to her unchanged feelings about the Princess. 'Princess Louise arrived yest,' she told her mother, 'we all tremble but I think she hates us all about equally so there is safety in numbers!'[30] Sadly, the person who had most valued Princess Louise's presence at Court was no longer there. Sir Henry Ponsonby had suffered a stroke in the New Year which left him semi-paralysed. He never recovered and would die in November. He had been succeeded as the Queen's private secretary by Arthur Bigge.

Princess Louise missed Sir Henry very much; life at Balmoral that autumn seemed duller than ever and the evenings were interminable. Princess Louise and Princess Beatrice played patience after dinner while the gentlemen and Prince Henry stood at the end of the room and Queen Victoria was read to. At about eleven, the princesses would stop the cards and collect the 76-year-old Queen from her chair. Prince Henry would kiss the Queen's hand at the door as she left the room, Princess Louise and Princess Beatrice following behind her.

It is not surprising that when the opportunity arose to escape from this stifling atmosphere Prince Henry seized it. He joined a military expedition to depose the Ashanti King and stop cannibalism and slave trading. He had volunteered against the Queen's wishes but with her reluctant permission. Prince Henry told Princess Louise: 'You know I want to show on this occasion that I am fit to be thought of for something in the future should an occasion arise.' Princess Louise thought he had 'great courage and a cool head' and, as an African enthusiast, she encouraged him in his adventure.[31] He was one of the few bright spots in her life. She valued his companionship and adored 'dear, merry Liko'; 'his dash, good looks, his interest in everything new and progressive' appealed to her and together they had tried to enliven the Court.[32]

Marie Mallet, who was in-waiting when he set off, wrote, 'It is the climate I fear, *not* the enemy'.[33] On January 11th, Princess Beatrice heard that he had a fever at Sierra Leone. News reached Osborne that he was out of danger but then the cable lines broke. Nothing was known until, on January 22nd, they heard he had died. 'How soon his efforts to prove himself useful were ended & he was brave up to the last fighting the fever!' Princess Louise wrote to Mrs Gladstone on February 1st.[34]

She felt his death greatly: 'he was almost the greatest friend I had – I too miss him more than I can say'.[35] When, at last, she had found a kindred spirit, who was also family and who helped to fill the void left by Prince Leopold's death, he had been taken from her. The arrival of the rest of the Royal Family, all with their own fond recollections of 'Liko', caused her to behave badly. In one of those inexplicable *'moments d'humeurs'*, perhaps brought on by her time of life, she snapped at everyone.

It seems she announced to Princess Beatrice 'that *she* . . . was Liko's *confidante* & Beatrice nothing to him, indicated by a shrug of the *shoulders*!' And, according to the Duchess of Teck, she was unkind to Princess Helena 'after doing her utmost to set Uncle Wales against Helena, she – on going away – ignored her . . . the whole place is ringing with it'.[36]

However, sisterly relations were quickly re-established. Princess Louise started work on a reredos for the memorial chapel dedicated to Prince Henry, which Queen Victoria commissioned as a gift for Princess Beatrice. Whippingham Church is a simple, little country church with a large tower in the centre, which had been designed by Prince Albert. The plan was to turn the Household pew at the side into a memorial chapel where Prince Henry would be buried.

Alfred Gilbert was commissioned to do the chapel decorations, which included a bronze screen to stand between the chapel and the chancel. The Princess also worked her design for the reredos in bronze. It was a Crucifixion with the draped Angel of Resurrection protectively supporting the arms of Christ on the cross. Lorne saw the finished result the following Christmas and thought it looked very effective. He described it as 'more mediaeval German than anything else . . . the cross springing into boughs and roots' of life;[37] it was, like Gilbert's screen, in the *art nouveau* style.

Before she had done more than start work on it, Princess Louise caught another of her 'chesty' colds and went to join Princess Beatrice in the South of France. It is some measure of the closeness of the sisters that, despite Princess Louise's disparaging remarks, on the one occasion Princess Beatrice was away from Queen Victoria, she chose to have Princess Louise with her when she was in deep mourning at Cimiez.

Since it was Lorne's first parliamentary session, he was unable to get away to celebrate their silver wedding anniversary in Cannes. While he passed it at Sandringham with the Princess of Wales, his wife celebrated it at Cannes on the royal yacht *Britannia* with the Prince of Wales. On March 26th, the Prince wrote to Lorne that Princess Louise was 'not looking well and is so drawn and thin – that I much regret that she leaves here today'.[38] The Princess was leaving because she had to go to Rosneath with Lorne.

The previous year, Lorne had managed to save Rosneath from being sold. With Princess Louise's help, he had arranged to take over £170,000 of the Duke's debts 'so the place is purchased by me and is in the meantime safe'.[39] He thought it was well worth the financial sacrifice to retain it in the family, who had held it for five centuries. The Princess told Lord Ronnie she could not bear the place, which was not strictly true, but said to emphasize her disapproval.

She wanted to live at Inveraray and was concerned lest, by buying Rosneath which also needed extensive restoration, they would be unable to afford Inveraray when the time came. Nevertheless, now they were committed to Rosneath, the Princess was determined to make the best of it. Her first step was a tour of inspection with Lorne in June 1896. The house and policies were badly in need of repair, for Rosneath had either been let, or left empty, since Duchess Elizabeth's death in 1878.

It was in the autumn of 1896 that another death in the family took them back to Rosneath. On September 23rd, Lady Libby died from pneumonia. Because of Duchess Ina the funeral service was held at Rosneath, which now became a regular port of call for the family. 'Great sense of rest in the old Home,' noted Lady V at the time.[40]

'As if by magic Aunts appeared,' recalled the motherless Lesley Clough-Taylor, who now frequently stayed at Kensington Palace.[41] The Kensington enclave was shrinking; by 1897 only Kensington Palace and Addison Road kept open house for the family. Argyll Lodge was under Duchess Ina's management and the Vicarage no longer housed the Glyns.

Teddy Glyn had been Vicar of Kensington for eighteen years 'and had done very well and is much liked and a very hard working man,' Princess Louise wrote of him.[42] She thought he deserved promotion and recommended his name to the Prime Minister, who appointed him to the Bishopric of Peterborough. Although the Glyn girls cried for an hour about leaving Kensington and Lady Mary thought 'no happier work or house could ever be found,' Princess Louise rejoiced that recognition of Teddy Glyn's work had come.[43] From 1897 onwards, it became something of a tradition for the Lornes to see in the New Year at Peterborough.

When the Glyns consulted Princess Louise about renovation work to the long, rambling Bishop's Palace, she arranged for an aspiring young architect she was employing to undertake it. Edwin Lutyens first went down to Peterborough on 23 March 1897. The following week Princess Louise sent for him. Apparently, Lady Frances had warned Lady Mary and Lorne that Lutyens could only build 'cottagey things' and insisted he must not make Peterborough look cottagey. Lorne had passed this on to Princess Louise and blamed her for recommending Lutyens.

Princess Louise was furious. She told Lutyens 'she wd never help the Glynns more – blew up Lady Mary' who 'led the Bishop – "a dog of a life"' and put it down to Eustace Balfour, also an architect, being impossible and interfering and Lady Frances being jealous.[44] Having aired her views, the Princess then became all smiles again and proceeded to smoothe everyone down, so that Edwin Lutyens retained the commission and the Glyns were content with him and his work.

The Princess had been introduced to him by Miss Gertrude Jekyll, a lady of remarkable accomplishments who designed textiles for the Princess and advised her on the gardens at Dornden, where she is said to have laid out the rhododendrons. Considered by Christopher Hussey as 'perhaps the greatest *artist* in horticulture and garden planting that England has produced',[45] Miss Jekyll was never in formal partnership with Lutyens; she nevertheless created many of the gardens which surrounded his houses.

Miss Jekyll was part of an interesting circle, which included Barbara Bodichon, founder of Girton, the artist Brabazon and the musicians Hubert Parry, Lionel Benson and the Blumenthals, to whom Lorne's Uncle Westminster had introduced Princess Louise when she was first married. It was during the seventies that she came to know them well. When the Princess was taking the waters every summer, she used to break her journeys at the Chalet Blumenthal in Switzerland. She delighted in the informal parties where the mornings were passed in sketching or practising music, the afternoons in walks and the evenings in impromptu theatricals, composing limericks, games and singing; the light-hearted approach to serious artistic output thoroughly suited her.

Hercules Brabazon or 'Brabby', whom Ruskin thought was 'the only person since Turner at whose feet I can sit and worship and learn about colour,' was the resident art instructor.[46]

'HRH seems to enjoy herself immensely,' Brabazon wrote home during one holiday, 'she enters into all our games and surprises with great zest'. She also painted 'rather well'. Owing to the Princess's wish to be incognito, the party confined their activities to the chalet and saw no one else. This was no hardship as 'there is no *gêne* or formality of any sort so we are all a most pleasant party'.[47] As the participants grew older and were preoccupied with other responsibilities, the parties were given up, but each retained fond memories of them and continued to keep in touch at home.

An introduction to Princess Louise was obviously of enormous value to the, then almost unknown, architect. Lutyens found her 'witty and downright' in conversation, while she enjoyed his irreverence and whimsy and respected his great talent. He also possessed for her, the advantage of not being known at Court. Having consulted him about alterations to Kilkatrine House near Inveraray, she had commissioned him to build an additional wing to the Ferry Inn at Rosneath and to carry out improvements at the Castle, which she inspected in April 1897.

Lutyens found the Princess rather exhausting as a client. She seemed pleased with his work 'only she do worritt about the little outside things with which I shd having nothing to do. The kitchen gardens – the woods – the field for the cow' and all sorts of extraneous matters.[48] Although Lutyens' commission was for Rosneath, he soon found himself seeing the Ministry of Works about 'some mantel piece' at Kensington Palace, looking for houses in Surrey and Berkshire and doing other 'little odd and ends' for her. Then, on May 7th, the Princess took him down to Guildford for the second meeting of the Old Guildford Society of which she had become Vice-President. This conservation society owed its existence to William Morris and the Society for the Protection of Ancient Buildings, through whom Princess Louise had heard about it. At the meeting, she recommended Lutyens to the Society 'as a person who was likely to make his mark'.[49]

Dashing all over the place with Princess Louise was not quite what Lutyens' fiancée associated with work on the Rosneath commission. Lady Emily Lytton became a little jealous of the amount of time her 'Ned' was spending with the Princess and complained. He immediately reassured her, 'I squirm at the thought of the Princess fascinating me! I have only eyes, soul and body for Emy.' 'Hoheit', as they called Princess Louise, might be 'helpful and does good and gets me work,' but real friendship was impossible with a Royalty; 'one makes believe and has jokes innumerable,' that was all. Yet, he admitted, he found it difficult to refuse the Princess: 'she is so grateful and says such pretty things'.[50]

Like all her family, once the Princess had confidence in someone then she tended to use them for everything. Princess Louise's collaboration with Colonel Bigge over Henry Campbell-Bannerman's interview with Queen Victoria had led her to turn to him for help with other matters; in the same way as her collaboration with Mr Lutyens over Rosneath had done. Both cases aroused talk and, on the part of some people, jealousy.

Princess Louise had first met Arthur Bigge, later Lord Stamfordham, through Lady Sophie. In the seventies he was a subaltern in a Battery of the Royal Artillery led by her brother, Captain the Hon. Ralph Hare. It was to report upon the death of a fellow officer, the Prince Imperial, that Captain Bigge first appeared at Court in 1879 and began his meteoric rise in the Household hierarchy. Princess Louise had championed him to the Queen solely because of his friendship with the Hares.

When, surprisingly, he was appointed Assistant to Sir Henry Ponsonby and Assistant Keeper of the Privy Purse, talk about him had been rife in the Household for some time. 'It is likely the Queen may make Capt Bigge Privy Purse – he is so very well spoken of,' wrote Lady Agnes Wood, '– & when they do take fancies, they take such violent ones.'[51]

A slim, unassuming, courteous man, Bigge lacked one of Sir Henry's qualities, that of evenness of temper. On one occasion he 'exploded with rage' when brought yet another of the Queen's messages on military matters by one of her ladies.[52] As with the Queen's previous private secretaries, he became a great friend of Princess Louise and she turned to him for advice on everything from theatricals to her latest political crusade. Soon, there was talk about how much she saw him. No such gossip had attached itself to her relations with General Grey or Sir Henry, but then they were older men whose wives were close to Princess Louise. This was not so with Lady Bigge, a 'rather jumpy . . . curious woman, too nervous to be really pleasant,' who became jealous.[53] Moreover, instead of confining her complaints to her partner, as Lady Emily Lytton had done, Lady Bigge broadcast them to the Court.

Princess Beatrice now spoke to Sir James Reid, who was Sir Henry Ponsonby's successor as Court confidant, and said 'something must be done' about Princess Louise.[54] If the Queen heard about it, she would use Bigge less, which would involve extra duties for the princesses. Princess Helena, considered 'not quite safe' by Marie Mallet because of 'her violent opinions and very often absurd tirades',[55] also took up against her sister: 'She had ruined relations of others before and must not be allowed to do so again.'[56] Princess Helena may have been indulging in a short-lived explosion and exaggerating the drama, since the rivalry between the sisters remained undiminished. Yet, equally, she genuinely may have been worried by the rumours.

Certainly, as the most beautiful woman then at Court, Princess Louise undoubtedly attracted more comment than anyone else. In any woman's life there is a period when she is at her most alluring; in Princess Louise's case it was the eighteen nineties. Photographs taken of her reveal a woman at the height of her beauty, looking no more than twenty-five though in fact in her forties. The clinging fashions of the nineties showed off her slim figure, while the curly, fringed hairstyles softened her strong face. Less shy and more confident in manner than formerly, her sense of fun and intelligent conversation were considered charming, especially by men, and she was not beyond exercising her charms in a little flirtation.

When Lady Wolseley passed a Friday to Monday at Osborne, she joined the Royalties and Household to hear Miss Kentish Moore sing. '"Louise" was there too and most charming to her,' she wrote to Lord Wolseley, 'but made the Queen angry because at the Music she wd not sit with the Royalties but – with the Court. To flirt I daresay.'[57] An Edwardian, who knew the Princess, remembers hearing that she flirted divinely from behind her beautiful, hand-painted, lace fans. Marie Mallet naturally put it more strongly when she described how Princess Louise invited Annie Yorke's yachting party to tea during Cowes week, adding 'I am sure she will admire Jack and pounce on him at once.'[58]

Like her mother, Princess Louise was susceptible to beauty in everything, but especially in the form of good-looking men. It is one thing, however, to admire good looks and to flirt and quite another, to indulge in illicit affairs. It seems unlikely that Princess Louise indulged in them. In the nineties, her name was linked with a series of men. With the exception of her old master and father-figure Boehm and John McNeill, these men were all younger than her and, more significantly, they were all employed either by her or her family: Bigge, Lutyens, later Probert and even an unknown music master. Yet, though she visibly enjoyed the company of young, attractive men, it was the maternal, domesticated *hausfrau* which predominated in her character. She might flirt with men but, as a mother *manqué*, it was sons she sought, rather than lovers.

Although she was the most unconventional member of her family, she possessed a highly developed sense of duty and of the position of royalty *vis-à-vis* everyone else. She could be 'very informal and chatty but one had to be on one's guard not to forget oneself and be too familiar in return. The barrier always remained in spite of the friendliness and affection.'[59] Only with her own and with Lorne's family was the barrier removed. It would have been wholly out of character for her to have risked bringing disgrace upon her family by conducting affairs with people who were, for the most part, Household employees. Even in fast Society circles, affairs were always conducted with members of the same set.

In fact, no evidence suggests that she ever had a sexual relationship with another man, apart from her husband; Lorne was always her 'darling boy'. His diary and the letters between them show that they were close and affectionate throughout the forty-three years of married life; even in the mid-eighties, when their marriage was under a great strain.

Her position placed her like a specimen under the microscope of the world, hence her mostly unsuccessful attempts to retain her anonymity and her horror at having her name bandied about. When she discovered that tittle-tattle was still rife about her and Bigge, she felt it dreadfully. She had to be put to bed 'suffering from nervous troubles', as Lord Ronnie described it.[60] 'I am so distressed about Louise,' Queen Victoria wrote to Lorne on 11 May 1897. She asked Sir James Reid, who was attending another patient in London, to call and see Lorne about the Princess: 'Pray consult him as to some safe clever doctor to see her and where she should go to and rest. I am in dreadful distress.'[61]

However, the Princess recovered and the talk about her was soon superseded by some new topic. She continued to see Arthur Bigge at

Court; just as she continued to see Lutyens, who was still searching for a home for her near the Connaughts in Surrey. He gave Lady Emily an account of one such May outing in which he and the Princess appear as two schoolchildren thoroughly enjoying themselves on an exeat. 'Charged to Paddington . . . and no Princess! . . . got tickets and one minute after 11 HRH arrived. Jumped into train how we laughed. I forget what at. She was without Lady so we hid when a Queen's messenger was seen . . . too funny!' To the Princess's delight they bought some lunch in a shop: 'buns and ginger beer 6½d for 2 lunches, not bad' and returned shamefacedly late for a regular lunch at three o'clock when Colonel Collins was 'rather stuffy being kept so late'.[62] This was exactly the sort of occasion, innocent as it was, which excited censure in Court circles; for Princess Louise was ignoring her position, and innocently enjoying herself as any commoner would.

In June 1897 the Princess's appearances in public were of a more formal kind when she played her part in the Queen's Diamond Jubilee. For her, the most important event of the Jubilee Year was the performance of Lorne's opera, *Diarmid*, at Covent Garden on October 23rd. It was based on an old Celtic legend of thwarted love, yet for some reason Queen Victoria found it very funny. When Lord Ronnie had dined with her at Cannes in the spring, she had laughed uproariously at the idea of it. Nevertheless, it was a proud moment for Princess Louise, who occupied the Royal Box with the Princess of Wales. 'A big house and all a great success,' Lord Archie recorded in his diary. 'Lorne crossed the stage hand in hand with the prima donna.'[63]

In the spring of 1898 Gladstone fell seriously ill. Princess Louise had asked his daughter, Mary Drew, for reports of his health, writing, 'Please give him my love. He knows what an admirer I have always been of his and do say how much I think of him and how I wish it were in our power to do anything to take his pain away.'[64] Gladstone was aware of Princess Louise's fondness for him. It was entirely due to her efforts, that a reconciliatory meeting had occurred between him and Queen Victoria at Cannes in 1897. On March 24th, Princess Louise had called on the Gladstones after tea, when she had hatched a plan with Mary Drew for 'Our Grand Old People' to meet. The Gladstones were staying near the Hôtel du Parc, where a batch of Hanoverian Royalties were housed. The Queen was going to call upon these so that it would be easy to include the Gladstones in the party. Mr Gladstone remained unconvinced; he refused to force himself upon his

Queen. 'I was quite able to conceive the Queen's desire to see my wife; but most sceptical as to any corresponding wish about myself.'[65]

However, it soon became evident to Gladstone that Princess Louise had 'set her heart upon this meeting' and had enlisted the support of the Prince of Wales and the Duke of Cambridge. Two days later a message was sent to the Gladstones, inviting them to tea with Princess Louise at a quarter past four.

Princess Louise and the Prince of Wales received the Queen at the entrance of the hotel and escorted her upstairs to the Queen of Hanover. Later, the Princess sent for the Gladstones and, as they stepped out of the lift, ushered them into a room 'tolerably but not brilliantly' lit and led them up to the Queen, who sat in the inner part of the room. During their talk, the Princess stood chatting to Mary Drew, while they watched the proceedings.

'Notwithstanding my enfeebled sight,' wrote Gladstone afterwards, 'I became at once conscious that there was a change in the Queen's appearance . . . compared with . . . last year.' She seemed much weaker. What surprised him was the change in her manner towards him: it was 'decidedly kind, such as I hadn't seen it for a good while before my resignation'. Furthermore, the Queen gave him her hand, 'a thing . . . rather rare with men, and wh had never happened with me during all my life'.[66]

Princess Louise and Mary Drew were delighted with their success. 'All went off really particularly well,' recorded Mary Drew; only the look on the Queen's face saddened her, 'speaking of the mind, less there than of old'.[67]

Mr Gladstone, however, read more significance into the meeting. He knew that the Queen had cataracts, he now saw a physical and mental deterioration. The Prince of Wales seemed 'a more substantive person' and he wondered if the Queen was really a cypher as Sovereign. The Queen, however, thought it was Mr Gladstone who looked old and feeble. To the last, they could not agree and, in the event, it was Mr Gladstone who proved the frailer of the two, for he died on 19 May 1898. Even Princess Louise was unable to persuade the Queen to express royal regret. She would only comment, 'I am sorry for Mrs Gladstone; as for him I never liked him, and I will say nothing more about him.'[68]

Unfortunately, even the Princess's efforts at mediation could not change relations between Lorne and his father which had deteriorated greatly since 1896. They disagreed over Douglas and Lilah, who were brought up by the Duke but whose affairs were managed by Lorne. In June 1896 the Duke discovered from Coutts that Douglas had overspent by £500. In a great rage, the Duke blamed Lorne, who felt this most unfair. To make matters worse, the Duke also blamed Lorne for remarks about Lilah: 'Don't *you* join the feminine spites who abuse Lilah *solely* because she is attached to Ina.' Angry and upset by this 'extraordinary outburst', the mention of 'his tiresome wife's name [Ina],' only added salt to Lorne's wounds.[69] For, although Princess Louise made Lorne accompany her to call on the Duke on his birthdays, Lorne otherwise avoided Duchess Ina. So he only saw the Duke occasionally at Argyll Lodge, for he never went to stay at Inveraray. At the same time, Lilah's conversion to Catholicism and Douglas's marriage to a Catholic were great shocks to the strictly Presbyterian family, who still included clauses in their wills to disinherit Papists or those who became Papists.

It was against this atmosphere of 'feelings' that Lady Frances travelled to Inveraray in the New Year of 1900 to see the Duke, who had been ill with gout for over six weeks. The bitter January wind howled round the turrets 'and the rooms [were] peopled with ghosts and haunted with memories'.[70] She found the Duke altered and very frail looking. She returned to London to inform the family, who had not been told of the serious nature of the Duke's condition by their stepmother.

His condition had still not improved at the beginning of March but Princess Louise could not persuade Lorne to see him. 'I fear it is hopeless to suggest it,' wrote their nephew, Niall. *'Trop de baguerre en serait le resultat.'* Nevertheless, Lorne continued to write to the Duke as usual every week; though it seemed that the Duke did not see his letters since he continually asked Lady Frances for information about Lorne. On March 24th, Lady V reached Inveraray and four days later sent news of a bad relapse and that rooms were ready for any of the family who chose to go. Niall wrote, 'Uncle Ian [Lorne] absolutely refuses to set foot in the house as long as Duchess Ina is in it.'[71] Princess Louise thought he had a duty to be with his father, which ought to override any personal feelings he might have. She could neither understand nor accept his obstinate refusal to do what was right. Lorne's reluctance to see his father was provoked not just by Duchess Ina; he also could not bear to face the reality of his father's awful illness. The Duke was not only ill, but 'absolutely insane'. One moment he knew his children, the next he believed he was dead and Lorne was in possession.

Moreover, instead of allowing the Duke to slip peacefully away, the Duchess fought ferociously to prolong his life. 'He wd have died hours before,' wrote Lady Frances, but every ten minutes when 'the respiration stopped they put the oxygen on double force, and he was literally air pumped into life' although remaining unconscious. One of the Duke's last conscious sayings was, 'it is mere brutality'.[72]

The Queen received daily accounts from Princess Louise with several distressing *cris du coeur* about Lorne's refusal to go to the Duke. The Queen believed that if Lorne did not go to his father now 'he would never forgive himself hereafter'. She did not wish to interfere herself, but said that 'Only if Frances likes she may tell him how much I hope he will go.'[73]

Two days later Princess Louise and Niky joined Lorne and Niall at the Clachan, the small Rosneath dower house. The next day Teddy Glyn arrived from Inveraray with the latest news of the Duke's deplorable state: 'He is as much shocked as we were at Uncle Ian having despatched a coffin for Grandpapa to Wyllie's office. Can anything be more comically indecent?' wrote Niall.[74]

Apparently Lorne, unsure of the exact size required, had ordered a selection of coffins. They had arrived in the middle of the night and were found by Chamberlain Wyllie the next morning. The whole town heard about it, as it took nine or ten men to carry them into Wyllie's office. He was horribly frightened at having them there and stood wringing his hands in despair in full view of everyone. It made a fine scandal since the Duke was still alive.

On April 17th, Queen Victoria addressed herself directly to Lorne in a long letter imploring him to forgive the past and go to his dying father, even though he had been 'monstrously treated' by him. Lorne composed a reply beginning with his usual 'Dearest Madam and Mama', but continuing with language 'so violent' that Princess Louise 'just tore it up in his face'. She did the same to a vehemently worded postscript he added to a more reasonable second letter. Even Queen Victoria could not change Lorne's mind: he still flatly refused to go to Inveraray while Duchess Ina was there.

In an effort to mediate, Princess Louise wrote to Duchess Ina that she was ready to come whenever the Duchess wanted her. Her idea was that if she went, Lorne might perhaps follow. But Lorne forbade her to go at all. Unfortunately, any attempts by Princess Louise to reason with him were thwarted by further accounts from Inveraray of Duchess Ina's appalling behaviour, which immediately sent Lorne into a rage. Meanwhile, Princess Louise was herself being subjected to pressure from her own family, who blamed her for being unable to make Lorne go to Inveraray.

Niall found 'Aunt Looloo nearly crying over the Queen's violent telegrams', two more of which arrived through the Post Office on April 20th.[75] The Queen peremptorily wrote, 'If you do not go you will forever afterwards regret it' and then, in the evening, 'We deeply deplore your decision.'[76] Princess Louise was caught in the middle; she could not avoid disobeying either her mother or her husband.

Her mother proved the more understanding of the two. 'It is all most distressing,' Queen Victoria told Lady Frances, 'I have tried all I can to persuade Lorne to go . . . & Louise has done the same, and is quite ill from it all. She is deeply attached to the dear Duke and wd at once have gone to see him, but Lorne made difficulties.'[77] He now declared that he meant never to take the name of Argyll; it had become contaminated and degraded by Duchess Ina, who would still bear the name as the Dowager Duchess.

News of this reached the Prince of Wales, a real stickler about such matters. He immediately wrote to Princess Louise, saying that he hoped Lorne was not going to make such a fool of himself. Princess Louise confided to Niall that Lorne blithely declared he would 'ask the Queen to let him be something else'. He had already written out a communication to the press, for publication on the Duke's death. Niall predicted, 'He will make himself the joke of the whole kingdom if he does any such thing' and doubted the legality of it.[78]

On Monday, April 23rd, Lord Archie wired from Inveraray that the Duke was sinking fast. Time was running out, yet Lorne still refused to go. More telegrams arrived from the enraged Prince of Wales. The distraught Princess declared that if Lorne committed such a bêtise she would leave him. This had the effect of pulling Lorne up short; all talk of changing the Argyll name ceased. Sadly, before Princess Louise could act upon his change of mood, Lord Archie wired that the Duke 'poor old dear, passed peacefully away at 2.30 a.m.' on April 24th.

A further blaze of family rows followed. In a codicil to his will the Duke had desired to be cremated and his ashes buried in the ancestral mausoleum at Kilmun, on the Holy Loch, next to his first wife,

Elizabeth. Lorne was appointed sole executor but the arrangements for the funeral were left with Duchess Ina or 'Bitchina' as Niall now called her. The trouble that ensued stemmed from this division. Lorne, as executor, had a duty to carry out the Duke's wishes. Duchess Ina did not want the Duke buried next to Duchess Elizabeth and so refused to settle a date for the funeral until Lorne agreed to her wishes to have the Duke buried elsewhere.

The first moves were made by Duchess Ina, who was reported as being so overcome with grief that she was unable to speak of parting with the Duke's body. 'I am so prostrate that I can hardly write,' she wrote to Bishop Boyd-Carpenter on April 25th, 'but I am trying to do all I know He wd wish'[79] and promptly proceeded to ask him to do what the Duke had clearly not wished. This was to ascertain if he could be buried in the Henry VII Chapel in Westminster Abbey. Anxious that the family should not learn of her request and aware of the steadfast loyalty of the townspeople towards them, Duchess Ina enclosed a code for the Bishop to use for his reply. Simultaneously, she sent Lord Archie off to Rosneath with a letter written in a shaky scrawl saying that a few months ago the Duke had stated his desire to be buried at Iona where she too wanted to be laid. 'Uncle Ian hearing this *tantum iratus est*, that we feared he would get a stroke,' Niall wrote.

It took only two days for Princess Louise to discover Duchess Ina's request for Westminster Abbey. 'Fancy desiring to be buried in an English Abbey with which we have absolutely no connection,' Niall exclaimed. 'For 500 years we have buried our dead on the shores of the Holy Loch, and for 1,000 years before that . . . at Innishael, and Kilchrenan . . . and Iona before that.' Princess Louise immediately concocted a long telegram in French to the Queen to ask her to stop Dean Bradley from offering the Abbey.[80] This the Queen agreed to do.

By May 1st the Queen was 'shocked and grieved' and Princess Louise 'wild' about being kept in suspense, owing to Duchess Ina's refusal to settle a date. After all, 'The Queen cannot be expected to go into retirement for all the time a lunatic widow choses to keep her husband's body above ground.'[81] The Duke had not only been a public figure, he was also related by marriage to the Royal Family. Mourning etiquette decreed that certain formalities be observed.

Her Westminster Abbey plot having been scotched, Duchess Ina now threatened to remove the Duke's body to some unknown place.

The idea of their father's body being carted around the country by a mad woman in search of a burial place seemed macabre in the extreme to his children. When Lorne met his lawyer, he told him emphatically that he would call the Sheriff to turn the Duchess out of Inveraray if she did not settle a date to bury his father.

On the evening of May 3rd, a bewildered Chief Constable of Argyll showed John Campbell of Kilberry a message from the Dalmally policeman, who asked for instructions about an anonymous telegram, handed in at Rosneath, worded, 'if Dss attempts secret removal of Duke's remains by Dalmally have her arrested by force'. Kilberry thought it must be a hoax but another wire reached them late that night: 'Hope no bother take no notice Niall Campbell.'[82] Niall had sent the wire as support for the instructions given by Lorne to the Sheriff to be ready to act at a moment's notice 'in case the Dss tries anything'. Lorne had become so enraged that he threatened to go to Inveraray by sea to carry off the Duke's body by force to Kilmun. Princess Louise now became very frightened. She tried to get Niall and Niky to prevail on Lorne to allow the burial outside the family Chapel as a compromise acceptable to the Duchess. 'There shall be no compromise,' he thundered, 'but an end put to her insolent ways.'[83]

To try to influence Lorne, Princess Louise secretly sent for Dr MacGregor. Unable to see him at Rosneath, she was reduced to arranging a furtive meeting in a dingy temperance hotel room at Helensburgh. The Princess's plan was for Dr MacGregor to try to stop Lorne carrying away the Duke's body by force, and he agreed to help.

By now, the County were speaking their minds 'with great freedom' about the delay in burying their Chief. The estate people took Lorne's part with great ferociousness. The clergy were aghast, and Professor Storey called the Duchess 'that infamous Hell-Cat'. On May 9th, Princess Louise heard that Duchess Ina had again sent for the embalmers, and had instructed them to cut out the Duke's heart late on the night of the 7th. They had sent downstairs for a pickle jar and enclosed something in it in a square lead box. 'It is all filthy and disgusting,' wrote Niall when told of it by Princess Louise, 'and I should not have thought it possible that such things could take place in the end of the 19th century.'[84]

At last, after receiving what was tantamount to an order from Queen Victoria, Duchess Ina agreed to have the funeral on May 11th, eighteen days after the Duke's death, on condition none of the family attended the Kilmun burial service. To avoid scenes, the family arranged to go secretly by special steamer to Kilmun where they would join the funeral party too late for Duchess Ina's objections to matter. Niall said there would be a scene in any case. 'But it won't matter . . . as it will be dark by the time the body arrives . . . at Kilmun,' Princess Louise sagely pointed out.[85]

Until the very morning of the funeral, it was feared that Duchess Ina would make off with the body or cancel everything. Lorne did not attend his father's funeral and his absence did not pass unnoticed. Duchess Ina had allowed only three wreaths to be placed on the coffin in Inveraray Kirk: those from the Queen, the Prince of Wales and her own. After the service the coffin was carried outside, placed on a shooting brake, covered with a tarpaulin and driven to Kilmun. Only the Duchess in a closed carriage followed it. Lord Archie and Niall took the boat across to St Catherine's and thence went by carriage to Kilmun.

Princess Louise and the rest of the family arrived there in great secrecy from Rosneath just before seven o'clock in the evening. They hid inside the church near the mausoleum to avoid being seen by Duchess Ina. Outside, a large crowd lined the path from the landing place up to the mausoleum. At a quarter to eight, Lord Archie and Niall met Duchess Ina and escorted her to the mausoleum, leaving her to follow the coffin inside, while they rejoined the others in the church. Princess Louise then asked the Minister to begin the service, whereupon Duchess Ina heard it and said if he continued she would leave immediately for the Pier Hotel, which she did. After laying her wreath on the Duke's coffin inside the mausoleum, Princess Louise asked to see Duchess Ina, but was refused.

It was an extraordinary and most painful experience for the Duke's family to have to hide away in order to see him decently buried. After returning to The Clachan, Princess Louise went straight to bed. Only after she heard the following morning, that Duchess Ina had left Inveraray for the South, was it possible to feel safe. As Lorne told Lord Dufferin, 'Number three's are such trials!'[86] Now, at last, the Princess could consider her long-awaited position as the new Duchess of Argyll.

PART III

The Duchess of Argyll

1900–1939

CHAPTER XXIV

A Bittersweet Succession

'1900, strange to write!' commented Lady Frances as the new century came in. 'It is awful to begin the year with the knowledge that we are at war.'[1] While the Duke of Argyll lay dying at Inveraray, the attention of the family was also directed towards South Africa. For the Boer War had broken out on 11 October 1899.

During the Crimean War, the last major war to involve Great Britain, women's contribution had been confined to the pioneering work of Florence Nightingale. During the Boer War, women again turned to nursing, but in a more organized and professional way. And the princesses provided the leadership, which inspired others to greater efforts. While Queen Victoria reviewed troops or visited hospitals and Princess Helena continued her work with the Nursing Association, Princess Louise contributed to the war effort on three fronts.

She first became involved through helping Lady Randolph Churchill provide an American women's hospital ship, the *Maine*, to care for the wounded in South Africa. Jennie Churchill had formed a committee a fortnight after war was declared to raise £30,000 through concerts, matinees and general entertainments. She and Minnie Paget had approached Princess Louise for help in organizing some of the fund-raising entertainments with her musical and artistic friends. Princess Louise thought the project 'a splendid thing to do' and was most anxious to know all about it.[2] She agreed to talk to Sir Lawrence Alma-Tadema at whose soirées she regularly met all the painters and musicians of the day.

The Princess also worked with Prince Arthur to ensure recognition from the War Office for the ship. Queen Victoria was persuaded to donate a Union Jack to the *Maine*, which was presented at a ceremony attended by Princess Louise and the Connaughts. In his speech Prince Arthur said, 'Never has a ship sailed under the combined flags of the Union Jack and the Stars and Stripes; and it marks, I hope, an occasion which brings out the . . . affection that the two countries have for each other.'³

However, Princess Louise's wish to serve her country was not satisfied by her small part in the *Maine* project. Her main contribution to the war effort came through her position as President of the County of London branch of the Soldiers and Sailors' Family Association, which later added Airmen to their title to bear the initials S.S.A.F.A. On December 18th, she launched an appeal for funds in *The Times*; with her second-in-command, Lady Wolseley, she also began a programme of radical reorganization. Princess Louise met her four Vice-Presidents informally and arranged that they should send her regular monthly reports of the families helped by the S.S.A.F.A. East London District. As she told Lady Wolseley, 'I am very anxious to have more uniformity.'⁴ The Princess saw her task as setting up the organizational machinery; much of what is now taken for granted in the simple daily routine of such a charity was introduced by her in 1900.

'I trust that Comt Rooms are established in each Division and that certain days are fixed for the attendance each week of the Presidents, V-P's and Hon. Sec. to receive applicants and give relief,' she told them. She also introduced a system of report cards listing visits paid, cases relieved and expenditure. The Princess was most careful not to detract from the founder, Colonal Gildea, 'a very hard working and well meaning man' since S.S.A.F.A. was 'a wonderful creation of his'; but 'I think he is overworked' she tactfully told Lady Wolseley, and thus unable to introduce these reforms.⁵

In addition, Princess Louise was involved in an even more exciting project. As the disasters mounted over Christmas 1899, she was preparing a plan to organize Hospital Homes for wounded soldiers sent home from South Africa. Early in 1900, she approached General Lord Wolseley, who had succeeded the Duke of Cambridge as the Commander-in-Chief of the Army, and sent him her proposals for the sick soldiers. The first hospital would be at the Savoy Hotel in London.

'I have been carefully over the rooms, and they seem very suitable and comfortable having 2 lifts to the kitchen and a still room. A serving room. Two bathrooms, a room to store all necessaries for the patients and nurses' rooms close at hand,' as well as bedrooms for six officers and NCOs and two night nurses and a ward woman. The rooms, which overlooked the Thames, had been handed over to her by the directors of the Savoy and would be ready to receive patients in two to three weeks.

Princess Louise assured Lord Wolseley that the nurses were experienced after three years thorough hospital training and that she would obtain the services of 'some of the best London medical men'. She had also arranged special railway coaches to convey the wounded men from Southampton Docks to London.[6] Lord Wolseley recognized the professionalism of her proposal and gladly undertook to support it.

Enclosed with the proposal for the Savoy was another for a hospital at Rosneath. The Princess wanted to devote the new wing of the Ferry Inn to the wounded soldiers of the Highland Brigade. In 1897, Edwin Lutyens had supervised the building of this wing with its tall Elizabethan chimneys and small mullioned windows set into gleaming white walls beneath a hipped roof of stone slates. She had always intended this wing of the Ferry Inn as a convalescent home for patients from nearby Glasgow hospitals. Its proximity to the pier meant that patients could be wheeled off the steamers and into the wards; furthermore, meals for them could be prepared by the inn. So, with the outbreak of war, the Princess had a ready-made hospital waiting to be used and was well-prepared to meet the stringent conditions of the War Office. She had arranged for Professor William Macewen, a well-known Glasgow surgeon, to act as medical consultant and engage the three doctors, two nurses, sister and ward woman for the fifteen men and three officers she could accommodate there. Her plans were given approval by the War Office. As the military ships from South Africa began to offload the wounded at Southampton in the spring of 1900, Princess Louise was at Rosneath, simultaneously trying to persuade Lorne to go to his dying father at Inveraray and preparing to receive her first batch of soldiers at the Ferry Inn Hospital. One of the disadvantages of her involvement was that, 'Of course all eyes are on the hospital – it needs therefore double care,' especially since in her opinion, 'Soldiers are rather like children and require looking after more than usual patients.'[7]

On April 16th, she discovered to her horror that the rain pipes were defective. 'There is so much rain here that the water shoots down peoples necks, and for sick people . . . this is not desirable,' she informed Lutyens' partner, Baynes Badcock.[8] He was instructed to make it good 'as soon as possible' for, on April 27th, General Chapman was coming from Edinburgh to inspect her hospital 'and I don't want the place all untidy then'.[9] Mr Badcock must have acted quickly for the inspection went off well.

While Princess Louise was attending to her Hospital Homes, Lorne, as he continued to be called generally, had begun to investigate the condition of his inheritance. It was assumed by everyone that changes would be introduced by the new Duke and Duchess. Mrs Dawkins prophesied that 'When the Princess comes to her Kingdom there will be a tremendous clear out.'[10] Apart from discovering that Duchess Ina or the 'Black Duchess', as the family now called her, had performed a 'clear out' of her own by carrying off a tremendous amount of family memorabilia as well as valuable furniture, pictures, guns and flags, Lorne also learnt that much of his inheritance was, in his own words, 'nothing but a fraud'.[11]

'The position of the estate is deplorable,' Lorne informed Lord Archie on May 22nd. Out of his nominal annual estate income of £7,000, Duchess Ina received a £4,000 widow's jointure and £6,300 per annum for eight years went to death duties and interest. This left an annual deficit of £3,300. 'It is all a humbling and vain show & the beauty of the place can't hide the cancer,' Lorne continued. At fifty-five, he felt that he had to try to clear the death duties of £45,000; if he died before full payment, it would 'smash you and Niall up altogether to pay succession duties'.[12]

The annual deficit on income meant that it was impossible to maintain farm buildings and cottages, let alone the many piers and boats. Added to this was the discovery that, in addition to the interest payments on mortgage debts, the old Duke had left £38,000 of personal debts and bank loans of £15,000. 'Nobody in the family,' according to Niall, 'seemed to have the slightest notion that *any* of this large sum went to any other but Ina'. Their worst fears about the Black Duchess seemed confirmed when it was found that 'Ina, who had sedulously depicted herself as a grief-struck widow lying on a sofa,' was sufficiently business-like to write out, and later cash, a cheque for £500 only a few hours after the old Duke had died.[13]

When Niall went round to Kensington Palace on June 2nd he found Princess Louise 'full of Ina's further wickedness'.[14] Apparently, she was pestering Princess Louise about some family busts at Argyll Lodge, which Lorne had ordered to be returned to Inveraray but which Duchess Ina had declared were her own property. She had pursued his valuer all over Argyll Lodge, raving against the whole family in terms of such violent abuse that he came to the conclusion that she was drunk and refused to return.

The family had hoped that if Princess Louise used her money to pay for the upkeep of Inveraray, it could still be saved as 'the old home'. Unfortunately, they had forgotten that she was already using her money, at Lorne's request, to save and restore Rosneath. When Lorne decided that Inveraray had to be let to a rich American in order to clear the massive debts, Princess Louise's worst fears were realized. She had always feared that by saving Rosneath she would end up by forfeiting Inveraray; now it was to happen. Lorne told her he had already approached the rich Mr Astor about it.

All 'this comes rather hard on Princess Louise, who is very fond of the old place,' wrote Lord Ronnie on hearing about it.[15] Having had to wait all these years to live in Inveraray, it was a cruel blow of fate that denied her the pleasure when, at last, she was able to become its chatelaine. It was almost more than she could bear to go there with Lorne to arrange it for a tenancy. 'It is a very beautiful spot as you know,'[16] she told Louisa, Duchess of Buccleuch, and to see the 'dear fey place', radiant with the beauty of early summer: the parterre of blue hyacinths, the white and purple lilacs, the white and crimson rhododendrons, the sheets of bluebells in front of the Castle, all set against the lush green of the surrounding hills, made her unutterably disappointed.

Nevertheless, she had to accept that Lorne was right and, as Lord Archie said, 'we must just sit tight and grin and bear it all'.[17] Still, 'The worry and anxiety about all these properties and nothing to meet them with makes me very miserable in every way,' she wrote.[18]

On her return to Kensington Palace, she found that the talk in London was all of Inveraray and whether it was really going to be let. Some of the family were also muttering that the Lornes' plea of poverty was 'a dodge to keep the Queen's purse open to them' and to keep a host of relations at bay.[19] This was unfair, since Lorne had met all the jointures usually paid to his younger brothers and sisters from the estate and was still paying Lord Archie's insurance premiums and Lady Evey's debts.

As if this was not enough, the Prince of Wales was 'in such a rage' about Lorne's obstinacy in not going to see his father at Inveraray that he had told Princess Louise he did not wish to meet Lorne 'in case they should have words'.[20] Furthermore, Lord Salisbury had said that, owing to the scandal of Lorne not going to his father's deathbed, the Lord Lieutenancy of Argyll, which otherwise would naturally have passed to him, must now lie in abeyance for a year or so.

On June 22nd, the Princess had to go to Hertford House without Lorne, since the Wallace Collection was being opened by the Prince of Wales. There she met Mrs Dawkins to whom she passed on the news that Sir Walter Phillimore had bought the rest of the lease of Argyll Lodge where he intended to live, thus saving it from developers, and that Inveraray was let 'to Mr Lawson-Johnson who makes extract of meat! *Sic transit gloria mundi* . . . the Princess told me Ian wanted to let for 2 years at £8,000 a year,' wrote Mrs Dawkins, which would enable them to be, according to Princess Louise, 'poor, but out of debt'.[21]

It might be all for the best but it was, nonetheless, painful to think of Inveraray Castle being let to a compressed meat manufacturer. 'Loch Fyneside seems all under a cloud at present, let us hope it will lift by and by,' commented one of the Callanders.[22] With only The Clachan or Kilkatrine available, both of which were too small and only suitable for letting, the Lornes decided to take over Rosneath Castle from the tenant and live there while supervising improvements. An advantage for Princess Louise was its proximity to the Ferry Inn Hospital, where the first six wounded soldiers from the Boer War were now in residence.

Unfortunately, the Princess had become run down 'from these many months of worry and trouble', and was advised to rest in bed as much as possible.[23] With her spirits at a low ebb, she heard by telegram on July 31st that Prince Alfred had died in his sleep at Coburg. It was, as Queen Victoria wrote in her journal, 'a horrible year, nothing but sadness and horrors of one kind and another'.[24] Despite British victories in the spring, the Boers continued to fight on using guerrilla warfare and the lists of dead and wounded continued to mount. Princess Louise lost a nephew in the war when Prince 'Christle' of Schleswig-Holstein died from enteric fever and pneumonia.

It was clear that the Queen herself was far from well; she had lost her appetite and, unable to sleep at night, would fall asleep at odd times throughout the day. In failing health, she seemed less able to withstand the shock of bad news. She took Prince Christle's death badly 'rocking herself with her head in her hands'; another sign of her deteriorating health was the refusal to do her worsted work and an inability to follow the routine of a lifetime.[25]

There was a good deal of government business for the Queen to transact in consequence of the recent election in which Lord Salisbury had routed a divided Liberal party. Cabinet changes had to be discussed and military matters agreed. It was Princess Louise who undertook to help the Queen with these duties. Princess Beatrice seemed self-absorbed whereas, as even Marie Mallet admitted, Princess Louise was 'affectionate and kind' and 'is at her best when people are in real trouble and this is a redeeming feature in her most complex character'.[26]

Another who could testify to Princess Louise's kindness was the Queen's resident physician, Sir James Reid. In 1899 he had become engaged to a maid of honour, Susan Baring. The Queen was shocked at the *mésalliance* and annoyed that her doctor was marrying, since she believed a man told his wife everything. Queen Victoria showed her displeasure by refusing to allow him to live with his wife. Unlike her mother, Princess Louise was full of sympathy and immediately offered nearby Kent House for their use whenever the Court was at Osborne. The Reids eventually found a house of their own near Osborne, and Princess Louise again came to their rescue when it became uninhabitable after a fire.

The Princess's depressed state was increased by the unexpected death from heart failure of Lady Churchill on Christmas morning. Princess Louise heard the news at Sandringham: 'After her *son* I think I am the one who will miss her most and in some ways even more! She was all to me in my very lonely and sad life,' she confided to Sir James on December 29th.[27]

The first 'horrid' year of the new century was over, but the outlook for 1901 did not seem much brighter to the Princess. The news from Osborne of her mother was all of failing health. On January 19th the Prince of Wales, now reconciled with Lorne, lunched at Kensington Palace. Their conversation was of the way the Prince 'was rigidly excluded from affairs, especially by Salisbury, and that it was not dignified he should learn everything through Bigge'.[28] This had become even more serious with the Queen unable to cope and the boxes piling up unseen.

If it was galling to the Queen's private secretaries to receive messages through mere maids of honour, it was worse for the Prince of Wales to realize that the reins of Monarchy were in the hands of his least able or qualified sisters, Princesses Helena and Beatrice. Princess Louise no doubt agreed with her eldest brother. She sometimes spoke with 'a sense of the ludicrous', about these two sisters to Niall, 'and poor Mama so deluded by Beatrice my dear, and by Helena,' she would say.[29]

Late that Friday afternoon, Princess Louise returned to Kensington Palace to find Lady Frances sitting with Lorne and Niky. As she left a committee meeting, Lady Frances had noticed the appearance in the streets of broadsheets bearing the words 'Illness of the Queen'. She had rushed over to Kensington Palace to discover their meaning. Princess Louise said the newspapers had got their information from the fact that Sir James Reid had called in Sir Douglas Powell, a heart and lung specialist, for a second opinion. Of her mother's condition, Princess Louise said 'it is a thing that may end any moment or go on for a long time'. She and the Prince of Wales were not contemplating any immediate call to Osborne. In answer to her wire, 'Wld you like me to come to Osborne – I am ready for anything,' she had been told to keep to her original plan of arriving on Monday. It seemed 'there was great outward secrecy being kept, but that things were v serious'.[30] That night Queen Victoria became confused in her speech and did not seem to know where she was. She had now lived longer than any other British Sovereign.

On Saturday the 19th, the first bulletin issued by the Queen's doctors spoke of 'grave symptoms'. When Lady Frances travelled home from King's Cross in a bus, she was struck by the atmosphere around her. 'The absorbed look, the questions of working men in the bus, the universal buying of papers, all the signs of rapid & great anxiety.'[31] A day of rain and high winds, it was hardly the one to choose for crossing the Solent to Cowes. Nevertheless, the summons came for Princess Louise to be ready at forty minutes' notice to leave at four o'clock with the Waleses for Osborne. For once Princess Louise was punctual.

She arrived to find the Queen had rallied. She telegraphed to Lorne that the Queen had been quite collected that day. Apparently, when asked what day it was, she had replied, Saturday, and added 'then Louise will come on Monday'.[32] There was no clot or stroke as was rumoured, just general weakness and thickening of the brain vessels. The royal sisters had a few skirmishes over which of them was to be called in to see the Queen; but the doctors diplomatically decided she must be kept quiet and see nobody. Queen Victoria was conscious but so weak she could not turn in bed and had to be given oxygen.

On Monday afternoon, with the family gathered round the Queen,

Princess Louise and the Kaiser slipped out for some fresh air. Everyone had remarked how the normally ebullient Emperor Willie was 'totally sinking his "bossy side" and emphasising his presence as a grandson and not as the Emperor of Prussia'.[33] Princess Helena and Princess Beatrice had been strongly against his coming and were rather 'hostile' but Princess Louise and her nephew had always got on well. As he later fondly recalled, 'My favourite aunt, Princess Louise, . . . spoilt me from the time I was a tiny child; she was of a joyous, sunny temperament and had as keen a sense of humour as her mother . . . the very sort that wins the heart of a child at once.'[34]

Not even fully dressed, Princess Louise hurriedly went to her mother at eight o'clock the following morning. There in the Queen's bedroom, where the wide, high windows looked out on the arboretum and the sea, she knelt with her family round her mother's great canopied bed. Queen Victoria was breathing with difficulty. The Bishop of Winchester, Randall Davidson, tried to say prayers, but it was difficult with so many people in the room 'some of them giving way a good deal to emotion'.[35] Little Prince Maurice of Battenberg cried so loudly he had to be removed.

After a while the Queen grew quieter, and Princess Louise left the room with everyone else to allow her mother to sleep. The Prince of Wales summoned Lorne by telegram to Osborne. Lorne became very upset and told Lady Frances that the Queen had been a second mother to him, so he 'greatly feared' what he might find. But where he could refuse to go to his father's deathbed, he could not refuse a royal command to attend Queen Victoria's.

While Lorne was on his way to Portsmouth, Princess Louise was summoned again to the Queen's bedside. From a quarter past two until half past five, she knelt by her mother and stroked and held her hand, while the Princess of Wales supported the Queen. Lorne had only just arrived when, at six o'clock, the family was told she was sinking fast. They wished to see her alone one by one so, as each entered her bedroom, they spoke to her in turn. 'I think she heard the names of us all called to her singly . . . before the end,' Lorne wrote. Then, there was complete calmness and the whole family gathered around the Queen. Lorne found it 'horribly painful, the breathing sounding so horrid at intervals, & the poor dear being held up sitting in bed – most distressing'.[36] As Randall Davidson said the words of 'Our Father' and gave the Aaron's blessing, Queen Victoria died.

At half past six, leaving Princess Louise and the rest of the family alone with Queen Victoria, the Prince of Wales came out and composed a message: 'My beloved Mother the Queen has passed away surrounded by her sorrowing children.'[37] It was the greatest change that had occurred in the lives of three generations. Few people living could really remember a king.

Princess Louise passed the next day discussing arrangements and coping with a vast correspondence which threatened to overwhelm her. When Fritz Ponsonby heard she was in difficulties, he volunteered to help her deal with her telegrams. Princess Louise went through them and dictated the replies, which he took down in shorthand. He found that she had no difficulty in expressing herself and dictated 'some really first-rate answers'. They developed such an efficient system that Princess Louise complained of having nothing to do, while her sisters remained hard at work writing their answers out in longhand.[38]

Queen Victoria left Osborne on February 1st, 'in Queen's weather to the last' as people said of that clear, bright, winter's afternoon. At one o'clock, Princess Louise, clad in the deepest mourning with her crêpe veil falling almost to the ground, left Osborne, walking alongside the new Queen and Princess Helena; their black figures in contrast to those of the King, the Kaiser and the Duke of Connaught and three of her nephews, all in uniforms of blue, scarlet and gold, who walked in front of her and immediately behind the gun carriage bearing the coffin. As the royal procession reached the gates, the piper's strains were replaced by the massed bands and muffled drums of the soldiers playing Chopin's 'Funeral March'. It was now that tenants of the estate fell in behind the royal party and Households, and the whole cavalcade walked with stately simplicity to Admiralty Pier in Cowes.

Here, Queen Victoria was carried to a chapel on the quarter deck of the smallest royal yacht, the *Alberta*. Princess Louise boarded the second yacht, the *Victoria and Albert*, with the King and Queen. As the crowd on the shore waited in reverent silence, the music and muffled drums faded away before the deep boom of the minute guns of the fleet, which heralded Queen Victoria's progress on her last voyage.

The Channel Fleet and naval battleships had formed a vast avenue, stretching across the Solent to Portsmouth, through which the tiny *Alberta* now passed. It was a glorious scene as the frosty sunlight glinted upon the brass buttons of full-dress, naval uniform, upon the wreaths of smoke and upon the tiny, white coffin, which glided across the calm blue waters to the opposite shore.

It was, however, only the beginning of the funeral ceremonial. The next day Princess Louise and the Royalties landed at Portsmouth and processed, in the sleet, to the platform of the Great Western Railway; here the coffin was placed in a coach specially painted white and draped in purple and white velvet for the occasion, and they boarded the train for London.

At a quarter past eleven, the booming of the first minute gun announced the arrival of the cortège at Victoria station. Led out by a long array of soldiers and the officers of the Household, the gun carriage bearing the white, palled coffin was drawn by cream-coloured horses. After over forty years clad in black, Queen Victoria had ordered a white funeral. Next came the King, Kaiser and Duke of Connaught on horseback, followed by all the male Royalties and Princess Louise in the second carriage with her sisters and the infirm King of the Belgians.

It took them two hours to reach Paddington and, from the carriage window, Princess Louise could see through the grey haze of sleet, the purple drapings of horses, the lamp posts wreathed in ivy and the flags at half-mast. In the intense and solemn hush that surrounded the procession, nothing could be heard except the tramp of horses' feet; yet all around there was an immense crowd standing in sombre black who, as the gun carriage and Royalties passed, lifted their hats and bowed their heads. It was the absolute dead hush of one of the mightiest crowds ever assembled that was the most moving aspect of Queen Victoria's funeral.

On arrival at Windsor at two o'clock, Princess Louise joined the procession, walking with Queen Alexandra and Princess Helena through the familiar town to St George's Chapel. At the Castle gates they were received by Lorne in his capacity as Governor of Windsor Castle.

The scene inside St George's Chapel was in brilliant contrast to the grey skies and dark hue of the streets outside. All was splendid ceremonial, glittering gold and silver, scarlet and blue and grey and white. Everyone of title and power was assembled in their robes of State in the Chapel. Princess Louise and the women members of her family provided the only sombre touch. Afterwards, to the sound of Beethoven's 'Funeral March', the Royalties passed out of the Chapel, leaving Queen Victoria to lie in state until the burial service on Monday.

Tired and no doubt hungry, they repaired to the Castle for a buffet lunch.

The final committal service, on Monday, February 4th at the mausoleum, was a simple, family one. This time Princess Louise walked with her sisters and sisters-in-law, each of them holding the hand of a little nephew, niece or grandchild. As he walked down the hill from St George's, little Prince Edward of York, who was representing his sick father, said in an audible voice to his grandmother, Queen Alexandra, 'What a pity Father has missed so much fun.'[39] Inside the mausoleum there were tears as Queen Victoria was laid beside Prince Albert. On this day Princess Louise grieved not for her Queen, but for her mother.

It was the closing scene not only in a chapter of English history but in her own family life. It was now that Princess Louise began to realize the loss of her mother's 'continuing authority and counsel'. It had been with her for over half a century. Now, like Princess Beatrice, she could not imagine 'what life will be like without her, who was the centre of everything'.[40]

On the whole, Queen Victoria had been a loving, sympathetic mother. In the days following her death, Princess Louise felt she had lost the one person who had always loved her and could always be relied upon to know what ought to be done. 'The sorrow . . . never wears off,' she told a friend. 'And I can never realise that she is gone, only for a bit I cannot see her.'[41]

It is hard to change the habits of a life-time. H. G. Wells said that Queen Victoria was like a great paperweight that had sat upon men's minds and, when she was removed, their ideas began to blow haphazardly all over the place. Princess Louise must have felt a little like this; her first thought about everything, a funny story, an item of news or an idea for a picture was still to write and tell the Queen: 'She was always waiting to hear and to know.'[42]

CHAPTER XXV

Sister to the King

King Edward VII ascended the Throne in his sixtieth year; at an age when most of his subjects looked towards retirement rather than innovation and an increase in duties. The King said that twenty years before he would have liked it immensely but, now he had settled into his life, he could not wish for the change. Despite this, he seized the long awaited opportunity to set in motion a series of radical changes in the organization of the Monarch's way of life.

More significantly, he redefined the function of royalty as a ritualistic and ceremonial one through magnificent and increasingly popular public appearances; he also re-established the Crown in a position of social pre-eminence. All of this, he believed, would enhance the popularity of the Monarchy. 'It is like beginning to live again in a new world,' Lord Esher wrote of the new reign.[1]

His first innovation was to revive the ceremonial of the State Opening of Parliament on 14 February 1901. On the rare occasions when Queen Victoria had performed this function a very simple ceremony had been followed. The State Glass Coach, which had cost George III £7,000, was now unearthed and restored; magnificent robes were designed for the King; and a throne was made for the Queen.

It was a cold, grey day yet crowds of people, clad in black, lined the streets as the Argylls drove from Kensington to Westminster. Lorne was in red ducal robes but Princess Louise was heavily veiled and in black, except for the broad, white ribbon of the Victoria and Albert Order across her chest. Within the Lord's chamber, peers in scarlet robes 'like a brilliant bed of geraniums' had begun to assemble; around them waited a black fringe of ladies 'sparkling with diamonds, nodding with feathers and fluttering with veils'. The low buzz of talk suddenly hushed as the Royal Family entered. When the Duke of Connaught led in the princesses, Lady Battersea thought that, 'Amongst them all Pss Louise was distinguished by her fine expressive face and graceful figure.'[2] After the faithful Commons had been summoned, the King rose, put on his plumed hat and read his first speech to the first British Parliament of the twentieth century.

The accession of King Edward had naturally affected Princess Louise. She was now no longer daughter of the Queen, but sister of the King. One of her nieces recalled her early life with nostalgia, 'we were just like one big family until Grandmama died, when we became the "old royal family", replaced by the new Waleses'.[3] Princess Beatrice, who had lived entirely in royal circles, found herself at forty-five having to make a life outside the Court. Princess Louise was much more fortunate; she had made the transition upon her marriage. As for Princess Helena, she had never been especially close to her eldest brother; indeed she was not invited to sleep at Windsor once during King Edward's reign.[4]

Princess Louise, however, had always been close to the Wales family and now saw, if anything, more of the new King and Queen. The fatal illness of the Empress Frederick, who would die that summer from cancer of the spine, left Princess Louise as the King's favourite sister. In many ways, she was nearer to the Monarch than she had been in her mother's lifetime.

On April 4th, by the King's invitation, she returned to Windsor for the first time since the funeral. Although many of her mother's servants were still in place, such as the piper Campbell and the Indians, there were many changes. All the Household dined so that, when she entered the Green Drawing Room with the King and Queen, she found a large assembly. They dined in the large White Dining Room at half past eight, instead of a quarter past nine. It was just like an ordinary dinner party, with none of the whispered conversation found at Queen Victoria's table.

After dinner everyone went to the Green Drawing Room where smoking became general, Princess Louise lighting her cigarette with the rest. This was a great break with tradition. Smoking indoors for gentlemen had only been permitted in a special, isolated smoking-room. No one was ever allowed to smoke elsewhere; indeed to escape detection by Queen Victoria, visitors had had to smoke with their heads up the chimney.

Yet if smoking was difficult for men, it had been considered impossible for women; the only permissible use for a cigarette was to keep the midges away out on the hills. The Empress Frederick had hated smoking and thought it unfeminine of Princess Louise to smoke; 'It is neither pretty, nor clean, nor wholesome, nor like a woman,' she had told Lady Agnes Wood in 1891.[5] Such views never deterred Princess Louise, who had started smoking in Canada. But she never smoked in public, nor on her own at Rosneath or Kensington Palace except in her boudoir or bedroom: 'a very private Smoker,' recalled one of her housemaids.[6]

Princess Louise took the opportunity of discussing several matters of concern with the King during this visit. There was the scheme for a public memorial for Queen Victoria for which an inter-party committee had been formed. Lord Esher had suggested a statue in front of Buckingham Palace and an arch in the Mall, which found favour with the King. However, Princess Louise felt aggrieved that she had not been consulted. In Queen Victoria's lifetime, she had always been consulted about artistic projects; indeed Lord Esher had himself sought her advice over the Clarence Memorial.

The Princess suggested placing the memorial in Green Park to prevent it replacing Trafalgar Square as a meeting place for demonstrators; it would not be seemly for Queen Victoria's statue to be used in this way and it was important to avoid the danger of mobs in front of the Palace. The King thought her idea sensible and, like his mother, was guided by her opinion. He told Lord Esher that he no longer supported his proposal and mentioned Princess Louise's alternative.

Lord Esher was a wily opponent and a far greater schemer than Princess Louise. He did not agree with the King but did not say so; he merely sent off a strongly worded letter to Lord Knollys to enlist his help in opposing Princess Louise. He also successfully lobbied Arthur Balfour and other members of the Committee. Princess Louise was soon outnumbered; it was no longer enough to have a quiet word in the Monarch's ear even though, in Lord Esher's words, the new King 'showed in this as in other matters, a slight tendency to yield to the pessimistic attacks of his sisters'.[7] The King could not ignore the united decision of his Committee in favour of Lord Esher's plan. The scheme adopted, despite Princess Louise, resulted in the present day Mall with the Brock Memorial in front of Buckingham Palace and Admiralty Arch.

Although close to Princess Louise, the King was not above reprimanding her. When she had asked him if he would open a wing of one of her pet projects, the Charing Cross Hospital, he administered a smart rap on her knuckles. Through Lord Knollys, he reminded her that he did not undertake any public ceremonies between the end of the London Season and the meeting of Parliament. Nor was he prepared 'to open or lay the first stone of the wing of an Institution, especially if it were not a very large and important one'. The King believed that the Monarch should confine his work 'to the new main buildings'.[8]

King Edward was a great stickler for protocol and sometimes Princess Louise must have wished for the simpler ways of Queen Victoria. When a message arrived that the King was coming to lunch, Princess Louise would rush round Kensington Palace, saying 'Hurry up, we must take all the Holland covers off the chairs.' She seemed excited and nervous; everything had to be just right for the King.[9] And, although she was his closest sister, she still had to write to ask if she could leave Windsor on November 17th rather than the 18th; on behalf of the King, Lord Farquhar replied that King Edward gave his permission.

The Princess and the King also discussed Lorne's latest literary project. Spottiswoode had given him £1,300 to write extracts in resumé form of Queen Victoria's life, which they planned to publish in monthly parts. To date three numbers had appeared, to the King's dismay. He was not the only member of Princess Louise's family to disapprove; the Kaiser had sent a long letter to his 'Dearest Aunty Loo' about it: 'I am most astonished at what you tell me about Argyll's intention,' he wrote. While admitting that Lorne was well able to undertake such a project, the Kaiser argued that 'it should only be for the *family* itself' in the form of a manuscript to be kept for historians of the future. But 'on *no account can a real "Life" of* Grandmama be *published* before the *next 20 years* are over'. Many political issues remained unresolved and too many people were still alive.[10] The Kaiser's letter arrived too late to affect the publication of Lorne's work but his views found favour with the King, who suggested to Princess Louise that Lorne restrain himself in future.

Another issue concerned the future of Osborne. In her will, Queen Victoria had bequeathed Osborne to the King but allowed her daughters certain proprietary rights. However, the King had no need of a further country house and was anxious to find some other use for it without offending his sisters. It was again Lord Esher who made the suggestion that was eventually adopted. Osborne should be handed to the nation; Queen Victoria's apartments should remain private, 'as a shrine'; the remainder of the house should be divided into State Apartments and an Officers' Convalescent Home.

Princess Louise was in favour of such an excellent use for the place and welcomed the opportunity of helping impoverished, sick officers. She continued to take a deep interest in its affairs; perhaps too much so for the Governor of Osborne's liking. Whenever Princess Louise was at Kent House, she would pop over to visit the patients and later, when it became a junior naval college, the boys at the school. 'The sea, the Garden, the School Boys, the sick officers shd give entertainment. *Croyez vous?*', was how she described the delights of Kent House when inviting friends to stay.[11]

Until now, Kent House had been used more as an overflow for nearby Osborne than a separate country house. Friends in need, like the Reids, found refuge there. Numerous nephews and nieces with their nannies and governesses also passed seaside holidays there at Princess Louise's open invitation. With Osborne no longer available Princess Louise decided it was time to redecorate and improve Kent House and, in 1901, she employed Baynes Badcock, as being cheaper than Lutyens, to carry out the work.

When Mr Badcock's young wife, Ethel, accompanied him on a visit of inspection, she expected to find a grand house worthy of a princess. True, everything including the blotter was stamped with VR, but this was the only sign of grandeur. 'But inside! My dear, the furniture! and the decorations! They baffle description,' Ethel exclaimed in a letter to her sister. Comfort, chintz covers and white walls did not find favour with her, perhaps because she had been brought up in France and expected something smarter.

If Ethel had met Princess Louise she would have known the Princess was more concerned that the beds were comfortable, that she could see the sea, that the garden should be lovely and that the birds should continue to fly indoors to be fed. 'There are a tremendous quantity of wild birds,' Ethel found, 'and a robin comes into the sitting room and perched on the loaf this morning.'[12] Kent House was a children's paradise; which was exactly what Princess Louise wanted it to be.

Since Lorne had decided to let Inveraray and live at Rosneath, the Princess also had to set about making that place habitable. In the autumn of 1901, she asked Badcock to go to Rosneath to supervise further alterations. By now he and Lutyens had dissolved their rather informal partnership, as a result of Badcock's preference for fishing over inspection of building sites. The Princess used him, rather than Lutyens, because she wanted a technician who would execute her designs rather than his own ideas.

The Princess was also anxious to rebuild the Post Office at Rosneath and had drawn up designs for Lutyens, which she now gave to Badcock to complete. The present Rosneath Post Office is the one designed by her. Mr BB, as she called Baynes Badcock, then began work on the Castle, which was shabby when the Lornes took it over that summer. There were hardly any bathrooms and no hot or cold water systems; all that was required was carried up the stairs. There was no electricity and the house was heated by stoves in the passages with fires in every room. Nevertheless, it was much more to Ethel Badcock's taste than Kent House. 'Our bedroom is a very grand just like a room at Versailles,' she wrote to a sister on November 5th.[13] She had established herself there in the absence of the Argylls, after Mr BB had explained he could not be separated from his wife. Then 'Take her with you', they had urged him. Over the next two years, the Badcocks passed a great deal of time at Rosneath.

Princess Louise was soon bombarding Badcock with instructions. Although she was funding the work, Lorne felt that he had every right to interfere since Rosneath belonged to him. Not surprisingly, the restoration became the cause of many conflicts between them.

Princess Louise soon found herself piggy-in-the-middle between Lorne and Mr BB. 'I am exceedingly worried to find out that the workmen have not begun with the stove and hot-water,' she wrote on October 11th. 'The Duke is most anxious the Things should be progressed with,' and then she confided, 'if I do not take care he will take it all out of my hands & then there will be endless confusion'. She also warned him 'Lorne is very angry with me and more so with Jones for his heavy charges of freight –, *monst* [monstrous]!'[14]

Lorne, who could be extremely stubborn and domineering with his wife, did not appear so to Ethel Badcock, who thought him charming. 'There is something also very pathetic about the poor man; somehow he gives one the impression of being neglected, & rather lonely,' she thought.[15] Ethel Badcock was then twenty-six and an extremely pretty, vivacious woman. She had inherited the considerable talents of her father, the painter Frank Davis, and passed much of her time at Rosneath painting landscapes of the loch.

Lorne had arrived at Rosneath ahead of Princess Louise and was soon a great admirer of Ethel's. She amused him playing billiards one evening after dinner. Her shot had misfired; she impulsively whipped up her ball to make a fresh start, to the protests of her two opponents: 'Oh no, Mrs Baynes,' said Lorne, 'no going back. *Nulla vestigia retrorsum*

– you know what that means, of course?' 'Of course,' replied Ethel, 'not a vestige of trousers!'[16] As Lorne was wearing the kilt, this sally was well-received.

Princess Louise first met Ethel Badcock at Rosneath in mid-November. It was a blustery, wet afternoon and, clad in a mackintosh, Princess Louise, with her dogs and Anna Alma-Tadema, clambered into an old waggonette hired from MacPhee at the inn and was driven by Lorne up to the house. Despite the weather, Princess Louise looked immaculate, her hair perfectly dressed. Ethel was presented to her and thought 'HRH was strikingly handsome, indeed her features were beautiful.' She wore large pearl earrings on her ears, and carried herself superbly. What most impressed Ethel 'was the gracious poise of her head' which 'when she addressed anybody, was beautiful to see'. The Princess's deep, slow, penetrating voice could be heard, floating along the passage, throughout the house. After being presented, Ethel retired into an adjoining room and heard Princess Louise say in a penetrating whisper to Mr BB, 'Your wife is charming . . . charming'.[17]

Once the Princess discovered Ethel's artistic talents and sense of humour, she quickly adopted her as an unofficial lady and companion. Apart from Lady Sophie and Colonel Collins, whom she loved, the Princess preferred to use people not usually associated with royalty, rather than people from the Court; in this way she could mould them to suit herself. This was easier with Niky Campbell or Ethel Badcock, who were much more natural and unaware of the excessive formality of a Court, than any courtier, who inevitably became over-conscious of 'the solemn trifles of etiquette' and dress, and was also used to a highly disciplined '*vis inertia*', which was never a mark of Princess Louise's Household.[18]

In those early years of the present century there was a great change in Princess Louise's life as she began to assume a more public role. The divide between her public and private lives became greater. She might lead a simple, unconstrained life and be the only Royalty to accompany her visitors to the front door to see them out, yet now, wherever she changed trains in Britain, she was recognized and must promenade along the platform and bow to the people at the station. For the corollary of more public appearances and greater participation in cere-monial was that she became an instantly recognizable figure. Nor, any longer was that favourite royal convention 'the incog', universally observed.

Now, when she left Rosneath, there were crowds of people to see her off, '& the poor thing hates being stared at so. She gets quite nervous,' Ethel wrote. All the wounded soldiers now stood to attention at the pier and saluted the King's sister as she passed to the waiting boat. Then they rushed 'at her piles of luggage, each seizing something and putting it on board in no time'.[19]

She had to attend the first 'Court' of the King's reign on February 11th. Instead of the afternoon Drawing Rooms of Queen Victoria's day, the King had introduced evening Courts held in the Ballroom at which the presence of Royalties was no longer voluntary. From now on Princess Louise would be expected to attend all similar functions. Two days later the Princess was in Manchester for the unveiling of her statue of Queen Victoria, which she had completed the previous summer in her studio at Kensington Palace. It was unveiled by her nephew, George, Duke of York, who, as Prince of Wales, would unveil another of her works. For the Princess had long been occupied by a project to commemorate colonial soldiers, who had fallen in the Boer War; she had almost finished it and was currently arranging to have it placed in St Paul's Cathedral.

In addition to public engagements and long sessions in her studio, Princess Louise was also involved in the preparations for the Coronation. Decoration of the streets of London was planned, hotels booked, houses rented and immense sums of money changed hands over the purchase of seats and window space. Whilst the public read daily about every detail of the ceremony, details about one item were zealously kept hidden from them; these concerned Queen Alexandra's Coronation dress.

Nobody knew the correct dress for a Queen Consort to wear since the last such dress had been worn by the wife of William IV in 1831. When pressed about it, Queen Alexandra had made her views clear. 'I know better than all the milliners, and antiquaries,' she wrote to Sir Arthur Ellis and, 'I shall wear exactly what I like, and so shall all my ladies – Basta!'[20]

The person to whom the Queen turned for help and who received the commission to design and work her robes was Princess Louise, who used the Ladies' Work Society. Behind locked doors at Sloane Street, a bevy of her best embroiderers worked the design of gold embroidery into a Cross of St George entwined with the rose, the shamrock and the thistle. It was the ultimate honour for her little

Society and the Princess's own dress and train, to be embroidered in silver thread, was very much 'a last minute' job.

By June, all was in readiness for the great festivities of Coronation Week. On the evening of the 23rd, Princess Louise went to a dinner party and reception at Buckingham Palace for all the foreign Royalties, at which over two hundred people dined. The Princess knew something was wrong when only Queen Alexandra received the guests. Her daughter, Princess Victoria of Wales, moved through the crowds, whispering to immediate family, 'Dear Papa is very ill.'[21]

The doctors had examined the King and taken the decision to operate for appendicitis the next morning. The Coronation must be postponed indefinitely. Many people made up their minds that the King would not get over it. For, in those days, the operation was extremely serious and one from which few over thirty recovered. Princess Louise stayed with the Queen during the operation which, thankfully, proved a complete success.

While the King was convalescent aboard the royal yacht, Princess Louise, like other Royalties, attended various functions which he had ordered should take place as planned. She presided at the King's Dinner for the 12,000 poor of Hammersmith, Kensington and Paddington where she was cheered wildly; there was a march past of 2,500 school children in Battersea; and, most moving of all, a dinner for the blind of London at Chelsea Town Hall, where she went among her guests, grasping at each of the hundreds of outstretched hands.

After the King had recovered and the postponed Coronation had taken place, the King and Queen set off on a cruise along the west coast of England to Scotland, where they intended to call at Inveraray. Lorne had been unable to find a replacement tenant for the compressed meat manufacturer and was extremely concerned about the financial condition of his estates. Even though he had put in £20,000 of his own money since he inherited, he found that he 'cd not expect to live in Scotland at all without L's help'.[22] Nonetheless, the King having expressed a wish to see Inveraray, Lorne was happy to oblige and even organize a grouse drive of twenty guns for him. News of this leaked out and Niall rushed to Inveraray to help with arrangements, only to find that the King was not coming. The official excuse was that he had had to hurry North. Lorne, however, explained to Niall that Princess Louise 'forbade' the King to come in her absence. Niall thought this a strange reason and surmised that 'there has been a slight shindy' between his uncle and aunt.

In fact, as he learnt the next day, a disappointed Princess Louise had had to explain to the King that he could not be entertained in the usual way at Inveraray. When Niall was there on August 15th he found it 'looking terribly sad and deserted'. Instead of the seventy servants, who used to sit down to dinner in Duchess Elizabeth's time, there were only four: a hired manservant, a cook, a housemaid and Mrs Robb, the housekeeper. 'One could scarcely do with *less*!'[23] Where there used to be seventy-four dogs in the kennels, there were now two. With annual interest on the old Duke's debts of £19,000 alone, there seemed no alternative.

However, Princess Louise had not dissuaded the King solely owing to the lack of creature comforts at the Castle. To her mind, a far more important reason was to avoid hurting the feelings of all the estate people, who had been let go in consequence of Lorne's economy drive. 'I am most anxious Lorne shd not attempt to entertain as otherwise all the dear good people – who have had to be turned away – wd feel it doubly,' she had told the Duchess of Buccleuch, when asking if she knew of anyone who might like to rent it, even for a nominal amount, just to keep the place going. 'It would be good for the place, the people and everyone'; it would also make Lorne 'more contented'.

He did not seem to understand 'how in these days things can't be done shabbily, people can't understand it . . . as no one attempts to live in gt big houses when they have not the means'. To her it looked 'like want of hospitality, not want of means!'[24]. It was a sorry state of affairs that the principal Chieftain in Scotland and laird of what, one hundred years before, had been one of the largest estates north of the Tweed, had nothing to offer his guests. The Princess was more realistic than Lorne; she preferred not to entertain at all rather than offend people with half-measures. This was certainly wise in the case of the King. On his way to Balmoral he went to Tyninghame for tea. 'They had to provide *pâté de foie* sandwiches and curaçoa – if he reigns long it will be surprising!', commented Lady Frances from nearby Whittinghame.[25] Inveraray could certainly not run to such luxuries.

The greater part of the Princess's energies were now taken up with Rosneath. From wherever she was, scribbled letters of instruction were hastily sent off, often countermanding previous instructions, to the patient Badcock, who had been at Rosneath for the past year. 'Have windows been painted white a nice warm *white* not as dark as *cream* white?' she asked. Then there were the Argyll family portraits to contend with: 'those old men are so dull'. As for the prints, 'Please take down the old prints on stair they won't do', etc., etc.[26]

Her scribbles often ended with 'Excuse scribbles H[is] G[race] disturbing all the time'. For, as she wrote, Lorne would be reminding her not to forget to tell Mr BB something completely different and often contrary to what she had already arranged. The Princess found that, after nicely rehanging all the pictures, Lorne would change them. After one of his fleeting visits to Rosneath, he wrote plaintively to Ethel, 'I missed the *Landscape Pictures* I saw in the Hall last time I came here, very much.'[27]

Unfortunately, Lorne's temper had not improved with age; the Princess lived in constant fear of another explosion. 'You wrote first "Safe Key" and I was in trouble as HG wd have had an attack at once if I had asked him for that,' she explained to Badcock. She begged him to lock everything up after him and put the keys back as found, 'otherwise I shall get into trouble & am not well enough for that'. It was the same with the unpaid bills which 'bombarded' her for Rosneath: 'said not to be paid, made out to the Duke and he says I am to pay'. Surely, she had paid them, but could Mr BB find out quickly because 'I am catching it hot'.[28]

When Niall paid his first visit for two years, he found 'many changes, all great improvements'. The lovely circular library, which when Princess Louise was first married had been the gathering place for the family but was changed by Duchess Mimi, was restored to its former glory and was once more full of books. The old billiard room now boasted 'a lovely parquet floor'. Two of the hitherto unfinished rooms had been 'beautifully done; hot water everywhere'; there was a new entrance into the garden and 'The greatest improvement of all is the cutting away of the steep bank fosse so that cars can come up to the house door' on the diverted carriage drive.[29]

Nevertheless, it was a great disappointment for Princess Louise not to be able to keep open house for Lorne's family at Inveraray, where she had looked forward to recreating the old family life of Duchess Elizabeth's time. Now that she was Duchess, she wanted to be able to mother the large circle of nephews and nieces which would have compensated for the lack of children of her own. Still, she did the best she could for the family. Since the Eustace Balfours had neither a great deal of money, nor a large house, she lent Kensington Palace and gave the wedding breakfast for her niece Baffy's marriage.

This wedding was especially noteworthy because the bride and groom went away in a motor car. Lord Salisbury had resigned as Prime Minister in July and his nephew and successor, Arthur Balfour, became the first Prime Minister to go to Buckingham Palace in a motor car. He now lent it to take his niece on honeymoon; it seemed an extraordinarily fast and dangerous way to start married life. Motor cars were regarded as great adventures. The Princess was still at the bicycle stage and often complained of injuries or sprains suffered after some spill; yet she avidly entered into discussions, as did everyone, about motors. They seemed to form, in Lady Frances's opinion, 'an inexhaustible and dreary topic of conversation, as tedious as the noise of an exhaust pipe'.[30]

The Princess also arranged a Christmas gathering of the Clan, albeit at Kensington Palace instead of Inveraray. The Archies, Niall and Niky were staying at Kensington Palace and, with the Glyns and Balfours at Addison Road, and the Georges across the Park, it was quite like a return to old Argyll Lodge days. Then, in January 1903, the Lornes paid a long promised visit to Somerleaze, near Wells, where Mr BB's mother and sisters lived. Ethel had assured them that Princess Louise was so simple 'she would be charmed with everything'.[31] Mrs Badcock, nevertheless, remained apprehensive about entertaining royalty, especially when she heard that Princess Louise had only once in her life stayed in a non-aristocratic house.

The Princess, however, made it clear that she did not want her hostess to go to any additional trouble. Her only instructions were that they should not tell anyone that she was coming: 'as she wants to come here and not be troubled by having the people stare at her, a fate which she hates and has generally to endure'.[32] The family were thus put to little extra expense; indeed 'Bis' Badcock was rather proud that the flowers for the table arrangements 'looked quite pretty at very small expense,' being violets, daffodils and primulas from the garden and three tall pink orchid blooms costing one shilling for the three.[33]

There was no need for extra servants either, for Lorne's manservant, George, carved at the sideboard and the stable boy was brought in to wait at table with the parlourmaid and housemaid. Mrs Grant, Princess Louise's beloved old Aberdonian housekeeper, acted as her maid-cum-dresser and saw to the breakfast, which the Princess always had in her room. The only out-of-the-ordinary person at Somerleaze during the four day visit was a local nightwatchman to guard the Princess's jewels.

'We are getting on quite nicely,' wrote a relieved Mrs Badcock that evening. 'The Princess is certainly very attractive and simple and puts us all at our ease.'[34] The only etiquette observed was the obeisance upon greeting her in the morning and on bidding good night at half past ten when she retired. 'Of course she always went first into dinner and lunch and was the first to rise from the table and to sit down in the drawing room,' Bis recorded. However, at tea, it semed 'both strange and natural' for the Badcocks to see the Princess kneeling on their hearthrug warming herself and looking at the books by Mrs Badcock's chair.[35]

After dinner, the Princess and Lorne talked at length to Captain Probert, who was married to Mr BB's sister, Mary, and had recently fought in the Boer War. It was the beginning of what was to be a highly satisfying, mutual admiration between the Argylls and the Proberts in general, and the Princess and Will Probert in particular. Since his return from the Boer War a few months before, Will Probert had been seeking employment with little success; with a wife and young family and a manor house to support, he needed a fairy godmother. Princess Louise was delighted to mother such a good-looking, dark-haired, charmer. After her return to London she set about trying to get him a position through the War Office.

'I do not think she likes to be beaten in anything she undertakes,' old Mrs Badcock wrote in a shrewd assessment of Princess Louise.[36] In the absence of a military appointment, Princess Louise decided to employ Captain Probert on a temporary basis to help with her correspondence. Unlike her previous equerries, Captain Probert had no experience of royal Households. Even his family thought 'he was not the ideal sort of equerry,' for he was 'awfully vague and often late'.[37] Since Lorne was increasingly vague and the Princess notoriously unpunctual, Captain Probert did not seem a promising addition to the Household. Fortunately, his charm eased the task of organizing a somewhat temperamental royal mistress.

While Princess Louise was in the middle of arranging matters for Captain Probert, she became unwell. In a letter to Mr BB from Bath, Lorne wrote that she had caught a chill and was 'suffering much from teeth'. The next day he allowed her to add a few words to the letter, when she corrected his diagnosis. 'It's not a chill on teeth it's merely being worried and fussed at, all the day long has pulled me down when taking the baths,' she told Mr BB. 'There are hourly fits of temper one never knows what about.'[38]

The trials of the last eighteen years had affected Lorne's temperament. The chivalrous, easy-going, sweet-tempered, young man with the promise of a golden future had become a sometimes crusty, often hot-tempered, fussy, old gentleman with rather sad memories. He required all the sympathy and understanding which Princess Louise could give him. The strain of coping with him told upon her own precarious health, yet, when Lorne was in a good humour, she vastly enjoyed being with him, believing still there was 'no one like him'.

It did not make life easier to be told by Lorne that he did not have long to live. In April, when negotiating to let Inveraray for seven years, he insisted that this 'will see me out'; if so, Princess Louse would never have her wish to live at Inveraray.[39] However, Lorne was delighted to let it to a rich Mr Cresswell from near Alnwick, who was no longer received in Northumberland because he had run away with a married woman. He had since returned to his wife, and they arranged to take Inveraray from June. Niall thought it would be all right since 'there is nobody for him to elope with round this part of the world'.[40]

After the Lornes went to Inveraray to do the inventory, Niall was surprised to receive a wire from Princess Louise on May 30th, asking him to join her immediately at Rosneath. He arrived to find Lorne absent and Princess Louise in her bedroom. She wanted his help to pacify Lorne, who was in the most fearful rage about Mr Cresswell's lease. There had been an awful row with tears and Lorne shouting he would never be able to live in the house again.

The cause of this violent dispute was exceedingly trivial. Lorne had given orders that the old tapestries at Inveraray should be packed away before the new tenants arrived. At supper that night he had thrown his plates across the room in a rage saying he was off to dismiss his new Chamberlain, Mr Lowis, who had disobeyed him. Princess Louise tried to reason with him, to no avail. He was up at six the next morning saying that the tapestries had not been taken down and that he had been defied.

More than likely, the real cause of the tantrum was that Lorne was distressed at having to make way for a stranger. It was upsetting for him to see Inveraray in such contrast to all his fond memories of it. However, when he returned to Rosneath two days later, he was in good humour and had forgotten all about it.

On June 24th, the Princess was back in London for a series of functions with Captain Probert in-attendance for the first time. She presided at the largest meeting ever held of the District Nursing Association in Battersea Park. Crowds enthusiastically cheered the Princess and people cried 'Loo' and 'Good old Loo', as she went by. When Princess Louise asked what they were shouting, Captain Probert pretended he did not know but Lorne had no hesitation in telling her. Princess Louise 'got very red but almost immediately began to laugh as if she enjoyed it immensely'.[41]

The Princess also had to receive in audience new ambassadors and state visitors. There was less urgency about the ambassadors, whom she liked to invite to lunch or to dine, than the state visitors who had limited time and a busy programme. Her unpunctuality was often the cause of missed appointments. The Khedive of Egypt had twice been left 'kicking his heels' at her non-appearance. Only a peremptory note from the Master of Ceremonies on behalf of the King could ensure the Princess's presence the next time he called.

While she remained at Kent House, Lorne left on October 14th for Kensington Palace to prepare for a visit to France. Two days later he wired that he 'was laid up by temporary illness'.[42] Since he did not specify the extent of his illness, the Princess assumed it was a cold and made no plans to go to him. It then transpired that Lorne had been taken ill 'with severe bleeding from the lungs' and was not allowed to see anyone.[43]

Lorne was not the easiest of patients, Princess Louise wrote to Lord Ronnie on October 20th. Lorne 'will fuss and write and do things and so that he shd get quickly well, I must not let him', she explained.[44] Niall did not think him looking as ill as he had expected, when he found him sitting up in the library for the first time on October 29th. Princess Louise was out for a function but Mrs Grant told Niall that he was convinced he had had a stroke. They were both getting old, yet the Princess could hardly preach to Lorne about following doctor's orders; she rarely obeyed them herself. 'I am never to be cured of my pain,' she admitted to a friend about her bad, rheumatic knee, which had troubled her since her engagement, 'save by a horrid screwed machine wh is a gt weight – shan't use it I know.'[45]

As Lorne's health improved, hers deteriorated; by the beginning of November, it was Lorne who begged her to postpone her engagements and remain quietly at home. The Princess could be as stubborn as her husband. She refused to cancel her functions in the North of England and disappoint everyone; even though, as she admitted, 'I shall be dead, as I am suffering continually from violent headaches & sleeplessness.'

The Princess was also concerned about Lady Sophie, who had developed heart trouble but had not been told the truth about her condition. The Princess was 'frightened abt [the] fatigue for her and taking cold in nasty weathers'. She felt certain that 'any hurry or agitation' would be bad for her heart.[46] Her predicament was how to dissuade Lady Sophie from going without causing offence. In the end, the Princess detailed Captain Probert to attend Lady Sophie, who no doubt thought his behaviour rather odd.

On November 4th, the Princess opened an orphanage in Prescot near Liverpool and, Lorne being absent, was able to make 'a capital little speech'. After the ceremony, she made one of her surprise visits to the workmen's houses. Captain Probert was amused to see that 'the inhabitants were considerably "took aback" to see her dive into the kitchen and coal-hole', and, after several searching questions about their domestic arrangements, to be told 'the *best* way of cooking cabbages'.[47]

When the schoolchildren carried in flowers to present to her, she was unused to see them deposit their offerings everywhere but with her. For Captain Probert was too busy watching Lady Sophie, whose hat kept slipping off, to direct the children towards the Princess. On her return home, Princess Louise was put to bed in a state of exhaustion.

She had always found the fatigue of her ceremonial duties most severe as each public appearance was a test of nerves. The continual bows and smiles, until her head was dizzy and her face ached with the strain, were borne because it was her duty. Even when unwell and advised to rest, the Princess would rise from her bed for a function. Lord Ronnie was once involved with the organization of a large charity fair. On the first day Princess Beatrice attended it: 'HRH looked cross and extremely bored and produced an unfortunate impression'; on the last day Princess Louise came with Lorne: 'HRH was in every way a contrast to her younger sister, being most gracious and charming everyone and creating a capital impression.'[48]

The public never knew the cost to her health of these appearances; of how she would have to recuperate from them by passing several days in a darkened room. Nor would she have wanted them to know.

CHAPTER XXVI

A Royal Career

The 'headship of philanthropy' was how Prince Albert had defined the function of royalty;[1] his daughter, Princess Louise, had striven all her life to live up to his ideal of royalty as a source of disinterested counsel and encouragement in the effort to achieve a better life for the people. Yet, whereas in the middle of the previous century there were no girls' day schools, no evening classes, no women's teacher training colleges and university colleges, by the early years of the present century all these institutions had become established. Thus the Princess's pioneering role had been diminished by the increasing intervention of the State.

This is not to say that there was no room for improvement; there undoubtedly was. Yet now the role of the individual in such matters was less powerful. Decisions were more often taken by large committees than by a few women gathered in a drawing room. However, there remained one area in women's lives where pioneering work was still necessary. Women continued to clamour for their rights; the battle for political rights consumed the energies of many young women who could ride bicycles, earn their living and wear divided skirts but who could not vote in an election. Unfortunately, Princess Louise's status prevented her lending any support to their movement. Thus, she devoted more of her energies to cottage hospitals and homes for children, which were still the preserve of the philanthropist rather than the politician. At the same time, despite her more frequent appearances in public, she was leading a more domestic life.

The death of Queen Victoria had removed the last Monarch whose whole family were actively involved in the political life of the country. The Prime Minister, be it Balfour, Campbell-Bannerman, or Asquith, no longer sought Princess Louise's advice and intermediacy with the Monarch as Gladstone had done. She discussed political affairs with the King but she was no longer in the mainstream of the political life of the country. Her influence was confined to artistic and conservation matters and to the organizations in which she was still active.

One of these was an organization which is now called the National

Trust. In the summer of 1894 a meeting at Grosvenor House had decided to form a society which would 'provide open air sitting rooms for the poor' and save commons from industrial development. Princess Louise knew about it through the Duke of Westminster and Octavia Hill. In January 1895, she had become a Vice-President after the official foundation of the Trust.

After helping the National Trust acquire Brandlehow, their first property in the Lake District, in 1902, the Princess performed the opening ceremony. While talking to Octavia Hill in the committee tent, the Princess asked who was going to replace Lord Dufferin as President of the Trust. When told that nothing had been settled she asked, 'Would there be any objection to *my* becoming President?'[2] Her suggestion was immediately accepted.

She was also busy putting the finishing touches to her St Paul's Memorial. She had arranged for a Mrs Lloyd, a new model, to sit for her. 'She has a splendid head, beautiful arms and is quite nice. No Hs, but really refined,' was how Sir William Richmond had recommended her.[3] The Princess was using her for the Angel and had to work hard to complete everything by the beginning of May, when Lorne wanted to go to Dalchenna. 'My arm is terribly bad from working at the statue so much,' she told Ethel, 'It has improved a lot – the wings finished but not the rest alas.'[4]

Dalchenna House, about two miles south of Inveraray on Loch Fyne, was one of the estate houses Lorne could use instead of the Castle. Princess Louise found it most depressing: 'continual torrents of rain and mist up to the windows and absolutely dark . . . Rain, rain, dark, cold,' she moaned to Ethel, 'My hand is so bad I can hardly hold the pencil.' She bore it because Lorne was 'so pleased with the place that of course I seem pleased for his sake.' It was also pleasant to be able to visit old friends in Inveraray. She had forgotten how the locals made her feel at home. 'The inhabitants dont look at us but just fr under a half shut window or if standing at door when we pass, with their backs turned. This is the height of politeness to their minds, as staring they think rude.'[5]

There were also the latest improvements at Rosneath to inspect. She hated the cold and had instructed Mr BB to install central heating on all three floors, so that the servants need not have fires in their rooms; this was most unusual, since servants' rooms were usually bereft of all comforts. When Niall arrived on May 21st, he found Rosneath a bower of bluebells and primroses and Princess Louise weeding in the garden. 'I thought the house . . . very much improved but overheated with hot water pipes to a ridiculous extent'.[6]

Princess Louise felt at last that the place was 'getting a little into shape'. As she told Lord Ronnie, 'everything is on such a large and unfinished scale that it is difficult and costly to do anything really satisfactory'. It would have been much easier to have started from scratch for 'old Bonomi [the original architect] was a Terror, with just clapping in rooms, staircases, windows and the like, where he could; only thinking of the exterior – the inside plans having to shift for themselves',[7] so that it was extremely inconvenient and uncomfortable by Princess Louise's standards.

The Princess had to be in Scotland at the end of November to receive the honorary degree of LLD from Glasgow University; 'the highest honour the University can bestow,' Dr Story told Lorne.[8] The University had decided to confer it as recognition of her Presidency of Queen Margaret College from its inception. The College had recently been incorporated into the University of Glasgow after a long campaign on the part of the women staff and students to be fully recognized by the University.

On November 28th the Princess, accompanied by Lorne and Ethel, arrived at Glasgow station where Sir William Macewen was waiting to take them to the Samaritan Hospital. There was such an enveloping black fog that a policeman had to walk in front of them; Princess Louise was quite frightened and was sure people would get hurt. After inspecting the hospital, the party went to dine with the Storys. The Kelvins were staying there and the Princess was distressed to hear that Lord Kelvin had a bad cold, especially since he was to deliver an address at his installation as Chancellor of the University the next day.

The Princess had arranged to go to the Storys the next morning 'to fit cap and gown' and to go to the University Building with them. 'I shall be much less shy that way,' she had explained.[9] The Storys were surprised when she called soon after breakfast, since it was much too early to begin dressing up. It transpired that she was anxious that Lord Kelvin would not be able to make his speech and had called to suggest a remedy, which she proceeded to make up herself. She asked for some eggs to be brought to her and then beat them while adding some ingredients from her bag. Lord Kelvin was then made to swallow the frothy mixture and the Princess departed.

When she returned at a later hour, she was wearing a pale, grey, velvet gown; 'beautiful she looked and with her college gown over it and her cap', Ethel thought her an absolute delight.[10] The Princess found the whole ceremony 'most imposing' as well as 'touching'. She was particularly pleased when Lord Kelvin gave a marvellous address in good voice. After the ceremony, she and Ethel lunched at Mrs Story's with a large assembly of ladies 'great & would-be-great'. Ethel felt they curtsied and bobbed and fawned about far too much.

The Princess had another engagement to attend in the afternoon, when she went to preside at a meeting of the Ladies' Committee of the Maternity Hospital, which was also a teaching hospital. By the time she boarded the train for Rosneath, the 56-year-old Princess was cross and tired. The rain had ruined her dress, which was also dirty from climbing in and out of carriages. According to Ethel, Princess Louise bad-temperedly crushed the voluminous, velvet skirt under her arm and finally pushed its train through the hanging arm-strap in the compartment. Her feelings soothed, the Princess was now all smiles again and entered into a cheerful discussion about the day's activities.

When the Princess returned to Kensington in the New Year of 1905, she found Ethel Badcock's present of two miniatures, one of Princess Louise for Lorne and the other of Lorne for the Princess. 'Both miniatures are really excellent,' wrote Lorne to Ethel on January 9th. 'The Princess says "my nose too long. *Yours* is excellent." I say she's the only person who ever understood yr nose.'[11] Princess Louise was always sensitive about the length of her nose. Much as she admired the miniatures, she could not restrain from a little criticism: 'mine you must just alter a little, one eye comes too close to the nose and is a little to [sic] warm in tone all over,' she told Ethel on January 10th.[12] To soften her criticism, the Princess sent the artist a present of a lovely, opal necklace.

Another artist, her aged tutor, Edward Corbould, who was well over ninety, lay dying in his son's house in Victoria Road. She went to see him every day, sitting at his bedside and 'caring in every way for his comfort', and would go home in tears. His old servant was most impressed with her baskets of provisions: 'Aye, the Princess used to bring him new laid eggs with a coat of arms stamped on each.'[13] Such is the stuff of royal legends, for the eggs bore not a coat of arms but a dairy stamp.

Lorne attended Corbould's funeral service at St Mary Abbot's and

Princess Louise sent a wreath, which was placed at the head of the coffin with Corbould's paint brushes arranged in it like a sheaf of arrows. The King was irritated to learn from her that the Kaiser had sent a nice telegram of condolence. According to Lorne, 'our King . . . is apt to get very impatient with Emperor Willie's impulsive pieces of patronage. "I don't see what he had got to do with such messages,"' the King told the Lornes.[14]

The Princess had been advised by her doctors to go to the South of France in early January but had been delayed by Lorne who, as she told Mrs Probert, 'expects me always to be doing things for him so I cannot get my things together'.[15] The Princess had assumed Lorne would remain in London, since he did not wish to accompany her. Suddenly, he announced 'in a fit of excitement' that he was going to Rosneath with Lady V 'to keep house' and, whilst there, he would complete all the unfinished rooms. He had already instructed Robinson, the carpenter, to begin work, which he would supervise.

This was not at all agreeable to the Princess. She had tried to keep the restoration work within their means yet up to a high standard; this had necessitated a certain amount of juggling and the decision to close off a few rooms. The thought of Lorne impulsively ordering them to be finished did not please her. Since Lorne kept telling her it was hers to do with as she liked, she now told him, 'I shd gtly dislike it to be bigger, I cd not live there if that was done.' 'Then you need not,' was Lorne's reply.

The Princess realized that he was in one of his 'regular bad moods' which put him beyond reasoning. Upset, she saw 'misery in this new impetuocity'. When she pleaded, 'Don't do anything without [consulting] Mr Badcock,' he answered 'Oh! he don't want to come I am sure.'[16] In despair, the Princess wrote off to Mr BB, explaining, 'I am the wife and I have devoted my time, energy, health and money to this difficult place to make it a credit to *him* and so *indeed* have you.' She was going to send Mrs Grant to Rosneath to guard her interests and now asked Mr BB if he would also go for three weeks and find out what Robinson's orders were, since Lorne would not tell her himself. This Mr BB agreed to do.

Although Lorne remained largely unaffected by these domestic squalls, Princess Louise suffered badly from them: 'These boisterous agitations do for me & take me weeks to recover'. After this one, she confided to Mr BB, 'It is sad when he knows that my violent headaches and sleeplessness came from this continual fussiness and perpetual agitation I am made to live in.'[17] It was not until March 4th, when Mr BB joined Lorne at Rosneath and Princess Louise had recovered her equilibrium, that she was able to consider leaving and that Captain Probert was instructed to make all the travel arrangements for the 8th.

Ethel came to help sort out costumes for the journey. She remembered the occasion when the Princess gave her an exquisite, red, silk blouse, a Paris model; however, it was not a perfect fit. To Ethel's horror, the Princess insisted upon altering it herself: 'she kneels down, & pulls & pinches & tugs & digs pins into me & roars with laughter'.[18] She now insisted upon giving Ethel a brown dress, another *crêpe de chine* blouse, and a number of lovely boards to paint on. 'She really is extraordinarily kind – like a sister – but at times gets very cross, for a few minutes at a time'.[19] Packing for the Princess meant a running battle with her maids, as she recounted to Ethel: 'And the moment my back is turned Miss Williams and Miss Goodison go and fill my box so crammed full – FULL – and of what? Garbage! and then I come back and empty it all out and then they cry!', ending her tale with a peal of laughter.[20]

Having been joined by the Proberts, the Princess and Ethel journeyed to Paris where they put up in great comfort at the Hôtel d'Athenée in the rue Scribe. 'This is a beautiful and quiet hotel,' recorded Ethel. She shared a room with Mary Probert while Princess Louise was next door and Will Probert on the floor below. It proved to be anything but quiet and peaceful for the ladies. Princess Louise became as overexcited as a child on a surprise outing: 'Pss is *terrible*, not leaving us a moment in peace, popping in and out without any . . . warning, so that M and I are nearly beside ourselves. Very tired'.[21]

At last, they caught the sleeper to the South. The Princess was just like Queen Victoria in the way she asked constantly, for windows to be opened and closed. At Mâcon in pitch dark, Ethel had to get up to close the window 'and as there was not a convenient hole in the tongue of leather she made me cut one with a penknife, in the inky darkness! I did it somehow.' Unfortunately, the rest of the party caught colds at Hyères. Ethel thought Princess Louise was 'so sympathetic and sweet' to them. 'She has a wonderful kind heart and sympathetic character,' which more than made up for her fussing and unpunctuality.[22] When Will Probert caught cold, Princess Louise plied him with drugs and remedies, most of which he refused. She 'worries herself to death over him . . . with her incessant admonitions and drugs,' wrote Ethel, so that 'he gets furious and then she gets offended and then they squabble most absurdly' and finally make it up again.[23]

Travelling with royalty was a constant source of entertainment for Ethel; Princess Louise did not seem to understand the difference between staying with friends and staying in an hotel. Sitting out on the terrace before tea with Ethel, Will Probert, Mr Pears, an elderly guest, and his nurse, Princess Louise suddenly decided that Will Probert was catching cold. Without further ado, she walked into the nearest room, which was a bedroom with windows opening on to the terrace, removed a quilt from the bed and spread it over his legs. 'Will and I were aghast and he furious and the Pears people evidently surprised,' recorded Ethel. 'The dear thing absolutely forgets that these rooms are private, and that she is not at Kensington Palace or Inveraray!'[24]

It was a relief to them when the Princess decided to move along the coast to St Raphael. Unfortunately, she was in terror of being recognized and so the rest of the holiday was spent dodging in and out of hotels and restaurants like criminals on the run. With so many of her relations on the Riviera 'we dare not go to any place where they might be,' Ethel wrote home.[25]

The incognito Princess was furious to be spotted by 'some people called Bonham Carter', who had recognized HRH and asked to speak to her. As a result, she decided they must flee to Cannes. While there, she received letters from Lorne which did little to pacify her about Rosneath affairs. According to her, Lorne was 'so angry that I am away he is doing *all* that he knows I wd rather not'.[26]

At Cannes, Princess Louise took Ethel into Nice to watch the battle of the flowers. After a busy day, the Princess was exhausted and dined alone in her room. Then, while Ethel was undressing, Princess Louise joined her, clad 'in her knickers and danced reels *beautifully*' just 'like a madcap which she is, and finally flew out of the room with a military salute and a kick-up behind'. All evening she had looked 'fagged and quite old,' then, suddenly, she had turned into a girl of eighteen again.[27]

At the beginning of April they travelled to Florence; Princess Louise adored the city regarding it with almost a proprietorial air. She would set off through the streets at a cracking pace, Ethel almost running to keep up with her. Wherever Princess Louise saw any repair work or new building, she would cry out loudly: 'Isn't it *shameful. Shameful!*

Ruining everything! That's just what they do – Destroy all the old things.' The museums were accorded the same treatment. Amidst crowds of people, the Princess would stop in front of a picture, say the Medici Venus, and begin to criticize it at the top of her voice: 'anyone with a trained eye could see – he hadn't taken any trouble over the bosom as there was no modelling' – and then triumphantly produce the reason: 'He *must* have been in a hurry.'[28]

While in Florence, the Princess heard from Arthur Bigge, now the Prince of Wales's private secretary, that May 24th would be the best day for the unveiling of her bronze Memorial in St Paul's. The Princess agreed to the date and settled to return home in order to complete the final arrangements.

The Memorial had been initiated by the Colonial Troops Club, in conjunction with Princess Louise, and a Memorial Committee formed whose members included Sir Arthur Birch, the Dean of St Paul's and Sir Lawrence Alma-Tadema. In October 1903, the Memorial Committee had gathered in St Paul's to judge the site chosen by the Princess. A cartoon, painted by her, had been fixed immediately above the statue of Sir Ashley Cooper. It depicted a life-size Angel of Mercy leaning protectively over an effigy of Christ on the cross and supporting his hands. The Angel's robes tumbled down on each side of the cross and billowed round Christ's feet, while the large outstretched wings rose high, converging almost to a point above the bent head of the Angel, and swept low forming a frame for the trailing robes around Christ's feet. Once the Committee had seen the cartoon and the way the light from a westerly window touched it, they unanimously supported the Princess's choice of site and design. Since then, the Princess had worked hard but, a perfectionist, she was never completely satisfied and so delayed announcing its completion.

Now, in April 1905, she hurried home from Italy to attend to it. On May 2nd Ethel wrote, 'Went with HRH to the Foundry at 12.30. She stayed at the Foundry an hour and worked at the crown on Christ's head.'[29] On May 5th, the Dean of St Paul's reminded Captain Probert that they were waiting to install the statue, but it had not yet arrived.

The Princess passed the next four days 'in a fearful rush' to get everything ready for the service at St Paul's. Crowds gathered outside to watch the Royalties and notables arrive at the Cathedral on May 24th. The Princess thought the ceremony was beautiful: 'I was horribly nervous and of course feeling my work *not* nearly good enough for such a place and for all the fuss that was made . . .'[30] The work can still be seen high up on a wall in the South Transept at St Paul's Cathedral.

Throughout the remainder of the year, she was dejected; family difficulties taxed both her strength and patience. Their nephew, Douglas Campbell, had turned out to be what Lady Frances termed, 'such a ne'er do well'. In the summer they had discovered that Douglas had been speculating heavily, signing dishonoured cheques and then asking for large sums of money from Lorne. When he refused to give him yet more funds, Douglas had made a determined effort to commit suicide. Lorne decided to exclude Douglas and his infant son Ian from the succession to the entailed estates. 'D has again gambled, and the estates must not pass to gamblers,' he wrote in his Journal.[31]

In November 1905, Princess Louise heard that Douglas and his wife had gone to stay with people she knew in France and were still there a month later. She was sure that he would misrepresent them because he was angry with Lorne. Douglas was also airing his relationships more than ever by telling everyone he was the future Duke, using Princess Louise's name and then extracting credit on the strength of it. It was a great worry, yet they were powerless to stop Douglas without harming his innocent wife and child. The outside world, indeed most of the family, knew nothing of these worries. When John Campbell of Kilberry dined at Kensington Palace on December 16th, he thought Princess Louise was 'as she always used to be, full of fun and laughter and does not look much older than she did 30 years ago'.[32]

Ethel had been trying to persuade the Princess to winter in Ceylon, where her sister was living; instead, the Princess decided to go to Egypt. 'We are off on January 11th a large party – the Duke comes too, so thank goodness we shall be spared the incognito and enjoy ourselves enormously more in consequence,' wrote a delighted Ethel on December 17th.[33] Lorne was so excited by the prospect that he rushed out to buy innumerable cummerbunds, helmets, 'cellular' clothing and duck suits as protection against the heat; he was convinced he would die of sunstroke. Princess Louise was equally excited, although her preparations were different. 'Yes I do want lessons in Arabic Tell Ethel,' she scribbled to Mr BB, 'There is so little time and so much to do.'[34]

Soon after their arrival in Cairo, the Khedive called on Princess Louise, and the Princess then paid a visit to the Khediva. Accompanied by two runners, she drove with Lady Cromer, the High Commissioner's wife, and Ethel to a brand new palace where they were received by a giant Black 'who must have been 8 feet high'. In the hall were two rows of women of every shade from fair to black, wearing gorgeous, Parisian, brocade, ball dresses with equally gorgeous bonnets. The Khediva and her mother-in-law stood in the middle of this enormous hall and received them. The Princess was led into an inner room where everyone sat down; then, there was dead silence.

Eventually, Princess Louise was offered a cigarette, which she smoked, after which the women brought in coffee served in cups decorated with enormous diamonds, which were placed on a tablecloth encrusted with thick gold and with a huge, diamond star in the centre. The Princess found it heavy going as the Khediva's mother-in-law was deaf and the Khediva was not expected to talk in the presence of her mother-in-law, who was considered a much grander personage. Ethel did not dare look at Princess Louise for fear of making her laugh.[35]

On January 20th, the party borded a dehabiyeh (steamboat) for their journey up the Nile to Luxor. 'Our steamer is perfectly delightful. We ladies have each quite large cabins, . . . and the whole thing is exactly like a houseboat on the Thames,' Ethel wrote home.[36] They steamed at about five miles an hour sedately up the Nile with plenty of time to sketch, shoot duck or go for a row when the boat anchored.

Whenever they stopped anywhere, Lorne refused to land, declaring it was too hot. The party concocted a poem to coax him out. It went, in part, as follows:

> There was a Duke who went abroad
> He sat on deck, profoundly bored.
> While others took good healthy walks
> And daily plied their knives and forks
> Oft times asleep, oft yawning wide
> He was content with Murray's guide.
> The rivers nothing but a ditch
> The country neither fair nor rich
> 'Oh for my own beloved braeside
> Compare this river with the Clyde!!'[37]

The poem met with universal approval, but Lorne refused to accompany them further than Aswan and said he would wait there while they travelled on to Wady Haifa and Khartoum.

From Aswan they made excursions to Philae, to see the partly flooded temple; then to Abu Simbel which Lorne loved because it was so cool inside. After several uncomfortable days of sandstorms, when their mouths were 'worthy of a newly elected MP after an Irish Wake,' they left Aswan for Thebes and Luxor.[38] Ater two weeks recuperating at the Ghezirah Palace Hotel in Cairo and a visit to the pyramids by moonlight, the party left for Italy on March 15th. They were tired and prickly except for Lorne, who was all smiles and vagueness; he was delighted to be leaving Egypt: 'I think it is a beastly country.'[39]

Cool, balmy Italy was much more to his liking. This time he joined all their excursions, the first being to Pompeii with Frederick Rolfe, the Consul-General and author of *Hadrian the Seventh*. 'Very interesting, and delightful Mr Rolfe wonderful in all he knows about the place as if he had lived at the time it all happened and was one of the survivors,' Princess Louise wrote in Ethel's Journal on March 20th.[40]

On her return the Princess was busier than ever with charitable work. A room had been set aside at Kensington Palace solely for the purpose of sorting through clothes and other articles for her charities. Each charity had a different part of the room; the Princess gave strict instructions to her helpers that they were not to muddle the charities up, nor were they to give people the same thing twice. She used to kneel on the floor to sort the clothes into different piles, while her helpers moved between her and each corner, like runners on the floor of the stock exchange.

Princess Louis of Battenberg assisted the Princess with many of her charities. Another helper, Mrs Thesiger, thought her clever, but she obviously paid little attention to her clothes. On one occasion, the three of them were visiting a charity, where a large box was kept in the hall for donations of old clothes. When they came to leave, Princess Louis' hat and coat could not be found. A helper had assumed, quite reasonably in view of their condition, that the hat and coat were donations and dumped them into the box. It may have been after this visit that Princess Louise gave her niece a 'nice looking' coat for her birthday and assured her it was '*le premier cri*'.[41]

The Princess was triumphant in the spring of 1907 to catch the press out on a story. 'The kind papers state that "I never give a single bit of my clothing away that therefore I have a perfect example of all fashions! Like my Mother had!" Lovely is it not,' she told Mary Probert, whose family were regular recipients of clothes and presents from her.[42] The Princess had a large wardrobe, a certain amount of which she gave away every year. But she was not an extravagant dresser and most of her clothes were made at home by her ladies' maids and her dressmaker with a tailor for coats and tweeds.

Her life seemed to become more hectic every year. In May and July she was opening bazaars, visiting hospitals and exhibitions and attending prize givings nearly every day. 'I am dead beat on the go! 10 o'clock am to 8pm,' was how she described it.[43] It was not just the engagements but the huge correspondence entailed in undertaking them. In July, Will Probert's letters mention '3 or 4 functions tomorrow', and 'We got back yest and had to do a function immediately and I found such a pile I have been at it all day with Mrs Colver typewriting'.[44] The Princess was beginning to feel she was on a treadmill: 'I fear I cannot write more,' she apologized to a friend, 'I do nothing but write all day I dont rest or sleep or walk.' It did not help that her glasses were troubling her. 'Are you comfortable with your glasses,' she asked Mary Probert, 'I hope so I am not. The[y] slide up and down my nose, then mine seem a troublesome shape'.[45]

Even the Royal Drawing Society caused her extra trouble these days. Sir Lionel Cust, the King's Surveyor of Pictures, who was Chairman of the Council, resigned because Mr Ablett, the Secretary, believed he had a special right of access to the Princess, and Sir Lionel felt this undermined his authority as Chairman. The Princess had to smoothe ruffled feelings and arrange for Sir Lionel to retake his place on the Council without embarrassment.

Then there were constant worries about the Ladies' Work Society, which Princess Louise felt she had to keep 'up to the mark'. When the Princess had started the L.W.S. in the seventies, she had been the first in the field, but now there was great competition. This was aggravated by an ex-manageress, whom the Princess had taught from scratch – 'she knew nothing when she came' – who abused the L.W.S. and enticed customers away to her own business. Nor could Princess Louise counter this by putting examples of the best work in the shop windows; 'We found people with drawing books copying our designs in the streets and "spies"', probably trained by the art schools to walk by and then go home and copy. 'That is why I put so little in the windows,' she explained. It was the same at Exhibitions: 'my designs and inventions were copied by other Societies,' so she stopped exhibiting work. 'As soon as I invent a thing in come the customers buy them and give them to other Societies. That ribbon work wh is now done everywhere

I started entirely no one knew how to do it then,' she grumbled.[46] Yet her helpers in the L.W.S., indeed in all her charities, learnt to pay little attention to her occasional grumblings; it was usually a passing phase and was soon overtaken by a mood of enthusiasm. '*Surtout pas trop de zèle*' was a favourite motto of Queen Victoria's, which Princess Louise tried to remember; she rarely succeeded.[47]

Lorne tried to stop her taking on more engagements, but she could never resist anything to do with children and agreed to open the children's ward of the Essex County Hospital in Colchester on June 24th. The Mayor wanted to invite all Colchester to lunch to meet her. Forewarned, she suggested a small informal tea, but he nonetheless submitted seventy names of those he wished to present individually to her. It was tactfully pointed out that perhaps the hospital staff and their wives could be omitted since the Princess would already have met them at the hospital. The Mayor agreed, but only because he had twelve ex-Mayors and their wives up his sleeve for presentation in their place. It is said this method of conducting official visits would have been wholly unacceptable to Queen Victoria. After being presented to her at a library, the Librarian seized the opportunity to make an introduction: 'Your Majesty, this is my daughter.' 'I came to see the library,' said the Queen as she swept by.[48]

There was a great sense of change and of the old order dying at the end of the first decade of this century. The Duke of Devonshire died in 1908 as did Campbell-Bannerman, while Joseph Chamberlain lay paralysed. Public life seemed to be managed now by people the Princess and Lorne did not know. Lorne religiously attended the Lords; yet even here he felt the changes. He noted in his Journal: 'The country seems gradually to be forming only two parties Tories and PredaTories.'[49]

One of the 'PredaTories' Lorne had in mind was David Lloyd George, the new Chancellor of the Exchequer in the Liberal Government led by C.B.'s successor, Henry Asquith. Politically, the great issue of 1909 was the Lloyd George Budget 'aimed against landowners'. Lloyd George campaigned throughout the land during the summer, and represented the Lords as rapacious landlords trying to evade taxation: 'A fully equipped Duke costs as much to keep as two Dreadnoughts.'[50]

One duke, who would not have met Lloyd George's financial expectations, was Lorne. A patriarch of the feudal school, he was opposed to the Budget. Lorne, who would always help an old woman carry her pail of water from the well to her bothy but who never thought of laying on water from the mains to the bothy, believed this was the end of the Argyll estates.

*   *   *

In May 1910, Princess Louise took her niece, Joan Balfour, to a play. As they came out of the theatre, they saw broadsheets announcing the King was ill. Princess Louise knew nothing of this and, alarmed, bought the paper. The newsboy standing on the step of her carriage said, 'Give us sixpence for luck.' In great agitation, Princess Louise answered, 'Yes, Duckie'.[51]

She urged the coachman to drive fast, 'calling him fool!'. At a canter they swept through the Park and through the gates of Buckingham Palace, where Princess Louise left Joan in a sitting room while she saw Queen Alexandra. The Princess learnt that her brother was 'very bad' with bronchitis; he could not lie down or speak for coughing and wheezing. After sleeping at home, she returned the next day to Buckingham Palace.

Determined to behave as if he was not ill, the King had insisted upon getting up that morning as usual. He dressed in a frock coat, rather than the more informal clothes his valets had laid out and even, with great effort, arranged his tie at the glass. After a light luncheon in his bedroom, he collapsed and had to be helped to an armchair by nurses. There, he suffered a series of heart attacks. Nevertheless, he resisted any attempts to move him to his bed.

There was something unbearably poignant about the way the King, propped up in an armchair and clad in his smart frock coat, fought for breath, yet retained his dignity to the end as he gave his farewell audiences in that bedroom. Friends were ushered in during the afternoon to say their goodbyes. Throughout the day and into the night his closest family remained near him: his wife, his children and Princess Louise.

When the Archbishop of Canterbury was called into the room, at about half past ten, he found Queen Alexandra standing by the bed and administering oxygen, while the Prince of Wales knelt on one side of the bed with the Duchess of Fife, Princess Victoria, the Princess of Wales and Princess Louise on the other side. As the King's breathing grew weaker, the Archbishop said the Commendatory Prayer 'and a few moments afterwards he simply ceased to breathe'. It was fifteen minutes before midnight on 6 May 1910. The little group of family remained quietly kneeling for a minute's silence after the doctors and Archbishop left. A few minutes later, the Prince of Wales came out, as his father had come out of the bedroom at Osborne nine years before, and once more Randall Davidson was the first one to greet the new King, George V.[52]

The suddenness of it left everyone stunned. 'I am heartbroken. It's been too awful,' the Princess wrote to Niky, 'will the country understand? Oh! . . . Ah! dear my suffering is terrible. Love and kisses sweet darling'.[53]

Mourning was still strictly observed. Mrs Thesiger passed an old tramp standing outside Kensington Palace as she entered the gates. In contrast to his shabby looking coat and trousers, he sported a clean, new, black mourning tie around his neck. When she told Princess Louise about him, the Princess burst into tears: 'It was so touching,' she would tell Queen Alexandra.[54]

Back from the funeral at Windsor, Lorne told Niall of his last words with King Edward. Just before his death, the King met him at the Academy where a new portrait of Lorne writing a foreign telegram was on exhibition. Seeing it, the King said with a laugh, 'Lorne is asking where Louise is.'[54]

CHAPTER XXVII

Lorne

Once the large group of foreign Royalties, who came over to attend King Edward's funeral, had departed, the Princess retired gratefully to Rosneath for a month. At sixty-two, she was less able to withstand the strain and fatigue of a royal funeral. Now that the main building work had been completed and tranquillity had returned, Rosneath was a great restorative.

She liked to hear the sound of boys' singing float across the water from the training ship, anchored in the bay. There were walks to the Green Isle by the woods and then across the fields, calling in at the keeper's cottage on the way home. Long hours were passed weeding in the garden; when it became too hot, she would sit in the laburnum pergola and admire the honeysuckle, which scented the air and which she had trailed up the trees.

On one of her walks into the village she inspected the new bicycle shed erected in the laurel grove by the church. A dark, green, wooden structure with a corrugated iron roof, it had been a gift to the parish and erected after consultations between Lorne and the minister, Alfred Warr. They thought it unobtrusive; the Princess declared it a monstrosity. Greatly incensed at this 'blot on the landscape', she insisted upon its immediate demolition. In its place she would build an attractive stone shed, which would at least harmonize with the surroundings. Mr Warr pointed out that to demolish it would be an insult to the donor; this he could not allow. The battle of the bicycle shed had begun.

One fine morning, the beadle came to the manse to say the carpenters from the estate were about to demolish the shed on Her Royal Highness's instructions. Mr Warr promptly sent for reinforcements. The Rosneath constable was instructed to arrest the first man who dared to lay a hand upon the shed. The village were agog and the factor, Mr Stewart, reported the goings-on to Princess Louise. She laughed till the tears ran down her cheeks. 'I'd have pulled it off,' she said, 'if only I'd had a different sort of person to deal with!'[1]

For the Warr family, she, nonetheless, remained 'that sweet and gracious lady' who 'worked wonders with Rosneath'.² They were equally fond of the Duke; now sixty-five, stocky and white-haired, he was imbued with a strong, feudalistic spirit and great kind-heartedness. After seeing Mrs Warr catch her heel in a loose board of otherwise perfect flooring, he had the halls of the manse laid with mosaic tiles to ensure her safety; he deemed it not so much his duty as the heritor but his privilege to do so.

In June of 1910, Lorne was himself concerned not so much with the present as the future; in particular that of the Argyll Estates. A death in the family, like King Edward's, always renewed his belief that his own death was imminent. He was, therefore, all the more anxious that Niall should marry and have children, which would cut Douglas out of the succession; it was galling to Lorne to hear that Douglas already called his son 'the young Duke'. But although Lorne thought Douglas 'a confirmed criminal lunatic', he said there was no use 'troubling oneself on the subject'.³ It was important to look ahead. If Niall would not marry, then Douglas's son, Ian, must be prepared for eventual succession. When he and the Princess went South, they would meet him for the first time.

However, other family events soon overshadowed the Douglas problem. First Lady V died and then came a sad tale concerning Lord Ronnie who was immensely rich but quite incapable of looking after business affairs. He had fallen in with Francis Shackleton, younger brother of the explorer Ernest, and had been somehow persuaded to give him power of attorney to invest large sums of his own money. It now appeared, according to Princess Louise, that Shackleton had embezzled Lord Ronnie's money and had 'bolted to the Continent or to America with the whole of his fortune, or most of it £80,000 or so'.⁴

Owing to Shackleton's activities, Lord Ronnie had already been involved in investigations concerning the theft of the Dublin Crown Jewels from Dublin Castle in 1907. Suspicion fell upon the Ulster-King-at-Arms, Sir Arthur Vicars, and his Heralds, one of whom was Francis Shackleton. In the police enquiry, all were cleared except Vicars and Shackleton. However, in the absence of any proof, neither could be arrested and the mystery has remained unsolved.

Rumour, however, has persisted that the robber or robbers were highly placed. Shackleton's homosexuality was known, as was his friendship with Lord Ronnie; this had led to the circulation of some curious stories. The only one to concern Princess Louise was that Lorne and Lord Ronnie were involved in the robbery, and that both were homosexuals. In support of this theory, it is said that Lorne was 'on friendly terms' with Shackleton and, in order to shield him, the King 'hushed up' the enquiry.

None of the evidence bears this out. On the contrary, the King ordered the enquiry, first in private and then in public. Furthermore, Lorne was not on friendly terms with Shackleton; he never entertained him and only met him when he visited Lord Ronnie, whom he had warned against Shackleton, but to no avail. Lord Ronnie remained under Shackleton's influence even after the Dublin enquiry. It is, presumably, the close family tie, which has led to Lorne being tarred with Lord Ronnie's brush.

For no evidence has come to light to show that Lorne was homosexual. In his youth, it was maids and landladies' daughters he ran after. In Scotland, the rumours that linger are that, far from being a homosexual, it was rather a case of the opposite: that he had an eye for a girl and, like the old Duke, even fathered the odd child. In the family, there was never a hint of Lorne's homosexuality, although later generations knew of Lord Ronnie's.

Although Lord Ronnie had been ostracized by several members of the family over Shackleton, his relations with the Lornes remained unchanged. Now, when he was ruined and would have to sell Hammerfield and his art collection, it was the Lornes who stood by him. On March 4th, Lord Ronnie's case for bankruptcy was heard. That afternoon the Princess arrived to see hin 'very amiable – as she always is and I think she really feels for one in one's trouble,' he wrote.[5]

The Princess was also worried about Lorne's health. He did not look well and seemed breathless. When called in, the doctors told him he must reduce his weight. Princess Louise, immediately, put him on a diet and stipulated no drink at meals. This regime was difficult to follow during Coronation week. Two days before her nephew King George V's Coronation on June 22nd, Lorne had received the Order of the Garter in the Coronation Honours List. Their faithful, stately butler, Tolchard's comment to the Princess was, 'I am so glad We have got the Garter.'[6]

Instead of passing the autumn of 1911 in Scotland, she remained at Kensington Palace nursing Lorne, who had severe bronchitis. The Princess had to cancel numerous functions because of his health. Nor did the demands on her lessen with Lorne's partial recovery in the New Year. For his memory was failing, which meant she had 'constantly to help and remind' him over his affairs, while he continued to chatter on, blithely repeating himself. Lord Ronnie, who used to look forward to Lorne's visits, began to find them wearing. Lorne was 'full of talk but nothing fresh. He hacks on the same subjects, Scotch land troubles principally and one feels one has heard of all, time after time.'[7]

If Lord Ronnie found Lorne trying after an hour's visit, it can be imagined how exhausted Princess Louise was after months of looking after him. 'My health and vitality have been so undermined,' she admitted to Will Probert, who had left her Household to return home after his wife's serious illness, 'after each public entertainment . . . I am ordered to keep my bed one or two days as I am so thoroughly done by them.'[8]

Unfortunately these days, she seemed to be worried all the time. 'Poor Uncle Ian is a great Trial, with his queery memory it always was queer,' she told Niky.[9] When Lord Curzon was collecting portraits of former Presidents of the Royal Geographical Society and asked Lorne for one of himself, Lorne sent one of the old Duke, having forgotten that he was the President, not his father. The difficulty about Lorne was that 'one never knows sometimes he remembers *everything* and others everything is a hopeless jumble and tangle which puts one into despair'.[10] Lady Battersea was full of admiration for the way the Princess coped with him. She 'really bears well with her tiresome, prosy, poor old Duke who repeats himself a dozen times a day and asks the same questions over and over again,' Lady Battersea wrote to her sister. Princess Louise looked 'worn and tired and indeed it is a wearing life – Poor woman'.[11]

The Princess had developed a heart condition, 'nothing organic only great weakness', was how she described it.[12] Although she began to tell a few close friends about it, she begged them to say nothing to Lorne, who was not in a fit state to have any additional anxieties. The doctors had advised as much rest as possible and 'I have to eat ever so often wh is most unpleasant,' she wrote to Mrs Probert in October.[13]

It hurt her to the quick, when Lady Sophie wrote to Lorne to complain that his wife had forgotten her. 'Oh! but! *how*! CAN you say I never let you cross my thoughts,' the Princess immediately wrote. 'I *constantly* do that you really *do* know and I am very devoted to old Friends. So please do assure me you don't really think as you wrote. It pains me dreadfully as its unjust.'[14] Lady Sophie's death, on December 11th, made it an especially sad Christmas for the Princess, who always found Christmas-time unbearably sad; it brought back not only memories of her childhood, but also her misery over not having any children of her own. 'How I long I had a house full of young voices and cheery faces no one knows – I just love children at Xmas time,' she confided to a friend before Christmas.[15]

The Princess could not give up her duties, nor would she lessen her work load; in her eyes, it was more important than ever for royalty and the aristocracy to be seen to be working for the people. As she explained on one occasion to Lady Sophie: 'the Upper Classes have to work *very very* hard to keep things going. The whole state of things has been rendered so difficult and complicated through this movement of advocating Class hatred.' The volatile, international situation and especially the defeat of Russia by Japan made her anxious about Great Britain. 'When in unity we are unassaleable,' she wrote, 'May God help us in all our difficulties and dispell a chance of ruction & fighting.'[16]

She had been responsible for some spirited ruction and fighting herself. Five years previously, the Princess, ever in search of a simple rustic retreat, had purchased the old Wool Hall in Lavenham, Suffolk. Built in the fifteenth century by the Guild of Our Lady, it had been converted into a wool hall after the Reformation and, in 1907, was divided into three cottages and a bakery. In May 1912 the sole tenant had been given notice to quit for arrears of rent and Sidney Seymour-Lucas, whose firm were building a new house for the Princess at Ribsden in Windlesham in Surrey, advised her not to re-let it, which could further damage the fabric, but to restore it to a single dwelling.

By the beginning of December, the local conservationist, the Revd Henry Taylor, had noticed various architects 'sketching, and measuring etc.' but was unable to discover the reason for such activity, 'the whole affair [being] shrouded in mystery'. When the tiles were removed from the roof of the timbered hall, he wrote a letter of protest to the *East Suffolk Free Press*. 'Boiling over with grief and indignation' at what appeared to be the imminent demolition of the building, he also approached Mr Powys, the secretary of the Society for the Protection of Ancient Buildings (S.P.A.B.), who was spearheading a national campaign to prevent the, then fashionable, sales of medieval, timbered, Suffolk houses for rebuilding elsewhere.[17] Meanwhile, he was mustering the might of the village to save the Wool Hall. Two local lads, armed only with bicycles, were deputed to follow, in secret, the lorry loads of roofing tiles in order to discover their destination and the name of the owner.

Once the lads had followed the lorries to their final destination, they sped back to Lavenham where they triumphantly reported to the Vicar. 'House nearly all down, destination Pss Louise Ribsden Windlesham Sunningdale Please act immediately', Mr Taylor wired to Mr Powys on the afternoon of December 15th. In desperation, he followed this up the next day with a letter in which he threatened to 'tell such stories as would please Lloyd George when he visits Limehouse'. Nevertheless, he could not believe that Princess Louise was aware of the true state of affairs, for 'she is the last person in the world to do any such thing', he wrote.[18]

His revelations about the Princess caused consternation at S.P.A.B. headquarters. Powys was just able to stop the letter to *The Times* condemning the removal, but it was an awkward business. Not only was Princess Louise a member of S.P.A.B. and a leading conservationist but a Bill then before Parliament which S.P.A.B. ardently supported, was aimed at preventing just such acts of vandalism as the Princess appeared to have perpetrated. S.P.A.B. enlisted the support of the National Trust to restrain its Royal President, who might be 'rather sore on the subject'.[19]

Aghast at what had been undertaken in her name, once the Princess heard the whole story from Canon Rawnsley, she immediately sent her solicitor down to Lavenham to stop all work on the Wool Hall and to make arrangements for its sale to the villagers, as they requested. Simultaneously, she asked the National Trust builder and architect, William Weir, to arrange not only the re-erection of the roofing tiles and timbers but the complete restoration of the building to its original medieval form. When she learnt that the villagers were too poor to raise the £1,200 necessary to purchase the Hall, she convened a special private conference of the National Trust and, apart from herself footing the £500 repair bill together with further large sums for the preservation of the Hall, she offered to place the Wool Hall at the disposal of a charity. Her offer was accepted and the Hall became a convalescent home for female employees of the railways. The Princess was praised for such public-spirited action and for 'saving' the best example of a Suffolk wool hall. Few realized that its saviour had so nearly been its destroyer.

The gales were so bad that the roof was almost off Kensington Palace too. 'The storm here is terrible,' wrote the Princess, 'a row as if one were at sea raging and storming, crying through the chinks of the old honny [honey] combed place'.[20] She also had to contend with the resident ghost, who scared her visitors more than herself but then, she pointed out, he was a relation, even if a naughty one. On one occasion, Hilda Montalba was dining with her. After dinner they were going up to the Princess's boudoir on the first floor, when Princess Louise forgot something and rushed back for it. As Hilda climbed the stairs alone, a clear young voice called out commandingly from below, 'Who is there?' Startled at anyone calling out in Kensington Palace, she stopped to wait for the Princess, who soon appeared saying, 'Did you hear anything?' When Hilda told her, the Princess said reassuringly 'Yes, others have heard it too, it is George IV.'[21]

The Princess accepted ghosts, as she accepted the second 'sightings' of the Campbells. When Lord Archie died at Rhudnacraig, a little house near Inveraray, the Princess passed on Janey's sightings to Niky, who was at her father's deathbed. Janey had heard 'beautiful music abt the time he went'. Like Niall and Niky, the Princess believed that Lord Archie was alive, just invisible to them. He had always been her favourite Campbell and she grieved not to have been with him when he died. 'Don't I just know *all* you have gone through, it breaks the very heart,' she comforted Niky and Niall. 'But God will help and comfort you both dear things. You know how I love you both darling, I feel sure Budie [Lord Archie] is very happy and quite at peace only the relations must not bother and make trouble, of course he wd be miserable at that'.[22]

There had been talk in in the London papers of a strange German airship floating above Loch Fyne; the Argyll Campbells, including Princess Louise, knew better. It was, of course, the phantom Galley of Lorne, which always appears when a Chief, or one closely connected with him, such as Lord Archie, passed from his people. When Niall returned South he told the family that the phantom galley had been seen everywhere, even by a foreigner who called it a 'funny airship,' coming up Loch Fyne, floating over Inveraray and Glen Aray before it sailed away to Inischonain. 'It is filled with glittering figures . . . and is managed by the very early generations of the Clan, right back in the Celtic Ages who do it regularly as a compliment.'[23]

With Niall and Niky in deep mourning, the Princess had to rely upon the two official members of her Household to accompany her to functions. Her new equerry was George Lane, 'very tall and good looking', whose uncle was an old friend of the Duke of Connaught's.[24] Lady Victoria Russell, a daughter of Lord Granville, was her lady-in-waiting, a position she had held unofficially since the beginning of King Edward's reign when Lady Sophie's health began to decline.

The Princess had been accustomed to attend the annual Birmingham Music Festival, when she stayed nearby at Hewell Grange with Wally Paget's daughter, Lady Plymouth. On April 22nd, Princess Louise travelled to Hewell Grange, which had been built by Bodley. One of the guests invited by HRH's command was Charles Ashbee, who twenty years previously had worked on the drawings as Bodley's assistant. The Princess was arriving at five o'clock and the house party was asked to be ready to meet her by a quarter to five. Ashbee was amazed at the way everyone was in tweeds and caps and flannels one minute, until at '4.45 when hey presto! we were all turned out into dark navy blue town suits with grey squash hats to meet the Princess'. The only person who let the side down was George Lane: 'Lord bless you, by the look of the equerry's clothes I shrewdly suspect . . . a reach me down from Moss [Brothers],' wrote Ashbee.

Even Lord Plymouth seemed rather nervous at the Princess's arrival but she soon set everyone at ease. She gaily tucked into the cucumber sandwiches while Lorne drank his tea out of the saucer; Ashbee was riveted by the turn of conversation, which seemed to be of the period of Thackeray. While the Princess ate, Lorne talked incessantly. Ashbee thought him 'really rather a dear old boy, lots of quaint stories . . . talks . . . indistinctly, blurs the ends of his sentences . . .' Ashbee tried to bring the conversation more up-to-date by mentioning Lloyd George. Lorne 'twinkled kindly' and continued to talk in an anecdotic way of 'everything under Heaven'. Princess Louise, however, was very ready to talk of the present and the future. She wanted to discuss Ashbee's book on the Arts and Crafts' Movement, and showed great enthusiasm and interest in his plans for a gallery.[25] Princess Louise felt quite at home, even though the mantel of aestheticism and Arts and Crafts had passed to a new generation.

Ashbee thought Princess Louise at sixty-five, 'guelphic and a bit conventional, not so hop-eyed as the rest of the family, but very kindly'. She had the royal gift of manner 'which is so taking when you are bowed to and thanked . . . or your hand is gently pressed when you are given your *congé*. He had gathered that 'her immediate circle adore her but find her rather a "trying" lady'.

At eleven o'clock on the 23rd the Princess travelled into Birmingham in her motor car. For the first time, Ashbee had the experience 'rare I suppose to the ordinary mortal and socialist – of riding in a royal procession and being shouted at by a gaping populace'.[26] First there were the flags, ever more flags on houses, in streets, in the hand of each child lining the kerb so that, as one maid of honour put it, 'I have much fellow feeling with the Spanish bull whom everything red infuriates.'[27] Then there was the continuous noise of the roar of the crowds, the shrill screams of children, the crash of the military bands, the general, never-ending uproar of public interest and enthusiasm, which beat ruthlessly upon the senses of the representative member of the Royal Family in their midst.

One of Queen Mary's ladies wrote that she could imagine few things more shattering or fatiguing than a royal visit: with the blaze of publicity, the emotional strain of mass loyalty and the deprivation of all privacy and peace. Yet, throughout the day, Princess Louise had to rise to the level of enthusiasm of those about her and to meet dignitaries and people, who were flustered in the presence of royalty and anxious about the successful outcome of their many weeks of preparation. The only noticeable difference between this visit to Birmingham and her official visits elsewhere was that, for the first time, the Princess and her party were cinematographed to the sound of a great clicking.

At the Town Hall the Princess was received by civic Birmingham standing in scarlet splendour on the red baize carpet. At lunch Mr Ashbee sat next to an old Birmingham alderman who had once heard him speak 'too socialistically and been shocked, he had treasured this up and was puzzled how in the world I could have got into the royal train'. At last, unable to contain himself any longer and helped on by the champagne, he said, 'Really I can't think what's come over Lord Plymouth to take up with a chap like you?!'

After lunch and speechifying the Princess was taken at her request round the city's art gallery. While most of her party were in a state of complete exhaustion and the aldermen were either drowsy or slightly inebriated, the Princess 'was most energetic, tired everybody out and left no picture unlooked at'. On the return journey to Hewell, as everyone sank thankfully back into their seats, she vivaciously discussed a sign board Mr Ashbee must design for her. Only after the party reached Hewell did she retire to her bedroom to rest before dinner.[28]

During the spring and summer of 1913 the Princess carried out the largest number of public engagements she had ever undertaken. Yet her family were not neglected. Widowed Janey was incapable of managing her affairs so Princess Louise arranged for her secretary to help under her personal supervision. When she heard Mrs Dawkins was unwell, she called with 'a bouquet the size of a house'. The family loved her dearly; yet they recognized that Princess Louise in good health was not the same person as Princess Louise in bad health. 'She is a dear kind thing' but 'as her health is bad ... what pleases her one day, displeases her another'.[29]

In February 1914 the Princess and Lorne attended a family wedding. When twenty-four-year-old Maysie Glyn had become engaged to Lieutenant John Wynne Finch the previous autumn, she had jokingly told Lady Mary that he deserved their thanks for preserving her from 'adding another to the old maids in the family,' such as Niky and Lilah Campbell.[30] Princess Louise arrived at the Guards' Chapel at two o'clock; she looked exceedingly handsome swathed in dark furs and a small black toque, with her lovely pearls and a long diamond chain glistening against the emerald green of her velvet dress. The Chapel was absolutely packed with the Argyll aunts, uncles and vast cousinhood. It was such an enjoyable occasion that, somewhat unusually, many of the family lingered on after the 'going away', as if they did not wish to leave. It was the last great gathering of the Argyll family before war and death came suddenly upon them.

Lorne's memory became steadily less reliable. He would pick up some object or document, wander about with it, and then put it behind a bookshelf or in a cupboard. Suddenly, there would be an explosion of rage when he could not find it, and Princess Louise would have to search everywhere. Yet there was something endearing about his devotion to, and dependence upon his wife. For her part, she lavished care and affection upon him, as upon a child.

In April, she went down to Kent House. Lorne joined her after attending an outdoor function with Ralph Glyn, who had a bad cold. By the next morning he was extremely unwell and Dr Hoffmeister diagnosed double pneumonia. On the 28th, Princess Louise wired to Niall at Inveraray, 'Uncle Ian very ill pneumonia quite suddenly. Alas no room here for anyone but you should come.'[31] Lady Frances was also sent for and arrived with two nurses to help Princess Louise nurse Lorne round the clock.

Niall arrived at Kent House on the 29th when Princess Louise, 'looking very tired', ran out to meet him. At midnight, the doctors thought he might be dying and Lady Frances and Niall were called to his bedside. There they found Princess Louise holding and stroking Lorne's hand, 'quite distraught'. His breathing became dreadfully laboured owing to his blocked lungs; Princess Louise held fresh, cold water compresses to his forehead to prevent him leaning forward and choking. During these long hours of the night and into the dawn, Princess Louise and Niall knelt on either side of his bed watching him sink and rally. The only comfort for her was that he felt no pain; nor did he appear to realize how ill he was.

The doctors were astonished at his vitality over the next two days as he sat up in bed, at times speaking distinctly and asking about lunch; at other times rambling, 'talking of faces and seeing roses and something about Glenshira and mosquito nets'.[32] Princess Louise refused to leave him and had to be forced to go and lie down for the odd hour.

When Lorne indistinctly demanded some unspecified picture, Princess Louise immediately sent Niall off in her carriage to Osborne to find a picture by one of the Italian masters in Queen Victoria's bedroom as quickly as possible. Apart from a bronze tablet placed at the head of the bed by her children with a crucifix below it, this room was exactly as Queen Victoria had left it. Unfortunately, for Niall's purposes, the pictures were too heavy for him to move. Suddenly he saw a small one and, tearing it off the wall, returned in great haste to Kent House. Princess Louise recognized it as one of Raphael's but said it was too small for Lorne to see. In the event, Lorne was comatose throughout the night.

Everyone present was impressed by the way in which Princess Louise coped with the constant fluctuations in Lorne's condition. 'She is wonderfully well and on the spot and manages him perfectly,' Niall wrote to Niky, who was confined to Rosneath with a cold. 'All these days the breathing has been dreadful to listen to accentuated in his case as Aunt L remarks, by the fact that he was always a loud breather and snorer at night.'[33]

On Saturday May 2nd, it was 'so painful a sight' that Lady Frances could not bear to remain in the room and Niall also came in and out, finding Lorne's appearance 'more and more painful'; only Princess

Louise bore up and, apart from some sleep before lunch, stayed continually with him. The newly-arrived Princess Louis of Battenberg joined the others for a sad silent dinner. It was clear by that evening that Lorne was sinking rapidly. At half past ten with Princess Louise holding him, Lorne's head slipped sideways towards her, as he died. She became very tearful, and Lady Frances had to lead her gently away to her room.

On the morning after Lorne's death, Kent House assumed a national importance for the first and only time in its history. Although it was a Sunday, postmen, messengers and delivery boys endlessly made the short journey from East Cowes up the hill to the house to deliver letters, wires and even the first wreaths. Within the house, the advent of the telephone was felt to be anything but a blessing. 'The telephone from the Lord Chamberlain and from Aunt Looloo's sisters is incessant,' Niall recorded in exasperation.[34]

Princess Helena learnt from Princess Louis that 'Louise is comparatively quiet and calmer this morning but has a bad throat and is afraid of a return of laryngitis – they are endeavouring to keep her as quiet as possible.'[35] In spite of this and of what she described as the 'exquisite torture I have been going through these past weeks,' the Princess allowed herself no rest.[36] Although made to stay in bed, she nevertheless answered the Lord Chamberlain's endless enquiries about the funeral service; ran through the details with Niall; and arranged who was to answer the telegrams and less important letters with which they were deluged. She also arranged for the little lich lights which were used at Queen Victoria's funeral to be sent over from Osborne. These were lit with unbleached candles and placed around Lorne's bed.

Only then did she begin to break down under the strain. The worst moment came when she went to Lorne's room to see him, having almost forgotten that he was no longer alive, and found him lying dead. He looked 'so altered and strange' that she could not bear to see him again.[37] She cried and was painfully upset for the rest of the day. In this over-wrought state, she turned on those she loved. Mrs Grant was the first, as Princess Louis recorded: 'Aunt Louise was horrid to Mrs Grant this morning,' although Mrs Grant 'gave as good as she took and said she would go and actually has done so . . . Aunt Louise feels an injured martyr and speaks about the selfishness of Mrs Grant.' Princess Louis was glad that her own lady-in-waiting had always resisted any bullying, 'I don't want to grow like "the Aunts",' she declared.[38]

The Princess's next victim was Ralph Glyn, who had wanted to be at Kent House with her. She refused to allow him to come, because she irrationally blamed his cold as the cause of Lorne's illness. Nothing could persuade her otherwise. So Ralph, who was the nearest she and Lorne had to a son, was kept away. With considerable insight into Princess Louise's character, Princess Helena explained to him: 'There are natures – who when trials and griefs come to them – somehow shrink from the *very* ones who are most dear to them!'

Princess Helena could enter into Ralph Glyn's feelings; for she was also one of those excluded from Kent House. Princess Louise had let it be known that she did not want Princess Helena to come; mainly because she thought her elder sister would start interfering and reorganizing everything. 'Poor, poor Louise . . . my heart aches for her,' Princess Helena had written to Lady Mary on May 3rd. 'I . . . wd go any moment if she wd have me but you *know* the *difficulties* and I don't want to put myself forward in *any* way'.[39]

The Princess became much more herself, though voiceless and weary, over the next few days. Niall's help was invaluable. 'All day telegrams in hundreds, and messages of all kinds to be answered,' he recorded in his diary. There were several every day from the King, Princess Helena and Princess Beatrice. Then there were the arrangements to settle with the Chief of Police, Westminster Abbey and the Commander-in-Chief, and such taxing issues as whether uniform or mourning dress should be worn. 'All very tiring. How glad I shall be when it is all over,' wrote Niall.[40] It was the first time he had come into direct contact with royal ceremonial. Lorne, who in life had done his best to avoid the regalia and fuss of royalty, was in death surrounded by it.

On the afternoon of May 7th, the body of the 9th Duke of Argyll was taken on a gun carriage drawn by sixty bluejackets to Trinity Pier. That morning Princess Louise had gone into the garden to gather bay leaves and lilies of the valley, which she used to compose her wreath. This now lay on the coffin with Lorne's coronet and decorations. At the pier used for Queen Victoria, the coffin was taken aboard the royal yacht, which steamed slowly away to the sound of the 'Last Post'.

In London the people had turned out as if to watch a royal funeral. Princess Louise, accompanied by Princess Helena, travelled in a royal carriage through great crowds, who lined the route to Westminster

Abbey. As they entered St Faith's Chapel, the choir sang 'Lead Kindly Light' and Princess Louise took her place at the prie-dieu near the bier; many of the Argyll family kneeling behind her. After a brief service, Bishop Boyd-Carpenter led Princess Louise to the altar to pray and then escorted her out with the family.

She had wanted Lorne's body to lie in Kensington Palace until they left for Scotland, but the King had written to say it would not do to have it in the house when the King of Denmark called, even though he would not come in. 'It is against some curious custom it appears,' Niall wrote.[41] Instead, the body was stealthily transferred to Kensington Parish Hall. On the afternoon of May 9th, Princess Louise and Niall walked over there. The vicar's sons were playing tennis outside in the gardens, unaware of the sombre scene within.

Princess Louise also had to receive visiting Royalties like her nephew, Prince Henry of Prussia, who was representing the Kaiser. Yet when Princess Beatrice came in to see Niall and then moved upstairs to see Princess Louise, Mrs Grant told her that she had orders to forbid her even to enter the corridor. Princess Beatrice took this very calmly. She had already had to obtain all the details of Lorne's death from Princess Louis and Lady Mary, since 'when I meet dear Louise I dare not ask her much, for she seems to be in such a prostrate and excited condition'.[42] Princess Beatrice knew this 'cloud' would blow over and Princess Louise would once more be her loving, affectionate, old self. Niall concluded her behaviour was 'all nerves I suppose'.[43]

On the night of May 12th, Princess Louise boarded the night sleeper from King's Cross bound for Glasgow. Travelling with her were Niky, Joan Balfour, Ralph and Niall; the coffin was in a separate compartment. After breakfast, the party travelled on to Craigendoran and thence by special steamer across to Rosneath, all the church bells tolling up the loch.

The tenants pushed the coffin on a hand bier from the pier to the little church, followed by Princess Louise leaning on Niall's arm as they walked. Mr Warr said a short prayer and the tapers were set out and lit around the coffin. Both Princess Louise and Niall now became tearful as they stood in the church Lorne had loved best and 'where he used to appease me with picture books,' Niall remembered. Later that evening Princess Louise slipped back into the church to lay a simple wreath of sea lavender and white heather with a card bearing the words 'His Wife L'.

The burial service at Kilmun took place on May 15th. Princess Louise drove to Rosneath pier where all the family were gathered before boarding the steamer. The sun was blazing on loch and hills, the gorse making the near slopes a mass of yellow and gold against the dazzling blue waters of the Holy Loch. As the steamer approached Kilmun pier, the shore loomed up crowded with people. Niall later heard that 9,000 had arrived on foot and by land. Many had travelled overnight from the far flung Western Isles, from Tiree and Iona and Lismore. Despite their large numbers, the crowds were so well-ordered and quiet, that they were almost unobtrusive. They had come to bury not some great public figure but a man known to all of them, the Mac Cailein Mor. And, as Princess Louise stepped ashore to the skirling of the pipes – 'and the pipes are calling, calling, Lochaber no more' – she came, not as a princess of the royal blood but, as his wife, who had come among friends and family to bury their Highland Chief.

The sun beat down upon the heralds in their tabards on either side of Teddy Glyn, Provost Gilmour carrying the heraldic banner, Chamberlain Lowis with the baton, the pipe band in their kilts, the gun carriage and pallbearers, who were all Campbell lairds; and upon the coffin covered with a great banner upon which rested Lorne's bonnet, claymore and plaid, with a single wreath, a great bunch of the blue hyacinths Lorne loved to see at Inveraray and which had been specially brought from the gardens there. The sun beat down upon the black, veiled figure of Princess Louise on Duke Niall's arm, with Lord George on her other side; and Lady Mary, Alan Percy and Niky, followed by Lady Frances, Sybil and Lady Connie, and then four nephews and nieces; all of whom now walked for the last time with Lorne among them.

When the long procession started, minute guns fired and the noise flew over the water and was repeated again and again in fainter echoes among the surrounding wooded hills. As Princess Louise, near the head of the procession, reached the turning before the long climb up to the church, a halt was made and Lord Archie's Inveraray pipe band took its place at the head of the line. As they played, the tolling bell of Kilmun mingled with the dirge of the pipes and the hot sun glinted everywhere. 'The pipe band made one's heart ache as they started away and we followed [up] that dusty winding road through crowds who stood on each side, silent, bareheaded, and heads bowed,' wrote Lady Mary's daughter, Meg.[44]

When they turned into the churchyard, the procession halted. Only the family continued along the path. For one moment the coffin halted against the green sunlit hill and then the family went into the mausoleum, a haven of coolness from the scorching heat of that May day in 1914.

'I have been wandering where "the wild river fed from the hills of Ben More, encircles the island of graves",' Lorne had written forty-six years before. 'There is certainly no burying place in the world like it – and one feels as if the rush of the waters on either side were a cromach to be wailed by them for ever.'[45]

CHAPTER XXVIII

The End of an Era

The first few months of Princess Louise's widowhood made little outward change to her daily life. She was, if anything, busier than ever for there was a vast correspondence, and a great deal of estate business to transact. On May 18th, copies of Lorne's will and codicils arrived from Edinburgh, followed on the 19th by the family lawyers, with the result that the Princess passed the next few days discussing trusts, settlements and taxes. Although she had been left Rosneath for life, it was so heavily mortgaged that she would have to maintain it and spend far more than she would ever receive as income from the farm and rents at Inveraray. Together with Dalchenna and Hardelot in France, Rosneath would pass back into the entail at her death.

In the afternoons, the Princess escaped from trustees and lawyers into the gardens, where the bluebells were out in sheets, or on walks with Niall, Niky and Ralph. After the lawyers left, the Princess and Niky began the task of marking furniture and pictures in preparation for the valuers. This was complicated by the presence at Rosneath of family heirlooms from Inveraray, which had been brought over for safekeeping after it was let.

Ralph left on May 21st and Princess Louise walked with Niall to the Point to wave to him as he passed by. Ralph, who did not share the family's propensity for 'sightings' and hearing voices, had heard a voice saying, 'You must ask MacDuff.' The Princess triumphantly told Niall that she had the solution: the voice was King Edward's. Whereas Lorne called the Duke of Fife 'Fyffie', the King always called him 'MacDuff'. She was worried about estate matters and the King was reminding them that the Duke of Fife was the person to consult.

It seemed much more unnatural to receive 'crank' letters from strangers claiming they were descendants of Lorne. There was a woman in Peterborough, who had long plagued the Princess with letters in which she declared Lorne was her father. After Lorne's death, she wrote, 'now calling herself joint progeny of Aunt Looloo and Uncle

Ian . . . There appear to be lots of bedlamites running about loose,'
Niall concluded.[1]

The Princess had planned to journey South on May 25th or 26th
but, when it came to it, she could not bear to leave Rosneath, which
was so loved by Lorne and so full of memories of him. 'Never leave
Rosneath,' Lorne had once said, 'for there is but one step upwards
which is worth leaving Rosneath for . . . The step to heaven'.[2] As
Queen Victoria had done from Windsor in 1861, so Princess Louise
now postponed her departure again and again from Rosneath in 1914.

'I cannot get over my loss at all – the dear Duke was so tied up in
my life,' she confided to Ethel. 'My every thought and interest was tied
up in him. I am, apart from the sorrow, utterly lost and desolation is
all around me now.'[3] The Princess's feelings did not lessen with time.
In 1916 she wrote, 'My loneliness without the Duke is quite terrible, I
go on for a bit determined to choke down all feelings and then I utterly
break down. A book, or a paper or letters, I come across just finishes
me – 40 years I was married and you know how he depended on me,'
adding with characteristic curiosity, 'I wonder what he does now!!'[4]

On May 26th, she and Niky went over to Kilmun to lay fresh
flowers in the mausoleum. The smell of rotting flowers from the
hundreds of wreaths – there had been almost four hundred from
Scotland alone – was so overpowering that they spent most of the visit
carting them out for disposal. They inspected the Princess's own
memorial to Lorne, a verse she had composed, which was inscribed on
the marble door of his sepulchre:

> His was a noble heart, with ready will
> He stretched a kindly hand to those in need.
> Champion of right, he fought against the wrong
> With swift and eager pen, perfect and pure
> His faith in God: lofty the goal he sought
> Beside the chosen comrade of his love,
> Labouring to make the Empire Nations one
> His best was given to serve his country's cause.
> Loving, high-souled, and valiant, he now lives
> In death, as in earthly days, Beloved.[5]

Princess Louise's absorption in the concerns of widowhood was
interrupted by the outbreak of war with Germany. She was sixty-six
and in deep mourning at Kensington Palace when war broke out. Her

reaction was remarkably different from the majority of the country. Crowds gathered along the Mall and outside Buckingham Palace to sing patriotic songs; Lord Esher noted that Society people 'mostly looked upon war as a sort of picnic'.[6] Unlike them, the Princess felt only horror at the prospect. It was fifty-nine years since she had been taken to visit the wounded soldiers back from the Crimea; in the intervening years she had seen too much of hospitals and convalescent homes to be able to view another war with any feelings other than revulsion and sadness. Her immediate concern was for the wounded servicemen, who would require medical attention and nursing facilities.

To this end, she ensured her Rosneath Hospital was in readiness to receive more patients, and then offered it to the War Office, who gladly placed it under the direction of the Army Medical Officer at Glasgow. The Princess did not understand this to mean that she had relinquished her powers of control. On August 23rd, she let her old colleague, Sir William Macewen, now also Surgeon-General for the Royal Navy in Scotland, know that the local doctor 'has no right whatsoever to send' men to Rosneath, 'as my hospital is directly under the War Office now,' and was for the wounded above all other cases.

Some authorities considered the Territorials, who had enlisted as an auxiliary home force, as third class soldiers well behind the Army and Kitchener's new Army of men and that they fell outside the scope of Army medical attention. When the Princess was told that Territorials would not be sent to her hospital, she made the point that 'Territorials are now for this war counted as belonging to the Army and expected to do the same work as regular troops.' They constituted 'the reinforcements of our forces and therefore, it is most important they should be fit, not only with reference to drill, but also in their general physical health, as so much may depend on them, when their time comes'.[7]

In addition to organizing her hospital and her normal hospital work and visits, the Princess also turned her hand to market gardening. Concerned at the prospect of food shortages, she instructed the few older gardeners, who remained at home, to plough up a good deal of her gardens and some of the neighbouring fields in order to grow vegetables. She also began to publicize the need to grow vegetables. Two years later, her market gardens at Rosneath and Kensington Palace were flourishing. She wrote to Wally Paget: 'I am so glad the vegetables are of use . . . I always send whatever I have that will carry and am growing first for our beloved sailors & troops.'[8]

These were not the only changes effected in Rosneath during the War. When Niall visited Princess Louise there in September, he found the place 'all covered with entrenchments etc to protect the Fort there, blockhouses all across the moors connected by telephones'.[9] Owing to its position on the Clyde, Rosneath had become strategically important to the Navy; the fear of German spies meant that troops were placed there as a 'look-out' and Princess Louise had to help with providing accommodation and extra supplies.

She was busier than ever, what with looking after Lorne's properties left in her charge, 'Troops stationed there and I don't know what all. My Hospital & the Red X,'[10] but she also missed Lorne more than ever, although she was thankful that he, who had been a leading light in the Anglo-German Society and had worked to promote unity between the two countries, had been spared 'these terribly anxious times'. To Ralph she wrote, 'dear Uncle Lorne's chair empty its very dreadful here without him & I feel so lost'.[11]

One effect of the war was that, for the first time in her life, Princess Louise was without a Household and found herself almost alone; this was not only a novelty but, coming on top of her recent widowhood and the outbreak of a world war, also something of a shock. She wrote about it to Mr BB from Rosneath in October: 'I am absolutely alone – no Gentleman wh is sadly needed with all these various works with W.O. etc no Lady and v inexperienced Sec. Dear Mrs G breaking down so I am overwhelmed often but peg on'. Her high sense of duty and the belief that, in her own small way, she could be of use to her country, saved her from succumbing to depression and grief: 'but duty says go on . . . so I do'.[12]

Once again, the Princess found herself with relations fighting against each other, this time on the battlefields of Mons, Ypres, and the Somme. Her sister Vicky's children were naturally on the German side, led by that nephew who had fondly spoken of her as his favourite 'Aunty Loo'. Her brother Leopold's family were in a dreadful position, for Charles Edward, now the Duke of Saxe-Coburg & Gotha, fought for Germany while his mother, Helen, and sister, Alice, were in England. It was the same with her sister Alice's children: Irene, the Kaiser's sister-in-law, in Germany, while Ella and Alicky were on the Allies' side in Russia and Victoria was in England.

Matters were still worse for Princess Helena. After the death of Prince Christle in the Boer War, her second son, Prince Albert, had been groomed to manage the family estates in Silesia and had joined the German Army with whom he now fought: 'Our only boy is with the German Army on the wrong side!!' All she knew of his whereabouts was that he was not on the Belgian frontier but they could have no communications with him. 'Oh! the sickening anxiety for so many dear ones out on the front – on *both* sides.'[13]

Princess Helena wrote these words before she became a victim of the xenophobia which swept Britain in the autumn of 1914. The anti-German crusade claimed a more public victim when Prince Louis of Battenberg, who had been christened 'the Germhun' by *John Bull*, was forced to resign as First Sea Lord. It was on this same day that he heard that his nephew Princess Beatrice's son, Prince Maurice of Battenberg, had died from wounds received in the battle of Mons. Those who vilified Prince Louis forgot those Royalties, who had served and died for their English country; they also forgot that two of his sons were serving in the Royal Navy.

After Prince Louis's resignation, the Battenbergs were homeless and almost like refugees; it was Princess Louise who came to their rescue. She had bequeathed Kent House in her will to Princess Louis. She now gave them Kent House outright, for she could not bear the thought that 'they had no home to go to'.[14] It was yet another change in her life and a great wrench for her. Sometimes the Princess longed to be in the Isle of Wight and she admitted to missing her old home, 'but of course I was glad to help' she would remind herself.[15] Just as she reminded herself the war was all the Kaiser's fault.

Princess Helena thought he 'must be *quite* mad to have lit such a conflagration'[16] and when Niall called at Kensington Palace on November 24th he found 'Aunt Looloo . . . most violent against the Kaiser.'[17] The war was going badly for the Allies and the wounded from the battlefields of the Somme were being transported home in droves. At Rosneath the Princess's hospital was full and she had begun to take in soldiers from 'her regiment' at Kensington Palace on a sort of half-way-house arrangement between hospital and convalescence.

Some of the Argyll family, their ranks sadly depleted by the war, gathered in London before Christmas for the wedding of Lord George's daughter, Enid Campbell. The Princess attended it with Niall and they arrived early. This gave her the opportunity to have a good look round, accompanied by her usual running commentary. She said in a loud voice just before the service began, 'My dear, *do* look at the pommade

on the choir boys' hair!'[18] She was also delighted to see several members
of 'Her Regiment,' the Argylls, outside the church. Lord George was
even more delighted to see one of them, his old valet. He greeted him
with the words, 'Hector, I'm verra glad to see you. I haven't been able
to find my bath sponge since you left.'[19]

Princess Louise felt the blank of her first Christmas without Lorne
terribly. 'I tried to forget the time altogether,' she wrote to a friend on
11 January 1915. 'My husband was always like a little child about it,
enjoying the time so much. After 43 years to be quite alone, it is no
thing to hold up ones head.' She always tried to remember the 'charming
words' of a piece of verse she was fond of quoting:

> Time there was – but it is gone;
> Time there may be – who can tell?
> Time there is to act upon
> Help us Lord, to use it well.

For as she readily admitted 'to try and help others is . . . the only way
one can live on'.[20]

By 1915 khaki was ubiquitous in London and military searchlights
sent staggering gleams across the sky. Lorne's old chum, Henry Lucy,
wrote, 'The very multitude of names of killed, wounded or missing
does something to blunt the sharpness of sympathy.'[21] For Princess
Louise who, day after day, year after year, visited hospitals, canteens
and servicemen's clubs and who comforted and encouraged with an
ever-smiling face, the sharpness of sympathy for those who suffered
was never blunted. One of her pet London hospitals was the Weir
Hospital at Balham. 'I have 40 Australians and one or two New
Zealanders at my Balham Hospital such nice fellows and we make a
great fuss of them,' she wrote to her other 'darling boy', Ralph, on
September 2nd. The Dardanelles business made her not only sad but
angry: 'one muddle and waste of life after another'.[22]

Her Campbell nephews at the Front received regular letters of
sympathy and encouragement. Oswald Balfour was wounded several
times and sent home on sick leave. On one occasion, when he had
returned to London after convalescence, Princess Louise greeted him
with, 'Oh! but you are safe. This is dreadful. I'm having you prayed
for.'[23]

Lady Mary lunched with Princess Louise at Kensington Palace on
February 6th and told Ralph that 'she looked well but thin, and older

& with such a strange look of her mother I had never seen before'.[24]
Shortly afterwards, Ralph was sent home on the sick list. Princess
Louise was beside herself with anxiety and hoped that he would
eventually convalesce at Rosneath, 'Your table in library always ready
and dear Uncle Lorne's chair empty.' Her great worry was that he
would grow bored and not follow the doctor's treatment: 'You are very
good I hope and do all which Dr Blacket thinks necessary . . .'[25]

The Princess, in common with everyone else, was beginning to feel
the effects of the Zeppelin air attacks. She would have preferred to be
near the hospital at Rosneath, but duties kept her in London. 'I have
been really so frightfully busy, letters, letters, functions, meetings,
laryngitis, late to bed, no sleep, constant worries,' was how she
described her days to Ralph.[26]

Many of these letters were concerned with her latest project. Sir
William Macewen had hatched the idea of starting a Scottish hospital
for the treatment of limbless sailors and soldiers and the supply of
artificial limbs. After the Red Cross had intimated that it would not
help, Sir William had arranged a meeting of influential citizens in
Glasgow, gained the co-operation of the Lord Provost and asked
Princess Louise to be their Patron. She was delighted to be involved
in such an undertaking and thought it a first-rate idea. However, before
her letter of acceptance was posted, she mentioned it to the King. To
her surprise, he was most anxious that nothing should be done which
would compete with the Roehampton hospital work. 'It seems that the
King has been approached, and the hope expressed that such a Scottish
institution would not be started, which would in any way hinder the
success of Roehampton,' Princess Louise explained. King George had
been told that 'the only people in the world able to make artificial
limbs' were three Americans, who were also demanding 'ridiculous
sums for their limbs'. He feared that if the price was not paid, wounded
men would go limbless.

Having warned Sir William of the opposition, Princess Louise
suggested that any announcement about the Scottish hospital should
emphasize that the object was 'merely to take off pressure and give
quicker assistance', not to cause rivalry. 'We must go carefully to work,'
she cautioned him, and enclosed a cheque for £1,000.[27] Sir William
turned to the Clyde shipbuilders, showed them an artificial leg and
asked if they could produce a replica. One of them, a Mr Yarrow,
returned two days later with an exact copy of the leg. All that was

required was an unlimited supply of willow trees, which people all over Scotland willingly began to sacrifice for the hospital. Mr Yarrow even developed a rapid method of drying wood and standardized the manufacture of limbs for arm and leg.

On March 30th, a meeting in Glasgow formally approved the establishment of the hospital at Erskine House in Renfrewshire. In a press statement the Princess said, 'I entirely approve of such a hospital being started in Scotland, and I will be very proud to become its patron'. She was rarely a mere titular patron of any organization and Erskine proved no exception; she was soon one of its guiding lights. 'A deep personal interest in its equipment and administration' were the words chosen by Erskine to describe the Princess's involvement in the day-to-day running of the hospital and her regular tours of inspection whenever she was at Rosneath.[28]

The Heritage Craft Schools at Chailey in Sussex constituted another organization which knew the benefit of her interest. Opened in 1908 as 'The public school of crippledom', the Heritage aimed to train children in self-sufficiency, particularly through the teaching of crafts. During the Great War, the Boy's Heritage became the Princess Louise Military Hospital. Here, soldiers who had been crippled in action convalesced whilst learning a remunerative trade under the supervision of the Schools' trained assistants and with the help of the crippled boys, who acted as their orderlies and provided encouragement by showing how much they had achieved despite severe disability. The Princess worked indefatigably to promote the Schools; she helped to raise funds and designed and sculpted the Schools' War Memorial which was dedicated on 24 November 1925. She also carved and donated the altar pieces for the Girls' School Chapel in 1931 as well as the oak panels in the Chapel and in the Dining Hall.

Another wartime concern for the Princess was the fate of her Regiments, the Princess Louise's Kensington Regiment, formerly the 13th London Regiment, whose colours she had helped to embroider in 1909, and her Argylls, whose colours she took into her own keeping for the duration of the war. 'The anxiety we live in for what is going on is great,'[29] she wrote, and the accounts she received from the Argylls at the Front strengthened her desire to be fighting alongside them: 'It makes me only long more than ever that I were a man and could be with you all,'[30] she told Colonel Tweedie. To compensate, she kept open house for soldiers home on leave and cared for shell-shocked men at Kensington Palace and at Rosneath. She ignored fatigue: 'I am awfully tired but that dont matter one must help *all* one can'[31] and was furious when, in the autumn of 1917, her 69-year-old body collapsed under the strain: 'I have been so ill again it is most trying, there is no time to be ill.'[32]

She soon returned to her duties, which the Armistice did little to diminish. On 6 December 1918, after a tiring day opening an Edinburgh bazaar in aid of the Argylls and passing the afternoon at a naval refreshments hut, she heard that a contingent of released prisoners of war were disembarking at Leith. She immediately hurried down to the large shed in the dockyards, where she went from table to table, shaking hands and talking to each of the thousand suffering men, 'deeply interested, making enquiries, and getting at the root of their experiences' well into the dark and wintry evening. Afterwards, when a companion asked if she was tired, she said she would not have missed for the world, the opportunity of welcoming the soldiers back after what they had done and been through.[33]

The Princess clung to her work as to a life-raft throughout 1919, the first full year of peace. As she explained to Lady Victoria Richardson, 'I have lost all my friends *nearly*, old, middle aged & young, and life is very lonely but I work as much, and more than my health enables me to and it is the only thing which makes life worth living.'[34] It was also stimulating, and kept her active and young at heart. Unlike her sister-in-law, Queen Alexandra, whose mind and body were failing fast, and her nephew and niece, King George and Queen Mary, who resisted all change and passed most of the 'gay twenties' in comparative, staid seclusion, Princess Louise welcomed change and innovation in the world around her, as she had always done. Despite her seventy years, she was considered by the younger generation to be 'a modern thinker', who 'smoked and laughed and knelt on the floor'.[35]

Her curiosity about life remained undimmed and her habits were found endearing by younger people; in particular, her obsessive desire for anonymity, which led her to refer to herself as 'A Lady' and everyone else to call her thereafter 'The Lady'. Letters between her friends contain phrases like: 'I hear The Lady has gone abroad' or 'in case The Lady asks,' while presents would arrive with a card bearing the tell-tale message 'From A Lady'.[36] Her Campbell great-nephews and nieces always knew when she was on the telephone because she would say, 'A Lady wishes to speak with' so-and-so.[37]

She was unfailingly interested in the activities of her family. To one nephew-in-law, bound for the Sudan, she wrote, 'I have been finding out what would be helpful for you to take out with you to Khartoum' and to combat any feverish attack she enclosed a bottle of tablets with the instructions 'one *every* 2 or 3 [hours] till temp normal then stop them at once'.[38] She possessed a huge medicine chest, which accompanied her everywhere, and news of family or friends' illness always resulted in a home remedy being posted off from her store.

As an aunt, her sympathy was unvarying, yet she was never over-indulgent. In the middle of tea, the Prince of Wales (later Edward VIII) suddenly remembered that it was Aunt Louise's birthday the following day. Rifling through a drawer for a suitable present, he found a pretty snuff box, which was hurriedly sent to her. The next day he received a little parcel containing his snuff box and a note: 'Dear David, Do look inside this box.' Inside, he found a card inscribed 'To David from Aunt Louise'.[39]

Despite close contact with the younger generation, the nineteen twenties were a depressing period for the Princess. There was in Queen Mary's words, 'a perfect epidemic of deaths' to bear: first Prince Louis of Battenberg, then Princess Helena and Janey in June 1923; then, in 1925, Queen Alexandra, 'the very dearest of sisters and Friend to me';[40] Lord Ronnie had died during the war, and Lady Connie in 1922. The loss of loved ones left the Princess even more depressed and isolated. She missed Lorne increasingly; Lady Frances came across her standing under his portrait at Rosneath in tears and she continually referred to him. 'Lorne wd I know have been much interested,' she wrote to Mary Drew when thanking her for a book of reminiscences. 'It is so hard to see hear & read things always alone now, & yet I know so well all he wd have said & felt.'[41]

Her own health was poor: 'First sciatica a torture in itself & *synovitis* wh is inflammation of the covering of the bones of the knee that is a pain no one can understand who has not had it. Real vile pain that makes you shout, where your strength is nearly worn out,' she explained to Laurence Alma-Tadema.[42] During these attacks she 'just screwed' herself up to attend a function and then collapsed again.[43] It was at such times that her thoughts turned to the dispersal of her belongings. She devised a system whereby anything very breakable, of historical interest or great value was donated to the Victoria and Albert Museum. Other odds and ends were given in a haphazard fashion to visiting family and friends. Jewellery, small items and her greatest treasures, especially those of sentimental value, were put away in cupboards for distribution after her death. She found making a will most troublesome as 'one gets so bewildered & worried'. She confided to a friend: 'Earthly goods are a trouble when one knows one may be called away any day – and with no children makes it yet more difficult.'[44] She bequeathed Lorne's scrapbook, 'one of the most precious things there is', to Lady Mary early on because 'I cannot bear to think if it was my lot suddenly to be called the dear little old Book wd be discarded or thrown away or got into the wrong hands, & the sight of it nearly breaks my heart'. She could see Lorne 'breathing heavily over it gumming things in like a child so happy with it'.[45]

However, her feelings about the dead were never morbid. She believed strongly in the afterlife: 'those that leave us are not far off'.[46] Nor did she fear her own death. To her, death was a form of emigration and 'Many are the surprises that await the emigrant' she would say, as if anticipating an exciting adventure.[47]

Until such time as this particular adventure began, she busied herself with charitable work and enthusiastically took on board a new project, the building of a hospital for children in Kensington. She had long been a patron of the Kensington Dispensary and Children's Hospital, which offered medical and surgical aid to the poor of the parish from premises in Kensington Church Street. However, since its inception in 1840, the neighbourhood had so increased in wealth that, by the 1920s, the poorer residents were more often densely packed into North Kensington, an area which lacked medical facilities. The Princess decided it was time to re-establish the dispensary elsewhere. In 1924 she convened a meeting of the Dispensary Committee, which agreed to her proposal to move the premises to North Kensington and to appoint a Re-establishment Committee of which she became President. A public meeting the following month officially brought into existence the Committee and an appeal to raise £80,000 for a new hospital to be called, The Princess Louise Hospital for Children.

That autumn, the Princess bustled about in search of a suitable site: for, now that she had a worthwhile project to occupy her, she meant to manage everything to do with it herself. A shortlist of sixteen possible sites was compiled and her energy was 'like a bracing wind' to those who accompanied her as she tramped through North Kensington to make a careful examination of each site and its surroundings. In and out of houses, slums and mewsways she went, before deciding on a site by the playing fields in St Quintin Avenue. Two years later, on 2 November 1926, she returned to the site to lay the foundation stone: 'The name "Hospital" was derived from hope and every hospital ought to be a centre of hope to sufferers,'[48] she told the audience. 'We want to build up all these children to become strong, healthy citizens. That is a privilege everyone has a right to.'[49]

Over the next few years she regularly inspected the building works and attended the bazaars held to increase the building fund, to which she had donated £1,200. Finally, at her request, the King and Queen opened the hospital. The Princess's connection with her hospital did not end here, for she liked to feel she was part of it and often dropped in to see patients and staff. Her only stipulation was 'No Fuss'. Dr Taylor, a young woman doctor, was once examining a patient when the Princess came past her with the usual, 'Don't let me interrupt your work.' Dr Taylor continued when suddenly she heard a crash. Princess Louise had caught her foot on one of the protruding legs of a screen and 'come down, Crash, on her bottom on the wooden floor'. She did not cry out, so that the doctor thought she had sustained a serious injury. But the 84-year-old Princess was soon halfway down the corridor, walking smartly along, brushing down her right hip. The doctor had to run after her to enquire if she was all right: 'Yes, yes, oh yes, I'm all right,' she answered. Dr Taylor thought she had 'all the guts in the world' for it had been a bad fall for an old lady: the Princess 'must have been brought up to be tough' or else 'she'd learnt to grin and bear it'.[50]

During her time at the hospital, Dr Taylor came to respect and admire the Princess, who was not only very interested in medicine but also knowledgeable about it, especially about children's diseases. At an open day, the Princess was showing people round as part of the hospital team when her group arrived at the cot of a child with pyelitis. None of her guests knew what the condition was but the Princess explained that it was an infection of the kidneys, commoner in girls than boys and gave them a thorough description of its treatment. Dr Taylor was impressed both by her 'practical, matter-of-fact manner' and by her easy, affectionate way with the child patients.

The hospital was not the only local cause she served. Indeed, she had long been thought of as 'the fairy godmother' of Kensington. More than one mayor and local MP had been told 'Be sure you let me know of any scheme the object of which is to benefit Kensington, and I will do what I can to further it.'[51] It was in recognition of her many years of invaluable support that, on 31 July 1928, the Kensington Borough Council availed itself of a recently conferred power to admit the Princess as their first Honorary Freeman of the Royal Borough. It was not until 1949 that they admitted as their second Freeman, Winston Churchill.

Princess Louise certainly considered it a great honour and was pleased by the award. Two years later, she was very hurt when Glasgow ignored her and, like Edinburgh, awarded the Freedom of the City to young Princess Mary, who had married Viscount Lascelles in 1922. 'Glasgow she felt bitterly, and spoke of the years of service she had given it,' recorded Lady Frances, who wrote to Charlie Warr to ask if nothing could be done by Edinburgh in recognition of the Princess's work. Although Glasgow afterwards offered the Freemanship to her, she refused it. 'When she says Princess Mary has done nothing for either (compared to her) she speaks the truth,' Lady Frances assured Charlie Warr.[52]

There were now only three surviving members of the 'old' generation of royalty: Princess Louise, Princess Beatrice and the Duke of Connaught. Their stamina and interest in life made it easy to forget that they had great-grandchildren and great-great-nephews and nieces; nor did they seem to relish their exalted status. When Princess Louis introduced her granddaughters to their 'Great-Great-Uncle', the Duke of Connaught replied in a horrified voice, 'My dear Victoria, you are making an ancestor of me![53] In her old age, Princess Louise remained as close as ever to him: 'The wonderful tie of brothers and sisters, *when they understand each other* is unique,' she wrote when staying with this 'beloved brother' at Bagshot Park.[54] The attraction of Ribsden, her small house in Surrey, was its proximity to Bagshot. He and Princess Louise shared many interests, the most abiding of which was gardens.

The Duke had also created a marvellous garden at his villa, Les Bruyères, in Cap Ferrat where she used to join him for the winter months in the late nineteen twenties and thirties. On the first occasion that her butler James arranged the journey, it included an overnight stop in Paris, where he had reserved rooms by letter, under his own name, for the Princess wished to be incognito. When she arrived at the hotel, she was welcomed by the proprietor: 'You are Madame James I believe.' After a second's hesitation, she replied, 'Oh, yes.' She made a point of telling James, 'so I am Mrs James now'. The incident did not end there for, during a family party after her return home, King George loudly condemned some peer who had been seen in a Paris hotel with a lady who was not his wife. Everyone agreed with him except Princess Louise, who pleaded the possibility of mistaken identity. When the King countered with 'Surely you cannot uphold a man who has done such a terrible thing?', she replied 'No', adding with relish, 'but I have stayed more than once in an hotel in Paris under the name of a man who was certainly not my husband!' As she had anticipated, this greatly shocked the company. She then went on to explain James's mistake.[55]

While wintering on the Riviera in 1931 the Princess heard of the death of Lady Frances: 'I shall miss her too terribly, she was really just the one only friend I could go to and know I would be able to have interesting talk with, give and get sympathy.'[56] It left her 'more than ever lonely' and she realized more and more, 'that there is One Friend who will ever be near and never does leave us, and then the loneliness goes'.[57] On her return home, she journeyed North to Rosneath which, of all her houses, gave her the most solace, because there she felt nearest to Lorne. At Rosneath, she donned her Campbell tartan skirt and blouse like a uniform and was rarely seen in the usual black.

Rosneath bore little evidence of the passage of the years; tucked away on the Clyde and cocooned by surrounding waters from the great changes wrought elsewhere in these inter-war years, it was a haven for the Princess. It had remained a feudal village and her coming was a great event, which some of the older inhabitants recall with pleasure today.

The Castle staff would have been notified of her arrival in advance and Mr Wyburn, the joiner, would be detailed to prepare the rooms by removing dust sheets and organizing furniture. Only certain rooms were opened up for the Princess: the library, small drawing room and dining room, the billiard room for its close association with Lorne since she never used it, and her blue bedroom and dressing room. If guests were expected then bedrooms would be specially opened up for their stay. The Princess kept a large outdoor establishment to maintain the estate: she certainly did not need to, but she could not bear to re-enact the sad days when Lorne had had to economize at Inveraray after the old Duke's death.

The Household was down to a skeleton, permanent staff consisting of the housekeeper, the handyman who also carried coal and chopped sticks, and the housemaid, Marjorie Macfarlane, who came to Rosneath in 1931. She recalls that the Princess was 'quite deaf' by then 'and you had to shout when speaking to her'.[58] This never resulted in any loss of speech on the part of her mistress. The present Queen is said to recall from her own childhood how Princesses Louise and Beatrice 'talked sometimes until their audience was stunned by the outpouring of words'.[59] With age, Princess Louise's features had sharpened but with her 'almost white' hair tucked up behind and her upright yet graceful carriage, she seemed to the young housemaid 'quite nice looking for an old lady'.

To augment the Rosneath people, the Princess brought key staff from Kensington Palace including her secretary, Miss Lucy James, 'a very nice' grey-haired woman in her sixties whose passion was shell collecting; the butler, Mr James; her Scottish nurse-companion, Miss Furneaux, then in her fifties; and her ladies' maid, Miss Francis, who had been with her for years. Her staff stayed with her a long time as they enjoyed working for her, even though she could be a 'bit temperamental'. This tendency revealed itself in her habit of shying cushions or any object to hand at people when she was in a tantrum. The faithful Miss Francis was the usual recipient of such treatment as she was of the subsequent charming apology which accompanied it.

The Princess's habits in old age were strangely at variance with her earlier life. Formerly notoriously unpunctual, her days were now ordered with the precision of a time-piece. Breakfast of two Huntley and Palmers biscuits, or sometimes two Marie ones, with a little watercress, or piece of lettuce, was brought to her bedroom every morning at eight. She slept in a large, brass bed with a light coverlet as she hated the weight of sheets and blankets. The morning was passed in reading and writing, varied only by sketching which she continued to do from her bedroom window, standing at her easel even when aged ninety. She lunched in her bedroom, where a tray, often bearing her favourite dish of 'bangers and mash' was taken up to her.

The afternoons were reserved for gardening with a drive after tea. She loved to potter about the beautifully kept gardens. The hedges were trimmed by Mr Wingate, the travelling hedger, and she also employed one of the estate workers as a path-keeper. Once, shortly after her arrival, she came upon him hacking away at undergrowth. 'You're very busy,' she commented. 'Oh yes,' he replied, 'we've been very busy ever since we aheard you was comin'!' He was quickly removed from path-keeping before her next visit. The south-facing, rose garden was her especial love and here she would put into practice her belief that 'if you can't get things done right, do them yourself', by taking the secateurs off a gardener and mounting the ladder to trim the climbing roses herself.[60] It required three gardeners under Mr Dawson to maintain the gardens as she liked them, and it was not the easiest billet on the estate, for her standards were high.

She always dined at eight and remained on in the dining room afterwards to listen to music on the wireless. She liked plain, simple fare and rice pudding was a particular favourite. Marjorie Macfarlane recalls how one Sunday evening they were at the pudding stage in the Servant's Hall when the footman came rushing in to say the Princess would like the creamed rice she did not eat at lunch. This was unfortunate as the staff 'were just digging into it', so they had to stop while the plates were removed to salvage the remains for the Princess.[61]

The orders of twenty years continued unchanged despite the diminished demand. She ate very little, yet large supplies of groceries were delivered every week. Each day the Helensburgh steamer off-loaded the cargo of one, fresh, cottage loaf for Miss James, despite the adequate supplies in the village bakery. 'Fancy foods' like pistaccio nuts and little boat-shaped pastries, which cook regularly requested, were never touched by the Princess; instead the staff feasted on the exotica. The only item the Princess insisted upon was farm butter from Calderwood, off the Clachan Farm. In bad weather, or if he had run out, cook would use ordinary butter and mould it to look like his.

The Princess's 'hermit existence' at Rosneath was punctuated by church on Sundays, and by tours of the village. In general, the villagers welcomed her visits for she was immensely approachable and 'Nothing ever happened except she gave her consent, [even] like a tree being cut. Anyone could go over the factor's head to her.'[62] Her habit of walking into a house unannounced could cause consternation if, as sometimes happened, she caught a villager ironing underclothes. Mrs McColl, one of the older inhabitants, had no hesitation in rebuking her: 'You knock before you come in here again!'[63]

According to a local farmer, Princess Louise 'did more for the place' than anyone else: 'She was handing out all the time and always doing something for somebody.'[64] The Rosneath children were the object of her especial attention and she looked after the guides and the scouts, who were entertained regularly for tea. On one occasion, as the boys were led downstairs, they noticed two cords hanging down and

mischievously gave one of them a pull. Immediately, a loud bell
sounded and the Princess came rushing down. 'She thought it was a
huge joke. And then she had a go too. And everyone was running
about and she was laughing.' The bell turned out to be the fire alarm.[65]

Despite her approachability, the Rosneath inhabitants were never
left in any doubt as to her wishes. The telephone poles were all moved
to the back of the village so as not to spoil its appearance. Signs and
advertisements were her pet hates. McPherson, the grocer, had long
despaired of the schoolchildren's habit of perching on the stone window
ledges of his shop. He, eventually, found some sloping brass plaques
containing advertisements which were too slippery for the children to
use. Princess Louise, however, thought they spoilt the look of her
village and ordered their removal. McBraynes, the steamship company,
had a workshop by Rosneath and, as a young lad, Douglas Haig used
to be sent down to the pier to check if the Princess was on the steamer
so that the signboards could be removed before her arrival.

Yet Rosneath affairs were one of the few areas of interest the
Princess could continue to dominate. For the influence of the older
generation of royalty had greatly diminished. As early as 1930, Lady
Frances had observed that the Princess's hospital at Erskine was 'going
to be completely under the Board of Health and her influence will
go'.[66] Another case in point was that of the Edinburgh College of
Domestic Science (now Queen Margaret College) of which she had
been patron since 1875. It would have been a much simpler matter to
obtain the use of the title 'Royal' for it before the Great War than it
was in the nineteen thirties. The Princess could not approach the King
directly but had to submit an application through the Scottish Office.
Although the College was the oldest, largest and foremost in reputation,
her application was refused owing to the existency of another smaller
institution in the West of Scotland.

There were further irritations to bear from the Ministry of Works,
who quibbled over the cost of a bronze plate by Alfred Gilbert for her
statue of Queen Victoria in Kensington Gardens. In 1925, instead of
incurring a charge of £10-15-0 to replace the plate, the Ministry chose
to remove the original plate and to incise the inscription 'HRH Princess
Louise sculpt' in the stone pedestal at a cost of £2-5-0. The matter was
raised again in 1933 as, according to the Princess, 'so many people are
continually asking which daughter is referred to. Showing that the
name which is cut in the base is evidently not visible enough – Some

people were heard to remark "that is the one who is dead".[67] But the Ministry of Works 'made difficulties' as they disliked Gilbert's design and the expense.

It was, however, partly owing to the Princess's influence that the King agreed to give the Queen Alexandra memorial commission to Gilbert. She proved 'a splendid friend' and, when he fell ill, she constantly visited him 'full of encouragement & hope & brightness'.[68] His death left yet another gap in her life but there were other, younger faces to give her pleasure. She shared a love of art and music with her great-nephew, Prince George, Duke of Kent whom she thought 'wonderfully thoughtful in everything just like his Grandfather [King Edward VII] in doing kindnesses'.[69]

It was through Princess Louise that, in 1934, the beauty of his fiancée, Princess Marina, was immortalized in the photographs of Cecil Beaton. Princess Louise was Beaton's first royal sitter and was, as ever, extremely specific about the commission. She was photographed in his drawing room at Sussex Gardens 'in a variety of conventional poses', her ropes of pearls gleaming against the grey of her embossed tea-gown. Cecil Beaton thought the 86-year-old Princess 'a charming old lady with pale hair and features, but it was difficult to register her personality with my Folding Kodak'. Like Queen Victoria, the Princess was an exacting client; after a lengthy exchange of correspondence, Miss James conveyed the Princess's opinion that 'the alterations have been beautifully done', nevertheless, 'the cheek should not be so light against the deep shadow left side . . . the bone above eye requires slightly toning down; the right eye should be a tiny bit bigger towards the nose, upper lid . . . The hair to be a wee bit lighter,' not to mention the fact that 'The nostril on left hand side would not show in that position, and makes the nose look a little out of drawing . . .' and there should not be 'too much light on the nose as it is inclined to make it too prominent'.[70]

The Princess encouraged the Duke as a collector of *objets d'art* and bequeathed many of her treasures to him. He had inherited 'an eye for beauty' from his mother, Queen Mary, whose acquisitiveness is well known. It was Queen Mary who organized and catalogued the Royal Collections and who searched through the storerooms and attics of royal residences for missing pieces of furniture and china. Such activity did not, however, always please Queen Victoria's surviving children. Hunting through Kensington Palace, Queen Mary came across a roomful of furniture. Luckily, before she could arrange for its dispersal, Princess Louise heard about it and put a stop to such plans. For the items were old wedding presents and pieces from Dornden. Now on her guard, the Princess was quick to resist any further designs upon her belongings. During a visit the Queen paid her at Kensington Palace, she noticed a beautiful clock on the mantel-piece and, as she advanced towards it, commented upon how much she liked it. But Princess Louise was there before her and, standing between the clock and the Queen, she firmly told her niece-in-law, 'The clock is here, and *here* it will stay.'[71]

During the King's long illness over the winter of 1928–9 she had been quick to offer her support to Queen Mary, who had to carry out engagements on her own. 'To my surprise', the Queen wrote to King George, 'I hear that dear At Louise at 81 is actually coming to the Court tomorrow, too nice of her and I feel much touched.'[72] The King's death and the abdication of her great-nephew, Edward VIII, made 1936 'a sad year' for Princess Louise.

She did not see her great-nephew George VI crowned. At eighty-nine she lacked the stamina to withstand the long, trying hours of ceremonial. 'I was quite unable to go to any of the Coronation things and cannot tell you anything about it and my headache too bad to hear much of the wireless which was very disappointing,' she wrote to Niky.[73] All her thoughts were with King George and Queen Elizabeth, and also with Princess Marina. When Charlie Warr telephoned to her that evening, as promised, the first thing Princess Louise wanted to know was how the Duchess of Kent had looked. 'Radiantly beautiful as always,' he told her. To which Princess Louise answered: 'Of course! She was wearing my train.'[74]

The Princess found her great age tiresome and hated the fuss it entailed. On her eighty-ninth birthday she had two favourite people, Louisa Antrim and Ralph, to luncheon, which was all she wanted as her 'entertainment'. Nevertheless, there was a great deal of fuss which did not meet with her approval, as she told Princess Louis: 'People were very kind with flowers and messages etc . . . Of course I missed you. Lots of silly people bothered doing silly things meaning to be kind but really to please themselves.'[75]

She also found the interest of the press in her illness unbearable. 'A Lady's illness is her own affair, poor thing,' she would say. All the press did was create 'endless worry, papers etc. ringing up'; she did so hate it.[76] All her letters, written by the faithful Lucy during her long months of illness in 1938, contain the request to keep it secret in case the press heard; 'a comfort not to have a fuss,' she told Arthur Ponsonby in a rather rambly letter in May 1938.[77]

Her interest in current affairs was as intense as ever; it was her physical strength which annoyingly let her down. She felt the same at ninety as she had done at eighty-four. 'I am near the time when I shall be called away, but life has many interests,' she had written then, 'one still feels keen, and longs to help, or save.'[78] In May 1938, as Churchill was urging the Government in the House of Commons to expand the Royal Air Force which was lamentably inadequate, he had one supporter in Princess Louise. She believed that Germany could not be trusted: 'It was the same . . . country – wish to come and dictate to us and take our children from us,' she wrote.[79]

She was no better in 1939 and gave her devoted Household a very anxious time, but there were compensations. When her country entered a second world war, the anxieties of the time were understood only hazily at Kensington Palace. The wireless was unusually silent in her bedroom and, for the first time, her power of speech deserted her. 'This last week end [she] has not had strength enough to say much,' Lucy James wrote to Charlie Warr on 22 November 1939.[80] It was clear that the Princess was failing.

On November 30th, Lucy thought 'The Lady' was gradually improving but Princess Louise knew she was dying. Ralph came twice to see her. He thought there had been a rapid change since the week before: 'She was quite clear and very affectionate to me and was more demonstrative.' When he came again on the 30th, he gave her some carnations and she said with a smile, 'You will never need to bring any more flowers for me.' The Princess took the flowers and held them to Ralph's nose and lips, then pressed them to hers and held him down to be kissed over and over again.

'It was dreadful to leave her,' he told Lady Mary, 'and I knew . . . it was improbable I cd see her again'.[81] Princess Louise looked a tiny, wasted figure in her huge four-poster bed. She, who had suffered for over fifty years from insomnia, now slept right through the remaining days.

At ten to seven on 3 December 1939, Princess Louise died. As graceful in death, as in life, she slipped away with no effort. 'She must have had an easy sundering of soul from body and one cannot wish it to be otherwise,' wrote Ralph later that morning.[82]

In her will she had left instructions that if she died in Scotland she wished to be buried beside Lorne in Kilmun, but if she died in England then it should be beside her parents at Windsor. As it happened in wartime, Kilmun presented insuperable difficulties. The Holy Loch was part of the protected inner basin used by submarines and, as Lady Mary wrote, the alarms and raids and boat hunts would interfere with the funeral, while access by road was impossible with all the snow and ice. So the Princess would have had to be buried at Windsor, wherever she had died.

She had asked to be cremated, which was unusual in the Royal Family. Niall, with his High Church views, was shocked at this departure: 'I dislike cremation and none of my ancestors have practised it and certainly none of the Royal Family either,' he wrote sharply in his diary.[83] The Princess had become interested in cremation through Lord Ronnie, who had written a pamphlet about it for the Cremation Society in 1910. He had sent a copy to Princess Louise, much to Lorne's annoyance, and she had become converted to it. On December 8th, she was cremated at Golders Green with only Ralph, Oswald, Frank Balfour and Ian Campbell present. Afterwards, Ralph put her wedding and engagement rings, with her ashes, in a silver box she always used. The box was sealed and placed in her coffin which was taken straight to the Albert Memorial Chapel at Windsor to await the funeral.

Unlike Lorne's great ceremonial funeral, the Princess was buried quietly and simply, owing to the exigencies of wartime Britain. It was, however, exactly the way she would have wanted it – without any of that hateful fuss. On a cold, frosty day in December her 'dear' Argylls, followed by the Royal Family, bore her coffin from the Albert Memorial Chapel along the North Aisle to the choir. A huge assortment of the Argyll family were also there, seated in the stalls. Princess Louise had arranged her own funeral service, so that her favourite hymn 'Abide With Me' was sung and, after the blessing, 'God be in my Head'. As the Garter King of Arms ended his proclamation of her Style and Titles, the first notes of that poignant lament 'Flowers in the Field' floated up from the nave as the pipers bade her farewell.

'I never remember her being angry and unkind to me. I am grateful to her for more than anyone – even you – know,' Ralph wrote to his mother. There were many who shared his sentiments, for Princess Louise had never believed in advertising her deeds. Many would remember her, especially those she had loved. 'When I pass Aunt

Louise's door without going in,' Princess Louis wrote, 'I feel I miss her affectionate pleasure at seeing me very much.'[85]

It was, as Ralph wrote, the end of an era. Those who had received 'unbroken love and affection' for over fifty years, now had to face the inevitable changes that would follow her death. Yet those who were with Princess Louise when she died, or saw her in death, could not wish otherwise. She lay there with her face framed by the exquisite, billowing lace of her wedding veil. Her lovely features were smoothed out, as if someone had stroked away the lines of age and pain to leave her looking as beautiful as on her wedding day sixty-eight years before. Those who saw her would never forget how beautiful she looked, with the beginnings of a smile playing about her mouth. And all about her, an air of great peace.

NOTE ON THE TEXT

Princess Louise remained a notoriously bad speller throughout her life. Her letters are sprinkled with misspelt words and bereft of punctuation. I have decided not to alter them but to retain the mistakes, since their meaning is clear and flurries of [sic]s would only distract the reader. This also applies to the letters of members of her family.

ACKNOWLEDGEMENTS

I wish to thank Her Majesty the Queen for gracious permission to reproduce material in the Royal Archives of which she owns the copyright and to reproduce pictures, drawings and photographs from the Royal Collections. I should also like to thank Mr Oliver Everett and his staff for advice and for the careful attention given to the text; Sir Oliver Millar, Surveyor of the Queen's Pictures; Mr Geoffrey de Bellaigue, Surveyor of the Queen's Works of Art; the Hon. Mrs Roberts, Curator of the Print Room; and Miss Frances Dimond, Curator of the Royal Photograph Collection.

I am profoundly indebted to the Duke of Argyll, Mac Cailein Mor, for allowing me to make use of his papers and to him and the Duchess for welcoming me with such interest and kindness on my visits to Inveraray. Nor can the contribution of other members of the family be overstated; with their personal recollections and their exceptional courtesy and patience with my questions, Mr Ian Anstruther, the Hon. Mary Percy, Miss Elisabeth Brodrick, Frances, Lady Fergusson, Mr Adam Fergusson, Mrs Jocelyn Gibb, Mrs Michael Babington-Smith, Mr and Mrs John Meade, Mr Charles Wynne Finch, Mrs Alec Malcolm and Mrs Olwen Wake brought the past to life.

For their extensive help and many kindnesses, I especially thank Mr Alastair Campbell Yg of Airds, whose knowledge of Campbellania is prodigious, and the Proberts, the late Colonel Oliver Probert and Mrs Probert, Major and Mrs Ynyr Probert, Lt.-Colonel and Mrs Richard Probert and Mr Geoffrey Probert.

Many others have helped me along the way and been equally prodigal of their time and hospitality. To them, to those who allowed me access to papers in their care and to all mentioned below, I am extremely grateful: the late Mr Hugh Anderson (St George's Hospital); the Marquess of Anglesey; Lady Aubrey-Fletcher; the Duke of Atholl; the Earl of Balfour; Lady Eve Balfour; Mrs Georgina Battiscombe; Mr Frank McLeod Black; Mr Michael and Lady Evelyn Brander; Mr Gordon Brook-Shepherd; the Duchess of Buccleuch; Mrs Shirley Bury; Mr Esmond Butler; Mr Richard Brand (Princess Louise's Kensington Hospital for Children); Mrs

Georgiana Blakiston; Mrs Richard Ballantine; Lt.-Commander Hugh Campbell-Gibson; Miss Marion Campbell of Kilberry; Mr Matthew Calderwood; Mr Alan Cameron; Mrs Arabella Carter; Major Hamish Clark; Mr Vere Collins; the Hon. Mrs Cunnack; Captain North Dalrymple-Hamilton RN; Mr Richard Dorment; Mrs Grace Duckworth; Mr Maldwin Drummond of Cadland; Mrs Marjorie Duncan; Mr Colin Easden; Sir Seymour Egerton; Mr H. G. Evans (Girls' Public Day School Trust); Mr Alwyn Compton Farquharson of Invercauld; Mr Stuart Fairley; Dr Terry Friedman; Lady Gainford; Dr Cecil Gilbert; Miss Mary Goldie; Miss Maryel Greenhill Gardyne; Revd P. J. Garralt; Mr R. H. Harcourt Williams; Mr Gerald Hadoke; Mr Duncan Haig; Miss Susan Hamilton; the late Miss Eileen Hose; Mr H. Montgomery Hyde; the Hon. Lady Hayes; Mrs Gay Hilleary; Mrs Verena Hanbury; Lady Rosemary Jeffreys; Miss Faith Lascelles; Mr Harry Lee; the Countess of Longford; Mr Jeremy Maas; Mrs John Macarthy; Mr Donald McKechnie; the Hon. Hector McDonnell; the late Roger Machell; Miss Jessie McGruer; the late General Sir Gordon Macmillan of Macmillan; Dr Anthony Malcolmson; Mr & Mrs Philip Mallet; Mrs Elfrida Manning; Mrs Betty Massingham; the late Sir Iain Moncreiffe of that Ilk; Mr Victor Montagu; Mrs E. J. Montgomery; Mr Hugh Montgomery-Massingberd; Mr James Morris; Mr Iain Murray; Mr D. Maxwell-Macdonald; Mr Michael Moss; Miss C. L. Morgan (Queen Margaret College); Mr Brian Nodes; the Earl of Northesk; the Revd E. Neale; Mr John Noble; Major Murrough O'Brien; Group Captain D. G. F. Palmer (SSAFA); Mr Hugh Parrott (Heritage Craft School, Chailey); Mr Anthony Dugard Pasley; Captain R. H. Parsons RN; Mr John A. L. Phillips; Lord Ponsonby of Shulbrede; Mrs Anne Piggott; Mr Benedict Read; Lady Reid; Mr E. B. Richardson; Mr Cosmo Russell; Mr Rex Riley; Commander Charles Shears; Dr Honor Smith; Mr Mark Stocker; the Countess of Sutherland and Mr Charles Janson; the Dowager Lady Strathcona; Mr and Mrs James Smith; Lady Salisbury-Jones; the Very Revd Dr Ronald Selby Wright; Dr J. S. Taylor; Miss Patience Thesiger; Mrs Mollie Travis; Lady Turner; Brigadier John Tweedie; Mrs Patrick Twist; Miss Sarah Twist; Mr Philip Venning; Mr Hugo Vickers; Mr Christopher Warwick; Mrs Wilber; Mr David Williamson; Mr John Wardroper; Mrs Enid Wilson; Lt.-Colonel G. P. Wood; Lady Victoria Wemyss; the Earl of Wemyss.

I should also like to thank the staff of the London Library and of the Royal Commission of Manuscripts and the many archivists and librarians who made my work easier: in particular, Mr F. B. Stitt, former County

Archivist of Staffordshire Record Office, and Dr Peter Anderson, Mr George Mackenzie and Mr Donald Galbraith of the National Register of Archives (Scotland).

For permission to use copyright material and to quote letters I must thank the Duke of Abercorn; Miss Felicity Ashbee; the Duke of Atholl; Berkshire Record Office; Mr B. Babington-Smith; the Bodleian Library, Oxford; the Earl of Bradford; the Marquess of Bristol; the Trustees of the British Library; the Trustees of the Broadlands Estate; Sir Walter Bromley-Davenport; the Duke of Buccleuch; Central Region Archives, Stirling; the Earl of Cranbrook; the Earl of Derby; the Drummond of Cadland Archives; the Marquess of Dufferin and Ava; The College, Durham; East Sussex County Library; Mr J. W. O. Elliot; the Trustees of the Fitzwilliam Museum; the Hon. Mrs Crispin Gascoigne; Sir William Gladstone; the Glasgow University Archives; the Librarian of Glasgow University Library and the University Court of the University of Glasgow; the Earl of Halifax; Viscount Hambleden; Baron Hatherton; the Controller of Her Majesty's Stationery Office; the Clerk of the Records, House of Lords; Lady Mary Howick; the John Rylands University Library of Manchester; Keele University; the Kent Archives Office; the Earl of Kimberley; the Trustees of Lambeth Palace Library; the Marquess of Londonderry; the Earl of Minto; the Trustees of the National Library of Scotland; the National Trust; the Public Archives of Canada; the Deputy Keeper of the Records, Public Records Office of Northern Ireland; Jane Ridley; the Harveian Librarian of the Royal College of Physicians; the Royal Borough of Kensington & Chelsea Libraries and Arts Services; the Earl of St Aldwyn; St Andrew's University; the Marquess of Salisbury; the Scottish Record Office; the Earl of Selborne; Staffordshire Record Office; Suffolk Record Office; the Surrey Local Studies Library; the Tennyson Research Centre, Lincoln by permission of Lincolnshire Library Service; Test Valley Borough Council; the Master and Fellows of Trinity College, Cambridge; the University of Glasgow; the University of York.

My thanks are due to Philip Ziegler, my editor, whose informed criticism and practical assistance were invaluable at every stage. I also thank Carol O'Brien, Vera Brice and, especially, JoAnne Robertson of Collins who nursed the book to completion. I am grateful to Susan Morris for art research, Jeanne McKechnie and Sonia Lochner for Canadian research and Edward Turner for American research.

This book would never have been finished without the boundless help of family and friends, including Jamie and Morag Mellor; Deirdre

Livingstone; Catriona Livingstone; Annabel Huxley; Neil McWilliam; Colum Scott; Louise Williams; Felicity Dix; Penny Carrega; Zelfa Hourani; Susie Wake; Margaret Turner and Cornelia Manocci; and the late Brian Meadows helped in countless ways. Carolyne Mazur and Drew Parnell took the photographs and Helena Beaufoy supervised the picture research; Janie Griffiths re-typed an indecipherable manuscript. My warmest thanks to Mercury Hare who compiled the index and bore with equanimity the associated crises. His intelligence and niceness were no small part of the unlimited support he so readily gave throughout the final stages. To Jane Meadows I owe an especial debt. This book was her idea and throughout its long gestation she gave unfailing support and the benefit of her knowledge of Victorian royalty. Above all, my husband William endured the presence of Princess Louise and numerous Campbell ancestors in his life with great patience and understanding. His knowledge together with his own literary and editorial skills have been invaluable. I could not have written this book without his help and I cannot thank him enough.

LIST OF MANUSCRIPT COLLECTIONS

ABERCORN PAPERS, Public Record Office of Northern Ireland.

THE ARGYLL AND SUTHERLAND HIGHLANDERS' (PRINCESS LOUISE'S) PAPERS, Stirling Castle, Scotland.

ALMA-TADEMA PAPERS, Bodleian Library, Oxford.

THE ASHBEE JOURNALS, King's College, Cambridge.

ASTOR PAPERS, University of Reading.

ATHOLL PAPERS, Private Collection at Blair Castle.

BALFOUR PAPERS, British Library and Private Collection.

LADY FRANCES BALFOUR PAPERS, Private Collection at Whittingehame.

BATTERSEA PAPERS, British Library.

BEVILLS PAPERS, Private Collection.

BLACKWOOD PAPERS, National Library of Scotland.

BLUNT PAPERS, Fitzwilliam Museum, Cambridge.

BOYD-CARPENTER PAPERS, British Library.

BRADFORD PAPERS, Staffordshire Record Office.

BROADLANDS PAPERS, Private Collection.

BROMLEY-DAVENPORT, John Rylands University Library of Manchester.

BUCCLEUCH PAPERS, Scottish Record Office.

BUTLER PAPERS, St Andrew's University Library.

CADOGAN PAPERS, Record Office, House of Lords.

CAMPBELL-BANNERMAN PAPERS, British Library.

CAMPBELL-GIBSON PAPERS, Private Collection.

CAMPBELL OF KILBERRY, Private Collection.

CAMPBELL OF ISLAY, National Library of Scotland.

CLARK PAPERS, Royal College of Physicians, London.

CRANBROOK PAPERS, Suffolk Record Office, Ipswich.

DALHOUSIE PAPERS, Scottish Record Office.

DALRYMPLE-HAMILTON OF BARGANY PAPERS, Private Collection.

DAVIDSON PAPERS, Lambeth Palace Library.

DE BUNSEN PAPERS, Private Collection.

DERBY PAPERS, Liverpool Record Office.

DUFFERIN PAPERS, Public Record Office of Northern Ireland.

MARY DREW PAPERS, British Library.

DRUMMOND OF CADLAND, Private Collection.

DUCKWORTH PAPERS, Private Collection.

BLANCHE DUGDALE PAPERS, Private Collection.

ARTHUR ELLIOT PAPERS, National Library of Scotland.

EASDEN PAPERS, Private Collection.

ERSKINE PAPERS, Erskine Hospital, Scotland; University Archives, Glasgow.

ELPHINSTONE PAPERS, Private Collection and Royal Archives, Windsor.

FARQUHARSON OF INVERCAULD PAPERS, Private Collection.

GLADSTONE PAPERS, British Library.

GLYNNE GLADSTONE PAPERS, St Deiniol's Library, Harwarden.

GLYN PAPERS, Berkshire Record Office, Reading.

GRANVILLE PAPERS, Public Record Offices, Kew.

GOWER PAPERS, Private Collection.

GREY PAPERS, Department of Paleography and Diplomatic, The College, Durham.

HALDANE PAPERS, National Library of Scotland.

HALIFAX PAPERS, Borthwick Institute of Historical Research, York.

HAMBLEDEN PAPERS, W. H. Smith and Son, London.

SIR EDWARD HAMILTON PAPERS, British Library.

HAMILTON PAPERS, Private Collection.

HARCOURT PAPERS, Bodleian Library, Oxford.

HATHERTON PAPERS, Staffordshire Record Office.

HERVEY PAPERS, Suffolk Record Office.

HOLLAND PAPERS, British Library.

KNIGHTLEY PAPERS, British Library.

HUGHENDEN PAPERS, Bodleian Library, Oxford.

INVERARAY PAPERS, Private Collection.

LEE PAPERS, Private Collection.

LONDONDERRY PAPERS, Public Record Office of Northern Ireland.

LONGLEY PAPERS, Lambeth Palace Library.

LEIGHTON PAPERS, Kensington and Chelsea Public Library.

LUTYENS PAPERS, Royal Institute of British Architects' Library.

MACDONALD PAPERS, Public Archives of Canada, Ottawa.

MACEWEN PAPERS, University of Glasgow Archives.

MACGREGOR OF MACGREGOR PAPERS, University of Glasgow Archives.

MALLET PAPERS, Private Collection.

MEADE PAPERS, Private Collection.

MELVILLE PAPERS, Strathclyde Regional Council.

MINISTRY OF WORKS PAPERS, Public Record Office, Kew.

MINTO PAPERS, National Library of Scotland.

MYERS PAPERS, Trinity College, Cambridge.

CATHERINE PAGET PAPERS, Bodleian Library, Oxford.

PAC PAPERS, Public Archives of Canada, Ottawa.

PAGET PAPERS, British Library.

PONSONBY OF SHULBREDE PAPERS, Bodleian Library, Oxford.

POORE PAPERS, Andover Public Library.

PROBERT PAPERS, Private Collection.

REID PAPERS, Private Collection.

RICHARDSON PAPERS, Private Collection.

SPAB PAPERS, Society for the Protection of Ancient Buildings Archives.

SIEVEKING PAPERS, Royal College of Physicians.

SANDWICH PAPERS, Private Collection.

ST ALBANS PAPERS, Dept of Paleography and Diplomatic, The College, Durham.

ST ALDWYN PAPERS, Gloucester Record Office.

SALISBURY PAPERS, Hatfield.

SELBORNE PAPERS, Lambeth Palace Library.

SMITH OF JORDANHILL PAPERS, Strathclyde Regional Archives.

SNEYD PAPERS, Keele University Library.

SPRING RICE PAPERS, John Rylands University Library of Manchester.

SPRELMANN PAPERS, Royal Academy Library, London.

STIRLING-MAXWELL OF POLLOK PAPERS, Strathclyde Regional Archives.

STORY PAPERS, University of Glasgow Archives.

SUTHERLAND PAPERS, Staffordshire Record Office.

TENNYSON PAPERS, Tennyson Centre, Lincoln Public Library.

THORNTON PAPERS, Public Record Office, Kew.

THURSTON PAPERS, Private Collection.

TREVELYAN PAPERS, Newcastle University Library.

TWEEDIE PAPERS, Private Collection.

TWIST PAPERS, Private Collection.

VOELAS PAPERS, Private Collection.

WARR PAPERS, National Library of Scotland.

WATERPARK PAPERS, British Library.

WEIGALL PAPERS, Kent County Archives Office.

WEMYSS PAPERS, Private Collection.

WHISTLER PAPERS, Special Collections, University of Glasgow Library.
WILLIAMSON PAPERS, Guildford Public Library.
WOLSELEY PAPERS, Hove Central Library.

ABBREVIATIONS USED IN
SOURCE NOTES

BL	British Library.
D of Argyll	George, 8th Duke of Argyll.
Dss of Argyll	Elizabeth, his wife.
FB	Lady Frances Balfour.
INV	Inveraray Castle Archives.
Leaves	*Leaves from a Journal of Our Life in the Highlands*, edited by Arthur Helps (1868).
Letters	*The Letters of Queen Victoria, A Selection from Her Majesty's Correspondence*, First Series, 1837–61, edited by A. C. Benson and Viscount Esher, 3 vols. (1907); Second Series, 1862–85, edited by G. E. Buckle, 3 vols. (1926); Third Series, 1886–1901, edited by G. E. Buckle, 3 vols. (1930).
Lorne	Ian, Marquis of Lorne and, later, 9th Duke of Argyll.
Dearest Child	*Private Correspondence of Queen Victoria and the Princess Royal 1858–1861*, edited by Roger Fulford (1964).
Dearest Mama	*Private Correspondence of Queen Victoria and the Crown Princess of Prussia 1861–1864*, edited by Roger Fulford (1968).
Your Dear Letter	*Private Correspondence of Queen Victoria and the Crown Princess of Prussia 1865–1871*, edited by Roger Fulford (1971).
Darling Child	*Private Correspondence of Queen Victoria and the Crown Princess of Prussia 1871–1878*, edited by Roger Fulford (1976).
Beloved Mama	*Private Correspondence of Queen Victoria and the Crown Princess of Prussia 1878–1885*, edited by Roger Fulford (1981).
Passages	*Passages from the Past* by the Duke of Argyll, 2 vols. (1907).
PL	Princess Louise.
PRO	Public Record Office.
RA	Royal Archives.
QV	Queen Victoria.
QVJ	Queen Victoria's Journal.

SOURCE NOTES

CHAPTER I

1 QV to King Leopold, 11 January 1848, *Letters*, 1st Series, vol. 2, p. 172.
2 General Grey to his wife, 9 December 1847, Grey Mss V/2.
3 King Leopold to QV, 26 February 1848, *Letters*, op. cit., p. 176.
4 QV to King Leopold, 11 March 1848, ibid., p. 194.
5 *Correspondence of Sarah Spencer, Lady Lyttelton 1787–1870*, ed. Hon. Mrs Hugh Wyndham, 1912, pp. 373–4.
6 QV to Baron Stockmar, 6 March 1848, cit. Reginald Pound, *Albert*, 1973, p. 178.
7 Elizabeth Longford, *Victoria R.I.*, 1964, p. 195.
8 Pr. Albert to Stockmar, 18 March 1848, cit. Sir Theodore Martin, *The Life of The Prince Consort*, 1882 edition Vol I, p. 81.
9 Pr. Albert to his brother, Duke Ernest, 18 March 1848, *The Prince Consort and His Brother*, ed. H. Bolitho, 1933, p. 103.
10 Tyler Whittle, *Victoria and Albert at Home*, 1980, p. 38.
11 Disraeli to Ly Londonderry, 1 May 1848, *The Life of Benjamin Disraeli*, ed. W. F. Monypenny & G. E. Buckle, 1914, vol. III, p. 178.
12 Ld John Russell to QV, 11 April 1848, cit. Cecil Woodham Smith, *Queen Victoria, Her Life and Times*, Hamish Hamilton, 1972, p. 291.
13 QV memo to Gen. Grey, n.d., Grey Mss, Royal Correspondence XIII/6.
14 Ibid.
15 Pr. Albert to Baron Stockmar, 11 March 1848, *Letters of the Prince Consort 1831–1861*, ed. Dr Kurt Jagow, tran. E. T. S. Dugdale, 1938, p. 135.
16 J. T. Ward, *Chartism*, 1973, p. 202.
17 QV to King Leopold, 11 July 1848, *Letters*, op. cit., p. 218.
18 Col. Phipps to Pr. Albert, 9 April 1848, cit. Woodham Smith, p. 288.
19 Lyttelton, p. 378.
20 Ld John Russell to QV, 10 April 1848, *Letters*, op. cit. p. 200.

21 QV to King Leopold, 11 April 1848, cit. Woodham Smith, p. 289.
22 Lyttelton, p. 381.
23 QV to Crown Princess, 4 May 1859, *Dearest Child*, p. 191.
24 Ibid., 1 August 1860, p. 267.
25 Lyttelton, p. 381.
26 QV to Harriet, Dss of Sutherland, 2 May 1848, INV Mss.
27 QV to King Leopold, 16 May, 1848, *Letters*, op. cit., p. 206.
28 Ernest Stockmar, *Denkwurdigkeiten aus den Papieren des Frhm Christian Stockmar*, 1872, p. 391.

CHAPTER II

1 *The Prince Consort and His Brother*, op. cit.
2 Lyttelton, p. 372.
3 Ibid., p. 368.
4 Pr. Albert to Herr Florschutz, n.d., 1846, cit. Hector Bolitho, *Albert Prince Consort*, 1964, p. 108.
5 *Letters of Lady Augusta Stanley 1849–1863*, ed. The Dean of Windsor and Hector Bolitho, 1927, p. 23.
6 Gen. Grey to his wife, 18 March 1849, Minto Mss 13181 f10.
7 PL to Mrs Thurston, n.d., Thurston Mss.
8 Note on QV, n.d., INV Mss.
9 Lyttelton, p. 326.
10 QV Memorandum, 4 March 1844, cit. *Alice Grand Duchess of Hesse, Princess of Great Britain and Ireland*, ed. Princess Christian, 1884. Preface.
11 *20 Years at Court*, from the correspondence of the Hon. Eleanor Stanley, ed. Mrs Steuart Erskine, 1916, p. 115.
12 Gen. Grey to his wife, 2 November 1849, Minto Mss 13181 f17.
13 Eleanor Stanley, p. 129.
14 Ly Frances Balfour to Ly Betty Balfour, 28 January 1901, FB Mss TD 84/53 Box 4.

15 Catherine Paget's diary, Bodleian Ms Eng misc d. 244 f204.

16 Baron Stockmar Memorandum, cit. Andrew Sinclair, *The Other Victoria*, 1981, p. 10.

17 Ld Ronald Leveson-Gower's journal, 11 January 1855, Dunrobin Mss.

18 QV to Crown Princess, 21 July 1858, *Dearest Child*, p. 123.

19 Mary Howard McClintock, *The Queen Thanks Sir Howard*, 1945, p. 38.

20 Louisa, Countess of Antrim, *Recollections*, 1937, p. 139.

21 Frances, Ly Fergusson to author, 12 May 1983.

22 *The Queen's Reminiscences*, January 1862, cit. Woodham Smith, p. 333.

23 QV to Pr. of Wales, 26 August 1857, cit. Philip Magnus, *King Edward the Seventh*, 1964, p. 17.

24 *Later Letters of Lady Augusta Stanley 1864–1876*, ed. The Dean of Windsor and Hector Bolitho, 1929, p. 153.

25 Ly Augusta Stanley, *Letters*, pp. 84–5.

26 Pr. Albert to QV, 1 October 1856, cit. Woodham Smith, p. 330.

27 QV to Crown Princess, 10 February 1871, *Your Dear Letter*, p. 319.

28 McClintock, p. 36.

29 *Seventy Years: Being the Autobiography of Lady Gregory*, ed. Colin Smythe, 1974, p. 175.

30 *Mary Ponsonby*, ed. Magdalen Ponsonby, 1927, p. 17.

31 Princess Friedrich Leopold of Prussia, *Behind the Scenes at the Prussian Court*, 1939, pp. 7–8.

32 QV to Ld Melbourne, 3 April 1845, *Letters*, op. cit. p. 42.

33 Eleanor Stanley, p. 167.

8 QVJ, 14 March 1855, cit. Longford, p. 249.

9 PL to Louisa Knightley, 22 December 1866, Knightley Mss 46361.

10 R. H. H. Davies, *Victorian Watercolours at Windsor Castle*, 1937, p. 50.

11 Eleanor Stanley, pp. 299–300.

12 HRH Princess Alice, Countess of Athlone, *For my Grandchildren*, 1966, p. 68.

13 QV to Princess Augusta of Prussia, 8 April 1856, cit. *Further Letters of Queen Victoria*, ed. Hector Bolitho, 1938, p. 64.

14 Pr. Albert to Crown Princess, 29 January 1859, cit. Egon C. C. Corti, *The English Empress*, 1957, p. 62.

15 Louisa Antrim, p. 144.

16 QV to Crown Princess, 24 November 1858, *Dearest Child*, p. 146.

17 Archbishop of Canterbury to Catherine Longley, 2 July 1862, Longley Mss 1840 f23.

18 Pr. Albert to Pr. of Wales, 20 November 1861, cit. Woodham Smith, p. 417.

19 Gen. Grey to Ld. Dalhousie, 19 December 1861, Dalhousie Mss GD45/14/726/10.

20 QVJ, cit. Marquis of Lorne, *V.R.I. Her Life and Empire*, 1902, p. 259.

21 The accounts of the eyewitnesses differ: QVJ: 'But he was dozing and did not perceive them.' Ly Augusta Stanley: 'He smiled at her but did not speak.' Gen. Grey: 'I don't think he knew or noticed them.'

22 QV's account, 14 December 1861, RA Z142, cit. Longford, p. 301.

23 Mrs Caroline Grey to Maria, Countess Grey, 16 December 1861, Maria Grey Mss.

24 Ibid.

25 Ly Augusta Stanley, *Letters*, p. 246.

CHAPTER III

1 Queen Mary to George V, December 1910, cit. James Pope-Hennessy, *Queen Mary*, 1959, p. 432.

2 Ld Ronald Gower, *My Reminiscences*, 1883, vol. I, p. 82.

3 Eleanor Stanley, p. 258.

4 QV to Crown Princess, 9 April 1859, *Dearest Child*, p. 175.

5 Ld Ronald Gower's journal, 18 March 1858.

6 Ibid., 2 & 14 March 1855.

7 Ibid., 31 January 1855.

CHAPTER IV

1 Harriet Sneyd to Ralph Sneyd, 24 December 1861, Sneyd Mss S1248.

2 Charlotte Sneyd to Ralph Sneyd, 27 December 1861, ibid.

3 Victoria Stuart Wortley to Ly Elizabeth Drummond, 23 December 1861, Drummond of Cadland Mss B6/92/3/1.

4 Gen. Grey to Ld Dalhousie, op. cit.

5 Eleanor Stanley, p. 401.

6 PL to Edgar Boehm, n.d., Easden Mss.

7 Harriet Sneyd, op. cit.

8 QV to Harriet, Dss of Sutherland, 29 December 1861, INV Mss.

9 Ly Augusta Stanley, *Letters*, p. 254.

10 Col. Phipps to Ld Dalhousie, 24 December 1861, Dalhousie Mss GD45/14/681/11.

11 Victoria Stuart Wortley, op. cit.

12 Eleanor Stanley, p. 395.

13 Gen. Grey to his wife, 16 February 1862, Grey Mss V/3.

14 Pr. Albert to QV, 1861, *Dearest Mama*, p. 12.

15 Ly Augusta Stanley, *Letters*, p. 251.

16 McClintock, p. 49.

17 QV to Pss Augusta, 26 May 1862, *Further Letters*, p. 127.

18 *Life and Letters of George Earl of Clarendon*, ed. Sir Herbert Maxwell, 1913, vol. 2, p. 256.

19 QV to Crown Princess, 1 July 1863, *Dearest Mama*, pp. 238–9.

20 Ibid., 2 May 1862, p. 59.

21 A. MacGeorge, *William Leighton Leitch*, 1884, pp. 53–4.

22 QV to Crown Princess, 28 June 1862, *Dearest Mama*, p. 84.

23 Ibid., p. 108.

24 Ly Augusta Stanley, *Letters*, p. 272.

25 G. K. A. Bell, *Randall Davidson*, 1938, vol. 1, p. 119.

26 QV to Crown Princess, 8 November 1862, *Dearest Mama*, p. 127.

27 Ly Augusta Stanley, *Letters*, p. 229.

28 QV to Crown Princess, 11 & 18 February 1863, *Dearest Mama*, pp. 175 & 179.

29 *The Correspondence of Priscilla, Countess of Westmorland*, ed. Ly Rose Weigall, 1909, p. 440.

30 Ly Augusta Stanley, *Letters*, p. 282.

31 QV to Crown Princess, 18 March 1863, *Dearest Mama*, p. 182.

32 Pss of Wales to PL, RA/Add/A/17, cit. Georgina Battiscombe, *Queen Alexandra*, 1969, p. 82.

33 *A Victorian Canvas*, ed. Neville Wallis, n.d., p. 112.

34 *Diaries and Letters of Mary Drew*, ed. L. Masterman, 1930, p. 10.

35 Pss Helena to Major Elphinstone, 4 June 1863, Elphinstone Mss.

36 *Mr Gladstone to his Wife*, ed. A. Tilney Bassett, 1936, p. 153.

37 QV to King Leopold, n.d., *Dearest Mama*, p. 16.

38 Dss of Argyll's journal, 29 November 1863, INV Mss.

39 Sybil Grey's diary, 22 February 1864. Grey Mss, Box 403.

40 Sir Charles Phipps to Gen. Grey, 10 January 1864, Grey Mss X1/4.

41 *The Diary of Lady Frederick Cavendish*, ed. John Bailey, 1927, vol. 1, p. 197.

42 QVJ, 16 February 1864, cit. E. Darby & N. Smith, *The Cult of the Prince Consort*, 1983, p. 108.

43 A.M.W. Stirling, *Victorian Sidelights*, 1954, p. 211.

44 'Personal Relics of the Queen', *The Strand Magazine*, p. 540.

45 PL to Edward Corbould, 25 October 1869, PAC Mss, M927, F.51.

46 MacGeorge, p. 65.

47 QV to Crown Princess, 28 April 1866, *Your Dear Letter*, pp. 70–1.

48 PL to Louisa Bowater, 16 September 1865, Knightley Mss. BL 46361.

49 QV to Gen. Grey, 28 August 1863, Grey Mss XIII/4.

50 Sybil Grey's diary, 17 October 1864.

51 QV to Gen. Grey, 19 November 1864, Grey Mss XIII/6.

52 QV to Crown Princess, 23 March 1864, *Dearest Mama*, p. 311.

53 PL to Louisa Bowater, op. cit.

54 Gen. Grey to Sir Charles Phipps, 14 August 1865, Grey Mss X1/3.

55 QV to Crown Princess, 18 July 1866, *Your Dear Letter*, p. 81.

56 Pr of Wales to Gen Grey, 29 October 1865, Grey Mss III/5.

57 QV to King Leopold, 25 October 1865, cit. *Princess Alice*, Gerard Noel, 1974, p. 120.

58 Sybil Grey's diary, 1 December 1865.

59 QV to Crown Princess, 5 March 1866, *Your Dear Letter*, p. 59.

60 Ibid., 24 January 1866, p. 56.

61 Archbishop of Canterbury to Catherine Longley, 15 July 1866, Longley Mss. 1840.

62 *The Journals of Lady Knightley of Fawsley*, ed. Julia Cartwright, 1915, p. 117.

63 Longley Mss, op. cit.

64 PL to Louisa Knightley, 20 July 1866, Knightley Mss.

CHAPTER V

1 QV to Crown Princess, 21 July 1866, *Your Dear Letter*, p. 82.

2 *Lady Lytton's Court Diary 1895–99*, ed. Mary Lutyens, 1961, p. 123.

3 QV to Crown Princess, 28 April 1866, *Your Dear Letter*, p. 70.
4 Knightley Mss, op. cit.
5 QV to Crown Princess, 1 April 1858, *Dearest Child*, p. 83.
6 Sybil Grey's diary, 21 January 1865.
7 Ibid.
8 Charge delivered in Whippingham Church at the Confirmation of HRH the Princess Louise, Priv. Pr.
9 QVJ, 21 January 1865, p. 44.
10 QV to Crown Princess, 1 March 1865, *Your Dear Letter*, p. 18.
11 QVJ, 28 February 1865, p. 77.
12 Lady Mary Meynell, *Sunshine and Shadows*, 1933, pp. 46–7.
13 PL to Louisa Knightley, 21 March 1866, Knightley Mss.
14 PL to Ethel Badcock, n.d., Probert Mss.
15 Louisa Antrim, p. 202.
16 PL to Col. Elphinstone, 11 February 1869, Elphinstone Mss.
17 Ly Frederick Cavendish, vol. 1, p. 198.
18 QVJ 1867, cit. *The Woman At Home*, vol. 1, 1894.
19 Ly Frederick Cavendish, vol. 1, p. 214.
20 Ly Knightley, p. 69.
21 Ly Frederick Cavendish, vol. 1, p. 180.
22 QV to Gen. Grey, February 1863, Grey Mss XIII/4.
23 QV to Pss Victoria of Hesse, 8 December 1880, cit. James Pope-Hennessy, *Advice to a Grand-daughter*, 1975, p. 29.
24 Louisa Antrim, p. 96.
25 Ibid., p. 128.
26 Arthur Ponsonby, *Henry Ponsonby His Life from His Letters*, 1942, p. 36.
27 Paul Emden, *Behind the Throne*, 1934, pp. 225, 154.
28 William Gladstone's diary, 3 December 1868, Gladstone Mss BL 44756 f65.
29 PL to Louisa Antrim, 9 November 1928, p. 102.
30 QV to Gen. Grey, 15 October 1863, Grey Mss XIII/4.
31 Mary Bulteel to Gen. Grey, 18 December 1863, ibid.
32 QV to Gen. Grey, 16 December 1863, ibid.
33 Sir James Clark to Sir Charles Phipps, 30 December 1864, ibid. XI/1.
34 Sir James Clark's diary, 5 February 1856, Clark Mss.
35 Gen. Grey to Phipps, 4 September 1863, Grey Mss XIII/4.

36 E. Denison to Lady Elcho, 27 August [October] 1865, Wemyss Mss, TD83/77.
37 QV to Gen. Grey, 6 February 1866, cit. Nina Epton, *Victoria and her Daughters*, 1971, p. 114.
38 Gen. Grey to QV, 18 February 1866, Grey Mss XIII/8.
39 QV to Gen. Grey, n.d., ibid.
40 Sybil Grey's diary, 5 February 1867.
41 Ibid., 6 February 1867.
42 QV to Crown Princess, 5 February 1867, *Kronberg Letters*, cit. Longford, p. 351.
43 *Letters*, 2nd Series, vol. 1, p. 466.
44 QV to Major Elphinstone, n.d., Elphinstone Mss.
45 Gen. Grey to his wife, 14 October 1867, Grey Mss 95/1.
46 QV to Crown Princess, 11 January 1868, *Your Dear Letter*, p. 169.
47 PL to Major Elphinstone, n.d., Elphinstone Mss.

CHAPTER VI

1 Catherine Paget's diary, February 1868.
2 Ld Clarendon, vol. 2, p. 249.
3 QVJ, 18 March 1868.
4 Ly Hardy to Sir Malcolm MacGregor, 21 May 1868, MacGregor of MacGregor Mss Bdl 478.
5 Sir Henry Lucy, *Diary of a Journalist*, 1920, vol. 1, pp. 52–3.
6 Gen. Grey to Disraeli, 22 & 24 May 1868, Hughenden Mss. B/xix/D/59-60.
7 PL to Louisa Knightley, n.d., Knightley Mss.
8 Gathorne-Hardy's diary, 5 June 1868, Cranbrook Mss T501.
9 Sybil Grey's diary, 16 November 1868.
10 Henry to Mary Ponsonby, 4 August 1868, Ponsonby Mss, cit. Longford, p. 356.
11 PL to Col. Elphinstone, 8 August 1868, Elphinstone Mss.
12 Gen. Grey to his wife, 26 September 1868, Grey Mss V/3.
13 PL to Col. Elphinstone, 23 May 1869, Elphinstone Mss.
14 Letters between PL and the Dean, and QVJ, cit. *Letters*, 2nd Series, vol. 1, pp. 536–9.
15 Gen. Grey's journal, 21 Nov & 3 December 1868, Grey Mss D6/25.
16 Ibid., 29 December 1868.

17 Gen. Grey's Memo of 2 June 1869, Grey
    Mss XIII/11.
18 QV to Gladstone, 31 May 1869, ibid.
19 Princess Helena to Ly Bradford, 27
    February 1877, Bradford Mss 18/1A.
20 PL to Gen. Grey, Memo, 29 May 1869,
    Grey Mss XIII/11.
21 Ibid.
22 Gen. Grey to Gladstone, 1 June 1869,
    Grey Mss IV/2.
23 Ibid., 5 June 1869.
24 QV to Dean Wellesley, 3 July 1869,
    Gladstone Mss BL 44339.
25 Henry to Mary Ponsonby, 28 October
    1870, cit. Longford, p. 380.
26 QV to Gen. Grey, 17 February 1866,
    Grey Mss XIII/7.
27 Sybil Grey's diary, 26 March 1867.
28 Elfrida Manning, *Marble and Bronze*,
    1982, p. 27.
29 Pr. Albert to Crown Princess, 13 April
    1859, cit. Martin, vol. I, p. 323.
30 Pr. Albert to Ly Bloomfield, 20
    December 1860, ibid., vol. IV, p. 16.
31 QV to Crown Princess, 16 April 1859,
    Dearest Child, p. 178.
32 Benedict Read to author, 7 January
    1983.
33 M. Pullan, *Maternal Counsels to a
    Daughter*, 1855, p. 81.
34 QVJ, 24 May 1864, p. 203.
35 Catherine Paget's diary, 23 January 1858.
36 F. Palgrave, *Handbook to the Fine Arts'
    Collections in the International
    Exhibition of 1862*, p. 91.
37 QV to Crown Princess, 7 December
    1867, *Your Dear Letter*, p. 164.
38 QVJ, 25 February 1868, p. 52.
39 Catherine Paget's diary, op. cit., & albums
    of PL and Ly Sophia Macnamara.
40 Ibid. Catherine Paget; Ly Susan Leslie
    Melville's diary, 22 January 1868, Stirling
    Maxwell of Pollock Mss TPM/121/1.
41 QV to Gen. Grey, 17 September 1864,
    Grey Mss XIII/6.
42 Ly Augusta Stanley, *Later Letters*, p. 75.
43 Dow Dss of Atholl to Emily
    MacGregor, 4 March 1869, Atholl Mss
    Box DRB.
44 Carlyle, to sister, 11 March 1869, Atholl
    Mss. Bd/1541.
45 QVJ, 18 March 1868.
46 PL to Mrs Grey, 11 December 1867,
    Grey Mss IX/10f.
47 PL to Ld Dufferin, n.d., April 1870,
    Dufferin Mss. D.1071.

48 R. Strachey, *Millicent Garrett Fawcett*,
    1931, p. 116.
49 PL to Josephine Butler, 22 March 1869,
    Butler Mss.
50 Sir Theodore Martin, *Queen Victoria as
    I Knew Her*, 1908, pp. 69–70.
51 Ibid. and Philip Guedalla, *The Queen
    and Mr Gladstone*, 1933, vol. I, p. 271.
52 Elizabeth Longford, *Eminent Victorian
    Women*, 1982, p. 127.
53 QV to Theodore Martin, 29 May 1870,
    op. cit.
54 PL to Josephine Butler, 27 March 1869,
    Butler Mss.
55 *The Lancet*, 1870, vol. I, p. 680.
56 Jo Manton, *Elizabeth Garrett Anderson*,
    1965, p. 168.
57 Louisa G. Anderson, *Elizabeth Garrett
    Anderson 1836–1917*, 1939, p. 130.
58 Manton, op. cit.

CHAPTER VII

1   Magdalen Ponsonby, p. 64.
2   Emily Becher to D of Argyll, 15 October
    1870, INV Mss.
3   *Memoirs of Edward, Earl of Sandwich*.
    ed. Mrs Steuart Erskine, 1919, p. 89.
4   Baroness Burdett-Coutts to D of
    Argyll, 13 October 1870, INV Mss.
5   William Gladstone to his wife, 18
    September 1869, Glynne Gladstone Mss,
    Box 29/3.
6   QV to Crown Princess, 1 January 1869,
    Your Dear Letter, p. 215.
7   A. M. W. Stirling, p. 93.
8   QV to Ld Granville, 5 August 1869,
    Granville Mss PRO 30/29, vol. 31.
9   Gen. Grey to Sir Augustus Paget, 18
    September 1863, Paget Mss, BL 51205.
10 Queen of Holland to Ly Westmorland,
    19 October 1870, Weigall Mss. U.1371.
11 QV to Crown Princess, 25 October 1872,
    Darling Child, p. 65.
12 Sybil Grey, and Gen. Grey's journal, 18
    November 1868, Grey Mss D6/25.
13 Pss of Wales to PL, n.d., November
    1868, RA/A/17/288 cit. Battiscombe,
    pp. 101-2.
14 QV to Ld Granville, op. cit.
15 *A Guardsman's Memories*, p. 252, cit. Pss
    Friedrich Leopold of Prussia, p. xix;
    Maurice FitzGerald to his mother, 17
    February 1878, Spring-Rice Mss 1190.
16 PL to Col. Elphinstone, 12 April 1870,
    Elphinstone Mss.

17 Richard Hough, *Louis and Victoria*, 1974, p. 10.
18 Walter Bagehot 'The Income of the Prince of Wales', *The Economist*, 10 October 1874.
19 QV to Gladstone, 15 February 1870, Philip Guedalla, *The Queen and Mr Gladstone*, 1933, p. 267.
20 Louisa Antrim, p. 227.
21 Hon. Mary Percy to author, 25 October 1983.
22 W. Greg, 'Why are Women Redundant', *National Review*, April 1862.
23 QV to Ld Granville, 27 July 1869, Granville Mss.
24 Ly Gregory, p. 103.
25 Boehm to Alfred Gilbert, cit. I. McAllister, *Alfred Gilbert*, pp. 32–3.
26 QV to Crown Princess, 3 March 1869, *Your Dear Letter*, p. 227.
27 *Magazine of Art*, 1880, p. 335.
28 QV to Crown Princess, 17 July 1869, *Your Dear Letter*, p. 240.
29 QV to Ld Granville, 27 July 1869, Granville Mss.
30 Ibid., 29 July 1869.
31 Ibid., 28 & 31 July 1869.
32 Ly Frederick Cavendish, vol. I, p. 235.
33 QV to Dss of Argyll, 27 October 1868, INV Mss.
34 QV to Crown Princess, 25 February 1858, *Dearest Child*, p. 59.
35 *Leaves*, p. 52.
36 Ld Lorne to Mrs Paisley, 15 January 1900, Smith of Jordanhill Mss TD1/501.
37 Dss of Argyll to Ly Emma McNeill, n.d. 1849, INV Mss.
38 QV to Ld Granville, 2 August & 29 July 1869, Granville Mss.
39 Ibid., 31 July 1869.
40 Lorne's journal, 16 August 1869, INV Mss.
41 Granville, 31 July 1869, op. cit.
42 Ibid.
43 *Mrs Story's Reminiscences*, J. Story, 1913, p. 12.
44 Ly Frederick Cavendish, vol. I, p. 162.
45 Lord George Hamilton, *Parliamentary Reminiscences and Reflections 1868–85*, 1916, vol. I, pp. 97–8.
46 Georgina Battiscombe, *Mrs Gladstone*, 1956, p. 110.
47 Niall, D of Argyll to Maysie Wynne Finch, 8 October 1940, Voelas Mss.
48 Henry Lucy, p. 115.
49 D of Argyll to Ld Granville, 11 August 1869, Granville Mss.
50 Ibid., 16 August 1869.
51 Lorne's journal, 16 August 1869.
52 D of Argyll to Ld Granville, 18 August 1869, Granville Mss.
53 QV to Ld Granville, 9 August 1869, ibid.
54 Dean Wellesley to Ld Granville, 15 & 17 August 1869, ibid.
55 Ibid., 14–17 August 1869.
56 D of Argyll to Ld Granville, 18 August 1869, ibid.
57 Lorne's journal, op. cit.
58 D of Argyll to Ld Granville, op. cit.
59 Lorne's journal, op. cit.
60 Ld Granville to D of Argyll, 21 August 1869, Granville Mss.
61 Ibid.

CHAPTER VIII
1 QV to Ld Granville, 18 December 1869, Granville Mss.
2 Ibid., 28 July 1869.
3 Ibid., 12 March 1870.
4 Dean Wellesley to Ld Granville, 15 March 1870, ibid.
5 QV to Ld Granville, 22 March 1870, ibid.
6 Ibid., 12 March 1870.
7 Ibid., 29 March 1870.
8 Sybil Grey's diary, 2 April 1870.
9 PL to Mrs Grey, 29 April 1870, Grey Mss IX/10f.
10 Mrs Duckworth to the author, 8 March 1984.
11 QV to Crown Princess, 26 June 1867, *Your Dear Letter*, p. 141.
12 Mrs Duckworth, op. cit.
13 PL to Col. Elphinstone, 12 April 1870, op. cit.
14 A. D. Duckworth's family notes, 15 June 1960.
15 Dean Wellesley to Ld Granville, 11 August 1869, Granville Mss.
16 QV to Ld Granville, 29 April 1870, ibid.
17 Ibid., 14 January & 14 May 1870.
18 PL to Col. Elphinstone, op. cit.
19 Ibid., 25 May 1870.
20 QV to Ld Granville, 16 May 1870, Granville Mss.
21 Ibid., 19 June 1870.
22 Ibid., 15 July 1870.
23 QV to Pss Victoria of Hesse, 19 June 1883, Broadlands Mss.

24 QV to Ld Granville, 26, 25, 24, 31 July 1870, Granville Mss.
25 Ly Clifden to QV, 13 August 1870, ibid.
26 QV to Ld Granville, 14 July, 17 September 1870, ibid.
27 QV to Crown Princess, 20 July 1870, *Your Dear Letter*, p. 287.
28 Ibid., 1 August 1870, p. 289.
29 PL to Mrs Gladstone, 19 September 1870, Mary Drew Mss, BL 46220.
30 Lord Halifax to his wife, 22 September 1870 Halifax Mss A2/43 Pt vii.
31 QV to Ld Granville, 12 & 17 September 1870, Granville Mss.
32 George Poore to his sister, Ellen, 3 October 1870, Poore Mss. F.30.
33 Mrs Olwen Wake to author, 15 February 1984.
34 George Poore to Dr Beck, 13 October 1870; Ly Frances Balfour, vol. 1, p. 85.
35 Mary Ponsonby to Ld Granville, 11 October 1870, Granville Mss.
36 QV to Ld Granville, 1 October 1870, ibid.
37 Mary Ponsonby to Ld Granville, op. cit.
38 QV to Ld Granville, 3 October 1870, ibid.
39 Mary Ponsonby to Ld Granville, op. cit.
40 QV to Ld Granville, op. cit.
41 Lorne to D of Argyll, 3 October 1870, INV Mss.
42 D of Argyll to Ld Granville, 24 October 1870, Granville Mss.
43 Lorne to Ly V Campbell, 7 October 1870, INV Mss.
44 Lorne to D of Argyll, op. cit.
45 QV to Ld Granville, 5 & 26 October 1870, Granville Mss.
46 Lorne's journal, op. cit.

CHAPTER IX
1 Pl to Mrs Thurston, 12 October 1870, Thurston Mss.
2 D of Argyll to Ld Dufferin, 7 October 1870, Dufferin Mss D, 1071/HBF/1– 159.
3 Ibid., to Gladstone, 10 October 1870, Gladstone Mss, BL 44101, vol. xvi.
4 D of Argyll to Ld Granville, 24 October 1870, Granville Mss.
5 Ibid., 28 October 1870.
6 D of Argyll to Ld Halifax, 19 October 1870, Halifax Mss A4/82.
7 Ibid., to Ld Granville, op. cit.

8 Henry to Mary Ponsonby, 15 October 1870, cit. Longford, p. 368.
9 QV to Ld Granville, 18 & 19 October 1870, Granville Mss.
10 D of Argyll to Ld Granville, op. cit.
11 Ibid., to Ld Dufferin, 20 October 1870, Dufferin Mss.
12 Ibid., to Dr Cumming, 18 October 1870. Inv. Mss.
13 Ibid., to Gladstone, 19 October 1870, Gladstone Mss.
14 Ibid., to Dr Cumming, op. cit.
15 Ibid., to Ld Granville, op. cit.
16 Ibid., 11 October 1870.
17 QVJ, 10 October 1870, p. 234.
18 QV to Crown Princess, 3 & 11 October 1870, *Your Dear Letter*, pp. 301–2.
19 Ly Ely to Disraeli, 21 October 1870, Hughenden Mss B/XIX/D/152.
20 QV to Ld Granville, 18 October 1870, Granville Mss.
21 QV to Crown Princess, 1 November 1870, *Your Dear Letter*, p. 305.
22 David Duff, *The Life Story of HRH Princess Louise, Duchess of Argyll*, 1940, p. 121.
23 Pss of Wales to PL, n.d., Battiscombe, p. 110.
24 QV to Ld Granville, 26 October 1870, Granville Mss.
25 Pr. of Wales to QV, n.d., RA/Add A/ 17/39, cit. Georgina Battiscombe, *Shaftesbury*, 1974, p. 303.
26 QV to Ld Granville, op. cit.
27 D of Argyll to Ld Granville, 24 October 1870, Granville Mss.
28 Ly Frederick Cavendish, vol. 2, p. 91.
29 Ly Jocelyn to Ly Elcho, 14 November 1870, Wemyss Mss.
30 Queen of Holland to Ly Westmorland, 19 October 1870, Weigall Mss U. 1371.
31 *Letters*, 2nd Series, vol. 1, pp. 632–3.
32 Lorne to Ld Granville, 7 October 1870, Granville Mss.
33 D of Argyll to Ld Granville, 10 October 1870, ibid.
34 PL to Dow Dss of Atholl, 26 October 1870, Atholl Mss.
35 PL to Mrs Gladstone, 18 October 1870, Drew Mss BL H6220.
36 *The Times*, 14 October 1870, p. 9.
37 PL to Dow Dss of Atholl, op. cit.
38 PL to Ld Dufferin, 19 October 1870, Dufferin Mss.
39 Mary Ponsonby to Ld Granville, op. cit.

40 QV to Ld Granville, 24 October 1870, Granville Mss.
41 Lorne to Ly V Campbell, op. cit.
42 Ibid.
43 Arthur Ponsonby, p. 91.
44 QV to Ld Granville, op. cit.
45 D of Argyll to Gladstone, 21 & 24 October 1870, Gladstone Mss. BL 44101 f307–8.
46 Ibid. to QV, copy, 21 October 1870, INV Mss.
47 QV to Crown Princess, 25 October 1870, *Your Dear Letter*, p. 305.
48 George Poore to his mother, 9 November 1870, Poore Mss.
49 Ibid. to Dr Beck.
50 Ibid., to his mother, op. cit.
51 D of Argyll to Ld Dufferin, 14 November 1870, Dufferin Mss.
52 QV to Ld Granville, 11 November 1870, Granville Mss.
53 Henry to Mary Ponsonby, 27, 29 October & 11 November 1870, cit. Longford, pp. 331–2.
54 QV to Pss Victoria of Hesse, 21 October 1883, Broadlands Mss.
55 QV to Ld Granville, op. cit.
56 Dss of Argyll to Ld Dufferin, 9 November 1870, Dufferin Mss.
57 Sybil Grey's diary, 15 November 1870.
58 QV to Ld Granville, op. cit.
59 Ibid.
60 Dss of Argyll to Ld Dufferin, 2 December 1870, Dufferin Mss.
61 QVJ, 10 December 1870 p. 286; Granville Mss 8 January 1871.
62 *The Times*, 2 February 1871.
63 Sybil Grey's diary, 13 February 1871.
64 QVJ, 15 March 1871, p. 57.
65 QV to Dow Dss of Atholl, 16 March, 1871, Atholl Mss.
66 QV to Dss of Abercorn, 2 October 1869, Abercorn Mss D623/A/257/19.
67 QV to Annie, Dss of Sutherland, 14 & 18 March 1871, Sutherland Mss.
68 Ly Frances Balfour, vol. 1, p. 101.
69 Ian Campbell of Islay to Ly Ruthven, 24 March 1871, Campbell of Islay Mss, Adv. Mss 50, 4, 6.
70 Ld Ronnie Gower's journal, 21 March 1871, Dunrobin Mss.
71 Sybil Grey's diary, 21 March 1871.
72 D of Argyll to Ly Emma McNeill, 25 March 1871, INV Mss.
73 Lorne to Ly Emma, 19 March 1871, INV Mss.

74 *Memoir of Robert Herbert Story* by his daughters, 1909, p. 108.
75 Ian Campbell of Islay, op. cit.
76 Lorne to Ly Emma, op. cit.
77 QV to Ld Granville, 23 March 1871, Granville Mss.

CHAPTER X

1 Ian Campbell of Islay to Lady Ruthven, op. cit.
2 Lorne to Dss of Argyll, 22 March 1871, INV Mss.
3 Rt. Revd W. Boyd-Carpenter, *Some Pages of My Life*, 1911, p. 300.
4 Lorne to Dss of Argyll, op. cit.
5 Mary Drew, p. 50.
6 QV to Dss of Argyll, 8 April 1871, INV Mss.
7 QV to Ld Granville, 24 February 1871, Granville Mss.
8 PL to Col. Elphinstone, 3 February 1871, Elphinstone Mss.
9 Lorne to Dss Argyll, 4 April 1871, INV Mss.
10 Pss Alice to QV, 8 April 1871, *Alice Letters*, p. 265.
11 Lorne to Dss of Argyll, 8 April 1871, INV Mss.
12 PL to Dss of Argyll, 17 April 1871, INV Mss.
13 Lorne to Dss of Argyll, n.d., INV Mss.
14 Walburga, Lady Paget, *Embassies of Other Days*, 1923, vol. 1, p. 260.
15 PL to Walburga Paget, n.d. & 20 September 1922, Paget Mss BL 57238.
16 Lorne to Dss of Argyll, 8 May 1871, INV Mss.
17 Lorne to Dss of Argyll, 19 May 1871, ibid.
18 Pss Alice to QV, 8 June 1871, *Alice Letters*, p. 267.
19 George, Eighth Duke of Argyll, *Autobiography and Memoirs*, 1906, vol. 1, pp. 391–2.
20 Ly Mary Campbell to Lorne, 23 May 1880, INV Mss.
21 Lorne to Dss of Argyll, n.d., 1871, op. cit.
22 Mary Drew, p. 59.
23 QV to Ld Granville, 18 October 1870, Granville Mss.
24 QV to Dss of Argyll, 19 June 1871, INV Mss.
25 Henry Ponsonby to Ld Granville, 28 July 1871, Granville Mss, Box 32, vol. 2.

26 QV to Ld Granville, 10 August 1871, ibid.
27 Henry to Mary Ponsonby, 17 September 1871, cit. Longford, p. 386.
28 D of Argyll to Mr Gladstone, 18 August 1871, Gladstone Mss. BL 44102.
29 Ian Campbell of Islay to his mother, 21 August 1871, Campbell of Islay Mss.
30 Ly V. Campbell to Aunt Dot, 24 August 1871, INV Mss.
31 QVJ, 18 August 1847, *Leaves*, pp. 51–2.
32 Dss of Argyll to Aunt Dot, Ly Frances Balfour, vol. 1, p. 104.
33 Ibid.
34 *Oban Times*, 26 August 1871.
35 John Campbell of Kilberry's diary, 23 August 1871, Campbell of Kilberry Mss.
36 Ly Mary to Ly Frances Campbell, 29 May 1872, Meade Mss.
37 Campbell of Kilberry's diary, 25 August 1871.
38 Ly V. Campbell to Aunt Dot, op. cit.
39 Press clipping, n.d., Glyn Mss.
40 Lorne to Ld Dufferin, 29 September 1871, Dufferin Mss.
41 *Oban Times*, 30 September 1871.
42 Dss of Argyll's journal, 15 April 1863, INV Mss.
43 Ly Frederick Cavendish, 10 September 1871, vol. 2, p. 112.
44 PL to Mrs Grey, n.d., October 1871, Maria Grey Mss.
45 Albert Grey to Victoria Grey, 7 October 1871, Grey Mss.
46 QVJ, 8 December 1871, cit. David Duff, *Victorian Travels*, 1970, p. 223.
47 PL to Gladstone, 13 December 1871, Gladstone Mss. BL Loan 73.
48 Maurice Fitzgerald to his father, 13 December 1871, Spring-Rice Mss.
49 QV to Crown Princess, 16 December 1871, *Darling Child*, p. 19.

CHAPTER XI
1 Lorne to Dss of Argyll, n.d., January 1872, INV Mss.
2 PL to Ly Mary Glyn, 9 January 1899, Meade Mss.
3 Patrick Howarth, *When the Riviera Was Ours*, 1977, p. 51
4 PL to Dss of Argyll, n.d., 1872, INV Mss.
5 Lorne to Dss of Argyll, 13 January 1872, INV Mss.
6 Ibid., 2 February 1872.

7 PL to Dss of Argyll, op. cit.
8 Lorne to Dss of Argyll, op. cit.
9 PL to Dss of Argyll, 21 May 1871, INV Mss.
10 Lord Ernest Hamilton, *Old Days and New*, 1923, p. 47.
11 PL to Mary Probert, 31 May 1905, Bevills Mss.
12 Lady Knightley, p. 233.
13 Ibid.
14 Lorne to Dss of Argyll, 26 May 1871, INV Mss.
15 Josephine Butler to Maria Grey, n.d., Butler Mss.
16 Robert Collins to Frederick Myers, 26 July 1871, Myers Mss. M/124.
17 Josephine Kamm, *Indicative Past*, 1971, p. 30.
18 *Passages*, vol. 2, pp. 402–6.
19 Sir Wyndham Dunstan, 'Tribute to Work for Women's Education', *The Times*, 8 December 1939, p. 11.
20 Kamm, p. 45.
21 Dorothy Beale, *Girls' Schools Past and Present, Nineteenth Century*, 1888, vol. XXIII.
22 Kamm, p. 43.
23 *Pall Mall Gazette*, 16 May 1875.
24 Lady Knightley, p. 247.
25 PL Speech, cit. Epton, p. 227.
26 Janey to Ld Archie Campbell, 27 March 1875, INV Mss.
27 PL to Henry Ponsonby, Ponsonby Mss, cit. Epton, p. 133.
28 Lorne to Dss of Argyll, 16 April 1870, INV Mss.
29 D of Argyll to Ld Dufferin, 13 October 1872, Dufferin Mss.
30 Dss of Argyll to Ld Dufferin, 30 August 1872, ibid.
31 Niall Argyll to Maysie Wynne Finch, 30 October 1940, Voelas Mss.
32 Arthur Ponsonby, pp. 116–19.
33 Blanche E. C. Dugdale, *Family Homespun*, 1940, pp. 41–2.
34 Lesley Brodrick's notes, *Nothing But the Truth*, p. 15.
35 A. V. Baillie, pp. 41–2.
36 Mrs Baldwin to Archie Baldwin, 3 October 1875, Campbell-Gibson Mss.
37 Blanche Dugdale, p. 39.
38 Lady Frances Balfour, *Lady Victoria Campbell, A Memoir*, 1911, p. 69.
39 Olwen Wake to the author, 15 February 1984. Elizabeth Brodrick to the author, 26 April 1983.

40 Ly Mary to Ly Frances Campbell, 29 May 1872, Meade Mss.
41 D of Argyll to Lorne, 28 July 1874, INV Mss.
42 Blanche Dugdale, p. 39.
43 Sir William Richmond to his mother, n.d., September 1867, R Acad Mss R1/1/48.
44 Ibid. and A.M.W. Stirling, *The Richmond Papers*, 1926, p. 240.
45 Ly Frederick Cavendish, vol. 2, p. 27.
46 Leslie Brodrick, p. 9.
47 Ibid., p. 18.
48 Ibid.
49 Lorne to Niky Campbell, 29 December 1884, INV Mss.
50 Ly Frances Balfour, vol. 2, p. 89.
51 Ethel to Baynes Badcock, n.d., March 1905, Probert Mss.
52 The Richmond Papers, p. 239.
53 Dss of Argyll to Ld Dufferin, 18 December 1872, Dufferin Mss.
54 Lorne to Ld Dufferin, 12 February 1873, Dufferin Mss.
55 *Oban Times*, 31 January 1874.
56 *Oban Times*, 7 February 1874.
57 D of Argyll to Lord Northbrook, 13 February 1874, INV Mss.
58 QV to Crown Princess, 14 February 1874, *Darling Child*, p. 129.

CHAPTER XII

1 Queen of Holland to Ly Salisbury, 2 March 1874, cit., *A Great Lady's Friendships*, ed. Ly Burghcleve, 1933, p. 391.
2 QV to Disraeli, 20 March 1874, Hughenden Mss B/XIX/B/18B.
3 Ibid., 17 March 1874, B/XIX/B/20.
4 QV to Crown Princess, 18 March 1874, *Darling Child*, p. 133.
5 Lorne to Ld Archie Campbell, 24 October 1873, INV Mss.
6 D of Argyll to Sir John McNeill, 14 October 1873, INV Mss.
7 Lorne to Ld Archie Campbell, op. cit.
8 PL to Ly Holland, 4 December 1873, Holland Mss BL 52114.
9 PL to Ld Archie Campbell, 24 February 1874, INV Mss.
10 Dss of Argyll to Ld Dufferin, 16 February 1874, Dufferin Mss.
11 Ld Ronnie Gower's journal, 4 April 1874.

12 PL to Ld Archie Campbell, 24 February 1874, op. cit.
13 Lorne to Dss of Argyll, 22 May 1874, INV Mss.
14 Ld Ronnie Gower, n.d., July 1874, *My Reminiscences*, 1883, vol. 2, p. 91.
15 D of Argyll to Lorne, 21 June 1874, INV Mss.
16 D of Argyll to PL, 24 June 1874, INV Mss.
17 D of Argyll to Lorne, 15 July 1874, INV Mss.
18 PL to Ly Holland, 12 April 1874, Holland Mss.
19 PL to Ld Archie Campbell, op. cit.
20 Ld Ronnie Gower's journal, 29 July 1875.
21 Ly Frederick Cavendish, vol. 2, p. 175.
22 Pss Alice of Athlone interview, cit. Epton, p. 233.
23 Henry Ponsonby to Monty Lowry Corry, 28 & 30 December 1874, Hughenden Mss B/XX/D/99.
24 PL to Ly Knightley, 22 December 1866, Knightley Mss.
25 Henry Ponsonby to Corry, 3 January 1875, op. cit.
26 Robert Collins to Frederick Myers, 7 February 1875, Myers Mss. M/146.
27 Dss of Argyll to Ld Dufferin, 22 January 1875, Dufferin Mss.
28 Robert Collins to Frederick Myers, op. cit.
29 PL to Ld Archie Campbell, 23 January 1875, INV Mss.
30 Robert Collins, op. cit.
31 PL to Janey Campbell, 15 November, n.d., INV Mss.
32 Arthur Ponsonby, p. 90.
33 QVJ, 10 March 1875, cit. D. Hudson, *Kensington Palace*, 1968, p. 102.
34 PL to Ly Holland, 4 December 1873, Holland Mss.
35 PL to Ld Archie Campbell, n.d., INV Mss.
36 Dss of Argyll to Lorne, 14 July 1875, INV Mss.
37 D of Argyll to Mr Wyllie, 20 July 1875, INV Mss.
38 Lorne to Ld Archie Campbell, 4 September 1875, ibid.
39 QVJ, 22 September 1875, cit. David Duff, *Victoria in the Highlands*, 1968, p. 308.
40 Henry to Mary Ponsonby, cit. Epton, p. 148.

41 D of Argyll to Gladstone, 11 October 1875, Gladstone Mss. BL 44103.
42 *Memoirs of R. H. Story*, p. 142.
43 QVJ, 25 September 1875, cit. David Duff, *Queen Victoria's Highland Journals*, 1980, p. 191.
44 Mrs Baldwin to Archie Baldwin, op. cit. Campbell-Gibson Mss.
45 QVJ, cit. Duff, p. 304.
46 Henry to Mary Ponsonby, cit. Epton, p. 150.
47 Ly Ashburton to Thomas Carlyle, September 1875, Virginia Surtees, *The Ludovisi Goddess*, 1984, p. 172.
48 Henry to Mary Ponsonby, op. cit., p. 149.
49 Ld Ronnie Gower's journal, 29 July 1875.
50 D of Argyll to QV, 3 October 1875, INV Mss.
51 Lorne to D of Argyll, 13 January 1876, INV Mss.
52 Robert Collins to F. Myers, n.d., Myers Mss.
53 Dss of Argyll to Ld Dufferin, 18 December 1872, Dufferin Mss.
54 D of Argyll to Lorne, 12 July 1874, INV Mss.
55 Lorne to Dss of Argyll, 27 August 1876, INV Mss.
56 Ld Ronnie Gower's journal, 20 September 1876.
57 Dss of Argyll to Lorne, 11 September 1877, INV Mss.
58 Ly Mary Campbell to Ld Ronnie Gower, 12 October 1877, Dunrobin Mss.
59 D of Argyll to Dr Cumming, n.d., October 1877, INV Mss.
60 Ly Connie Campbell to Ly Alex Leveson Gower, 1 November 1877, Sutherland Mss, D.593/P/29/1/10.
61 Ly Mary Campbell to Ld Ronnie Gower, op. cit.
62 Ibid.
63 D of Argyll to Dr Cumming, op. cit.
64 Ibid.
65 Ly Mary Campbell to Ld Ronnie Gower, op. cit.
66 Ly Connie to Ly Alex Leveson Gower, op. cit.
67 Dss of Argyll to Ly Emma McNeill, 15 October 1877, INV Mss.
68 Dss of Argyll to Ld Dufferin, 22 October 1877, Dufferin Mss.

CHAPTER XIII

1 Ly Frances Balfour, vol. 1, p. 142.
2 ibid.
3 Ly Mary Glyn to Maysie Wynne Finch, 17 October 1940, Voelas Mss.
4 Ly Libby Campbell to Norah Callander, 17 December 1877, INV Mss.
5 PL to Ld Dufferin, 10 November 1877, Dufferin Mss.
6 QV to Crown Princess, 19 December 1877, *Darling Child*, pp. 3, 271.
7 Lorne to Dss of Argyll, 6 December 1877, INV Mss.
8 Maurice Dreyfous, *Dalou, sa vie et son oeuvre*, 1903, p. 86.
9 E. F. Benson, *As We Were*, 1930, pp. 250–1.
10 George Lewes to Mrs Stuart, 12 July 1877, *The George Eliot Letters*, ed. Gordon Haight, 1956, vol. VI, p. 394.
11 *Grosvenor Gallery Notes*, ed. Henry Blackburn, 1878, no. 233.
12 Disraeli to Ly Bradford, 4 March 1878, Bradford Mss B778.
13 Lorne to Dss of Argyll, 29 December 1877, INV Mss.
14 Walburga Paget, *Linings of Life*, 1928, pp. 264–5.
15 PL to Ld Archie Campbell, 23 November 1874, INV Mss.
16 Walburga Paget, op. cit.
17 Disraeli to Ly Bradford, 4 August 1878, Bradford Mss B.919.
18 Boehm to PL, 22 April 1879, RA/Vic. Add. A/17 1772.
19 Ld Ronnie Gower's journal, 21 February 1878.
20 Ly Frederick Cavendish, vol. 2, pp. 217–19.
21 Ld Archie Campbell to Molly Sartoris, 29 May 1878, INV Mss.
22 Pl to Dss Annie Sutherland, 25 May 1878, Sutherland Mss D/593/P/28/7/5.
23 PL to Minnie Paget, 29 May 1878, Paget Mss BL 51248.
24 Pss Beatrice to Lorne, 26 May 1878, INV Mss.
25 PL to Lorne, 4 June 1878, ibid.
26 Ibid., 5 June 1878.
27 Lorne to Dean Stanley, 6 June 1878, ibid.
28 PL to Aunt Dot, 11 June 1878, ibid.
29 D of Argyll to Ld Selbourne, 31 May 1878, Selbourne Mss 1866 f315.
30 Stanley Weintraub, *Whistler*, 1974, p. 173.

31 James Whistler to Godwin, n.d., June 1878, Whistler Mss G112.

32 Whistler to PL, n.d., November 1878, Whistler Mss L169.

33 Frederick Campbell to Whistler, 15 November 1878, Whistler Mss CII.

34 QVJ, 21 July 1878, *Letters*, 2nd Series, vol. 2, p. 631.

35 QV to Ld Dufferin, 16 September 1878, Dufferin Mss.

36 Lorne to Ld Dufferin, 29 July 1878, Dufferin Mss.

37 QV to Disraeli, 28 July 1878, Hughenden Mss B/XIX/B/1381.

38 Ibid., 30 July 1878, B/XIX/B/1383.

39 PL to QV & QV to Disraeli, 20 August 1878, Hughenden Mss B/XIX/B/1403.

40 Sir M. Hicks Beach to Disraeli, 26 August 1878, St Aldwyn Mss D2455 PCC/13.

41 QV to Disraeli, 11 September 1878, Hughenden Mss B/XIX/B1411.

42 Admiralty to First Sea Lord, 4 October 1878, Hambleden Mss p. 56/216.

43 Disraeli to James Daly, 25 September 1878, Hughenden Mss B/XIX/B/1420.

44 Disraeli to Ly Bradford, 8 November 1878, Bradford Mss B.838.

45 Ld Ronnie Gower's journal, 13 November 1878.

46 Lorne to Ld Dufferin, 30 August 1878, Dufferin Mss.

CHAPTER XIV

1 Viscountess Byng of Vimy, *Up the Stream of Time*, 1946, pp. 9–10.

2 Foreign Office Memos: no. 93, 1 & 5 November 1878, C.O. 694 Secret Register No. 3 Domestics PRO.

3 *Passages*, vol. 2, pp. 407–8.

4 Ibid., p. 409.

5 Lorne to D of Argyll, 25 November 1878, INV Mss.

6 J. E. Collins, *Canada under the Administration of Lorne*, 1884, p. 45.

7 *St John Morning News*, 2 December 1878, p. 2, col. 1.

8 Ibid., & Collins, op. cit. pp. 45–7.

9 Ld Dufferin to Dss of Argyll, 31 July 1872, Dufferin Mss.

10 Lorne to Ld Lansdowne, 5 June 1883, Albert Grey Mss 204/2.

11 *Passages*, vol. 2, p. 415.

12 Lorne to D of Argyll, 4 December 1878, INV Mss.

13 Ibid.

14 Lorne to Sir Edward Thornton, 11 December 1878, Thornton Mss.

15 Lorne to Ld Dufferin, 7 December 1878, Dufferin Mss.

16 QV to Crown Princess, 12 December 1878, *Beloved Mama*, p. 29.

17 Gwen Stephenson to Ld Dufferin, 16 December 1878, Dufferin Mss.

18 PL to Ly Cadogan, 5 February 1879, Cadogan Mss CAD/229.

19 QVJ, 1 January 1879, *Letters*, 2nd Series, vol. II, p. 4.

CHAPTER XV

1 Lorne to Ld Dufferin, 30 August 1878, Dufferin Mss.

2 Ibid., 5 January 1879.

3 *London Advertiser*, 8 April 1880, *Canadian Scrapbooks*, vol. II, p. 182, INV Mss.

4 Viscountess Byng, pp. 11–12.

5 S. W. Silver & Co., *Handbook to Canada*, London, 1881, p. 24.

6 *Passages*, vol. 2, p. 419.

7 Sir Edward Thornton to Ld Salisbury, 13 August 1878, Salisbury Mss.

8 Maurice de Bunsen to his mother, 19 January 1879, de Bunsen Mss MB/I/C.

9 C. Berry, *The Other Side*, 1880, pp. 174–6.

10 Lorne's journal, 21 January 1879.

11 Ld Frederick Hamilton, *Days Before Yesterday*, 1920, p. 272.

12 Ly Frances Balfour to Arthur Balfour, 22 February 1882, FB Mss.

13 Eva Langham to Ly Alfred Paget, 29 February 1880, Paget Mss BL 51243.

14 Ly Frances Balfour to Revd Robertson, 20 February 1882, FBMSS.

15 Lorne to Ld Dufferin, 6 March 1879, Dufferin Mss.

16 Henry James to Mr Hoppin, n.d., November 1880, cit. L. Edel, *The Conquest of London*, 1962, p. 351.

17 Ly Frances Balfour to Arthur Balfour, 6 February 1882, FB Mss.

18 Ly Frances Balfour to Revd Robertson, op. cit.

19 C. Berry, p. 252.

20 J. E. Collins, p. 309.

21 Mary Melgund to Mrs Grey, 27 February 1884, Minto Mss 13182 f171.

22 Lorne to Ld Lansdowne, 13 June 1883, Albert Grey Mss.

23 Lorne to Mr O'Brien, 8 June 1879, Records of the Founding of the Royal Canadian Academy by the Marquis of Lorne and HRH Princess Louise, PAC M.6.28.I 126, vol. 14, p. 9.
24 G. Grant, *Picturesque Canada*, 1882, vol. 1, p. 187.
25 Maurice de Bunsen to his mother, 3 February 1883, de Bunsen Mss MB/I/f.
26 PL to Minnie Paget, 1 August 1879, Paget Mss BL 51248.
27 Viscountess Byng, pp. 13–14.
28 D of Argyll to Ly Frances Balfour, 22 June 1879, INV Mss.
29 W. Stewart MacNutt, *Days of Lorne*, 1955, p. 212.
30 D of Argyll to Ly Frances Balfour, op. cit.
31 Ly Frances Balfour, *Life and Letters of the Reverend James MacGregor*, 1912, pp. 375–6.
32 D of Argyll to Dr Cumming, 29 June 1879, INV Mss.
33 MacNutt, op. cit.
34 *Passages*, 14 August 1879, p. 432.
35 Berry, p. 184.
36 Prof. Goldwin Smith to Mrs Hertz, 17 September 1879, *Goldwin Smith's Correspondence*, ed. Arnold Haultain, p. 83.
37 *Passages*, vol. 2 p. 438.
38 PL to Minnie Paget, op. cit.
39 Lorne to Ld Dufferin, 6 October 1879, Dufferin Mss.
40 Lorne to Ld Archie Campbell, 22 September 1879, INV Mss.
41 Ly Mary Campbell to Lorne, 23 October 1879, INV Mss.
42 Disraeli to Ly Bradford, 2 September 1879, Bradford Mss.

CHAPTER XVI

1 Lorne to Ld Dufferin, 20 January 1880, Dufferin Mss.
2 Lady Glover, *Life of Sir John Glover*, 1897, p. 264.
3 Eva Langham to Ly Alfred Paget, op. cit.
4 Maurice to Marie de Bunsen, 22 January 1881, de Bunsen Mss MB/I/f.
5 Marie de Bunsen, *The World I Used to Know*, 1930, p. 132.
6 Eva Langham, op. cit.
7 Ibid.
8 *Passages*, vol. 2, p. 444.

9 Ibid.
10 QV to Dss Annie Sutherland, 7 January 1885, Sutherland Mss.
11 *The Montreal Gazette*, 16 February 1880.
12 Collins, pp. 326–7.
13 A. Mackenzie to his wife, 18 February 1880, PAC Mss A40 MG26B, vol. 15.
14 QV to Crown Princess, 18 February 1880, *Beloved Mama*, p. 65.
15 Ld Ronnie Gower's journal, 2 March 1880.
16 Ly Mary Campbell to Lorne, 12 March 1880, INV Mss.
17 PAC Mss MG27/I A4 Bdl PC/B/2e.
18 Lorne to D of Argyll, 18 March 1880, INV Mss.
19 Ibid.
20 PL to Mrs Thurston, n.d. 1880, Thurston Mss.
21 Robert Collins to Frederick Myers, 13 June 1880, Myers Mss. MI 141.
22 Berry, p. 113.
23 *Chicago Tribune*, 5 June 1880, p. 9.
24 Lorne to D of Argyll, 10 June 1880, INV Mss.
25 Press clippings, 5 June 1880, Atholl Mss Box 75.
26 PL to Minnie Paget, n.d., 1880, Paget Mss.
27 Lorne to D of Argyll, 4 December 1879, INV Mss.
28 Ibid., 2 July 1880.
29 Augusta Hervey's account of Cascapedia, Hervey Mss 941/62/8.
30 Lorne to Ld Granville, 2 July 1880, Granville Mss Official Corresp. A–L.
31 Lorne to D of Argyll, 18 March 1880, op. cit.
32 QV to Pss Victoria of Hesse, 17 July 1880, Broadlands Mss.
33 Lorne to D of Argyll, 18 March 1880, op. cit.

CHAPTER XVII

1 Lady Waterpark's diary, 21 December 1880, Waterpark Mss BL 60750.
2 Lady Frederick Cavendish, vol. 2, p. 275.
3 Lorne to Dr Cumming, 16 January 1881, INV Mss.
4 Lorne to Ld Archie Campbell, 3 May 1881, ibid.
5 Ld Ronnie Gower's journal, 15 May 1881.
6 Lorne to Sir Edward Thornton, 17 May 1881, Thornton Mss FO 933/109.
7 *Passages*, vol. 2, p. 467.

8 MacNutt, pp. 218–19.
9 Lorne to Col. Littleton, 28 December 1881, Hatherton Mss D1121/P/4/5.
10 Sir Henry to Mary Ponsonby, n.d., cit. Epton, p. 163.
11 Lorne to Aunt Dot, 29 December 1881, INV Mss.
12 Ld Ronnie Gower's journal, 11 March 1882.
13 Lorne to Aunt Dot, op. cit.
14 MacNutt, p. 139.
15 Lorne to Sir John Macdonald, 22 June 1882, Macdonald Mss MG 26A, vol. 62, PAC.
16 British Consul to Ld Granville, 11 July 1882, No. 11 Political FO Mss, PRO.
17 Lorne to Sir J. Macdonald, 13 August 1883, Macdonald Mss, op. cit.
18 Gwen Stephenson to Ld Dufferin, 26 May 1883, Dufferin Mss.
19 Ibid.
20 *The Englishman's Guide Book to the United States and Canada*, 1879, p. 81.
21 Oliver Jensen, *The American Heritage of Railroads in America*, 1975, p. 121.
22 Lorne's journal, n.d., INV Mss.
23 *San Francisco Chronicle*, 14 September 1882, p. 1.
24 *San Francisco Exchange*, 16 September 1882.
25 *The Colonist*, 24 December 1882.
26 Ibid., 27 October 1951, p. 11.
27 Ld Kimberley to Lorne, 3 January 1883, PAC MG27, I A4 Bdl PC/B/6 Reel A/313.
28 British Columbia Archives, c. 1976, Government House in British Columbia, p. 4.
29 *The Colonist*, 24 December 1882.

CHAPTER XVIII

1 *Passages*, vol. 2, p. 488.
2 *San Francisco Examiner*, 11 December 1882.
3 *Passages*, vol. 2, pp. 489–90.
4 *Santa Barbara Daily Press*, 26–8 December 1882.
5 Lorne to D of Argyll, 2 March 1883, INV Mss.
6 *A Victorian Diarist, Extracts from the Journals of Mary, Lady Monkswell 1873–1895*, ed. Hon. E. C. F. Collier, 1944, vol. 1, p. 81.
7 *Passages*, vol. 2, p. 505.
8 D. F. Jones to Sir John Macdonald, 28 March 1883, PAC MG 26 A, vol. 392.

9 *Bermuda Journey*, William Zuill, 1946, pp. 299–300.
10 Jones to Sir John Macdonald, op. cit.
11 *Montreal Gazette*, 18 April 1883.
12 Gwen Stephenson to Ld Dufferin, 26 May 1883, Dufferin Mss.
13 Josceline Bagot to Ld Melgund, 25 August 1883, Minto Mss 12385 f95.
14 Dufferin Mss, op. cit.
15 Ibid.
16 PL to Ld Granville, 5 June 1883, Granville Mss.
17 Sir Robert Herbert's note, 28 March 1883, Derby Mss 920 DER (15) 20.
18 Lorne to Ld Derby, 17 April 1883, ibid.
19 QV to Ld Granville, 25 April 1883, Granville Mss.
20 PL to Ld Granville, op. cit.
21 QV to Ld Granville, 13 June 1883, Granville Mss.
22 Ibid.
23 Ibid., 25 April 1883.
24 Ibid., 15 June 1883.
25 Lorne to Ld Derby, 16 July 1883, Derby Mss.
26 Lorne to D of Argyll, n.d., INV Mss.
27 *Mark Twain – Howell's Letters*, ed. H. N. Smith & W. M. Gibson, 1960, p. 439.
28 S. Clemens to Lorne, 31 May 1883, INV Mss.
29 *Mark Twain's Notebooks & Journals*, ed. F. Anderson & M. B. Frank, 1979, Vol 3, p. 329.
30 Ld Melgund's diary, 8 October 1883, Minto Mss 12490.
31 Mary Melgund to Arthur Elliott, 19 October 1883, Elliott Mss 19483 f75.
32 Albert Grey to Mrs Grey, 15 October 1883, Minto Mss 13181 f186.
33 *A Victorian Diarist*, vol. 1, p. 99.

CHAPTER XIX

1 Lady Mary Campbell to Lorne, 10 February 1879, INV Mss.
2 Ld Archie Campbell to Lorne, 11 July 1879, INV Mss.
3 Disraeli to Ly Bradford, 4 August 1879, Bradford Mss.
4 Lorne to Ld Archie Campbell, 22 September 1879, INV Mss.
5 D of Argyll to Ld Dufferin, 24 July 1881, Dufferin Mss.
6 Ld Ronnie Gower's journal, 13 August 1881.

7 Gerald Balfour to Ly Frances Balfour, 5 December 1882, FB Mss.

8 Molly Sartoris to Norah Callander, 11 April 1878, INV Mss.

9 D of Argyll to Ld Dufferin, 13 January 1880, Dufferin Mss.

10 Ld Ronnie Gower's journal, 16 July 1880.

11 Ibid., 13 April 1882.

12 D of Argyll to Ld Dufferin, 8 June 1882. Dufferin Mss.

13 John Meade to author, 17 April 1983.

14 Ly Frances Balfour, vol. 2, p. 247.

15 Ly Mary Campbell to Lorne, 9 June 1881, INV Mss.

16 D of Connaught to Minnie Paget, 22 January 1883, Paget Mss, BL 51247.

17 Ld Granville to Gladstone, 24 April 1883, BL 44175 f136.

18 QV to Ld Granville, 25 April 1883, Granville Mss.

19 Ld Granville to Gladstone, 19 May 1883, BL 44175 f146.

20 Ld Granville to Ld Derby, 19 May 1883, Derby Mss.

21 Ld Granville to Gladstone, op. cit.

22 QV to Ld Granville, 11 October 1883, Granville Mss.

23 D of Argyll to QV, 11 October 1883, INV Mss.

24 QV to Crown Princess, 2 January 1884, *Beloved Mama*, p. 155.

25 Ly Knightley, 26 March 1884, p. 371.

26 PL to Aunt Dot, 30 March 1884, INV Mss.

27 PL to Ld Tennyson, 12 April 1884, Tennyson Mss.

28 Ly Knightley, 14 May 1884, p. 373.

29 Ld Ronnie Gower's journal, 22 July 1884.

30 Pss Alice to QV, 24 September 1874, Alice letters, p. 327.

31 PL to Minnie Paget, 29 May 1878, Paget Mss.

32 QV to Crown Princess, 27 July–30 September, 26, 29 November 1884, Kronberg letters, cit. Longford, p. 480.

33 Ly Frances Balfour, vol. 1, p. 87.

34 Lorne to D of Argyll, 11 May 1884, INV Mss.

35 QV to Crown Princess, 22 September 1884, *Beloved Mama*, p. 170.

36 Crown Princess to Lorne, 6 January 1885, INV Mss.

37 QV to Ld Granville, 10 July 1884, Granville Mss.

38 *The Diary of Sir Edward Hamilton*, 1880–1885, ed. Dudley W.R. Bahlman, 1972, vol. 2, p. 656.

39 Ld Granville to Ld Derby, 20 August 1884, Derby Mss 920 DER(15)21.

40 Ld Ronnie Gower's journal, 14 & 15 December 1884.

41 QV to Lorne, 13 January 1885, INV Mss.

42 Ld Ronnie Gower's journal, 23 August 1888.

43 Ly Frances Balfour to Henry Callander, 15 May 1879, INV Mss.

44 Ld Ronnie Gower's journal, 9 May 1879.

45 Ibid., 24 September 1879.

46 Ly Agnes Wood to her husband, 11 March 1880, Halifax Mss A2/124 part IV.

47 Ly Frances to Henry Callander, op. cit.

48 Ly Evey Campbell to Lorne, 12 October 1880, INV Mss.

49 Ld Ronnie Gower's journal, 26 October 1880.

50 Lorne to Mary Probert, 26 October 1904, Bevills Mss.

51 Lorne to Dr Cumming, 16 January 1881, INV Mss.

52 D of Argyll to Lorne, 26 April 1881, INV Mss.

53 *The Diary of Sir Edward Hamilton*, vol. 2, p. 586.

54 Lorne to Ld Archie Campbell, 1 August 1885, INV Mss.

CHAPTER XX

1 Ly Frederick Cavendish, vol. 1, p. XVI.

2 Lorne to Ld Archie Campbell, 5 November 1884, INV Mss.

3 Ibid.

4 Lorne's electoral address, 9 September 1885, ibid.

5 Gladstone to Lorne, 17 September 1885, INV Mss.

6 Sir A. Richmond, *Twenty-six Years 1875–1905*, 1961, p. 10.

7 Sir R. Ensor, *England 1870–1914*, 1952, p. 87.

8 R. Shannon, *The Crisis of Imperialism 1865–1915*, 1974, p. 185.

9 Lorne to Ld Dufferin, 11 April 1880, Dufferin Mss.

10 PL to Connie Flower, 28 November 1885, Battersea Mss BL 47909.

11 PL to Ld Granville, 5 June 1883, Granville Mss.

12 Battersea, op. cit. and Ld Ronnie Gower's journal, 9 October 1885.
13 Ly Victoria Campbell, p. 189.
14 Lorne to D of Argyll, 27 April 1886, INV Mss.
15 P of W to Henry Ponsonby, 2 February 1886, RA T9/62, cit. Magnus, p. 245.
16 Henry Ponsonby to Lorne, 4 February 1886, INV Mss.
17 Lorne to Gladstone, 20 September 1885, BL 44492 f104.
18 *London Letter*, G. Smalley, 1890, p. 370.
19 Ld Granville to Gladstone, 5 March 1886, BL 44179 f43.
20 Ly Frances Balfour, vol. 2, p. 65.
21 Lorne to D of Argyll, 17 March 1886, INV Mss.
22 Ly Frances Balfour, vol. 2, p. 56.
23 PL to Ly Salisbury, 2 July n.d., Salisbury Mss A19/9.
24 Lorne to D of Argyll, 27 April 1886, INV Mss.
25 PL to Ld Cadogan, 22 May 1886, Cadogan Mss CAD/226.
26 Lorne to Ld Archie Campbell, 22 September 1886, INV Mss.
27 D of Argyll to Lorne, 11 October 1886, INV Mss.
28 Ibid., 7 February 1885, INV Mss.
29 Henry Ponsonby to his wife, 24 April 1889, Ponsonby Mss.
30 Ly Frances Balfour to Sabina Smith, 26 December 1885, Smith of Jordanhill Mss.
31 Ld Ronnie Gower's journal, 5 December 1886.
32 Augustus Hare, *In My Solitary Life*, ed. M. Barnes, 1953, p. 199.
33 Lorne to D of Argyll, 26 January 1887, INV Mss.
34 Henry to Mary Ponsonby, 24 April 1887, Ponsonby Mss.
35 Pss Friedrich Leopold of Prussia, p. 39.
36 Ld Ernest Hamilton, *Forty Years On*, 1922, p. 8.
37 Henry to Mary Ponsonby, op. cit.
38 Ibid.

CHAPTER XXI

1 PL to Ly Battersea, 11 September 1889, Battersea Mss, BL 47909.
2 Lorne to Ld Dufferin, 6 May 1889, Dufferin Mss.
3 Ld Ronnie Gower's journal, 19 August 1892.
4 Note of Lilah Campbell of Argyll, INV Mss, p. 37.
5 Ibid., p. 2.
6 Ibid., p. 37.
7 Connie de Rothschild, *Reminiscences*, 1922, pp. 378–83.
8 PL to Ld Ronnie Gower, 29 June n.d., INV Mss.
9 PL to Cyril Flower, 10 January 1887, Battersea Mss.
10 PL to Ly Battersea, 10 September 1890, Battersea Mss.
11 Ibid., 6 October 1890.
12 Charles L. Warr, *The Glimmering Landscape*, 1960, pp. 37–8.
13 Marie Mallet to her husband, 8 November 1895, Mallet Mss.
14 Henry to Mary Ponsonby, 1 November 1890, Ponsonby Mss.
15 Ibid., 3 November 1890.
16 Ibid., 2 November 1890.
17 Ibid., 29 September 1878, cit. Longford, p. 570.
18 Ly Battersea to her mother, 23 May 1886, Battersea Mss BL 47910 f74.
19 QVJ, 13 December 1890, p. 109.
20 Lorne to Ld Ronnie Gower, 20 December 1890, Dufferin Mss.
21 Ly Abercromby to Mrs Haldane, 16 December 1890, Haldane Mss 6093 f142.
22 Wilfred Blunt, 14 June 1809, *General Memories*, vol. 1908–9, Blunt Mss, f237–243.
23 QVJ, 13 December 1890, pp. 177–8.
24 PL to Dowager Dss of Atholl, 3 January 1891, Atholl Mss.
25 Boehm to Mrs Edwards, 20 June n.d., Alma-Tadema Mss. Autogr. 6. 9.
26 Atholl Mss, op. cit.
27 QV to Pss Louis of Battenberg, 19 December 1890, Broadlands Mss.
28 F. Horner, *Time Remembered*, 1933, p. 118.
29 QVJ, 20 December 1890.
30 F. Leighton to George Watts, n.d. 1890, Leighton Mss 12755.
31 Ly Battersea to her mother, 15 April 1891, Battersea Mss BL 47910 f140.
32 Ibid., 12 April 1891, f137.
33 Ibid.
34 Marie Mallet to her husband, 28 March 1891, Mallet Mss.
35 Battersea Mss, op. cit. 137.
36 Marie Mallet, 4 & 16 April 1891, op. cit.
37 Ibid., 11 April 1891.
38 E. Smythe, *Streaks of Life*, 1924, p. 95.

39 Marie Mallet, 5 April 1891, op. cit.
40 Ly Battersea's journal, 11 April 1891, Battersea Mss BL 47940.

CHAPTER XXII

1 Lorne to D of Argyll, 3 February 1892, INV Mss.
2 Ibid., 19 August 1892.
3 Janey to Niall Campbell, 7 November 1892, INV Mss.
4 Sir Frederick Ponsonby, *Recollections of Three Reigns*, 1951, p. 51.
5 Fritz Ponsonby to PL, 7 December 1904, Bevills Mss.
6 Lorne to Ld Archie Campbell, 23 August 1887, INV Mss.
7 Ibid., 5 November 1884.
8 *Letters of Roger Fry*, ed. Denys Sutton, 1972, vol. I, p. 146.
9 J. A. Symonds to Edward Gosse, 18 September 1891, The Brotherton Collection Mss.
10 Caroline Holland *Notebooks of a Spinster Lady*, 1919, p. 131.
11 M. Spielmann, *British Sculpture and Sculptors of Today*, 1901, pp. 160–1.
12 Caroline Holland, op. cit.
13 Lorne to Ld Archie Campbell, 13 July 1890, INV Mss.
14 Lesley Brodrick, pp. 23–4.
15 QVJ, 28 June 1893, cit. Derek Hudson, p. 103.
16 *Morning Post*, 29 June 1893.
17 Dowager Ly Stanley of Alderley to PL, 29 June 1893, INV Mss.
18 Press clipping, n.d., INV Mss.
19 Spielmann, op. cit.
20 Arthur Byron, *London Statues*, 1981, p. 375.
21 Inspector Hogan's report, 8 August 1893, PRO WORK 20/77.
22 Board of Works memo, 21 August 1893, ibid.

CHAPTER XXIII

1 Lesley Brodrick, pp. 28–9.
2 D of Argyll to Sabina Smith, 30 August 1893, Smith of Jordanhill Mss.
3 D of Argyll to Ld Selborne, 9 January 1894, Selborne Mss 1876 f270.
4 D of Argyll to Ld Dufferin, 10 January 1894, Dufferin Mss.
5 Molly Dawkins to Norah Callander, 4 April 1894, INV Mss.
6 Ibid., 10 May 1894.
7 Frances, Lady Fergusson to author, 12 May 1983.
8 Molly Dawkins to Norah Callander, 24 May 1894, INV Mss.
9 Ly Frances Balfour to Ly Salisbury, 29 March 1894, Salisbury Mss.
10 Molly Dawkins, 24 May 1894, op. cit.
11 Ibid., 9 July & 20 June 1894.
12 Ibid., 4 & 30 July 1894.
13 QV to Ld Salisbury, 25 October 1894, RA A/70/70, copy cit. John Wilson, *CB*, 1973, p. 550.
14 CB to his wife, 7 November 1894, Campbell-Bannerman Mss BL 52520 f52.
15 Ibid., 2 November 1894, f38.
16 Ibid., 3 November 1894, f42.
17 Ibid., 5 November 1894, f44.
18 Ibid., 6 November 1894, f51.
19 Ibid., f50.
20 Ly Frances to Ly Betty Balfour, 17 November 1894, FB Mss.
21 Ibid., 19 January 1895.
22 Ibid., 7 December 1894.
23 Ld Ronnie Gower's journal, 24 & 31 May 1895.
24 QVJ, 27 May 1895, cit. Ly Lytton, p. 26.
25 Ld Ronnie Gower's journal, op. cit.
26 Lilah Campbell, p. 50.
27 PL to Ld Ronnie Gower, n.d., INV Mss.
28 Harriet Phipps to Marie Mallet, 11 May 1896, Mallet Mss.
29 Ld Ronnie Gower's journal, 18 June & 12 August 1895.
30 Marie Mallet to her mother, 26 October 1895, Mallet Mss.
31 PL to Lord Minto, 26 June 1896, Minto Mss 12389 f109.
32 E. H. Cookridge, *From Battenberg to Mountbatten*, 1966, p. 115.
33 Marie Mallet to her husband, n.d., 1895, Mallet Mss.
34 PL to Mrs Gladstone, 1 February 1896, Drew Mss.
35 PL to Ly Minto, 26 January 1896, Minto Mss.
36 Dss of Teck to Dss of York, 9 February 1896, RA cit. James Pope-Hennessy, p. 317.
37 Lorne to Bp Boyd-Carpenter, 25 December 1896, Boyd-Carpenter Mss BL 46721 f145.
38 P of Wales to Lorne, 26 March 1896, INV Mss.
39 Lorne to Ld Archie Campbell, 27 March 1895, INV Mss.

40 Ly Victoria Campbell, p. 275.
41 Lesley Brodrick, pp. 36–7.
42 PL to Ly Salisbury, 26 October n.d., Salisbury Mss.
43 Ly Mary Glyn to Sir William Harcourt, 11 November 1896, Harcourt Mss.
44 Edwin Lutyens to Ly Emily Lytton, 5 April 1897, Lutyens Mss LUE/1/5/5.
45 Christopher Hussey, *Life of Sir Edwin Lutyens*, 1953, pp. 24–5.
46 Betty Massingham, *Miss Jekyll*, 1966, p. 37.
47 Ibid., p. 40.
48 Lutyens to Ly Emily, 21 April 1897, Lutyens Mss LUE/1/6/15.
49 Dr Williamson to F. Norris, 5 July 1935, Williamson Mss.
50 Lutyens to Ly Emily Lytton, 5 May 1897, Lutyens Mss LUE/2/1/4.
51 Ly Agnes Wood to her husband, 5 & 30 March 1880, Halifax Mss A2/124, part IV.
52 Marie Mallet to her husband, 18 February 1900, Mallet Mss.
53 Ibid., 9 February 1900.
54 Sir James Reid's diary, n.d., December 1895, Reid Mss.
55 Marie Mallet to her husband, 18 June 1896, Mallet Mss.
56 Reid, op. cit.
57 Ly Wolseley to her husband, 4 February 1891, Wolseley Mss LW/P17/14a.
58 Marie Mallet to her husband, 3 August 1898, Mallet Mss.
59 Patience Thesiger to the author.
60 Ld Ronnie Gower's journal, n.d., 1896.
61 QV to Lorne, 11 May 1896, INV Mss.
62 Lutyens to Ly Emily Lytton, 10 May 1897, Lutyens Mss LUE/2/1/9.
63 Ld Archie Campbell's diary, 23 October 1897, INV Mss.
64 PL to Mary Drew, 29 March 1898, Drew Mss.
65 Gladstone's account, 4 April 1897, Gladstone Mss BL 44791 f57–63.
66 Ibid.
67 Mary Drew, pp. 435–7.
68 Longford, p. 551.
69 D of Argyll to Lorne, 11 June 1891, INV Mss.
70 Ly Frances to Ly Betty Balfour, 22 June 1900, FB Mss.
71 Niall Campbell's diary, 9 March 1900, INV Mss.
72 Ly Frances to Ly Betty Balfour, 4 & 10 April 1900, FB Mss.

73 QV to Ly Betty Balfour, 8 April 1900, ibid.
74 Niall Campbell's diary, 26 April 1900.
75 Ibid.
76 Ibid.
77 QV to Ly Frances Balfour, 23 April 1900, FB Mss.
78 Niall Campbell's diary, 21 April 1900.
79 Dss Ina Argyll to Bp Boyd-Carpenter, 25 April 1900, B-Carpenter Mss BL 46723 f205.
80 Niall Campbell's diary, 25 & 27 April 1900.
81 Ibid., 3 May 1900.
82 John Campbell of Kilberry's diary, 4 May 1900, Kilberry Mss.
83 Niall Campbell's diary, 4 May 1900.
84 Ibid., 9 May 1900.
85 Ibid., 8 May 1900.
86 Lorne to Ld Dufferin, 3 May 1900, Dufferin Mss.

CHAPTER XXIV

1 Ly Frances Balfour, vol. 2, p. 309.
2 PL to Minnie Paget, 1 December 1899, Paget Mss.
3 *Reminiscences of Lady Randolph Churchill*, 1908, p. 320.
4 PL to Ly Wolseley, 9 March 1900, Wolseley Mss WA 334.
5 Ibid., 8 March 1900.
6 PL to Ld Wolseley, 22 January 1900, Wolseley Mss 330.
7 PL to Sir William Macewen, 3 December 1902, Macewen Mss DC7/9/73.
8 PL to Baynes Badcock, 16 April 1900, Probert Mss.
9 Niall Campbell's diary, n.d., April 1900.
10 Molly Dawkins to Norah Callander, 12 October 1894, INV Mss.
11 Lorne to Ld Archie Campbell, 23 May 1900, INV Mss.
12 Ibid., 22 & 24 May 1900.
13 Niall Campbell's diary, 27 May & 4 December 1900.
14 Ibid.
15 Ld Ronnie Gower's journal, 23 May 1900.
16 PL to Dss of Buccleuch, n.d., Buccleuch Mss GD224/82/11/128.
17 Ld Archie Campbell to Ld Dufferin, 14 May 1901, Dufferin Mss.
18 PL to Dss of Buccleuch, op. cit.

19 Molly Dawkins to Frances Callander, 29 June 1900, INV Mss.
20 Niall Campbell's diary, 19 June 1900.
21 Molly Dawkins to Frances Callander, op. cit.
22 Frances Callander to Ld Archie Campbell, 16 July 1900, INV Mss.
23 PL to Ly Battersea, n.d., July 1900, Battersea Mss.
24 QVJ, cit. Lady Lytton, p. 150.
25 Ly Frances Balfour's diary, 31 January 1901.
26 Marie Mallet to her husband, 9 November 1900, Mallet Mss.
27 PL to Sir James Reid, 29 December, 1900, Reid Mss.
28 Ly Frances Balfour's diary, 18 January 1901.
29 Niall Argyll to Maysie Wynne Finch, 17 October 1940, Voelas Mss.
30 Ly Frances Balfour's diary, op. cit.
31 Ibid., 19 January 1901.
32 PL to Lorne, n.d., FB Mss.
33 Randall Davidson to his wife, 21 January 1901, Davidson Mss, vol. XIX.
34 Kaiser William II, *My Early Life*, 1971, p. 76.
35 Memo on QV's death and funeral, 22 January 1901, Davidson Mss XIX f101.
36 Lorne to Ld Archie Campbell, 23 January 1901, INV Mss.
37 Press clipping, n.d., FB Mss.
38 Sir Frederick Ponsonby, *Recollections of Three Reigns*, 1951, p. 83.
39 Niall Campbell's diary, 9 February 1901.
40 Pss Beatrice to Dr Story, 15 March 1901, Story Mss P/CN 49,21 f66.
41 PL to Audrey Tennyson, 23 April 1901, Tennyson Mss 4754.
42 Ibid.

CHAPTER XXV
1 *Journals and Letters of Reginald Lord Esher*, ed. M. V. Brett, 1934, vol. 1, p. 275.
2 Ly Battersea's diary, 14 February 1901, Battersea Mss BL 47943.
3 Pss Alice of Athlone, p. 78.
4 Ly Minto's diary, 1 July 1911, Minto Mss 12459.
5 Ly Agnes Wood to her husband, 6 June 1891, Halifax Mss A2/124, part V.
6 Marjorie Duncan to the author.
7 Ld Esher to Arthur Balfour, 16 April 1901, Balfour Mss BL 49718.

8 Ld Knollys to PL, 5 July 1904, Bevills Mss.
9 Patience Thesiger to the author.
10 Kaiser William to PL, 17 March 1901, Bevills Mss.
11 PL to Ethel Badcock, n.d., Probert Mss.
12 Ethel Badcock to Beatrice Dunsmure, 13 May 1901, ibid.
13 Georgina Lee's history of the Davis family, p. 70, Lee Mss.
14 PL to Baynes Badcock, 11 & 23 October 1901, Probert Mss.
15 Ethel Badcock to Lydia Davis, 5 November 1901, ibid.
16 Georgina Lee, op. cit.
17 Ibid.
18 Lord Ribblesdale, *Impressions*, 1927, pp. 106–8.
19 Ethel Badcock to Lydia Davis, 7 October 1902, Probert Mss.
20 Ld Esher, vol. 1, p. 318.
21 Georgina Battiscombe, pp. 245–6.
22 Lorne to Ld Archie Campbell, 31 August 1902, INV Mss.
23 Niall Campbell's diary, 15 & 27 August 1902.
24 PL to Dss of Buccleuch, op. cit.
25 Ly Frances to Ly Betty Balfour, 15 October 1902, FB Mss.
26 PL to Baynes Badcock, n.d., 1902, Probert Mss.
27 Lorne to Ethel Badcock, 27 August 1903, ibid.
28 PL to Badcock, op. cit.
29 Niall Campbell's diary, 20 October 1902.
30 Ly Frances Balfour, p. 373.
31 Ethel Badcock to Mary Probert, 23 December 1902, Bevills Mss.
32 Kate Badcock to Mary Probert, 21 January 1903, ibid.
33 Elizabeth Badcock to Aunt Ellen, 2 February 1903, ibid.
34 Mrs Badcock to Mary Probert, 28 January 1903, ibid.
35 Elizabeth Badcock, op. cit.
36 Mrs Badcock to Mary Probert, 11 March 1903, ibid.
37 Col & Mrs Oliver Probert to the author, 25 June 1983.
38 Lorne & PL to Baynes Badcock, 11 & 12 February 1903, Probert Mss.
39 Lorne to Ralph Glyn, 17 April 1903, Glyn Mss/D/EGL-C14.
40 Niall Campbell to Frances Callander, 1 June 1903, INV Mss.

41 William to Mary Probert, 30 June 1903, Bevills Mss.
42 Ld Archie Campbell to Niall, 16 October 1903, INV Mss.
43 Ld Ronnie Gower's journal, 17 October 1903.
44 PL to Ld Ronnie, 20 October 1903, INV Mss.
45 PL to Baynes Badcock, 20 November 1903, Probert Mss.
46 PL to Marie Mallet, 7 March n.d., Mallet Mss.
47 William to Mary Probert, 4 November 1903, Bevills Mss.
48 Ld Ronnie Gower's journal, 7 & 8 July 1894.

CHAPTER XXVI
1 F. H. Myers. *The Duke of Albany, In Memoriam*, Myers Mss.
2 *Forty-Fifth Annual Report of the National Trust*, p. 1.
3 Sir William Richmond to PL, n.d., 1904, Bevills Mss.
4 PL to Ethel Badcock, 13 May 1904, Probert Mss.
5 Ibid.
6 Niall Campbell to Frances Callander, 3 June 1904, INV Mss.
7 PL to Ld Ronnie Gower, 17 October n.d., INV Mss.
8 Dr Story to Lorne, 4 November 1904, Bevills Mss.
9 PL to Mrs Story, 17 November 1904, Story Mss Gen 510(42).
10 Ethel Badcock to Beatrice Dunsmure, 1 December 1904, Probert Mss.
11 Lorne to Ethel Badcock, 9 January 1905, ibid.
12 PL to Ethel, 10 January 1905, ibid.
13 A. M. W. Stirling, p. 213.
14 Lorne's journal, n.d., (1900s) INV Mss.
15 PL to Mary Probert, n.d., Bevills Mss.
16 PL to Baynes Badcock, 17 February 1905, Probert Mss.
17 Ibid.
18 Ethel Badcock to Beatrice Dunsmure, 3 December 1902, ibid.
19 Ethel Badcock's diary, 6 March 1905, ibid.
20 Ibid., 7 March 1905.
21 Ibid., 8 March 1905.
22 Ibid., 13 & 17 March 1905.
23 Ethel to Baynes Badcock, n.d., March 1905, ibid.

24 Ethel Badcock's diary, 19 & 20 March 1905, ibid.
25 Ethel to Beatrice Dunsmure, 28 March 1905, ibid.
26 PL to Baynes Badcock, 30 March [1905], ibid.
27 Ethel Badcock's diary, 30 March 1905 and to Baynes Badcock, 30 March 1905, ibid.
28 Ethel to Baynes Badcock, 12 April 1905, Probert Mss.
29 Ethel Badcock's diary, 2 May 1905.
30 PL to Mary Probert, 25 May 1905, Bevills Mss.
31 Lorne's journal, 29 October 1905.
32 John Campbell of Kilberry's diary, 16 December 1905.
33 Ethel Badcock to Beatrice Dunsmure, 17 December 1905, Probert Mss.
34 PL to Badcock, 28 December 1905, ibid.
35 Ethel to Baynes Badcock, 18 January 1906, ibid.
36 Ibid.
37 Ethel Badcock's diary, 26 January 1906.
38 Ibid., 12 February 1906.
39 Lorne to Ld Archie Campbell, 26 November 1906, INV Mss.
40 PL in Ethel's diary, 20 March 1906, Probert Mss.
41 PL to Pss Victoria of Battenberg, n.d., Broadlands Mss.
42 PL to Mary Probert, 25 March 1907, Bevills Mss.
43 Ibid., 26 April 1907.
44 William to Mary Probert, 2 July 1907, ibid.
45 PL to Mary Probert, 25 March & 26 August 1907, ibid.
46 Ibid., 29 September 1904.
47 Ibid., 19 November 1907.
48 Longford, p. 568.
49 Lorne's jottings, 1 August 1907, INV Mss.
50 R. Shannon, p. 399.
51 Ly Frances to Frank Balfour, 5 May 1910, FB Mss.
52 Randall Davidson, Memo of death and funeral of Edward VII, Davidson Mss vol. XX f17.
53 PL to Niky, 12 May 1910, INV Mss.
54 Patience Thesiger to author.
55 Niall Campbell's diary, 12 May 1910.

CHAPTER XXVII
1 Charles Warr, pp. 36–7.

2 C. L. Warr, *Alfred Warr of Rosneath*, 1917, p. 126.
3 Lorne to Ld Archie Campbell, 27 July 1910, INV Mss.
4 Niall Campbell's diary, 13 July 1910.
5 Ld Ronnie Gower's journal, 4 March 1911.
6 Niall Argyll to Maysie Wynne Finch, 6 July 1944, Voelas Mss.
7 Ld Ronnie Gower's journal, 10 March 1912.
8 PL to Will Probert, 15 June 1912, Bevills Mss.
9 PL to Niky, n.d., INV Mss.
10 Ibid.
11 Ly Battersea to Annie Yorke, 29 January 1913, Battersea Mss BL 47963 f207.
12 PL to Elizabeth Badcock, 18 September 1912, Bevills Mss.
13 PL to Mary Probert, 11 October 1912, ibid.
14 PL to Ly Sophia Macnamara, n.d., Twist Mss.
15 PL to Mary Probert, n.d., Bevills Mss.
16 PL to Ly Sophie, op. cit.
17 Bertha Taylor to Powys, n.d., SPAB Mss.
18 Ibid., 15 & 16 December 1912.
19 Thackeray Turner to Canon Rawnsley, 18 December 1912, ibid.
20 PL to Ethel Badcock, n.d., Probert Mss.
21 Lady Gregory, pp. 173–4.
22 PL to Niky Campbell, 2 April 1913, INV Mss.
23 Niall Campbell to Frances Callander, n.d., April 1913, ibid.
24 Molly Dawkins to Frances Callander, 13 July 1913, ibid.
25 Charles Ashbee to his wife, 22 April 1913, Ashbee Mss, vol. 15.
26 Charles Ashbee to his wife, op. cit.
27 The Hon. Katharine Villiers, *Memoirs of a Maid of Honour*, p. 188.
28 Charles Ashbee, op. cit.
29 Molly Dawkins to Frances Callander, op. cit.
30 Maysie Wynne Finch to Ly Mary Glyn, 10 September 1913, Voelas Mss.
31 Niall Campbell's diary, 28 April 1914.
32 Ibid., 1 May 1914.
33 Niall to Niky Campbell, 2 May 1914, INV Mss.
34 Niall Campbell's diary, 4 May 1914.
35 Pss Helena to Ly Mary Glyn, 3 May 1914, Meade Mss.

36 PL to Ethel Badcock, n.d., Probert Mss.
37 Pss Victoria of Battenberg to Nona Kerr, 4 May 1914, Broadlands Mss.
38 Ibid.
39 Pss Helena to Ly Mary Glyn, op. cit.
40 Niall Campbell's diary, 6 May 1914.
41 Ibid., 8 May 1914.
42 Pss Beatrice to Ly Mary Glyn, 7 May 1914, Meade Mss.
43 Niall Campbell's diary, 9 May 1914.
44 Meg Meade to Maysie Wynne Finch, 16 May 1914, Glyn Mss. D/EGL/f31/1.
45 Lorne to Dss of Argyll, 23 February 1868, INV Mss.

CHAPTER XXVIII
1 Niall Argyll to Niky Campbell, n.d., June 1914, INV Mss.
2 Alfred Warr, p. 123.
3 PL to Ethel Badcock, 4 December 1914, Lee Mss.
4 Ibid., 12 March 1916, Probert Mss.
5 John James, *Memoirs of a House Steward*, 1949, p. 43.
6 Ld Esher, vol. 3, p. 180.
7 PL to Sir William Macewen, 23 August 1914, Macewen Mss.
8 PL to Walburga Paget, n.d., Paget Mss.
9 Niall Argyll to Ly Londonderry, 26 September 1914, Londonderry Mss D3099/3/2/48.
10 PL to Bp Boyd-Carpenter, 26 February 1915, B-Carpenter Mss. BL 46721 f136.
11 PL to Ralph Glyn, 23 September 1915, Glyn Mss D/EGL/C15.
12 PL to Baynes Badcock, 16 October 1914, Probert Mss.
13 Pss Helena to Ly Agneta Montagu, 20 August 1914, Sandwich Mss f324B.
14 PL to Mary Probert, 14 April 1917, Bevills Mss.
15 Ibid., 14 April 1917.
16 Pss Helena to Ly Agneta Montagu, op. cit.
17 Niall Argyll's diary, 24 November 1914.
18 Ibid., 9 December 1914.
19 Hon. Mary Percy to the author.
20 PL to Mary Probert, 28 December 1908 & 11 January 1915, Bevills Mss.
21 Sir Henry Lucy, p. 218.
22 PL to Ralph Glyn, 2 September 1915, Glyn Mss.
23 Ly Eve Balfour to the author, 31 January 1984.

24 Ly Mary to Ralph Glyn, 8 February 1916, Glyn Mss D/EGL/C/2/3.
25 PL to Ralph Glyn, n.d., ibid.
26 Ibid., 14 April 1916.
27 PL to Sir William Macewen, 22 March 1916, Macewen Mss.
28 Erskine Hospital Mss.
29 PL to Ralph Glyn, op. cit.
30 PL to Col. Tweedie, 4 September 1916, Tweedie Mss.
31 PL to Ralph Glyn, 3 October 1915, Glyn Mss D/EGL/C15.
32 PL to Mary Probert, 14 April 1917, Bevills Mss.
33 *Oban Times*, 23 December 1939, p. 5.
34 PL to Ly Victoria Richardson, 19 October 1919, Richardson Mss.
35 Patience Thesiger to the author.
36 Lucy James to Charles Warr, 12 March 1939, Warr Mss ACC.7566.
37 Frances, Ly Fergusson to the author.
38 PL to John Wynne Finch, 21 March 1932, Voelas Mss.
39 Anon to author.
40 PL to Walburga Paget, 13 December 1925, Paget Mss.
41 PL to Mary Drew, 27 February 1918, Drew Mss.
42 PL to Laurence Alma-Tadema, n.d., Alma-Tadema Mss.
43 PL to Col. Tweedie, 22 May 1922, Tweedie Mss.
44 PL to May Hamilton, 3 July 1922, Hamilton Mss.
45 PL to Ly Mary Glyn, 21 September 1919, Meade Mss.
46 PL to Charles Warr, 20 June 1916, Warr Mss.
47 John James, p. 79.
48 *The Scotsman*, 3 November 1926.
49 *The Daily Telegraph*, ibid.
50 Dr Taylor to the author, 16 August 1983.
51 Sir William Davidson, cit. *Kensington News*, 15 December 1939.
52 Ly Frances Balfour to Charles Warr, 7 October 1930.
53 R. Hough, *Louis and Victoria*, p. 274.
54 PL to Charles Warr, 15 September 1936, Warr Mss.
55 John James, pp. 34–5.
56 PL to Ly Battersea, 29 February 1931, Battersea Mss.
57 PL to Charles Warr, 12 April 1931, Warr Mss.
58 Marjorie Duncan to the author.
59 R. Hough, op. cit., pp. 49–50.

60 Matthew Calderwood to the author, 2 July 1983.
61 Marjorie Duncan, op. cit.
62 Mrs McKay to the author, 2 July 1983.
63 Duncan Haig to the author, ibid.
64 Matthew Calderwood, op. cit.
65 Duncan Haig, op. cit.
66 Ly Frances Balfour to Charles Warr, op. cit.
67 Lucy James to Sir Patrick Duff, 20 October 1933, PRO WORK 20/176.
68 Isabel McAllister to Marion Spielmann, 6 June 1935, Spielmann Mss SP/8/179/1–3.
69 PL to Charles Warr, 14 January 1936, Warr Mss.
70 Cecil Beaton, *Photobiography*, 1951, p. 129.
71 Frances, Ly Fergusson. Interview.
72 James Pope-Hennessy, p. 547.
73 PL to Niky, 30 May 1937, INV Mss.
74 Charles Warr, p. 276.
75 PL to Pss Victoria of Battenberg, 2 April, n.d., Broadlands Mss.
76 Lucy James to Charles Warr, 25 February 1939, Warr Mss.
77 PL to Arthur Ponsonby, 17 May 1938, Ponsonby of Shulbrede Mss. Eng. Hist. C.680 f44–6.
78 PL to Charles Warr, 29 September 1932, Warr Mss.
79 PL to Arthur Ponsonby, op. cit.
80 Lucy James to Charles Warr, 22 November 1939, Warr Mss.
81 Ralph to Ly Mary Glyn, 3 December 1939, Glyn Mss D/EGL/09/10.
82 Ibid.
83 Niall Argyll's diary, 4 December 1939.
84 Ralph to Ly Mary Glyn, op. cit.
85 Pss Victoria of Battenberg to Nona Kerr, 14 December 1939, Broadlands Mss.

SELECTED BIBLIOGRAPHY

Adam, Eve, *Mrs J. Comyns Carr's Reminiscences*, 1932.

Adamson, J. W., *English Education 1789–1902*, 1930.

Archer, R. L., *Secondary Education in the Nineteenth Century*, 1921.

Argyll, The Duke of, *Yesterday and Today in Canada*, 1910.

Bamford, Francis and Viola Bankes, *Vicious Circle*, 1965.

Beattie, Susan, *The New Sculpture*, 1983.

Benson, A. C., *Memories and Friends*, 1924.

Benson, E. F., *Queen Victoria's Daughters*, 1939.

Bentinck, Lady Norah, *My Wanderings and Memories*, 1924.

Bobbit, Mary Reed, *With Dearest Love to All, life and letters of Lady Jebb*, 1960.

Campbell, Marion, *Argyll The Enduring Heartland*, 1977.

Canziani, Estella, *Round About Three Palace Green*, 1939.

Cheekland, E. O., *Philanthropy in Victorian Scotland*, 1980.

Clark, R. W., *Balmoral, Queen Victoria's Highland Home*, 1981.

Clayton, Ellen C., *English Female Artists*, 2 vols, 1876.

Cooke, A. B. and John Vincent, *The Governing Passion*, 1974.

Cowan, John, *Canada's Governor-Generals 1867–1952*, 1961.

Crum, Major F. M., *The Isle of Rosneath, Notes for Scouts and Guides*, 1948.

Delamont, Sarah and Lorna Duffin (eds.), *The Nineteenth Century Woman*, 1978.

Digby, Anne and Peter Scarby, *Children, School and Society in Nineteenth Century England*, 1981.

Dorment, Richard, *Alfred Gilbert*, 1985.

Dyson, Hope and Charles Tennyson, *Dear and Honoured Lady*, 1969.

Reid, John (ed.), *Erskine House – The Princess Louise Scottish Hospital for limbless sailors and soldiers at Erskine House*, 1917.

Fawcett, Millicent Garrett, *What I Remember*, 1924.

Fine Arts Society, *Catalogue of British Sculpture 1850–1914*.

Fitzmaurice, Lord Edmond, *Life of the Second Earl Granville 1815–1891*, 1905.

Fitzroy, Sir Almeric, *Memoirs*, 2 vols, n.d.

Frechette, Annie Howells, 'Life at Rideau Hall', *Harper's New Monthly Magazine*, vol. 163, 1881.

Matthew, H. C. G., *The Gladstone Diaries*, vol. VI, 1861–1868 and vol. VII, 1869–1871, publ. 1978 & 1982.

Ramm, Agatha (ed.), *The Political Correspondence of Mr Gladstone and Lord Granville*, vol. II, 1883–1886, 1962.

Gleichen, Lady Helena, *Contacts and Contrasts: Reminiscences*, 1940. *Life and Work of Feodora Gleichen*, priv. printed, 1934.

Gower, Lord Ronald S. L., *Old Diaries 1881–1901*, 1902.

Grant, Col. M. H., *A Dictionary of British Sculptors*, 1953.

Gardyne, Lt.-Col. C. Greenhill, *Records of a Quiet Life*, 1915.

Grosskurth, Phyllis, *John Addington Symonds*, 1964.

Halifax, Viscount Charles, *Lord Halifax's Ghost Book*, 1936.

Halle, C. E., *Notes from a Painter's Life*, 1909.

Halle, C. E. and Marie Halle, *Life and Letters of Sir Charles Halle*, 1896.

Hamilton, Rt. Hon. Lord George, *Parliamentary Reminiscences and Reflections 1886–1906*, 1922.

Hardie, Frank, *The Political Influence of Queen Victoria 1861–1901*, 1935.

Hobsbawm, Eric and Terence Ranger, *The Invention of Tradition*, 1983.

Hoge, James O. (ed.), *Lady Tennyson's Journal*, 1981.

Hubbard, R. H., *Rideau Hall*, 1967.

Hubbard, R. H., 'Viceregal Influences on Canadian Society', *The Shields of Achilles, Aspects of Canada in the Victorian Age*, ed. W. L. Morton, 1968.

Hubbard, R. H., *Ample Mansions*, Canadian Royal Society, vol. 15, 1977.

Hutchinson Horace, G. (ed.), *Private Diaries of the Rt. Hon. Sir Algernon West*, 1922.

Laver, James, *Whistler*, 1930.

Lees-Milne, James, *Ancestral Voices*, 1975.

Lindsay, Ian G. and Mary Cosh, *Inveraray and the Dukes of Argyll*, 1973.

Lindsay, Mrs Patricia, *Recollections of a Royal Parish*, 1902.

Lorne, The Marquis of, *Canadian Pictures*, n.d.

Lorne, The Marquis of, *V.R.I. Queen Victoria Her Life and Empire*, 1902.

Lucy, Henry W., *A Diary of the Salisbury Parliament 1886–1892*, 1892.

Lutyens, Lady Emily, *A Blessed Girl*, 1953.

Lutyens, Mary, *Edwin Lutyens*, 1980.

Maclean, John, *Royal Visits to Inveraray*, Priv. printed, 1933.

Maclean, Kate S., *The Coming of the Princess and other Poems*, 1881.

Matson, John, *Dear Osborne*, 1978.

Maugham, W. C., *Rosneath, Past and Present*, 1893.

Maugham, W. C., *Annals of Garelochside*, 1897.

Maxwell, Gavin, *The House of Elrig*, 1965.

Millais, John Guille, *The Life and Letters of Sir John Everett Millais*, 1899.

Owen, David E., *English Philanthropy 1660–1960*, 1965.

Paget, Lady Walburga, *Scenes and Memories*, 1912.

Panton, Mrs Jane, *Leaves from a Life*, 1908.

Percy, Eustace, *Some Memories*, 1958.

Ponsonby, Sir Frederick, *Sidelights on Queen Victoria*, 1930.

Pratt, E. A., *Pioneer Women in Victoria's Reign*, 1897.

Rait, R. S., *Royal Palaces of England*, 1911.

Randal, Florence Hamilton, 'Rideau Hall Past and Present', *Canadian Magazine*, vol. 12, 1898.

Read, Benedict, *Victorian Sculpture*, 1982.

Ritchie, Hester, *Letters of Anne Thackeray Ritchie*, 1924.

Evans, J. and J. H. Whitehouse (eds.), *The Diaries of John Ruskin*, vol. 3, 1874–1879, 1959.

Story, J. J., *Later Reminiscences*, 1913.

Stuart, Dennis, *Dear Duchess*, 1982.

Sullivan, Herbert and Newman Flower, *Sir Arthur Sullivan, His Life, Letters and Diaries*, 1927.

Sutherland, Duke of, *Looking Back – The autobiography of the Duke of Sutherland*, 1957.

Vansittart, Peter, *Voices 1870–1914*, 1984.

Van der Kiste, John and Bee Jordan, *Dearest Affie . . . Alfred Duke of Edinburgh*, 1984.

Wagner, Gillian, *Children of the Empire*, 1982.

Walvin, James, *A Child's World*, 1982.

Warwick, Rt. Hon. the Earl of, *Memories of Sixty Years*, 1917.

Williamson, Dr G. C., *Memoirs in Miniature*, 1933.

Woolfield, T. R., *Life at Cannes*, 1890.

INDEX